BIOLOGICAL FOUNDATIONS OF BEHAVIOR

BIOLOGICAL FOUNDATIONS OF BEHAVIOR

AN INTEGRATIVE APPROACH

D A N I E L   W.   L E G E R

University of Nebraska

HarperCollins*Publishers*

Sponsoring Editor: Laura Pearson
Project Editor: Steven Pisano
Design Supervisor: Heather A. Ziegler
Text Design Adaptation: Robin Hoffmann/Brand X Studio
Cover Design: Armen Kojoyian
Cover Photo: © Clayton Fogle/Allstock
Photo Researcher: Feldman & Associates
Production Manager/Assistant: Willie Lane/Sunaina Sehwani
Compositor: Circle Graphics Typographers
Printer and Binder: R. R. Donnelley & Sons Company
Cover Printer: The Lehigh Press, Inc.
Insert Printer: Southeastern Color Graphics, Inc.

Biological Foundations of Behaviour: An Integrative Approach

Library of Congress Cataloging-in-Publication Data

Leger, Daniel W.
    Biological foundations of behavior : an integrative approach /
Daniel W. Leger.
        p.   cm.
    Includes index.
    ISBN 0-06-043894-0
    1. Psychophysiology.   I. Title.
QP360.L43   1992
591.1'88—dc20
                                                91-18278
                                                CIP

91 92 93 94   9 8 7 6 5 4 3 2 1

To my parents, George and Ann Leger

. . . We are witnessing the fusing of many sciences, all concerned with one or another aspect of behaviour, into one coherent science, for which the only correct name is *biology of behaviour.*

—Niko Tinbergen

CONTENTS

PREFACE

In setting out over a decade ago to teach my first course in biopsychology, I faced the daunting task of choosing a textbook. The primary focus, of course, had to be behavior, but the "biological" part was tough to pin down. Biology is a large and diverse field, and it seemed to me that all the biological disciplines that could shed light on behavioral processes should be given their "say." But the biopsychology texts never did so. They covered neural anatomy and physiology, but rarely had much to say about genetics, evolution, ecology, or even development.

Texts in animal behavior were better, but tended to cover these fields in isolation—one chapter on neurophysiology, one on evolution, another on hormones—almost like a collection of 15 to 20 "mini-books" lacking a unifying theme.

I wrote this book not only to educate students about the findings and methods of the biological disciplines that contribute to behavior, but to show how these disciplines contribute to a unified, integrative approach to behavior. To choose just one example, an understanding of memory is enhanced by a combination of how experience affects later behavior; how these experiences affect the nervous system; how the changeable nervous system is a product of genetic-developmental processes; and how certain memory abilities help adapt animals to their ecological conditions and therefore facilitate reproduction, leading to evolution. All the behavioral processes long studied by psychologists and ethologists are amenable to such integrative approaches.

One other major goal in my writing was to integrate studies of human behavior with studies of animal behavior. Although it seems obvious that the same *principles* that apply to animal behavior also apply to human behavior, there is often a reluctance to mix the two. Human behavior is relegated to the back of the book, almost as an apology for including humans in a text about animal behavior—or, equally distressing, as though we need to wade through material on lesser creatures before we can begin to understand ourselves. Humans are indeed unique— but so are platypuses and aardvarks—and an integrative approach requires that as full a range of similarities and differences in as many species as possible be considered.

In sum, then, this book attempts to integrate the diverse contributions of biology and psychology to behavior in all animals, including humans. As such, it should work quite well in courses dealing with animal behavior, whether taught in departments of psychology or biology. Further, courses on biopsychology, psychobiology, or biological bases of behavior will find this book concerned with many of the issues traditionally treated in texts on physiological psychology, but with the added benefit of placing physiological processes into a modern evolutionary/ecological context.

I owe my interest in integrative thinking to my graduate school mentors at the University of California at Davis: Donald Owings, William Mason, and Richard Coss. Their encouragement of my work laid the early groundwork for this book.

More recently, earlier drafts of this text were greatly improved by the careful reading and detailed comments provided by several reviewers, including: Charles Blaich, *Eastern Illinois University*; William Buskist, *Auburn University*; Richard Burright, *State University of New York,*

Binghamton; David Chiszar, *University of Colorado;* Paul Cornwell, *Pennsylvania State University;* Terry Deacon, *Harvard University;* Robert Dooling, *University of Maryland;* Charles Flaherty, *Rutgers University;* Owen Floody, *Bucknell University;* Russell Grant Foster, *University of Virginia;* William Gibson, *Northern Arizona University;* Gary Greenberg, *Wichita State University;* David Gubernick, *University of Wisconsin;* Leonard Hamilton, *Rutgers University;* Marilyn A. Houck, *University of Arizona;* Wendy James-Aldridge, *Pan American University;* Timothy Johnston, *University of North Carolina;* John E. Kelsey, *Bates College;* Mark Kristal, *State University of New York, Buffalo;* Paul J. Kulkosky, *University of Southern Colorado;* Robert Lickliter, *Virginia Polytechnic Institute;* Linda Mealey, *College of St. Benedict/St. John's University;* Daniel J. Moriarty, Jr., *University of San Diego;* David S. Olton, *Johns Hopkins University;* Ronald H. Peters, *Iowa State University;* Charles Snowdon, *University of Wisconsin;* and Kenneth Wildman, *Ohio Northern University.*

The people at HarperCollins have been most generous of their time and support of this project. Judy Rothman and Laura Pearson originally saw merit in my ideas, and Marla Johnson arranged for most of the reviews. Michelle Steir handled many details, and Steve Pisano led the book through production. I am grateful to them all.

Daniel W. Leger

COLOR PLATES

CHAPTER 1

To understand behavior, such as this elephant's aggressive display, we must know how it *develops* in individuals, the various *mechanisms* that produce the behavior, how behavior aids in *adaptation* to ecological conditions, and how the behavior *evolved*. These are the four components of an **integrative approach** to behavior.

CHAPTER 2

Behavioral development is driven by a continuous transaction between an individual's genes and its environment. This young leaf monkey (*Presbytis obscura*) is unique because of genetic and environmental differences from other individuals.

CHAPTER 3

The behaving individual can be thought of as a machine, having **mechanisms** that need to be explored. For example, the foraging behavior of this ruby-throated hummingbird depends on the workings of its nervous system, the release of hormones, and the contractions of muscles. How sensory systems monitor the environment and how the animal learns and becomes motivated are other examples of behavioral mechanisms.

CHAPTER 4

Behavior is an important element in the **adaptation** of animals to their ecological problems. Female Belding's ground squirrels give loud calls when they detect predators, warning offspring and other relatives of danger and thereby enhancing the callers' reproductive success. Living animals are the descendents of successful ancestors, so **evolution** helps us understand behavior.

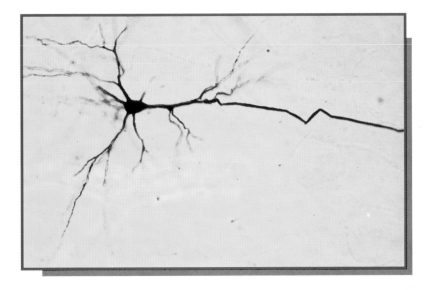

CHAPTER 5

How does the **nervous system** generate behavior? Nervous systems develop from a few generalized neurons early in life. Chemical and electrical signaling processes allow neurons to communicate with one another and with glands and muscles. This neuron has been stained, allowing us to see the fine branching structures so critical to neural communication.

CHAPTER 6

The **structure** and **functioning** of nervous systems helps adapt animals to their ecological conditions. Nervous systems also evolve, and many of the chemicals, physiological processes, and structures found in the nervous systems of primitive animals are retained in modern nervous systems such as the human brain.

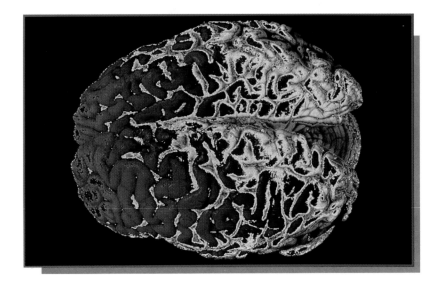

CHAPTER 7

Sensory systems link animals with their environment. Vision and hearing are used to illustrate the mechanisms of sensation, how they develop in the individual, and how ecological problems have shaped the form and function of sensory systems. This barn owl, for instance, has exceptionally good hearing, an invaluable aid in capturing prey.

CHAPTER 8

Integrative systems forge a link between sensory input and movement output. Learning, memory, and motivation are examples of processes that acquire, analyze, and store information. Species differ enormously in their specific abilities, largely because of differences in their ecological conditions. Bees are good at learning the locations and characteristics of flowers, for instance.

CHAPTER 9

Behavior is **movement**, and movement is produced by muscle contractions. This leaping squirrel monkey shows how movements change the animal's relationship to its environment, often in beneficial ways. Some movements require specific individual experience before they can be performed effectively, but others require little or no specific experience.

CHAPTER 10

These copulating lions illustrate the many processes involved in **reproduction**. Hormonal conditions in early life direct the development of sexual anatomy, physiology, and behavior. Neural and hormonal conditions influence the motivation for sexual activity in adulthood. Animals copulate in various ways and these variations are linked with their reproductive physiology and with the diverse functions of copulation.

CHAPTER 11

Sexual reproduction requires **mate acquisition**, as this male sage grouse is attempting to do. The distribution of male and female mates is a **mating system**, and these systems are adapted to the ecological conditions in which the animals live. Reproduction is timed to increase the odds of successfully rearing the offspring, which often entails extensive **parental care**.

CHAPTER 12

Animal **societies**, such as this school of reef fish, differ in many ways, such as the number of individuals in a group and their spacing patterns. The behavioral mechanisms involved in these social arrangements are varied and complex, but they tend to be adaptive in ecological context. Social behavior patterns develop in individuals, often due to interactions with the parents or peers. Learning in a social context can produce culture in nonhuman animals.

CHAPTER 13

Communication is often essential for adaptive success. The song of this western meadowlark, for example, attracts mates and repels other males. Signals—the sounds, odors, and movements used to communicate—are adapted to ecological conditions and can change over time due to individual experience, or evolve as conditions change. **Language** is a form of communication that shares many features in common with the systems used by other animals, but it has some other features that may be unique. Language-like processes in apes may shed light on the evolution of language.

CHAPTER 14

These wolves devouring their prey illustrate the survival implications of **feeding and anti-predator behaviors**. How animals recognize their food, and make choices among food sources are key issues. How much to eat and when to eat are other important concerns. There are intricate neural systems devoted to these tasks. Antipredator behaviors ranging from remaining hidden to counterattack have evolved in diverse animal species.

CHAPTER 15

Aggression, in this case involving two male elk, often is used in the acquisition or defense of limited resources, such as food or mates. The neural and hormonal systems that contribute to aggression are complex and varied, but they generally are successful in their ecological contexts. Human aggression tends to employ the same mechanisms used by other animals. Organized warfare, however, may be unique to humans.

CHAPTER 16

Biological clocks are used to time the behaviors that adapt animals to their ecological problems which recur on regular cycles. The daily cycle of **sleep** and waking is a good example. Sleep changes with age, and is governed by an intricate set of neural systems. Sleep helps animals, such as these bear cubs, deal with their ecological problems by conserving energy and reducing the risk of predation.

BIOLOGICAL FOUNDATIONS OF BEHAVIOR

Chapter 1

BIOLOGY AND BEHAVIOR

When a person suffers a stroke (blockage of a blood vessel serving the brain) the brain cells that receive their oxygen and nutrients from that vessel will soon die, impairing normal functioning. Depending on the site of damage, muscular paralysis, sensory deficits, and other problems may occur. One of the most common effects of stroke is aphasia, a language disorder involving speech production or comprehension. In most cases, aphasias occur only if the stroke damaged certain portions of the left side of the brain. Comparable damage to corresponding parts of the right side of the brain seldom lead to language problems. Why is language localized to the left side? Can the right side perform these tasks if the left side does not? Are other behavioral processes also localized to specific brain regions?

When laboratory mice are given two drinking tubes, one supplying water, the other alcohol, one typically finds substantial individual differences in the amount of alcohol consumed. When males and females with the highest alcohol preference are bred, and their adult offspring are tested for alcohol preference, they tend to prefer alcohol even more than their parents did. Continued selective breeding for alcohol preference results in a population of mice with extremely high alcohol preference scores. In contrast, selective breeding for low alcohol preference results in mice who absolutely avoid alcohol. Thus, there seems to be a strong genetic component to alcohol consumption. How do genes influence this behavior? Do genes contribute to human behavior? How could we find out if selective breeding experiments are not feasible with humans? Could alcoholism be prevented through genetic screening programs?

When white-crowned sparrow eggs

Young male white-crowned sparrows will sing their species' song only if they first hear an adult male white-crowned sparrow singing it. They usually avoid imitating the songs of other species, however.

are removed from their nests and incubated in the laboratory, the young birds can be raised in individual soundproof chambers so that their auditory experience can be carefully controlled. Males raised without hearing white-crowned sparrow songs grow up to sing a nonmelodious cacophony bearing almost no resemblance to normal songs. However, males raised hearing white-crowned sparrow songs played to them in their chambers sing perfectly well as adults. It appears that they need a song to imitate. But males raised hearing only the song of the closely related song sparrow do not sing song sparrow songs. Their songs resemble those of males who heard no songs at all! How do these birds recognize the songs of their own species and imitate them so precisely, but fail to imitate the songs of similar species? How does song learning occur? Can we learn anything about language acquisition in humans by studying song learning in birds?

The three examples above are only a few of the topics being investigated by researchers concerned with the biological foundations of behavior. Behavior is the externally observable movements and postures of humans and other animals. How can biology help us understand behavior? Biology is the study of life processes, many of which are directly related to behavior. For instance, the anatomical features of an organism will dictate the sorts of movements it can perform. The physiology of the nervous system is largely responsible for initiating and coordinating the organism's behavior patterns, and its sensory systems monitor the external environment to which its behavior is directed. Genes contribute to the structures and physi-

ological systems involved in behavior. Finally, because behavior helps animals adapt to their environments, behavior is an important element in studies of ecology.

The scientists who study the biological foundations of behavior typically affiliate themselves either with biology or psychology, but some come from chemistry, anthropology, medicine, and other disciplines. They refer to themselves by a wide variety of discipline names, such as neurobiologists, comparative psychologists, behavioral ecologists, animal behaviorists, behavior geneticists, and so on. *Behavioral biology* is a convenient, generic term for those disciplines that attempt to understand the biological bases of behavior. As we will see throughout this book, this field is highly interdisciplinary and some of the most creative and enlightening research is conducted by people who attempt to merge their primary field with one of the others, for example psychology and chemistry, or anthropology and genetics. As bridges continue to be built between disciplines, new and important insights are generated. To encourage these insights it is useful to map out the domain of behavioral biology. By doing so we will not only see where the traditional disciplines (psychology and biology) are working, but also find points of interchange between them and note areas that are largely unexplored.

The Dimensions of Behavioral Biology

The "map" of behavioral biology has two dimensions: The temporal dimension of cause and consequence, and the level of organization dimension, ranging from molecules to ecosystems. We will cover them separately before combining them into a single system.

THE TEMPORAL DIMENSION: CAUSES AND CONSEQUENCES

Causation Behavioral scientists, like all other scientists, are concerned with causation. We want to know what causes behavior. When investigating causes, however, we find a wide assortment of events and conditions that influence behavior. Some of these immediately precede the behavior but others occur substantially earlier in the organism's life. The entire array of causal factors is important. Let us review an example.

When a male laboratory mouse is placed in the cage of another male, the resident usually approaches and sniffs the "intruder," and then, more often than not, attacks and bites him. What causes the resident's behavior? First, there are several types of external stimuli that provoke and direct his behavior: The sight of the intruder leads to approach by the resident. The resident probably will attack if the intruder smells like a male, but not if it smells like a female. The form of the attack itself depends on moment-to-moment changes in the intruder's behavior. If he runs, the resident chases; if he rears up, the resident lunges forward, and so on.

Ernst Mayr

*"Behavior constantly interacts with both the living and the inanimate environment and is thus constantly the target of natural selection." [Mayr, E. (1974). Behavior programs and evolutionary strategies. American Scientist **62**, 650–659 (p. 658).]*

What about earlier causal conditions? Several have been identified. First, the resident male's housing conditions prior to the intruder's appearance will influence his behavior. If the resident was housed with a group of males he is less likely to attack than if he had been housed in social isolation, or only with females. The resident is also more likely to attack if he has been deprived of food. Second, the resident's behavior is influenced by his previous experience in similar situations. If he has won fights in this context before, he is more likely to attack and will be bolder in his attack than if he has frequently lost these fights. Further, conditions early in the resident male's life influence his adult behavior. The concentrations of certain hormones before and shortly after birth shape the structure and activity of his nervous system, making him more or less prone to attack. Going back further in time, his adult behavior can be traced to the genes he inherited at the moment of conception. Behavior geneticists have discovered that individual differences in genes have a strong influence on the aggressiveness of their bearers, probably through their role in shaping the nervous system. (These topics are covered in greater detail in Chapter 15.)

The causes of behavior can be arrayed on a temporal continuum from the immediate to the distant past. The ends of this continuum are called *proximate* and *ultimate* (or distal) *causes* (Mayr, 1961). The most proximate causes are those that occur immediately before the behavior. These include the stimuli that initiate and guide behavior, and aspects of the organism's internal state. The most ultimate causes are those with a lengthy history, particularly the genetic constitution of the organism and the long-past evolutionary forces that shaped them. Of course, many causal events and conditions, such as early experience, occur between the proximate and ultimate extremes.

Causal events that occurred earlier in life have their effect because of their impacts on the organism as it currently exists. So, for instance, the hormonal milieu that helped shape the mouse's brain took place several months before the aggressive episode. However, the brain structure is part of the mouse's current make-up and it is this brain that directs its present behavior.

Consequences   The consequences of behavior are just as important as the causes. What happens as a result of a behavior? Following up on our example, the resident male mouse experiences several *proximate consequences*: The exertion of the fight expended energy, left him in a temporary oxygen debt, changed the concentrations of various hormones, and may have left him with wounds. If the encounter had taken place in the wild, he might have become more vulnerable to predators. There are also long-term or *ultimate consequences* of his fighting. Wounds may become infected, leading to diminished health and vigor. If the fight was lost, the male was probably driven from his home territory, making food and mate acquisition more difficult, and death due to predation more likely. On the other hand, if the fight was won he may have protected his resources and mates, increasing his chances of survival and fathering offspring (Table 1.1).

Proximate and ultimate consequences are those changes brought about by behavior that affect the animal's well-being, survival, and reproductive success (i.e., the number of offspring

Behavior is often controlled by its (proximate) consequences. For example, if a blue jay eats a monarch butterfly, which is nauseating, the jay will in the future refrain from eating other monarch butterflies. Thus, a proximate consequence of one behavioral episode becomes a cause of subsequent behavior.

Table 1-1

SOME CAUSES AND CONSEQUENCES FOR ATTACK IN THE MOUSE

Ultimate Causes:	Genes contributing to development of the nervous system and other structures and physiological processes
	Evolutionary–ecological conditions that favored aggression
Proximate Causes:	Gender of intruder (as determined by odor)
	Reaction of intruder (flee or rear)
	Housing conditions
	Food deprivation
	Resident's previous fighting experience
Proximate Consequences:	Energy expended during fight
	Wounds or injuries sustained
	Protection of territory and/or mates
Ultimate Consequences:	Diminished health or even death
	Either more offspring/greater reproductive success OR
	Fewer offspring/lowered reproductive success

produced). These consequences may be positive or negative, and small or large in magnitude.

The consequences of a behavioral episode can act as causal influences on later behavior. For example, suppose a blue jay eats a toxic monarch butterfly and then becomes ill (Brower, 1969). The jay subsequently refrains from eating monarch butterflies when it encounters them. The bird's earlier behavior (eating a monarch butterfly) had consequences (illness) that had a causal effect on its later behavior (avoiding monarch butterflies). Much of the psychology of learning is concerned with how consequences affect subsequent behavior (Skinner, 1981).

THE ORGANIZATIONAL DIMENSION:
MOLECULES TO ECOSYSTEMS

The second dimension of behavioral biology is the level of organization. The individual organism is one level of biological organization, albeit the most familiar one. The individual, however, is a collection of organ systems, the organs are comprised of tissues, and so on. In the other direction the individual is a member of a social group, the social group is part of a population, populations comprise a species, and several species constitute an ecosystem (e.g., the plants and animals of a forest or an intertidal zone).

Each level in this scheme is a product of the lower levels, but with properties of its own. An *emergent property* is a characteristic of a higher level of organization that is not predictable on the basis of observations of its component parts (Salt, 1979). Water possesses emergent properties because its characteristics are not predictable simply by knowing the properties of its components, hydrogen and oxygen. Similarly, a social group may have characteristics, such as dominance relationships and division of labor, that are derived from the interactions of its members and therefore constitute emergent properties of this level of organization (Fig. 1-1).

Figure 1.1
Social groups often have dominance relations among the group members, and these relations are often reflected by who is groomed, as is occurring in these baboons. Dominance is an emergent property because it is found in social groups but not in individuals. Dominance influences the individuals but arises through individual behavior.

The existence of emergent properties means that each level of organization is important in its own right (Thomson, 1984; Sherman, 1988). Further, all levels are related to the others in that the higher levels are assembled from the lower ones, and the higher levels act to constrain or control the lower levels (Grene, 1987). For example, an organ such as the brain is affected by the condition of the organism as a whole, and a pack of wolves can influence the behavior of the individual members. To understand behavior, which is a phenomenon that occurs at the level of the individual, we need to investigate not only the individual itself, but its lower and higher levels of organization.

THE BIOTEMPORAL SPACE

A map of the domain of behavioral biology is made by superimposing the temporal and organizational dimensions to form the *biotemporal space* (Jensen, 1987; Fig. 1-2A). The point of intersection of the two dimensions represents an individual's current behavior. However, our understanding of behavior cannot advance very far if we stay at that point. We need to look at its causes and consequences; at lower levels, such as the physiological workings of the nervous system; and at higher levels such as the interaction of predators and prey at the ecosystem level.

The disciplines that contribute to behavioral biology have traditionally specialized in different portions of the biotemporal space (Fig. 1-2B). Much of psychology, for instance, is concerned with proximate causes and consequences (such as sensation, perception, and learning) at the individual level. Physiology, too, is primarily a proximate science but it operates at the organ to molecular levels. On the other hand, evolutionary biologists tend to be more concerned with ultimate issues, such as the long-term survival and reproductive consequences of individuals' actions, usually at the social group to ecosystem levels. The point to remember is that although various scientific disciplines specialize in different parts of the biotemporal space, their subject areas often overlap, and each discipline has important contributions to make to our total understanding of behavior. The biotemporal

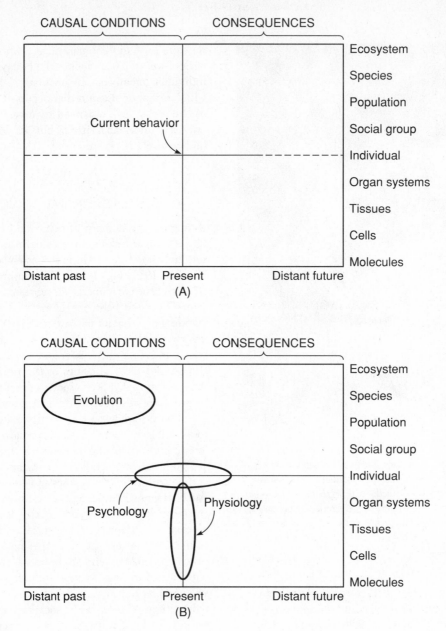

Figure 1.2
Diagram of the biotemporal space. (A) The horizontal axis is the temporal dimension, ranging from distant causal conditions to distant consequences. The behaving individual's lifespan is indicated by the solid portion of the central line. Behavior is an individual-level phe-nomenon. (B) The scientific disciplines that contribute to behavioral biology tend to specialize in various parts of the biotemporal space. Physiology, for instance, investigates phenomena primarily at the organ system level or below and close in time to the present.

space concept emphasizes that behavior that is being performed now is an individual-level phenomenon that is fully understood only if we look at insights obtained through more molecular and more molar levels of analysis. Behavior is also more fully understood if we know about its evolutionary and individual histories and its short- and long-term consequences.

An Integrative Model of Behavioral Biology

The biotemporal space defines the breadth and scope of behavioral science. However, it is not immediately obvious how various regions of the space are related to one another. For example, how can the interactions of predators and prey in

evolutionary history contribute to our understanding of brain cell activities in a modern organism? Can these diverse areas be linked? The genetic–evolutionary model, shown in Fig. 1-3, attempts to illustrate, in succinct form, the relationships among the topics of behavioral biology.

MAJOR COMPONENTS OF THE MODEL

The genetic–evolutionary model consists of four major components and their interrelationships. These four components (development, mechanisms, adaptation, and evolution) are the primary areas of study in the behavioral sciences (Tinbergen, 1951, 1963). We will discuss each of them in the process of describing the model.

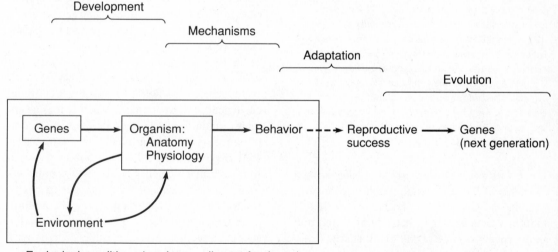

Figure 1.3
The genetic-evolutionary model of behavior, which forms the focus of the text, is shown here in simplified form. There are four major components to the model: development, mechanisms, adaptation, and evolution. These components are closely interrelated. Solid arrows *indicate that some influence exists in the direction of the arrow. The dashed arrow from behavior to reproductive success means that reproductive success is not always achieved. See the text for additional explanation.*

NIKO TINBERGEN

" . . . *Behaviour is part and parcel of the adaptive equipment of animals; that, as such, its short-term causation can be studied in fundamentally the same way as that of other life processes; that its survival value can be studied just as systematically as its causation; that the study of its ontogeny is similar to that of the ontogeny of structure; and that the study of its evolution likewise follows the same lines as that of the evolution of form.*" [Tinbergen, N. (1983). On aims and methods of ethology. Zeitschrift für Tierpsychologie *20, 410–433 (p. 430).]*

Development *Development*, (also known as *ontogeny*) is the lifelong process of change in individuals. Growth, the attainment of sexual maturity, acquisition of behavioral skills, and senescence are some of the many changes that occur during an individual's lifespan. These changes are due to the animal's inherited genetic material acting in concert with its environment. Together, genes and environment produce and continually modify the structure and physiology of the organism. Behavior, which depends on the animal's structure and physiology, also

changes during development. Developmental studies seek to understand the dynamic processes that govern behavioral changes across the lifespan.

Mechanisms The behaving organism can be viewed as a machine with processes that make it work as it does. Studies of the mechanisms of behavior typically involve examination of the neural and hormonal processes that influence behavior, the means by which environmental energies (e.g., light, sound, heat) are sensed by the animal, how memories are formed and influence later behavior, and so on. We probably know more about the mechanisms of behavior than about development, adaptation, and evolution, largely because mechanisms are more amenable to experimental investigation. For example, parts of the nervous system can be removed or stimulated to determine their effects on behavior; rewards can be provided to probe processes of learning and memory; and sensitivity to sensory stimuli can be measured using sophisticated equipment. These and many other procedures are designed to answer questions about how the animal produces its behavior.

Adaptation Behavior takes place in an ecological context including such things as climate, predators, social companions, and competitors for food. The animal's behavior is evaluated by the ecological conditions in which it lives. For instance, if a toad's prey-capture behavior is not adequate for it to meet its needs, the toad will not survive long and will not reproduce many offspring. The study of adaptation seeks to understand how behavior patterns assist animals in solving their ecological problems and how effective these solutions were in dealing with the animal's ecology. Adaptive behaviors are those that tend to increase the number of offspring that an individual bears, either because the behavior contributed to reproductive success *directly* (e.g., mate acquisition or parental care), or *indirectly* by enhancing survival (e.g., finding food, evading predators, or hibernating).

Evolution (phylogeny) When animals reproduce, they pass on copies of their genetic material to their offspring. This is important to understanding behavior because behavior is partially determined by the individual's genetic endowment. Further, if individual differences in reproductive success are due to individual differences in anatomy, physiology, or behavior that arise through genetic differences, then those genes that contribute to the more successful forms will be represented in the following generation in greater numbers than will the genes that contribute to less successful forms. Change in the commonness of genes is the foundation of evolution. The evolutionary component is largely concerned with historical changes that occurred due to differences in reproductive success of the individuals of earlier generations.

No simple diagram can fully depict the full flavor of a complex phenomenon, and Fig. 1-3 is no exception. Because the model represented by Fig. 1-3 plays a pivotal role in the organization of this text, let's consider a few points that are important to remember, but which are difficult to include in a diagram. First, although the figure gives the appearance of a chronological sequence, it is only loosely associated with the passage of time. Development is a lifelong process, and the organism's anatomy, physiology, and behavior continually change. Similarly, mechanisms of behavior are operating continuously: Sensory stimuli are always being detected and processed, the organism is always influencing its environment and vice versa. The adaptive value of the organism's structure and behavior are also continuously assessed by environmental features that affect survival and reproduction. The animal may perish early in life or much later, and its reproductive success may range from none to a great deal. The ecological assessment of an individual's adaptive status is not a "final exam." It is more like the accumulation of many daily "pop quizzes." Evolution, of course, implies the passage of many generations, only one of which is shown in the figure. Many important details are omitted from the figure. These will be provided in the chapters that follow.

A Case Study: Sexual Behavior in Unisexual Lizards

Before closing, a case study of a behavior system will be presented that illustrates the genetic–evolutionary model. Seeing how it all fits together will make more detailed treatment of the parts of the model more straightforward.

Whiptail lizards of the southwestern United States and northern Mexico are fascinating animals because several species do not have males (Fig. 1-4). During the breeding season females lay eggs that later hatch into female offspring that are genetically identical to one another and to their mother (Cole, 1984). Reproducing asexually is rare among vertebrates, so it is interesting in its own right. However, whiptail lizard sexual behavior is also fascinating. Although there are no males in the unisexual species, sexual behavior occurs just before ovulation (release of eggs). A female engages in the same sort of behavior patterns that males of other whiptail species use during courtship and copulation (Crews, 1982). At other times the same female behaves like a female. A captive pair of females may exchange these roles several times during the course of a breeding season.

Although little is known of the development of sexual behavior in these lizards, studies of its mechanisms have shown how the behavior is initiated by various hormones. Just prior to ovulation, females have large concentrations of

Figure 1.4
Some lizard species, including Cnemidophorus neomexicanus, *are unisexual, consisting only of females. They nevertheless engage in mating activities.*

estrogen and it is this hormone that leads to female copulatory behavior, presumably through its affects on the nervous system. Following ovulation, estrogen concentration drops dramatically and another hormone, progesterone, rises. Progesterone brings on male copulatory behavior (Crews, 1987). The cycling of these hormones begins with the lengthening days of spring. Thus, sexual behavior in this species illustrates how an environmental variable (increasing day length) affects hormones and how hormones influence behavior. Other mechanisms involve the sensory stimuli (odors, movements) that coordinate the mating behaviors of the two individuals.

The adaptive value of copulatory behavior in this species is obviously very different from what it is in species that reproduce sexually, where copulation serves to unite eggs with sperm. Female whiptails can lay viable eggs without engaging in sexual behavior. However, females housed alone laid fewer and smaller eggs than did females who were housed in pairs (Crews, 1982). Apparently, copulatory behavior affects reproductive physiology in ways that increase fertility. This is also true of other lizards and some mammals (Crews & Moore, 1986).

Finally, what about the evolution of this behavior? Fortunately for the study of behavioral evolution, the species which were ancestral to the unisexual species are still alive, reproducing with both males and females. The similarity of the sexual behavior patterns of the unisexual species and their duosexual ancestors suggests that the genes that influence the behavior have changed very little, if at all, since the evolutionary divergence of the species. As genes change over time, so do behavior and anatomy. The existence of sexual behavior in a species that reproduces asexually is understandable only in light of the evolutionary history of the species.

Summarizing, the genes that a whiptail lizard inherits are descended from a long evolutionary lineage. These genes contribute to the development of the neural and hormonal systems that are sensitive to day length and that are important controls over sexual behavior and reproductive physiology, as well as many other behaviors that contribute to individual survival, such as predator avoidance, food-finding, and shelter-seeking. These behaviors are adaptive to the extent that they lead to reproductive success, and reproduction passes on to the next generation those genes that contributed to the lizard's adaptive success, yet another installment in the evolution of the species.

Summary

Behavior has both short-term (proximate) and long-term (ultimate) causes and consequences. The continuum ranging from ultimate causes to ultimate consequences is known as the temporal dimension of behavior. Another dimension, that of organizational level, ranges from molecules to individuals to ecosystems. Although behavior occurs at the individual level of organization, studies at other levels help us understand behavior. Because the scientific disciplines that contribute to behavioral biology tend to emphasize different parts of the temporal and organizational dimensions, an integrated approach is necessary. The integrative approach to behavioral biology requires four areas of study: development of individuals through the combined actions of genes and environment; mechanisms of behavior; the adaptive significance of behavior, that is, how the behavior affects survival and reproductive success; and, finally, the evolution of behavior by means of gene perpetuation through reproduction. The integration of these areas is accomplished by the genetic–evolutionary model, a case study of which involves the sexual behavior of certain lizard species which consist only of females.

Recommended Readings

MAYR, E. (1961). Cause and effect in biology. *Science,* **134,** 1501–1506.

SKINNER, B. F. (1981). Selection by consequences. *Science,* **213,** 501–504.

TINBERGEN, N. (1951). *The study of instinct.* New York: Oxford University Press.

TINBERGEN, N. (1963). On aims and methods of ethology. *Zeitschrift für Tierpsychologie,* **20,** 410–433.

Chapter 2

GENES, ENVIRONMENTS, DEVELOPMENT, AND BEHAVIOR

The genetic–evolutionary model begins with individual development, or ontogeny. A lifelong process, development is influenced by the individual's genes and by its environment. But the simple phrase "is influenced by" scarcely begins to do justice to the highly dynamic interaction that goes on among genes, environment, and the organism itself. That is, each of these elements affects the others in very important ways.

These elements and their interactions are shown in Fig. 2-1, which expands the first section of the genetic–evolutionary model presented in Chapter 1. We begin with genes, because these specialized molecules not only are the basis of inheritance from one generation to the next, they also provide the code for the synthesis of thousands of different proteins. These proteins are incorporated into the organism's ever-changing structure and physiology. Behavior changes accordingly.

The environment figures prominently in this process. Various environmental variables can activate or inhibit the protein-making machinery, a few genes at a time or many at once. "Environment" is best viewed from the perspective of the genes. Thus, such organismic entities as hormones, nutrients, or body temperature may influence gene activity. The environment also exists "outside the skin" of the animal, of course, but can still affect gene activity through its influence on the organismic (internal) environment. The environment also affects the way the anatomy is constructed from the protein "building materials."

There are important feedbacks among many of these elements. The protein produced by a gene becomes

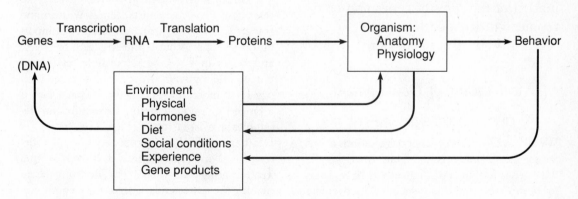

Figure 2.1

The first block of the genetic-evolutionary model is concerned with the processes of development. These processes include the production of proteins according to a code specified in the genes. Production is influ- *enced by the environment, as is the construction of the anatomical features of the phenotype. Genes, environments, and the phenotype have important effects on one another.*

part of the environment for that gene and others, often affecting further protein output. The developing individual changes its environment through its behavior, its chemical discharges, and so on. These environmental changes can then re-influence the organism directly or through their impact on gene activity.

It is important to remember that developmental processes go on continuously throughout the lifespan. Although it is often tempting to think of development as equivalent to the changes of early life, in reality the changes that occur then are only part of the bigger picture of lifespan development (although often a rapidly changing part).

With this brief overview complete, we now begin a more detailed examination of the roles of genes and environment in the development of organisms and their behavior.

Mechanisms of Development

GENES AND DEVELOPMENT

We all have heard everyday conversations about genes and characteristics: That some people have genes for blue eyes, but others have genes for brown eyes; that scientists have discovered a genetic cause for some vexing disease; or that Jim is taller than Bob because Jim has more genes for tallness, and so on. The common misconception in these statements is that there is a one-to-one correspondence between a gene and a *phenotype* (any attribute of the organism, including anatomical structure, physiological processes, or behavior). This simply is not true. There is no eye color gene, no curly hair gene, no intelligence gene, no introversion gene. Although it is tempting to think of genes as producers of phenotypes, that is much too simple.

But if genes don't code for eye color and such, then what do they do? The answer is that genes direct the synthesis of proteins. And why are proteins important? For three reasons: A great number of different proteins are incorporated into the structure of the body. They are the building materials of muscle, nerves, glands, and so on. Other proteins, the *enzymes,* regulate thousands of biochemical events ranging from digestion to the production of chemicals used by nerve cells to communicate with one another. Finally, some proteins regulate the genes' synthesis of other proteins. Proteins are important because, in many ways, we are what our proteins are and do (Doolittle, 1985). Our first task, then, is to delve into the mechanisms of protein synthesis by genes.

Genes and protein synthesis Nearly 40 years ago, two biochemists, James Watson and Francis Crick (1953a,b), answered two important questions: What is the structure of DNA, and how can DNA be responsible for inheritance? Their answer, which revolutionized biology (Baltimore, 1984), suggested that DNA is arranged in a double helix, a structure that resembles a twisted rope ladder. The "ropes" of DNA are made of two components, a sugar (deoxyribose) and phosphoric acid, linked together in alternating order (Fig. 2-2). The "rungs" connecting the two strands of deoxyribose phosphoric acid are known as *bases* of which there are four types: adenine (A), thymine (T), guanine (G), and cytosine (C). The bases are attached to the main strands and to each other (Strickberger, 1986; see Fig. 2-2). The intercon-

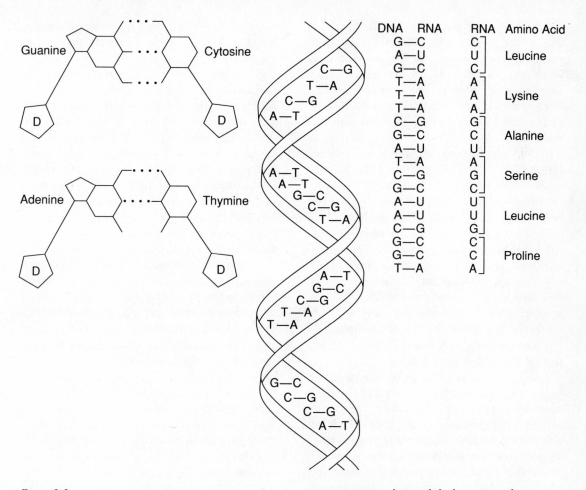

Figure 2.2
(Left) DNA is constructed of four bases joined in pairs with hydrogen bonds (dots). The structures labeled D are molecules of deoxyribose. The paired bases are chemically bonded in long series, and the complete structure is twisted around the long axis to form a double helix (center). Strands of DNA periodically serve as templates for the production of messenger RNA which in turn contains the code for the linkage of specific amino acids that form the protein (right).

nections are specific: adenine connects only to thymine, and guanine connects only to cytosine.

Nearly all the DNA in animal cells is found in the nucleus, arranged in one or more chromosomes. Chromosomes consist of complexly folded DNA and an assortment of protein molecules attached to it. The chromosomes are separated from the cytoplasm (fluid inside the cell) by a porous nuclear membrane through which DNA regulates cellular physiology (Felsenfeld, 1985).

Periodically, the DNA molecule "unzips," that is, the A–T and G–C connections break and the chains unravel. Each chain is copied when enzymes attach As, Ts, Gs, and Cs to the complementary bases on the chain. Thus, the DNA molecule replicates itself, and these replicates emerge in new cells being formed in the body.

DNA also makes a related type of molecule called RNA. RNA differs from DNA in two ways. Ribose replaces deoxyribose and, instead of thymine, RNA has a different but similar base, uracil (U). Unlike DNA replication in which the entire DNA strand is duplicated, RNA production occurs along relatively short segments of DNA. In other words, stretches of DNA are exposed from time to time and serve as templates for the construction of RNA. This is accomplished in much the same way as DNA synthesis, by attaching bases to the complementary base on the DNA strand (Fig. 2-2). This process is called *transcription.*

When a chain of RNA is completed it leaves the nucleus and drifts to one of the cell's *ribosomes,* specialized subcellular structures where protein synthesis occurs (Lake, 1981). At a ribosome, the RNA molecule (known as messenger RNA because it is carrying the "message" provided by DNA) is in a position to direct the construction (synthesis) of a protein molecule, a process known as *translation* (Darnell, 1983, 1985; Nomura, 1984).

Proteins are complex molecules. Consisting of strings of up to 20 different types of amino acid, thousands of different proteins are constructed every minute of our lives. How are proteins made? The process begins with a strand of messenger RNA at a ribosome. The RNA is a string of up to about three thousand bases linked together in a line. A sequence of these bases might be: A A C C C G U U G U G U C G C U U A. (Of course, the actual RNA strand would have a much longer series of bases.) A fascinat-

ing property of these bases is that sets of three in a row make up a code specifying the various amino acids (Fig. 2-2). For example, AAC is a code for the amino acid asparagine, and CCG codes for proline. Each of the amino acids has at least one unique triplet code of RNA bases; most have two codes, and some have up to six.

Amino acids, which are either synthesized by the body or which must be consumed in the food we eat (essential amino acids), are present in the cytoplasm and are brought to the ribosomes where enzymes attach them in a sequence specified by the RNA's triplet code. Each protein "species" has its own unique arrangement of amino acids, usually 100 to 1000 in total.

Each of the thousands of different proteins that make up our bodies and regulate their activity can be traced to a linear code of DNA bases, a gene. Genes occur at particular locations on one of the chromosomes. Because most cells contain two copies of each type of chromosome, most genes occur twice in each cell. However, the two copies of a gene need not be identical. Genes often exist in two or more forms called *alleles.* Alleles produce the same type of protein, but in somewhat different form. Take the human blood type gene as an example. It has three alleles (labeled A, B, and O), and an individual can have any two of them or a double set of one of them. (If an individual has two copies of the same allele, it is said to be *homozygous* for that allele. If it has two different alleles, it is *heterozygous.*) Other genes may have more or fewer alleles, although no individual will have more than two of them. Alleles are important because the differences in their proteins may affect the bearer's ability to survive and reproduce in its environment. Changes in the commonness of alleles in a population is the essence of evolution.

New alleles arise through *mutation,* a process in which the base sequence of an existing gene is changed. This can occur when extra bases are spliced into the series, when existing bases are deleted, or when bases substitute for other bases. Many substitution mutations have no effect on the protein because of the redundancy of the amino acid code. Other substitution mutations will lead to a different amino acid being placed into the resulting protein. When this occurs, the protein's characteristics *may* be modified sufficiently to affect the resulting phenotype. Some mutations (especially insertions and deletions) are lethal, others may be slightly detrimental relative to the previous form of the gene, but others may be beneficial to varying degrees. A mutation may be localized to a small number of cells or spread to many cells as those cells replicate themselves. A mutation will enter the next generation, however, only if it exists in the gametes (sex cells) that produce offspring. Thus, mutation is the *source* of modified gene structure, but the *retention* of that modified structure depends on reproduction of those genes from one generation to the next.

Cellular differentiation and development
We have learned how genes direct the synthesis of proteins. But how do we get from proteins to bodies, physiological processes, and behavior, the three components of phenotypes? Furthermore, because all the body's cells are derived from the same fertilized egg and thus contain the same genes and alleles, why are not all cells alike? Why aren't we great globs of cells, each identical to all the others?

The answers to these questions depend on one very important phenomenon: Although each cell contains the full complement of genes, not all genes work all the time in all the cells (DiBerardino *et al.*, 1984; Gehring, 1985; Ptashne, 1989). If each gene is thought of as a light bulb that is either on when the gene is directing the synthesis of its protein, or off when it is not, then we would see a twinkling of lights. Some genes in certain cells work around the clock, other genes in the same cells turn on

momentarily, but many others may never turn on. In other cells, the same genes may be on or off for varying periods.

What regulates the timing and amount of gene activity? At the molecular level there are proteins that bind to the DNA, thereby influencing its activity (Takeda *et al.*, 1983; Ptashne, 1989). Chromosomes consist of two parts: the DNA itself and an array of proteins attached to it. One class of these proteins, the histones, has a generalized inhibitory effect. That is, once chemically bound to DNA, histones block transcription (Stein *et al.*, 1975). In contrast, nonhistone proteins have specific activating effects. They appear to do this by dislodging histones from a specific stretch of DNA, permitting transcription. Thus, a cell's complement of nonhistone proteins, which are themselves products of gene expression, determines the sort of protein-generating activity that the cell will conduct. In fact, molecular biologists have succeeded in altering cell structure and physiology by changing the cell's nonhistone proteins (Stein *et al.*, 1975).

In addition to the histone and nonhistone proteins, gene activity is regulated by various hormones, temperature, light, and the chemical environment of the cell. Because these conditions vary from cell to cell, the subset of possible proteins that is synthesized varies among cells. Consequently, cellular structure and physiology diverges, a process called *differentiation*. Differentiation is the core of development, and as it proceeds, the body begins to take shape, largely due to the workings of certain genes operating within their cellular environments (DeRobertis *et al.*, 1990).

ENVIRONMENT AND DEVELOPMENT

Genes figure prominently in development, but it is important to remember that the environment also plays a critical role. Environments consist of

The phenotypic sex of the American alligator is determined by the incubation temperature while it is developing in the egg. Relatively cool temperatures result in the development of a female; warmer temperatures lead to development of a male.

numerous variables, including the chemical composition of the cells and the fluids surrounding them, physical variables such as temperature, and the presence and activities of other individuals. Environments exert their effects prenatally and throughout the independent life of the organism, strongly influencing the development of the phenotype. We will now review some examples of environmental effects on development.

The physical environment   Temperature, wind, light, and other aspects of the physical environment often influence developing organisms. For example, American lobsters typically have one large claw, the crusher, and one smaller claw, the cutter. This phenotype, however, depends on the kind of substrate to which the lobster is exposed during its larval development. In laboratory research, the presence of crushed oyster shell in the trays in which the young lobsters were growing led to the crusher and cutter phenotype, but young lobsters reared in trays without crushed shells developed two claws of the small, cutter variety (Lang *et al.*, 1978). The shells, or other objects that can be manipulated by the young lobsters, led to differential use of the two claws. The more extensively used claw developed into the crusher. Thus, behavior had an impact on anatomic development (Govind, 1989).

Another example comes from the American alligator, a creature whose sex is determined by its incubation temperature while in the egg. If the temperature is less than 30° C, the alligator becomes a female, but if the temperature is greater than 34° C, a male is produced (Ferguson & Joanen, 1982). In this case, two courses of development are available, and, depending on the temperature during prenatal development, the animal's sex is indelibly determined.

Hormones   *Hormones*, chemicals produced by the body that influence tissues elsewhere in the body, can have enormously important impacts on development. Hormones are said to have *organizational effects* when their presence alters the form (organization) of the phenotype. The hormone testosterone has been especially well studied in this regard. Its presence often leads to cellular differentiation of nerve cells and other tissue in a manner characteristic of males. For example, injections of testosterone into newborn female mice leads to the development of male-typical brain structure and physiology. These females later behave in a manner resembling that of normal males rather than normal females (vom Saal, 1983). Further examples of the organizational effects of testosterone are provided in Chapters 10 and 15.

Diet The popular media has made us abundantly aware of the impacts of our diets on such phenotypic features as obesity, cardiovascular condition, and even behavioral characteristics such as activity levels and mood. Less well known are some other cases of diet influencing development. The caterpillars of a southwestern moth eat the leaves and catkins (flowers) of oak trees. Spring caterpillars eat the catkins and develop anatomical features that make them closely resemble the catkins. Summer caterpillars eat leaves and develop anatomical features resembling oak twigs. The phenotypic outcome depends on tannin, a chemical which is scarce in catkins but high in leaves (Greene, 1989; Fig. 2-3).

Diet can also affect the *timing* of developmental events. For instance, puberty in girls depends on having a minimum amount of body fat which, in turn, is partly due to diet (Frisch,

Figure 2.3

Caterpillars (Nemoria arizonaria) *develop into two very distinct forms depending on the amount of tannin in their early diets. On the left is a caterpillar that resembles the catkins (oak flowers) it has been eating (the caterpillar is difficult to see because of its effective* camouflage). *On the right is a caterpillar of the same species which resembles a twig. It ate leaves early in life. This example is a striking illustration of how environmental conditions can influence phenotypic development.*

1984). The metamorphosis of tadpoles into frogs depends on food availability, with abundant food retarding metamorphosis (Wassersug, 1986).

Social environment   Social conditions may also influence development. A good example of this occurs in the platyfish, a fresh-water, neotropical species. Young males grow more slowly in environments in which adult males are common (Borowsky, 1978; Sohn, 1977).

The sorts of social interactions to which an individual is exposed also affects the developing phenotype. Cleaner wrasses, small coral reef fishes that pluck parasites from larger fish that visit their "cleaning stations," live in groups of several individuals, all but one of which are female. Females are socially subordinate to the larger male, who aggressively guards them. However, if the male disappears, the largest female of the group changes into a male, behaves like a male and breeds with the remaining females (Robertson, 1972). Apparently the aggressiveness of the male suppresses the transition to the male phenotype (Shapiro, 1983).

Other forms of experience   Most of the examples cited above are concerned with gross anatomic features such as body form or body size. Anatomy contributes to behavior, of course, so such examples are appropriate for a text whose main concern is behavior. However, there are numerous other examples of environmental features that influence anatomy in more subtle ways, or at least in ways that are not readily observed. For instance, learning and memory depend on microscopic changes in nerve cells and in their physiological processes (Squire, 1987). Learning and memory both involve experience with the environment. These issues are explained more thoroughly in Chapter 9.

Similarly, exposure to certain stimuli affects the development of connections among nerve cells and later behavior. The visual parts of the mammalian brain are influenced by light patterns early in postnatal life (see Chapter 7). Experience, then, helps shape the structure of the brain and therefore influences the individual's behavior.

Developmental paths   Environmental factors manifest themselves throughout the course of development. In some cases the nature of an important environmental variable results in the development of a phenotypic form that falls into one of a small number of discrete categories. The alligator's sex or the caterpillar's shape (catkin *vs.* stem) are examples of this sort of effect, known as *conversion* (Smith-Gill, 1983). The environment, in essence, works like a railroad switch, moving the developing phenotype to one or another track.

Environmental factors can influence development in another way, known as *modulation* (Smith-Gill, 1983). In modulation, the environmental variable influences the degree to which the phenotypic feature develops. Body size, for instance, grades along a continuum from small to large depending on food intake, and the aggressiveness of male mice is influenced by the number and gender of other mice with whom they live. Most of the individual differences in behavior with which we are familiar are due to modulation effects of the environment in conjunction with individual genetic differences.

These examples and many others that will be presented throughout this book illustrate the crucial point that development depends in large measure on the characteristics of the environment. Many people have the erroneous idea that gene action is rigid and predetermined, that "biology is destiny." This simply is not true. Although genes are absolutely essential for the phenotype, gene action and development are regulated by environmental conditions.

THE DEVELOPMENTAL SYNTHESIS

That development is affected by both genes and environment is abundantly clear. To understand why an individual is the way it is we need to know both its genetic composition and its environment. By itself, neither can ever be sufficient. But knowing about the genes and the environment is only the beginning. Because development is an ongoing process, we need to understand the dynamic, reciprocal influences of genes and environment throughout the lifespan. Great strides are being made in the developmental sciences of psychology and biology that are leading to a more complete understanding of development (Oyama, 1985; Bonner, 1988). This section will describe the major features of this important area of study.

A transactional approach to development The central feature of a transactional approach to development is that there is a constant interchange, or reciprocal influence, between genes, environment, and the organism. That is, the individual at time 1 influences its environment, which in turn affects the genetic material and the organism at time 2, and so on. Consider the following example. A newborn mammal obtains milk from its mother by suckling. Suckling changes several things. As the milk fills the newborn's stomach, physiological changes associated with digestion and thermoregulation occur. The nutrients in the milk are incorporated in the growing body and antibodies in the milk help combat disease-bearing organisms that may be present. Further, the suckling of the newborn affects the mother. Her physiological status changes as the milk supply is depleted, and hormonal changes occur that have impacts on her behavior toward the offspring and on her reproductive physiology. While nursing is going on, the newborn is subjected to stimuli emanating from the mother, such as her odor and sound,

which the infant uses later on to identify the mother.

As anatomical changes occur in the infant as a result of nursing, its behavior begins to change. It becomes more mobile as its size and strength increase, and as its nervous system matures. The newfound mobility exposes it to new experiences which change the infant even more. It eventually encounters and consumes food other than milk which in turn changes the nature of its relationship with the mother. This ongoing pattern of change in the organism which brings on change in the environment which produces still more change in the organism is the central core of the transactional model of development. This differs from an approach that sees development as an "unfolding" of a "plan" residing in the genes, and from an approach that sees the environment as all-important, "writing," if you will, on the blank slate of the developing individual.

Similarities and differences in development Perhaps the most striking feature of development is its regularity. Comparing several individuals of the same species as they progress through their lives, one observes similar changes in anatomy, physiology, and behavior. This regularity is the basis for the "stages" so often recognized by developmental psychologists and others. Of course, individual differences exist: some individuals attain "developmental milestones" such as walking, talking, metamorphosis, or flight earlier than others, and some become larger, faster, more aggressive or more active than others. Nevertheless, the regularity of development is profound. How can it be explained?

The transaction of genes, organism, and environment helps explain developmental regularities. Usually, individuals encounter roughly the same environmental conditions at a particular period of development and therefore tend to change in the same way at about the same time. This tendency is fostered by hierarchical patterns of gene activity. The timing of protein synthesis (gene expression) is frequently influenced by environmental features, and when a gene is expressed it may affect the expression of one or more other genes (Gehring, 1985), and so on. Thus, a hierarchy of gene expression may contribute to the regularities in development between individuals brought on by predictable environmental conditions.

Individual *differences* in development are also predicted by the transactional approach. Rarely will two individuals have precisely the same genes, and their environments are likely to differ. Plomin (1989) has argued that children in the same family are likely to differ (sometimes extensively) because of their idiosyncratic environments.

The transactional approach predicts that phenotypic similarities should be greatest in those individuals who are most alike genetically *and* environmentally. Wilson (1978) provided support for this prediction. Tests of mental development were administered periodically to sets of monozygotic (identical) and dizygotic (fraternal) twins beginning at three months of age and continuing until they were six years old. This is an interesting comparison because both types of twin share similar prenatal environments and, because they are the same age, are more likely to share similar postnatal environments. The monozygotic twins were more similar than the dizygotic twins in the patterns of "ups and downs" in their mental development scores (Fig. 2-4). One would expect to find even less similarity in nontwin siblings and, of course, in unrelated individuals.

Gene–environment interaction   The transactional approach recognizes the importance of reciprocal influences between genes, environ-

ment, and the changing individual. We say that genes and environment interact in producing the phenotype. In this sense, the term "interact" means a joint, reciprocal influence. (When people interact, as in conversation, they influence each other.)

The term *gene–environment interaction* is also used in another, more restrictive sense. Here, it means that a given environmental feature influences one gene or set of genes differently from the way it influences some other gene or set of genes (Plomin *et al.*, 1977). An example of gene–environment interaction comes from studies of inbred strains of mice. (An *inbred strain* consists of individuals who are virtually identical to one another genetically, due to many generations of interbreeding close relatives with one another.) Mice and other rodents will often bury an object that is dangerous or painful by piling soil or bedding materials on it (Pinel & Treit, 1978). In the lab, researchers have used an electric prod which, when touched, gives a moderately painful shock. Strains of mice differ in their defensive burying behavior. When mice were placed in a tunnel-like runway of three different lengths containing a prod at one end, one strain showed only weak burying tendencies regardless of the length of the runway. Another strain buried the prod only if the runway was short. A third strain buried vigorously at short and medium runway lengths, but not with a long runway. The fourth strain buried the prod regardless of the runway length. Thus, the environment (length of runway) led

Figure 2.4
Congruence in mental development scores for four sets of identical or monozygotic (MZ) twins (A–D), and four sets of fraternal or dizygotic (DZ) twins (E–H). Although each individual is unique, the MZ twins are more similar over time than are the DZ twins.

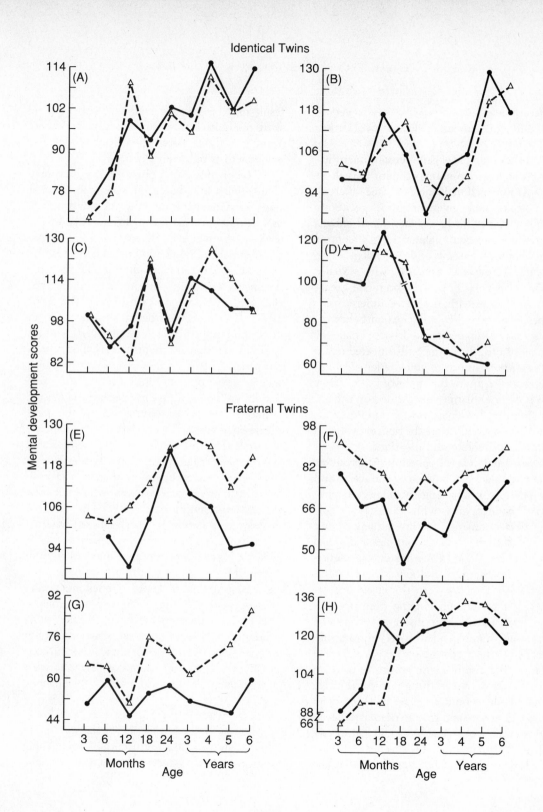

Identical Twins

Fraternal Twins

Mental development scores

Age

Months   Years

to different defensive burying patterns in genet-ically different animals (Maggio & Harder, 1983).

Another example of gene–environment interaction comes from an experiment by Vale *et al.* (1974) in which male mice of three different inbred strains were given hormone injections immediately after birth. As mentioned above, certain hormones exert organizational effects on the developing anatomy and physiology. The male mice were tested, as adults, with sexually receptive females. The early hormone treatments interacted with the three different genotypes as measured by adult sexual behavior. For instance, compared to noninjected males of the same strains, the hormonally injected males were faster or slower to mount the females, depending on the strain. In other words, the effect of the hormone treatment depended on the genetic strain of the mouse. Gene–environment interactions again illustrate the notion that gene action is not absolute and invariant.

Open and closed phenotypic systems
The environment can influence gene action and shape phenotypic development. However, phenotypic features vary with respect to how strongly environmental factors influence their form. This is the concept of *open and closed systems* (Mayr, 1974). Open systems are sensitive to environmental conditions; closed systems are relatively impervious to the environment. (There is a continuum ranging from open to closed, not merely two discrete categories.) Even closely interdependent parts can vary substantially in their openness to environmental influence. For instance, the growth of teeth in young mammals is surprisingly impervious to environmental conditions. The teeth erupt at the appropriate age and grow to normal size even when environmental factors, such as dietary calcium, are far from normal. However, the jaws are stunted by an inadequate calcium supply. The result may be a young mammal with normal-sized teeth in undersized jaws (Pond, 1977). Tooth growth is a closed phenotypic system, but jaw growth is relatively open.

The openness of a phenotypic system may change with age, being relatively closed for a time, open for awhile, and then closing again. A useful analogy is that the organism is like a train with opaque windows. When a window opens, the occupants (the phenotypic system) may be influenced by external conditions. But the window may close again, shutting down the potential for environmental influence (Bateson, 1979). The process of being influenced by an environmental variable more strongly at certain times (ages) than at other times is called a *sensitive period,* one of the most important phenomena in development. Unfortunately, sensitive periods are not as simple as opening and closing windows. We will encounter some of the complexities of sensitive periods in later chapters.

It is tempting to slip into the comfortable mistake of concluding that open systems—ones heavily influenced by environmental factors—have little or no genetic basis, whereas closed systems are heavily gene-dictated. This is the old dichotomy of nature (genes and closed systems) *vs.* nurture (environment and open systems). However, diverse phenotypes may result from different environmental inputs influencing a particular system of genes. Genes are always involved with phenotypes but we must recognize that their involvement can occur in many ways. Thus, the outdated question of whether phenotype X is under genetic or environmental control does not make sense. *Phenotypes are always a joint product of genetic and environmental factors.*

HERITABILITY

There is always a joint contribution of genes and environment in producing phenotypes. It would be nice if we could partition an individual's phenotype, such as height, into a fraction due to genes and a fraction due to environment, but unfortunately, this is impossible. The two components are as completely enmeshed as the ingredients of a cake (Bateson, 1983a). Is there any sense in which we can properly ask about the relative importance of genes and environment in a phenotype?

One approach is to focus our attention on *differences* between individuals. Instead of asking how much of a person's height is due to genes, we begin with a set of individuals that differ phenotypically and then attempt to discover how much of the phenotypic difference is due to genetic differences. This value is known as *heritability*.

Understanding heritability begins with differences in a phenotypic trait. For example, if we weigh each of 200 mice, we obtain a distribution of body weights. The population has a mean (average) value, but it also has variability and this is what we want to explain. Why are the individuals different? There are several environmental reasons, such as diet or exercise, that might cause body weight to differ; or the weight differences could be due to genetic differences; or, most likely, to some combination of environmental and genetic differences. This is expressed in the following equation:

$$V_P = V_G + V_E$$

where V stands for variance, and P, G, and E refer to phenotypic, genetic, and environmental, respectively. In these terms, heritability is the proportion of total phenotypic variance in the population that is due to genetic differences among the population members.

How is heritability measured? The most direct approach would be to control the environment, making it as identical as possible for each individual. Any variance in the phenotype must then be due to genetic differences among the population members. But in most cases, such complete control of the environment is impossible. For instance, behavioral geneticists often want to know the heritability of behavioral or cognitive phenotypes in humans. This is extremely difficult owing to the impossibility of controlling environments and problems in measuring environmental influences. Although there are techniques for minimizing these troubles (such as adoption studies; see Plomin *et al.*, 1977; Plomin, 1989), some geneticists see absolutely no use for the heritability concept, especially for human studies (Feldman & Lewontin, 1975). Despite its detractors' complaints, heritability studies continue to be done on humans, and some intriguing results have been obtained on such important attributes as intelligence, personality characteristics, and psychopathology. In brief, these studies generally find that genetic differences between people account for appreciable amounts (20% or more) of the variability in the characteristic of interest (Plomin, 1990).

Proper interpretation of heritability scores has always been troublesome. For instance, all heritability estimates are limited in their generality. If we are interested in the heritability of human IQ scores, as many behavioral geneticists are (Plomin *et al.*, 1980), and draw our sample of subjects from a limited environmental range (say, white, middle-class families of a particular community), heritability will tend to be higher (i.e., more IQ variance would be attributed to genetic differences) because of restriction of the range of environmental conditions that may be relevant. Conversely, if heritability were measured in a genetically homogeneous group, heritability scores would tend to be smaller. Thus, we must be constantly aware that heritability scores are limited to the group and environmental conditions in which they are measured. However, comparison of the heritabilities of different attributes in the same population can give us insights into the relative importance of genetic variation in accounting for phenotypic variation.

Genes and Behavior

The first half of this chapter attempted to illustrate how genes and environment come together in producing the organism and the changes it undergoes during its lifetime. Thus, I approach this part of the chapter, on genes and behavior, with apprehension. My worry is that there will appear to be an imbalance between the two co-equal entities (genes and environment), that genes will seem to be more important than environment.

I am willing to run this risk because *most* people have more trouble seeing the relationship between genes and behavior than the relationship between environment and behavior. We each have long histories of perceiving environmental effects on behavior—the way a bird changes course as it pursues an insect, or a dog sniffs a fencepost and then urinates on it—and therefore do not need to be convinced of the role of environment in behavior. That is not true of genetic effects on behavior. Let us proceed, then, with a review of the ways that genes affect behavior, followed by a discussion of the evidence linking genes and behavior.

HOW GENES AFFECT BEHAVIOR

The connection between genes and behavior is always indirect. Genes direct the synthesis of proteins, but because proteins do not make behavior, we must look for the intervening connection between genes and behavior. That connec-

tion is provided by anatomical structures and physiological processes.

Neural anatomy and physiology The nervous system is the primary control mechanism in behavior. It follows that any genetic difference that results in nervous system differences may affect behavior. For example, an allele found in many mammalian species produces abnormalities in development of the visual system. In cats, some of the nerve fibers leading from the eyes to other parts of the brain end up in unusual places relative to individuals with other alleles. This may produce a cross-eyed condition and inferior vision (Guillery, 1974).

Gene products can influence behavior through their effects on neural physiology. For example, the marine snail *Aplysia* has several behavior patterns associated with egg-laying (Fig. 2-5) that can be traced to activity of clusters of neurons located within the animal's abdomen. Scheller and Axel (1984) located a gene whose product instigated the behavior by acting directly on specific neurons, thereby affecting the animal's egg-laying movements. In other words, when these genes are active, egg-laying behavior commences.

Sensory systems Sensory systems are responsible for detecting energy sources in the environment or within the body that may be useful for the organism's survival and well-being. Sensory stimuli frequently initiate behavior or are used in directing ongoing behaviors. Genes whose products affect sensory function will therefore indirectly affect behavior.

An example of genetic effects on sensory systems comes from a study of genetic mutations in crickets. Bentley (1975) exposed young crickets to a chemical known to induce mutations. Later, he discovered a small number of crickets that failed to jump away in response to a puff of air. This response is also found in one of the most abhorred (but nevertheless fascinating)

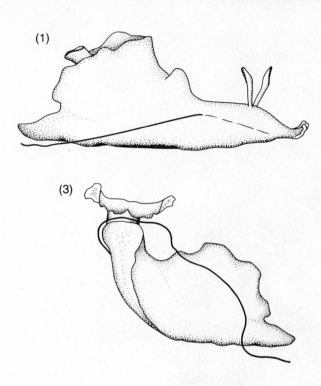

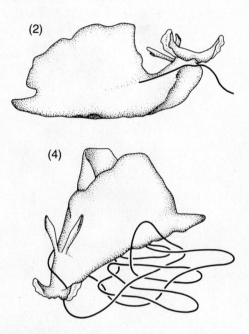

Figure 2.5
The component acts involved in egg-laying of Aplysia, a large marine snail, include the extrusion of a string of eggs (1), grasping the string by the mouth (2),

head-waving which helps pull the string out of the body (3), and attaching the string to the substrate (4). These behaviors have been linked to the products of certain genes of the snail's neurons.

creatures, the cockroach, and is controlled by sensory hairs on projections from the animal's abdomen (Fig. 2-6). Bentley noticed that in the crickets with the mutation the sensory hairs gradually disappeared with age. These crickets fail to escape-jump because they lack the sensory receptors required to detect the air currents that initiate the behavior.

Human sensory systems also are influenced by genes. Two well-known examples illustrate this. First, color "blindness" is easily traced to genes on the X chromosome. The most common form of color blindness is due to reduced sensitivity in the red end of the visible spectrum, but

not in the violet end. The sensitivity difference is due to a protein in the retina that absorbs light (Nathans *et al.*, 1986). Another sensory system with known genetic effects is the ability to taste certain substances, such as PTC (phenothiocarbamide). Some people are unable to taste PTC except at very high concentrations, but those who can (a majority as it turns out) report an unpleasant, bitter taste. The difference between tasters and nontasters is due to allelic differences. Other chemicals, many of which appear in our foods, are tasted more or less readily due to genetic differences among people (Dixon & Johnson, 1980).

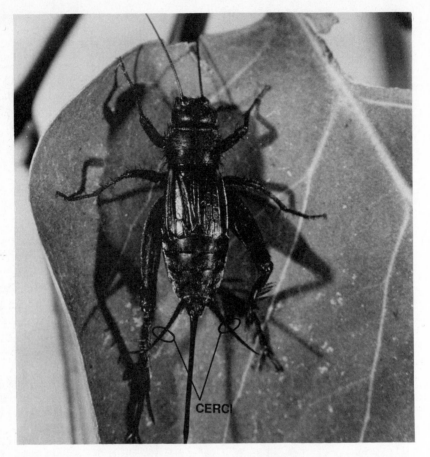

CERCI

Figure 2.6
Cricket cerci contain sensory "hairs" that detect air movement. Their location on the cricket is shown. Certain mutations cause the sensory hairs to disappear as the cricket ages. Consequently, the cricket does not jump away in response to air puffs.

Effectors   Effector tissues and organs, such as muscles and limbs, are those that are involved in the execution of behavior. Genetic differences that influence effectors will indirectly influence behavior.

Benzer (1971) describes a case in the fruit fly, *Drosophila*, in which the wings are constantly held straight up, rather than down to the side as is usual. This behavior was traced to one of the sets of muscles responsible for wing movement. Another example comes from a tiny round-worm. Some individuals fail to produce a coordinated series of muscle contractions that move them through the environment. This is due to an allele that affects myosin filaments, a protein component of muscle cells (Ward, 1977).

EVIDENCE OF GENETIC INVOLVEMENT IN BEHAVIOR

There is often considerable resistance to the notion that genes are involved in behavior, largely because the link between genes and behavior is poorly understood. Although we have reviewed the ways by which genes influence behavior, a review of the sorts of evidence used in behavior genetics is called for.

Single gene mutations Probably the most convincing evidence for genetic involvement in behavior comes from the effects of changing just one gene. If two animals are genetically identical except for one gene and if their environments are the same, any behavioral differences must be due to that single gene difference.

The effects of single gene mutation on behavior involve study of *inbred strains* of laboratory animals. Inbred strains are produced by allowing only brother–sister matings for at least 20 generations. If such a breeding program is successful (often the breeding "line" dies out), the individuals share 100% of their genes in common. Phenotypically, these individuals are as alike as identical human twins. Occasionally a mutation occurs in one of these strains that affects some aspect of anatomy, physiology, or behavior. When this happens the modified behavior pattern can be traced to the effects of the mutated single gene. Examples of single-gene mutations that affect behavior are common. One is known that changes the courtship "song" of male *Drosophila* (von Schilcher, 1977). Male fruit flies court females by approaching toward one side of her head, extending the wing closest to her, and rapidly flapping that wing. The resulting buzz is the courtship song. The female either moves away or accepts the male's advances. Males with altered songs due to a single mutation have more difficulty attracting females.

GREGOR MENDEL

"That no generally applicable law of the formation and development of hybrids has yet been successfully formulated can hardly astonish anyone who is acquainted with the extent of the task and the difficulties with which experiments of this kind have to contend. It requires a good deal of courage to undertake such a far-reaching task; however, this seems to be the one correct way of reaching the solution to a question whose significance for the evolutionary history of organic forms must not be underestimated." [Mendel, G. (1865/1966). Experiments on plant hybrids. In C. Stern & E. R. Sherwood (Eds.), The origin of genetics: A Mendel source book. *San Francisco: Freeman (p. 2).]*

Chapter 2 Genes, Environments, Development, and Behavior

Mendelian analysis Another method of investigating gene effects on behavior begins with behaviorally different animals. They are interbred in ways that permit us to decide whether the behavioral difference is due to a single gene difference. To understand this approach, we will quickly review Mendelian studies of genetics. Gregor Mendel performed his famous research on lines of peas that breed true for various traits such as round, smooth seeds or wrinkled seeds. ("Breed true" means that a mating between two individuals of the same phenotype produces progeny with that phenotype only.) When round-seeded and wrinkle-seeded plants were cross-bred, all the offspring had round seeds. When these were interbred, their offspring had about 75% round seeds and 25% wrinkled seeds. This is the expected result if one gene with only two alleles is involved. In this case, the allele that produces protein *R* is dominant over the allele that produces protein *r*. That is, if an individual has at least one *R*, all its seeds will be round. Only if it has two *r*'s will its seeds be wrinkled (Fig. 2-7).

Mendel's work was on plants and did not involve behavior. Can the same process occur in animal behavior? Definitely. In mice, a true breeding line of "waltzers" (a behavior condition in which the animal spends a good deal of time walking in circles while shaking the head) was bred with a line of nonwaltzers. None of the progeny waltzed. When the progeny were interbred, however, the usual 3 to 1 ratio (nonwaltzer to waltzer) was obtained. In this case the nonwaltzer allele was dominant over the waltzer allele (van Abeelen & van der Kroon, 1967).

Mendel's research has been both a blessing and a curse. It advanced our understanding of the mechanisms of inheritance, but it also instilled a deceptively simplistic notion of what genetic effects look like. Generations of genetics students have come to believe that genetic ef-

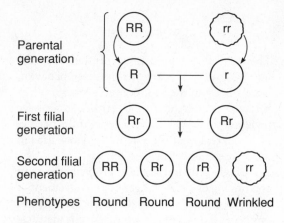

Parental generation

First filial generation

Second filial generation

Phenotypes Round Round Round Wrinkled

Figure 2.7
Mendelian analysis of a single gene for pea shape with two alleles is illustrated here. Two parents (top) homozygous for the two alleles, can contribute only that allele to their gametes (second row). However, all their offspring (first filial generation) will be heterozygous. Because heterozygous individuals can contribute either allele to their gametes, their offspring (second filial generation) will have four different genotypes. If one allele is completely dominant, their phenotypes will be of two types in the ratio of 3 to 1.

fects should be simple, categorical ones, and if a phenotype fails to match this expectation then the phenotype must not be "genetic." However, as we have seen, there is abundant evidence for environmental modification of gene activity and thus even genetically identical individuals are unlikely to be perfectly similar. Even Mendel accepted this (his round peas could be "roundish" according to his original report [see Plomin et al. (1980) for a translation]), so at the very least, minor phenotypic variation within categories should not be troublesome.

A more important issue, however, concerns the number of genes and alleles that influence a phenotype. Mendel worked with single gene effects and those genes typically had only two alleles each. But many genes can be involved in some aspect of the phenotype, and each of those genes may have many alleles. Therefore, when the combined effects of those genes and alleles are considered in populations of freely interbreeding organisms, the resulting distribution of phenotypes may not resemble in the least the simple categorical distributions that classic Mendelian analysis would lead us to expect.

Consider the following hypothetical case involving two genes with three alleles each. Assuming independent assortment, nine distinct genotypes are possible, as shown in Fig. 2-8. If the alleles have different effects on the phenotype, that is, if allele 1 of each gene produces 1 unit in the phenotype (say, body length in worms, in centimeters), allele 2 produces 2 units and allele 3 produces 3 units, the distribution of phenotypic units that would result from the nine genotypes is shown in Fig. 2-8. This exercise shows how a simple gene system can produce a normal distribution of phenotypes within a population. There are other ways to make this analysis match the continuously distributed phenotypes (such as height, weight, extraversion, or intelligence) with which we are familiar. One way is to increase the number of genes or the number of alleles, both of which increase the number of phenotypic categories. Another way is to remember that environmental effects on the phenotype will tend to blur the phenotypic categories, smoothing the distribution. Finally, for simplicity we assumed that alleles X1 and Y1 have equal impacts on the phenotype. That assumption certainly is not necessary and is probably unrealistic. In fact, the form of a phenotype may be strongly affected by one or two genes, and by the relatively small effects of several "modifier" genes.

The conclusion to draw from this exercise is that differences in behavioral phenotypes that are distributed in a continuous fashion rather than categorically can still be due, in large mea-

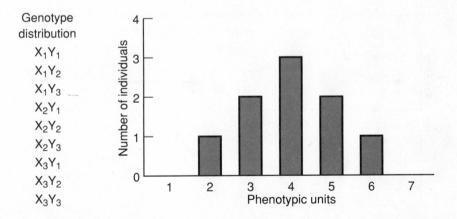

Figure 2.8
Mendelian genetics applies to two or more genes with two or more alleles each. Here, two genes (X and Y) each with three allele forms (1, 2, and 3) are illustrated. On the left, all possible combinations are listed. Each genotype has a phenotypic score associated with it. In this hypothetical case, X1 and Y1 produce 1 unit each; X2 and Y2 produce 2 units each; and X3 and Y3 produce 3 units each. In a population of nine individuals (one for each of the genotypes), one of five phenotypic unit scores is found. When plotted (right), their distribution is normal with an average score of four units.

sure, to individual differences in genetic materials. Mendelian analysis, when expanded to multiple alleles of several or many genes, can produce graded phenotypic distributions.

Hybridization experiments   Some pairs of species, when interbred, produce healthy offspring. If the parental species differ behaviorally, we can compare the hybrid offsprings' behavior with that of the parents. For example, a captive pair of gibbons, small Asian apes, consisting of a female whitehanded gibbon and a male Bornean gibbon, produced a hybrid daughter. Female gibbons are well known for their spectacular "great calls," fast-paced, booming songs given early in the morning, usually accompanied by wild swinging through the branches. Each species has a distinctive great call. The hybrid daughter's songs were intermediate to those of the parent species (Fig. 2-9). She could not have learned her song because the daughter had only her mother to listen to, and the males sing a completely different song (Tenaza, 1985). Other

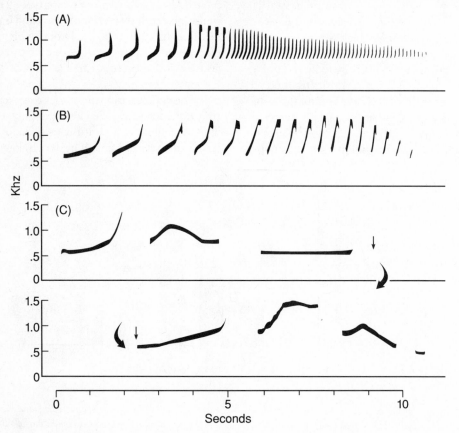

Figure 2.9
The "great calls" of female whitehanded and Bornean gibbons (A and C) are quite different. A female hybrid sang great calls (B) that were intermediate to those of the parental species. The arrows on C indicate where the call continues from one panel to the next.

gibbon species produce hybrid offspring, even in the wild, and they sing intermediate songs (Brockelman & Schilling, 1984). The hybrid offspring of other species have also been found to be intermediate to the parental species in their vocalizations. This is the case in frogs (Gerhardt, 1974), birds (Ficken & Ficken, 1967), and ground squirrels (Koeppl *et al.*, 1978).

A final example deals with "migratory restlessness" in birds. In the fall, birds in captivity that would normally migrate south for the winter become unusually active. Berthold and Querner (1981) found that the restlessness of blackcap warblers varied according to the distance migrated: Populations in northern Europe have farther to fly to their wintering grounds in Africa than do populations from southern Europe; an African population is nonmigratory. When they interbred blackcaps summering in Germany with ones summering in Africa, they found that the offspring were intermediate to the parents in fall restlessness. Because all the birds were maintained in captivity in a standard environment, the results can be attributed to genetic differences.

Selective breeding experiments If variation in a behavior has a genetic basis we should be able to breed for the trait in the same way that animal breeders select for egg-laying capacity in hens, or for weight gain in livestock. The logic of artificial selection experiments is simple: Breed a line of high-scorers for several generations, selecting the highest scoring individuals from each generation for mating. To be most convincing, however, one should also breed a low-scoring line, and a line of randomly chosen individuals. (The reason for breeding the other lines is to lessen the chance that an environmental change is producing the phenotypic change. If, during the course of the selective breeding experiment, the environment changed in a certain direction, the phenotypes of the animals might change, too, without a genetic change.) If the phe-

notypic differences between high-scorers and low-scorers are due to genetic differences, we should expect to find that their scores will diverge as generations of selective breeding continue. This is usually the outcome.

Numerous experiments of this sort have been performed on a wide variety of species, especially fruit flies and mice. An example is an experiment in which lines of mice were selected for high or low activity levels. After several generations of this breeding the lines diverged dramatically into active and lethargic groups (DeFries *et al.*, 1974).

The amount of time per night that male crickets spend calling has also been subjected to artificial selection. From a starting population that averaged about three hours of calling per night, Cade (1981) selected a line that spent a great deal of time calling, and another line that called only sparingly. In just a few generations the lines differed dramatically (Fig. 2-10).

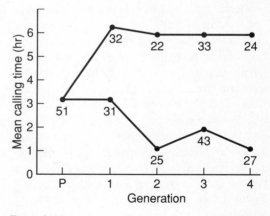

Figure 2.10
The amount of calling by male crickets is subject to artificial selection. Notice how quickly the two lines diverge. The numbers by each data point indicate the number of males who were scored that generation for the particular line.

Summarizing, several research procedures illustrate the link between genes and behavior. Interestingly, these procedures have produced results like those obtained on anatomic phenotypes. This should not be surprising. Behavior is a product of the animal's anatomy and physiology. Careful attention to the organisms subjected to selective breeding or hybridization studies, for example, are likely to yield indications of differences in neural anatomy or physiology.

Summary

This chapter covers the first phase of the genetic–evolutionary model: the development of individuals' phenotypes and the intertwined roles of genes and environment in this process.

Genes regulate the production of diverse proteins. The protein produced by a particular gene depends on the ordering of its DNA bases because the bases specify the sequence of amino acids that are strung together to form the protein molecule. Although each gene can produce only one kind of protein, the gene's action can be switched on and off by environmental conditions and by other genes. Slight environmental differences between cells lead them to develop different anatomic and physiologic properties. This cellular differentiation is central to organism development.

Various environmental conditions are known to influence the anatomical, physiological, and behavioral characteristics of organisms. Among these conditions are the physical environment (temperature, light, and so on), hormones, diet, social conditions, and individual experience.

Genes, environment, and the individual are engaged in a dynamic, reciprocally influencing system. To understand why an individual is the way it is, one would need to know the complex interplay that has gone on between genes, environment, and the organism throughout the individual's lifespan. This transactional approach to development accounts for both similarities and differences in phenotypic outcomes among individuals.

Differences in individuals' phenotypes are partly attributable to genetic differences among them, a concept known as heritability. Heritability is not a measure of genetic involvement in an individual's phenotype, but rather is a measure of how much of the differences between individuals' phenotypes is accounted for by their genetic differences.

Some phenotypic characteristics are highly influenced by the environment, others less so. The former are referred to as "open," the latter as "closed."

The products of gene activity can affect behavior through several routes. These include influences on the anatomy and physiology of the nervous system, modifications of the sensitivity and tuning of sensory systems, and the structure and action of effector systems such as muscles and limbs.

Four forms of evidence for the role of genes in behavior were presented. These include: (1) the effects of single gene mutations, (2) Mendelian analysis of behavioral differences, (3) studies of hybridization in which different species or different populations of a species are interbred and the hybrid offsprings' behavior compared to that of the parental species, and (4) selective breeding experiments in which high- and low-scoring lines are produced. All these forms of evidence provide compelling reasons to accept the link between genes and behavior.

Recommended Readings

DIXON, L. K., & JOHNSON, R. C. (1980). *The roots of individuality: A survey of human behavior genetics.* Monterey, CA: Brooks/Cole.

EHRMAN, L., & PARSONS, P.A. (1981). *Behavior genetics and evolution.* New York: McGraw-Hill.

OYAMA, S. (1985). *The ontogeny of information: Developmental systems and evolution.* New York: Cambridge University Press.

PLOMIN, R., DEFRIES, J. C., & MCCLEARN, G. E. (1980). *Behavioral genetics: A primer.* San Francisco: W. H. Freeman.

VALE, J.R. (1980). *Genes, environment, and behavior: An interactionist approach.* New York: Harper & Row.

Chapter 3

MECHANISMS OF BEHAVIOR

In the preceding chapter we saw that a wide variety of variables, such as genes, external environmental features, and hormones can influence the developmental processes that contribute to individual differences in behavior. But to understand behavior we need to understand, at a more proximal level, the *mechanisms* that produce it. Metaphorically, organisms are living machines, and one of the outputs of such machines is behavior.

If we wish to understand the actions of a nonliving machine such as a clock, we would be only partially satisfied if our investigation were limited to its raw materials and manufacturing procedures. We would also want to study the internal workings that make the hands move as they do, chime each hour, and so on. In short, the second component of the genetic–evolutionary model of behavioral biology is concerned with the workings of the body-machine that contribute to behavior.

What Is Behavior?

Before we can really begin a consideration of behavioral mechanisms, we need to consider what is meant by the word "behavior." **Behavior** refers to any movement or posture produced by an individual animal that influences the animal's relationship to its environment. Thus, a turn of the head is a behavior, but a beat of the heart is not. Speaking, walking, and nest-building are behaviors, but digestion, thinking, and hearing are not. Behavior, then, is intimately concerned with the activities of muscles. Movements of the entire body relative to the surrounding environment and of limbs and appendages relative to the rest of the body are brought about by contractions and relaxations of various muscle groups. Postures also involve muscular activities, but they are of the sort that resists the pull of gravity or the push of wind or water. In other words, although postures do not involve movement, they are active processes relative to the surrounding environment and are therefore behavioral (Reed, 1982).

If behavior consists of movements and postures brought about by patterns of muscular contraction, then why doesn't behavioral science just focus on muscle physiology? The answer lies in the fact that numerous nonbehavioral processes influence the emission of behavior. Memory of a previous event, detection of a strange odor, and changes in the concentration of oxygen in the bloodstream may all influence an animal's behavior. These and many other processes are part of the causal conditions, both internal and external, that influence the behavior of animals. As such, it is imperative that behavioral scientists study the relationships between such processes and behavior.

Systems of Behavioral Mechanisms

Most behavioral scientists would agree that we know more about the mechanisms of behavior than we know about behavioral development, adaptive significance, or evolution. This is probably because mechanisms occur closer in time to the behavior of interest and therefore are more readily studied than are the other three elements of behavioral science. For instance, in studying the behavior of wolves who hear the howls of a neighboring pack, we can relate their responses to such variables as the location of the howling pack within its territory, whether the pack that hears the howling has recently made a kill, weather conditions, and so on (Harrington & Mech, 1979). Although field work on wolves is no simple task to say the least, it would be even more difficult and time consuming to relate responses to howls to reproductive success (adaptation), or to investigate the important conditions during the lives of individual wolves that affect the ways that they respond to howls (development). Although development, adaptation, and evolution are as important as mecha-

Communication among wolves seems a simple enough behavior, but it is a complex process influenced by both proximate mechanisms (e.g., the presence of other wolves in its territory, weather conditions, and so on) and ultimate mechanisms (e.g., adaptation). However, we know more about how proximate mechanisms influence such behavior than we do about its evolution and development.

nisms to our comprehension of behavior, the fact remains that we know more about mechanisms than about the other three elements of behavioral science.

AN OVERVIEW OF
BEHAVIORAL MECHANISMS

Classifying the diverse mechanisms of behavior is no simple task. The scheme depicted in Fig. 3-1, however, is a good place to start. The major elements of the figure include (a) the external and internal stimuli that affect the organism, (b) the sensory systems that detect, filter, and enhance the stimuli, (c) integrative systems that compare and contrast sensory inputs, learn and

remember, motivate, think, and make decisions, and (d) the motor or effector systems, such as muscle contractions, that produce movement or change postures, and nonmuscular physiological systems such as glandular secretions, digestion, and respiration, that can affect behavior. Finally, behavior results in some proximal consequences for the organism, such as a change in its location or orientation, the acquisition of various "commodities" (food, water, and so on) or stimulation (an attack by a predator, escape from adverse weather conditions). These proximal consequences change the array of stimuli to which the sensory systems are exposed, beginning the cycle over again. In brief, behavioral mechanisms consist of those processes that influence the way that individual animals initiate, maintain, and change their behavior.

Although the "flow" (solid arrows) depicted in the diagram is from stimulus reception to behavior and back again, there are some important feedback processes (dashed lines) embedded within this network. Integrative systems can have direct feedback on the sensory systems. An animal that gets a whiff of a predator may not only respond by increasing its behavioral vigilance (a decision made by integrative systems), but its sensory organs themselves may become temporarily more sensitive. Similarly, one type of integrative process may affect others. Remembering a previous experience may affect that individual's decisions about what to do. Finally, movement will not only change the sorts of stimuli to which the animal is exposed, but it may also change the organism's integrative systems. For example, a behavior may result in a stimulus change that is beneficial to the organism and this behavior–consequence association may be remembered. Further, execution of a behavior may affect the sensory systems. For example, sexual behavior tends to change hormonal secretions that can modify the sensory

Systems of Behavioral Mechanisms

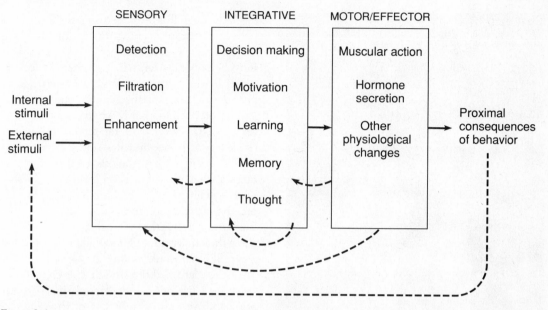

Figure 3.1
The mechanisms of behavior consist of three main components (sensory, integrative, and motor/effector systems) and their feedbacks. Sensory systems detect, filter and sometimes enhance stimuli. Integrative sys- *tems process sensory information along with other information stored in memory. Motor and effector systems execute movement and hormone changes. Movement changes the stimuli that impinge on the organism, thereby changing behavior.*

systems, changing their sensitivity to certain stimuli (Gandelman, 1983). The various patterns of influence within the elements of behavioral mechanisms are indicated in Fig. 3-1 with arrows. You may find it valuable to take an example of behavior and work through the mechanism system to better appreciate its features.

The goal of this chapter is to explain, in general terms, the nature of behavioral mechanisms. The details of how some of these mechanisms work will be explained in later chapters. For example, the workings of the nervous system are extremely important to behavior. This chapter only briefly reviews the "nuts and bolts" of neural processes, although enough, I hope, to provide a feel for the ways that nervous systems operate. A more detailed, thorough treatment

appears in Chapter 5. Similarly, sensory, motor, and integrative systems receive one chapter each (6, 7, and 8, respectively). Mechanisms receive attention in all the other chapters as well.

BEHAVIORAL MECHANISMS: OPENING THE BLACK BOX

A controversy exists about the sorts of mechanisms that should be studied to further our understanding of behavior. One perspective, most forcefully espoused by Skinner (1987), advocates restricting our investigations of behavioral mechanisms to those which can be observed directly by the scientist. Thus, using terms found in Fig. 3-1, Skinner and others claim that we

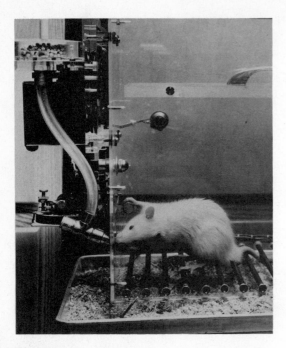

Is this rat pressing the lever because of a particular re-inforcement history or because it is hungry? Which explanation provides the more useful explanation of the animal's behavior?

Although it is possible to create a science of behavior without opening the organismic black box, Skinner's position is not very popular with most behavioral scientists. Consider the following example. Suppose that a rat has learned to press a lever to obtain food pellets, and that lever presses produce food only when a small light is on above the lever. The rat sometimes presses the lever and sometimes does not. Its lever pressing is partly under stimulus control (i.e., it presses when the light is on but rarely does so when the light is off). But even when the light is on, the rat does not always press the lever. Further study reveals that if much time has elapsed since the rat last ate, it is more likely to press the lever. Skinner would claim the task is complete: We have identified the stimuli that control the behavior (light and time elapsed since the rat ate), and we know the history of the relationships between these conditions, behavior, and consequences. Would a physiological notion of "hunger" add anything to our knowledge? Would anything be gained by invoking concepts such as motivation, thought, or decision-making?

The answers to such questions depend on one's orientation. To some, nothing is gained because they add unnecessary, unobservable concepts to what can be explained by readily observed phenomena. For instance, the scientist does not directly observe hunger or motivation, only feeding behavior. However, I feel that such concepts, although sometimes difficult to study, are necessary for a complete understanding of behavior. To follow up on our example, the mere passage of time is not adequate to account for lever-pressing and feeding by the rat, although it may be so in the artificial confines of the laboratory cage. In the real world, the passage of time is complicated by what occurs during that time. Did the sun set, did the rat nurse her pups, or get chased by a predator? The expenditure of energy

should only study external stimuli, behavior, and the consequences of behavior, including the influences that these three components have on one another. This perspective does not deny the existence of internal, physiological processes, but instead suggests that they do not further our understanding of behavior. According to this approach, if one can accurately *predict* the behavior of an animal by knowing what it has done before, what the stimulus circumstances were when it behaved, and the consequences of its behavior, the behavioral scientist's job is complete. Skinner's position treats the organism's internal workings as something of a "black box" which need not be opened in order to understand behavior.

will vary as a function of what happens during a particular time interval. Skinner's perspective would have to add these and many other variables in order to predict the rat's behavior with appreciable accuracy. When these additional variables are added and measured, I doubt that the system is any simpler than what we have with such concepts as motivation and decision-making. In the final analysis, perhaps it is more straightforward to use a physiological measure of the rat's energy reserves to predict its behavior than it is to try to measure so many variables that influence behavior through their effects on food reserves.

In conclusion, behavioral scientists should always strive to seek the simplest (most parsimonious) explanation for a phenomenon (as is true of other sciences as well), but a parsimonious explanation is without value if it fails to account for the whole phenomenon (Dunbar, 1980). In most cases we need to understand what is going on inside the organism to understand its behavior.

AN INTRODUCTION
TO NEUROPHYSIOLOGY

Although nervous systems are not required for behavior, as evidenced by the behavior of protozoa and plants, there is no doubt that the behavior of animals with nervous systems is considerably more varied than it is in species lacking nervous systems. And it is the nervous system to which we must turn to understand many of the mechanisms of behavior. In fact, because neural processes form the core of sensory, integrative, and motor systems, the basics of neurophysiology are presented here before we review these elements of behavioral mechanisms.

A typical neuron is illustrated in Fig. 3-2, where its most important parts are labeled. First, the *cell body* or *soma* is the part of the neuron that

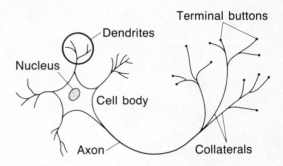

Figure 3.2
A typical neuron consists of a cell body, dendrites (which are specialized for the receipt of signals from other neurons), and an axon, which is specialized for sending signals.

contains the nucleus. The nucleus consists of the DNA that was discussed at length in Chapter 2, and is thus ultimately responsible for controlling the physiological processes of the cell. Second, projecting from the soma are two types of filaments. The more numerous, shorter branches are the *dendrites*, specialized for the reception of signals from other neurons. The other type of filament is a single *axon*, specialized for conveying signals to other neurons, or to muscles and glands. The axon may be short or extremely long, but is almost always longer than the dendrites. Some neurons in the giraffe's spinal cord have axons that stretch all the way to the animal's foot, a distance of two to three meters. Axons typically branch toward the terminal end (the end farthest from the cell body); these branches are known as *axon collaterals*. The collaterals often subdivide further with each filament ending in a single *terminal button*. Finally, the entire neuron, including the cell body, dendrites, and axon, is surrounded by a continuous membrane. Neurons differ in size and shape depending on where they are found in the nervous system and what they do. Some examples of neurons are illustrated in Fig. 3-3.

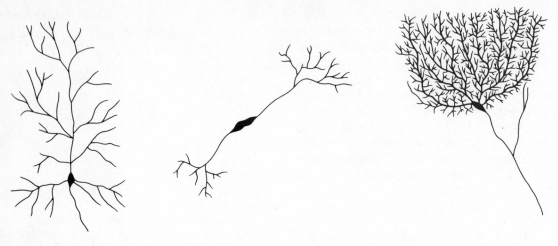

Figure 3.3
Neurons are highly varied in size and branching pattern. Several examples illustrate this variability.

What makes neurons so important to behavior is their ability to communicate with one another and with muscles and glands. They do this through electrical signaling. The chemical composition of the fluid inside the neuron's membrane (*cytoplasm*) differs from the fluid outside the membrane, the *extracellular fluid*. When a neuron is stimulated, either by another neuron or by a stimulus (such as light or pressure), chemicals from the extracellular fluid pass through the membrane into the neuron, and some pass through in the opposite direction a moment later. The movement of these electrically charged atoms or *ions* produces an electrical signal that moves rapidly along the axon toward the terminal buttons.

When the electrical signal, called an *action potential*, reaches a terminal button, a chemical *neurotransmitter* is released. The neurotransmitter molecules drift briefly in the extracellular fluid and some of them may contact the membrane of another neuron nearby. Depending on the type of neurotransmitter and the characteristics of the neuron that it contacts, the second

neuron may be stimulated to fire its own action potential, or it may be inhibited. The system consisting of a terminal button, the small space separating it from the next neuron, and the portion of the membrane on the receiving neuron that is adjacent to the terminal button is known as a *synapse*. Communication between neurons occurs at synapses.

Neurons communicate with nonneural cells in the same way. Because all cells are sensitive to certain chemicals, it is not surprising that neurotransmitters can be used to influence other cells. For instance, synapses occur on muscle cells. When an action potential reaches such a synapse, a neurotransmitter is released that causes the muscle cell to contract briefly. Similarly, synapses onto cells of the endocrine system may lead those cells to secrete certain hormones.

The interconnections of neurons with other neurons and with muscles and glands forms the core of behavioral mechanisms. Consider an example illustrated in Fig. 3-4. This hypothetical case involves a sensory neuron, let's say a temperature-sensitive neuron in the skin. When the temperature of the skin in the vicinity of the neuron reaches a certain level, the neuron initiates an action potential that moves swiftly along its axon, synapsing onto two other neurons. One of these neurons, when activated by the incoming action potentials, sends action potentials back out to the sensory neuron, inhibiting it. This inhibition would tend to reset the sensory neuron so that further heat will instigate another action potential. The other neuron controls two others that, in turn, are connected to some muscles in the vicinity of the sensory neuron. One set of these muscles, when contracted, causes the part of the body where the sensory neuron is located to move away from the heat source. The opposing group of muscles is prevented from contracting because the neuron that would cause them to contract has recently been inhibited. This example, which is far simpler than most real neurobehavioral systems, illustrates the role played by neurons in the control of behavior.

These few, basic ideas concerning neurophysiology will be expanded and clarified in Chapter 5. For now, it is sufficient to realize that the same basic processes occur in sensory, integrative, and motor systems. Our attention will now turn to each of those systems and to their roles in behavior.

SENSORY SYSTEMS

Our definition of behavior emphasized its relationship to the environment. Behavior operates on the environment, or at least changes the animal's relationship to the environment. It is not surprising, then, that animal behavior is greatly influenced by the environment and that systems exist for monitoring the environment. Investigation of sensory systems helps us understand why animals do what they do. Although there are numerous sensory systems that are

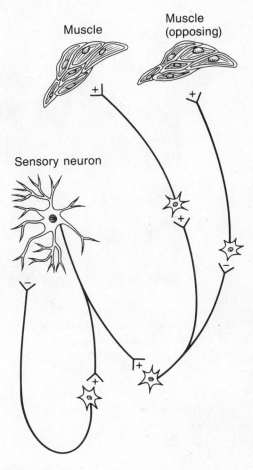

Figure 3.4
The connections that form among neurons and other cells, such as muscle cells, are fundamental to the production of behavior. In this example, a sensory neuron, when stimulated, sends action potentials along its axon, synapsing on two other neurons, generating action potentials in each of them. One of them inhibits the sensory neuron; the other influences two more neurons that produce muscle contractions. One of these last two neurons produces contractions in a muscle that opposes the other.

Sensory systems are specialized for detecting and enhancing sources of energy that are important for survival and reproductive success. The sensory systems of predators and their prey, for example, are good at detecting stimuli emanating from the other.

tuned to different forms of physical energy in the environment (light, sound, chemicals, and so on), our treatment of sensory systems will, for now, be restricted to what sensory systems do in a general sense. How they do these things will be covered in Chapter 6.

Transduction   *Transduction* is the process of converting one form of energy into another form. For instance, an electric blanket transduces electricity into heat. Sensory systems consist of specialized neurons that transduce various forms of physical energy into physiological activities such as action potentials. There are numerous *sensory modalities* that correspond to the type of physical energy that is transduced. Many of these modalities, such as vision, taste, and audition, are widespread in the animal kingdom. Others, however, are more restricted in their distribution. For example, some fishes can detect electric energy in the environment, and some birds can detect magnetic fields. The diverse ecological circumstances in which various species have evolved have led to equally diverse sensory systems.

Detection, filtration, and enhancement To the extent that sensory receptors can transduce even minimal levels of certain forms of energy, we say that the animal is sensitive to the stimulus. Shark olfaction (smell) is capable of detecting minute quantities of blood in water, and insect visual systems are extremely sensitive to movement (which makes flyswatting a nontrivial matter!). Sensory systems that are sensitive to certain forms of energy enhance the probability of stimulus detection. In some cases, detection is extremely important (e.g., predators by their prey), so those features of sensory systems that enhance detection are adaptive and the alleles that contribute to those features will tend to become more common in the population.

On the other hand, some sensory systems cannot detect certain forms of energy, or can detect them only at relatively high intensity levels. For example, although human vision is quite sensitive to a rather wide range of wavelengths (colors), we cannot detect ultraviolet light. Other species, such as honeybees, can do so. Sensory systems act as filters when certain forms of energy cannot be detected, or when they can only be detected when very intense. Stimulus filtering is also adaptive. The world (both inside and outside the organism) consists of a potentially overwhelming supply of potential stimuli, many of which are unimportant to the survival of the animal. Filtering out such extraneous stimuli helps control the amount of input such that the neural tissue can work more effectively on the more important forms of input. In the same way that forms of energy that are important to survival are capable of being detected even at very low intensity, forms of energy that are of lesser importance are filtered out. Stated differently, sensory systems are adaptively tuned to relevant forms of energy in the environment.

Finally, sensory systems sometimes act to enhance certain stimuli. When you look at a dark edge next to a light background, for instance, the *apparent* contrast exceeds the actual physical contrast (or difference) between the dark and light. In essence, the greater apparent contrast is constructed by the visual system. Similar constructive processes occur in other sensory systems and in other species. For instance, it appears that frogs' perception of moving insects is enhanced through processes that contrast dark and light edges and moving versus stationary features.

In sum, the world as it appears through the sensory systems is not an altogether faithful rendition of physical energy. Some aspects are "played up" and others are "played down." Nevertheless, this version of the world that is constructed by the sensory systems is what much of our behavior is directed toward. How sensory systems operate, then, is an important part of the study of behavioral mechanisms.

INTEGRATIVE SYSTEMS

Several important processes stand between sensory and motor/effector systems (in a functional sense) and coordinate their actions. Classifying these integrative systems is difficult because they are hopelessly interwoven. Some examples include such cognitive processes as decision-making, thought, learning and memory, and motivation. Of course, other categories could be identified, and each of these can be subdivided into several or many subprocesses. In fact, these processes, which are often called "modules," are thought to be involved in a wide variety of information-processing tasks. These modular systems can operate independently, but their actions are so coordinated that it is difficult to distinguish among them. Further, their operations are frequently not apparent even to the individual engaging in them (Kihlstrom, 1987).

As an example of such modular processes, consider a task in which a person is shown two letters and asked to decide whether the letters are the same or different. To complicate matters, the letters may be capital or lower case. This task is conducted by different parts of the brain depending on the stimuli. For instance, EE is quickly recognized as being the same, but Ee takes longer and calls other brain structures into action.

Posner *et al.* (1988) have pioneered the use of cognitive and neural research methods to localize these modules within the nervous system.

They point out that any cognitive task, such as reading or recalling a previous event, depends on many of these discrete modular processes acting in unison. We are far from knowing how many modules there are, or how they work. Therefore, the categories of integrative systems discussed below must be viewed as rather large sets of modules. Within each of them there are several or many subcategories, each of which may be divided again. In other words, there may be a hierarchy of integrative processes which nevertheless operate closely with one another.

Decision-making Suppose that a fox has recently killed a rabbit and is beginning to eat it when another fox approaches. Does the first fox continue to eat, or does it threaten its rival? This is a case of decision-making. Sensory inputs initiate processes that culminate in one of two or more mutually exclusive behaviors. Animals can emit a wide variety of behaviors, and they can orient or direct them in different ways (e.g., a hen can peck the hen on her right or on her left), and with different intensities. The amount of time spent engaging in various behaviors, and the effort and timing of these behaviors, are all elements of the decision-making process. These decisions seem to be based on stimuli currently acting on the organism (both internal and external) and on information gleaned earlier but stored in memory. Depending on the particular mix of these sources, the behavioral output of the animal varies. Going back to the example of the fox, if the rival is one that the fox has met and lost to before, it may relinquish its prize and run away. However, if the fox has not eaten in a long time, it may be more inclined to stay and defend its catch.

The term "decision-making" does not imply that animals use the same sorts of mechanisms that humans use in choosing among available options, or even that the same process is used in all decision-making contexts in a given species.

Motivation An integrative process related to decision-making is motivation, a catch-all term referring to processes that affect the probability, form, direction, or intensity of a certain behavior pattern. Behaviors that have previously succeeded in acquiring food are more likely to be performed, or are performed more vigorously, if one has not eaten in a long time. Motivation is an integrative process because it takes sensory input (which can arise from within the organism as well as from outside it) and then influences behavior in some fashion. Although we tend to infer motivation from the nature of the behavior that the individual emits, technically motivation has to do more with the totality of the individual's physiological status. Thus, although I may infer that my cat is thirsty because of the nature of his drinking behavior, thirst as a motive is best left to statements about the physiological status of the animal relative to its environmental context. The physiological status influences the probability of drinking, and its vigor and duration. The environmental context includes such variables as the availability of resources necessary to perform a behavior, and the presence or absence of conditions that may make other behaviors more useful at the moment. A sparrow that has had little to eat will emit food-searching behaviors until food is found, and will then switch to food consumption activities. It will not do so, however, if it detects a predator in the vicinity. The study of motivation is concerned with the interplay between certain physiological conditions and environmental variables that affect the profitability of certain behaviors.

Learning and memory As animals engage their environments, changes may occur in their nervous systems that may influence the way that the animal later behaves in similar circumstances. In many cases, the sort of interchange between the individual and the environment consists of the animal emitting a behavior followed by the receipt of some sort of consequence. For example, if a robin turns over a fallen leaf and discovers an earthworm, the robin may increase its probability of turning leaves. Consequences of behavior may also be aversive to the animal. A dog that scraps with a skunk may be hit with a spray of stinging fluid, and the dog may thereafter avoid skunks. In both cases, a behavior produced a consequence that altered the animal's subsequent behavior. There is ample evidence that the nervous system changes in subtle but important ways when learning occurs, that these changes can last for a very long time, and that these neural changes are the basis for the behavioral change (Squire, 1987; Alkon, 1988).

Learning and memory can also occur in the absence of overt consequences of behavior. For instance, mice learn the characteristics of complex mazes even when there is no apparent consequence for exploration (Brant & Kavanau, 1964), and you may cease noticing the household sounds that kept you awake for a few days after you moved to a new home. Again, changes in behavior occur as a result of interaction with the environment.

Although there are several forms of learning as defined by the nature of the interaction between the animal and its environment, they share the common element of a change in the organism that influences its subsequent behavior. Types of learning and the processes that occur in the nervous system that underlie memory are treated in more detail in Chapter 8.

Thought *Thought* is any self-contained activity of the nervous system of which one is aware. Self-contained means that thought does not depend on stimuli from the environment, although thought may be influenced by such stimuli. This provision distinguishes thought from the neural systems set in motion by sensory stimuli. Awareness is an agonizingly difficult concept to define or describe although we all know what it is. (Awareness is not the only such difficult term. Any privately perceived phenomenon is equally difficult. How would you define sweetness or pain without resorting to typical behavioral responses to them?) Many neural processes occur without our awareness, such as monitoring the concentrations of oxygen or glucose. These are important, but are not examples of thought.

Although there are behaviors that are often associated with thinking (just watch a class of college students taking an exam), like other integrative systems thought is a process that links stimulus reception with behavioral output, rather than a behavior *per se*.

If an organism's nervous system is such that it can manipulate information, make predictions about the consequences of certain actions, or recall important events from earlier in its life, the organism stands to gain. Cognitive psychologists study such activities, but it is important to note that they invariably use behavioral or neurophysiological measurements to investigate thought processes. Thought itself is not directly observable, but the behavioral change due to thought can be observed and it is this change that is used to infer thought processes.

There is probably no integrative system that is more controversial than thought. What is thought? What produces it? Do animals think? If they do, what form does it take? Donald Griffin (1976, 1984a, 1984b) has been a leader in the debate about animal thinking and awareness. He argues that because we do not directly observe thought in other humans, but only infer it from their behavior, when we observe "thoughtful" behavior in other animals we should be willing to accept the notion that a thought process can and does occur in other animal species. There is no claim that the nature

DONALD GRIFFIN

"The hypothesis that some animals are indeed aware of what they do, and of the internal images that affect their behavior, simplifies our view of the universe by removing the unparsimonious assumption that our species is qualitatively unique in this important attribute." [Griffin, D. R. (1976). The question of animal awareness: Evolutionary continuity of mental experience. *New York: Rockefeller University Press* (p. 101).]

of thinking is the same in all species; indeed, there is the possibility that thinking may change with age as it almost certainly does in humans after the acquisition of language.

A caution about integrative processes Although I disagree with Skinner's opinion about not opening the black box to investigate physiological processes associated with behavior, there is a way in which I must agree. That agreement concerns the need to avoid the temp-

tation to use integrative systems as a shortcut explanation for behavior. It is altogether too easy to attribute an animal's emission of a particular behavior to its decision-making apparatus or to its thought processes. Such claims are easy to make, but decidedly more difficult to investigate. Integrative system concepts are not meant to cover gaps in our understanding of behavior. They need to be studied directly and they need to be linked with sensory and motor processes.

MOTOR AND EFFECTOR SYSTEMS

Behavior Motor or effector systems are the output side of integrative and sensory systems. The most obvious of these processes is behavior itself, which was defined as self-produced movements or postures that change the animal's relationship to its environment. Behavior may affect the environment, as when a toad flicks out its tongue and captures an insect, or when a dog growls at an opponent that then retreats. But if behavior is heavily influenced by sensory and integrative systems, why is there so much emphasis placed on behavior? The pivotal position given to behavior is justified because it is *behavior* that operates on the environment, and thus influences survival and reproductive success. The most finely tuned sensory system, the fastest decision-making process, and the shrewdest thinking are all for naught if the individual does not *escape* from the detected predator, *capture* the chosen prey, or *build* the nest. Action is the essence of adaptation. Both sensory and integrative systems are in the service of behavior.

Two different and formerly adversarial scientific disciplines have championed the study of behavior. One of them, *ethology*, studied the naturally occurring behavior of animals under (usually) undisturbed conditions in the animal's

Behavior operates on the environment and thus is critical to an organism's survival and reproductive success. (Left) A male baboon directs a "threat yawn" toward a rival. (Below) Musk oxen protect themselves from predators by circling. (Above) A bear emerges with a salmon that it will soon consume.

native habitat. Ethologists attempted to describe and categorize the full range of behavior, and to understand behavioral evolution and its adaptive significance. Although some ethologists studied the development and mechanisms of behavior, the emphasis was on the other two components of the integrative model outlined in Chapter 1.

In contrast to the ethologists, *comparative psychologists* typically studied behavior in the confines of the laboratory. Although such conditions did not permit the richness of behavior that could occur in the field, the laboratory permitted investigations of development and mechanisms that could not be accomplished in the field (Timberlake, 1990). Careful control of the animal's environment permitted psychologists to study such phenomena as stimulus control, physiological processes of motivation, sensation, and so on. Although the two camps occasionally expressed their dissatisfaction with one another, it became clear that the two perspectives were complementary, not competitive. Today, it is difficult to distinguish between ethology and comparative psychology. Indeed, many behavioral scientists have argued that neither term does justice to the breadth of contemporary research in animal behavior and that both terms may carry historical "baggage" that is no longer appropriate. Thus, the more neutral term *animal behavior* is generally preferred, regardless of the discipline in which the researcher was educated (Snowdon, 1983).

Physiological systems   Many of the sensory and integrative systems that affect behavioral processes may also influence various physiological systems other than those that are strictly behavioral. For example, a form of stimulation that has reliably preceded feeding may come to alter the actions of the digestive system, or the odor of a prospective mate may change the amounts of certain hormones released into the bloodstream. These physiological systems may then influence behavior and, of course, behavior itself may affect these other systems. Feeding results in food coming into the digestive system which will modify its activity, for instance.

Consideration of the full range of physiological systems that are not strictly behavioral is beyond the scope of this chapter. Instead, let's focus on one system, the endocrine system, that has long been of interest to behavioral scientists. Hormones are chemicals secreted by cells that affect cells elsewhere in the body. Such intercellular communication is ancient and influences many physiological processes, including behavior.

Hormones affect behavior in three ways. *Organizational effects* are those that influence the developing structure of the organism in long-lasting ways. Testosterone, for instance, influences the development of the sex organs and parts of the nervous system responsible for sexual behavior. Organizational effects of hormones were discussed in Chapter 2.

Our concern with hormones in this chapter is with their two roles in activating behavior, roles known as *priming and feedback effects.* That is, hormones often prime the organism for responding to certain stimuli, and they may be released following behavior or other stimulation and in this way modify subsequent behavior. Some of the ways that hormone secretion occurs during or around the time of behavior are discussed by Leshner (1979). Their relationships to one another and to behavior are illustrated in Fig. 3-5. Before we discuss them, however, let us briefly review how hormones affect the nervous system, because it is the nervous system that is the most proximal director of behavior.

There are several ways in which hormones can affect behavior by influencing the physiological conditions of neurons (Gandelman, 1984). First, hormones influence neurons by acting directly on neuronal membranes. For instance, hormones may affect the sensitivity of neurons to neurotransmitters, and the capacity of neurons to produce neurotransmitters (Wingfield *et al.*, 1987). These hormones sometimes have fast-acting but brief neuronal effects (lasting only seconds), through to effects that have slow onsets but which are long-lasting (hours or days).

Hormones may also affect neural activity by altering neuronal gene expression (McEwen, 1981). Because neurotransmitter receptors are made of protein, it follows that modification of the genes involved in receptor–protein synthesis can affect neural functioning. Of course, this mode of action takes longer than direct action on the membranes.

Hormones can also influence nonneural tis-

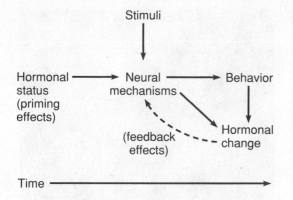

Figure 3.5
The activating roles of hormones occur before and after behavior. The baseline hormonal state influences neural mechanisms, which therefore affects the way the nervous system responds to a certain stimulus; the behavioral response will therefore vary. This part of the system is called the priming effect of a hormone. Activation of a behavior or a neural system may produce a hormonal response that in turn may affect the neural system, and therefore behavior.

sues that may indirectly influence behavior. Several effects of hormones on sensory systems are known, for instance. In male rats, testosterone maintains penile spines (Fig. 3-6), microscopic projections that are probably involved in tactile sensation (Phoenix *et al.*, 1976). In females, including humans, olfactory and visual sensitivity are known to wax and wane with hormonal changes associated with the ovulatory cycle (Gandelman, 1983). Presumably these sensory changes make certain forms of stimulation more salient or more rewarding, thus influencing behavior.

Let us return now to the priming and feedback effects of hormones. When hormone concentrations change, as they do, for instance, when day length increases in the spring, the nervous system's sensitivity to various stimuli increases, tending to modify the type of behavior or its strength or duration. Such hormonal changes that occur for reasons other than the emission of a particular behavior are called *priming effects*. For example, female cowbirds in the spring have increased levels of estrogen, secreted by their ovaries. When so primed, they are likely to respond to male song by assuming the species-typical copulatory posture (West *et al.*, 1981). Similarly, the hormonal changes that occur at birth in female rats makes them respond to the distress calls of newborn pups. Without these hormonal changes, adult female rats typically ignore these calls (Bridges *et al.*, 1985). Both of these examples involve hormonal changes that precede certain forms of behavior, and exert their influence by altering the animal's perception of certain stimuli.

In some cases, when an animal engages in a behavior or is subjected to certain forms of stimulation, its hormone concentrations may change. For example, male birds on their breeding territories respond aggressively to the songs or approaches of other males. This behavior leads to increased amounts of testosterone, which, in turn, makes the males even more prone to aggression (Wingfield *et al.*, 1987). Similarly, we have all been in situations in which a startling or frightening event produces a surge in the release of adrenalin (epinephrine), leading to rapid heart rate, dryness of the mouth, and so on. Following the epinephrine release, we are unusually sensitive to all sorts of otherwise innocuous stimuli. In both cases, the release of the hormone *followed* certain behaviors or stimuli, and these changes influenced the sorts of behaviors emitted afterwards. So, although one might see such changes as having something of a priming effect, the cause of the initial hormone change relative to the stimuli that provoke behavior differs from that in priming.

Figure 3.6
Hormones may affect behavior by modifying sensory systems. These photographs illustrate the effect of testosterone on penile spines in male rats. The photo- *micrograph on the left shows the well-developed spines of a male rat with normal amounts of testosterone. On the right, the surface of a castrated male rat's penis shows the absence of spines.*

Behavioral Disorders

Our primary concern throughout this book is with the normal adaptive behavior of animals. Nevertheless, we will occasionally inquire about forms of behavior that are clearly not in the individual's best interests. Many scientists study such abnormalities, particularly in humans, and treating these disorders occupies much of the time of some psychologists, psychiatrists, and neurologists. Although the humanitarian aspects of treating behavioral disorders clearly justifies the effort expended on them, we can also gain insights into normal behavior through studies of abnormal behavior.

WHAT ARE BEHAVIORAL DISORDERS?

Some conditions may impair an individual's ability to cope with reasonable demands placed upon it. Whether such conditions are called diseases, disorders, pathologies, or injuries, their underlying commonality is their impairment of coping (survival) ability. Behavioral disorders, then, are ones that reduce coping because of their impact on behavior, broadly defined to encompass not only movement, but also sensory and integrative systems.

By this definition, then, a person who walks with a limp due to an ankle sprain has a behavioral disorder. So does one who walks with a limp because of having too little of the neurotransmitter responsible for initiating movement or muscle contractions. And so does one who walks with a limp because she has found that others give her lots of attention and sympathy when she walks this way. But most people would not be comfortable labeling all of these as behavioral disorders. The first person has something wrong with her ankle; the second person has something wrong with her nervous system; and the third has something "wrong" with what she has learned. Clearly, the treatments that would be appropriate for the three cases would be vastly different. They are all behavioral disorders, however, although their causes are quite different.

Traditionally, behavioral disorders (or mental disorders) were limited to those states that had no organic basis that could be identified. By organic, we mean anatomical or physiological processes. The ankle injury and the neurotransmitter deficiency cases above would be considered to have organic bases; the learning problem case would not. For most of the history of medicine, the organic bases of behavioral disorders, especially of those, such as schizophrenia or depression, that impaired thought or emotional processes were unknown. Because they were unknown, they were sometimes relegated to supernatural powers such as demons or ghosts, and were therefore considered incurable. One by one, however, medicine and psychology have discovered organic bases for many of these problems. Now, instead of offering incantations to rid the person of the demon inside, chemicals that help restore functional levels of neurotransmitters are taken that are ever so much more humane and effective (Berger, 1978; Snyder, 1984b).

DISORDERS AS INSIGHTS INTO MECHANISMS

In the same way that diagnosing and fixing a malfunctioning automobile can enhance one's understanding of the way engines work, the diagnosis and treatment of behavioral disorders has furthered our understanding of normal behavior. Two examples will help to clarify this concept.

Parkinson's disease is characterized by muscle tremors and difficulty initiating movement. Something as simple as reaching over to pick up a coffee cup is very difficult for a person with Parkinson's disease because of the trouble in be-

ginning the movement and in completing it successfully. For many years, Parkinson's patients were placed in mental hospitals or nursing homes where nothing could be done about the condition. However, work on the disease revealed that the problem was with a neurotransmitter, dopamine (Hornykiewicz, 1966). Specifically, there was too little dopamine, and this was due to too little of an enzyme involved in its synthesis. Bypassing the missing enzyme was found to be possible by giving the patient the substance that the enzyme normally produced. In this way, dopamine rose to more appropriate levels, initiation of movement problems declined, and the person could resume a more

MICHAEL GAZZANIGA

"An emerging view is that the brain is structurally and functionally organized into discrete units or 'modules' and that these components interact to produce mental activities." [Gazzaniga, M. S. (1989). *Organization of the human brain.* Science **245,** 947–952 (p. 947).]

normal life (with continued medication, however).

The information about movement initiation that was obtained through investigations of Parkinson's disease has contributed enormously to our understanding of normal movement patterns. With the neurotransmitter identified, studies of the neural systems of movement were facilitated.

Gazzaniga (1989) has used studies on humans who sustained brain damage to investigate the modular organization of integrative systems mentioned earlier. *Neuropsychology* investigates the relationships between brain disorders and behavioral abnormalities. Neuropsychologists, then, are in a position to notice when a module is impaired, and therefore to investigate the modular organization of the brain. For instance, Gazzaniga reports on a woman who, after suffering a stroke, was unable to name the color of red fruits, but who could name the color of other fruits and even name the color "red" when it appeared on other nonfruit objects. Our knowledge of such specific disorders is meager, but with advances in neuropsychology and neurology, they should help us understand the functional organization of the brain. Studies of normal behavior and of behavioral disorders will no doubt continue to have mutually advantageous effects.

Summary

Behavior is defined as any form of self-generated movement or posture of an animal that changes the animal's relation to its environment. Although this definition is somewhat narrow due to its restriction to movement, it does not restrict the behavioral sciences just to movement. Rather, many other processes that are not strictly behavioral contribute to our understanding of behavior.

The mechanisms of behavior are those processes that are involved in production and regulation of behavior. These processes are classified into three main groups: Sensory systems receive, filter and sometimes enhance stimuli in the external environment and from inside the organism. Integrative systems, such as decision-making, motivation, learning and memory, and thought, use sensory information and stored information in coordinating sensory inputs with behavioral output. Finally, motor/effector systems include behavior itself, and various physiological processes such as hormone secretions. Sensory, integrative, and motor systems involve neural processes. Some of the basics of neurophysiology are reviewed briefly.

Although most behavior patterns and the processes that generate them are adaptive to the organism, some are not. Behavioral disorders are conditions that reduce the individual's ability to cope with normally occurring demands. Behavioral disorders need to be studied not only to facilitate their treatment, but also because they can increase our understanding of normal behavior patterns.

Recommended Readings

COLGAN, P. (1989). *Animal motivation.* New York: Chapman and Hall.

GOLDSTEIN, E. B. (1984). *Sensation and perception.* Belmont, CA: Wadsworth.

LEAHEY, T. H., & HARRIS, R. J. (1989). *Human learning.* Englewood Cliffs, NJ: Prentice Hall.

LESHNER, A. I. (1978). *An introduction to behavioral endocrinology.* New York: Oxford University Press.

SHEPHERD, G. M. (1988). *Neurobiology.* New York: Oxford University Press.

SLATER, P. J. B. (1985). *An introduction to ethology.* London: Cambridge University Press.

Chapter 4

THE ADAPTIVE SIGNIFICANCE AND EVOLUTION OF BEHAVIOR

Animals spend every moment of their lives in intercourse with their environments. The environment is diverse, consisting not only of physical variables such as temperature and wind, but also a whole host of biological conditions such as predators, competitors, and foods. In many respects, these environmental conditions can be seen as "problems" that may adversely affect survival and reproduction. Numerous characteristics help animals deal with environmental problems. Cryptic coloration helps avoid predation, and sharp senses help the individual acquire food. Behavior can be of great importance in dealing with environmental problems. Shelter-seeking helps counter the difficulties posed by inclement weather, bluffing an opponent may mean acquiring a scarce food resource, and caring for the body surface may remove parasites that carry disease. Behavior, being quick to change, is of critical importance in dealing with environmental conditions which themselves can change in an instant. Behavior, then, is of great adaptive significance.

Individuals differ in the degree to which they solve their environmental problems. Although one could measure success by means of longevity (an individual that dies in old age being more successful than another that dies earlier in life), there is a good reason to use a different measure, namely, reproductive success. Each offspring that an individual leaves carries some of the parent's genes. These genes contributed (along with many environmental conditions) to the development of the anatomical, physiological,

and behavioral features that led to the parent's reproductive success. In other words, because of individual differences in reproductive success, some genes (and the phenotypes that they influence) will become more common, and other genes and phenotypes less common. Individual differences in reproductive success are the raw material for evolution.

This chapter will discuss the primary elements of the study of adaptation and evolution, the last two components in the genetic–evolutionary model. We treat them together because they are so closely interrelated. An animal is adapted to its environment due, in large measure, to the genes that it inherited from its ancestors, its evolutionary lineage. Further, to the extent that the animal reproduces, it influences its offspring, their offspring, and so on. Each individual animal stands as a bridge linking the evolutionary past with the future.

Adaptation

The study of adaptation seeks to understand the relationship between features of the animal, its environment, and reproductive success. Out of the lifelong process of dealing with the environment, the individual animal has some degree of reproductive success, ranging from none at all to a great deal (relative to others of its species). We can therefore ask two questions about adaptation. First, what are the environmental problems facing an animal species? Second, how do characteristics of the animal contribute to solving environmental problems as measured by reproductive success? These questions are illustrated in Fig. 4-1.

METHODS OF STUDYING ADAPTATION

The study of behavioral characteristics that contribute to adaptation is a rapidly growing field. *Behavioral ecology,* as this field is known, scarcely existed a few decades ago. Now, behavioral ecology is growing rapidly (see, for example, texts by Krebs & Davies, 1987, and Morse, 1980). There are three basic methods employed in studying the adaptive value of behavior, the same methods used in studying the adaptive value of nonbehavioral features (Curio, 1973).

Correlational method At the heart of this method is the notion that phenotypic traits are, in effect, solutions to environmental problems. If we can identify a gradient of some problem, we should expect to find a gradient of solutions to

the problem. For example, canids (dogs, wolves, foxes, and so on) prey on many different species ranging from very small (mice, insects) to extremely large (moose, bison). The size of the canids does not vary over nearly so great a range (the smallest foxes and the largest wolves are much more similar in body size than are their prey, mice and moose). Canids adapt to such different prey by hunting in groups to bring down large animals. The larger the body size of the prey species, the greater the number of animals in the canid's pack. Wolves, who frequently prey on large animals, live in large packs; foxes, who prey on small animals, tend to live in pairs and frequently hunt alone. Other species are intermediate (MacDonald, 1983). This is an example of an *interspecific correlation* because different species are used in the analysis. Although distantly related species may be used in such comparisons, a better approach is to work with a set of closely related species, preferably members of the same genus (Jarman, 1982). In canids, an analysis of prey size and pack size has been conducted on jackals. The same relationship that

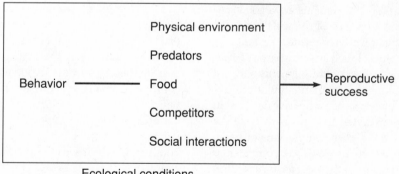

Figure 4.1
Adaptation is concerned with the "fit" between the organism and the environmental conditions in which it exists. The fit is measured by the organism's reproductive success. These conditions act as "filters" or obstacles to reproductive success. Individual differences exist in how well these filters are handled.

Canids that prey on large animals tend to hunt cooperatively in large packs, as these wolves have done. Canids that prey on smaller animals hunt in smaller packs or individually.

was found in the canids in general was noted in the jackals (Moehlman, 1987).

We can apply the correlational method to populations of a species residing in ecologically diverse circumstances. Humans are a good species for such work because of the wide variety of habitats in which we have resided for long periods. An example of such an *intraspecific correlation* in humans concerns skin pigmentation and ultraviolet (UV) light. Human populations living in high UV regions typically have darker skin than populations living in areas with less UV. This explains the darker complexions of equatorial peoples and the lightening of complexions in peoples farther from the equator (Quevedo *et al.*, 1985). UV light is known to break down folate, a vitamin necessary for maintaining pregnancy. Melanin, the primary component of human skin pigmentation, helps block the entry of UV light through the skin (Branda & Eaton,

1978), thereby reducing folate loss and enhancing reproductive success. Thus, population differences in skin pigmentation appear to be adaptive given variations in UV light.

To reiterate, the correlational methods measure two variables: an ecological variable (such as prey size or UV light) and a phenotypic variable (such as pack size or skin pigmentation) that, in theory, is an adaptation to the ecological condition. However, correlational results can never be used to infer that the environmental variable caused the evolution of the phenotypic variable. No significant correlation, even when combined with other relevant information, can prove that varieties of the phenotypic variable were caused by variations in the ecological condition. However, if that causal connection were true, we would expect them to be correlated. The correlational technique, then, is a good "first test" of the hypothesis that an ecological condition caused the evolution of genes that influence an adaptive phenotype.

Experimental method   The only way to determine cause and effect is to manipulate either the phenotypic characteristic or environmental condition and then measure the effect of the manipulation. For example, flocking in birds is thought to aid in predator avoidance. The idea is that having more eyes and ears helps detect predators sooner, thus giving the birds greater opportunity for escape. This suggested an experiment in which 1, 5, or 10 starlings were placed in an aviary over which, without warning, a stuffed hawk was "flown" on a wire. As expected, the larger the flock, the faster the hawk was detected (Powell, 1974). This has been confirmed in field experiments on other birds and mammals (Harvey & Greenwood, 1978).

As a second example, McKillup (1983) noticed that some individuals of an Australian intertidal snail twisted their shells from side to side when they contacted another snail. To find out if twisting aided snails in crowded conditions, McKillup placed snails together in aquaria. Some aquaria had a single small food source but others had the same total amount of food scattered in several locations. Twisters grew faster and lived longer than did nontwisters in the single food-source condition, but the two types did equally well in the distributed food condition. The conclusion was that food distribution patterns (an ecological condition) affected the survival and reproductive success of snails, with restricted distributions favoring snails with the "twister" behavioral phenotype.

Optimality method   The third method in the study of adaptation takes a fundamentally different perspective. First, a selection problem is defined precisely. Second, the best or optimal solution is devised. Finally, the species faced with the problem is studied to ascertain whether its behavior corresponds to the "designed behav-

ior." To the extent that it does, we conclude that the behavior is an adaptation to the problem.

For example, if a bird species that feeds on berries has many bushes to explore for food, an optimal solution to the problem of obtaining berries efficiently is to devote time to bushes in proportion to the yield of the bush. A bird should spend twice as much time in a bush with 200 berries as it does in one with 100 berries, for instance. Many animals that forage in discrete patches allocate their foraging time in this way, leading to the conclusion that matching persistence in a patch to the food value of a patch is an adaptation to varying patch quality (Pyke *et al.*, 1977).

Quite often, the proposed optimal behavior may not match the observed behavior. This could be because the animal is coping with two or more opposing problems. For instance, efficient foraging may conflict with watching for predators so a pure solution to either problem may not be possible, and the optimal behavior may be some compromise between them. If the observed behavior does not match the prediction, the researcher should redefine the problem and collect a new set of data (Lewontin, 1979).

In summary, correlational, experimental, and optimality analyses, applied in numerous and diverse cases, have led to the identification and understanding of numerous adaptations in many species. Because of the availability of these techniques we should not be content with armchair speculation, however clever, about the adaptive significance of any phenotypic trait. All of these techniques will be used in later chapters for analyzing adaptations.

IS EVERYTHING ADAPTIVE?

Nature is replete with wonderful adaptations: Insects that look like sticks or leaves, marine mammals that can stay submerged for many minutes without resurfacing, hawks that can see the scurrying of a mouse in the grass hundreds of feet below, and the complex societies of some insects and primates are just a few of the many examples. When we see these adaptations, especially when they are juxtaposed to our knowledge that natural selection is always continuing its relentless removal of relatively ill-suited forms, it becomes tempting to slip into the notion that everything we see in nature is adaptive, otherwise it would have been eliminated long ago. However, this sort of reasoning is circular: A trait exists today because it is adaptive, and it must be adaptive because it exists. The way out of the circular trap is not to equate existence with adaptiveness. We must instead ask "Is this trait adaptive?", and be fully prepared to answer "no" in some cases.

Not all existing traits are adaptive. Some are definitely maladaptive. The following section reviews some reasons why maladaptive features may persist despite their often detrimental effects on reproductive success.

Changes in selection conditions We must not succumb to the idea that evolution was something that happened a long time ago but which has now ceased. Natural selection is always operating, even on humans, so traits with negative consequences may be in the process of elimination. If we could observe long enough, we might witness total elimination of the maladaptive phenotypic feature.

Environmental conditions do not remain constant. The climate may go through long cycles of temperature change, new predators may appear, and so on. Ecological conditions probably change faster than the populations they influence, so traits in existence today may be maladaptive in today's selection conditions, but may have been adaptive some time ago. Natural selection and evolution take time and populations are nearly always behind the times in terms of their adaptations.

Geographic variation in selection conditions Species that occupy a widespread range may be subjected to somewhat different selection conditions in different parts of the range. If there is movement of individuals from one area to another, they may be ill-suited for the new conditions. For instance, the common mussel has a physiological mechanism for coping with water salinity. This mechanism is directly tied to a gene that exists in several allelic forms. One allele is well-suited to high salinity conditions; another is well-suited to low salinity. When the mussels reproduce, some of their offspring end up in salinity conditions that they are not well suited for, and suffer poorer condition and higher mortality (Koehn & Hilbish, 1987). If we knew about only one salinity condition, we might be puzzled about the existence of the alleles that contribute to the disadvantageous characteristic.

Heterozygote advantage If a gene has two alleles, the phenotypes that result can be of three forms: one typical of one allele when it is homozygous, another form that is typical of the other allele when it is homozygous, and a third form that is typical of the heterozygous genotype. Depending on environmental conditions, heterozygous individuals may out-reproduce both types of homozygous individuals. If so, Mendelian genetics dictate that homozygotes will still be produced. For example, with two alleles, X and x, pairing of two heterozygous individuals will result in the following offspring genotypes: XX, Xx, xX, and xx. Consequently, heterozygote advantage will constantly produce less-adapted offspring (along with the better-adapted homozygous offspring).

An example of heterozygote advantage occurs in *Colias* butterflies. Heterozygous males have stronger flight (used in courting females), live longer, and achieve more matings than do homozygous males (Watt *et al.*, 1986). The less adaptive forms nevertheless persist because they are unavoidable whenever heterozygous individuals mate with one another.

Pleiotropism More often than not, a protein may influence more than one trait, a phenomenon known as *pleiotropism*. For example, a single gene in mice influences such diverse phenotypic features as fur color, kidney enzymes, and visual sensitivity (Balkema *et al.*, 1983). When multiple traits are influenced by a single gene, the chance is good that these traits will vary with respect to their effect on the individual's reproductive success. So, for example, if the fur color is disadvantageous, but the kidney enzymes are so advantageous that they outweigh the fur color effects, individuals will still have the disadvantageous fur color because it comes as part of the package. Some counteradaptive traits may exist because of their pleiotropic association with adaptive phenotypic attributes.

The existence of pleiotropisms maintaining maladaptive traits leads to a very important point: Natural selection can only operate on whole individuals. It cannot remove a bad trait in the same way that a bruised spot can be cut from an apple. If an individual reproduces, *all* its genes are reproduced, including the ones that may contribute to disadvantageous phenotypic forms. Similarly, the beneficial genes of a superb specimen that nevertheless has one fatal flaw will perish, unreproduced, along with the detrimental genes. Selection on the whole organism must be considered whenever the adaptive significance of phenotypic traits is under study.

Frequency-dependent selection The adaptiveness of a phenotypic form sometimes depends on its frequency relative to other forms. If the reproductive success of bearers of less common phenotypes exceeds that of the more common phenotypes, diversity will be maintained. For example, Gross (1985) reported that coho salmon of the Pacific Northwest develop into one of two male forms: large, pugnacious "hooknose" males, specialized for fighting on the spawning grounds for females, and small, nonaggressive "jacks," specialized for surreptitiously fertilizing females. Jacks hide behind rocks to get close enough to fertilize eggs; therefore, if there are too many jacks, some will have to fight for proximity, a task for which they are poorly suited. If there are few jacks, each can get closer and have more success. Therefore, there is a self-regulating mechanism influencing the relative numbers of the two phenotypes. It would be difficult to conclude that one type was more or less adaptive than the other because the adaptiveness depends on its frequency in the population.

We began this section by asking whether all traits are adaptive. Clearly not. Changing selection conditions, heterozygote advantage, pleiotropism, and frequency-dependent selection are good reasons for the existence of characteristics that may seem to be less than ideal. Nevertheless, some find the allure of adaptation irresistible and claim that phenotypic traits are adaptive even if that means concocting speculative accounts about how adaptation may have arisen. Gould and Lewontin (1979) have criticized the practice of using "adaptive stories" as substitutes for evidence regarding adaptation. Plausible ideas about adaptation must be subjected to appropriate scientific scrutiny.

WHAT IS THE LEVEL OF ADAPTATION?

In any animal population, some individuals will leave more offspring than others. The number of offspring that an individual produces during its lifetime is known as its *individual fitness*. By definition, the best adapted individuals are the ones with the greatest fitness. They have the characteristics that led to survival and reproductive success in the ecological context in which they led their lives. In essence, then, there is a "competition" going on among individual animals for genetic representation in the following genera-tion. Of course, the term "competition" does not imply that the animals understand what is happening. Rather, some individuals just have more offspring than others, and whatever ge-netic material contributed to the characteristics that led to this success will be more prevalent in the next generation, at the expense of the genes that contribute to less successful forms.

There is another way that genes can be passed along to the next generation besides di-rect, personal reproduction. Individuals can contribute to the reproductive success of rela-tives. Imagine an allele that affects an individ-ual's behavior in such a way as to promote the reproductive success of close relatives. This could come about through diverse means. For instance, a lioness may allow cubs other than her own to nurse; a person may adopt their niece, nephew, or grandchild after his or her parents become unable to care for the child; or a rodent may "brood" a litter of younger siblings while the mother is off looking for food. If such activities mean that the relative has more sur-viving offspring than they would have had with-out the assistance, then the genes that contrib-ute to such aid-giving behavior will tend to increase in frequency in the population.

The reason why such genes would increase ("spread") in the population is because of the genetic similarity that exists among relatives. For example, full siblings (individuals who have the same mother and father) share, on average, 50% of their alleles. (The reason that this is an average figure is explained in Fig. 4-2.) Less closely related individuals share less than 50% of their alleles (again, on average). The percentage of alleles that two relatives have in common can also be expressed as the probability of having a certain allele in common. So, full siblings have a probability of .5 of sharing a particular allele. The allele in question is the one that contributes

---

Genotypes of Parents

Female	Male
$A_1 A_2$	$A_3 A_4$
$B_1 B_2$	$B_3 B_4$

Genotypes of Offspring

1	2	3	4	5
$A_1 A_3$	$A_1 A_4$	$A_2 A_3$	$A_1 A_4$	$A_2 A_3$
$B_1 B_3$	$B_1 B_3$	$B_1 B_3$	$B_1 B_4$	$B_2 B_3$

Genetic Similarities of Offspring Pairs

Offspring Pair	Genetic Similarity
1 and 2	75%
1 and 3	75%
1 and 4	50%
1 and 5	50%
2 and 3	50%
2 and 4	75%
2 and 5	25%
3 and 4	25%
3 and 5	75%
4 and 5	0%

Figure 4.2
The genetic similarity between various relatives is sometimes expressed as an average value. This concept is illustrated using full siblings. Assume that the mother and father share no alleles of the A or B genes (top). Of the 16 possible genotypes of their offspring, five are shown (middle). The percentage of alleles held in common in the offspring pairs are also shown (bot-tom). When expanded to include all possible pairs of genotypes, comparison of genetic similarity averages to be 50%. If the parents share alleles in common (which is most likely the case), the genetic similarity among full siblings increases.

to the aid-giving behavior. Thus, the rodent that broods a set of four full siblings is likely to be giving assistance to two copies of the aid-giving allele. (Our discussion of this phenomenon, for simplicity, will refer to a single gene or allele that contributes to aid-giving activities. This is undoubtedly too simple, but the logic is identical regardless of the total number of genes and alleles that are involved.)

Would not an individual be better off reproducing directly? After all, offspring *always* have 50% of the parent's genes, whereas other relatives have fewer alleles in common. Would not aid-givers reproduce more copies of their genes by having and caring for their own offspring rather than assisting others? Such questions imply that there is a cost in aid-giving, and frequently there are such costs. The lioness who nurses another's cub runs some risk of being unable to feed her own cubs when they need milk, and a ground squirrel that gives an alarm call when a predator appears is risking its own life and its remaining reproductive output, presumably for the good of its relatives that happen to be within earshot. These alleles can indeed spread in a population provided that the costs (as measured by lost personal fitness) are less than the benefits to the relatives (as measured by enhanced reproductive success in the relatives). The notion that evolutionary changes in gene frequency can occur through contributions to the reproductive success of relatives is known as *kin selection.*

W.D. Hamilton (1964) developed the concept of kin selection and showed its implications. He proposed that evolution could proceed by individuals promoting their *inclusive fitness,* a term that encompasses the individual's personal fitness plus its contribution to its relatives' reproductive success. One of the great benefits of Hamilton's kin selection concept was the clarity that it bestowed on some otherwise puzzling ob-

W. D. HAMILTON

" . . . A gene causing altruistic behavior towards brothers and sisters will be selected only if the behavior and the circumstances are generally such that the gain is more than twice the loss; for half-brothers it must be more than four times the loss; and so on." [Hamilton, W. D. (1963). The evolution of altruistic behavior. American Naturalist **97,** 354–356 (p. 355.]

servations. For example, female lions allow other females' cubs to nurse from them. Raising cubs to maturity is by no means simple for lions: Cubs grow rapidly and require a good deal of food. Many die of starvation each year. On the basis of individual selection alone one would expect lionesses to be selfish, allowing only their own cubs to nurse. However, lions live in groups consisting of female relatives (Bertram, 1975). When a female nurses her relatives' cubs she increases her inclusive fitness. Hamilton proposed that such assistance to relatives would be scaled according to the relatedness of the aid-giver to the benefactor. For example, the benefit derived by nursing a sister's cubs would be greater than the benefit from nursing a cousin's cubs. In either case, the cost must be less than the benefit over the long run for the genes that contribute to such behavior to spread in the population. In Hamilton's terms: $Br > C$, where B is benefit to the recipient, C is cost to the actor, and r is their coefficient of relatedness.

Let us work through this important formula. Benefit and cost are ideally measured by the effect of an act on inclusive fitness. Giving an alarm call when a predator appears entails some risk of being attacked and killed. Suppose that calling results in an average cost of 2% (0.02) when averaged over the caller's lifespan. That is, alarm callers produce 2% fewer offspring, on average, than those individuals who do not call. However, predators are more likely to kill one of the caller's close relatives living nearby if they are not warned. If, for example, a sister is killed, the loss is measured by her expected remaining reproductive success. Alarm calling in the presence of predators, then, has the benefit of increasing inclusive fitness by that amount, say 20%. The formula states that benefit (0.20) times relatedness (0.50) ($=0.10$) is greater than cost (0.02). Therefore, given these values, genes that contribute to alarm calling will increase in frequency in the population.

Does all this seem far-fetched? When first exposed to the concept of kin selection, most people wonder how the animal knows how many relatives there are in the vicinity, how closely related they are, and how individually costly their behaviors are. Such questions, however, confuse the mechanisms of the behavior with the effect of the behavior. There is no need for ground squirrels to understand costs and benefits of their behavior to behave adaptively. All that is needed is a reliable proximate cause for the behavior such that, when the behavior is performed in appropriate circumstances, the benefits exceed the costs. *If* ground squirrels live in

close proximity to relatives, and *if* their alarm calling in the presence of predators saves more copies of their genes (that reside in those relatives) than it costs in terms of lost direct reproductive success, then those genes that contribute to alarm calling will spread in the population. These conditions are indeed met (Sherman, 1977), and alarm calling is common. Ground squirrels need not be probability calculators nor understand kin selection theory in order to behave in ways that enhance their inclusive fitness. Neither do people.

Let us review briefly before going on. Individuals can reproduce directly (personal fitness) and by assisting relatives to produce more offspring than they could have otherwise produced (inclusive fitness). The common denominator in both cases is gene perpetuation. Because one's genes reside in others as well as in oneself, either form of reproduction is favored. Self reproduction is a special case of gene perpetuation, albeit the most familiar one.

Relatives share genes, but all members of a species have genes in common. If Hamilton's kin selection idea is correct, shouldn't we expect to find individuals doing things that are individually costly but which benefit the species as a whole? The notion of incurring some reproductive cost to oneself for the benefit of the population or species is known as *group selection*. V.C. Wynne-Edwards, a Scottish ecologist, published a book in 1962 listing numerous examples of behaviors that seemed to be individually disadvantageous, but which supposedly aided the population or species (for a synopsis, see Wynne-Edwards, 1964). A common observation that would support Wynne-Edwards's thesis is that of *reproductive restraint*, i.e., individuals having fewer offspring than they seem capable of producing. According to Wynne-Edwards, if all the members of a population reproduced at the maximum rate, the population would quickly grow too large, overexploit its resources, and then all would suffer. Reproductive restraint, then, would be good for the species, although disadvantageous to the individuals themselves.

For example, David Lack (1966), a British ornithologist, noted that European swifts usually laid three or fewer eggs per pair, even though they seemed fully capable of laying four. Does this qualify as group selection? Lack followed up his observations with data on offspring survival. He found that in most years those pairs that had three eggs had more surviving offspring than did those pairs that had four eggs (Fig. 4-3). In most years the food supply was not sufficient to provision four chicks well enough for them to be sufficiently strong and healthy; thus, mortality

was greater in these chicks. In short, Lack's swifts were not holding back, they were producing as many offspring as possible given their ecological constraints. Again, no suggestion is being made that the birds understand the relationship between the food-producing abilities of their environment and the food needs of their offspring. If there are genetic differences among swifts that account for some of them laying more eggs than others, and if those swifts that lay three eggs have more surviving offspring than swifts that lay more eggs, then the "three-egg-genes" will become more common in the swift population.

To sum up, it appears that group selection may not exist. This is because the benefit derived by assisting unrelated individuals is not sufficient to offset the costs. In other words, natural selection has favored those individuals whose characteristics lead to the highest rates of gene perpetuation. In most cases this occurs through self reproduction, but in cases in which the act results in individual harm, the benefits to close relatives may outweigh the costs, and genes influencing the trait may spread via kin selection. No cases of group selection have been confirmed, although theoretical work suggests that it might exist under certain, unlikely circumstances (Grafen, 1984).

There are some common expressions that should be avoided because they imply the action of group selection when there is no evidence of group selection. For instance, in an interesting account of winter hibernation in garter snakes and their early-spring breeding activities, Lynch (1983) used several group selectionist terms. Males emerge from hibernation before females, and wait around the hibernation den for females to emerge. When they do, males immediately mate with them, and it is common for many males to participate in a mating swarm with a single female, each male trying to be the one to

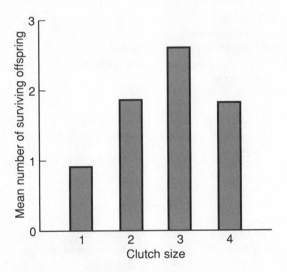

Figure 4.3
The number of offspring surviving their first year in the European swift is associated with the number of eggs in the clutch. Swifts usually lay two or three eggs, rarely more (four-egg clutches were produced by moving eggs from one nest to another). Swifts are not restraining their reproduction; they are producing as many offspring as can be raised, dispelling the notion of group selection. (Data from Lack, 1966.)

When a female garter snake emerges from her hibernation den, many males attempt to mate with her. However, once she is inseminated, other males will stop their mating activities because of an odorant in the male's semen that has an "anti-aphrodisiac" effect on them. From the standpoint of individual fitness, these males have a better chance at reproduction if they seek other females with whom to mate.

copulate with the female. This is precisely what one would expect from the perspective of individual fitness. When a male from the swarm copulates with the female, the other males cease their mating attempts due to the presence of an odorant in the male's semen that has an "anti-aphrodisiac" effect on the males. Lynch claims that the other males giving up is "for the good of the species" because the now-fertilized female needs to get on with the business of finding food, and further pestering by males could only reduce her reproductive success. A more feasible explanation is that the other males have a better chance of reproducing if they seek out a female that has not yet been fertilized. The semen coagulates in the female reproductive tract, and even if another male copulated with her the chances are slim that his sperm could fertilize any of the female's eggs. Males, then, are acting in their own personal interests, not in the interest of the species.

Evolution

An organism's life is spent interacting with its environment. It eats, excretes, seeks shelter, fights, hides, and communicates. Each of its behavioral episodes has some consequence for the organism's well-being and reproductive success. The cumulative effect of these interactions can be expressed by the organism's lifetime reproductive success. How many surviving offspring did it produce? How many grand-offspring or other relatives did it contribute to? Individuals differ in their reproductive success, and

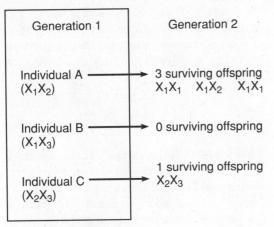

Ecological conditions

Figure 4.4
The essentials of evolutionary change are illustrated in this diagram. A population in Generation 1 consists of three individuals, each of whom has a different combination of alleles of the X gene. The three alleles are equally common in this generation. The population members leave different numbers of surviving offspring, a measure of reproductive success. The genotypes of the offspring are also shown. Note that in Generation 2 the frequencies of the three alleles have changed from what they were in Generation 1.

much of this variation is attributable to the effectiveness of interactions with their environments. If individual differences in reproductive success are due to phenotypic variations that are attributable to genetic differences between individuals, then those genes that contribute to the more successful individuals will become more common in the next generation. The essence of evolution is change in gene frequencies over generations (Fig. 4-4). To understand an individual's behavior we must understand the evolutionary process that led to the presence of particular genes in that individual. That is one of the goals of this section.

DEFINITIONS OF EVOLUTION

The term "evolution" has been around for many years, and, like many terms, has been defined in many ways, which can lead to confusion. There are two definitions of evolution in addition to the one that will be adopted. We will review the first two briefly before presenting the final one in more detail.

First, evolution is often used synonymously with history, especially if long-term, gradual trends are implied. Astronomers study the evolution of the universe, historians research the evolution of political philosophies, and geologists explore the evolution of mountain ranges and coral reefs. Second, evolution is defined as the origin of life. In this sense, the term does not pertain to the historical changes that have occurred in living organisms, but with how life originated. [In many ways, the original wigglings of life have no important bearing on evolution as we will use the term. That is, a creator or God could have "breathed life" into one or more original creatures, but this is not particularly relevant to the evolution-as-change definition that we will use. We will have little to say about the origin of life, although the topic is a fascinating one (Dickerson, 1978).]

The third definition of evolution is the one that we will use throughout this book. It deals with changes in gene (allele) frequencies over time: *Evolution is any long-lasting change in the genetic composition of a population* (Mayr, 1978). Three features of this definition must be stressed so that it is absolutely clear.

First, the definition only applies to populations, not to individuals. Barring occasional mutations, the genetic material of each individual remains constant throughout its life and thus does not evolve. Individuals *develop*, they do not evolve. (By the same reasoning, populations or species evolve, they do not develop.)

Second, "long-lasting change" is superior to "change" because of the widespread occurrence of transient or cyclical changes in gene frequency. For example, Dobzhansky (1950), one of the foremost authorities on evolutionary genetics, described a cyclical change in a species of European ladybird beetle. In Germany, the insect occurs in two forms, either black with red spots, or red with black spots. The two forms change in frequency over the year with the red-spotted form more common during the summer and the black-spotted form more common during the winter. Because there is a genetic basis to this color difference we have a case in which one set of genes increases in frequency in the population, to be replaced later by the other. This certainly is an interesting genetic change in a population, but because the change is temporary, it does not qualify as evolution.

Finally, our definition stresses *genetic change*. This criterion is perhaps the most difficult of all to demonstrate, and often cannot be. For example, paleontologists—scientists who study the ancient, historical changes of organisms—are unable to observe the genetic make-up of extinct species. All they have available are body parts (usually bones or shells) and sometimes remnants of their activities such as burrows, tracks, or nests (Hunt *et al.*, 1983; Horner, 1984). Yet paleontologists point to successions of organisms based on fossil remains and speak confidently of evolution. Their confidence is not entirely justified because, as we have seen, variation in phenotypic traits is not entirely due to genetic differences. Nevertheless, it is generally safe to talk about successions of organisms as examples of evolution because genetic transformation probably determined at least some of the anatomical changes. *Phenotypic evolution* is the best term to use in cases such as these. Genetic evolution and phenotypic evolution may proceed at different rates. For example, A. C.

Wilson (1985) has pointed out that various species of frogs, although phenotypically similar, are more divergent genetically than are humans and apes, which differ a great deal from each other phenotypically.

CAUSES OF EVOLUTION

How does evolution occur? There are three causes of evolution (chance events, artificial selection, and natural selection) that will be reviewed. Natural selection is generally regarded as the most important cause of evolution, so we will save it for last and treat it in greatest detail.

Chance events   A variety of events, operating solely on chance, can cause evolutionary change. For example, a catastrophic event may decimate a population except for a few lucky survivors. Assuming their survival was due purely to chance, the surviving population, because of its small size, may not be representative of the gene composition of the original population. If so, the genetic composition of the population was transformed and evolution occurred (Gould, 1980). Similarly, a small number of individuals may become separated from the main population. Like the individuals spared from a calamity, this *founder population* may have a nontypical sample of the genes from the main population (Fig. 4-5). If the founder population persists, the gene composition of its subsequent members may differ from the original population, and thus would qualify as evolution.

Another form of chance as a cause of evolution is known as *genetic drift* (Fig. 4-5). Drift may occur due to the random assortment of chromosomes and their accompanying genes during sexual reproduction. For example, consider a gene with two alleles, Q and q. Suppose that all members of the population are heterozygous, having Q on one chromosome and q on the

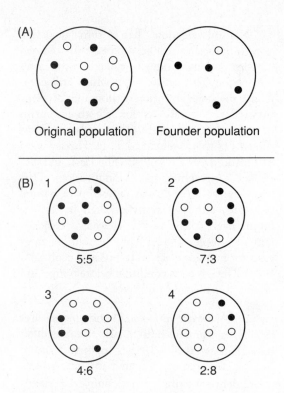

(A)

Original population   Founder population

(B)

1
5:5

2
7:3

3
4:6

4
2:8

Figure 4.5
(A) The frequency of alleles may change suddenly due to the establishment of a founder population (right) apart from the original population (left). The filled and open circles represent two different alleles. In this example the filled circles change from 50% (5 of 10) to 80% (4 of 5). (B) Random changes in allele frequency from generation to generation is known as genetic drift. Filled and open circles represent two different alleles. The frequency of the filled circle allele is indicated beneath each large circle which represents a separate generation.

other (an unlikely event, but bear with me!). They can pass along either Q or q depending on which member of the chromosome pair ends up in the egg or sperm that make up the zygote. It appears that the assortment of chromosomes is random. Thus, for example, Q could be lost from

this population in only one generation if each individual by chance contributed only the q-bearing chromosome to the zygotes that produce the next generation. If two alleles have equal effects on the reproductive success of their bearers, their frequencies in a population may change randomly from generation to generation, perhaps leading to elimination of one of them (King & Jukes, 1969).

The likelihood of such an event occurring in a fairly large population is small. To follow up on our example, if there are only five individuals, the chance of losing Q in one generation would be 0.5^5 or about 3%. (This is the same probability as flipping a coin five times and getting tails each time.) However, if there are 10 individuals, the chance of losing Q completely in one generation drops to less than one-tenth of one percent. But this is an artificially stringent example. An allele need not be completely eliminated for genetic drift to produce evolutionary change. We merely need a long-lasting change in gene frequency, and drift can do this.

Evolution does not necessarily imply the advent of new species. A founder population may be entirely capable of breeding with the main population's members [interbreeding is the criterion for species status (Mayr, 1970)] even though the two populations may differ genetically. In other words, evolution can and does occur without formation of new species.

Artificial selection Artificial selection or selective breeding is another way of producing long-lasting changes in gene frequencies. This is the familiar process of breeding for desired traits in livestock, plants, and so on. From a starting population the breeder selects those individuals demonstrating the valued characteristics. They are interbred and the best offspring are retained for subsequent breeding. All others are discarded. If there is a genetic basis to variation in the desired trait (which usually is the case), the

CHARLES DARWIN

"There is grandeur in this view of life, with its several powers, having been breathed into a few forms or into one; and that, whilst this planet has gone on cycling according to the fixed law of gravity, from so simple a beginning endless forms beautiful and most wonderful have been, and are being, evolved." [Darwin, C. (1859/1979). The origin of species. *New York: Avenel Books (pp. 459–460).]*

alleles contributing to the favored form will comprise an ever larger proportion of the population. In this way, we have produced docile livestock, homing pigeons, sheep-herding dogs, and anatomical traits valued in agriculture. Underlying the whole process, however, are human decisions about which phenotypic forms will be favored reproductively.

Natural selection   Let us turn our attention to natural selection, a process that earned Charles Darwin worldwide acclaim in the latter half of the 19th century and which still commands the eager attention of thousands of scientists today. Natural selection is both elegant in its simplicity ("how extremely stupid not to have thought of that!" remarked T. H. Huxley upon first reading Darwin's *Origin of Species*), and subtle and far-reaching in its ramifications. Darwin's theory of evolution by means of natural selection, although hotly debated in its fine points even today, is still viewed as basically correct (Gould, 1982). Three conditions must exist for natural selection to produce evolution. We will review each condition before tying them together as a single package.

1. *Phenotypic Variation.* Phenotypic features usually vary among individuals. Humans differ in such traits as blood type, leg length, intelligence, brain size, temperament, and so on. Even identical twins are not completely identical in their phenotypes! Animals and plants also vary greatly if we care to look carefully enough. Snails of the same species have different colors, markings, and twists in their shells (Clarke, 1975); flounders may have both their eyes on the left side, or both on the right (Policansky, 1982); birds have individually distinctive voices (Beer, 1970); and individuals of many species have different enzyme varieties (McDonald, 1983), to mention just a few. Without phenotypic variation as a starting point, natural selection cannot proceed to produce evolutionary change.

2. *Heritability.* The second requirement is that at least some of the individual differences in the phenotype must be due to genetic differences among the individuals (see Chapter 2 for an expanded discussion of heritability). Although many people find it relatively easy to envision heritability with reference to anatomi-

cal traits, in fact, many individual differences in behavior are heritable (Plomin, 1989).

3. *Differential Reproductive Success.* Individuals differ with respect to their reproductive success. Whether we measure reproductive success as the number of offspring produced, the number of offspring surviving to adulthood, or the number of grandoffspring, we always find that some individuals are more successful than others. For example, among the !Kung bush people of southern Africa, women may have from zero to nine children in their lifetimes (Howell, 1979; Konner & Worthman, 1980), and in a population of ground squirrels 89% of the animals present in 1967 were descendants of only 20% of the 1963 population (McCarley, 1970).

Reproductive success must be associated with the form of the phenotypic trait. For example, McGregor *et al.* (1981) correlated lifetime reproductive success of male chickadees with the number of songs in their repertoires. In general, males with more songs left more descendants than did males with fewer songs (Fig. 4-6).

Researchers often encounter difficulties in measuring relationships between phenotypes and reproductive success. First, keeping track of how many offspring an animal produces in its lifespan may be very difficult, although this has been done in baboons (Altmann, 1980), deer (Clutton-Brock *et al.*, 1982), and other species. Second, there may be a lengthy delay between the occurrence of a behavior and its effects on reproduction. For instance, young monkeys play with each other, and like other phenotypes, play is variable. If we wanted to know whether variation in amount of play is correlated with reproductive success we would need to wait several years before the animals became old enough to breed. Third, male reproductive success is almost impossible to measure in many species. Because there is almost always a possibility that

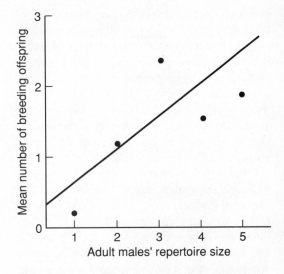

Figure 4.6
Reproductive success (number of young who survived to reproduce) is correlated with the number of songs that male great tits (a species of European chickadee) have in their repertoires.

some other male fathered the offspring that a particular male is caring for, we can rarely be certain of male reproductive success, even though paternity analysis methods are being developed for some animal species (Sherman, 1981).

As a result of such difficulties, researchers often correlate phenotypic forms with *indirect* measures of reproductive success such as number of copulations, efficiency in gathering food, health and vigor, or dominance status. Many of these measures are known to be related to reproductive success, and, to the extent that they are, they may serve as acceptable substitutes. We must remember, however, that the currency of evolution is reproductive success, and that is what should be measured whenever feasible.

The synthesis When these three requirements—phenotypic variation, heritability of the phenotype, and reproductive success correlated with phenotypes—are all met, natural selection produces evolutionary change. If variations in a phenotypic form are due (at least in part) to individual genetic differences, and if some phenotypic forms are more successful at reproducing than are other forms, then the next generation will have more copies of the gene(s) that contributed to the more successful forms. Evolution will have occurred.

Put another way, evolution will *always* occur whenever these three conditions exist. *Evolution is inevitable* whenever genetic differences contribute to phenotypic differences that lead to differences in reproductive success. This inexorable march of evolution is occurring now as it always has; it is occurring in humans as it is in other species; and it will continue to occur as long as these three conditions are satisfied. This does not mean, however, that the ecological conditions that are exerting themselves now are the same ones that operated in earlier times. Although we humans have often succeeded in reducing the magnitude of some age-old selective conditions (predators, diseases, starvation, or exposure to cold), we have not eliminated them entirely and we have increased the importance of other conditions. The society, for instance, acts as an important selective condition, favoring some phenotypes over others.

The Victorians, such as Herbert Spencer, talked of "the struggle for existence," and "nature red in tooth and claw," and so forth, implying that evolution proceeded through violent contests among animals. These aphorisms are still with us today, and the picture they portray has led many to disparage the concept of evolution because what they see going on does not fit their preconceived notions of evolution. However, evolution can be as peaceful as some plants producing a few more seeds than others, or as quiet as a mouse allowing her pups to nurse a while longer thus sending them out better nourished and prepared to deal with their world. Evolution is all around us. We must understand it.

Plans and Progress in Evolution

If most evolutionary change is brought about by environmental conditions favoring certain characteristics over others, it is tempting to think of evolution as a goal-directed process that attempts to increase the adaptive fit between animals and their environments. Evolution often looks as though it is planned or directed. Certainly, the supreme adaptations that are around us scarcely look as though they could have come about by "blind chance." Indeed, this is the sort of argument frequently used by religious fundamentalists who object to evolutionary theory (see Numbers, 1982; Dawkins, 1987). This section will attempt to show that sophisticated adaptations can arise without goal-orientation, that there is no evolutionary plan, and that progress in evolution is, like beauty, in the mind of the beholder.

POPULATION CHANGES
AND NATURAL SELECTION

Evolution is a historical process, and the changes are often gradual and tend to be in one direction. This is the sort of observation that leads some people to see a plan to evolution and therefore to seek out an "evolutionary agent" that oversees the process. This section will review some of the changes that occur in populations when they are exposed to a new selection problem. Using that as a base, we can then consider the questions of planning and progress in evolution.

Directional selection   Imagine a population of some organism, say, a species of goose, whose members vary in some feature of their phenotype such as migratory distance. If we measured enough individuals we would find that migratory distance is probably normally distributed, i.e., in the familiar bell-shaped curve (Fig. 4-7A1). Suppose that environmental conditions began changing such that those geese who fly farther south for wintering have higher reproductive success than those who do not fly as far south. Further suppose that at least some of the variation in migratory distance is due to genetic differences between the geese. In time, if we again measured distance traveled in migration, we would find a change in the distribution with the mean (average) shifted toward the longer-flight end (Fig. 4-7A2). This sort of change, which is quite common, is known as *directional selection* because the mean value for the phenotype in the population shifts in a single direction.

Stabilizing selection Natural selection can operate on a population such that both extremes of the distribution are disfavored relative

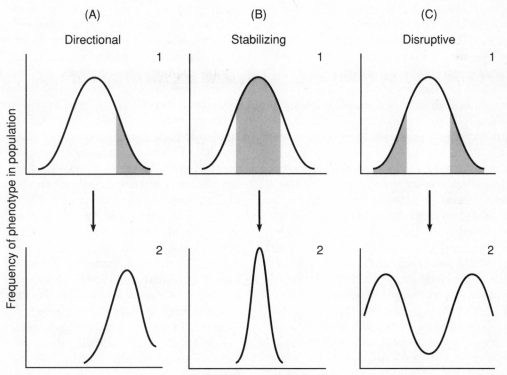

Figure 4.7
Beginning with a starting population (top) that may have been normally distributed, some individuals that have certain phenotypes will leave more offspring than do individuals with other phenotypes. The more successful segment of the population is indicated by shading. After selection has operated for several or many generations, the distribution of the phenotype changes.

to those closer to the midpoint (Fig. 4-7B1 and B2). For example, Belding's ground squirrels are residents of high mountain meadows in the far western United States. Because they hibernate through the long winter, these animals must commence their reproductive activities soon after emerging from hibernation if there is to be sufficient time for the offspring to mature enough to survive their first winter. Early spring breeding would appear to result in greater reproductive success than later spring breeding. However, environmental conditions can also penalize early breeding. Late spring snowstorms sometimes blanket the sparse food and subject the ground squirrels to added energy demands to keep warm. In short, these animals are selected in two directions simultaneously: to breed early, but not too early. The result is reduced variation in the date at which reproduction occurs. Virtually all animals of a well-studied population near Yosemite National Park in California breed within a two-week period (Morton & Sherman, 1978).

Stabilizing selection is probably the most common situation in nature. Even when directional selection is operating there will come a point where some other selection condition begins to exert itself. For example, one would expect directional selection to favor those individuals who commence reproduction a little earlier in life than others simply because that would provide more time to produce offspring. In humans, however, there is a cost to reproducing too soon (as well as too late). The incidence of Down's syndrome (a chromosomal abnormality which produces mental retardation and other congenital defects) is higher in babies born to very young mothers (less than about 15 years old) and to older mothers (about 30 to 35 years old) than to mothers in the intermediate age range (Erickson, 1978). Spontaneous abortions and other conditions that jeopardize the mother's health are also more common among very young mothers. Thus, although directional selection has undoubtedly favored early reproduction in humans and other species, there is a practical limit to which early reproduction can be pushed.

Disruptive selection   The third type of selection condition is probably the rarest. In this case environmental conditions favor those individuals who are toward the extremes of the starting population (Fig. 4-7C1). This results in a later distribution with two modes (Fig. 4-7C2).

An example of disruptive selection occurred in the common bluegill sunfish, in which two distinct male "strategies" can be observed each breeding season. In the "parental" strategy, males dig nest pits where they court females, fertilize the eggs, and defend the eggs and fry. These males are large, pugnacious, and drive away intruding males. In the "female-mimic strategy," males are small, nonaggressive, and colored like females. Further, they behave like females and may join females breeding with a parental male. The mimic discharges his sperm into the water when the female releases her eggs for fertilization by the parental male (Dominey, 1980). It is easy to see how an intermediate strategy would be disfavored. To be effective, a parental male must be large enough to protect his hard-won nesting territory. He must also diligently guard the eggs and fry against marauding intruders. But for female mimics to be effective, the match to real females must be very good (parental males will attack other males if they are detected). This fascinating dichotomy appears to have been the result of favoring both behavioral extremes, because weakly parental males or poor female mimics were probably unsuccessful at passing on their genes.

It is worth repeating at this point that the changes in gene and phenotype frequency that result from individual differences in reproductive success are not planned or directed. Variation is apparently random with respect to the selection problem, i.e., a disadvantageous change is just as likely as an advantageous one. Evolution by means of natural selection proceeds through a perpetual process of producing offspring that differ from the parents followed by those offspring experiencing varying degrees of reproductive success due to their dealings with the environment (Dawkins, 1987).

"FORESIGHT" AND EVOLUTION

Evolutionary biologists often use the term "selected for" when discussing characteristics of organisms. For example, one might hear that the ability of desert-dwelling rodents to retain water is selected for, or that choice of a safe nest site in birds is selected for. "Selected for" means that those individuals exhibiting the trait have greater reproductive success than those who do not, or those who have the trait in a different form or to a different degree. "Selected for" does not imply foresight. Breeders of animals and plants may select for a trait by deliberately breeding only those individuals that possess the desired trait, but among free-living organisms foresight is not implied. Desert rodents have good water-retention abilities because they are descended from parents who had such abilities, not because they or their ancestors recognized the need for such an ability. Natural selection has no way of *producing* individuals that might be better adapted. "Selected for" is used because it is less cumbersome than saying something like "the bearers of trait form X leave, on average, more descendants than do bearers of trait form Y." Foresight and planning definitely are not implied.

The absence of planning is often difficult to accept because humans engage in it all the time. We think about the future, about the best course of action, and plan according to our predictions of forthcoming events. Thus, we find it easy to think and speak in such terms. Furthermore, much of what animals do appears to be foresightful. However, as a general rule, it is wisest to think about natural selection in very different terms—of consequences of phenotypes, not planning of phenotypes. A genetic change occurs that results in a modified phenotype. Then the consequences are felt (either reduced or enhanced reproductive success). Most genetic change is either disadvantageous or neutral (King & Jukes, 1969).

Phenotypic variants arise first and then persist or not according to their reproductive success. Genetic changes are as likely (or more likely) to result in diminished success as in increased success. Change is random, not directed or planned, and from the random changes the best suited (most reproductively successful) come to predominate in later generations.

ADAPTIVE ROUTES

Species that may not be closely related phylogenetically may nevertheless face very similar selection conditions and consequently may evolve similar adaptations. This is known as *convergent evolution* because unrelated species have converged on the same solution to their common problem. (Convergent evolution can also occur among closely related species but it is more difficult to demonstrate.) An example of convergent evolution is the eye features that permit good night vision in owls, cats, and nocturnal primates. There are innumerable convergent adaptations and they reinforce the contention that natural selection is indeed a very powerful phenomenon.

The ubiquity of convergent evolution, however, should not lead us to the tempting conclusion that there is only one best adaptation for a given selection condition. In fact, there may be many different, although apparently equal, adaptations to a problem. Animal species, for example, that live in polar regions are faced with a big problem: winter. Yet there are several solutions. Most birds fly to more moderate climates, many rodents hibernate through the cold months, but humans and arctic foxes remain in the area, surviving by hunting and by consuming stored food. All are different ways of dealing with the same selection condition.

When alternative adaptations occur, can we explain why a species has a particular form of adaptation rather than another? What determines the structure of adaptations? The answer to this question begins with the realization that each species has unique genetic material that may constrain the range of adaptations that can be obtained. A useful analogy is that natural selection is more like tinkering than like engineering (Jacob, 1977). A tinkerer works by modifying existing objects. An engineer (at least theoretically) enjoys the luxury of building a new design from scratch. Natural selection can only act by weeding out genes that contribute to phenotypic variants that do not reproduce as well as other variants.

The tinkering metaphor allows us to understand some phenomena that don't make much sense for the engineering metaphor, namely, the existence of imperfection. To find such an example we need look no further than our own lower backs (Krogman, 1951). Humans evolved from quadrupedal mammalian ancestors. The skeletons of four-legged mammals work well because the weight of the abdominal region is suspended beneath the spinal column. As our ancestors stood more upright they had to make do with a skeleton originally adapted for a very different posture. Consequently, we suffer the problems associated with having a good deal of weight in front of and on top of the spine rather than slung

below it. Small wonder people suffer so many backaches: We are making do with a modified structure originally shaped by a different set of selection conditions. Imperfections in structure, physiological processes, and behavior are to be expected, and their presence provides clues to how natural selection and evolution have operated (Gould, 1979).

We have seen that organisms have similarities and differences. The analysis of similarities and differences is what is generally called the *comparative method*. There are many comparative sciences—including anatomy, psychology, embryology, and physiology—but they all have one thing in common: They seek to understand evolutionary processes by carefully comparing the similarities and differences among species. The great analytical power wielded by the comparative sciences is the best argument for studying nonhuman animals, even for those who are exclusively interested in humans. If we studied only humans we could not employ the comparative method to full advantage. But by comparing ourselves with other creatures, we gain additional insights into human adaptations. Thus, the attitude that "the proper study of man is man himself" leaves much to be desired. A valuable contribution to understanding our own species can be made by careful studies of other, diverse species.

PROGRESS AND EVOLUTION

In examining the great sweep of evolution, some researchers have been impressed with general trends: As a rule, animals have become larger, brains have become more intricate, and presumably, behavior has become more complex. Although these trends are interesting and probably true, there is a danger in making too much of them. The danger lies in concluding that

FRANCOIS JACOB

"It is natural selection that gives direction to changes, orients chance, and slowly, progressively produces more complex structures, new organs, and new species. Novelties come from [a] previously unseen association of old material. To create is to recombine." [Jacob, F. (1977). Evolution and tinkering. Science 196, 1161–1166 (p. 1163).]

bigger is better, that complexity is progress, and that evolutionary change is goal-directed.

There is a long history of interest in these evolutionary trends and their conceptual spin-offs, and they are still with us today. These ideas take the form of orthogenesis, and of evolutionary grades.

Orthogenesis There is an ancient notion, dating back at least to Aristotle, that humans are the culmination of a long series of lesser beings and that all organisms can be scaled from simple to complex. Man, of course, stands in grandeur at the highest point of this "great chain of being." It is as though humans are on the top rung of a very long ladder, with the great apes just behind, the monkeys below them, and so on

down to the protozoa, bacteria, or viruses on the lowest rung. The idea is that there is only one direction to evolution—straight up from simple to complex—and we humans lead this evolutionary parade. This is the notion of *orthogenesis*.

Although orthogenesis is false—evolution, as we will see in a moment, does not move linearly—it still exists in many forms. For example, I have been asked (quite seriously), "If evolution is true, why haven't chimpanzees evolved into humans?" Obviously, the questioner subscribed to the orthogenetic view. If chimps are on the second rung, why haven't they stepped up to the first? Who wouldn't become human if given the chance? A similar position was taken, although with different species, in 1981 by a state senator in Nebraska. The legislature had been debating the merits of a major water project and its opponents were stressing the detrimental effects that the project would have on wildlife, especially the whooping crane, an endangered species that stops in central Nebraska en route to its breeding and wintering sites. A vocal supporter of the project countered by stating that we needn't worry about whooping cranes. "After all," he said, "if they go extinct, they will just evolve again from the sandhill cranes." Apparently, sandhill cranes are just one notch down from the whoopers, and just waiting to step up!

Darwin thought of the relationships among living species as equivalent to the outermost twigs of a complex bush or tree, a metaphor that is infinitely superior to that of the chain or ladder. Although one could go around the evolutionary bush plucking off species here and there and arraying them according to some criterion such as brain size, the result would not necessarily reflect evolutionary descent among the species. This is because living organisms have had independent evolutionary histories. To reconstruct that history we need to get inside the bush and trace the various branches back to their

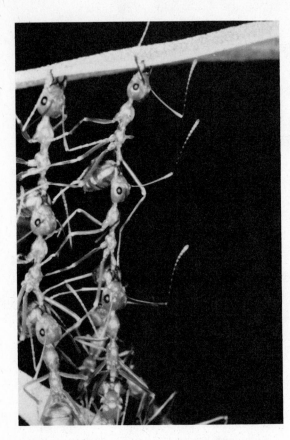 

Figure 4.8
Weaver ants construct a nest by bending a leaf down by a few ants (left) who are then joined by others who hold the leaves and some who manipulate the silk-excreting larvae (right).

common origins. In short, it is exceedingly difficult to work out the evolution of a trait such as brain anatomy by using living species alone because they have continued to evolve and may no longer be entirely representative of their ancestors. So, for example, when lizards, rats, cats, monkeys, and humans are arrayed in the context of the evolution of some characteristic, the sequence should not be taken as an approximation of evolutionary history (Hodos & Campbell, 1969).

Evolutionary grades   Although we know that evolutionary relationships among species are not linear, there is some support for the notion that evolutionary change involves greater complexity. In other words, as time passes and evolution proceeds, species become more complex and sophisticated. This notion, known as *anagenesis*, asserts that as evolution proceeds, new *evolutionary grades* (or levels) of complexity emerge (Yarczower & Hazlett, 1977). Consider the following example of anagenesis based on the nest-building behavior of weaver ants.

Weaver ants are a widespread group characterized by their habit of building nests in trees rather than using preexisting holes. Ants of the genus *Oecophylla* exhibit the highest (most complex) nest building grade. Periodically, worker ants line up along the edge of a leaf and pull it toward the opposite edge. Eventually they make contact and the now-curled leaf is held in position by the workers who strain to hold one edge in their mandibles and the other edge by their hind legs (Fig. 4-8). When this step is reached, other workers scurry off to bring larvae to the leaf. Holding a larvae in its mandibles, a worker swings it back and forth between the two leaf edges as the larvae expels a strand of silky material. Touching the larvae to one edge and then the other, a sheet of silk forms, binding the leaf edges together and forming a nest for the colony (Holldobler & Wilson, 1977, 1983).

Other weaver ant species build silk nests, but the process is substantially simpler. The workers do not cooperate in bending leaves, and the larvae do most of the work in placing the silk (larvae typically spin cocoons for themselves, and the cocoon-spinning movements are used in nest construction). In a third group of species, the workers do almost nothing except to place larvae on the spot where the nest will be built.

What can we learn from these interesting behavioral differences? Unfortunately, the evolutionary relationships among the species can not be deduced from these observations because the species evolved their behavior independently of one another. It may be the case that the species differ with respect to some selection condition, favoring one form of nest-building behavior more than the others. Unfortunately, the grading of these behavior patterns according to complexity is insufficient evidence to permit that conclusion. We need independent assess-

ments of what those selection conditions might be. All we are left with is a neat grading of traits according to their complexity. Although some see grading based on anagenesis as a potentially valuable activity (Yarczower & Hazlett, 1977; Yarczower & Yarczower, 1979; Gottlieb, 1984), there seems to be little value in it other than satisfying some esthetic impulse (Capitanio & Leger, 1979; Leger, 1989).

The primary point to remember is that evolution does not have a goal toward which it strives. Evolution need not move organisms toward greater complexity, greater size, or more sophistication. In fact, there are numerous cases where species have become less complex than their ancestors. Certain species of ants, for instance, that maintain other ants or aphids as "slaves" are anatomically and behaviorally less complex than their ancestral species that do not have slaves (Wilson, 1975a; Topoff, 1984), and some birds, owing to an absence of predators, have evolved the inability to fly. Less complexity is not necessarily bad or degenerate. In fact, any biases we may have toward complexity, plasticity, or size probably reflect our own prejudiced, anthropocentric (human-centered) view of nature. If one remembers that that which works is "best" and that simpler forms may work as well as or better than more complex forms, we will not get too enmeshed in empty philosophical arguments about progress and adaptation.

Summary

Ecological conditions influence animals' survival and reproductive success. Characteristics of the organism, including its behavior, that tend to increase reproductive success are said to be adaptations to certain environmental conditions. To discover whether traits are adaptations we can (a) correlate forms of the trait with the presumed selective condition, (b) experimentally manipulate the trait or the selective condition to assess its effect on reproductive success, or (c) see how well the phenotype compares with an independently derived optimal design.

Although most phenotypic traits are adaptive, many are not. Some traits may be in the process of evolving out of a population, others may be maladaptive yet persist because heterozygosity is favored, or because they are influenced by the same genes that contribute to adaptive phenotypic features. Finally, some traits may be more or less advantageous depending on their frequency in the population.

Adaptation most often occurs due to individual differences in reproductive success, that is, individual selection. However, individuals can perpetuate their genes by assisting relatives to reproduce, a process called kin selection. Individual selection and kin selection are merely two ways of achieving the same end: perpetuation of genes. A third level of natural selection, group selection, has also been proposed. This entails competition among populations or species for genetic representation. There seems to be no evidence for group selection.

Evolution (long-lasting changes in the genetic compositions of populations) can occur due to random events, artificial selection (selective breeding), or natural selection. Natural selection is the most important cause of evolution. Natural selection leads to evolutionary change when (a) there are phenotypic differences among individuals, (b) the phenotypic differences are due, at least partially, to genetic differences among the individuals, and (c) reproductive success is correlated with the form of the phenotype. Thus, when a heritable aspect of the phenotype confers on its bearer a greater than average reproductive success, the next generation will have relatively more copies of those gene(s) that were involved in that phenotypic form (at the expense of other genes that contribute to less successful forms).

Natural selection may produce changes in the distribution of phenotypes in a population. In directional selection, individuals at one extreme of the distribution are favored. In stabilizing selection, those individuals with an intermediate form of the phenotype have greatest reproductive success, but in disruptive selection the extremes are favored.

Evolution may appear to be foresightful, that is, there may appear to be a plan leading to this or that phenotype, but this is only illusory. What we see today may look planned only because we are seeing the products of previously successful individuals.

Species faced with similar selection conditions may converge on the same adaptation, but often they do not. This is because species start with different sets of genetic materials that constrain the kinds of changes that can occur or are most likely to occur in the face of changing ecological conditions.

The ancient notion that humans are the most advanced of all creatures and that everything else is striving to become human is known as orthogenesis. Orthogenesis itself, or in disguised form, is still common today and should be discarded. Biases we may have toward complexity, plasticity, or size have no bearing on the adaptive success of species. Each species exists in its own unique ecological context. Sometimes success in those contexts can occur because of the evolution of simpler phenotypic characteristics.

Recommended Readings

BONNER, J. T. (1988). *The evolution of complexity by means of natural selection.* Princeton, NJ: Princeton University Press.

DOBZHANSKY, T., AYALA, F. J., STEBBINS, G. L. & VALENTINE, J. W. (1977). *Evolution*. San Francisco: Freeman.

STEBBINS, G. L. (1982). *Darwin to DNA, molecules to humanity*. San Francisco: Freeman.

WILLIAMS, G. C. (1966). *Adaptation and natural selection*. Princeton, NJ: Princeton University Press.

Chapter 5

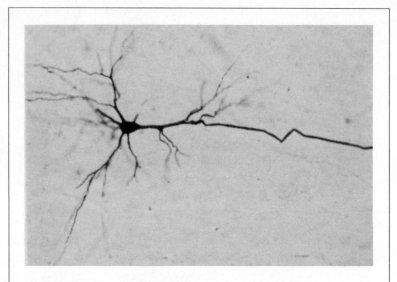

NERVOUS SYSTEMS AND BEHAVIOR

Successful dealings with the environment are crucial to survival and reproductive success. To be successful requires that the animal monitor important features of the environment (such as food, weather, social companions, potential mates, and predators) and then direct its behavior appropriately. Although this sounds straightforward, the mechanisms required to accomplish these things can become quite involved. This is where an understanding of nervous systems is so important. The four components of the genetic–evolutionary model—development, mechanisms, adaptation, evolution—apply as well to investigation of nervous systems as they do to any other topic in the biology of behavior. We will begin with a discussion of the processes involved in development of the nervous system, and then move on to their anatomy and physiology. The adaptive significance of nervous systems and their evolution are discussed in the next chapter.

Ontogeny of the Nervous System

The development of the nervous system is extremely complex and not fully understood. This is hardly surprising given that nervous systems may contain billions of neurons, most of which communicate with hundreds of others. But it is imperative that we understand neural development. Because of the importance of the nervous system to behavior, we cannot afford to ignore the processes that shape its form and function.

NEURAL GROWTH AND DIFFERENTIATION

Beginning with a small number of neurons in the fetus when it is only a few millimeters long, the human nervous system grows to contain billions of neurons collectively weighing over a kilogram in adulthood. In the process, subsets of neurons acquire different shapes, sizes, branching patterns, neurotransmitters, and physiological functions. These changes are referred to as *differentiation*. There are several processes involved in differentiation which are described below.

Neural proliferation Differentiation begins with expansion of the number of neurons through cellular replication processes. The number of neurons proliferates, as does their volume. Because of proliferation, the *neural plate,* a flat slab of tissue from which the nervous system develops, gradually folds inward and then closes, forming the hollow *neural tube* (Fig. 5-1). The interior of the tube eventually becomes the spinal cord's central canal and the brain's ventricles (Cowan, 1979).

The neural tube does not remain uniform along its length. Shortly after its formation, three swellings become apparent near the head end of the neural tube. The three swellings are due to unequal neural proliferation along the neural tube; disproportionate proliferation continues throughout development and varies across species. Proliferation is especially pronounced in the most anterior swelling in many mammals, resulting in paired structures, the cerebral hemispheres, that may dwarf the rest of the brain.

Neural movement Although the nervous system begins as a layer of cells around the neural canal, the final form is millions of cells thick, with cells on the outer surface that may be several inches away from the original layer. How do these cells get there? Unfortunately, the process is not as simple as adding layer after layer. Neurons often migrate considerable distances. How they do this and how they get to the correct location is the subject of considerable research in developmental neurobiology (Purves & Lichtman, 1985).

Neurons move by producing sheetlike extensions of their membranes that adhere to underlying tissue. When an adhesion is formed, contractile proteins (similar to those found in

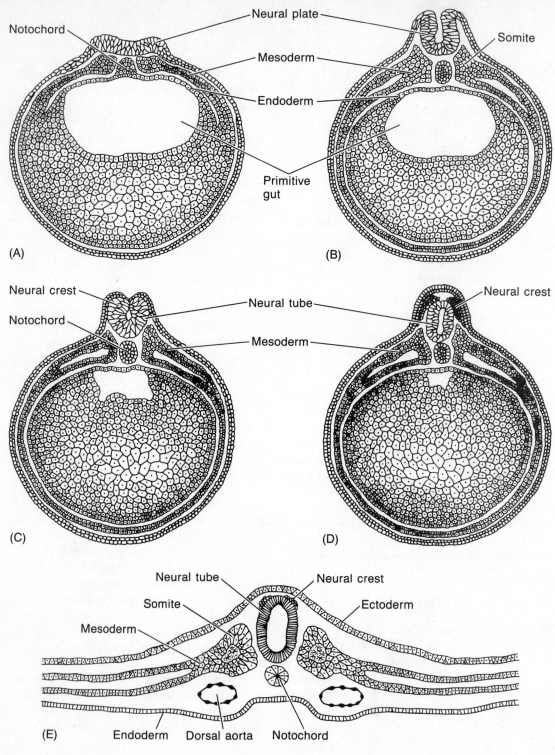

86

muscle) orient themselves along the sheet, pulling the bulk of the cell body toward the adhesion surface. New extensions form, the process is repeated, and the cell moves along the path of best adhesion.

Axon growth and synapse formation A process similar to the one above for the entire neuron occurs in the growth of axons and dendrites away from the cell body. At the ends of growing axons and dendrites are *growth cones,* flattened areas with numerous hairlike projections (Fig. 5-2). Growth cones adhere to surrounding tissue and contractile proteins pull the rest of the extension along (Bray, 1982). The importance of axon growth is that it is the first step toward synapse formation. As the growing axon tip reaches the neuron, muscle cell, or gland that it will influence, the axon tip undergoes modification and forms a terminal button.

The growth of axons from one area to another is precise in its timing and direction (Dodd & Jessell, 1988). Axons do not grow randomly in the nervous system; their growth seems to be guided in some way. For instance, Harris (1986) described the path taken by axons of a frog's retina to part of the brain known as the tectum. He also showed that these axons would "home" toward the tectum even when their starting point was artificially changed. This was accomplished by surgically removing one eye from a young embryo and transplanting it to another location on the other side of the head. The growing axons went straight to their target. Observations such as these raise the question of

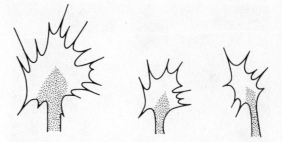

Figure 5.2
Growth cones of developing axons change in shape as the axon extends. Growth cone projections form adhesions to underlying tissue, pulling the axon along.

what guides the growth of axons. Three mechanisms are thought to be involved.

1. *Chemical Signals.* Chemicals sometimes are released by nerve and muscle cells that guide the growth of axons toward them. If there are enough of these signals and if neurons are selectively responsive to them, appropriate connections can become established. The best known chemical signal is a protein called *nerve growth factor* (NGF) (Levi-Montalcini & Calissano, 1979; Levi-Montalcini, 1987). NGF is produced and secreted by several types of nonneural cells. As NGF diffuses away from its points of synthesis, neurons with membrane receptors for it are stimulated to grow along the concentration gradient until contact is made with the target.

Other proteins that selectively induce growth in other populations of neurons are probable (Kuffler *et al.*, 1984; Morrison *et al.*, 1987) and may provide at least a coarse guide for axon growth. McKay *et al.* (1983) have found that bundles of growing axons in the leech nervous system have similar membrane proteins and that different sets of axons have different proteins. These unique proteins may be receptors for NGF-like molecules secreted by their target cells.

Figure 5.1
A series of drawings of the nervous system of a vertebrate as it develops (A is youngest, E oldest). Notice how the neural plate changes shape from a nearly flat slab to a tube.

RITA LEVI-MONTALCINI

"Studies in this last decade have not only provided new strong evidence of the most important contributions of NGF [nerve growth factor] in the field of neuro-embryology, but brought to the fore its significance in the more general field of neuroscience . . . " [Levi-Montalcini, R. (1987). The nerve growth factor 35 years later. Science 237, 1154–1162 (p. 1161).]

Another type of chemical guidance process involves the growth cone interacting with proteins embedded in the membranes of cells on which it is moving. Some of these proteins facilitate adhesion; others inhibit adhesion. Thus, the growth cone is guided in the correct path as it "feels" its way along (Dodd & Jessell, 1988).

Although chemically guided growth patterns can explain how axons reach their correct targets, this mechanism does not seem to be precise enough for the establishment of the specific contacts that we know exist (Easter *et al.*, 1985). For instance, axons from the retina syn-apse on neurons in a brain structure called the thalamus. The pattern of synapses that occurs is highly structured, i.e., the retina's surface is precisely "mapped" onto the thalamus. However, it seems unlikely that separate chemicals direct each of these synapses. It appears, then, that although there may be a chemical affinity between growing axons and their target cells (Sperry, 1963; Constantine-Paton & Law, 1982), other processes may be necessary to direct the highly precise synaptic connections that result.

2. *Glial Guides.* The second mechanism directing axon growth involves special glial cells. For example, just before development of the corpus callosum (a band of axons linking the two halves of the brain), a group of glial cells forms where the callosum will eventually be. The first axons grow along this glial structure. Later, as more and more axons appear in the callosum, the glial cells disappear (Katz *et al.*, 1983). Although such "pathways" probably are common, we know little about how the glial cells themselves appear in the proper place at the correct time.

3. *Mechanical Guides.* Some neurobiologists have emphasized the role of mechanical forces in determining patterns of neural growth (Horder & Martin, 1979). Mechanical guides include gaps, channels, or creases in neural tissue that make growth in some paths easier than in others. Horder and Martin (1979) review examples of such processes that undoubtedly shape neural growth patterns, at least in some populations of neurons. In brief, axons grow along paths of least resistance. Although this seems to be a risky way of building a nervous system, it works quite well and still results in great uniformity of neural structure among individuals because of the uniformity brought about by other developmental processes. Thus, the *same* paths seem to occur in each individual and

the growing axons end up reaching the same targets.

Neural differentiation As mentioned earlier, the first neurons to develop are all alike. Later, however, they begin to take on different sizes, shapes, and physiological characteristics. Because of their importance to behavior, we need to understand the processes of neural differentiation.

The different phenotypes of neurons can be traced to different patterns of gene expression (Chapter 2), which, in turn, are due to the products of other genes, the presence or absence of certain chemicals in the cytoplasm, and to hormones released by other cells (Barnes, 1986). In other words, the local environment acts in concert with the cell's DNA to shape neuronal phenotype. Although the "local environment" encompasses numerous factors, we will pay particular attention to just one: hormones.

Some hormones can enter cells and, together with a receptor protein, bind with a specific portion of a chromosome. Binding may either prevent synthesis of protein by one or more genes, or it may activate protein synthesis (see Chapter 2 for a more complete presentation of these processes).

Probably the best-studied hormone with neuronal differentiation ability is testosterone, the so-called male sex hormone (a misnomer that will be explained in Chapter 10). The presence of testosterone in the brain sometimes has dramatic effects on neurons. For example, a brain region called HVc in canaries contains many more neurons in males than in females (Paton & Nottebohm, 1984), apparently due to testosterone. The HVc neurons are critical to singing. This anatomic difference, then, is responsible for an important sex difference in behavior. Humans and other mammals are known to be sexually dimorphic due to the early effects

of testosterone (MacLusky & Naftolin, 1981; Swaab & Fliers, 1985; Breedlove, 1985). The number of neurons in a neural structure, the size of their cell bodies, and the length and branching patterns of their axons and dendrites are affected by hormones, often resulting in profound functional and behavioral differences.

Neural death and synapse loss Many of the neurons that develop early on will die and many of the synapses that form will eventually disappear. In monkeys, and probably in humans, most neurons are generated during the first half of gestation (Rakic, 1985), although some neurons continue to be added after birth. In humans, the maximum number of neurons is achieved at about 18 months of age (Winick, 1980). Thereafter, the number of neurons declines daily. On the average, about 50% of all neurons die, but in some neuronal groups the mortality may reach 85% (Cowan *et al.*, 1984).

Widespread early neuron cell death is common, but the loss of neurons is selective and seems to be driven by a competitive process (Jacobson, 1974). For instance, neural survival seems to depend on some form of input from the cells of the target field. In experiments in which additional target field cells were added (by grafting an extra limb onto a chick embryo) more spinal cord neurons survived than would normally be the case because they were able to form synapses. In contrast, when the size of the target field was reduced there was a corresponding decrease in the amount of neural survival. Cowan *et al.* (1984) have proposed that cells of the various target fields may secrete a substance that is necessary for the continued survival of the neurons contacting the field. These *trophic substances* are taken up by nerve terminals and transported back to the cell body. Currently, nerve growth factor (NGF) is the only trophic substance that has been identified, although indirect evidence strongly suggests that there are others (Johnson & Yip, 1985). Sympathetic system neurons grown in culture with NGF survive beautifully; without it they die. This is also true in the body. Antibodies to NGF were injected into rats, thus leading to the elimination of NGF. These animals developed without a sympathetic nervous system because the sympathetic neurons failed to survive without NGF (Levi-Montalcini & Callisano, 1979). Because the amount of NGF depends on the amount of target tissue present, the number of surviving neurons from a population varies according to the size of the target population (Cowan *et al.*, 1984).

Some hormones seem to act like trophic substances in that they prevent neural attrition. In rats for instance, the presence of testosterone prevents the loss of a spinal cord nucleus that innervates certain muscles used in male sexual behavior. Administering this hormone to young female rats prevents the loss of these cells (Breedlove, 1985). Bennett and Truman (1985) have demonstrated a similar process in insects, although with a different hormone, and the loss of HVc neurons in female canaries is due to lack of testosterone. In general, it appears that some of the excessive neurons that are originally produced in the developing nervous system will be lost selectively due to the absence of certain hormones.

Coinciding with periods of cell death is the selective loss of synaptic contacts and axon collaterals. For instance, in most adult mammals each muscle cell is innervated by a single neuron. However, earlier in life each muscle cell is innervated by five or six neurons. In the course of development these extra synapses are lost (Cowan *et al.*, 1984). Synapses and collaterals are lost because of cell death due to failure to acquire sufficient trophic substance, but in some cases the neuron does not die, it merely retracts the collaterals that fail to acquire adequate amounts of trophic substance.

Other synapses are lost because they occur on the wrong sort of cell. For example, neurons from the retina will form synapses on muscle cells, but these synapses soon regress and disappear. However, spinal cord neurons that normally synapse onto muscle remain viable. This implies that neurons somehow recognize appropriate and inappropriate contacts and strengthen the appropriate synapses while divesting themselves of inappropriate ones (Nirenberg *et al.*, 1983).

The loss of neurons and of synapses is a way for the nervous system to undergo adaptive modification during ontogeny. It is as though the particular patterns of use cannot be anticipated in advance, and so some initial overgrowth and overconnectivity occurs allowing unused portions to be pulled back. The other possible strategy would be to begin with fewer cells and synapses and then to add selectively to them. However, this strategy is less feasible because the growth of axons becomes more difficult the larger the nervous system and the more tangled it becomes internally. Thus, nervous systems are overdone at first. Those parts that are used remain and grow; those not used wither and die.

GENES, ENVIRONMENT, AND NEURAL DEVELOPMENT

In Chapter 2 we reviewed the interactive roles of genes and environment in the developmental process. This is as true of the nervous system as it is of other features of the organism.

Genetic differences and neural development Most of the research on the genetic effects on brain organization in mammals has been performed on laboratory stocks of inbred mice. This work has revealed that total brain size and the size of brain structures varies among strains (Wahlsten, 1977). In addition, several well-documented brain anomalies have been traced to heredity. First, the corpus callosum some-times fails to develop, or develops incompletely, in some mouse strains (Wahlsten, 1977), and occasionally in humans (Loeser & Alvord, 1968). Second, one or a few genes can affect patterns of connection in the visual system of mammals. Specifically, some retinal neurons have axons that synapse in the thalamus. In individuals with one of the several genes that produce albinism, these retinal connections are made incorrectly, resulting in inadequate binoc-ular vision (Kalil *et al.*, 1971). Finally, due to a single gene, the granule cells of the cerebellum of some mice fail to migrate, then degenerate en masse, resulting in a gross motor defect (Rakic & Sidman, 1973).

Genetic effects on neural development have been successfully studied in invertebrates such as the tiny roundworm, *Caenorhabditis elegans*. Be-cause these animals have only about 300 cells in their entire body, it is relatively easy to discern the effects of single gene mutations on neural form and function. For example, the worm nor-mally moves forward when touched on the tail, and backward when touched on the head. Sev-eral mutations are known that make them insen-sitive to touch, although they do move for other reasons. Touch insensitivity has been traced to a small number of neurons. The mutations that result in touch insensitivity affect the anatomy of these neurons in several ways (Chalfie, 1984).

These examples involve some sort of abnor-mal condition. Does this mean that genes are important only when they produce an abnormal-ity? No. The nervous system, like all complex biological systems, is the product of numerous genes acting with a wide array of environmental conditions. Thus, in terms of understanding the variation that exists among individuals, it is ex-tremely difficult to specify the contribution of any single gene. When a gene produces an ab-normal protein, however, its effects may be far-reaching and easier to discern. That is why we know more about abnormal genetic effects than about normal genetic effects.

Environmental effects on neural develop-ment Genes, of course, act along with envi-ronmental conditions in shaping the developing organism. Hormones were mentioned earlier as having an effect on neural differentiation. Three other environmental effects—nutrition, toxins, and experience—will be presented to further illustrate the role of the environment in neural development.

Nutrition can have long-lasting effects on neural differentiation. During periods of food deprivation the brain is given preferential treat-ment; that is, the brain obtains its nutrients at the expense of other organs if there is not enough for all. However, some nutrients may not be present even minimally, and so brain develop-ment is impaired.

Malnutrition's effects on brain differentia-tion depend on when it occurs, the nutrients involved, and the duration of the malnutrition. Timing is important because, as we have seen, neural proliferation is much more common at some ages than others. Malnutrition can se-verely disrupt proliferation. Thus, in humans, where proliferation is still occurring postnatally, malnutrition early in life has a greater effect than does the same amount and type of malnutrition later on (Winick, 1980). After they are in place and established, many neurons can "weather the storm" of malnutrition.

An interesting example of a specific form of nutritional impairment with profound effects on myelin production has been discovered by Lee and Moltz (1984a) who noticed that young rats became strongly attracted to and consumed ma-ternal feces for about two weeks beginning at about 14 days of age. Young rats who were denied access to maternal feces during this period devel-oped smaller brains for their body weight than did their peers who were able to eat maternal feces. The difference was due to significantly lower myelin content in the deprived animals. The effects have been traced to the presence of deoxycholic acid in the feces of mother rats during this period (Lee & Moltz, 1984b). Deoxycholic acid is not present before or after this period, nor is it present in the feces of nonmaternal rats. Significantly, myelination largely occurs between 15 and 30 days of age, and deoxycholic acid aids in absorption of long-chain fatty acids by the intestines. Myelin is largely fatty acid. Therefore, even though the young rats were apparently consuming enough fatty acid in the mother's milk and in their solid food, they were unable to absorb sufficient amounts of it to satisfy their brain growth requirements.

There are many toxic substances that can influence neural development, but one of them, alcohol, has received a great deal of recent research. Prenatal exposure to alcohol is one of the leading causes of mental retardation in humans. Some of alcohol's effects on the growing brain are quite obvious: Brain size is substantially smaller than in those individuals not exposed to alcohol. Miller (1986) has shown that, in the offspring of female rats who were fed alcohol during pregnancy, the period during which cortical neurons were generated was delayed, the number of cortical neurons was reduced, and their distribution was altered. Although several physiological systems buffer the nervous system against environmental perturbations, some things such as alcohol, other toxins, and inadequate oxygen can have severe repercussions, especially when they occur during periods of proliferation, migration, and differentiation.

Behavioral experience affects several aspects of neural development. Rosenzweig and his colleagues convincingly showed that rats' brains were anatomically affected by their rearing conditions (reviewed by Rosenzweig, 1984). The typical experimental strategy was to take three

MARK ROSENZWEIG

"Work in a number of laboratories has now demonstrated that many aspects of the nervous system's structure, chemistry, and physiology can be modified to a significant extent by exposure to differential environments." [Rosenzweig, M. R. (1984). Experience, memory, and the brain. American Psychologist *39, 365–376 (p. 367).]*

male rats from the same litter and randomly assign one to an "impoverished" environment (living alone in a small, bare, wire cage), one to a "standard" environment (living with a small group of rats in a larger, though still bare, cage), and one to an "enriched" environment (living with many rats in a large cage with many objects to climb on and manipulate). After living this way for several weeks the animals' brains were carefully measured. The enriched environment rats had significantly larger brains overall, and specific parts of the brain were larger than those of the other two groups (Rosenzweig *et al.*, 1972; Rosenzweig, 1984).

Although these findings were met with disbelief when they first appeared, they are now widely accepted. Numerous studies have not only confirmed the original findings, they have also added more detailed accounts of the neuroanatomical and neurochemical differences wrought by the rearing conditions, demonstrated that brain plasticity is present in older animals, and that other rodent species and a primate are similarly affected by rearing conditions (reviewed by Rosenzweig, 1984). Although rearing conditions can clearly affect brain size, this does not necessarily mean that intelligence is improved or impaired by these various experiences. The relationship between brain size and intelligence is complex and is treated in more detail in Chapter 6.

In summary, although a nervous system begins with just a few cells, it undergoes extensive changes during the course of development. Many neurons are added, they come to differ from one another both in structure and activity, and many die or become more limited in their contacts. Some neurons grow while others are being lost. Such changes, which continue throughout life, are affected by individual differences in genes and many environmental conditions such as hormones, nutrients, and experience.

Mechanisms: Anatomy and Physiology

As neural development proceeds, distinct groups of neurons appear and bands or sheets of axons emerge that connect neurons in these groups. Studies of neural mechanisms of behavior focus on the interrelated features of neural anatomy and physiology. We will begin by covering some of the major components of the vertebrate nervous system, and then switch to the physiology of neurons.

MAJOR COMPONENTS OF THE VERTEBRATE NERVOUS SYSTEM

Nervous systems can be very complex, so it is easy to be overwhelmed by the voluminous detail and the myriad unfamiliar terms. To facilitate your learning of neuroanatomy, we will cover only the major components of the vertebrate nervous system in this section. Additional details will be presented in other chapters. Invertebrate nervous systems are treated in Chapter 6.

Peripheral nervous system The vertebrate nervous system is generally discussed in two parts, the *central nervous system* (CNS) and the *peripheral nervous system* (PNS). The CNS consists of the brain and spinal cord; the PNS consists of all other nerves (i.e., bundles of axons) and neurons found outside the CNS (Table 5-1). Some of these peripheral nerves, the *cranial nerves,* carry sensory inputs (in the form of action potentials) to the brain, primarily from the head and neck. The cranial nerves also con-

Table 5-1

DIVISIONS OF THE VERTEBRATE NERVOUS SYSTEM

I. Central nervous system
    A. Brain
    B. Spinal cord

II. Peripheral nervous system
    A. Autonomic nervous system
        1. Sympathetic
        2. Parasympathetic
    B. Somatic nerves

vey action potentials away from the brain where they may cause muscle contractions, glandular secretion, or regulation of sensory system sensitivity. The 12 pairs of cranial nerves and their functions are listed in Table 5-2.

In addition to the cranial nerves, the PNS consists of the *spinal nerves* and the *autonomic nervous system.* The spinal nerves are arranged in pairs along the length of the spinal cord. They convey inputs from sensory receptors of the skin, muscles, and joints to spinal cord neurons, and send action potentials out to the muscles from neurons in the spinal cord. For example, the axons that form the sciatic nerve originate from neurons in the lower portions of the spinal cord, and branch off to contact muscles of the leg.

The autonomic nervous system is subdivided into the *sympathetic nervous system* and the *parasympathetic nervous system* (Table 5-1). The cell bodies of neurons of these systems are located in clusters known as *ganglia* that lie outside the spinal cord. Sympathetic ganglia are arranged in a "chain" near the spinal cord, but the parasympathetic ganglia usually are found farther away, near the target organ (Fig. 5-3). The autonomic ganglia neurons receive synaptic contacts from neurons of the spinal cord, and in turn synapse onto such organs as the heart, intestines, and glands. In general, the sympathetic system has activating or arousing effects but the parasympathetic system has slowing, inhibiting effects. For example, the parasympathetic system slows heart rate, but the sympathetic system increases heart rate. Most internal organs have such dual controls, although some organs have only sympathetic or only parasympathetic innervation (Table 5-3).

Central nervous system   The CNS is divided into two parts, the spinal cord and the brain. Although they have extensive intercon-

Table 5-2

THE CRANIAL NERVES AND THEIR FUNCTIONS

NUMBER	NAME	FUNCTION
I	Olfactory	Smell
II	Optic	Vision
III	Oculomotor	Eye movements, pupil contractions
IV	Trochlear	Eye movements
V	Trigeminal	Sensation from face, chewing movements
VI	Abducens	Eye movements
VII	Facial	Facial muscle contraction, taste
VIII	Vestibulocochlear	Hearing, balance
IX	Glossopharyngeal	Taste, sensation from tongue and throat, swallowing, salivation
X	Vagus	Sensation from throat and internal organs. Muscle contraction of throat and many internal organs
XI	Spinal accessory	Sensation from neck and shoulders. Muscle contraction of neck and shoulders.
XII	Hypoglossal	Tongue movements

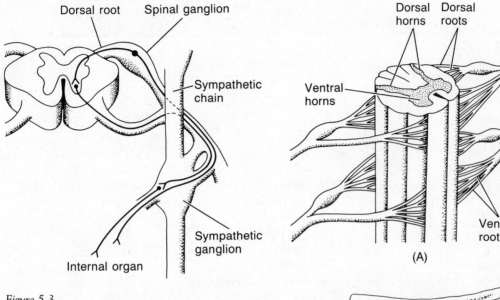

Dorsal root   Spinal ganglion

Sympathetic
chain

Sympathetic
ganglion

Internal organ

Dorsal   Dorsal
horns   roots

Ventral
horns

Ventral
roots

(A)

(B)

Figure 5.3
The sympathetic nervous system lies just outside the
spinal cord in a "chain" of ganglia (clusters of neuron
cell bodies) interconnected with axons. Sensory and
motor neurons are shown connected to a hypothetical
internal organ and to the spinal cord. The parasym-
pathetic system (not shown) has ganglia lying near the
target organ rather than near the spinal cord.

Figure 5.4
A simplified diagram of a spinal cord shows the dorsal
and ventral horns, where neuron cell bodies are lo-
cated, and the white matter (axons) surrounding the
horns. The central canal is filled with cerebrospinal
fluid and is continuous with the brain's ventricles.

nections, the spinal cord and the brain will be treated separately.

The spinal cord is nearly round in cross section (Fig. 5-4), with the central portions consisting mostly of neuron cell bodies (*grey matter*) and the surrounding regions made up mostly of axons (*white matter*). The grey matter of the spinal cord is shaped somewhat like a butterfly. The top or dorsal (toward the back) "wings" are known as the *dorsal horns*, and the lower wings are the *ventral horns*. The dorsal horn neurons receive synaptic input from sensory neurons but the ventral horn neurons are predominantly mo- tor (i.e., they synapse onto effector tissue such as muscles and glands). This dorsal-sensory and ventral-motor dichotomy does have exceptions,

Table 5-3
AUTONOMIC NERVOUS SYSTEM EFFECTS ON VARIOUS ORGANS

ORGAN	SYMPATHETIC EFFECT	PARASYMPATHETIC EFFECT
Pupil	Dilation	Contraction
Sweat glands	Perspiration	None
Heart muscle	Increased rate	Decreased rate
Coronary arteries	Dilation	Constriction
Bronchi of lungs	Dilation	Constriction
Lung blood vessels	Constriction	None
Lumen of gut	Decreased peristalsis	Increased peristalsis
Liver	Glucose release	None
Gallbladder	Inhibition	Excitation
Kidney	Decreased output	None
Penis	Ejaculation	Erection
Abdominal blood vessels	Constriction	None
Muscle blood vessels	Constriction (adrenergic) Dilation (cholinergic)	None
Skin blood vessels	Constriction (adrenergic) Dilation (cholinergic)	Dilation
Blood coagulation	Increased	None
Blood glucose	Increased	None
Basal metabolism	Increased	None
Adrenal cortical secretion	Increased	None
Mental activity	Increased	None
Piloerector muscles	Excited	None
Skeletal muscle strength	Increased	None

however (Chung *et al.*, 1983). The axons of the spinal cord primarily come from spinal cord neurons and synapse on neurons either higher or lower in the cord, or in the brain. As is the rule throughout the nervous system, the fiber tracts (groups of associated axons) of the spinal cord are labeled according to the location of their cell bodies and the location of their synapses. For example, the spino-cerebellar tract originates in the spinal cord and terminates in the cerebellum, an important part of the brain.

A diagrammatic sketch of some of the major regions of the brain is presented in Fig. 5-5. If one followed the spinal cord toward the brain, the first brain structure encountered would be the *medulla oblongata* or simply, *medulla*, a transitional area between spinal cord and brain. Several *nuclei* (groups of neuron cell bodies) are scattered throughout the medulla, and the neurons within these nuclei give rise to axons that make up some of the cranial nerves.

Ascending farther, additional brain struc-

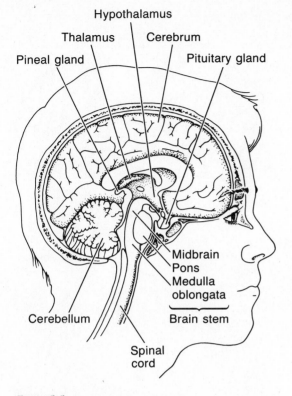

Hypothalamus

Thalamus   Cerebrum

Pineal gland   Pituitary gland

Midbrain
Pons
Medulla
oblongata

Cerebellum   Brain stem

Spinal
cord

Figure 5.5
Some of the principal brain structures mentioned in the
text are sketched here. In the top illustration of a
whole human brain (front is left), the bulk of the cere-
brum is shown only in outline to reveal the recessed
structures. The bottom outline shows the brain split
lengthwise along the midline.

and several nuclei (collectively known as the *tectum*) that process visual and auditory input or which control movements of the eyes and ears.

The *hypothalamus* is a small but extremely important part of the brain consisting of many discrete nuclei, each with its own rather unique function. The hypothalamic nuclei, in general, are involved in regulating physiological systems. For instance, blood oxygen and glucose concentrations, and hormone levels are monitored and adjusted by hypothalamic neurons. In addition, because of its intimate connections with the pituitary gland, the hypothalamus has indirect control of many hormones. It is not surprising, then, that hypothalamic neurons actively participate in neural systems that regulate feeding, drinking, aggression, and sexual behavior, to mention just a few.

The *thalamus* is another area composed of numerous nuclei. Located dorsal to the hypothalamus, the thalamus is involved in processing sensory input and in control of movement. In both cases the thalamus operates in close association with the outer surface of the brain, the cerebral cortex. Some thalamic neurons project their axons to specific cortical areas; others project more diffusely.

The *hippocampus* is involved in certain forms of learning and memory, particularly where spatial relationships are concerned. Also, in conjunction with several other brain structures known collectively as the *limbic system* the hippocampus participates in emotional processes.

The *cerebrum*, which is divided into two interconnected halves, the *cerebral hemispheres*, is what one normally thinks of as the brain. The human cerebrum is a massive region that overlies the deeper brain structures discussed above, although in most vertebrate species the cerebrum is much smaller.

tures are encountered. Overhanging the medulla is a large, deeply fissured structure, the *cerebellum.* The cerebellum is an important component of motor control systems because it participates in initiating and coordinating patterns of muscle contractions.

The *midbrain* consists of some major axon tracts involved in control of body movement,

The cerebral hemispheres have an outer layer of neurons called the *cerebral cortex* which is generally regarded as being the primary site of thought and other "higher-order" cognitive functions, such as speech production and comprehension, memory, and problem solving. Also, the cerebral cortex has areas devoted to sensory/perceptual processes such as vision and touch, and areas that participate in movement.

Each cerebral hemisphere is divided into four *lobes*, defined by the positions of certain grooves along the convoluted cortical surface or by microscopic cellular differences. The four lobes are the *frontal, parietal, temporal, and occipital* (Fig. 5-6). To some extent, the lobes are functionally distinct. The occipital lobe, for example, is primarily involved in visual information processing.

Beneath the cerebral cortex are extensive areas of fiber tracts that send action potentials to and from the cortical neurons. Other clusters of cell bodies within the cerebrum, such as the *basal ganglia,* which are involved in movement, are interspersed within the widespread fabric of the cortical axons.

The two cerebral hemispheres do not function independently. They are in constant communication with the other hemisphere via axons that cross the midline of the brain. There are several bundles of such axons, the largest of which is the *corpus callosum.*

The *cerebrospinal fluid* (CSF), a liquid similar to blood plasma, circulates around the outer surface of the brain, cushioning it from the inner surface of the skull. CSF is also found in the four *cerebral ventricles* of the brain and in the *central canal* of the spinal cord (Fig. 5-7). The CSF tends to remain stable in its chemical composition over time and it may buffer neural tissue, which is extremely sensitive to its chemical environment, against the relatively unstable com-

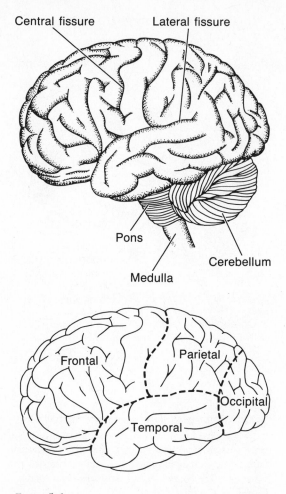

Figure 5.6
The cerebral cortex is heavily convoluted in the human brain. The central sulcus separates the frontal and parietal lobes; the lateral fissure separates the temporal from the frontal and parietal lobes. There is no sharp demarcation between the occipital and the other lobes.

position of the blood (Spector & Johanson, 1989).

Finally, the outer surface of the brain and

Third ventricle   Lateral ventricles

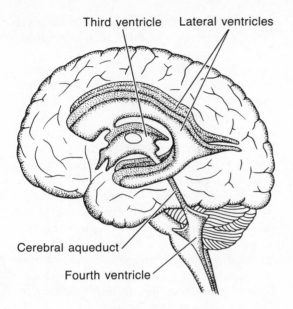

Cerebral aqueduct

Fourth ventricle

Figure 5.7
The brain's ventricles contain cerebrospinal fluid. Their
locations relative to the outer surface of the brain are
shown here. The circular space in the third ventricle
is where the two sides of the thalamus join at the
midline.

spinal cord are covered with three membranes, collectively called the *meninges*. The outermost of these is the *dura mater*, a tough, leathery material that lies adjacent to the skull. The two other meninges, the *arachnoid* and the *pia mater* lie next to the brain surface, separated from the dura by a layer of CSF. Infections of the meninges (meningitis) cause inflammation which can damage the underlying neural tissue.

Lateralization   An inspection of the vertebrate nervous system suggests that it is symmetrical, with right and left sides being mirror images of one another. However, careful measurements of both sides of the brain suggest that symmetry

is only superficial. The presence of asymmetry is referred to as *lateralization*. The presence of left–right asymmetry in the brain should not be surprising. Humans, like other animals, are asymmetrical from head to foot (Levy & Levy, 1978).

Brain lateralization is both anatomical and functional. The size differences in corresponding parts of the cerebral hemispheres are generally associated with differences in function. For example, parts of the left temporal lobe of humans are larger than the right. The left hemisphere is generally superior to the right in terms of language production and comprehension in adults. In contrast, the right hemisphere is superior at certain spatial and tactile processes. Human subjects who have had the corpus callosum surgically cut—thus severing most of the left–right neural connections—perform better on a block design matching problem when using the left hand (which is controlled by the right hemisphere) than when using the right hand (Gazzaniga, 1967). Finally, Witelson (1985) has shown that the size of the corpus callosum is about 11% smaller in exclusively right-handed people than it is in left-handed or ambidextrous people. Right-handers are generally more lateralized (i.e., have more functional asymmetry) than non-right-handers, and the relative paucity of interconnections may be the anatomical basis for this finding. The popular press has made "left-brain, right-brain" a major fascination. Although asymmetries certainly exist, their importance is often over-emphasized. The text edited by Geschwind & Galaburda (1984) is an excellent source for accurate information.

This brief introduction to the nervous system is now complete, although much more detail will be provided in some later chapters. Additional information on neuroanatomy can be found in Moyer's (1980) well-illustrated text.

BASICS OF NEUROPHYSIOLOGY

The physiological processes of neurons are quite complex. We will begin by reviewing physiological conditions in neurons that are neither sending nor receiving action potentials. Then we will tackle the mechanisms of action potential generation and reception.

Resting membrane potential The entire neuron is surrounded by a *lipid bilayer membrane,* so named because it is constructed of a double layer of lipid (fat) molecules. This membrane, although structurally simple, precisely regulates the neuron's activity (Knox, 1983). The membrane's regulatory ability comes from a large number of protein molecules (the *integral proteins*) embedded through it such that they are exposed to the extracellular fluid (outside the cell) and to the cytoplasm (inside the cell membrane). Some of the integral proteins are ion channels (an ion is an electrically charged atom—more on them in a moment). There are several types of ion channels in the membrane of most neurons (Stevens, 1984). They are like tiny, flexible tubes stuck through the membrane that can open and close, selectively allowing only certain ions to pass through the membrane (some channels, however, are more selective than others). Ion channels are named for the ion "species" that passes through them most readily. For present purposes the most important ions and their channels are sodium (Na^+), potassium (K^+), and chloride (Cl^-). The movements of these ions through the membrane can be regulated by opening and closing ion channels.

Let us begin by considering the distribution of ions when the neuron is at rest, i.e., neither sending nor receiving action potentials. At such times, Na^+ and Cl^- are more abundant in the extracellular fluid, but K^+ and sundry large, negatively charged protein molecules are more abundant in the cytoplasm (see Fig. 5-8). The interior–exterior difference in concentrations of these ions means that the neuron is polarized, something like a battery. Neural polarity is not very strong, only about -70 millivolts (mV; thousandths of a volt), with the interior negative relative to the exterior.

Anyone who has taken a chemistry course or who has seen how a drop of ink spreads through a glass of water knows that substances tend to flow from areas of greater concentration to areas of lesser concentration, i.e., down their concentration gradients. Moreover, substances tend to move along electrical gradients such that ions tend to move away from areas with the same charge. Concentration gradients and electrical gradients would both tend to reduce or eliminate the polarity that exists across the membrane by causing the various ions to reach equilibrium. Why does the polarity remain?

The membrane is polarized because it is not equally permeable to these ions. The large protein molecules cannot pass through the membrane. Potassium tends to leave the interior because of its greater internal concentration, but this is balanced by the greater positive charge outside the cell. Thus, although potassium ions cross the membrane, there is no net change in potassium concentration. Chloride will tend to flow into the neuron but this is countered by the electrical gradient. Finally, sodium will tend to flow into the cell both because of its concentration gradient and the electrical gradient. The usually strong impermeability of the membrane to sodium, however, effectively impedes movement of sodium into the cell.

Although permeability to sodium is low, some does enter, and as it does so, potassium will tend to exit. Neurons respond by expelling sodium ions from the interior and by pulling potassium in from the outside. Through this energy-consuming process, called the *sodium-potassium pump,* the resting membrane potential

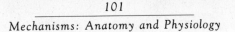
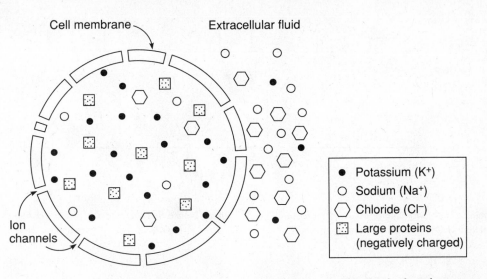

Figure 5.8
Ions, electrically charged atoms or molecules, are not evenly distributed across the neuronal membrane. Sodium and chloride ions are more abundant outside the *cell; potassium and negatively charged proteins are more common inside the cell. Movement of ions through the neural membrane occurs at a variety of ion channels.*

is maintained. These processes are covered in detail by Kuffler *et al.* (1984, chap. 8).

The neuron at rest is in a state of dynamic equilibrium. Ions are moving through the membrane in both directions, but the net change in polarity is zero. Disruptions of this dynamic equilibrium are responsible for the communication that goes on between neurons, a topic to which we now turn.

Most of the early work on the resting membrane potential was done with the giant axon of the squid because its diameter (nearly 1 mm) is much greater than that of most vertebrate axons. With a giant axon suitably prepared with recording microelectrodes, another electrode some distance away can deliver a tiny electric shock. As long as the shock is of low intensity, the interior of the cell momentarily becomes less negative (less polarized) than it was before. This change is called a *depolarization* because polarity

is reduced. Furthermore, the stronger the shock, up to a point, the greater the depolarization (Fig. 5-9).

What is responsible for these depolarizations? Think back to our discussion of the ions in and around the neuron. Temporary depolarizations can be achieved either by moving positively charged ions into the neuron, or by moving negatively charged ions out of the neuron. Through some elaborate experiments in which various drugs are used to inactivate ion channels selectively, it has been found that depolarizations usually are due to the opening of sodium channels, allowing more sodium than usual to enter the interior of the cell (Keynes, 1979). If the shock is brief and small, the sodium channels quickly close and the extra sodium is pumped out. Relatively little sodium movement across the membrane is required to produce these changes.

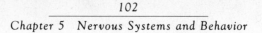

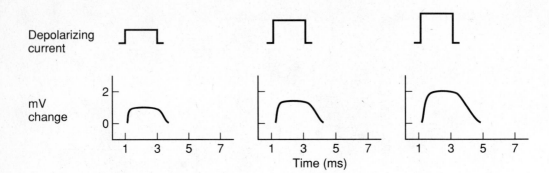

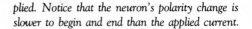

Figure 5.9
The amount of polarity change occurring in a stimulated neuron depends on the amount of current applied. Notice that the neuron's polarity change is slower to begin and end than the applied current.

ACTION POTENTIALS

As long as the intensity of the shock stays below a certain level, the amount of depolarization is tightly linked to the shock intensity. But when the intensity of the shock depolarizes the neuron to a particular value, known as its threshold, the neuron responds by generating an *action potential* (also known as a nerve impulse or spike) (see Fig. 5-10). Action potentials indicate a decidedly different physiological state, one characterized by a sudden loss of polarity with the cell interior even becoming positively charged. This sudden reversal is short-lived, however, and in the absence of further stimulation, the neuron quickly regains its polarized resting state.

What happens during an action potential? First, sodium channels open, and as they do so sodium moves into the cell, reducing polarity until the threshold value is attained. Sodium channels are also involved in the sudden loss of polarity. That is, up to threshold the channels open a little, and a little more, until the polarity is such that the channels suddenly open completely. This allows much more sodium to enter and the cell rapidly depolarizes. Sodium chan-

nels are *voltage gated*; that is, the extent to which they open depends on the difference between the interior and exterior of the neuron. For instance, the sodium channels are fully open at, say, −60 mV. They close completely shortly thereafter and remain "closed" for about one millisecond. It appears, then, that sodium channels can be almost completely closed (as during the resting membrane potential), partially open (during depolarization up to threshold), fully open (during the rapid upswing phase of the action potential), or inactivated and unable to be reactivated for a short time (during the falling phase of the action potential) (Keynes, 1979).

There is more to an action potential than these changes in sodium channels. Potassium channels also are involved. About the time that the sodium channels close, the potassium channels open. Potassium leaves the cell for two reasons. First, potassium is more concentrated inside the cell and thus tends to flow outward, along its concentration gradient. Second, because of the influx of sodium, the interior of the cell becomes positive and thus potassium tends to move out of the cell. The primary differences between potassium channels and sodium chan-

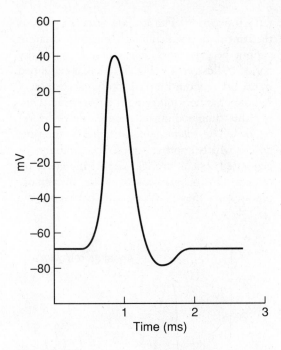

Figure 5.10
An action potential differs dramatically from graded potentials. Action potentials are characterized by rapid depolarization followed by an equally rapid return to the resting membrane polarity. Action potentials begin when a neuron is sufficiently depolarized by neurotransmitter molecules.

membrane. In some axons, the ionic changes described above occur repeatedly along the length of the axon. In other neurons, the action potential events recur periodically along the length of the axon, skipping places in between. In such axons an insulating material called *myelin* is produced by *glial cells* that wrap themselves around the axon. Adjacent myelin sheaths are separated by small, unmyelinated membrane segments called *nodes of Ranvier*. This process is called *saltatory conduction* because the action potential "jumps" from one node to the next. Action potential propagation is faster in myelinated axons because the density of sodium channels is much greater in the membrane exposed at the nodes than it is in membranes of unmyelinated

nels are that potassium channels are slower to become activated following the electric shock, and potassium channels are never fully inactivated, i.e., the membrane is much more permeable to potassium ions (Keynes, 1979). The involvement of sodium and potassium channels in the action potential is diagrammed in Fig. 5-11.

Action potentials spread along the neuronal membrane. This movement or *propagation* occurs because the polarity changes that occur at one point on the membrane are sufficient to open sodium channels of adjacent pieces of

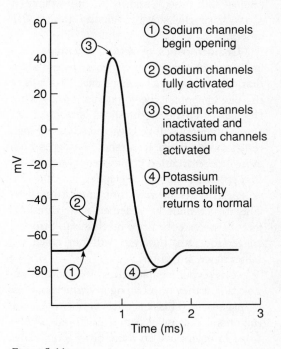

① Sodium channels begin opening

② Sodium channels fully activated

③ Sodium channels inactivated and potassium channels activated

④ Potassium permeability returns to normal

Figure 5.11
A simplified account of the molecular events underlying action potentials is shown here.

axons. Catterall (1984) estimated that sodium channel density in the nodes is about 2000 to 12,000 per square micron (a micron is one millionth of a meter), but density in the membrane of unmyelinated axons is only about 100 per square micron. This means that sodium ions can enter more quickly at nodes of Ranvier thereby creating a more rapid polarity change. This current quickly spreads, depolarizing one node and then the next down the length of the axon. This is much faster than the slower-onset depolarization that must occur micron by micron in unmyelinated axons. Action potential propagation velocity is also influenced by axon diameter, with larger axons propagating action potentials faster than thinner axons. Thus, large-diameter axons have the highest action potential velocity (about 120 m/sec) and thin, unmyelinated axons have the slowest velocity (about 0.1 m/sec).

Characteristics of action potentials   An important characteristic of action potentials is that they follow an *all-or-none law*. The basis of this phenomenon is the voltage gating of sodium channels. Whenever threshold is reached, an action potential will be triggered whose characteristics are uniform. If threshold is not reached, even if depolarization comes very close, an action potential will not be generated. An action potential is, in some ways, similar to firing a gun. The trigger must be squeezed with threshold force to activate the firing mechanism. Stronger trigger squeezes, however, will not make the bullet move any faster.

The second characteristic of action potentials is that they travel along axons without loss of magnitude. This *nondecremental conduction* is important because if action potentials diminished in magnitude en route down long axons, neural communication efficiency would be reduced.

Finally, action potentials have two types of

refractory period. The *absolute refractory period* is the time during which another action potential cannot be generated. The absolute refractory period is illustrated in Fig. 5-12 and is explained by the brief (about 1 millisecond) inactivation of sodium channels following their opening. During this time sodium channels cannot be reopened. The *relative refractory period* is the time during which another action potential can be generated, but a stronger depolarization is required. This occurs because of an "overshoot" past resting membrane potential; that is, the

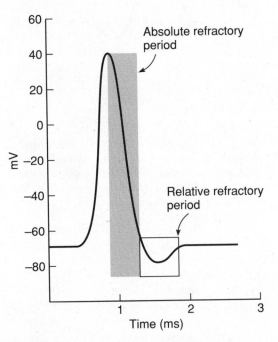

Figure 5.12
The shaded box represents the duration of the absolute refractory period, when another action potential cannot be generated in a particular piece of cell membrane. During the relative refractory period, shown by the open box, another action potential can be generated, but it requires more depolarization than usual to reach threshold.

polarity becomes more negative than usual after returning to resting membrane potential (Fig. 5-10). If depolarization is sufficient another action potential can be generated, but the amount of depolarization required to reach threshold is greater than it is while the neuron is at resting membrane potential.

Refractory periods are important to neurophysiological functioning because they prevent action potentials from retracing their path along the axon. If a microelectrode is used to stimulate an axon at its midpoint, the action potential will indeed travel in both directions. However, the membrane region that just had an action potential will be in its refractory period and thus cannot generate another one, so the action potential does not backtrack.

SYNAPSES

How do action potentials begin in normal tissue? The answer involves the stimulation provided by other neurons at points known as *synapses.* These are of two types: electrical and chemical.

Electrical synapses Electrical synapses occur at *gap junctions,* places where the axon of one neuron and the membrane of another neuron are connected by a few protein "pipes" called connexons (Unwin & Henderson, 1984). The connexons regulate the flow of substances between cells and may facilitate the flow of current from one neuron to the next when an action potential arrives.

Although electrical synapses are more common in invertebrates, they do occur in vertebrates, including humans. Electrical synapses are very fast. In crayfish and lobsters, for instance, electrical synapses control the muscles used in rapid escape where a millisecond could mean the difference between life and death. Also, electrical synapses are not as vulnerable to

the vagaries of temperature fluctuation as chemical synapses are. For "cold-blooded" species this can be important because some things need to be done even in cool conditions. Leeches that live in cool ponds can still respond because they have many electrical synapses (Nicholls & Van Essen, 1974).

Chemical synapses A chemical synapse is diagrammed in Fig. 5-13. Terminal buttons at the end of axons come close to other neurons, usually at their dendrites or cell body. The terminal buttons do not touch the next neuron, although they come exceedingly close. The space between the terminal button and the next neuron's membrane is the *synaptic gap* or *cleft,* which is continuous with the extracellular fluid. Because the terminal button comes before the cleft, it is known as the *presynaptic membrane;* the next neuron comes after the cleft, and is therefore called the *postsynaptic membrane.*

The terminal button under very high magnification (Fig. 5-14) can be seen to contain numerous spherical bodies known as *vesicles.* The vesicles are tiny packets containing chemicals called *neurotransmitters.* Neurotransmitters are responsible for bridging the cleft between the presynaptic and postsynaptic membranes.

When an action potential arrives at a terminal button, its calcium channels open, thereby allowing calcium ions to enter. The influx of calcium ions causes some of the synaptic vesicles to fuse with the presynaptic membrane, and to release their neurotransmitter contents into the synaptic cleft (Llinas, 1982; Zucker & Lando, 1986). The vesicles usually remain fused with the membrane only momentarily before the breach in the membrane is resealed (Fig. 5-14). The neurotransmitter molecules float in the extracellular fluid of the cleft; they are not transported across, nor are they "shot" out of the vesicles.

Some of the neurotransmitter molecules

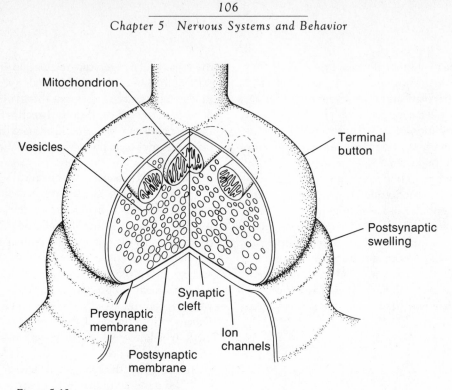

Mitochondrion

Vesicles

Terminal
button

Postsynaptic
swelling

Presynaptic
membrane

Synaptic
cleft

Postsynaptic
membrane

Ion
channels

Figure 5.13
A terminal button and postsynaptic swelling are illustrated in this drawing of a chemical synapse.

that come in contact with the postsynaptic membrane strike specialized integral proteins called *receptor sites*. The neurotransmitter molecule is a three-dimensional object, and the receptor site is a three-dimensional space conforming to the shape of the neurotransmitter. Associated with the receptor site is an ion channel that can regulate the movement of one or more ion species. Some channels are specific to sodium, potassium, chloride, or calcium, but others are more general, allowing several types of ion to pass. When a neurotransmitter fits into a receptor site, the ion channel opens, increasing the permeability to one or more ions.

The changes in membrane permeability brought about by a neurotransmitter may change the polarity of the postsynaptic neuron. Increasing permeability to sodium or calcium

will depolarize the neuron because these positively charged ions enter the neuron. In contrast, increasing permeability to chloride or potassium will hyperpolarize the neuron. When chloride, which is negatively charged, enters the neuron, it increases polarity. Potassium, which is positively charged, tends to leave the neuron when its permeability is increased. The loss of potassium therefore increases polarity.

Depolarizations of the postsynaptic neuron are known as *excitatory postsynaptic potentials* (EPSPs) because they excite the cell; that is, EPSPs push the postsynaptic neuron toward its action potential threshold. On the other hand, hyperpolarizations are known as *inhibitory postsynaptic potentials* (IPSPs) because they push the postsynaptic cell's potential away from threshold, making action potentials less likely. EPSPs

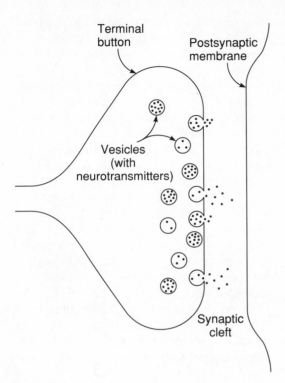

Terminal button

Postsynaptic membrane

Vesicles (with neurotransmitters)

Synaptic cleft

Figure 5.14
Within the presynaptic membrane, vesicles may either be full, fused with the membrane and releasing the neurotransmitter, or largely devoid of transmitter after a release. The latter will later be refilled.

and IPSPs together are known as *graded potentials* or *synaptic potentials*, and must not be confused with action potentials. Postsynaptic cells usually have two or more types of receptors, allowing both EPSPs and IPSPs to occur on the same neuron.

Graded potentials vary in magnitude depending on the number of active receptor sites and whether they produce EPSPs or IPSPs. Because EPSPs and IPSPs can occur on the same neuron, the net polarity change in that neuron will be determined by the number of EPSPs and

IPSPs occurring at different synaptic sites on its surface. This is called *spatial summation.* If there are enough EPSPs occurring on a neuron to cancel out the IPSPs and to depolarize it to its action potential threshold, an action potential is generated. This is the usual means by which action potentials are instigated in the nervous system.

There is another type of summation of graded potentials known as *temporal summation.* As action potentials arrive at a particular terminal button a quantity of neurotransmitter is released, causing a polarity change in the postsynaptic membrane lasting up to about 100 msec. If successive releases occur with little delay between them, their effects can summate. When EPSPs summate, they bring the neuron closer to its action potential threshold, but when IPSPs summate, the neuron is brought away from threshold.

In summary, each neuron is constantly integrating the depolarizations and hyperpolarizations occurring on its surface. If the net depolarization reaches threshold, the neuron generates an action potential that will be conveyed to yet other neurons to depolarize or hyperpolarize them.

NEUROTRANSMITTERS AND THEIR RECEPTORS

Let us take another look at the molecules used at chemical synapses, the neurotransmitters. There are numerous chemicals that function as neurotransmitters. Indeed, one estimate (Snyder, 1980) puts the total at over 200, some of which also have other functions elsewhere in the body. A few neurotransmitters are listed in Table 5-4.

Neurotransmitters After the discovery in the 1920s of acetylcholine, one of the most abundant neurotransmitters, other chemicals

Table 5-4

NEUROTRANSMITTER CHEMICALS
AND THE BIOCHEMICAL GROUPS
TO WHICH THEY BELONG

The neurotransmitters listed here are only a
fraction of those found in the nervous system.

Acetylcholine (ACh)

Monoamines
  5-Hydroxytryptamine (serotonin) (5HT)
  Histamine
  Dopamine (DA)
  Norepinephrine (NE)   } Catecholamines
  Epinephrine

Amino acids
  Gamma-aminobutyric acid (GABA)
  Glycine
  Glutamate
  Cysteine

Peptides
  Vasopressin
  Oxytocin
  Substance P
  Luteinizing hormone releasing hormone
    (LHRH)
  Angiotensin II
  Beta-endorphin
  Leu-enkephalin
  Cholesystokinin

have been found that mediate communication between neurons. The discovery rate has been extremely rapid in the past 10–15 years due to rapidly advancing biochemical and genetic techniques, and to well-funded research programs because of the involvement of these chemicals in health and disease. This area of neurobiology is advancing very rapidly. Rather than attempt an up-to-the-minute review of all

these substances, which could easily fill a book in itself, we will review the better-known neurotransmitters individually and some of the others as groups.

The neurotransmitters can be classified according to their chemical structure (Table 5-4). One of the most widespread neurotransmitters, acetylcholine (ACh), is used to initiate muscle contraction. ACh is also found throughout the central nervous system where it is excitatory at some synapses and inhibitory at others.

The monoamine group contains serotonin or 5-hydroxytryptamine (5HT). Cell bodies of neurons that produce 5HT are restricted to a small area of the brain but their axons extend widely. A subset of the monoamines is the *catecholamines* such as dopamine, norepinephrine, and epinephrine (adrenalin). Like 5HT, these neurotransmitters are produced by rather small clusters of neurons, but their importance is undeniable due to the widespread extension of catecholamine-releasing axons throughout the brain.

Several amino acids, the building blocks of proteins (Chapter 2), have been identified as neurotransmitters. The most widespread of them is gamma-aminobutyric acid (GABA). Although GABA is an amino acid, it is not incorporated into proteins, but instead is found at an estimated one-third of all synapses where it is usually inhibitory (Iversen, 1979; Gottlieb, 1988).

Finally, a large number of peptides influence neuronal communication (Snyder, 1985). Peptides are short chains of amino acids that occur in the brain and in many other organs such as the gut and liver. The neuropeptides occur in small quantities in many parts of the brain, and are the most recently discovered and therefore least understood of the neurotransmitters (Krieger, 1983). In fact, there are so many kinds of peptides that differ from one another only in chemical detail that neurobiologists are undecided about how many functionally distinct neuropeptides may exist. Several of them are listed in Table 5-4.

Synthesis and transport of neurotransmitters The production or synthesis of neurotransmitters occurs in two different ways, both of which are linked to the genes. One way, typical of the peptide transmitters, is most directly influenced by the genes. First, long chains of amino acids (polypeptides or proteins) are coded by a gene and assembled in the ribosomes (see Chapter 2). In most cases the polypeptide is cleaved into two or more shorter peptide units by special enzymes.

Some neurotransmitter synthesis is accomplished by enzymes. That is, an enzyme may change a molecule by adding or deleting components, rearranging their positions, or linking molecules together. The modified molecule may then be changed by yet another enzyme. In fact, several of these enzymatic series produce more than one type of neurotransmitter because the intermediate products are themselves neurotransmitters. The catecholamines provide an excellent example (Fig. 5-15).

Although it was long believed that each neuron synthesized only one type of neurotransmitter, it now appears that many neurons may synthesize two or more neurotransmitters (Hokfelt *et al.*, 1984). A neuron may produce both a peptide and a catecholamine, for example. When two transmitters are produced they tend to have complementary effects on the postsynaptic cell, such as a peptide producing a sustained EPSP and ACh producing brief, fast EPSPs.

Finally, neurobiologists are reporting cases of neurons changing their neurotransmitter(s). This appears to be common during early development of the nervous system, but probably also takes place in mature mammalian nervous sys-

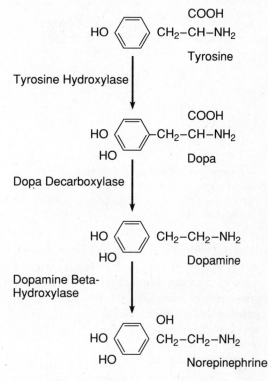

Figure 5.15
Neurotransmitters are often synthesized in a multistep process. This illustration shows the steps involved in the synthesis of catecholamine neurotransmitters.

tems (Black *et al.*, 1984). Changes in the neurotransmitter released by a neuron may not only affect the sort of polarity change occurring in a postsynaptic cell, but may also allow neurons to begin communicating with a new set of target neurons. This has some fascinating implications for developmental changes in behavior.

Regardless of how the neurotransmitter is produced, it must be present in the terminal button to be released. In some cases, such as the production of the catecholamines, synthesis occurs in the terminal buttons. In other cases, most notably the peptides, synthesis occurs only

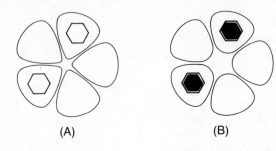

(A)   (B)

Figure 5.16
Looking down on a flat piece of postsynaptic membrane, the acetylcholine receptor and ion channel is thought to consist of a ring of five protein units, two of which have sites for binding an acetylcholine molecule (open hexagons, left). When ACh is not bound to these sites, the ion channel is closed (left), but when the sites are occupied, the protein units change shape, permitting ion flow (right).

in the cell body. Thus, the completed neuropeptide, or at least its precursor molecule, must be transported to the terminal button. This is accomplished by *microtubules* running the length of the axon (Schwartz, 1980). The movement rate ranges from less than a few millimeters per day to 50 mm or more.

Receptors   Although each neuron may produce only one or two neurotransmitters, it may have six or more types of receptor, some of which may be activated by the same neurotransmitter. Why would so many types of receptor occur on a single neuron? It would seem most efficient to have only two, one for EPSPs and one for IPSPs. The answer lies primarily in the different time courses followed by the various receptors. That is, some receptors produce fast but brief changes in polarity, while others are slower to begin but have longer-lasting effects. We will return to this topic in a moment.

For the time being, we need to review the receptors for some of the neurotransmitters listed in Table 5-4. Undoubtedly the best understood receptor is the one that was first discovered, the nicotinic ACh receptor, so called because of nicotine's ability to activate it. The characteristics of this receptor have been sum-marized by Changeux *et al.* (1984). The receptor is a ring of five proteins embedded through the membrane with a pore through the center (Fig. 5-16). Two of the proteins contain a receptor site for acetylcholine. When these sites are filled the receptor is activated and its conductance to sodium is increased (Fig. 5-16).

Neurotransmitters may have different receptors, each with its own characteristics and distribution within the nervous system. Some of these receptors are listed in Table 5-5.

Inactivation   After a neurotransmitter has engaged a receptor, it eventually leaves and its effect ceases. This phase is referred to as inactivation, and is usually accomplished by enzymes found in the synaptic cleft. For instance, acetylcholine is inactivated by acetylcholine-esterase (ACh-ase), an enzyme that decomposes ACh into its two component parts, acetic acid and choline. The components are taken back into the presynaptic neuron, a process called *reuptake*, where they are assembled into fresh ACh molecules. Other deactivating enzymes exist for the other neurotransmitters. Monoamine oxidase (MAO) and catecholamine-O-methyltransferase (COMT) inactivate monoamine and catecholamine transmitters.

Table 5-5

MANY TRANSMITTERS HAVE TWO OR MORE TYPES OF RECEPTORS, SOME OF WHICH ARE LISTED HERE

The receptors have different properties leading to EPSPs or IPSPs following different time courses (e.g., fast and transient to slow and long-lasting.)

NEUROTRANSMITTER	RECEPTOR NAMES
Acetylcholine	Nicotinic, muscarinic
Dopamine	D1A, D1B, D2
Norepinephrine	Alpha, beta
Histamine	H1, H2
Gamma-aminobutyric acid	A, B

WHY ARE THERE SO MANY NEUROTRANSMITTERS?

Neurotransmitters either cause EPSPs or IPSPs on the cells that they contact. Why, then, are there so many different neurotransmitters when it would seem that two would be sufficient, one to produce EPSPs and another to produce IPSPs? There are two reasons for the large number of neurotransmitters. One has to do with the duration of the effect of the neurotransmitter, and the other is concerned with control of different behavioral systems.

Temporal effects Synaptic transmission was originally described as a quick coupling of transmitter molecule and receptor with a consequent brief change in polarity. Although fast, brief effects are important, they are not the only way to run a nervous system. In fact, it makes adaptive sense to have slower-developing but longer-lasting changes in postsynaptic cells. We will cover a few examples of these longer-lasting effects.

ACh in frogs has at least two effects in addition to producing fast EPSPs (Kuffler, 1980). In one of them, ACh initiates a slow IPSP that lasts two to three seconds. It is controlled by a receptor that increases permeability to potassium. In another, a slowly developing EPSP lasting about 30 seconds is produced by decreasing potassium permeability.

Chemicals that produce synaptic changes lasting several seconds or longer are usually called *neuromodulators*. In essence, they change the "tone" of the neurons they influence by temporarily resetting the potential such that fast-acting neurotransmitters may be more (or less) effective. For instance, in the slow EPSP of the frog, the postsynaptic neuron is set nearer its action potential threshold for about 30 seconds. Thus, fewer standard EPSPs are needed to produce an action potential. The slow EPSP makes the neuron more sensitive to other EPSPs.

There are several reasons why neuromodulation may be beneficial. For example, if a hint of a predator is detected, the prey may benefit by being vigilant, and sensitive to all changes occurring in the surrounding environment. Although this could be accomplished by continuous release of fast-acting neurotransmitters, it would be more efficient to have a neuromodulator increase sensitivity for several minutes each time it is released. Neuromodulators accomplish this by activating a physiological process known as a *second messenger system* (Nathanson & Greengard, 1977). Here, in simplified form, is how a typical second messenger works: When the neuromodulator fits into its receptor site, permeability to calcium ions increases in the postsynaptic neuron. Calcium activates an enzyme system that adds or deletes phosphate groups on the proteins that comprise ion channels. This protein change is reversible, but while it is in effect the movement of ions through that channel is modified (either increasing or decreasing ion flow, depending on the change made to the protein). Thus, the neuromodulator does not appreciably change the postsynaptic neuron *directly*, but has an important effect by initiating another process (Marx, 1985; Bloom, 1981; Nestler *et al.*, 1984).

Long-lasting changes can be produced by other substances, such as some hormones. Hormones may fit into receptors on the membrane of the neuron, or they may pass directly into the interior of the cell where they interact with internal receptors, or attach directly to the DNA in the nucleus. In either case, the activity of the DNA may be modified (in ways discussed in Chapter 2) and, as a result, certain proteins may be synthesized. For example, the neurotransmitter receptors are proteins whose construction is under the control of DNA. A substance that acts on the DNA may lead to increased production of these receptors which could eventually mean that the postsynaptic membrane now would have more receptor sites than it previously had. This in turn would mean that a given amount of neurotransmitter would have a greater effect. Alternatively, the neuron's DNA might be stimulated to produce proteins that are cleaved to produce neuropeptides, or enzymes for synthesizing other neurotransmitters.

In summary, substances released by one neuron can have effects on the postsynaptic neuron that range from a few milliseconds, on up to seconds or minutes. The advantage of influencing postsynaptic neurons for varying amounts of time is one reason for having an abundance of neurotransmitters.

Behavioral control Another reason for having so many neurotransmitters is the specific control that they can exert on functionally dis-

tinct behaviors. For example, when very small amounts of vasopressin were injected into the medial preoptic area of the brain of freely moving hamsters, the animals almost immediately commenced grooming the eyes and snout, licking the fur of the flanks, and rubbing the flanks on the walls of their cages. (The skin of the flanks has glands whose product is used in olfactory communication.) When vasopressin was injected elsewhere in the brain, even less than a millimeter away, these behaviors did not occur. Moreover, other peptides (oxytocin and angiotensin II) injected into the medial preoptic area did not increase the grooming, licking, and flank-rubbing (Ferris *et al.*, 1984).

Unfortunately, each behavior category does not have its own transmitter. In fact, the same transmitter may occur at several places in the brain, and be involved in different behaviors or physiological processes at each one. Vasopressin, for example, not only influences grooming and scent marking, elsewhere it regulates blood pressure. If there were only two types of neurotransmitter, however, there might be a tendency for behavioral control systems to blur together. The synaptic cleft is continuous with the extracellular fluid and some neurotransmitter is sure to leak away from the vicinity of the terminal button where it was released, perhaps influencing neurons elsewhere. By using several transmitter chemicals, behavioral control systems can be kept more distinct.

DRUG EFFECTS AND NEUROTRANSMITTERS

Because of the many steps involved in chemical synapses, anything that affects one process can affect synaptic transmission and therefore behavior (Snyder, 1984a). Drugs are known that affect all aspects of synaptic activity; we will review a few of them.

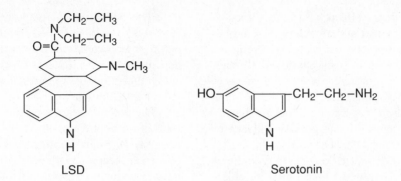

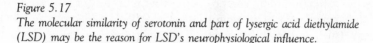

LSD   Serotonin

Figure 5.17
The molecular similarity of serotonin and part of lysergic acid diethylamide
(LSD) may be the reason for LSD's neurophysiological influence.

Transmitter agonists Some drugs are chemically similar enough to neurotransmitters to be effective at their receptor sites. Drugs with such effects are called *agonists* of the transmitter they "mimic." (Agonists should not be confused with *antagonists*, drugs that interfere with a particular transmitter.) Examples of agonists are common. LSD, an hallucinogenic drug, is structurally similar to serotonin (Fig. 5-17). LSD has a high affinity for one type of serotonin receptor, and mimics the effect of serotonin there. These receptors are widespread in the brain, and the activity changes brought about by the drug produce the well-known psychedelic effects (Jacobs & Trulson, 1979; Jacobs, 1987). The degree to which various drugs bind to serotonin receptors determines how effective the drug is in producing behavioral and perceptual changes (Glennon et al., 1984).

The opiates (a family of drugs that includes heroin, morphine, and codeine) are structurally similar to the recently discovered family of peptide neurotransmitters, the enkephalins and endorphins. These neurotransmitters are used in neural systems involved in the perception of pain, pleasure, and emotional expression (Snyder, 1977). A wide variety of opiate drugs have been produced that have varying affinities for one or more of the "internal opiate" receptors. Thus, the effect of opiate drugs depends on which receptors are activated and how strongly they are activated (Snyder, 1977, 1984a).

Transmitter antagonists Some drugs occupy receptor sites but interfere with synaptic action by preventing the neurotransmitter molecules from gaining access to the receptors. Strychnine, a common ingredient in rat poison, blocks GABA receptors. Because GABA initiates IPSPs, strychnine impedes a major inhibitory process, resulting in seizures. Another drug, curare, blocks ACh receptors at neuromuscular junctions, thereby causing paralysis. Because the diaphragm, the large sheet of muscle whose contractions help pull air into the lungs, uses ACh, curare can cause death due to asphyxiation. Finally, naloxone, an opiate antagonist, quickly binds with opiate receptors, even displacing drug molecules that may already be present. Naloxone, however, merely prevents receptor activation and thus is used for emergency treatment of opiate drug overdose (Snyder, 1977).

Other drug effects Although neurotransmitter agonists and antagonists are probably the most common mechanisms of drug action, drugs can affect neurophysiology through other routes. For instance, one of the effects of cocaine is slowing the reuptake of norepinephrine into the terminal button, thereby keeping the transmitter in great abundance in the synaptic cleft (Van Dyke & Byck, 1982).

The list of drugs with known synaptic effects is very long. Some of them, such as chlorpromazine, are useful in treating some psychological disorders that may result from neurotransmitter problems (such as certain forms of schizophrenia), but some have no known beneficial effects. The interested reader should consult a psychopharmacology textbook (e.g., Julien, 1981) for more details.

NEUROTRANSMITTERS AND BEHAVIORAL DISORDERS

Given the importance of neurotransmitters to neurophysiological processes and the relationship between neurophysiology and behavior, it is scarcely surprising that abnormalities of neurotransmitter systems will likely produce various behavioral disorders. Exciting discoveries are being made in the area of molecular reasons for psychiatric problems in people, and these discoveries not only help treat those who are afflicted, but further our understanding of normal forms of these behaviors (Snyder, 1984a). Two examples are presented here; others can be found in Snyder's (1980) excellent text.

Schizophrenia Schizophrenia is characterized by a variety of extreme thought disorders, including such hallucinations as hearing nonexistent voices telling the person what to do. Schizophrenics may be abnormally fearful, concoct far-fetched explanations of their actions, and so on (Snyder *et al.*, 1974). There is abundant evidence that schizophrenic symptoms are linked to dopamine, particularly to dopamine receptors (Ciaranello & Boehme, 1982). Schizophrenics tend to have elevated numbers of dopamine receptors (Seeman *et al.*, 1984; Farde *et al.*, 1986) relative to nonschizophrenics who are matched for age and sex.

The drugs that are used to treat the symptoms of schizophrenia affect the dopamine systems of the brain. Antipsychotic drugs block dopamine receptors; indeed, the effectiveness of a given amount of the drug is strongly correlated with the affinity of the drug for dopamine receptors (Nicol & Gottesman, 1983). Perhaps the genetic basis of schizophrenia (McGue *et al.*, 1986) is linked to the production of dopamine receptors or dopamine itself (Nicol & Gottesman, 1983).

Obsessive–compulsive disorder Obsessions are thoughts that recur at abnormally high rates, and compulsions are more overt behaviors that are repeated far more often than necessary. Some people who suffer from obsessive–compulsive disorder may wash their hands hundreds of times each day, others pluck out their hair strand by strand, and still others find themselves constantly thinking about spiders or other potentially harmful conditions (Rapoport, 1989). Ironically, people who suffer from these problems are usually aware that their behavior and thoughts are unjustified and they want to stop them, but seem unable to do so. Obsessive–compulsive disorders are now being treated with a drug, clomipramine, that blocks the reuptake of serotonin, meaning that more serotonin remains in the synapses longer after its release. In many cases, the obsession or compulsion ceases soon after the drug is taken and remains under control as long as the drug is taken in the appropriate dose (Rapoport, 1989).

Numerous other abnormal behavior patterns involving eating, sleeping, aggression, and so on have been linked to neurotransmitters. We may never be able to solve all of them chem-

controls of behavior will not only increase the chances of finding relief from these problems, but will also increase our understanding of normal, adaptive behaviors.

Summary

Nervous system development begins with only a few unspecialized cells, and then grows to include (in some species) billions of specialized neurons interconnected in precise ways. The processes involved in these developmental ically, but investigations of the neurochemical changes are reviewed. The section ends with a discussion of flexibility in brain organization, viewed from the perspective of gene-related brain structural differences, and from the perspective of environmental variables that can affect neural structure and physiology.

The mechanisms of the nervous system are presented in two major sections, one covering neuroanatomy and the other covering physiological principles. The primary components of the typical vertebrate nervous system are presented. Included in this discussion are the major structures of the peripheral and central nervous systems.

The resting membrane potential (the condition of a neuron when it is neither sending nor receiving action potentials) involves an unequal distribution of ions, with the inside of the neuron negative relative to the outside. When the neuron is stimulated the potential changes, either becoming more negative (hyperpolarization) or less negative (depolarization). If depolarization reaches a certain level (threshold) an action potential results.

Action potentials are propagated along the axon until they reach the terminal button(s). There, chemical neurotransmitters are released and drift across the synaptic cleft. The neurotransmitter molecules fit into receptor sites, which control ion channels, on the membrane of the next neuron. Depending on which channels are opened, the neuron's polarity is changed to be either more negative or less negative than before. In this way the next neuron may generate its own action potential, or it may be inhibited and thus unable to generate an action potential, at least temporarily.

Neurotransmitter molecules are numerous and their actions are complex. Some neurotransmitters have quick but short effects on other neurons, while others have slow but longer-lasting effects. The latter are called neuromodulators. Drugs can interfere with normal communication between neurons. They do this by mimicking neurotransmitters, blocking receptor sites, changing the amount of neurotransmitter released, and so on. Abnormalities involving neurotransmitters may produce behavioral disorders.

Recommended Readings

BRADFORD, H. F. (1986). *Chemical neurobiology: An introduction to neurochemistry.* New York: Freeman.

JULIEN, R. M. (1981). *A primer of drug action.* San Francisco: Freeman.

KUFFLER, S. W., NICHOLLS, J. G., & MARTIN, A. R. (1984). *From neuron to brain: A cellular approach to the function of the nervous system.* Sunderland, MA: Sinauer.

MOYER, K. E. (1980). *Neuroanatomy.* New York: Harper & Row.

PURVES, D. & LICHTMAN, J. W. (1985). *Principles of neural development.* Sunderland, MA: Sinauer.

SHEPHERD, G. (1988). *Neurobiology.* New York: Oxford University Press.

THOMPSON, R. F. (1985). *The brain: An introduction to neuroscience.* New York: Freeman.

Chapter 6

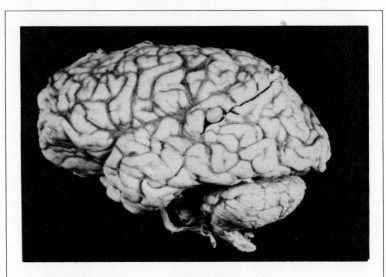

NERVOUS SYSTEMS: ADAPTIVE SIGNIFICANCE AND EVOLUTION

The preceding chapter discussed the development, anatomy, and physiology of nervous systems. We now examine the adaptive value of nervous systems and their evolution. How do nervous systems benefit animals as they go about dealing with their environmental problems? What processes are involved in the changes of nervous systems over evolutionary time?

Adaptive Significance of Nervous Systems

The complexity of nervous systems and their physiology is challenging and exciting, but it sometimes leads us to forget why they exist. As Shepherd (1983, p. x) has written "Nothing in neurobiology makes sense except in the light of behavior." Genes that affect nervous systems evolve because of individual differences in the adaptiveness of their behavior.

There have been two complementary approaches taken to the adaptive significance of nervous systems. One of them seeks to understand the neural processes underlying the natural, adaptive behavior of organisms. The second approach is more comparative in method and seeks to understand neural differences among species by relating features of neural organization to ecological circumstances.

NEUROETHOLOGY

Behavior helps organisms adapt to their environments, and because behavior is an outcome of neural processes, it follows that we can gain insights into behavior by examining neural processes. This field is known as *neuroethology* and is a rapidly growing interface between neurobiology and the behavioral sciences. Neuroethology concerns itself with neural mechanisms of naturally occurring animal behavior patterns, and with the development, adaptive significance, and evolution of these neural–behavioral systems (Camhi, 1984; Bullock, 1990). Neuroethology differs from other disciplines in the neurosciences that attempt to understand neural mechanisms without relating them to behavior. In this section we will review two case studies in neuroethology to illustrate its methods and objectives.

Escape behavior of cockroaches Escaping

THEODORE BULLOCK

"Neuroethology . . . is any ethology that explicitly seeks to make statements about the neural causation, ontogeny, and evolution of a behavior. . . . The field is inevitably both reductionist and integrative, both comparative and general . . . " [Bullock, T. H. (1990). Goals of neuroethology. BioScience *40,* 244–248 (p. 244).]

the attacks of predators is of obvious adaptive value. What are the neural bases of escape? This problem has been carefully researched by Camhi and his colleagues (e.g., Camhi, 1980, 1984). Cockroaches in darkness reliably move away from the attack lunge of a toad. They do not need visual cues to initiate or direct the escape, nor do they require auditory or olfactory information. Evidence indicates that the insects are responsive to air currents generated by the toad's movement. Air movement is detected by fine sensory hairs on the cerci (Fig. 6-1). When the cerci are removed or the hairs are covered by glue, the cockroach fails to turn away when stimulated by air puffs. The relevant neural elements are shown in Fig. 6-1. Each cercus has about 220 "hairs" that are responsive to wind-generated movement, each of which is associated with a sensory neuron. The sensory neuron sends action potentials along its axon to the central nervous system where synapses occur on the cell bodies of giant interneurons in the terminal ganglion. The seven pairs of giant interneurons have axons that extend along the nerve cord toward the head, synapsing on motor neurons governing leg movements.

The direction of the wind gust, and thus the location of the predator, is coded by the directional sensitivity of the wind-receptive hairs. Each cercus has nine long hairs arranged in a row. Each of the hairs on a cercus is most easily

bent in only a single plane. Recordings of action potentials of the sensory neuron of the cercus indicates that it is activated when the hairs bend in one direction, but inhibited when the hairs are bent in the opposite direction. Movements of the hairs in other directions produce less vigorous responses. The axons of the sensory neurons synapse, as mentioned above, on the giant interneurons. The directional specificity of the wind-receptive hairs and the sensory neurons is maintained (in modified form) by the giant interneurons. Then, through a process that is not well worked out, but which probably involves neuronal comparisons of opposite-side pairs of giant interneurons, appropriate amounts of leg muscle contractions are executed. Perhaps most astonishing of all is that these processes occur within a few milliseconds!

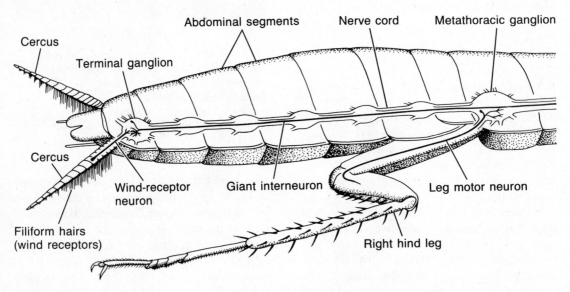

Figure 6.1
The cerci of cockroaches have rows of pliable wind-sensitive hairs which, when bent, depolarize a wind-receptor neuron. These neurons synapse with a giant interneuron in the terminal ganglion. Running along the *nerve cord, the giant interneurons can lead to muscle cell contraction by means of motor neurons in the metathoracic ganglion. The cockroach's legs move in appropriate ways, leading to escape from attacking predators.*

Mate attraction sounds of fish   In an evolutionary sense, mating successfully is as important as living a long life. For many species, successful reproduction requires attracting a mate, and this, in turn, may entail individuals of one sex producing signals that announce their location and readiness to mate. Bird songs sometimes do this, as do the chemical secretions of some insects and mammals. Another example of this phenomenon is the sounds made by males of some intertidal fishes, such as the midshipman of California (Bass, 1990). During the breeding season, males produce a loud, raspy "hum" that attracts females. The sound is loud enough that it can be heard by people outside the water, and can be quite obnoxious if one lives in a houseboat!

Bass (1990) has conducted an elegant series of studies on the development of the structures used in sound production, of the neural mechanisms involved, and even of changes that probably occurred in the evolutionary process leading to these adaptations from nonvocal ancestral species. Males vocalize but females do not, probably due to the early organizational effects of testosterone on males. The fish make their sounds by means of muscles that are attached to the swim bladder, an organ used by most fish to regulate their buoyancy as they change depth. Intertidal fish live in shallow water so the swim bladder is less useful in its traditional role. By tinkering (Chapter 4), evolution has modified this organ for sound production. (Think of the sound made by rubbing an inflated balloon.) Further, playback experiments indicate that females approach the sound source, and, in the presence of a male, proceed to lay eggs that he fertilizes.

These two examples serve to illustrate the basic approaches of neuroethology. Adaptive behaviors are linked to neural processes. Although the cockroach example is more detailed in the understanding of specific neurons and their interactions, the fish example shows a better understanding of developmental and evolutionary issues. Other examples of neuroethology drawn from a wide range of species will be presented throughout the text.

COMPARING BRAINS

The human brain is undoubtedly the feature that gives us the greatest pride. So much emphasis is placed on the brain that our proclivity toward comparison almost always centers on it. Illustrations such as the one in Fig. 6-2 are found in nearly all textbooks in which brain structure is discussed. Many of these brain comparisons are either useless or biased, largely because they imply that brain size directly reflects the intelligence of the species (or of the individual of a particular species).

There are, of course, enormous species differences in the size of the brain. The brains of some whales and elephants may weigh between five and eight kilograms, but the brains of some small birds and mammals weigh only a few grams. The human brain is toward the large end, weighing slightly over one kilogram on average. Is there any adaptive significance to these glaring differences? Are species with larger brains more intelligent than species with smaller brains? Although these are reasonable questions to ask, they are not easy to answer. This section will address the problems involved in comparing brains, and review some hypotheses that attempt to explain why species differ in the size of their brains.

Brain and body size correlation   Let us begin with the most obvious problem: the correlation between brain size and body size. Larger-bodied species tend to have larger brains. They also tend to have larger intestines, adrenal

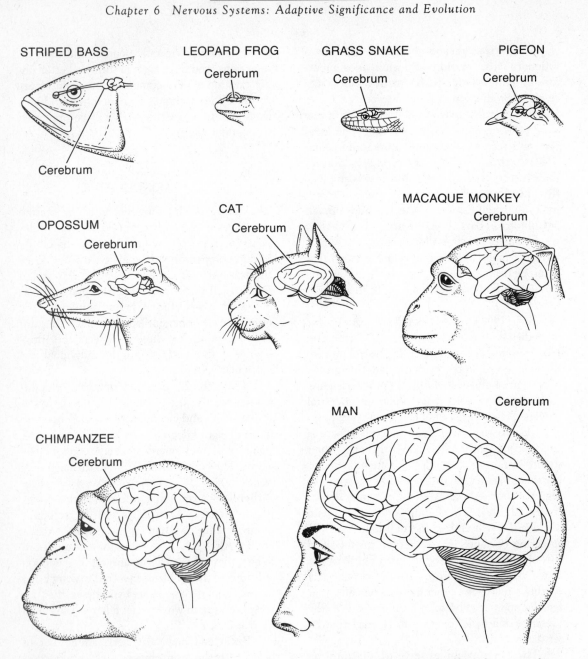

STRIPED BASS

LEOPARD FROG
Cerebrum

GRASS SNAKE
Cerebrum

PIGEON
Cerebrum

Cerebrum

OPOSSUM
Cerebrum

CAT
Cerebrum

MACAQUE MONKEY
Cerebrum

CHIMPANZEE
Cerebrum

MAN

Cerebrum

Figure 6.2
The brains of several vertebrates are frequently shown in ways that emphasize relative sizes, particularly of the cerebrum. This series should not be construed as an evolutionary sequence in that none of these species is ancestral to any other.

glands, hearts, and other organs. Because many of the neurons of all species are responsible for processing sensory input or for controlling motor output, it follows that larger animals, with more muscle mass and larger sensory surfaces, would have more neurons. For comparison purposes, we should at least express brain size relative to body size.

Body size, however, can be measured in several ways, including weight, length, volume, and surface area. Although body weight has been most commonly used in brain to body comparisons, weight (or any of the other measures) differs in importance among species, thereby biasing results. For example, because aquatic animals are supported by water, weight is probably of less concern to dolphins and whales than it is to bears and elephants.

However, even if weight is judged to be a good measure of body size, the body's composition should also be considered. For instance, some species routinely store a great deal of fat. Fat provides insulation for animals living in cold climates and is a good way of storing energy. Although fat adds to body weight, the amount of neural tissue devoted to fatty tissue is far less than the same amount of lean tissue. Thus, the ratio of brain weight to total body weight is probably lower in those animals, such as penguins and polar bears, for whom it is ecologically advantageous to store large amounts of fat. I know of no research in which brain weight is expressed relative to lean body weight.

In spite of its shortcomings, body weight has been the standard reference for expressing brain-to-body size ratios. In general, when brain and body weights are plotted on logarithmic scales, brain weight increases linearly with body weight. The slope between them has been estimated to be about 0.66 (Jerison, 1976) to about 0.75 (Harvey & Krebs, 1990). That is, for every unit of body weight increase, brain weight in-

creases about 0.66 to 0.75 units (see Fig. 6-3). The slope depends on the group of animals being studied. In primates, for instance, the slope is about 0.75 (Armstrong, 1985), but other groups have shallower slopes (Riska & Atchley, 1985). In birds, the slope is about 0.56 (reviewed by Harvey & Krebs, 1990). Generally, the more limited the group the shallower the slope (Pagel & Harvey, 1989).

Adaptive hypotheses about relative brain size Regardless of the slope relating brain size to body size, some species are relatively larger-brained than others. That is, some species lie above the line relating brain size to body size, but other species lie below it. The *encephalization quotient* is a measure of the average brain size of a species relative to a "typical" animal of the same body size (Jerison, 1976). If the EQ is 1.00 the species has a brain size precisely as expected for an animal of its size. If the EQ is greater than 1.00 the brain is larger than is expected for its size. Of course, the nature of the reference group is very important, and some controversy exists as to the most appropriate way of conducting such comparisons (Harvey & Krebs, 1990).

Having computed encephalization quotients using an appropriate reference group, can a hypothesis be devised to account for species differences? One hypothesis links relative brain size with intelligence. The hypothesis states that larger encephalization quotients mean that more neural tissue is available for "intelligent" functions such as learning, memory, and problem solving (Macphail, 1982; Jerison, 1985).

The evidence in support of this hypothesis is controversial because of the difficulty in deriving unbiased tests of animal intelligence. In the absence of such data, we often fall back on "common knowledge" to support the hypothesis. For example, encephalization quotients indicate that primates tend to have rather large brains compared to other mammals, that modern

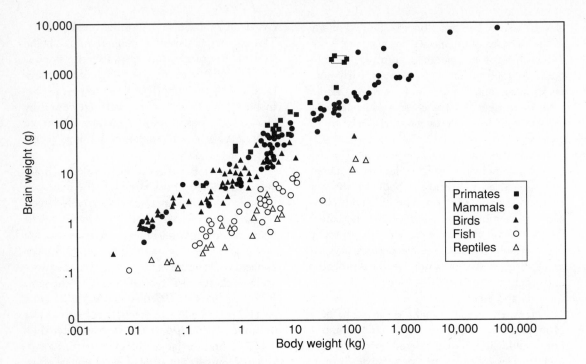

Figure 6.3
The relationship between brain weight and body weight is illustrated in this scatterplot based on many vertebrate species. Most of these groups have a slope of 2/3 when both variables are measured in log units. The four dots connected with lines represent the extreme scores for samples of humans.

mammals have larger brains than extinct mammals [although estimating body weights for extinct species is very difficult (Radinsky, 1982)], that reptiles have smaller brains than comparable-size mammals (Jerison, 1976), and that modern humans have larger brains than did our hominid ancestors (Passingham, 1975). Although it may seem plausible that primates are more intelligent than mammals in general, and that mammals are more intelligent than reptiles, plausibility is no substitute for hard data. Performance on a learning task is usually accepted as a measure of intelligence in animals, but the results here can be extremely fickle. Researchers tend to choose tasks that would seem to be a

reasonable gauge of human intelligence, and, not surprisingly, animals' performance on such tasks is almost perfectly predicted by their evolutionary closeness to humans. Is the superior performance of monkeys on a learning task due to their relatively large brains, or is it due to their sharing our bias about the chosen task, a bias that is not likely shared by fish, rats, or lizards? In other words, the tasks we set for animals may or may not tap their sensory, motor, and integrative abilities that have evolved in response to each species' ecological conditions. Some bird species that cache food in hundreds of hidden stores have superior memory abilities, for instance (Kamil & Clements, 1990), but this does not mean that these birds are more intelligent than other birds in some general sense. In Chapter 8 we will see more examples of species that are highly skilled in learning and remembering certain things, but not others. In other words, a general intelligence that is reflected in brain size may not exist.

Another adaptive hypothesis of relative brain size differences centers on species' diets. For a particular group of animals brain size tends to be relatively large in those species whose food is distributed in space and time in ways that favor the ability to remember the location from day to day. For example, fruit-eating bats have relatively larger brains than insect-eating bats (Eisenberg & Wilson, 1978). Tropical fruit trees do not ripen in unison. Therefore, within the flight range of the bats there may be only a few trees with edible fruit, but they may bear fruit for several days before it is depleted by the bats and other animals. The bats remember the locations of these trees and then switch to other trees after the fruit is depleted. Insects, in contrast, appear more sporadically and are not as predictable in their locations. Thus, there is less advantage to insectivorous bats to recall the locations of former insect swarms.

Relative brain size differences have also been linked to diet in primates (Clutton-Brock & Harvey, 1980) and dinosaurs (Gould, 1978c) in which leaf-eating or grazing is associated with relatively small brains compared to those species that ate fruit or preyed on other animals.

Another hypothesis to account for differences in relative brain size concerns metabolic rate. In general, as body size increases, metabolic rate decreases. Much of the total energy expenditure of an animal is accounted for by the brain, which consumes far more oxygen and glucose than comparable amounts of nonneural tissue. Armstrong (1983, 1985) has emphasized the necessity of having the bodily capacity to

power the brain. This can be done in two ways. First, a certain amount of neural tissue can be fueled by a relatively large body with lower metabolic rate. A larger body means a larger, more powerful heart, larger lungs for extracting oxygen, and more digestive system surface area for mobilizing energy sources. A second method for fueling the brain is to have a smaller body operating at a higher metabolic rate. Thus, the small heart beats faster, respiration rate increases, and so on.

Taking metabolic rate into account eliminates much of the relative brain size variability among species. This is true of mammals in general (Armstrong, 1983) and in a sample of 21 primate species (Armstrong, 1985), but not in a group of rodents (Hafner & Hafner, 1984). The primate results are particularly interesting. Primates are classified into three suborders, the apes, the monkeys, and the prosimians. Living prosimians (meaning "pre-monkey"), which are now found only in Asia and Africa, resemble the extinct forms that gave rise to monkeys. Prosimians have smaller brains for their body size than monkeys. However, when Armstrong (1985) took metabolic rate into consideration she found that brain:body size ratios were identical in the two primate groups! It appears that prosimians solved the brain-supply problem by evolving relatively large bodies with slower metabolic rates but that the monkeys increased metabolic rate instead. Thus, prosimians appear to have undersized brains.

A third hypothesis for relative brain size differences emphasizes the importance of ecological and behavioral specialization (Hafner & Hafner, 1984). That is, for a given group of species, some may live in ecological circumstances requiring elaborate sensory or motor skills, and these conditions may favor larger brains (or brain regions) for controlling these skills. For example, Mace & Eisenberg (1982) studied 32 species or subspecies of deermice. The brains of island and mountaintop forms were relatively smaller than those of peninsular and lower-elevation forms. Also, brains were relatively large in areas inhabited by many small rodent species than they were in areas with fewer species. Again in rodents, species that are adept climbers have relatively large brains for their body size compared to closely related species that do little or no climbing (Lemen, 1980; Meier, 1983).

Finally, relative brain size differences in birds have been explained by species differences in developmental rates. Precocial species are those which are relatively well-developed at hatching and can move around and acquire food on their own (e.g., chicks, ducklings). Altricial species, such as robins and sparrows, are far less developed at hatching. Their eyes are still closed, and they cannot move about or acquire their own food. Precocial species tend to have smaller brains for their body size than do altricial species (Bennett & Harvey, 1985).

In conclusion, species differences in relative brain size can be explained by several variables (diet, metabolism, ecological and behavioral specialization, and developmental rate) other than intelligence. Further, the importance of these other variables differs among various animal groups. This does not imply, however, that intelligence is *not* associated with relative brain size. Instead, these findings indicate that we should not automatically conclude that species with large brains for their size are more intelligent than species with smaller brains for their size.

Brain size and human intelligence The preceding discussion dealt with comparing different species in terms of their brain sizes. Such comparisons are difficult to accomplish because of the array of complications that are inevitably

present. Can we confine our analysis to a single species to circumvent these complications? Can we associate individual differences in brain size or brain–body ratios with differences in intelligence? This sort of approach has been attempted in humans, largely without success.

The question of whether brain size relates to intelligence in humans has had a long and infamous history. Nineteenth-century anatomists such as Broca and Cuvier in France, and Samuel Morton in America collected human skulls from all over the earth. They used the cranial volumes of these skulls as an index of brain size. They then used cranial volumes to rank human racial and ethnic groups in intelligence. There are obvious problems with this approach. First, they failed to account for differences in body size: the large-bodied Europeans tended to have larger brains than the smaller Asians, for example (Gould, 1978a). And, because men tend to be larger than women, men tend to have larger brains, although we know that, on average, there is no intelligence difference between men and women (Gould, 1978b). The net effect of this poor science was the perpetuation of racism and sexism, made the worse by its veil of scientific authority.

But Broca, Cuvier, and Morton worked a century ago. Certainly we have better data and methods now. What do they tell us? First, the data needed to answer the question of whether brain size is related to intelligence in humans simply does not exist. What we need is, first, the results of a professionally administered IQ test for a large sample of adults. (This assumes that the test is not culturally biased against any segment of the human population, an assumption that is probably not justified at this time.) Second, we need post-mortem brain weights that are not influenced by the cause of death nor distorted by tissue swelling that often occurs after death. Finally, we need other body measures such as body weight or height so that they can be corrected for. Even the best studies fall short of achieving these goals.

For instance, Passingham (1979) presented two studies on brain size and intelligence in humans. In the first he had IQ scores on hundreds of people, but no brain sizes. He used external measures of the skull to estimate brain size. (People may sometimes go to great lengths to help scientific research, but not many are willing to donate their brain, at least until they are finished with it!) When height was controlled for, there was no relation between intelligence and estimated brain size.

In his second study Passingham (1979) acquired data on brain weights obtained during autopsies on several hundred people. However, this time there were no IQ scores, so he used the occupational status of each person as a substitute, arguing that there is a rough correlation between occupation and intelligence. In this study there were slight differences in brain size between occupational categories even after accounting for body size. It held only for men, however. There may indeed be a relationship between intelligence and brain size in humans. Or there may not be. At this point the data are not available and they are unlikely to be available for a long time.

Other ways of comparing brains All the previous comparisons are based on brain weight relative to some measure of body size. There is another method of comparison that has merit. It involves comparing the amount of neural tissue found in a particular brain region with the brain as a whole. The idea is that a species can allocate its brain tissue to various structures based on its importance. We can then make comparative judgments of a structure's importance by examining the structure-to-brain ratio across species.

For example, the part of the cerebral cortex that controls movement of the fingers is very large relative to the rest of the brain in the racoon, an animal known for its manipulation of food and other objects. However, a close relative of the racoon, the South American coatimundi, has only a small area of motor cortex devoted to its digits. However, it has far more motor cortex devoted to control of its snout than does the racoon (Horel, 1973).

Another example of this sort of comparison comes from two populations of marsh wrens, one from California, the other from New York. Male marsh wrens are prolific singers, but on average the California birds sang nearly three times as many song varieties as the New York birds (158 vs. 54). Measurements of brain structures revealed that the California birds had significantly larger brain nuclei involved in song production and reception even though the New York birds had slightly larger brains overall (Canady *et al.*, 1984). In other words, the apparent importance of song in the two populations is reflected by the amount of neural tissue devoted to it.

Evolution of Nervous Systems

To understand why the nervous system of a species is constructed the way it is we must not only investigate the adaptive significance of its structure, but also its evolutionary origins. In Chapter 4 we discussed evolution as a tinkering process. Nowhere is this more evident than in the nervous system. Bundles of axons often take circuitous routes in getting from one structure to another, two or three synapses may intervene where one would suffice, and complex interconnections exist where simple ones would be more efficient (Dumont & Robertson, 1986). Evolutionary biology suggests that these conditions exist because nervous systems were not designed from scratch, but rather were built by a long series of modifications of earlier systems. As long as the behavior produced by the nervous system leads to beneficial reproductive consequences, these not-so-elegant neural systems will persist. The same behavior can be produced by several different neural arrangements (Dumont & Robertson, 1986).

The best metaphor for evolutionary relationships among animals is a tree whose largest limbs represent major related groups, and whose smaller limbs and twigs represent more discrete groups such as families, genera, and species. The vertical dimension of the tree represents time, so the lower a branch forks off, the earlier in evolutionary history a particular group diverged from its ancestral form. It is crucial to remember, however, that even though a group may have appeared early in evolutionary history, it does not necessarily follow that living descendants of that group are the same as their ancestors (Hodos & Campbell, 1969). In most cases, evolution has continued unabated. Today's rats are not unmodified representatives of the rodents of millions of years ago.

The reason for bringing up this cautionary note is that because soft tissues do not readily fossilize, we cannot directly study ancient nervous systems. Therefore, when investigating the evolution of nervous systems, we must, of necessity, study living species as representatives of their ancestors. If the living species closely resembles its fossilized ancestor we may use the modern form as an approximation of the ancient form. Thus, neuroanatomists have studied the brain of the living opossum because opossums are similar skeletally (and presumably, neuroanatomically) to early mammals (Sarnat & Netsky, 1981). Comparative neuroanatomy, then, uses findings on living species as the primary data for testing hypotheses about the past.

EVOLUTIONARY CHANGE AND STABILITY IN NERVOUS SYSTEMS

The comparative method is an approach used to deduce the evolutionary relatedness of animal species. It proceeds by searching for similarities and differences among species' phenotypic features, and then classifies the species based on how many features they share. The more closely related two species are, the more features they will have in common, and the fewer they will have that differ. To understand the evolution of nervous systems we need to look for similarities and differences in such surface features as total size, shape, and degree of convolution of the brain, and in internal features such as the size of various nuclei, patterns of connection among them, and even the presence or absence of entire brain structures. There may also be differences in the microscopic structure of certain neurons or in the chemistry of the brain that may shed light on the evolutionary relationships among animals. This section covers the processes that may have been responsible for differences between species in the structures of their nervous systems.

Neurons seem to work the same way regardless of the species in which they are found. In fact, the basic physiology of nerve cells seems to have been worked out very early in evolutionary history: Single-celled creatures such as *Paramecium* change their behavior by means of changes in permeability to various ions (Quinn & Gould, 1979) that cause their cilia to beat forward or backward, moving them around relative to biologically important stimuli.

As far as we know, all creatures possessing nervous systems, regardless of how many neurons they contain and how many contacts they make with one another, operate by means of graded potentials and action potentials. They all use synapses, and the neurotransmitters they release are common to species throughout the animal kingdom. Evolution seems to have been very conservative at this level. One gets the impression that once a useful process appeared, it remained that way thereafter. Thus, many of the peptide neurotransmitters found in humans are the same ones found in fish, insects, and squid (Krieger, 1983), and the enkephalins and endorphins that were once thought to be unique to humans have been discovered in earthworms (Alumets *et al.*, 1979)!

Although there are striking differences among vertebrate nervous systems (see below), there are also a large number of detailed similarities, some of which appeared in the earliest vertebrates, such as the jawless fishes, and persist in the most modern birds and mammals (Kavanau, 1990). Clearly, evolution of the nervous system has been highly conservative in that elements have been retained over enormous time periods.

The conservative nature of neural evolution does not mean that important changes have not occurred. New structures have been added, and old ones have changed in size, shape, and even function. Further, connections have appeared between structures that were formerly separated. A few examples of such changes follow.

One of the most conspicuous differences in nervous systems is the degree to which the cortical surface is convoluted. Some species' cortical surfaces are smooth, but others are far more convoluted (see Fig. 6-2 for examples). A smooth cortical surface seems to be the original form. Why is the cortex so wrinkled in some species? The convolutions seem to be a way of packing a large amount of cortex into a relatively small area. The skull of a dog or chimpanzee would have to be much larger to accommodate a smooth, stretched-out cortex containing the same number of neurons. Perhaps the advantage of keeping head size within limits to accommo-

date the birth process has placed an adaptive advantage on packing the same amount of cortical tissue into a smaller skull. This argument assumes that there was some selective advantage to having greater amounts of neural tissue (see the section on comparing brains, above), but that there was a disadvantage to large skulls.

Another change in nervous systems involves myelin. Although invertebrate nervous systems contain myelin-producing glia, they do not insulate individual axons, rather, they wrap bundles of axons. Only in vertebrates do we find individually insulated axons. Thus, the axons of vertebrates can be smaller and more energy efficient while obtaining fast conduction.

Probably the most striking evolutionary change is the appearance of a structure or connection not found in ancestral species. The appearance of a new structure is called an *invasion* (Northcutt, 1984). The corpus callosum is a good example of this process. Recall that the corpus callosum is a band of millions of axons that connect corresponding parts of the cerebral hemispheres. Only placental mammals have a corpus callosum; monotremes (such as *Platypus*) and marsupials (such as opossums and kangaroos), both of which evolved before the placental mammals, lack a corpus callosum. However, all mammals have another bundle of axons connecting the two half-brains, the anterior commissure. Thus, more recent mammals have a neural structure not found in species that are representative of more ancient mammals (Katz *et al.*, 1983).

Another neural difference distinguishes primates from other placental mammals. In nonprimates, axons originating from neurons in the retinas extend to the thalamus on the opposite side of the brain. In primates, however, about half of these axons synapse in the thalamus on the same side (Allman, 1982). Although this pattern was once thought to be explained by the more frontal placement of primate eyes, even nonprimates with frontal eyes, such as cats, have very little same-side projection. This difference between primates and nonprimates is so striking that it has been used as a basis for classifying animal species. For example, the large fruit-eating bats of Australia may be more closely related to monkeys than to the smaller, insect-eating bats because the fruit-eating bats have the primate retinal–thalamic projection pattern; other bats do not (Pettigrew, 1986).

INVERTEBRATE NERVOUS SYSTEMS

Although most of our attention to this point has been on vertebrates, the numerous and diverse invertebrates (animals lacking backbones) are important to a complete understanding of the biology of behavior. Young (1967) has emphasized the central role played by invertebrate neurons and nervous systems in our understanding of neurophysiology. Work on the action potential in squid axons is a case in point. In this section we will review a few invertebrate nervous system designs. There are, of course, numerous variations on these themes, as well as many others not presented here. Detailed treatments are available in Bullock and Horridge (1965) and Lentz (1968).

Nerve nets and rings Some nervous systems are quite diffuse. In some of the coelenterates, such as *Hydra,* the nervous system consists of a loose network of neurons around the body surface. There are no areas of greater density of neurons, and therefore no centralization of neural functions. When stimulated, the neurons interact with each other in simple but effective ways to bend the body or capture prey. In other coelenterates, such as the jellyfish, the nervous system has somewhat more centralization, with interconnected ganglia arranged in a ring

around the margin of the bell. When stimulated, the nerve ring neurons activate other neurons whose axons project up through the bell toward the top of the animal, producing muscle contractions. These contractions force water out of the bell, propelling the animal away from the source of stimulation (Roberts & Mackie, 1980).

Bilateral nerve cords Some invertebrates have two paired nerve cords running the length of the body. The flatworm *Planaria* has such a system (Fig. 6-4). The two cords have ganglia (clusters of neuron cell bodies) along their lengths and are interconnected at regular intervals by axons that extend across the animal. *Planaria* has a primitive brain in the head end formed by the fusion of the anteriormost ganglia.

Ventral nerve cord systems Many invertebrates, including the insects and annelids (segmented worms such as the earthworm and leeches) have nervous systems consisting of a single nerve cord (which is really two cords fused together) running the length of the body (Fig. 6-5). This ventral cord consists of a series of ganglia, which have an outer layer of neuron cell bodies and a core of dendrites and short axons,

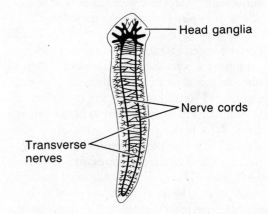

Figure 6.4
The nervous system of the flatworm, Planaria.

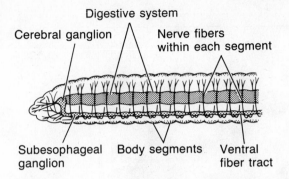

Digestive system

Cerebral ganglion   Nerve fibers
                      within each segment

Subesophageal   Body segments   Ventral
ganglion   fiber tract

Figure 6.5
The nervous system of the common earthworm is typical of the ventral nerve cord system found in many invertebrates. Each body segment has a ganglion along
the ventral cord. Neuron cell bodies in the ganglia in-
nervate the muscles of that segment. The head of the
animal, to the left, has larger, more specialized ganglia.

connected by axons. Some of the ganglia are
larger than others. For instance, there is a terminal ganglion near the rear of the animal, and
cephalic ganglia at the head end. The latter,
particularly in insects, can be quite large and
complex, and are appropriately referred to as a
brain. Such nervous systems can conduct a good
deal of sensory and motor processing independently of the brain, although the brain, because
of its heavier load of sensory inputs, is clearly the
most important feature of the nervous system
and behavior.

Summary

This chapter begins by reviewing the adaptive
significance of nervous systems from two perspectives. The first, that of neuroethology, relates neural processes to adaptive, naturally occurring behavior patterns of animals. The
second perspective involves comparing nervous
systems. Many of these comparisons have been
based on an attempt to link brain size with
intelligence. Brain size is difficult to measure in
unbiased ways, and brains may differ in size for
many reasons other than intellectual functions.
Conclusions about brain size and intelligence
may not be useful, and should be made cautiously.

The chapter reviews the principles of nervous system evolution. Although reconstructing
the past is difficult, we can get clues about the
probable structure of ancient nervous systems by
careful study of the brains of diverse living organisms. Entirely new structures occasionally arise,
but most evolutionary change involves the loss
of some connections and the embellishment and
specialization of others. The organization of several invertebrate nervous systems illustrates the
diversity that exists in neural structures.

Recommended Readings

ARMSTRONG, E. & FALK, D. (1982). *Primate
    brain evolution: Methods and concepts.* New
    York: Plenum.
BULLOCK, T. H., ORKAND, R., & GRINNELL,
    A. (1977). *Introduction to nervous sys-
    tems.* San Francisco: Freeman.
SARNAT, H. B., & NETSKY, M. G. (1981).
    Evolution of the nervous system. New York:
    Oxford University Press.

Chapter 7

SENSORY SYSTEMS: NEUROBIOLOGY AND ECOLOGY

Survival and reproduction depend on effective monitoring of biologically important conditions such as predators, food, mates, and weather, and on appropriate responses to them. Sensory systems have evolved because of the benefits of extracting information from physical energy in the surrounding environment. Sensory systems make *represen-*

tations of the environment. For example, although much has been gained by drawing an analogy between eye and camera, the fact remains that eyes are not miniature movie cameras, and retinas are not tiny screens on which the "mind's eye" views the passing scenery. Simply stated, sensory experiences are abstractions, condensations, and elaborations of physical energy (Hoffman, 1983). Natural selection has seen to it that these representations do not stray too far from reality and do not stray in detrimental ways. Natural selection, operating over countless generations, has led to the evolution of sensory systems that deemphasize or exclude some forms of physical energy, while emphasizing other forms of energy. This biased representation of reality is widespread, and each species seems to have its own biases. Thus a dog and a person walking along a mountain trail do not perceive the light, sound, and chemicals in the same way. Each senses a different form of the energy, emphasizing different aspects of it. The early German ethologist, J. von Uexkull, captured this notion with his concept of the *umwelt* (surrounding world). [Von Uexkull's ideas are summarized, in English, by Tinbergen (1951).] von Uexkull illustrated this concept with the common tick which, clinging to a limb, drops

when it detects butyric acid given off by a mammal below. The tick is superbly sensitive to this odor. Most other species are not. The tick's world, then, is vastly different from, say, the mammal walking below the tree. Their respective sensory systems create their own "real worlds" (Dethier, 1969). This chapter describes how organisms come to have their unique real worlds. In the process of describing the anatomy and physiology of vision and hearing, we will see how the processing of physical energy varies among species, imparting different values to various forms of energy. This is the important connection between sensory psychology and physiology on the one hand, and ecology and natural selection on the other.

Restricting this chapter to vision and audition should not be taken as a slight to the many other sensory modalities. Rather, it reflects the fact that we know more about these two systems than we do about the others, and that space is limited! The multiple volumes of the *Handbook of Sensory Physiology* take up over 3 feet of shelf space; obviously, a text such as this cannot do justice to the full range of sensory systems as they exist in diverse animal groups. Therefore, what I hope to accomplish in this chapter is to convey an appreciation of the integrative approach to sensory systems, using vision and audition as examples. Brief treatments of other sensory systems are found in other chapters.

Vision

Light varies in several ways, including intensity, wavelength, pattern, and movement. The importance of these features differs among species, and differences in their visual systems reflect these priorities (Lythgoe, 1979; Ali & Klyne, 1985). Species differ in terms of the constraints operating on their visual systems. For instance, nocturnal animals must see in low-illumination conditions, aquatic species encounter problems not found in air, and the depth and clarity of the water determines the spectral composition of the available light. Up in the air, birds that survive by gleaning cryptically colored insects from fluttering foliage face a very different visual problem from ones that suck nectar from brightly colored flowers.

The diversity that exists in visual systems reflects the diversity of visual worlds. The mammalian visual system will be used as a reference point for describing some of the variations that exist in other species. Thus, part by part, we will see how visual systems operate and begin to appreciate their specializations.

VISUAL SYSTEM ANATOMY

Vertebrate eyes, although sharing many features in common, differ in many ways. The anatomy of any vertebrate's eye is complex to say the least, so we will attempt to cover only the most basic features.

Cornea   The *cornea* is the clear, bulging, outer surface of the eye. The curvature of the cornea determines the degree to which incoming light will be bent or *refracted*. Light is refracted whenever it passes from one medium into another, such as from air into water. A straight stick, plunged halfway into clear water, appears to bend. This is because the part of the stick in the air reflects light that is not refracted until it reaches the cornea, but light reflected from the stick's underwater portion is refracted at the water–air surface, and again at the cornea.

The shape of the cornea depends on the medium in which vision occurs. In animals that see in air the cornea bulges and is responsible for the majority of refraction. In fish, the cornea is flattened. Why? The cornea in water can do very little refraction because light passes through water and the cornea in very similar ways. (The cornea, like most other tissues, consists mostly of water.) Fish, then, have nothing to gain by having a bulging cornea, but animals that see in air do.

Some special cases illustrate the difference between air and water vision. The Galapagos four-eyed fish lives a unique life, spending part of its time out of water, clambering about on tide pool rocks. The upper half of each eye has a curved cornea for vision in air, but the lower half of each eye has a flattened cornea for underwater vision (Weale, 1974). A similar arrangement exists in the Atlantic flying fish (Baylor, 1967).

Species that live in one medium (air or water), but which must make forays into the other (usually to obtain food), face the problem of refraction producing an illusion of where their target is located. For instance, birds such as herons, terns, pelicans, and ospreys capture fish. To a heron, for instance, the apparent image of its fish prey will be above its actual position (Fig. 7-1). Because fish are captured by a quick jab of the beak into the water, the bird's aim must be accurate or it will starve. Herons are remarkably accurate, however (Katzir & Intrator, 1987). Refraction problems also occur for aquatic animals seeing into air. The archerfish captures its insect prey by squirting a stream of water from its mouth onto an insect perched slightly above the water surface (Fig. 7-1). They, too, are highly accurate in spite of the discrepancy between the target's apparent and actual positions (Dill, 1977). Exactly how these compensations for refraction are made is unknown, but a learning mechanism is probable because in some species, such as herons, that hunt both in water and air, accuracy is maintained in both conditions.

Iris and pupil The *iris* is a double set of muscles behind the cornea that contract and relax, varying the size of the *pupil*, the opening

through which light enters. One set of iris muscles is under parasympathetic control, the other is under sympathetic control. Thus, pupil diameter variations, in addition to following changing amounts of ambient light, also indicate the status of the autonomic nervous system.

Species differ with respect to the maximum and minimum pupil openings. Nocturnal animals such as owls can enlarge their pupils enormously. Flash pictures taken of owls at night show eyes that look like enormous black dots due to their fully open pupils. Human pupils can vary from about 1.5 mm to 8.0 mm, permitting a 30-fold difference in the amount of light admitted (McCauley, 1971).

Lens Light passing through the pupil

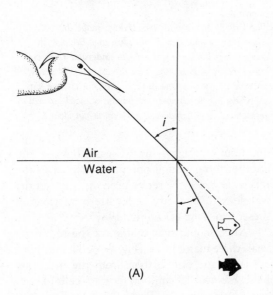

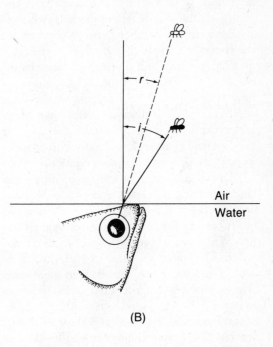

(A)   (B)

Figure 7.1
The refraction that occurs whenever light passes from one medium into another poses important problems for species whose prey are located in a medium other than the one in which vision is occurring. In the case of the heron (left) and the archerfish (right), the apparent position of the prey (in white) is higher than the actual position of the prey (black), so compensations must be made to be successful.

strikes the *lens.* In vertebrates that see in air, the lens does less refraction than the cornea. However, because the cornea's shape is fixed, the lens, which is adjustable, is responsible for fine-tuning refraction or focus. Lens adjustment or *accommodation* is achieved through contraction and relaxation of the ciliary muscles, causing the lens to flatten or to become more spherical (Koretz & Handelman, 1988). In fish, the lens is constantly spherical, and focus is achieved by moving the lens toward or away from the pupil (Fernald, 1984).

Photographers know that the depth of field of a lens (the distance between the nearest and farthest points that are in focus) is determined by the aperture (opening diameter) of the shutter (which is analogous to the diameter of the pupil) and the focal length of the lens (which is analogous to the distance between the front of the cornea and the back of the lens in the eye). Smaller apertures and shorter focal lengths increase depth of field. Nocturnal species tend to have poor depth of field because of the large pupil aperture, but diurnal species have much better depth of field. Whatever the species, depth of field changes dynamically with changes in pupil diameter and accommodation.

Lens accommodation can be used by some land animals to see clearly underwater. When a person opens their eyes underwater, the image is blurry because the cornea is ineffective at refraction. Thus, the image falls out of focus on the retina. The lens shape cannot be adjusted sufficiently to compensate. However, in some birds that see in water (not into water, as in the heron example above) the lens is sufficiently adjustable that the bird can see clearly (Waldvogel, 1990; see Fig. 7-2). Surprisingly, crocodiles do not focus underwater (Fleishman, *et al.,* 1988).

Retina   Light passing through the lens falls on a sheet of tissue, the *retina,* at the back of the eye. The retina is extremely important for two reasons. First, *transduction,* the conversion of

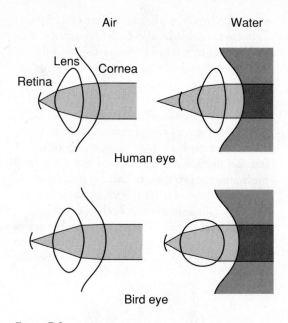

Figure 7.2
The lens of diving birds can change shape dramatically when seeing underwater, an advantage because the cornea does little refraction while underwater. In contrast, the eyes of animals that are adapted for seeing only in air, such as the human, can not change lens shape enough to compensate for the reduced corneal refraction. Thus, underwater vision is not clear.

one form of energy—in this case, light— into another form, neural potentials, occurs in the retina. Second, the retina processes some of the wavelength, intensity, and pattern information present in light (Dowling, 1987).

Microscopic examination of the retina reveals three major layers (Fig. 7-3). The *receptor-cell layer,* the one farthest from the incoming light, has over 100 million receptor cells in each adult human retina (Barlow, 1982). Receptors are of two types, rods and cones (Fig. 7-3). The 100 million rods are the first link in black and white vision, and the three to six million cones are responsible for color vision (Stryer, 1987).

The second or *intermediate layer* consists of

three cell types (the bipolar, horizontal, and amacrine cells) that are interconnected in complex ways (Fig. 7-3). The bipolar and horizontal cells have contacts with the receptors; the horizontal and amacrine cells synapse on the bipolars, on one another, and on the ganglion cells (to be discussed momentarily). The synaptic interactions among intermediate cells are important in forming contrasts, detecting motion, and so on (Masland, 1986).

The third layer of the retina consists of *ganglion cells*. Each of the one million ganglion cells in each human retina receives synaptic input from intermediate cells only. The ganglion cell

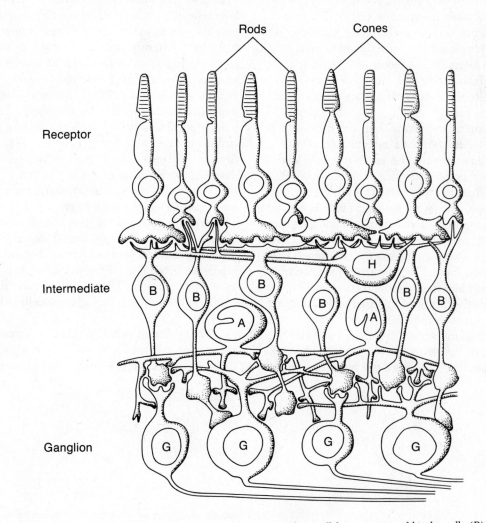

Figure 7.3
The retina consists of three primary layers. The receptor cell layer contains the rods and cones; the intermediate cell layer consists of bipolar cells (B), amacrine cells (A), and horizontal cells (H); and the ganglion cell layer consists only of ganglion cells (G).

axons collectively form the *optic nerves* that synapse in the brain. The ganglion cells' action potentials form the basis for visual perception, as well as providing input for systems that control pupil diameter, lens accommodation, and eye movements.

Although the flow of neural signals in the retina is from the receptor cell layer to the ganglion cell layer, the receptor cell layer is farther from the front of the eye than is the ganglion cell layer. This means that incoming light must pass through layers of cells before ever striking a receptor. Fortunately, the intermediate and ganglion cells are transparent so they do not interfere with passage of light.

Scanning the retina from the front of the eye reveals that it is not a uniform sheet of tissue. It is thinner toward the edges due to a lower density of receptors and ganglion cells (Lia *et al.*, 1987). Toward the center of each retina is a depression, the *fovea*. Its appearance is due to the fact that the intermediate cells and ganglion cells that serve the receptors of this area are displaced away, forming a dense, thickened ring around the fovea. Displacement of nonreceptor cells provides a freer path for incoming light. For this and other reasons (discussed below) sharpest vision occurs in the fovea.

The axons of ganglion cells from all over the retina exit the retina at a single place, the *optic disc* or *blind spot*. The optic disc has no receptors,

so light striking there cannot be seen. A simple demonstration of the blind spot is shown in Fig. 7-4.

Choroid layer   The last structure of the eye is a pigmented layer behind the receptor cell layer. This layer, the *choroid*, is specialized for preventing light reflection, or for enhancing it. In species that see in ample light, the choroid layer is heavily pigmented and any light that gets past the receptors is absorbed, reducing stray light that might otherwise impair image quality. In nocturnal animals the choroid contains a layer of light-reflecting material, the *tapetum lucidum* (Arnott *et al.*, 1970). This layer seems to benefit nocturnal animals by allowing as much light as possible to strike the receptors, even if it strikes on the rebound. The scatter of light reflecting off the tapetum lucidum reduces the sharpness of the image on the retina, but in the low-light worlds of nocturnal animals, this is the price paid for greater sensitivity.

Brain structures of the visual system
Vision begins in the eyes, but it depends on several specialized brain structures that will be briefly described here. They will come up again in more detail later. These structures and their relationships are illustrated schematically in Fig. 7-5.

The optic nerves are bundles of the axons of the retinal ganglion cells. In most vertebrates the axons of each retina synapse on neurons in

Figure 7.4
A simple demonstration of the optic disc or blind spot. Close the left eye and stare at the cat. Move the page

toward or away from you until the dog disappears. At that point light from the right circle is falling on the right eye's optic disc which contains no receptors.

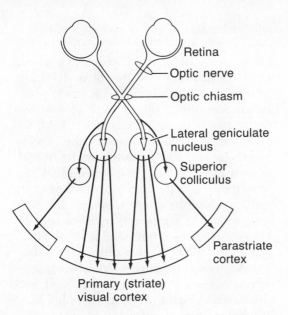

Figure 7.5
Primary structures of the visual system are diagrammed here along with their principal connections.

the other side of the brain. The cross-over point is called the *optic chiasm* (Fig. 7-5). Because the optic nerve axons are myelinated there is no interaction among the axons at the chiasm. In primates, including humans, about 50% of the optic nerve fibers cross over; in other mammals, nearly all cross over (Ali & Klyne, 1985).

Most of the optic nerve axons synapse in the two *lateral geniculate nuclei* (LGN) of the thalamus. The LGN neurons receive the optic nerve's action potentials, and send their own action potentials to other parts of the brain. Other optic nerve fibers synapse in the two *superior colliculi*. The superior colliculi control eye movements (such as to follow a moving object) and coordinate vision with other senses such as hearing and touch (Harris *et al.*, 1980).

Finally, axons from LGN neurons synapse on neurons in the *primary visual cortex* located in

the occipital lobes of the cerebral hemispheres. Although activity of visual cortical neurons is what we humans are consciously aware of as vision, in some animals such as fish, reptiles, and amphibians, the functions of the cortex are conducted by the *tectum,* a brain region that includes the superior colliculi.

VISUAL PERCEPTION

The preceding quick run through visual system anatomy can provide no more than a glimpse of how the system works and what it does. In its most basic form, visual systems operate in such a way that certain features of light energy are extracted, processed, and enhanced. These features—pattern, wavelength, intensity, location, and movement—vary in importance among species and thus the structural and functional characteristics of their visual systems differ (Lythgoe, 1979; Ali & Klyne, 1985)).

Transduction   Transduction is, in general terms, the conversion of one form of energy to another. In the visual system, light is transduced to neural potentials. Each rod and cone's outer segment is filled with photopigment molecules that change form when struck by light. In land animals and marine fishes, the rod photopigment is called *rhodopsin* and the cone photopigment is called *iodopsin.* They are constructed by linking a vitamin A_1 derivative, *retinal$_1$*, and a protein, *opsin.* In freshwater fishes and amphibians, the rod and cone photopigments use a different vitamin A derivative (A_2), and are called porphyropsin and cyanopsin, respectively (Ali & Klyne, 1985). We will discuss rhodopsin and iodopsin here, although the principles are the same for the other photopigments.

Although very few species have more than one type of rhodopsin, it is common to have two or more types of iodopsin. They all consist of the same retinal$_1$ component; they differ in the type of opsin attached to it (Dowling, 1987). Humans, for instance, have three types of cone photopigments. Some birds have four or five (Waldvogel, 1990).

When photopigment molecules are struck by light the retinal portion changes shape, initiating enzymatic activity in the opsin part of the molecule, which ultimately results in a change in the receptor's permeability to sodium ions (Knowles, 1982; Schnapf & Baylor, 1987; Stryer, 1987) (Fig. 7-6). This is the beginning of transduction.

Photoreceptors in total darkness have a resting potential of about −40 mV, much less

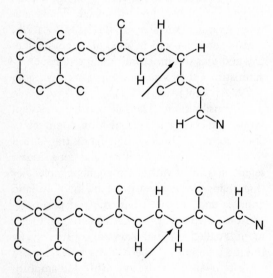

Figure 7.6
The structure of rhodopsin changes when struck by light. In the dark, rhodopsin consists of opsin (not shown) connected to retinal, whose chemical composition is shown on the top. It consists of numerous carbon atoms (C) attached to one another and to some hydrogen (H) and nitrogen (N) atoms. When struck by light, retinal changes shape (bottom) by rotating the portion of the molecule to the right of the arrow. This is the first step in the transduction process.

polarized than the resting potentials of typical neurons (usually −60 to −70 mV). This low resting potential seems to be due to a greater sodium permeability in receptors (O'Brien, 1982). Consequently, receptors in darkness constantly leak out small amounts of a neurotransmitter. Ironically, when struck by light, the permeability to sodium *decreases,* the receptor hyperpolarizes, and neurotransmitter release slows or stops (Barlow, 1982; Stryer, 1987). Because the effect of the transmitter on the bipolar cells on which the receptors synapse is inhibitory, when the receptor is hyperpolarized by light the bipolar cell is released from inhibition and is able to affect other cells of the retina.

Acuity and sensitivity   *Visual acuity* is resolving power or the ability to see detail, and *visual sensitivity* is the ability to detect dim light. We will treat these two processes together because, in general, acuity is obtained at the expense of sensitivity and vice versa.

Although receptors are found throughout the retina, they are not evenly dispersed. Toward the center of each retina is the fovea, the area with the greatest receptor density. Away from the fovea in the *periphery,* receptor density decreases. Acuity is greatest in the fovea and lower in the periphery. There are two reasons for this. The first reason is the receptor density difference just mentioned. When receptors are tightly packed, it is difficult for light not to strike a receptor. Acuity is lower in the periphery because more of the detail in the incoming light misses the receptors. Second, *retinal convergence,* the ratio of receptors to ganglion cells (connected via the intermediate cells), is much lower in the fovea than in the periphery. Because there are about 100 million receptors but only one million ganglion cells, the average ratio of receptors to ganglion cell is about 100 to 1. But this is only an average. In the fovea the ratio is much lower (often 1 to 1) than it is in the periphery, where the ratio can be hundreds to one (Barlow, 1982). When the brain receives action potentials from a foveal ganglion cell, the area on the retina where the light is falling is readily pinpointed. However, when the brain receives action potentials from a ganglion cell in the periphery, the light could have fallen anywhere in a relatively large area (see Fig. 7-7). In summary, because it has higher receptor density, and much lower convergence, the fovea is responsible for the most acute vision.

Such anatomical characteristics account for species differences in acuity. Falcons, hawks, and many other birds have two foveas in each retina (Meyer, 1977; Waldvogel, 1990). This allows the bird to have sharp vision in front of it and to the side or below without moving the eyes or head. Some birds that live in open country (e.g., prairies, shorelines) have foveas that are a horizontal strip rather than a circle. These birds have sharpest vision along the horizon. Receptor density is highly associated with acuity. Most birds have high receptor densities, and in some cases their visual acuity is more than twice that of humans (Fox *et al.*, 1976). Within a species, the packing of cones is positively correlated with

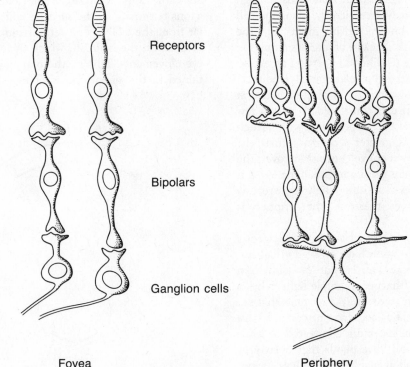

Receptors

Bipolars

Ganglion cells

Fovea

Periphery

Figure 7.7
Visual acuity differs between the fovea (left) where ganglion cells receive from only one receptor each, and the periphery (right) where ganglion cells receive from a large number of receptors scattered over a much larger area.

visual acuity. Hairston *et al.* (1982) found that as bluegill sunfish grew in body size their cone density increased and their ability to detect small prey at a distance improved.

Visual acuity seems to be correlated with the manner by which the species acquires its food. Falcons and hawks commonly detect their prey at great distances and have very high acuity (Meyer, 1977). Seed-eaters and others that detect their food at shorter distances, have less acuity (Waldvogel, 1990). Similarly, fish that "graze" on algae or other immobile food have poorer acuity than other fish in the same area that have to attack moving prey (Collin & Pettigrew, 1989).

The same organization that leads to high acuity tends to reduce sensitivity. Ganglion cell output depends on depolarizing inputs from the intermediate cells. Because of spatial summation (Chapter 5) the likelihood of getting an action potential from a ganglion cell that has (indirect) input from many receptors is greater than that from a ganglion cell connected to only a few receptors. Therefore, the periphery with its high convergence has greater sensitivity than the fovea with its lower convergence. Moreover, the periphery contains mostly rods but the fovea is exclusively cones. Rods absorb light more readily than do the cones; therefore, the periphery is more sensitive.

In general, nocturnal animals and species that live in deep water have evolved visual systems that are more sensitive but less acute than those of species that see in ample light. This is accomplished in several ways. Animals that see in the dark typically have few or no cones, have a large number of receptors connected to each ganglion cell, and have pupils that open very wide to admit all available light (Ali & Klyne, 1985).

Locating light sources   We have covered how the retina detects light. But how does the visual system recognize where in visual space the light is located? First, light from the visual field strikes the retina in a point-by-point fashion, albeit upside down and backward (Fig. 7-8)! This systematic organization is critical because if a particular ganglion cell is active it means that there is an appropriate amount of light in a particular area of the visual field. In short, the visual field is mapped onto the retina.

Second, retinal mapping is maintained in the visual structures of the brain. Ganglion cell axons extend to the lateral geniculate nuclei where they synapse on neurons in the same spatial arrangement as exists in the retina. That is, adjacent ganglion cells are likely to synapse on adjacent LGN neurons. Some ganglion cell axons terminate in the superior colliculus, not far from the LGN. The retinal surface is also mapped on the colliculi, which in turn govern eye movements. Finally, the mapping is maintained in the visual cortex. Thus, activity of

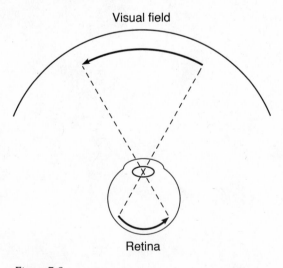

Figure 7.8
Light sources in the visual field are systematically arrayed ("mapped") on the retina.

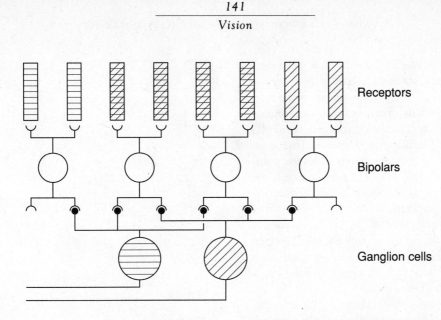

Receptors

Bipolars

Ganglion cells

Figure 7.9
The group of receptors to which a ganglion cell is connected is called its receptive field. Here, two ganglion cells are connected via bipolars to six receptor cells each, four of which provide input to both ganglion cells.

neurons in a particular part of the visual cortex is interpreted as the presence of light in the corresponding part of the visual field.

Form perception   The mapping of the visual world onto the retinas and from them to other neural structures is a necessary prelude to perceiving the form of the light stimulus. Let us see how that is accomplished.

Each photoreceptor cell receives light from its own unique part of the visual field. Because each ganglion cell receives its input from a set of nearby receptors, each ganglion cell responds to only a small part of the total visual field. The group of receptors to which a ganglion cell responds is called its *receptive field* (Fig. 7-9). (LGN and visual cortical neurons also have receptive fields. They will be discussed shortly.) Note that receptors often connect indirectly to two or more ganglion cells (Fig. 7-7). Thus, if a ganglion cell dies, a "hole" does not appear in the visual world. Overlapping receptive fields seem to be adaptive in coping with inevitable cell death.

Receptive fields are studied by inserting a recording microelectrode into the ganglion cell layer or, more commonly, into the optic nerve (because the optic nerves consist of ganglion cell axons). When the tip of the electrode is very close to an axon, its action potential can be discerned as discrete blips on an oscilloscope screen (Chapter 5). Next, a spot of light is projected through a translucent screen into one of the animal's eyes. By moving the light around the screen the researcher eventually finds the area where light changes the spontaneous firing rate of the ganglion cell. (The change can be either an increase or a decrease from the spontaneous rate, which is usually a few action potentials per second.) Note that each point on the screen corresponds to a point on the retina. The results of such studies indicate that ganglion cell receptive fields are circular and have *center-sur-*

round organization. This means that, for example, when light strikes the center of the receptive field, the ganglion cell increases its firing rate, but when light falls anywhere in the surrounding part of the receptive field, the ganglion cell's firing rate is significantly reduced. This is an example of an excitatory-center, inhibitory-surround receptive field. Other ganglion cells' receptive fields are inhibitory-center, excitatory-surround. The point to remember here is that the ganglion cell is affected by light in all parts of its receptive field, even though the effect is often inhibitory. This receptive field organization is achieved by the wiring organization of the intermediate cells (Fig. 7-10).

Species differences exist in the response characteristics of their ganglion cells (Rodieck & Brening, 1983). Frogs and toads, for instance, have some ganglion cells that fire briskly when a dark spot moves across a lighter background. These ganglion cells are appropriately known as "bug detectors." (In fact, toads will starve if small, moving prey are not available, even though edible, dead insects are strewn about.) Other ganglion cells respond only when the receptive field suddenly darkens, as it would when a shadow falls on the animal. Frogs and toads do more processing of visual input in their retinas than many mammals do, and some mammals, such as rabbits and ground squirrels, do more retinal processing than do the primates (Michael, 1969).

Receptive fields of LGN neurons can be measured by inserting a recording microelectrode near a LGN cell and repeating the procedure of moving a small spot of light around on the retina. LGN receptive fields are also circular and have center-surround organization. Note that although LGN neurons receive direct input only from the ganglion cells, we still refer to the LGN cells' receptive field as the group of *receptors* from which they receive their inputs.

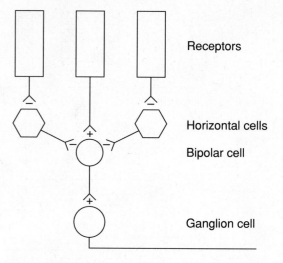

Figure 7.10

This is a simplified diagram of how receptors, bipolars, horizontal cells and ganglion cells may be synaptically connected to produce an on-center, off-surround receptive field for the ganglion cell. When light strikes the center receptor it depolarizes the bipolar which in turn depolarizes the ganglion cell, increasing its firing rate. When light strikes the left or right receptors, the horizontal cell is hyperpolarized. This removes the excitatory effect that they normally have on the bipolar. The bipolar therefore becomes less active and the ganglion cell reduces its firing rate. (+ = depolarization, − = hyperpolarization)

The LGN cells' input field, however, are the ganglion cells.

Finally, the LGN cells' axons project to neurons in layer 4 of the six-layered visual cortex. These neurons also have concentric circle receptive fields. Layer 4 neurons synapse on neurons in the other layers. However, their receptive fields are elongate (Fig. 7-11). These *simple cells* of visual cortex still maintain center-surround organization. In addition, each simple cell has a *preferred orientation* in its receptive field. In other words, maximal change in firing rate in the simple cell is achieved when a bar of light is

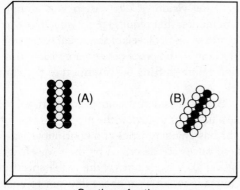

Figure 7.11
Simple cells in visual cortex have elongate receptive fields. Each circle represents a receptor in the retina. Open circles indicate that when light falls on these receptors the simple cell increases its rate of firing; closed circles mean that when light strikes the receptor the simple cell's firing rate is reduced. In A, the simple cell has an on-center off-surround receptive field with a vertical preferred orientation. In B, the simple cell has an off-center on-surround receptive field with a 45-degree preferred orientation.

oriented at a particular angle. Some simple cells respond best to a bar at 10 degrees, others at 94 degrees, and so on. These cells also respond to other angles, but such stimuli do not stimulate as many receptors that feed input into the simple cells, so the response of the simple cell is reduced.

How can simple cells have elongate receptive fields when everything else preceding them has round receptive fields? David Hubel and Torsten Wiesel (e.g. 1979), the Harvard neurophysiologists who were primarily responsible for discovering the workings of this system, suggest that a simple cell receptive field can be achieved by synaptic input to the simple cell by a set of layer 4 cortical cells that have partially overlapping circular receptive fields (Fig. 7-12).

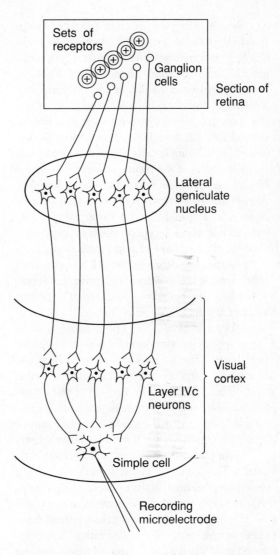

Figure 7.12
Simple cell receptive fields can be produced through a hierarchical set of connections beginning with retinal receptors. This particular simple cell has an on-center off-surround receptive field with 45-degree preferred orientation.

Simple cells are important to form perception in the following way. When an animal looks at a light rectangular object against a dark background (for example) there is a dark–light boundary between the object and the surrounding part of the visual field. The light stimulates the receptors, which, in turn, influence the intermediate cells, ganglion cells, LGN cells, and cortical cells. Simple cells whose receptive fields lie in the parts of the retina on which a vertical line of the rectangle falls (and whose preferred orientation is vertical) will have the greatest change in action potential firing rate. Other simple cells whose receptive fields lie away from the stimulus will not change their firing rates because these fields are not struck by light. Still other simple cells whose receptive fields are struck by light, but whose preferred orientations are not vertical, will also change their firing rates, but not as much. (The analogous argument applies to simple cells whose receptive fields are in the parts of the retina where the horizontal parts of the rectangular stimulus falls.) Thus, there will be a subset of the simple cell population that is quite active in this stimulus situation. If the rectangle is now moved across the retina, or if it is rotated, other subsets of the simple cell population will become activated. The forms of visual stimuli, then, are coded (represented) by the visual cortical cells that are active at any given moment.

Other neurons in the visual cortex have other receptive field characteristics. Some respond only when a bar of light moves across the receptive field; in others the movement must be in a certain direction. There are even some neurons in sheep that respond only to the features of a sheep's face (Kendrick & Baldwin, 1987)! The critical point to understand, however, is that the form of incoming light, that is, the angles, lengths, movements, and so forth, are perceived as they are because of the particular visual cortical cells that are active.

Color vision Color vision is a complex phenomenon that requires processing in the retinas and in higher levels of the visual system. We will examine the processes of color vision in the retina before shifting our attention to the brain itself.

Before considering color perception, we will take a moment to review the properties of light. Light has characteristics of a continuous wave. These waves are described by their wavelength (Fig. 7-13). Wavelengths of the visible spectrum in humans range from about 380 nm to about 650 nm (nm = *nanometer*, a billionth of a meter), but in other species the visible spectrum is different. We perceive short wavelengths as violet, and long wavelengths as red, with the rest of the spectrum arrayed between. Please note, however, that there is nothing about 400 nm light that makes it violet. Violet is a perceptual construction. Our objective is to understand how such constructions are formed.

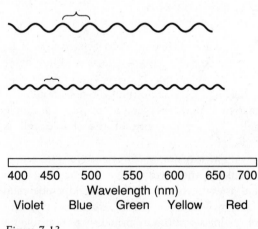

Figure 7.13
Light can be described by its wavelength in nanometers (billionth of a meter). One wavelength is shown by the bracket above each light. The visible spectrum (below) ranges from about 380 nm to about 650 nm. The approximate color assignments of the spectrum are shown.

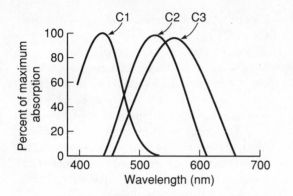

Figure 7.14

The absorption spectra of the three types of human cone photopigment (C1, C2, C3) are shown here. At each wavelength the cone absorbs a certain amount of light relative to its maximum absorption.

There are three varieties of photopigment in human cones, with each cone containing only one variety (Rushton, 1975; Mollon, 1982). The importance of having different photopigments can be seen when we examine the absorption spectrum of a photopigment (Fig. 7-14). An absorption spectrum, i.e., the amount of light absorbed by a photopigment across the visible spectrum, is obtained by a technique in which a living cone is pierced by a minute beam of light that is measured as it leaves the other side. The difference between light intensity as it enters and as it exits is the amount of light absorbed; absorption occurs when photopigment molecules are modified by light, and absorption is the first step in transduction (Mollon, 1982). This procedure is repeated many times, varying the wavelength of the input light. After many cones have been studied and their individual absorption spectra are averaged, we obtain three absorption spectra such as those of humans shown in Fig. 7-14 (Dartnall *et al.*, 1983).

One type of cone photopigment has an absorption spectrum that peaks in the short-wave-length end of the spectrum (420 nm); the other two cone photopigments peak around 530 nm and 560 nm, respectively (Fig. 7-14). (Rods, by the way, have peak sensitivity around 500 nm, but because rods do not figure in color perception, we will confine our discussion to cones.) Each photopigment absorbs light to some degree across a large portion of the spectrum. Although some researchers have labeled the three cone photopigments as blue, green, and red, respectively, these terms may be misleading because they suggest that only blue, green, and red lights are absorbed, or that activity of these cones is perceived directly as these colors.

Having only one type of cone photopigment will not permit color discrimination, that is, the individual will be "color blind." Here is why: Look at the absorption spectrum of Fig. 7-15. If a horizontal line is drawn at 50% absorption, the spectrum will be intercepted at two points representing two wavelengths that will hyperpolarize the cone equally. Consequently, the ganglion cells that derive their input from these cones will

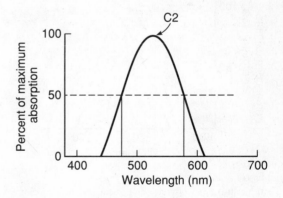

Figure 7.15

A single cone absorption spectrum (cone 2) is shown here. Two wavelengths (approximately 465 nm and 580 nm) are both absorbed equally at 50% of maximum. If we had only one cone photopigment these wavelengths (and many other pairs) could not be discriminated.

emit the same number of action potentials to the two wavelengths. To make matters even more difficult, the intensity of lights coming into the eyes varies enormously. So, for example, if 450-nm light is absorbed at 20% and 475 nm light is absorbed at 40%, identical amounts of cone hyperpolarization would occur if the 450-nm light is twice as intense as the 475-nm light. Color discrimination is therefore impossible when there is only one type of cone photopigment.

What will happen if there are two types of cone photopigment (which we will call C2 and C3) and their outputs are kept distinct? Because the two photopigments have different absorption spectra, they usually will not absorb a given wavelength equally. Look now at Fig. 7-16 in which two absorption spectra are plotted. Using the same two wavelengths as before, we now see that the activity ratio of the two cone types is different. You may want to try a few other pairs of wavelengths that are absorbed equally by C3

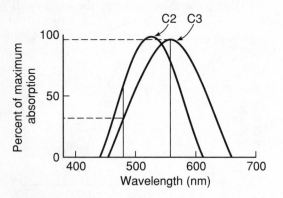

Figure 7.16

When two types of cone are present, the ratio of their activity will differ for most pairs of wavelengths. The two wavelengths from Fig. 7-15 that produced identical absorption in C2 cones have different amounts of absorption in C3 cones. Thus, 465-nm light produces 50%:40% (C2:C3 absorption), but 580-nm light produces 50%:85%.

cones to determine whether they yield different C2 to C3 ratios. If the two spectra overlap it is difficult to find pairs of wavelengths that yield identical activity ratios. However, by varying the intensities of two different wavelengths, many identical activity ratios can be produced, meaning that color discrimination will be imperfect. This problem can be overcome by adding a third, distinct type of cone photopigment (C1). Having three cone types makes it virtually impossible to confuse two dissimilar wavelengths.

A useful way of visualizing these processes is to shift away from absorption spectra to another kind of graph in which absorption is displayed for the three cone types for selected wavelengths (Erickson, 1984; see Fig. 7-17). The important thing to remember is that color discrimination can be obtained only by comparison of cone outputs, that is, the pattern of cone activities specifies wavelengths (color). The more similar two wavelengths are, the more similar their resulting patterns of cone activity.

Color "blindness" occurs in humans for two reasons. First, one of the cone photopigments may be missing. The missing photopigment is typically the middle- or long-wavelength pigment (the genes for which are located on the X chromosome), rarely the short wavelength pigment (the gene for which is on an autosomal chromosome) (Nathans, 1989). Although these individuals, known as *dichromats*, have a normal number of cones, they have only two types of cone photopigment rather than three, a condition similar to the situation depicted in Fig. 7-16. The second reason for color blindness is that two of the three cone photopigments have spectra that are very similar to each other. [This is probably due to differences in genes that code for the opsin part of the pigment (Nathans, 1989). As we have seen, as opsin molecules vary so do the resulting absorption spectra.] These people, known as *anomalous trichromats*, have

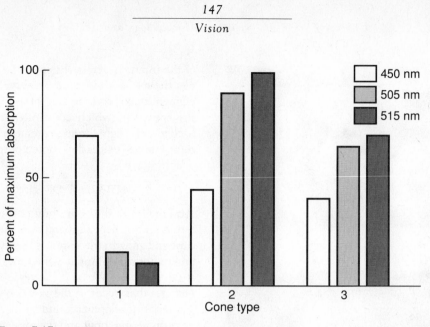

Figure 7.17
The closer two wavelengths are the more similar the C1:C2:C3 absorption pattern.

three cone photopigments, but because two of them respond in very similar ways, the brain essentially has only two types of information (Rushton, 1975).

The genetic basis for some types of color blindness is becoming better understood and apparently is more complex than was once thought (Nathans *et al.*, 1986). About 8% of Caucasian males have some form of color blindness, but within a type (such as anomalous trichromats) a wide variety of individual differences exist. These differences, however, are largely attributable to the genes that code for photopigment proteins (Nathans *et al.*, 1986).

The ecological conditions in which vision occurs have shaped the details of their visual systems. For example, species such as honeybees can see very well in the ultraviolet portion of the spectrum. This is adaptive because bees use the sun as an aid in navigating to food sources. Although the sun may be obscured to us by clouds, because UV penetrates clouds the sun is always visible to bees. Some hummingbirds can also see in the ultraviolet range (Goldsmith, 1980). Wavelength tuning also occurs in fish. The wavelengths available to fish depend on the clarity and depth of the water. Fish that inhabit parts of the water column where bluish light is prevalent tend to have absorption spectra that peak in that region (Levine & MacNicholl, 1982). Animals that have broader visible spectra than our own often have more than three cone types. For example, a species of Japanese fish has four types of cone photopigment (Harosi & Hashimoto, 1983), as does the mallard duck (Jane & Bowmaker, 1988).

Finally, oil droplets or other pigments are found in the receptors of numerous vertebrate and invertebrate species. Usually these droplets are colored yellow to red, and therefore absorb certain wavelengths from the incoming light before it strikes the photopigment. The functional significance of oil droplets in birds is not clear (Waldvogel, 1990), although there is good

DAVID HUBEL

TORSTEN WIESEL

"Innate mechanisms endow the visual system with highly specific connections, but visual experience early in life is necessary for their maintenance and full development." [Wiesel, T. N. (1982). Postnatal development of the visual cortex and the influence of environment. Nature **299,** 583–591 (p. 591).]

reason to believe that they may reduce glare (Ali & Klyne, 1985). In fireflies, oil droplets may enhance contrast. Lall *et al.* (1988) found that different firefly species are active at different times, ranging from dusk to complete darkness. The available light at these times differs in terms of the intensity across the spectrum. For example, the species that are active at twilight have a pigment that absorbs light from the green part of the spectrum (which constitutes most of the background light from vegetation), making their orange–red flashes more conspicuous.

ONTOGENY OF VISION

Attainment of the adult form of the visual system does not depend merely on the passage of time and growth; the system is highly dependent on environmental input, sometimes during sensitive periods. We will survey some of the changes that occur in the visual system during postnatal development, indicating the role of environmental input and the influence of sensitive periods.

Although there are developmental changes in the retina and LGN, most of our knowledge of environmental effects on visual system ontogeny comes from studies of visual cortex and the receptive field characteristics of simple cells. The cortical receptive field characteristics found in adult mammals seem to be present at birth, but patterned light input is required to maintain this organization. Wiesel (1982), summarizing two decades of research that led to his Nobel Prize in 1981, concluded that environmental input in the form of patterned light is required for mammalian visual cortex to develop normally. Monocular deprivation of patterned light has been imposed on young monkeys and kittens by suturing closed one eyelid. This procedure mimics the effect of a cataract: No clear pattern is formed on the retina, but the retina is not deprived of light. This procedure virtually eliminates visual cortical cells responsive to the deprived eye.

The loss of cortical cells responsive to the deprived eye is not due to disuse of the eye. Rather, there seems to be competition among LGN axons for synaptic contacts in visual cortex

(Barlow, 1975). With one eye deprived, inputs from the nondeprived eye come to predominate (Aoki & Siekevitz, 1988). This is also shown in the loss of binocularly-responsive cortical cells in animals and humans with *strabismus*, a condition in which the eyes are not properly aligned. Although both eyes may have good acuity, because their divergent orientation precludes forming a fused image, binocularly responsive cortical neurons fail to develop. The cortical neurons remain, but their input becomes monocular only.

Another example of the importance of patterned input for visual cortical development involves preferred orientations in cortical neurons. Recall that the receptive fields of simple cells includes a specific angle of light orientation. In kittens with normal visual experience, all preferred orientations are present.

What happens when animals are deprived of input? The result depends on the type of deprivation and its timing. Hirsch and Spinelli (1970) placed goggles over kittens' eyes. One eye saw only alternating black and white vertical stripes; the other eye saw only horizontal stripes. In studying the visual cortex of these kittens, Hirsch and Spinelli found very few binocularly-responsive neurons. Moreover, in the monocularly-responsive simple cells, the preferred orientations were exclusively at or near the orientation of the stripes seen by the eye providing input to the neuron.

Another way of producing visual deprivation was used by Blakemore and Cooper (1970) who raised kittens, without goggles, in large, upright tubes painted with black and white stripes, either vertical or horizontal. They found binocularly-responsive cortical neurons (to be expected since both eyes saw the same things), but preferred orientations only around the orientation in which the kitten was raised.

What can we conclude from these studies?

First, the visual system is largely organized at birth, but appropriate visual input is required to maintain that organization. A contrasting conclusion is that development is incomplete at birth (or at eye-opening in species like cats and rabbits that first open the eyes about two weeks after birth) and visual input helps guide subsequent development (Grobstein & Chow, 1975).

Both conclusions have merit, and probably both processes occur during development. Grobstein and Chow (1975) suggest that certain forms of visual deprivation, particularly binocular deprivation, retards the developmental process. The evidence for this position is stronger in rabbits and cats than it is in monkeys, however. Monocular deprivation, in contrast, means that development proceeds on schedule in one eye, but is retarded in the other. This leads to "unfair" competition and the nondeprived eye prevails in the final cortical arrangement.

Sensitive periods exist for the development of visual cortical systems. In kittens, the sensitive period lasts about three months and begins at eye opening. In monkeys, the sensitive period begins at birth and lasts for over two years (Harwerth *et al.*, 1986). In humans, the sensitive period begins at birth and lasts until three to five years, but is most pronounced during the first one to three years (Wiesel, 1982). Strabismus and other visual impairments are most damaging during the first three years in humans and so must be treated as early as possible (Banks *et al.*, 1975).

Why would it be adaptive to have the environment influence development of visual systems? The answer seems to be that there are unavoidable discrepancies in the size, shape, and orientation of the two eyes. In animals with extensive binocular vision it is imperative that the input from the two eyes be in register. As long as the disparity between the two eyes is slight, the system can use input to create that registry. Extreme disparity cannot be compensated for, however, and the system breaks down. The necessity for calibration makes environmental influences on visual development adaptive (Grobstein & Chow, 1975).

VISUAL DEFECTS

When something goes wrong with a complex system, the symptoms it exhibits will vary depending on what part of the system is dysfunctional. Dysfunctions occur in all parts of the visual system—from cornea to cortex—and depending on the site of dysfunction the symptoms will differ. In general, the impairments caused by damage to early parts of the system are more profound than ones farther along in the system. Receptor damage prevents input to the ganglion cells and thus eliminates input to the LGN and cortex. Blindness is complete. In contrast, cortical damage can leave other parts of the visual system intact and functioning. The visual abilities of people afflicted with cortical damage will differ according to the specific site of damage. Some examples follow.

Damage to the visual cortex may leave the person consciously unaware of vision, but able to perform visual tasks with surprising accuracy. Weiskrantz (1980) summarized work on several patients with visual cortical damage due to injury or stroke. A large majority of them were able to say whether a light flashed briefly into the blind area of their visual field was horizontal or vertical, and they could accurately point at the place where a spot of light had been flashed. Surprisingly, these people were astonished to discover the accuracy of their responses. They insisted that they saw nothing and treated the testing as though it were a guessing game. But they often "guessed" with over 80% accuracy. In other cases, they had only dim feelings that something was present in the visual field but couldn't elaborate on those feelings. Clearly, vision occurs and is available at some level even when the cortex is damaged. Perhaps activity of neurons in the LGN or superior colliculi are responsible for these abilities. Conscious awareness and verbal recognition, however, seem linked to the visual cortex (Weiskrantz, 1980).

Another interesting example of residual vision occurs in people with facial agnosia, a condition in which the person is unable to recognize faces, even of familiar people. People with facial agnosia may have normal visual acuity and can recognize people by other means, such as voice. When shown pictures of faces, some of whom were familiar and some not, the familiar faces were not described as being more familiar. However, by using a measure of autonomic nervous system activity, Tranel and Damasio (1985) showed that familiar faces did in fact elicit a different reaction than did unfamiliar faces. They suggest that the specific cortical lesions involved in this condition uncouple visual input from areas involved in conscious recognition, but not from other areas with input to the autonomic nervous system.

OTHER VISUAL SYSTEMS

Vertebrate visual systems are certainly remarkable in their variety and effectiveness, but they are not the only effective visual systems in the animal kingdom. Sensitivity to light is widespread even in those species that lack true visual systems. For instance, many single-celled animals have light-sensitive organelles that permit them to approach or avoid light even though image-formation is impossible (Diehn, 1979). Other types of visual systems (besides the lens eyes described above) are found in the animal kingdom. Three of them are presented below. They are thoroughly described by Land (1981).

Cup eyes   The simplest visual systems are

ones that detect the presence of light and provide some indication as to its direction. Cup eyes do exactly that. A cup eye is shown in Fig. 7-18. It is a light receptor-lined depression on the animal's surface. Although light from directly above illuminates the entire cup, light coming from one side will cast a shadow on part of the cup, a sort of visual sundial. The receptors that are exposed to light indicate the direction of the light. Flatworms have visual systems of this type, and the animal's movements with respect to light are controlled by these simple eyes.

Pinhole eyes An arrangement that can produce an image rather than just indicate direction consists of a spherical chamber with a small opening across from a sheet of light receptive

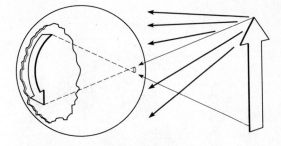
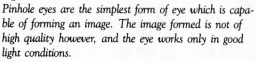

Figure 7.19
Pinhole eyes are the simplest form of eye which is capable of forming an image. The image formed is not of high quality however, and the eye works only in good light conditions.

cells (Fig. 7-19). The physics of such optical systems produces a point-by-point mapping of the light in the surrounding environment onto the receptive surface. Pinhole eyes work only in bright conditions because the pinhole admits only a small fraction of the available light. Enlarging the hole to admit more light degrades the sharpness of the image. You can see this effect by punching a small hole in a piece of paper (the tip of a pen will work) and, holding the hole close to one eye, looking at a distant object. If there is plenty of light the object will look sharper than it does with a larger hole. The chambered nautilus, an ancient mollusc, uses this sort of eye, but its acuity is thought to be poor.

Compound eyes Compound eyes are constructed of multiple tubes called *ommatidia*, each of which has a tiny lens at the end where light enters, and a set of light receptors at the other end. The ommatidia are packed together in a hemispherical bundle with each ommatidia pointing in a different direction and therefore seeing a different portion of the surrounding environment (Fig. 7-20). The resulting image is something of a mosaic of dots. Although the resolving power of compound eyes cannot match

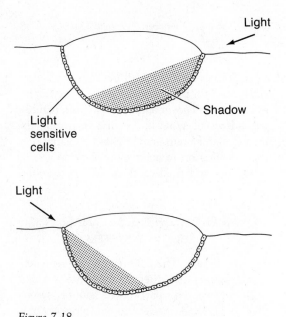

Figure 7.18
Eye cups can provide information about the direction of light striking their surface. Shadows cast on the receptive surface mean that some receptors will be inactive. Each direction relative to the animal will cast a unique shadow.

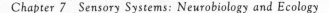

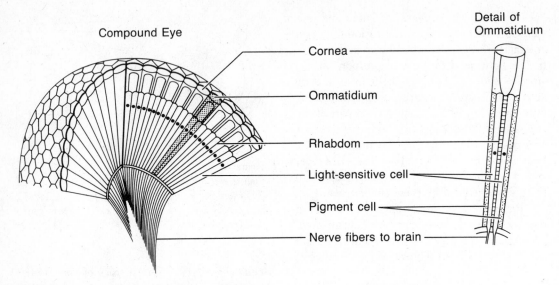

Figure 7.20
The compound eyes of arthropods such as insects (left) are comprised of a large number of ommatidia which are shown enlarged on the right.

that of lens eyes, they are superior in some ways. They are small and light—valuable for small-bodied animals— and they are exceptionally good at detecting movement.

Land's (1981) review of compound eyes illustrates their great diversity. They are found in a variety of invertebrate phyla that see in air or water, in bright or dim conditions. Some of them have even evolved fovea-like and pupil-like structures, making them somewhat more like the lens eyes of vertebrates.

Audition

Objects moving in the environment produce pressure changes that can be used by animals to adaptively direct their behaviors (Stebbins, 1983). These pressure changes are commonly referred to as sound, but vibrations of solid materials are of the same sort. Auditory systems of several types have evolved because they effectively monitor pressure changes in the environment. We will cover auditory systems much like we did visual systems, by first reviewing the mammalian system anatomy and its variations, then moving on to auditory perception and its ontogeny, and finally other auditory systems.

ANATOMY OF THE MAMMALIAN AUDITORY SYSTEM

Outer ear The outer ear or *pinna* is a flexible structure that directs sound into the true sensory (receptive) parts of the auditory system (Fig. 7-21A). Although human pinnae aid in some aspects of sound perception, such as locating the source of a sound (Shaw, 1974; Butler, 1975), their limited mobility makes them less effective than the pinnae of some other species, such as elephants (Heffner *et al.*, 1982), bats, rodents, and carnivores. Other vertebrates, including birds, fish, reptiles, and amphibians, lack pinnae entirely, although some birds such as the barn owl have a ruff of facial feathers that serves the same function (Knudsen, 1981).

The pinnae of some species have additional, nonauditory functions. For example, they are used as "radiators" for cooling blood in elephants, and may serve in gestural communication in many species. These other functions sometimes favor structural features of the pinnae that may compromise their auditory functions, thus complicating the search for adaptive variations based solely on auditory processes.

Middle ear Extending inward from the pinnae is a tube, the *external auditory canal,* that ends at the eardrum or *tympanic membrane.* This membrane is a thin piece of tissue, firmly anchored around its perimeter. Sound pressure conducted down the auditory canal causes the tympanic membrane to flex in and out slightly, like a windowpane rattled by thunder. Attached to the inner side of the tympanic membrane is the first of three small bones, the *malleus* (hammer). Connected to it in sequence are two other small bones, the *incus* (anvil) and the *stapes* (stirrup) (Fig. 7-21B). These three bones, which are hinged, are collectively known as the *ossicles.* The stapes is attached to another membrane, the *oval window.* Because the area of the tympanic membrane is greater than the contact area of the stapes on the oval window, slight movements of the tympanic membrane result in larger movements of the oval window (Evans, 1982). Nonmammal vertebrates do not have ossicles. Rather, a tube extends from the inside of the tympanic membrane (which is often on the surface of the head) to the oval window. This stiff tube moves as the tympanic membrane vibrates (Stebbins, 1983).

Variation in middle ear structure seems to correspond to species differences in their most sensitive hearing range. Mammals with relatively heavy middle ear structures (tympanic membrane and ossicles) hear best in the low frequencies, and species with less massive middle ears hear best in the high frequencies (Webster & Webster, 1980). Kangaroo rats, North American desert-dwelling rodents, have large middle ears and are very sensitive to low frequency sounds such as those produced by approaching snakes and owls. Surgically reducing the rodents' sensitivity to these sounds makes them significantly more vulnerable to predation (Webster & Webster, 1980). In contrast, insect-eating bats, which locate their prey by means of reflected high-frequency sounds, have small middle ear chambers and very light middle ear structures.

Cochlea Middle ear structures are devices for transmitting sound energy to the receptors. Now it is time to examine the cochlea, where the receptors are located (Fig. 7-21A).

The mammalian cochlea is enclosed in a hard, tapering tube that coils like a snail's shell (Fig. 7-21A). For simplicity, we will uncoil the cochlea to study its parts (Fig. 7-22). The interior consists of two fluid-filled chambers. One is the *scala media* (or *cochlear duct*) and the other is the *scala vestibuli/scala tympani* (or *vestibular* and *tympanic canals*). At the tip of the cochlea the vestibular and tympanic canals are continuous. The cochlear duct is separated from the rest of the cochlea by two membranes, the *basilar membrane* and *Reissner's membrane* (Fig. 7-22).

The oval window, at the base of the cochlea, moves the fluid of the vestibular canal when it is flexed by movement of the ossicles. The movement of the fluid causes the *round window* to bulge out whenever the oval window bulges in.

Movement of cochlear fluid occurs in the form of a *traveling wave* that progresses along the length of the cochlea causing movements of the basilar membrane. As a result, the hair cells,

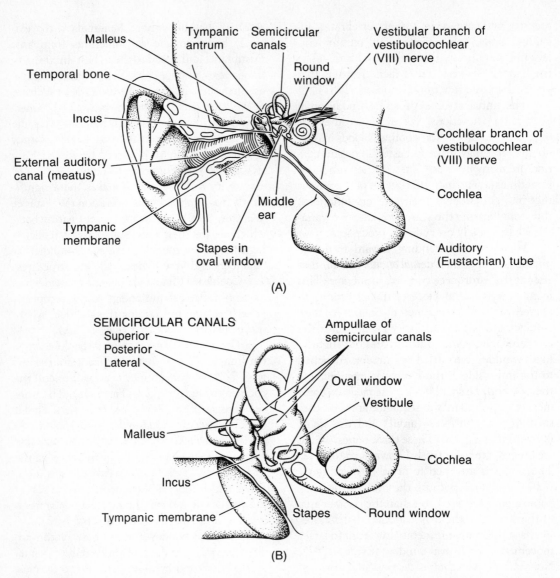

Figure 7.21
(A) Anatomical features of the human auditory system. (B) Detailed view of the ossicles and their relationship to the tympanic membrane and the oval window.

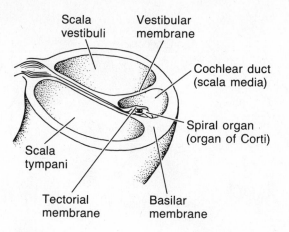

Scala vestibuli

Vestibular membrane

Cochlear duct (scala media)

Spiral organ (organ of Corti)

Scala tympani

Tectorial membrane

Basilar membrane

Figure 7.22
A cross-section through the cochlea showing the chambers.

which are attached at their base to the basilar membrane and which have bundles of hairlike cilia at the other end, move slightly. The hair bundles are sensitive to movement, allowing positively charged ions to enter, depolarizing the cell (Hudspeth, 1983, 1985). The hair cells, which have synaptic contacts with the auditory nerve neurons, are the transducers of the auditory system.

In the human cochlea, the hair cells are arrayed along the length of the cochlea in four rows. One row is formed by the 3000 *inner hair cells,* and the 12,000 *outer hair cells* make up the other three rows. The hair bundles of the outer hair cells are attached at their tips to the *tectorial membrane;* those of the inner hair cells are not attached, but nevertheless move as the basilar membrane vibrates. Each inner hair cell is represented by one fiber in the auditory nerve (to be discussed in a moment), but the outer hair cells are represented at a ratio of about 10 to 1.

Neuron cell bodies lie near the base of the hair cells and have dendrites that synapse with them. Depolarizations caused by hair cell activity are conveyed along the dendrites to the cell bodies whose axons project into the brain. These axons collectively form the *auditory nerve,* a branch of the eighth cranial nerve. The auditory nerve also contains axons that convey action potentials from brainstem neurons toward the cochlea. These axons synapse on hair cells but their effect is inhibitory, suppressing hair cell depolarization of the auditory nerve cells.

Brain auditory structures Several brain structures are involved in sound analysis. We will briefly describe them now, saving an account of their roles in auditory perception for the next section. A summary diagram of auditory brain structures is found in Fig. 7-23.

Neurons of each auditory nerve have their first synapse in the *cochlear nuclei* of the medulla oblongata. The two cochlear nuclei receive input from the cochlea on the same side of the head. However, the auditory nerve splits into three components as it enters the brainstem, each component proceeding to a different section of the cochlear nucleus. Each section is "cochleotopically" organized, meaning that cochlear output is systematically arrayed on the cochlear nucleus. The three regions of the cochlear nucleus contain neurons with different response properties; thus, they process, in parallel, different aspects of sound input (Evans, 1982).

The two *superior olivary nuclei* receive their synaptic input from both cochlear nuclei. That is, some axons from the cochlear nuclei cross the midline of the brainstem and synapse in the opposite-side superior olive (Fig. 7-23). This bit of anatomy is very important because it means that the superior olives are the first structures in which binaural comparison is possible. Sound localization, to be presented later, depends on binaural comparisons.

Axons of the superior olives extend to neurons in both inferior colliculi which, in turn,

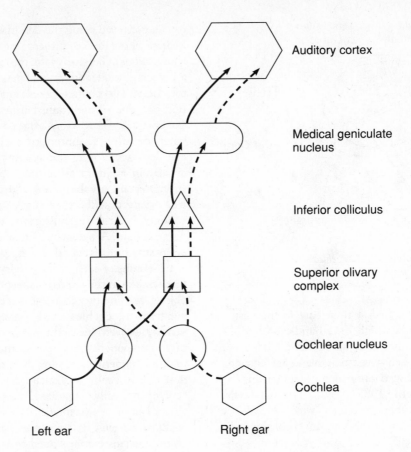

Auditory cortex

Medical geniculate nucleus

Inferior colliculus

Superior olivary complex

Cochlear nucleus

Cochlea

Left ear   Right ear

Figure 7.23
The auditory system has several brain nuclei. They are shown here, schematically. Solid lines indicate input from the left cochlea and dashed lines indicate input from the right cochlea.

project to the medial geniculate nuclei (MGN) of the thalamus. The MGN extends its axons to the auditory cortex. Thus, the role of the MGN is similar to that of the LGN in vision.

Located primarily within the temporal lobes, the auditory cortex is subdivided into regions based on microanatomical differences among neurons. These regions appear to have different roles in auditory perception. For exam-

ple, some parts of the human auditory cortex are specialized for speech perception.

AUDITORY PERCEPTION

As was true of light, sound energy is potentially informative in several ways. This section will describe how nervous systems are designed to extract information from sound, namely frequency (pitch), intensity (loudness), and location of the sound source.

Frequency Sound is a waveform phenomenon. Sounds are described by their frequencies, i.e., the number of cycles per second. This is expressed in a unit called the hertz (Hz). One Hz equals one cycle per second. (Sounds could be described by their wavelengths, as is done with light, but traditionally frequency is used.)

How do we discriminate sounds of different frequencies? The basilar membrane, which stretches the entire length of the cochlea, is not uniform along its length. Near the base of the cochlea (by the oval and round windows) the basilar membrane is relatively narrow (about 100 micrometers); toward the apex the basilar membrane becomes wider (about 500 micrometers) (Evans, 1982). Through ingenious experiments first performed by von Bekesy (1957) it was discovered that different sound frequencies produce traveling waves on the basilar membrane that have their peak movements at different places on the membrane. Specifically, the highest frequencies cause maximal movement of the basilar membrane near the cochlear base, but progressively lower frequencies cause maxi-

mal movement nearer the cochlear apex (Fig. 7-24). This *place theory* of frequency coding stipulates that the place (i.e., the region of the basilar membrane) of maximal movement depends on the frequency of the sound entering the ear. Further, we perceive movements of different places of the basilar membrane as different pitches. Another way to express this phenomenon is to say that the cochlea is *tonotopically organized*.

Each auditory nerve cell has a limited range of frequencies to which it responds by firing action potentials (Fig. 7-25). Because the basilar membrane can move at several points simultaneously, several frequencies can be heard and processed concurrently.

In addition to coding sound frequency along the basilar membrane, another coding scheme operates for low frequencies (below about 200 Hz in humans). For low frequencies the basilar membrane as a whole vibrates slowly enough that auditory neurons can follow each wave with an action potential. This process is not well understood, however.

The tonotopic organization of the cochlea is maintained in higher brain centers of the auditory system. In other words, the full range of

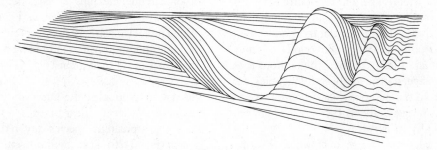

Figure 7.24
Movements of the oval window set up traveling waves along the basilar membrane. As frequency changes, the maximum amplitude of the wave changes location on the membrane.

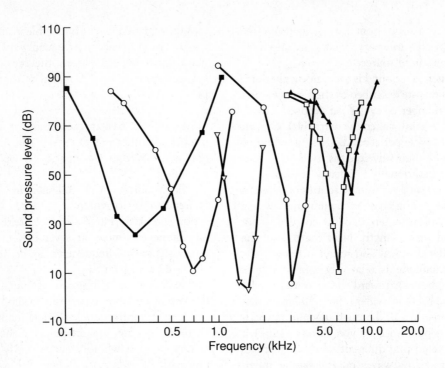

Figure 7.25
Each auditory nerve cell is "tuned" to a narrow best frequency (the bottom point of each curve), meaning that relatively soft sounds are sufficient to generate action potentials. However, louder sounds of a wider frequency range can also affect these cells.

frequencies is "mapped out" in other neural structures, just as spatial features are mapped in the visual system. The auditory cortex, for example, contains neurons that respond (by changing their action potential rate) only when the ear is exposed to a particular sound frequency (Pantev *et al.*, 1989). Further, the neurons that are responsive to the highest frequencies are farthest from the neurons that are responsive to the lowest frequencies, with the others arrayed systematically in between.

The frequency range over which hearing extends and the sensitivity within that range varies enormously across species. Humans, for instance, can hear sounds from about 20 Hz to 20,000 Hz, although most adults can only hear as high as 12,000 to 15,000 Hz. However, we do not hear equally well within this range: Sounds of some frequencies must be extremely loud to be heard, while others can be heard even if very soft. The relationship between sound frequency and minimum intensity required for detection is expressed in an *audiogram* (Fig. 7-26). Audiograms typically have a "V" or "U" shape, with the lowest points on the curve indicating the frequencies that are heard best.

Not surprisingly, species vary in their audiograms (Fig. 7-26) with the most sensitive hearing generally falling within the frequency range used in communication by that species. An intriguing example of this occurs in a tree frog, the coqui from Puerto Rico. The frog is named for the males' two-part call, a low-pitch "co" followed by a higher-pitched "qui." When exposed to a male's call, other males respond only to the "co" component, but females respond only to the "qui" component. Males' audiograms are sensitive to the frequency range of "co," but insensitive to the frequency range found in the "qui" (Narins & Capranica, 1976).

A special case of auditory tuning to the communication signals of the same species comes from the echolocating bats. Many bat species detect their prey by emitting high-frequency vocalizations that reflect off of nearby objects. These echoes tend to be rather soft, however, and bat hearing is highly sensitive to those frequencies (Suga, 1990). In fact, a disproportionate share of the auditory parts of the bat brain are devoted to this rather narrow range of frequencies that the bats hear.

In many cases, auditory sensitivity is especially pronounced in the range of frequencies used by predators or prey. For instance, moths hear best in the 25- to 50-kHz (= kilohertz) range, precisely the frequencies used in the echolocation calls of bats (Roeder, 1965; Fenton & Fullard, 1981). Indeed, many insects have auditory systems that, although simple in structure, are remarkably tuned to sounds made by bats. Praying mantises, for example, have only one ear, but it responds only to sounds in the frequency range employed by bats, and when it detects these sounds the flying mantis immediately contorts its body, making an erratic flight path (Yager & Hoy, 1986).

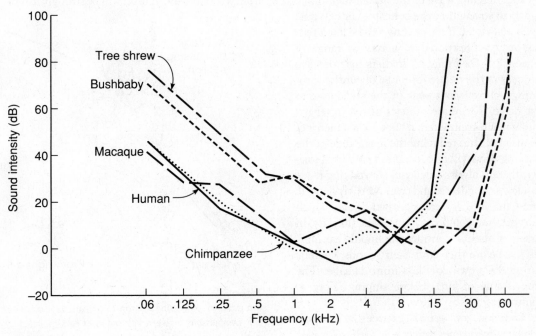

Figure 7.26
Audiograms of human and four other primate species.

Predators, of course, are expected to have the sensory abilities to detect their prey. Using bats again, Tuttle and Ryan (1981) found that the fringe-lipped bat, which preys on frogs by plucking them from trees or from the water surface, locates its prey by the frogs' own calls. The bats can even distinguish poisonous species from safe ones, and ignore the calls of frogs that are too large for them to capture.

Intensity The coding of stimulus intensity (loudness) is straightforward. The action potential rate of the auditory neurons codes sound intensity. As intensity increases, the action potential rate of the auditory nerve cells also increases.

Excessively loud sounds can permanently damage the cochlea. This is because the hair cells, like virtually all neurons, cannot be replaced. When an overly loud sound enters the ear, the traveling wave of the basilar membrane may be so strong that the delicate hair cell cilia may be damaged. If so, hearing will be impaired. This may be restricted to a narrow range of frequencies. For example, soldiers may damage hair cells in the frequency range of gunfire, producing a conspicuous peak in the audiogram in that range. There are muscles of the inner ear which, when contracted, dampen movements of the ossicles, thus reducing the magnitude of the traveling wave (Borg & Counter, 1989). However, there is always a delay in contracting these muscles, so sudden sounds can do their damage before the muscles can contract. Bats, which emit extremely intense sounds as they fly in pursuit of insects, contract the middle ear muscles just before they emit their sounds, thereby sparing their own cochleas from damage. The same is true of birds before singing (Borg & Counter, 1989).

Location of sound sources Although there are several cues that can be used to locate a sound source, most research has dealt with intensity and time-of-arrival comparisons between the two ears (Masterton & Imig, 1984).

Imagine a neuron somewhere in the brain that responds whenever a 500-Hz tone strikes either ear. Thus, it has two sources of input, one from the left and one from the right. Furthermore, imagine that its input source from the left causes EPSPs but its input source from the right causes IPSPs (Fig. 7-27). If a sound source originates from the left, the left ear will receive a more intense input than will the right ear because the head partially blocks sound waves, casting a "sound shadow." The neuron will therefore be stimulated to fire action potentials. A sound that originates from directly in front of the animal will strike the two ears with equal intensity and thus the neuron will receive equal input from both sides. The neuron's firing will be unaffected. Finally, if the sound source comes from the right, the neuron will be strongly inhib-

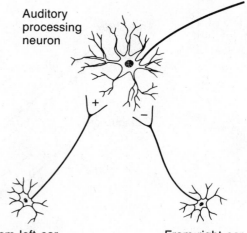

Figure 7.27
An auditory processing neuron (top) can make intensity comparisons between left and right ears provided both input cells respond to the same frequency and have opposite effects on the processing neuron.

ited. It appears that the brain uses this arrangement to locate sound sources.

Neurons of the lateral superior olive (LSO) receive excitatory inputs from the same side of the brain, and inhibitory inputs from the opposite side. Neurons that synapse on a given LSO cell respond to the same narrow frequency range. Thus, LSO neurons subtract opposite-side input from same-side input (Masterton & Imig, 1984). Of course, this system is not infallible. A sound source anywhere on the equidistance plane between the ears cannot be localized by this method alone because input would be equal in both ears. However, turning the head slightly (or the pinnae independently of the head) can create enough disparity to locate the sound source.

The use of intensity differences is most effective for relatively high frequency sounds. This is because the head more effectively blocks high-frequency, short-wavelength sounds than it does low-frequency, long-wavelength sounds. In other words, left–right intensity disparity is more pronounced at high frequencies thereby facilitating localization. Animals with small heads have difficulty localizing many sounds by intensity differences alone.

Another method for locating sound sources involves comparison of time-of-arrival of a sound at the two ears. A sound originating from the right will reach the right ear slightly sooner than it will reach the left ear. The medial superior olive (MSO) has neurons that respond when identical stimuli are presented to the two ears, but offset slightly in time. In some cases the output of these cells is facilitated by one delay and inhibited by another (Masterton & Imig, 1984). Unfortunately, little is known of the wiring of this system to accomplish this impressive feat.

Time-of-arrival perception improves when a sound begins or ends suddenly, or includes rapid

MASAKAZU KONISHI

" . . . We have found a region in the owl's midbrain . . . that contains units [neurons] that respond to sound only when it originates from a small area of auditory space (receptive field). . . . These units are systematically arranged . . . [so] that they form a physiological map of auditory space." [Knudsen, E. I., & Konishi, M. (1978). A neural map of auditory space in the owl. Science 200, 795–797 (p. 795).]

frequency changes. Such sudden events serve as good temporal markers, making comparisons crisper. This feature of auditory perception may have helped select for certain features of animal communication sounds. For instance, the mobbing calls of many birds and mammals is a rapid series of click-like sounds (Fig. 7-28A). This structure seems ideally suited for location by means of time-of-arrival. The individual who issues mobbing calls benefits by being joined by others who participate in harassing the predator. It should therefore provide ample clues to its location. In contrast, when a predator such as a hawk approaches suddenly, small birds and

(A)

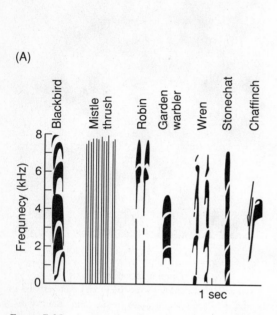

(B)

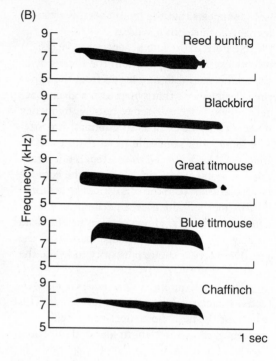

Figure 7.28

Sonagrams of the calls given by seven species of European birds while harassing owls (A), and of the calls given at the sudden approach of a hawk (B). Note that in (A) the calls start and stop abruptly and cover a wide frequency range, making localization easy. In (B) the calls begin and end more gradually and cover a narrow frequency range, making them more difficult to locate.

mammals often emit alarm calls that are difficult to locate (Fig. 7-28B): They fade in and out, and stay in a narrow frequency range. Thus, a warning can be issued without providing clues to the predator of the caller's position (Marler, 1959).

The intensity-comparison and time-of-arrival comparison circuits combine their outputs to map the surrounding world onto auditory centers. The medial geniculate nuclei (MGN) have such a map. It is analogous to the visual map of the nearby LGN, but the MGN's auditory map encompasses an entire sphere rather than a hemisphere as in the LGN. The barn owl has an incredibly detailed neural map of its auditory world. It is so precise, in fact, that they can land on a spot the size of a mouse in absolute darkness when provided with only a brief pulse of sound from that spot (Knudsen, 1981; Knudsen & Konishi, 1978).

ONTOGENY OF AUDITORY PROCESSES

Earlier in this chapter we reviewed some issues involved in the ontogeny of visual processes. Of primary concern was the role of certain forms of experience in attaining adult visual abilities. Although auditory system development has not been studied nearly as thoroughly as has visual development, the roles of experience seem to be much the same. That is, although auditory structures and processes come "on line" at certain ages, experience appears to be necessary to maintain them. For example, sound deprivation during the sensitive period in rodents and humans leads to significant reductions in the size of neurons of the cochlear nuclei (reviewed by Clopton, 1981). Similarly, sound deprivation in one ear only reduces the number of neurons that are binaurally sensitive (Silverman & Clopton, 1977), paralleling the findings on monocular deprivation described in the section on visual ontogeny. Further, sensitive periods operate in auditory development as they do in visual development. Rats, for instance, do not begin hearing until about 10 days after birth when their ear canals begin to open. The sensitive period for normal auditory development begins then and continues for about 10 more days (Clopton, 1981).

Developmental changes in auditory perception have been well documented in some cases, but the role of experience in such changes is not known. For instance, evidence from both mammals and birds indicates that low frequency perception is the first to develop, and that with age the system becomes better able to perceive high-frequency sounds (Harris & Dallos, 1984; Lippe & Rubel, 1983). The developmental sequence parallels the sound spectrum available to the developing organism. In mammals, the *in utero* sound spectrum is biased toward low-frequency components.

Along with the greater sensitivity to low frequencies, the tonotopic organization of the basilar membrane and of brainstem auditory nuclei shifts with age. Recall that the basal portions of the adult cochlea are maximally responsive to high frequencies. However, this part of the basilar membrane is originally responsive only to low frequencies. As the cochlea develops, the region of low-frequency responsiveness shifts toward the apex (Harris & Dallos, 1984). As this occurs, brainstem nuclei receiving neural input from the cochlea undergo a parallel shift in their tonotopic organization (Lippe & Rubel, 1983).

Although some aspects of auditory perceptual development appear to mature on schedule without obvious environmental inputs, there is a growing body of evidence implicating self-produced sounds as an important environmental determinant of normal auditory development. This topic has been elegantly studied by Gottlieb and his colleagues (reviewed by Gottlieb, 1981) using ducklings as their subjects.

Ducklings only a few hours after hatching readily approach a speaker playing a recording of the maternal call, a vocalization that aids in getting and keeping the brood together with the mother. So pronounced is the tendency to approach these calls that even ducklings who were incubated in soundproof chambers readily approach the first time they hear the sound. Although auditory experience seems unnecessary, in fact it is quite important.

Ducklings vocalize in the air space at the end of the egg a few days before they hatch. Could experience with their own sounds be necessary to develop the tendency to approach maternal calls? Gottlieb devocalized duck embryos while still in the egg through a delicate surgical procedure. Done shortly before the age at which vocalization commences, this procedure (combined with isolation in a soundproof incubator) ensures that the duckling lacks experience with its own (or other) duck sounds. When tested shortly after hatching, such ducklings fail to reliably approach the maternal call. However, devocalized ducklings incubated with nonoperated siblings did approach normally, indicating that merely hearing the sounds of other embryos, while still in the egg, is sufficient for normal auditory perceptual development (Gottlieb, 1981).

Studies such as these should make us cautious about claims that special environmental factors are unnecessary for the development of certain behaviors. Sometimes the relevant environmental features are self-produced and inconspicuous.

OTHER AUDITORY SYSTEMS

Mammalian auditory systems, while alike in basic form, differ in many ways that reflect the varied ecologies and evolutionary histories of the mammals (Stebbins, 1983). Equally diverse are the auditory systems of other vertebrates and invertebrates. This section briefly discusses some of these other auditory systems.

Insect hearing Invertebrates in general are not particularly responsive to sound (Michelsen, 1974). Although many are responsive to vibrations of the substrate, true hearing is uncommon. The insects, however, are truly auditory creatures which have evolved several methods for detecting sound.

One of these methods involves structures that resemble the mammalian tympanic membrane and ossicles. In this system a thin piece of cuticle (the insects' hard exoskeleton) is vibrated by airborne sound in a manner analogous to the tympanic membrane. Attached to the inner surface is a stiff, rodlike structure that moves as the membrane moves. Sensory cells are thereby activated, sending action potentials to other cells in the nervous system for processing. Such tympanal organs (Fig. 7-29) can be re-

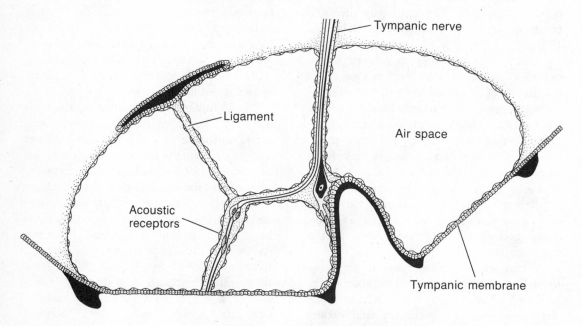

Figure 7.29
The tympanal organ of a moth consists of a cuticular "tympanic membrane" that flexes in response to sound. Its movement activates sensory cells which have synaptic connections to the nervous system.

markably adept at certain auditory tasks. For example, many moths effectively evade bats with only two sensory neurons in each of their two tympanal organs! This amazing system is treated in more detail in a later chapter.

Hearing in fishes Although the vertebrate classes (mammals, birds, reptiles, amphibians, and fishes) differ in many ways in terms of their auditory systems, the fishes are most unlike the others and vary most among themselves.

Fishes have two systems that may process waterborne sounds. The *lateral line system* consists of long, thin grooves running from head to tail, one on each side. These lines contain sensory cells that are responsive to water movement. Although underwater sounds generate water movement, the lateral line system does not seem to be sensitive enough to detect any but the most intense ones, or ones produced nearby.

The second system seems to be a better candidate for fish hearing. On each side of the head there is a three-part structure, the labyrinth, much like the vestibular apparatus of mammals (Chapter 9). It is thought that the cochlea evolved as an extension of the labyrinth, but that the labyrinth itself is capable of auditory sensations (Wever, 1974).

Although vertebrates that hear in air need structures for efficiently transmitting sound energy to the inner ears, sound in water readily passes through the fish's body to the labyrinth. By itself, however, the labyrinth is not very sensitive. But another structure, the swim bladder, provides some assistance. The swim bladder, a gas-filled flexible chamber, resonates in response to sound. In some fish species, extensions of the swim bladder come near the labyrinth and help transmit sound energy to it (Fay & Popper, 1980). In other fishes, the swim bladder works in conjunction with extended slim bones of specialized vertebrae near the head,

enhancing sound conduction to the labyrinth. Fishes with these accessories have the most sensitive and sophisticated auditory systems of all the fishes, and produce many communicative sounds in courtship and aggression (Stebbins, 1983).

Summary

Sensory systems extract, enhance, filter, and process certain forms of physical energy. Natural selection has operated in such a way that sensory systems are tuned to important forms of energy. Because species differ with respect to what is important, the structure and physiology of their sensory systems differ. To illustrate these concepts, the chapter examines two sensory systems: vision and audition.

Vision depends on special light-sensitive cells, the rods and cones of the retina. These cells transduce (convert) light into neural potentials. Transduction results in action potentials in axons of the optic nerves which lead from the retinas to the brain. Neurons of the brain integrate input from the optic nerve; brain activity in brain visual areas constitutes what we are consciously aware of as vision. There are several processes involved here. One of them is used to represent where light in the visual world is coming from. Others process color, movement, or form. There are species differences in the structure and physiology of the eyes and the brain visual areas that reflect their unique visual "problems." Synaptic connections in the visual systems of mammals are largely present at birth or shortly thereafter; however, patterned light must be present in both eyes for these connections to be properly maintained.

Audition begins with transduction of sound energy by hair cells of the cochlea of the inner ear. This leads to action potentials in the auditory nerve which leads to the brain where further processing is conducted. Auditory-processing regions of the brain determine where the sound source is located in space, the frequency of the sound, and the sound's intensity. As expected, species differ with respect to the structures and processes involved in audition, and these differences correspond to the exigencies of their respective environments.

Recommended Readings

ALI, M. A., & KLYNE, M. A. (1985). *Vision in vertebrates.* New York: Plenum.

BARLOW, H. B., & MOLLON, J. D. (1982). *The senses.* Cambridge: Cambridge University Press.

LYTHGOE, J. N. (1979). *The ecology of vision.* New York: Oxford University Press.

MASTERTON, R. B. (1978). *Handbook of behavioral neurobiology. Vol. 1: Sensory integration.* New York: Plenum.

PICKLES, J. O. (1988). *An introduction to the physiology of hearing.* London: Academic Press.

STEBBINS, W. C. (1983). *The acoustic sense of animals.* Cambridge: Harvard University Press.

Chapter 8

INTEGRATIVE SYSTEMS AND BEHAVIOR

The detection and processing of environmental energy, discussed in the preceding chapter, was the first of the three major elements of behavioral mechanisms. In this chapter we will take a look at the second element, the integrative systems that use some of the sensory input, learn and remember things about the environment and the animal's relationship to it, motivate the individual to engage in certain activities, make decisions about what to do, and so on. These integrative processes are neither strictly sensory nor motor, but are heavily influenced by them and, in turn, affect them.

The idea that integrative systems exist as more or less discrete "modules" was suggested in Chapter 3. That is, these systems (learning, memory, and so on) do not exist as single entities, but rather as sets of more limited subprocesses that together produce coordinated output. So, for instance, there are several memory processes, each working in its own unique way (Tulving & Schacter, 1990). Further, each of the major memory processes depends on the functioning of its subcomponents, much like the braking system of a car depends on the proper functioning of its parts. We are not yet at the point where we can confidently say how many of these modules there are nor how they are organized, but cognitive science is moving us toward that end.

The subject matter of this chapter has long been the province of psychology, but has more recently been entered by biologists interested in the neural mechanisms of integrative systems, and by ecologists who have come to realize the importance of integrative systems as adaptations to environmental conditions. There is an enormous literature on integrative systems from several perspectives, too much to cover in its entirety here. Therefore, we will examine three types of integrative systems to illustrate how they work in the total behavioral sphere of the animal.

Learning and Memory

For many species, one of the most valuable of all phenotypic traits is the ability to modify behavioral output on the basis of experience. Learning and memory boil down to that simple phrase: modification of behavior based on experience. We will approach this important ability by reviewing several types of learning. Second, we will cover the neural mechanisms of learning and memory. Finally, we will explore adaptive species differences in learning and its diverse functions.

TYPES OF LEARNING

Learning, contrary to popular opinion, is not a single process. Learning is a generic term used to label several related phenomena that share the common requirement that behavior change is due to experience. Further, the effects of the experience are somehow stored and therefore are capable of influencing the individual's behavior later on. "Experience," however, must be carefully defined: Muscular fatigue, motivational changes, and maturational effects must be ruled out because they can change the individual's behavior over time. For example, a marathon runner may run differently after 20 miles than she did after one mile, but the difference may be due more to fatigue than to learning. The fatigue will dissipate, but learning tends to be more lasting.

In many cases, the sorts of experiences linked with learning are the proximate consequences of behavior discussed in Chapter 1. That is, what happened to the individual following the emission of a behavior? Did it obtain food, get out of the cold, avoid a predator, or get attacked by one? Proximate consequences can increase or decrease the probability of a behavior reoccurring, at least in certain circumstances. Consequences also can modify the form, intensity, and orientation of the behavior. Other forms of learning and memory are not linked to behavioral consequences, but are instead more directly tied to exposure to environmental events, regardless of behavioral change. Following Mackintosh (1983), we will examine two major types of learning, each of which has two or more subtypes. Following them, we will look at the role of cognitive processes in learning.

Nonassociative learning Nonassociative learning involves behavioral change brought about by exposure to a particular stimulus. *Habituation* occurs when an individual ceases responding to an inconsequential stimulus after it has been presented numerous times. For example, terns living in the vicinity of hawks at first react strongly to them. If the terns are not attacked, however, they cease responding to hawks (McNicholl, 1973). Habituation has occurred. We habituate to the methodical ticking of clocks, and some unfortunate people who live near airports even habituate to thunderous jet takeoffs!

Another form of nonassociative learning is *sensitization*, which is, in many respects, the opposite of habituation. Following the presentation of an important stimulus, especially a noxious one, the individual responds more vigorously or at a higher rate than usual. For instance, if a puff of air is directed at the eye, eyeblinking occurs more frequently thereafter.

Associative conditioning Psychologists rec-

ognize two forms of associative conditioning. The first type, called *classical* or *Pavlovian conditioning*, was first reported by the Russian physiologist, Ivan Pavlov, early in this century. In classical conditioning a previously neutral stimulus (called the conditional stimulus or CS) precedes another stimulus (the unconditional stimulus or US) that reliably provokes a response (the unconditional response or UR). For example, a soft tone (the CS) precedes a puff of air to the cornea (the US) which produces an eyeblink (the UR). At first, the tone itself does not elicit an eye blink, but the air puff certainly does. If the tone and air puff are paired repeatedly (in that order), the tone alone eventually comes to elicit a response that resembles the UR (see Fig. 8-1). This is the conditional response or CR.

The CS comes to predict the arrival of the US, and the individual benefits from the preparation for subsequent action that this allows. For

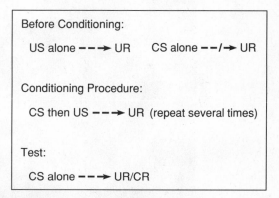

Figure 8.1
Summary of classical (Pavlovian) conditioning procedure. Before conditioning, the unconditioned stimulus leads to the unconditioned response; the conditioned stimulus does not. In conditioning, the CS and US are paired, in that order, several times. Later, the CS is presented alone. Generally, the subject emits a conditioned response that may closely resemble the unconditioned response.

example, Hollis (1984) presented male blue gouramis, a small fish, with a rival male (US). Half of the subjects received a CS, a red light, a few seconds before the rival appeared; the other subjects saw the same red light but it was not predictably paired with the rival. She found that the CS males directed more aggressive displays (fin erections) and bites toward the rival than did the no-CS males. This would translate into enhanced territorial defense, a requirement for successful reproduction in this species. Hollis (1982, 1990) has argued that the general function of Pavlovian conditioning is preparation for subsequent action. This is not only true of defensive responses (eyeblink, territorial defense), but also in feeding (anticipatory salivation, gastrointestinal motility), and sexual behavior (hormone release, changes in blood flow).

The other form of associative conditioning,

known as *operant conditioning,* occurs when a behavior is followed by some consequence that is either advantageous or disadvantageous to the individual. If the behavior reliably produces that consequence, the frequency of the behavior may change. For example, if a bird finds seeds by turning over fallen leaves, then leaf-turning will increase in frequency, and if a cat's jumping over the fence results in attacks by the neighbor's dog, the cat will soon cease jumping the fence.

If the consequences of a behavior increase the probability of emitting that behavior, the change is referred to as *reinforcement.* Reinforcement can occur in two ways. In *positive reinforcement,* the consequence itself is positive (e.g., a tasty morsel of food, money, praise). In *negative reinforcement,* the benefit comes from avoiding or escaping an aversive situation (e.g., flying from a predator, shooing away a mosquito, or

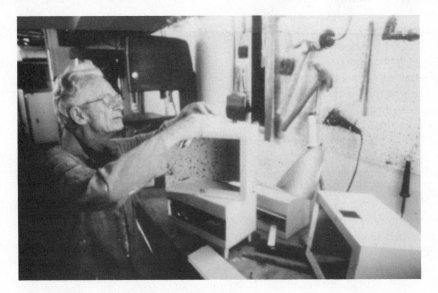

B. F. SKINNER

"It is now clear that we must take into account what the environment does to an organism not only before but after it responds. Behavior is shaped by its consequences."
[Skinner, B. F. (1971). Beyond freedom and dignity. *New York: Knopf.*]

getting out of the cold). Both forms of reinforcement increase the rate at which the behavior is performed, at least in those circumstances in which reinforcement has previously occurred (Catania, 1984).

If a behavior is followed by aversive consequences, the probability of emitting the behavior is decreased, and the process is referred to as *punishment*. Punishment can come about for two reasons. In the first case, the consequence is the reception of something that the animal would generally avoid if possible. A painful blow or a frightening sound might tend to decrease those behaviors that produce them. In the second case, the loss of something positive will also tend to decrease those behaviors that produce the loss.

Punishment and negative reinforcement are often confused because both of them involve aversive stimulation. The difference is that in negative reinforcement the behavior turns off the aversive stimulation (or avoids it if it has not yet appeared), whereas in punishment the behavior produces the aversive stimulation. The similarities and differences between positive reinforcement, negative reinforcement, and the two forms of punishment are shown in Fig. 8-2.

In addition to learning the relationship between behavior and consequences, animals may also learn that behavior produces those consequences only when certain conditions exist. In the laboratory, a rat may actively press a lever for food pellets when a light is on, but not press while the light is off because food is not forthcoming. We would say that the rat's lever pressing is under stimulus control. This is a very important ability because it permits the animal to engage in certain behaviors only when there is a reasonable chance of success. The environment, in essence, may "cue" the animal's behavior provided the animal can learn and remember the relationship between the environmental cue

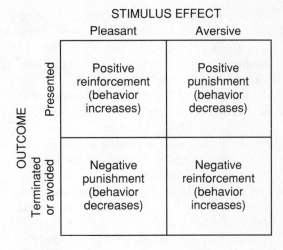

Figure 8.2
Four types of operant conditioning are derived from the combination of two variables: The sensory effect of the stimulus and whether the behavior brings about the stimulus or removes it. The change in the frequency of the behavior is also shown.

and the consequences of its behavior. Stimulus control need not be confined to positive reinforcement. If a stimulus reliably indicates that an aversive event is about to occur, the animal may perform a behavior that avoids the aversive event.

Cognition and learning There has been a long-standing controversy about what is learned during conditioning. Is it "merely" stimulus–response–consequence relationships, or is it something more abstract? There seems to be a consensus emerging that learning frequently goes beyond the specific learned associations (Roitblat, 1987). Some of the experiments that lend support to this conclusion are very simple ones. For instance, rats readily learn to turn correctly when they reach the choice point of a T-maze for food reinforcement. Does this mean that they have only learned that "turning right at the intersection leads to food?" Apparently not. When Tolman *et al.* (1946) turned the maze 180 degrees, the rats that had formerly been reinforced for turning right now turned left instead, indicating that they had learned the location of food, not simply a right turn.

In addition to learning specific associations, individuals may acquire "higher-order" associations. Harlow (1949) pioneered study of this subject. In his work a wooden tray with two recessed food cups was presented to a caged rhesus monkey. Each cup was covered by a wooden object (e.g., a circle and triangle), but only one of the cups contained a small food reward. If the monkey removed the correct block it got the food. The researcher then prepared the tray and conducted the test again, randomly positioning the food reward and its accompanying block. Monkeys usually make several errors before they reliably choose the correct block, but when they master the problem by getting, say, 9 out of 10 presentations correct, a new problem is instituted. This time, for instance, a red square and a blue square are presented, with blue always covering the food. Harlow persisted with this procedure until the monkeys had been exposed to about 300 separate problems. As you might expect, the monkeys gradually became more adept at this task until they almost always got the reward on the second exposure to the new problem. (Because the problem was new on the first exposure, the monkeys only scored 50% correct— chance—on the first attempt.) In other words, in addition to learning specific associations (blue block–food) they learned something abstract about the task itself. This can be summarized by the rule: If I win on my first guess, stay with that choice thereafter; if I lose, switch to the other option (Schrier, 1984). In human terms we would call this form of learning "concept formation." Other animals besides monkeys have been shown to develop similar concepts (e.g., Pepperberg, 1983).

Finally, according to a strict reinforcement view of learning and memory, behavior must be performed in order for learning to occur. However, memory can take place in the absence of overt behavior or consequences. You can probably remember what you ate for lunch yesterday, and some animals can remember to avoid an unpleasant experience by observing others in that situation (Mason & Reidinger, 1982). The presence of learning without obvious consequences to the individual was of great interest because the prevailing theories required consequences to strengthen the neural connections between stimuli and responses. Later in this chapter we will see how natural selection has led to some highly efficient learning and memory systems. Examples of learning without overt consequences would seem to be of this sort.

In summary, then, it is clear that learning and memory in animals frequently are of the "cognitive" variety, not just stimulus–response associations. This does not mean, however, that the cognitive process is the same in all species, or that conditioning is not important in its own right. Psychology spent over 30 years of its history working against the notion of cognition, particularly in animals (Epstein, 1985), but has since seen a remarkable turn in the other direction, with many influential researchers leading a return to cognitive explanations of behavior, even in animals (e.g., Griffin, 1984a, 1985). Conditioning and cognition are not competing theories of behavior. Rather, they complement one another.

NEURAL MECHANISMS OF LEARNING AND MEMORY

For many years behavioral scientists reasoned that structural or physiological modifications must occur in the nervous system during learning, and that these modifications must be long-lasting in order to account for memory. Several decades of intensive work have been devoted to understanding these processes. This work falls into three interrelated areas: gross brain changes in response to experience, structural changes in individual neurons, and neurochemical changes in synapses. Gross brain changes due to experience were discussed in Chapter 5 so we will focus here on the more microscopic changes.

Individual neuron structure What changes occur in neurons when learning and memory transpire? A particularly exciting line of investigation focuses on dendritic spines, small swellings on the surface of dendrites where synaptic sites are found (Fig. 8-3). Dendritic spines change in number and structure following specific forms of experience (Coss, 1985). For in-

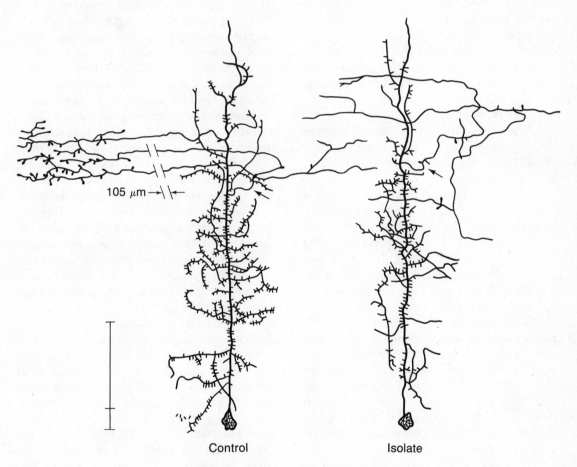

105 μm

Control

Isolate

Figure 8.3
Dendritic spines commonly show modifications due to individual experience. These two Golgi-stained neurons came from the same brain region of two jewel fish. The control fish was raised in an environment that al-

lowed it to see the eyes of another jewel fish. The isolated fish was raised in the same conditions but was not allowed exposure to eyes. The lower third of its neuron has significantly fewer dendritic spines, and they tend to be longer and thinner.

stance, Brandon and Coss (1982) examined the brains of bees that had just returned to the hive following their first foraging flight. They found that the dendritic spines in a particular part of the bee's brain were thicker and more numerous than the dendritic spines of other bees that were captured just before going out for their first flight. Similar changes in dendritic spines have been observed in jewel fish given specific visual experience (the opportunity to see the eyes of another jewel fish) compared to fish that lacked this experience (Coss & Globus, 1978, 1979). We are still far from being able to point out the dendritic spines that are modified when a person learns a new telephone number, but the progress toward that goal has been impressive and promises to continue in the near future.

Neurochemistry of learning and memory Several neurochemical processes have been implicated in learning and memory, some of which are described below.

One neurochemical process modifies the number of receptor sites available on postsynaptic membranes. Lynch and Baudry (1984) and Siman *et al.* (1985) noted increases in the number of receptors following stimulation of a postsynaptic membrane. Therefore, even if the amount of transmitter released per action potential were unchanged, having more receptors on the postsynaptic membrane would increase the magnitude of the neurotransmitter's effect. How does the postsynaptic membrane get more receptors? Lynch and Baudry argue that the receptors were there all along, but were occluded on the inside by a network of fodrin, a protein. Fodrin is decomposed by an enzyme that is activated by calcium ions. Calcium enters the postsynaptic membrane through channels activated by the neurotransmitter. Many action potentials in rapid sequence are required for enough calcium to activate this enzymatic process, which is summarized in Fig. 8-4. Interestingly, fodrin acts as a

sort of internal "skeleton" for the membrane, and as fodrin is removed, the dendritic spines swell, precisely the observation that Coss and others have made in microscopic studies of dendritic changes in response to experience.

The amount of neurotransmitter released with each action potential can change with experience as has been extensively studied in the marine mollusc, *Aplysia* (Kandel, 1979; Kandel & Schwartz, 1982). *Aplysia* retracts part of its body, the mantle shelf, when touched lightly. If touched repeatedly, retraction habituates. However, if a painful stimulus is applied to the tail before the animal is touched, retraction becomes more vigorous, an example of sensitization. Habituation has been linked to decreased neurotransmitter release from sensory neurons, but sensitization is due to increased transmitter release from the same neurons (Dale *et al.*, 1988). The neurons on which these cells synapse do not change their sensitivity to the transmitter.

A single painful stimulus results in sensitization lasting several hours. Four consecutive painful stimuli lead to sensitization that lasts a full day. More of these painful stimuli, spaced apart through time, produce sensitization lasting several weeks. In other words, the neurochemical events described above may be the basis of long-term memory (Kandel & Schwartz, 1982).

Associative conditioning has been traced to long-lasting changes in the regulation of ion flow across neuronal membranes. Alkon (1983) trained a species of marine snail (*Hermissenda*) to associate the onset of light with water turbulence. The snails normally approach light but avoid water turbulence; they quickly cease movement when light reliably precedes turbulence. Alkon's group mapped out the snail's relatively simple nervous system and eventually linked the learned response with changes in the membrane potential of a type of photoreceptor in the eyes. These photoreceptors became depo-

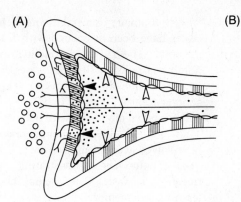

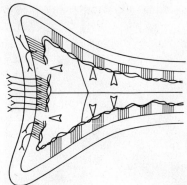

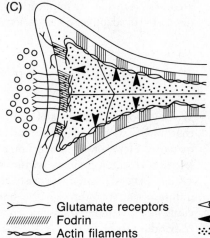

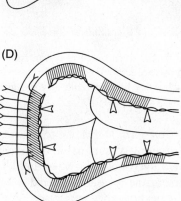

>——— Glutamate receptors
///////// Fodrin
~~~~~ Actin filaments

◁ Calpain (inactive)
◀ Calpain (active)
∴ Calcium

Figure 8.4
Lynch and Baudry's hypothesis about the mechanism underlying structural changes in dendritic spines is shown in a series of four steps. (A) A volley of neurotransmitter (glutamate, open circles) causes a calcium influx that activates calpain, an enzyme that degrades fodrin. This action uncovers more glutamate receptors.

(B) Shortly afterward, calcium is gone, and calpain is no longer active. (C) Another volley of glutamate leads to the entry of more calcium than before (due to the presence of more receptors) and this, in turn, leads to even more fodrin degradation. (D) So much fodrin has now been removed that the spine is permanently altered.

larized during training and remained depolarized relative to pretraining levels for several days after training, when they still exhibit memory of their experience.

Finally, hormonal responses to certain forms of experience can foster memory processes (McGaugh, 1983). For example, Gold (1987, 1989) reviews evidence for enhancement of memory by adrenalin. Emotionally arousing situations are typically remembered better than

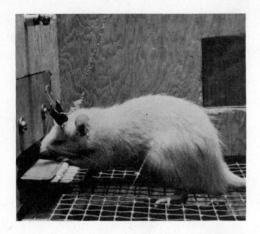

Stimulating electrodes, when placed in certain parts of the brain, can produce high rates of behavior, such as bar-pressing, when that behavior results in the delivery of a brief electrical stimulus.

nonarousing situations. Is this due to release of adrenalin in arousing conditions? In one experiment, rats were given footshock when they left a light-colored starting area and entered a dark chamber. The next day they were placed in the starting area again and the amount of time taken to enter the dark chamber was measured. Rats that received a stronger shock were slower to enter the chamber, indicating better recall of the previous day's event. However, when rats that were given mild shock got injections of adrenalin, their memory of the shock event improved and they were slower to enter the chamber (Gold *et al.*, 1982). Further, Gold suggests that adrenalin has this effect by stimulating release of glucose, a prime neural fuel. Injections of glucose can enhance memory independently of adrenalin. Finally, the generally poorer memories of aged humans and rats may be a consequence of lowered glucose regulation. When aged humans are given injections of glucose after a learning episode, they recall it better than others given a placebo injection (reviewed by Gold & Stone, 1988).

In summary, several neurochemical processes have been associated with learning and memory. These include modulation of the number of receptor sites, increases or decreases in the amount of neurotransmitter released per action potential, changes in polarity of neurons, and hormonal modification of neural physiology. There are undoubtedly other processes that may be involved even though we are still a long way from conclusively demonstrating causal relationships between some neural changes and learning and memory (Brown *et al.*, 1988). The wide variety of neurochemical processes associated with learning has implications for our later discussion of adaptive specializations of learning.

BRAIN STRUCTURES OF LEARNING AND MEMORY

We have covered the sorts of neuronal changes that appear to be responsible for learning and memory. However, we have not explored the location of these neurons within the nervous system. Several possibilities exist: They could be diffusely scattered through the brain, or they could be restricted to more discrete patches corresponding to brain nuclei. It appears that the latter possibility is more nearly correct in that some brain structures are much more crucial to learning and memory than other areas. We will review a few of them here. Before doing so, we need to examine a system that seems to be central to mammalian learning— the reward system of the brain.

Reward system of the brain   In the early 1950s, James Olds and Peter Milner were conducting an experiment that involved electrical stimulation of the brainstem through implanted electrodes. The electrode placement was off-target in one rat, however, and they noticed that the rat repeated behaviors that had occurred immediately before electrical stimulation. In fact, rats pressed a lever hundreds of times per hour for electrical stimulation (Olds & Milner, 1954). Three decades of research on this phenomenon followed and several brain regions have been identified that have these reinforcing properties (Olds & Fobes, 1981). Let us review this process.

Although electrodes placed in several brain regions are effective in producing self-stimulation, the most powerful effects are obtained through stimulation of the *medial forebrain bundle* (MFB), an axon tract connecting several midbrain structures with the base of the forebrain. It courses through the hypothalamus. The axons that comprise the MFB originate in several nuclei and terminate in several others. In fact, there are probably at least two populations of fibers in the MFB that contribute to the rewarding effects of self-stimulation. One of them uses ACh as a neurotransmitter (Gratton & Wise, 1985); dopamine (DA) is another. Drugs that increase DA facilitate the self-stimulation process, but DA-reducing drugs impede self-stimulation. Significantly, increased amounts of dopamine enhance memory, and the same drugs that increase self-stimulation also increase memory (Routtenberg, 1978).

Of course, observations such as these shed little light on the mechanism of learning and memory. How does DA enhance memory? Is it through modification of synapses or transmitter release? If so, which neurons are involved? If stimulation follows a left turn in a maze and the animal remembers this relationship, can we expect to find the modified neurons in the same area as those involved in remembering to push a lever when a light comes on? These are difficult questions to answer because the MFB may be only a part of the process. The neurons on which MFB axons terminate send axons to diverse regions, any of which could be involved in memory.

Returning now to the question of which neural structures are involved in memory, we will examine three that have received the most attention.

Hippocampus   The hippocampus, a forebrain structure, is gaining more and more attention as an important structure in memory. Much of the research on hippocampal involvement in learning has emphasized its role in spatial memory. Spatial memory is conveniently studied in a radial arm maze (Fig. 8-5). Rats placed in a radial arm maze with food at the end of each arm are adept at acquiring all the food without revisiting depleted arms very often (Olton, 1979). However, rats with hippocampal lesions are much less efficient: They revisit arms many times, apparently unable to remember where they have already explored (Olton & Samuelson, 1976). These rats have not forgotten everything: They apparently remember that the

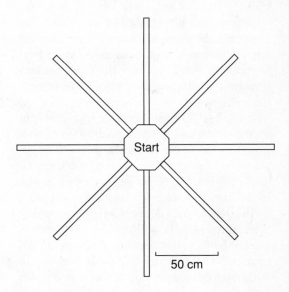

Figure 8.5
Radial arm mazes, such as this one, are widely used for studying spatial learning and memory. A rat is placed in the octagonal start area and allowed to visit the arms as often as it wishes. The arms usually contain a small amount of food at the end.

arms contain food. They also remember arms that *never* contain food, avoiding them consistently even though they make many mistakes among the arms that do contain food (Olton & Papas, 1979).

As expected, those species that rely heavily on spatial memory for survival have larger hippocampi relative to their body weight and brain size than do other species that are not as dependent on spatial memory. This relationship has been nicely demonstrated in food-storing birds, a group that will receive our attention again later (Sherry *et al.*, 1989).

Amygdala   The amygdala, a complex of neurons located in the anterior temporal lobes, is involved in memory formation in two ways. First, in conjunction with the hippocampus, the amygdala has a profound effect on memory formation (Mishkin & Appenzeller, 1987). When Mishkin and his colleagues lesioned both the amygdalas and hippocampi of monkeys, they found that the animals could not remember the solution to a simple problem even over a brief retention interval. However, the same monkeys remembered things acquired prior to the surgery, suggesting that memory was not stored in these locations but that they were critical for establishing the memories that were somehow stored elsewhere. Second, the amygdala seems to be involved in coordinating memories from different sensory modalities. A monkey, for instance, who learns that a square block covers a food reward and a circular block does not when the problem is presented visually, will not show evidence of recall when the problem is posed using only tactile cues if the amygdalas have been removed. An intact monkey readily makes the transfer, however.

Cerebellum   Classical conditioning of the eyeblink response in rabbits has been traced to a specific part of the cerebellum. McCormick and Thompson (1984) exposed rabbits to puffs of air

to one eye. The puffs were preceded by a brief tone. After conditioning was completed and the rabbits were reliably blinking in response to the tone alone, lesions were made within the cerebellum. Small lesions of the dentate–interpositus (D–I) nuclei abolished the conditional response, although lesions in other parts of the cerebellum had no effect. Other measurements indicated that D–I neurons became active just before the eyeblink was made, and electrical stimulation produced the eyeblink. Thompson (1986) presents more details on this work and on other studies of the cerebellum and memory.

There are two main conclusions to be drawn from these studies of brain structures involved in learning and memory. First, there are numerous brain regions involved, only a few of which are described here. Squire (1987) has written a comprehensive account of them. Second, the brain structures of learning and memory tend to have fairly specific roles. For example, monkeys were trained to perform delayed matching-to-sample tasks. In this task a stimulus comes on (e.g., a high-pitched tone) and then, after a delay, a second tone is played, either the same as the first, or different from it. If the second tone is the same as the first, one response is reinforced with food; if the second tone is different, another response is reinforced. Errors go unreinforced. Thus, the monkey needs to remember the first stimulus and compare the second with it. Colombo *et al.* (1990) lesioned the superior temporal lobes of monkeys who had mastered both auditory and visual versions of this task. The monkeys retained their performance on the visual problem, but lost their ability to solve the auditory problem. Their lack of performance was not due to an inability to compare sounds, but rather to remember them.

Neuropsychology has shown that damage to a structure often has very specific effects in humans. For instance, Tulving (1989) describes a case in which a man who sustained a head injury could not recall personal experiences from his own life, but could recall a great deal of factual information about the world at large. The human neuropsychological literature abounds with cases of specific deficits that bolster the conclusion that various aspects of learning and memory are localized to specific brain structures.

The neural structures and processes described above are expressions of the genes inherited by organisms as they interact with their developmental environments. Presumably, these genes have evolved because they contributed to a nervous system capable of being changed by certain forms of experience. But species differ with respect to their evolutionary histories, genes, and environments. Therefore, we expect to find differences in how learning occurs, what is learned, and so on. These are the topics to be addressed in the next section.

ADAPTIVE SPECIALIZATIONS OF LEARNING

Traditional ideas Learning has traditionally been viewed as a single phenomenon that obeys the same fundamental laws regardless of the species and the content of the learning (Roper, 1983; Leahey & Harris, 1989). This statement encompasses two ideas: The first of these is *general process theory.* This is the notion that all cases of a particular form of conditioning obey the same fundamental laws, regardless of the species. The second idea is the *principle of equipotentiality,* a cumbersome term meaning that all stimulus–response pairs (that the organism can perceive and execute) are equally likely to become associated.

Proponents of these ideas felt that the learning process was the same in all species and in all circumstances; therefore it was permissible to study learning in just a few species (usually rat and pigeon) using arbitrary tasks, all set in the confines of the laboratory. Although this may sound absurd in retrospect, the position had merit as it was being developed. First, other sciences have advocated similar ideas. Genetics has long depended on *Drosophila* as a standard organism, assuming that its genetic processes were applicable to other organisms; and in medicine and nutrition, lab rats fill in for humans as the subject of study. Second, this view is supported by the finding that neurophysiological processes are remarkably similar in highly diverse species. Because learning and memory depend on neural processes, it seemed reasonable to conclude that learning processes are the same throughout the animal kingdom. Finally, there is a historical reason for this thinking. Darwin had emphasized the importance of instinct and intelligence as adaptations in animals. Reasoning that if natural selection had produced organisms that were anatomically similar in some ways but different in other ways, behavioral similarities and differences also should be expected. Because differences between humans and other animals were obvious, early research sought similarities between humans and animals in the hope of demonstrating an evolutionary continuity of human intellect (behavioral capacities) with those of other animals (Kalat, 1983). Unfortunately, the emphasis on similarities became excessive and research soon lapsed into a search for general mechanisms of learning without the balance provided by studies of adaptive differences among organisms.

Constraints on learning The traditional perspective emphasized the great plasticity in behavior made possible by learning, a plasticity that was almost without limit. In contrast, another view of learning emerged in the early 1970s that questioned this great plasticity. It came to be called "constraints on learning"

SARA SHETTLEWORTH

"... *The study of learning [is] the study of how behaviour is fine-tuned to the details of the individual's environment and how the capacity for this fine-tuning influences fitness.*" [Shettleworth, S. J. (1984). Learning and behavioural ecology. In J. R. Krebs & N. B. Davies (Eds.) Behavioural ecology: An evolutionary approach (pp. 170–194). Sunderland, MA: Sinauer (p. 170).]

(Shettleworth, 1972), and it pointed out inconsistencies in the ability of an animal to learn two things that should have been equally difficult. Seligman (1970) reviewed examples of learning among animals and came to the conclusion that some things were readily learned, but that others were inordinately difficult. That is, an animal species is "prepared" to learn certain things, and "contra-prepared" to learn others. Three examples should clarify the distinction.

First, a highly influential experiment by Garcia & Koelling (1966) set the constraints on learning movement in motion. In their experiment, rats drank sweetened water from a spout and as they did so, sounds and flashing lights were on. The sounds and lights stopped whenever the rats were not drinking. Afterward, some of the rats were made ill by exposing them to large doses of X-rays; the other rats were given a painful shock. Next, the rats were given a choice between two drinking bottles. One contained sweetened water, as before, but it did not produce the sounds and lights. The other drinking bottle contained plain water, but produced the sounds and lights. Garcia and Koelling found that the rats that had been made ill avoided drinking the sweet water, but did not avoid the sounds and lights. In contrast, the rats that had been shocked avoided drinking from the bottle that turned on the sounds and lights, but did not avoid the sweet water. In short, there was a strong bias in rats' associations between environmental stimuli and behavioral consequences. These biases are not predicted in traditional views of learning.

Second, pigeons readily learn that when a light is turned on in the experimental chamber, key pecks will lead to food delivery. They are also adept at learning that a tone signals impending shock and do what is required to prevent the shock. However, the same pigeons are extremely slow at associating tones with food-getting activity and light as a signal for forthcoming shock (Foree & LoLordo, 1973). Finally, training an animal to avoid or escape a painful stimulus by moving toward it is extremely difficult; however, training proceeds rapidly if the animal is required to move away from the painful stimulus (Bolles, 1970).

The concept of preparedness need not be as dramatic as in the examples described above. It can be more subtle, on the order of biases or tendencies. Bees readily learn to associate colors with sugar water in test situations. This, of course, is highly adaptive because there may be many flower species that differ in color in the

bee's foraging area, and they produce nectar un-
equally. When a bee has had one or two successful visits to a particular kind of flower, it acquires
a stable memory of that flower type and visits it
preferentially thereafter. Although bees have
excellent color vision over a wide spectrum, they
are slower at associating blue-green with food
reward than they are at associating other colors,
especially violet and blue (Menzel & Erber,
1978). Blue-green is the predominant color of
the background vegetation (i.e., the nonflower
parts of plants) and thus is not "expected" to
yield nectar. Bees can learn to associate blue-
green with food rewards, but there seems to be
an initial bias against it. Biases, propensities,
and predispositions seem to be a built-in part of
many learning mechanisms.

Ecological perspectives The constraints
on learning approach made a significant contribution to our understanding of learning. Its emphasis was on limitations of the animal in the
learning situation. The ecological perspective,
although an outgrowth of the constraints approach, was more positive in that it emphasized
the value of learning as an adaptation to ecological conditions. This view asserts that species
differ in what is important for them to learn and
remember. Therefore, natural selection may
have favored different neural processes of learning and memory for their unique adaptive benefits (Kamil, 1988). We should expect to find
species differences in what is learned and remembered and in the ways that learning occurs
(Shettleworth, 1984; Gould & Marler, 1987).

According to the ecological perspective,
the most basic function of learning is coping
with environmental circumstances that cannot
be predicted far in advance. There is no way to
encode in the genes what a young monkey's
playmates will look like, what the landmarks
will be around a human's village, or where the
best berry bushes will be for a black bear. To

AL KAMIL

" . . . Traits with adaptive functions vary between
species, in ways that make sense in terms of the ecology and adaptations of the organisms they serve. If animal intelligence is adaptive . . . then intelligence must
vary between species. The variation may be qualitative
or quantitative; intelligence may consist of a complex
of processes. But differences there must be. [Kamil, A.
C. (1988). A synthetic approach to animal intelligence. In D. W. Leger (Ed.) Comparative perspectives in modern psychology. Nebraska Symposium
on Motivation, Vol. 35 (pp. 257–308). Lincoln:
University of Nebraska Press (p. 294).]*

make use of such details, the individual's phenotype must be modifiable on a short-term basis,
and at least some of the details must be retained
for later retrieval and use. Learning and memory,
then, are like other bodily processes that must
cope with the unforeseen: Heavily used muscles
strengthen to accommodate the load, and the
immune system responds to new pathogens and

even "remembers" them on subsequent reinvasions. Think of how disadvantaged an individual would be who could not learn and remember, whose muscle strength could not be changed, and who lacked an immune system with "memory." The world would seem to be constantly new and each recurring problem solved as though it were for the first time.

Let us follow up on the statement that learning and memory are adaptations for dealing with circumstances that cannot be predicted far in advance. Like all broadly encompassing statements, this one needs refinement. For instance, predictability of food sources is a very different problem for a long-lived monkey than it is for a short-lived insect. Monkeys may have hundreds of trees of different species in their home ranges. The trees vary in the quantity and quality of food they provide, and each fruit-bearing tree may yield food for only a week or so every few years. Monkeys who learn which trees are producing and know how to get "there" from "here" are at an advantage in the competition to perpetuate monkey genes. For an insect residing in the same forest, learning and memory may be a wasted expenditure, a luxury. Its lifespan may be so short that simply finding one fruiting tree may take care of its lifetime needs. The ecological perspective on learning does not say that the ability to learn is always more adaptive than an inability to learn; rather, learning may be adaptive in certain species–ecology combinations.

Long-lived species face problems that recur with unequal frequencies. Shortly after salmon hatch in the cold, shallow water of a Pacific northwest stream, they learn the idiosyncratic chemical flavor of that stream (Hasler *et al.*, 1978), and they remember it for years while living in open ocean. A salmon needs to learn this only once; it is set thereafter.

Other problems, of course, change on a short-term basis and therefore must be learned as

the occasion arises and relearned as conditions change. Interestingly, these situations also call for forgetting of outdated material. Although memory capacities may be enormous, they are not infinite, so forgetting may be necessary (or beneficial) for updating memory. Excellent examples of memory and forgetting come from studies of food-hoarding birds (Shettleworth, 1983; Sherry, 1984; Kamil & Clements, 1990). Some species, most notably Clark's nutcracker, a member of the crow family from western North America (Fig. 8-6), stashes nuts in small holes that it digs in the ground. When nuts are plentiful it stores hundreds of them, returning weeks or even months later to retrieve and eat them. The birds remember the locations of their hundreds of storage sites, using landmarks as memory aids (Kamil & Balda, 1985; Vander Wall, 1982). Food-hoarding birds do not have perfect memories, though. They forget. But they forget in an orderly fashion: The longer it has been since a nut was stored the more likely the bird is to forget it. This is adaptive because other animals may pilfer buried nuts, and the longer it has been since storage the greater the probability of pilferage. Birds that return to retrieve more recent stores first will probably recover more nuts than birds that attempt to retrieve in the order in which the nuts were stored.

Food-storing birds have remarkably good memories. Many animals are not so gifted, but even in their shortcomings there is adaptive sense. For example, some nectar-feeding insects remember which one of several flower species they have been visiting, and return to that type over and over. Butterflies become faster at finding nectar as they get more experience with that type of flower. However, they can not seem to remember the particular techniques required for more than one type of flower, so by specializing on one type they forage more efficiently (Lewis, 1986).

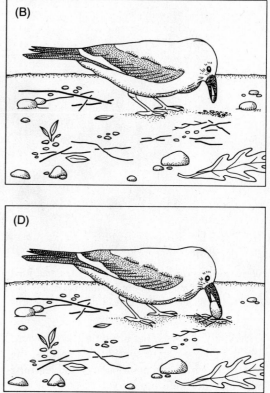

Figure 8.6
The Clark's nutcracker buries hundreds of nuts in the fall and recovers them during the winter and spring.

This sequences shows the bird digging a small pit (a), inserting a nut (b), and covering it with soil and plant material (c), and a pebble (d).

A CASE STUDY IN LEARNING: BIRDSONG

Summarizing thus far, it appears that long-lasting changes in the nervous system can occur due to an individual's experiences. Numerous genes undoubtedly participate in the development of the neural structures and processes that are involved in efficient learning and memory (Tierney, 1986). Such genes presumably evolved because of the positive contributions made to the reproductive success of their bearers. If these statements are correct, we should expect to find examples of learning whose neural and experiential processes are reasonably well understood and which contribute to reproductive success. One such example comes from birdsong. Although birdsong will be discussed again in a later chapter, we will quickly cover some aspects of it here to pull together the mechanisms and adaptive significance of learning.

Many bird species acquire their unique songs through individual learning. There is extensive variation in when songs are learned, how the learning is accomplished, and in the number

Singing in male canaries is influenced by seasonal variation in the size and activity of a brain region, HVc. As HVc waxes and wanes, so does the size of the song repertoire. Larger repertoires are favored by females, so genes that contribute to this behavior will spread in the population.

and variety of songs that are sung (Petrinovich, 1990). However, let us consider one species, the canary, in which the neurobiology and learning are especially well understood.

Male canaries, like many songbirds, listen to song while they are very young, but do not sing until they become adult at about one year of age. When they first begin to "sing," at about 40 days of age, they produce soft, highly variable sounds that bear little resemblance to the final adult song. After a few weeks of this "subsong," they begin to emit notes or syllables and repeat them reliably. This "plastic song" phase lasts until the birds are about eight months old, and the syllables they develop during this phase become the stable units of the fully adult song (Nottebohm, 1984).

The male's brain changes during the transition from subsong to plastic song. A particularly important structure, designated HVc, first appears in the brain just before subsong commences, and grows rapidly during the period of plastic song. As the male canary nears the end of the first breeding season, his song repertoire, which had been extremely stable and unique to him as an individual, becomes unstable and he eventually stops singing. The HVc at this point has declined to about half of its springtime volume. During the next season the male canary goes through a new plastic song phase in which he adds some new song elements, drops some old ones, and modifies others. HVc increases again during this phase. These seasonal increases and decreases in HVc size and in song repertoire continue throughout the male's lifespan (Nottebohm, 1984).

Clearly, neural processes are associated with song acquisition and change, although the precise details are not yet known. What about the adaptive significance of singing? Kroodsma

(1976) has shown that female canaries in captivity are more likely to commence nest-building and ovulation when they hear large song repertoires than when they hear smaller repertoires, so it would appear that individual differences in HVc volume might be associated with differences in male reproductive success. Species differences in song repertoire size and in the timing of song acquisition are also associated with differences in HVc. Thus, this neural structure and its physiology seem to have been shaped by evolutionary processes because of the impacts made on the singing behavior of males in diverse bird species.

Motivation

Animals do not respond to a stimulus the same way each time it occurs. In some cases, behavioral changes may be due to learning, but in others the behavioral differences are due to temporary modifications of the organism's state. *Motivation* pertains to those organismic variables that influence an animal's behavior with respect to a certain stimulus (Whalen & Simon, 1984). Motivational variables are used to explain behavioral differences that occur despite invariant stimulus inputs to the organism (Pfaff, 1982). For instance, a dog may greedily consume a bowl of food one time but ignore it the next. In common terms we would say that the dog was motivated to eat in the first case but not motivated in the second.

To say that an animal eats because it is hungry tells us nothing useful because we are using the behavior to infer the motivation, and the motivation to explain the behavior. Motivational terms such as hunger and thirst are used as substitutes for a variety of physiological conditions, but we should not assume that there is necessarily a single physiological process that corresponds to a motivational term. For instance, the physiological processes that we would label thirst are quite varied. Low water concentration in the blood, little water in the stomach, and dryness in the mouth may all lead to drinking. Obviously, "thirst" is a generic motivational term that comprises several physiological conditions. Other systems share this complexity.

MODELS OF MOTIVATION

Motivation entails several processes. We want to know why a behavior begins when it does, what keeps it going after it has begun, how vigorously it is performed, and what causes it to stop. Researchers have tried to answer these four interrelated questions with respect to many types of behavior, including feeding, drinking, sex, sleep, and aggression. No one imagines that the same mechanisms are involved in motivating these diverse behaviors; nevertheless, several principles have been found useful in attempting to understand motivational processes (Toates, 1983; Toates & Archer, 1978). We will describe some of these principles now; they will arise again when we discuss specific behaviors in later chapters.

Negative feedback and homeostasis When setting the thermostat on a heater one depends on a negative feedback device to keep the room at the desired temperature. The furnace switches off after the room temperature reaches the set point. When the temperature drops below the set point the furnace is reactivated.

Many physiological and behavioral systems use negative feedback processes. Various hormones are produced when their levels fall below a certain concentration and cease to be produced when they again reach set levels. Drinking ensues when the bodily store of water declines below a particular level. Negative feedback is one of the most common processes involved in maintenance of physiological and behavioral *homeostasis* or steady state.

Negative feedback models of motivation have been very popular among behavioral scientists. They form the basis for *drive reduction theories* of motivation in psychology, and for the so-called *hydraulic models* of classical ethology. The concept of drive in psychology dealt with deprivation states that could lead to tissue damage if not corrected. When water deprived, for instance, the animal engages in behaviors that have previously resulted in drinking. Drinking clears up the tissue needs, and the animal no longer searches for water or drinks it. According to drive theory, the most basic motivational conditions are those that can produce damage to the organism (reviewed by Colgan, 1989).

Drive theory, with its emphasis on tissue needs, could not account for some forms of behavior, such as sexual behavior, that would not produce damage to the individual if not satisfied. The hydraulic models of ethology sought to explain motivation as the build-up of *action-specific energy* that could only be released by engaging in certain activities called *consummatory responses*. Of course, action-specific energy could arise through food or water deprivation, but also through deprivation of other activities that would not necessarily endanger the animal if not executed. Such things as sexual behavior, parental behavior, sleep, or even flight were thought to be motivated through such processes (Eibl-Eibesfeldt, 1970; Lorenz, 1981). Once the consummatory responses had taken place, the individual would enter a refractory period in which it would be far less likely to engage in the behavior. Although the hydraulic models seem to explain a wider variety of behaviors than does

drive theory, they leave much to be desired. The notion of action-specific energy is quite vague. What is this energy? Can we measure it? Why does it build up?

Both drive theory and the hydraulic models suffer from their view of behavior as being a reaction to a condition, rather than as being in a position to avoid potentially costly departures from some optimal physiological levels. The next mechanism allows for solving problems before they arise.

Feedforward   In negative feedback, behavior occurs only after the organism strays from the relevant set point. If this were the only regulatory process we would not drink until depleted of water, warm up until cold, or eat until low on energy. Observations of animals and humans in their natural surroundings suggest that they act *before* straying from the set point (Collier, 1982). A feedforward (anticipatory) process helps prevent costly deviations from optimal conditions.

Feedforward can be accomplished by means of learning. If the sensory cues resulting from departure from the set point are aversive, the organism may learn to take whatever actions are necessary to avoid those sensory conditions. For example, if thirst is uncomfortable and the organism can recognize the situational cues that frequently precede thirst, drinking can ensue, thereby avoiding later thirst.

Positive feedback   If performing a behavior changes the organism in a way that increases the likelihood of continuing that behavior, positive feedback is operating (not to be confused with positive reinforcement). For instance, becoming sexually aroused leads to more sexual behavior and arousal, at least to a point (Beach & Whalen, 1959; Toates & Archer, 1978). Positive feedback tends to keep the behavior pattern going for some time after it begins. As such, it helps in the efficient allocation of behavior.

Otherwise, one might take a sip of water, wait for the effect to wear off, take another sip, and so on (McCleery, 1983).

TIME ALLOCATION

Animals usually have many behavior patterns that they can perform. Furthermore, these patterns can be varied in intensity, speed, duration, and direction. Given that there are so many behavioral variables, it is useful to think of organisms as behavioral decision-makers (McFarland, 1977). "Decision-making" is used here only metaphorically; we have no idea whether decision-making processes are similar in all species, or even from one situation to another within a single individual. Nevertheless, decisions are often based on information, and thus the decision-making metaphor spurs us toward analyses of the kinds of information that may be used in choosing among behavioral options.

Our treatment of time allocation will focus exclusively on decisions about which behavior to perform: whether to eat or drink, walk or run, study or sleep. Some researchers in this area prefer to work at a "microscopic" level of analysis, tracing moment-to-moment "switches" from behavior X to behavior Y, and attempting to understand why that switch occurred (rather than another) and why it occurred at that particular time (McCleery, 1978, 1983). Other researchers analyze behavior over longer time periods, preferring to measure the time allotted to each of the behavioral options. Time is finite; analysis of "time budgets" can provide important clues about an individual's priorities. The two approaches complement one another in a complete understanding of behavioral allocation.

The state–space approach The leading viewpoint on time allocation, particularly at the micro level of analysis, is the *state–space approach*

(McFarland & Sibly, 1975; McCleery, 1983). The idea here is that an organism's physiological conditions (states) influence its choice of behavior. There are numerous states that are relevant and an individual's current status on each of them defines its overall state or "state-space."

Consider a case in which only one state variable, water deprivation, fluctuates. As time proceeds without drinking, changes occur in the chemical composition of the body fluids. Because the body can operate efficiently only within a certain range of water concentration, the organism should do what it can to keep itself within that range. Dehydration increases the value of water consumption and, if water is available, drinking will occur. This is the idea of homeostasis presented earlier. In other words, the further an individual strays from its hydration set point, the higher the value of any behavior that moves the individual back toward the set point.

Rarely will only one state–space variable be away from its set point. In fact, many of the state–space variables are interrelated such that performing a behavior that influences one variable may also influence others. The best-studied two-variable example involves food and water consumption (e.g., N. P. Lester, 1984). When a food- and water-deprived animal is given access to both commodities, it will perform one behavior to acquire food and another to acquire water. The animal's food deprivation declines as it eats; eventually its food deprivation subsides enough so that drinking becomes more valuable and it will drink. This goes back and forth as the organism balances the two states (Fig. 8-7). The two behaviors and the state variables they influence are not independent, however. Eating may change the need for water, and foods differ in their effect on water requirements. (Protein is digested by means of adding water molecules, so protein-rich foods increase the value of drink-

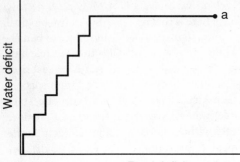

Figure 8.7
A hypothetical pattern of feeding and drinking in a lab
animal. The subject begins at point a, representing a
certain amount of food and water deprivation. It be-
gins by eating, which reduces its food deficit, than al-
ternates between drinking and eating until both deficits
are eliminated.

ing. Similarly, eating dry foods will clearly have a different effect on water requirements from eating moist food.) The point is that the state–space is a complex set of interrelated conditions. One variable may be so far from its set point that it requires immediate action, but more often the task is one of fine-tuning the constantly changing conditions of the organism.

External state–space variables Most state–space research has been concerned with internal, physiological variables. The animals are placed in laboratory testing conditions in which external conditions are held reasonably constant. There is no threat of predation, no offspring to care for, and no thunderstorms to contend with. But animals face such external conditions as well as their internal states. In some cases, such as the sudden appearance of a predator, the external state compels an organism to act; in other cases the external environment imposes constraints on what can be done or simply affords opportunities to perform behaviors efficiently.

Unfortunately, relatively little work has been conducted on behavioral choices of animals in their natural habitats, and none has been done at the micro level of analysis. Studies on time-budgeting in freely ranging animals suggest, however, that external conditions play a significant role in the behavioral decision-making process. For example, California ground squirrels have a number of important objects in their habitat, including burrows, rocks, and trees. Leger *et al.* (1983) investigated ground squirrels' time budgeting as a function of the number and proximity of these objects. Squirrels behaved differently as a function of their proximity to burrows, rocks, and trees. For instance, they were vigilant almost exclusively when they were in rocky areas, presumably because they could get up higher and therefore see farther and hear better. Most of their foraging occurred away from burrows, perhaps because most of the edible plants were quickly consumed in these high-traffic areas. In other words, the benefits to be derived from a particular behavior depend on the external circumstances in which the individual finds itself. In some cases the organism may move to conditions in which a behavior is most likely to be successful, as when birds fly to good foraging areas (Tinbergen, 1981); in other cases, the individual may be moving to or from a chosen area but must tailor its behavior to the conditions it encounters along its route. A deer, for instance, may have to cross a clearing to get to the stream to drink and it may be in greater peril in the clearing. Thus, it is highly vigilant while making the crossing.

Many species face a trade-off between two conflicting variables such as food acquisition and predator avoidance. This was clearly illustrated by a field study of marmots in Alaska (Holmes, 1984b). Marmots consume plants faster than the plants can grow. Therefore, after the marmots emerge from their hibernation burrows and begin eating the new spring growth, they must

Marmots must deal with their various physiological needs, such as food, within an ecological context that may contain complicating factors, such as predators. How these problems are resolved is a subject for motivational research.

tor appeared near the fertilized plots. Marmots certainly experience fluctuations in their internal state–space variables, but they must deal with these fluctuations within the larger context of constraints and opportunities of the external environment.

In conclusion, motivational processes alter the probabilities of certain behaviors. Some of these processes are internal to the organism but others are imposed by the external environment. Adaptive behavior occurs when these diverse conditions are weighed relative to all the others and the most profitable behavioral option is performed. "Profit" should ultimately be defined in terms of fitness, but its proximate units may be in terms of food consumption, hours of sleep, predator escape, temperature regulation, or any number of other important variables.

MOTIVATION AND GOAL ORIENTATION

Purpose and goal orientation are often closely associated with the concept of motivation. Most of us have no difficulty attributing purposiveness to ourselves or to other people. We do things with "goals in mind," and we know, or at least think we know, what we are doing and what our behavior is intended to achieve. Is it appropriate to attribute purpose to other animal species? Animals are often described as behaving instinctively or "blindly," implying no foresight. Although it is unwise to attribute human traits to other animals, a practice known as *anthropomorphism*, it is equally unwise to conclude that humans are alone in being able to foresee the consequences of our behavior. We saw earlier, for instance, that cognitive explanations for animal learning are certainly justified in some cases.

Animals clearly exhibit behavior that appears to be purposive, or goal-oriented, even if achieving the goal requires some sophisticated behavioral processes (Tolman, 1948). A jump-

move farther and farther from the safety of their burrows in search of food. They face an *approach–avoidance conflict*: A particular activity, area, or object has attributes that are both attractive and repellent. Holmes found that marmots shift their time budgets as they get farther from safety: They spend more time with their heads up, looking for predators. In a revealing case, Holmes applied fertilizer to a few plots in the marmots' meadow, causing particularly lush growth. The plots were far from burrows and thus were dangerous places to visit. The marmots responded to this predicament by hurriedly excavating refuge burrows (short, straight shafts) into which they could slip when a preda-

ing spider that sees an insect on another branch of a plant may need to take a convoluted path to get within striking distance, and its path may at times take it farther from its goal (Hill, 1979). Its behavior is strikingly similar to that of a person driving a roundabout path to get home around a detour. There is no reason not to call both of them goal-oriented. Similarly, chimpanzees open nuts by placing them on an "anvil" rock and pounding them with a hand-held stone. Goal orientation is obvious when one recognizes that the stones and nuts are often far apart. Chimpanzees carry stones great distances to nut trees.

Griffin (1984a, b), in his insightful works on "animal thinking," has concluded that if the terms cognitive, foresightful, and goal-oriented apply to human behavior, they should also apply to comparable behaviors performed by nonhumans. But there is a danger in concluding that just because the outputs are the same the processes that lead to the output must be the same (Kamil, 1988). Consider an example that comes, of all things, from a plant, scarlet gilia. Growing at high altitudes in the mountains of northern Arizona, scarlet gilia plants produce flowers that range from deep red through shades of pink to white. Flowers that bloom early in the season are red, but those that bloom later are lighter in color. Furthermore, many plants that start with red flowers switch to pink or white flowers at mid-season (Paige & Whitham, 1985). The timing of the color shift coincides with the departure of hummingbirds, which prefer to obtain nectar from red flowers, leaving only nocturnal hawkmoths, which prefer pale flowers, to pollinate the plants. (Hummingbirds and hawkmoths, like honeybees, inadvertently carry pollen from flower to flower while exploring for nectar.) The change of flower color seems to be oriented to the goal of attracting pollinators, and if plants had brains we might be

tempted to attribute the color shift to their cognitive capacities. The moral of the story is that sophisticated outcomes can arise through processes that do not involve motives, goal-orientation, or cognition. If a simpler process can explain a phenomenon, then invoking a more complex process, such as cognition, violates *Morgan's canon,* the notion that the best explanation is the simplest one that fully accounts for the phenomenon (Colgan, 1989). In other words, let us not invoke a complex process if a simple one will do. This is as true of human behavior as it is for other animals' behavior. Certainly, it seems reasonable to avoid attributing human behavior to sophisticated processes *just because* it is performed by humans, and attributing animal behavior to simpler processes *just because* it is performed by animals. Thought-provoking essays on these issues have been written by Terrace (1985), Griffin (1985), Epstein (1985) and Roitblat (1987).

Summary

Integrative systems include such processes as learning and memory, motivation, decision-making, and thought, that get inputs from the sensory systems and contribute to the execution of motor behavior. This chapter focuses on learning and memory, and motivation to illustrate some issues involved in the study of integrative systems.

There are several types of learning that seem to occur through separate physiological processes. All are adaptive in that they are ways of coping with environmental change and taking advantage of predictable features of the environment.

Neural changes occur when learning and memory transpire. These include rather gross changes in the size of the brain and of its parts;

changes in the structure of individual neurons, particularly the dendritic spines; and in the chemistry of synapses. Although many parts of the brain have been implicated in learning, the hippocampus, amygdala, and cerebellum have received most attention. Destruction of parts of these structures usually produces specific deficits in learning or memory.

Animal species differ with respect to what they learn and how readily they learn. These differences are related to their ecological conditions and seem to have been shaped by natural selection because of the benefits they bestow in those conditions.

A case study of the integration of neurobiology, learning, and reproductive success is presented. Male canaries learn their songs, and add song elements to their repertoires as a part of the brain, the HVc, increases in volume. The same males lose song elements as the HVc contracts later in the season. Female reproductive activity is known to be provoked by larger song repertoires, so having a large HVc, which apparently is necessary to learn a large repertoire, is adaptive for male canaries.

Motivation consists of several processes that regulate behavior. These processes are tuned to physiological (internal) conditions and to the external world. Animals appear to "decide" which behavior to perform at a given time, and these decisions are apparently based on the organism's current state (internal and external).

Recommended Readings

COLGAN, P. (1989). *Animal motivation.* New York: Chapman & Hall.

FLAHERTY, C. F. (1985). *Animal learning and cognition.* New York: Knopf.

GRIFFIN, D. R. (1984). *Animal thinking.* Cambridge: Harvard University Press.

STADDON, J. E. R. (1983). *Adaptive behavior and learning.* New York: Cambridge University Press.

TOATES, F. (1980). *Animal behaviour: A systems approach.* Chichester: Wiley.

Chapter 9

MOVEMENT AND
MOTOR SYSTEMS

Behavior is important because it is the primary method of affecting the environment. From an evolutionary perspective, operating on the environment is critical for survival and reproductive success. Food must be obtained, dangerous situations such as predators and excess heat must be avoided, and mates must be sought. Behavior, being quick to initiate and modify, permits coping with rapidly changing environmental conditions.

Because some forms of movement are more effective than others in accomplishing certain tasks, those genes that contribute to the development of the most beneficial movement patterns have evolved.

Motor systems are not limited to movements generated by muscle contractions. A wide variety of physiological changes, including hormone secretions, and changes in respiration, digestion, and cardiac output may be brought about by integrative systems in response to input from the sensory systems. Although we will not examine such physiological changes in much detail, they will be illustrated through the vehicle of emotion, which involves not only movements but a host of physiological events as well.

Neural Mechanisms of Movement

Whether movement is as simple as blinking an eye or as complex as a gymnastics maneuver, its underlying neural organization seems to be hierarchical. The most basic level of the hierarchy includes the neurons whose action potentials cause contractions of muscle cells. These motor neurons are controlled by other neurons, and so on up a hierarchical ladder. We will review this hierarchy by working up from the most basic element, the motor unit.

MOTOR UNITS

Movement occurs when muscles are contracted. In vertebrates, most muscle contractions are in-

stigated by the *alpha motor neurons* of the spinal cord. The alpha motor neurons' axons exit the spinal cord, extending toward a limb or the body wall. Near their termination, the axons form collaterals that synapse with muscle cells. Although these synapses are like those found between neurons, they are different enough to warrant their own name, *neuromuscular junctions* (Fig. 9-1).

Action potentials arriving at neuromuscular junctions release acetylcholine (ACh) which depolarizes the muscle cell. This would be called an EPSP on a neuron, but on muscle cells they are called *endplate potentials* (EPPs). EPPs in vertebrates are simpler than the graded potentials of neurons. First, EPPs are never inhibitory: Muscle cells can only contract, they cannot be inhibited directly. (As we will see shortly, preventing muscle contraction is accomplished by inhibiting the neurons that synapse on the mus-

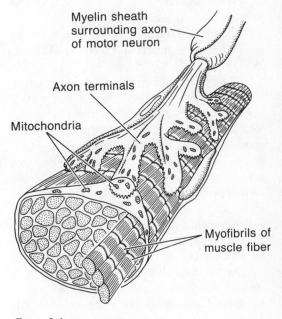

Myelin sheath surrounding axon of motor neuron

Axon terminals

Mitochondria

Myofibrils of muscle fiber

Figure 9.1
Illustration of the neuromuscular junction.

cle.) Second, EPPs are always above threshold. A single volley of ACh is sufficient to provoke an impulse that spreads along the muscle cell, causing contraction along its length. Contractions of striate muscle are brief. ACh usually detaches from the receptor site about 1 millisecond after binding to it, after which acetylcholinesterase (AChase), a deactivating enzyme, quickly breaks ACh into its component parts (Lester, 1977). The muscle cell is quickly readied for another contraction.

Disorders of the neuromuscular junction produce behavioral disorders. One such disorder, myasthenia gravis, is characterized by profound weakness, particularly of the head and neck. For example, the eyelids may chronically droop, and the muscles become fatigued even after minimal use. The person's tongue and face may become fatigued even after a short conversation. For persons whose lower body muscles are affected, even a walk across the room may result in severely weakened leg muscles. Myasthenia gravis appears to be due to decreased numbers of receptor sites on the muscles, apparently due to an autoimmune reaction (Kolb & Wishaw, 1985).

We are rarely interested in the contraction of a single muscle cell because behavior usually involves many muscle cells contracting in unison. However, each alpha motor neuron synapses with several or many muscle cells. Precision movements, such as those of the eyes, have as few as three muscle cells controlled by a single motor neuron (Evarts, 1979). Power movements, in contrast, can have about 2000 muscle cells controlled by each alpha motor neuron. This occurs in the gastrocnemius (calf) muscle, for example (Oster, 1984).

An alpha motor neuron and the set of muscle cells it controls are referred to as a *motor unit*, the most basic element of motor systems. All behavior depends on activity of specific motor units. A motor unit may be involved in the production of several different movements. A leg motor unit is used in walking, running, and jumping, for example. Different movement patterns are due to differences in which motor units are involved and the sequence in which they are activated. This control is accomplished by neurons higher in the hierarchy.

COMMAND NEURONS

For over two decades neurobiologists have known of individual neurons which, when stimulated electrically or by application of neurotransmitter, produce complete or nearly complete behavior patterns (Kupfermann & Weiss, 1978). Roosters have been made to crow and hens to scratch and peck at the ground (von Holst & von St. Paul, 1962), crayfish suddenly swim backward as if escaping (Zucker *et al.*, 1971; Krasne & Wine, 1977); and birds vocalize (Nottebohm *et al.*, 1976) by electrically stimulating parts of their nervous system. Observations such as these led to the conclusion that individual neurons or small sets of neurons controlled the coordinated pattern of muscle contractions involved in these behaviors. Such neurons came to be called *command neurons*. Command neurons occur at all levels of the motor hierarchy above the alpha motor neuron (Fig. 9-2), but the most dramatic demonstrations of this concept occur at the top of the hierarchy, those commanding complex movement patterns such as the ones mentioned above.

Some movements are initiated by *trigger command neurons* that fire briefly and then remain inactive while the movement occurs. When a crayfish is touched on the head, the medial giant axon is activated, causing a series of tailflips that carry the animal away from the stimulation (Krasne & Wine, 1977). The dura-

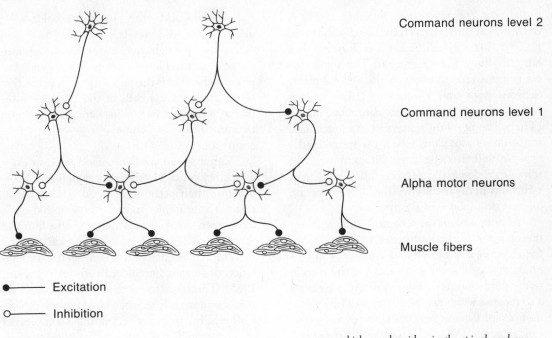

Command neurons level 2

Command neurons level 1

Alpha motor neurons

Muscle fibers

●—— Excitation

○—— Inhibition

Figure 9.2
Motor control systems are arranged in a hierarchy beginning with the alpha motor neurons which directly stimulate muscle contractions. Higher-order command neurons, which can be either in the spinal cord or brain, regulate alpha motor neuron activity, either directly, as the level 1 neurons do, or indirectly, as the level 2 neurons do.

tion of the tailflip movement outlasts the duration of the medial giant axon's signal.

Gate command neurons exert a different form of control. The movement persists while the gate command neuron is active, but ceases when it stops firing. Postural behaviors in crayfish are under the control of gate command neurons (Kennedy *et al.*, 1966). Stein (1978) gives other examples of trigger and gate command neurons.

The command neuron concept has been criticized (e.g., Kupfermann & Weiss, 1978). Although electrical stimulation of a neuron may be sufficient to produce a movement, it does not necessarily mean that that neuron is necessary to produce the movement, especially in an unconstrained animal. Also, there are undoubtedly many movements that are not commanded by a single neuron, but rather are under the control of several neurons at the same level of the hierarchy, a sort of "diffuse command" if you will. This is especially true in vertebrates (Stein, 1978). Despite these criticisms, the notion of neural command systems has been valuable in linking behavior to neurophysiological processes (DiDomenico & Eaton, 1988).

COMMAND NEURONS
OF THE SPINAL CORD

Alpha motor neurons and several types of command neurons are located in the spinal cord. Before describing them, let us briefly review the spinal cord (first presented in Chapter 5). A cross section through the spinal cord is shown in Fig. 9-3. Neuron cell bodies are clustered in a butterfly-shaped central region. The alpha motor neurons tend to occur in the ventral roots. Sensory input from the muscles, skin, joints, and other organs enters via the dorsal roots. (The cell bodies of the sensory neurons are found in the dorsal root ganglia near the spinal cord.)

We will describe three different types of spinal cord command neurons, all of which are rather low in the hierarchy; that is, they operate directly on alpha motor neurons.

Muscle cells have receptors that monitor their length. When lengthened a bit too much, the receptor is activated and signals the appropriate alpha motor neuron, causing the muscle to contract (shorten). Stretch receptor neurons also synapse with *interneurons* that cause inhibition of alpha motor neurons that control opposing muscles. (Muscle groups work in opposi-

tion. For instance, the biceps flexes the lower arm, the triceps extends it. To flex one's arm with a heavy weight held in the hand, the muscle cells of the biceps must be contracted, but just as important is the prevention of contraction of opposing muscle cells of the triceps.) Inhibitory interneurons are a form of command neuron, but they command inactivity, not contraction.

Other spinal cord command neurons exert excitatory control over groups of neurons, coordinating their activity in production of movement. For example, in cats whose spinal cords have been cut (eliminating the possibility of input from the brain), coordinated walking and running can be elicited through electrical stimulation of certain spinal cord neurons (Grillner, 1985). This is not to say that brain structures are unimportant, only that at a basic level the spinal cord is fully capable of generating a complex set of coordinated muscle activities.

Finally, another type of command neuron, the Renshaw cell, produces inhibition of alpha motor neurons whenever they fire. The alpha motor neuron's axon has a collateral that synapses on a Renshaw cell, causing EPSPs (Fig. 9-4). The Renshaw cell synapses on the same alpha motor neuron that excited it, producing IPSPs. Thus, whenever an alpha motor neuron fires, it activates a Renshaw cell that then inhibits it. This self-induced inhibition helps assure that the motor unit is not overworked.

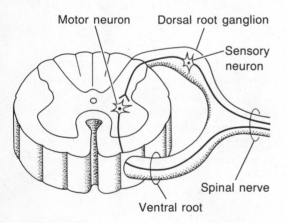

Motor neuron   Dorsal root ganglion

Sensory neuron

Spinal nerve

Ventral root

Figure 9.3
Schematic cross section through the spinal cord. Only one sensory neuron and one motor neuron are shown. The dorsal and ventral roots and spinal nerve also occur on the other side of the spinal cord, but are omitted here for clarity.

BRAIN STRUCTURES AND MOVEMENT

The alpha motor neurons and the spinal cord command neurons that control them are influenced by diverse brain structures, including parts of the cortex, subcortical forebrain structures, and parts of the brainstem. The interconnections among these structures are complex to

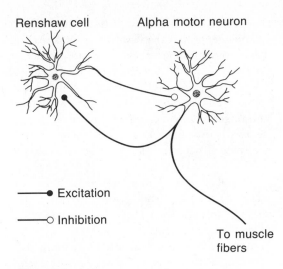

Renshaw cell   Alpha motor neuron

———● Excitation

———○ Inhibition

To muscle
fibers

Figure 9.4
Within the spinal cord an alpha motor neuron has a collateral fiber that excites an inhibitory interneuron called a Renshaw cell. It suppresses further activity by the alpha motor neuron.

say the least. Nevertheless, some of the major structures and connections of the vertebrate brain will be described. Additional details can be gleaned from other sources; I recommend Nauta and Feirtag (1986).

Primary motor cortex   The *precentral gyrus,* located at the posterior limit of the frontal lobes (Fig. 9-5), is often referred to as *primary motor cortex.* Electrical stimulation of these cells results in movement of various body parts. For instance, stimulation of one part produces chewing motions, but stimulation elsewhere produces flexion of a leg. The cells of the precentral gyrus have long axons that extend directly to the lower brainstem and spinal cord. Most of these axons decussate (cross over) to the opposite side at the level of the medulla. This means that the right precentral gyrus controls the left side of the body and the left precentral gyrus controls the right

side. This system is called the *pyramidal motor system*; the axon bundles are the *corticospinal tracts.*

Species differences in motor abilities are related to the structure of the precentral gyrus. The precision of movements of a body part is proportional to the amount of precentral gyrus devoted to that part. For example, the human

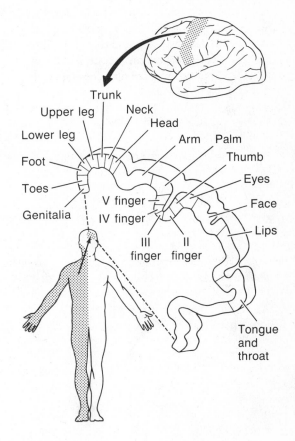

Trunk
Upper leg   Neck
Head
Lower leg
Arm   Palm
Foot
Thumb
Eyes
Toes
Face
V finger
Genitalia   IV finger
Lips
III   II
finger   finger
Tongue
and
throat

Figure 9.5
Primary motor cortex is located on both sides of the brain in a strip called the precentral gyrus (top). A section through it shows the location of neurons which produce muscle contractions in various body parts.

precentral gyrus has large sections devoted to the hands and face (Fig. 9-5), in keeping with our manual dexterity, complex facial expressions, and mouth and tongue movements of speech. Other species, of course, have different motor priorities. Monkeys with prehensile (grasping) tails devote a larger amount of motor cortex to the tail than do monkeys without prehensile tails.

Species differences in the corticospinal tracts are correlated with manual dexterity. Heffner and Masterton (1983), studying 21 diverse mammalian species, found that the abilities of these species to perform precise movements with their "hands" were strongly correlated with

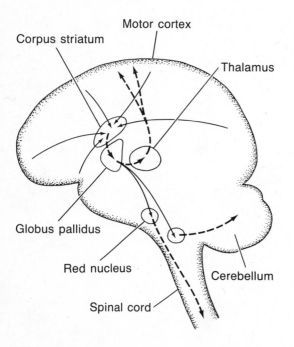

Figure 9.6
Relationships among brain structures involved in movement are shown in this simplified diagram. Arrows indicate the direction of action potentials. CS = corpus striatum, GP = globus pallidus. CS and GP together are called the basal ganglia.

the size of the corticospinal tracts (indicating the number of axons) and with how far down the spinal cord the axons extend. Primates, the most dexterous of the mammals, are alone in having corticospinal neurons that synapse directly onto spinal cord motor neurons controlling the hands and fingers. Other mammals have at least one neuron between precentral gyral neurons and the motor neurons (Heffner & Masterton, 1983).

Basal ganglia   Lying deep beneath the cerebral cortex, the *basal ganglia* are interconnected nuclei involved in the generation of movements. Complex behaviors can be performed by cats whose basal ganglia are intact but whose cortical connections have been severed. Thus, the cortex is not essential for initiating and executing movements (although the cortex undoubtedly plays a role). Decorticate female cats can give birth and rear their kittens, for example (Grillner, 1985).

The first step in this motor system, usually called the *extra-pyramidal motor system*, is input to the *corpus striatum* from widespread areas of cortex other than primary motor cortex. In turn, corpus striatum neurons synapse with neurons of another basal ganglion component, *globus pallidus*. Globus pallidus neurons synapse in the brainstem and in the thalamus. The latter synapse onto primary motor cortex. These relationships are summarized in Fig. 9-6.

The term "extra-pyramidal" implies that it is less important than the pyramidal system. This is probably only a historical artifact, however; the pyramidal system was discovered first, and the extra-pyramidal system was seen initially as supplementing it. Further, the unfortunate use of two terms (pyramidal and extrapyramidal) implies two distinct systems; in fact, their interconnections are extensive and it is not simple, in the light of current knowledge, to differentiate them (Nauta & Feirtag, 1986).

Studies of basal ganglia activity in monkeys

trained to perform a task (e.g., pulling a handle when a light comes on) for a reward indicate that basal ganglion neurons fire just before the movement is made. The delay between basal ganglia activity and arm and hand movement is due to the conduction time of action potentials, and to the transmission across several synapses (in the thalamus, motor cortex, spinal cord, and neuromuscular junction). All this takes about 40 milliseconds.

Damage to parts of the basal ganglia produce severe movement disorders. *Parkinson's disease* is due to loss of the dopamine-releasing neurons which synapse with basal ganglion neurons. Symptoms include severe difficulty in initiating movements and in rigidity of the limbs accompanied by tremor. The patient moves slowly and has difficulty changing a movement once it has begun. *Huntington's chorea* is another movement disorder linked to the basal ganglia. Degeneration of the corpus striatum neurons that use GABA or ACh seems to be the cause of this disease. The symptoms of this disorder usually appear in the fourth decade of life or later, and involve jerky, uncontrolled movements which, in a perverse way, resemble some dance movements. Huntington's chorea gets progressively worse over time and eventually is fatal. These disorders (among others) are nicely covered by Kolb and Wishaw (1985).

Cerebellum The cerebellum has important control over postural reflexes, and maintenance of balance and muscle tone. The cerebellum has a rich set of inputs including the vestibular system, which senses the position and movement of the head and body (more on this later in the chapter). Sensory input regarding tendon stretch and joint position arrives at the cerebellum from the spinal cord, and widespread input from the cerebral cortex reaches the cerebellum via a relay in the brainstem.

Output signals from the cerebellum are directed toward the red nucleus, whose axons synapse on spinal cord motor neurons, and to parts of the thalamus that project to motor cortex (Nauta & Feirtag, 1986). Thus, the cerebellum has indirect control over limb position and movement.

The cerebellum seems to coordinate and smooth movements. That is, most movements involve a precise sequence of contractions and relaxations of numerous muscle groups. Cerebellar damage severely disrupts this sequencing: Arm movements of reaching become clumsy, and walking may be virtually impossible, depending on the location and extent of cerebellar damage.

EXAMPLES OF NEURAL INVOLVEMENT IN MOVEMENT PATTERNS

Having examined some of the neural processes involved in movement, let us review some examples of movement in animals. The examples come from two major groups: rhythmic, repetitious movements and single, episodic movements.

Rhythmic movements Probably the best understood motor processes are rhythmic patterns consisting of a repeated series of movements. Examples include wing flapping of birds and insects in flight, and leg movements of walking and running. There are two major ways in which rhythmic movements can be produced, *chain reflexes* and *central oscillators*.

In a chain reflex, muscle contraction caused by one neuron is detected by another neuron, which leads to contraction of the next muscle, and so on. Leeches have a chain reflex that produces a weak swimming motion (Camhi, 1984). This flattened animal swims by generating waves of muscle contractions in the dorsal–ventral plane that move from front to back (imagine a piece of ribbon being shaken up and down). One way of generating this movement is illustrated in Fig. 9-7. Suppose the resting leech is provoked by sensory input to contract the dorsal muscles of a body segment. This flexes the animal ventrally (downward) at that point. Stretch receptor neurons of the ventral muscles detect this change, and via their connections to motor neurons, initiate contraction of the ventral muscles and relaxation of the dorsal muscles. Dorsal stretch receptors are then stimulated, leading to dorsal muscle contraction. As this pattern is repeated, the animal is propelled forward.

Another way of producing rhythmic movements is a *central oscillator* or *central pattern generator*, a command neuron that produces regularly paced signals that cause muscle contractions and relaxations via lower-order neurons. The central oscillator can be a master oscillator, solely in control of the entire movement, or there can be a series of oscillators, coupled together in sequence, each controlling a part of the total movement (e.g., movements of a single leg in a walking insect).

The running movements of mammals are under the control of oscillators. Once initiated, the synchronized contraction of many muscle groups is produced by oscillators. For example, horses change oscillators whenever they change gait (Bramble & Carrier, 1983). In contrast, human runners have only one oscillator which, however, can be varied in repetition rate.

Two or more oscillators may be synchronized to produce a useful form of behavior. Running and breathing in horses involve synchronized oscillators. Breathing occurs during a particular phase of the running movement, and is kept synchronized at a 1 to 1 ratio (stride per breath) at all running speeds. In humans, how-

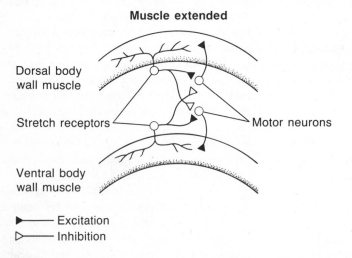
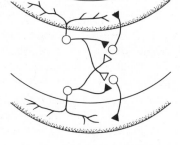

Muscle extended

Muscle contracted

Dorsal body wall muscle

Stretch receptors ← → Motor neurons

Ventral body wall muscle

▶—— Excitation
▷—— Inhibition

Figure 9.7
A chain reflex can produce rhythmic movement. When a stretch receptor is activated (top) it excites a motor neuron on the same side of the body while inhibiting a motor neuron which controls opposing muscles. The resulting contraction of the dorsal muscles reduces activity of the dorsal stretch receptor but increases activity of the ventral stretch receptor, leading to ventral muscle contraction (bottom).

ever, running and breathing are not as well synchronized. In inexperienced runners (even those who are in good condition) the ratio of strides per breath varies during a run from about 4:1 to 2:1 or even 3:2. Experienced runners, in contrast, maintain a stable ratio of about 2 strides per breath (Bramble & Carrier, 1983).

Episodic and nonrepetitive movements Many interesting behavior patterns are not repetitive; they occur singly, last for awhile, perhaps occurring again later. Rather than being controlled by a repetitious command, episodic movements are instigated by command neurons whose signals occur once, although the signal may be repeated if the initiating conditions remain in effect.

A nice example of episodic behavior is saccadic eye movements, the rapid, darting movement of the eyes from one fixation point to another, as in surveying a pictured scene. Saccadic eye movements are largely initiated by neurons of the superior colliculus, one of the neural structures receiving action potentials from the optic nerves (Wise & Desimone, 1988). The superficial (upper) layers of the colliculi consist of neurons that receive this sensory input, which is retinotopic, i.e., the retina is mapped onto the colliculus. Deeper layers of the colliculus, however, are motoric. These layers, too, are mapped, but they are movement maps. Stimulation of a given cell leads to movement of the eyes in a particular direction and distance (Robinson, 1972). This brings the fovea into position to fixate the object in the visual field (Collett, 1983).

Sensory Involvement in Movement

Most movements are modifiable on the basis of sensory feedback. For example, the precise pattern of muscle contractions involved in walking varies according to the conditions (e.g., going uphill, across a patch of ice, over a log bridge, or while hobbled by an injury). Variations in the details of walking are controlled by moment-to-moment changes in sensory feedback.

Although vision is an important form of sensory feedback for some movements such as reaching out to grasp an object, we shall focus instead on two other sensory modalities that we have not considered so far: the proprioceptive and vestibular systems.

PROPRIOCEPTIVE SENSES

An important source of sensory information comes from the muscles themselves. A muscle, such as the biceps, consists of thousands of muscle cells (or fibers, as they are often called). Muscle fibers are of two types. *Extrafusal fibers* are the power generators that are contracted by alpha motor neurons. In contrast, thin *intrafusal fibers* are interspersed through the muscle. They cannot generate much contractile power, and they are not controlled by alpha motor neurons. *Muscle spindles* are specialized sensory neurons that detect changes in muscle length. Their endings are wrapped around intrafusal fibers (Fig. 9-8). If the muscle lengthens beyond some set point the muscle spindles are activated causing additional contractions of extrafusal fibers via a reflex arc involving alpha motor neurons. These contractions shorten both the extrafusals themselves and the intrafusals lying nearby. This reduces activity in the muscle spindles. In other words, this system acts in such a way as to keep the muscle at a set length (Merton, 1972).

How is the desired muscle length established? The spinal cord has another type of motor neuron, the *gamma motor neuron*, that causes intrafusal muscle fibers to contract to a particular point. Any lengthening of the fiber leads to

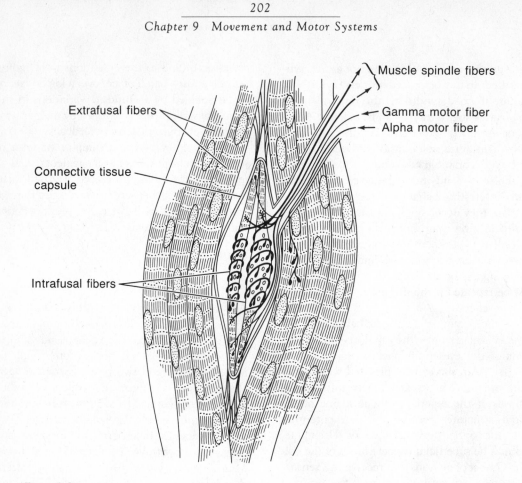

Extrafusal fibers

Muscle spindle fibers

Gamma motor fiber

Alpha motor fiber

Connective tissue capsule

Intrafusal fibers

Figure 9.8
Detailed view of muscle stretch receptors wrapped around intrafusal fibers and the relationship to the extrafusal fibers.

activation of alpha motor neurons, as described above. Finally, higher motor neurons influence gamma motor neuron activity, thereby determining the set point of muscle length.

Another important feedback mechanism is the *Golgi tendon organ* (GTO). The GTO is a true stretch receptor that is active whenever the tendon is subjected to stress. Thus, if the biceps is struggling to lift a too-heavy weight held in the hand, the GTOs of the tendons are strongly activated by the pulling.

VESTIBULAR SENSES

Another important form of sensory involvement in motor activity is the vestibular apparatus (Fig. 9-9). Composed of two related structures near the cochlea, the vestibular apparatus monitors head movements and changes in speed (Parker, 1980).

How do we sense changes in speed? The *otolith receptors* are carpeted with a layer of hair cells whose cilia support a free-floating membrane covered with tiny crystals. Some parts of the otolith receptors move whenever the head moves. However, the membrane/crystal structure, being supported in a viscous fluid, is slower to begin movement. Thus, the hair cells are bent away from the direction of movement, much like the bristles of a brush when they come in contact with a surface. Hair cell bending activates neurons that relay their information to the brain in the eighth cranial nerve (the vestibulocochlear nerve). The hair cells straighten when the mem-

brane/crystal structure catches up with the movement. This is why we fail to have a sensation of speed when a constant velocity has been achieved and we lack visual cues. One otolith receptor monitors forward–backward acceleration; the other responds to vertical acceleration.

The other part of the vestibular apparatus consists of the three *semicircular canals*. These ringlike tubes are oriented in three planes, roughly at right angles to one another. Filled with fluid and a set of hair cells, each canal

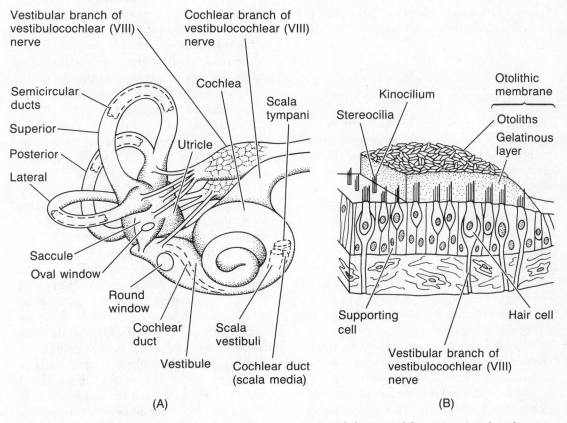

(A) (B)

Figure 9.9
(A) The vestibular apparatus consists of the three semicircular canals (superior, horizontal, and poste- *rior), and the two otolith receptors (utricle and sac-* *cule). The cochlea is at the bottom, right. (B)* *Detailed view of the interior of an otolith receptor.*

responds most vigorously to acceleration caused by head movements in a particular direction. Like the otolith receptors, the receptors of the semicircular canals respond best to *changes* in head position.

An important function of the vestibular apparatus is to provide information to motor control neurons so that compensatory muscle contractions can occur. For example, if you look at this page while moving your head from side to side the words remain clear. This is because the vestibular system detects changes in head position and signals the neurons that control the oculomotor muscles (Lisberger, 1988). The eyes remain fixated on their target in spite of the head movements.

SENSORY FEEDBACK DURING MOVEMENT

Although movement can be generated by the periodic output of command neurons even in the absence of sensory feedback (Delcomyn, 1980), a rich supply of sensory input during the movement is required to keep it proceeding smoothly and to compensate for variations in terrain while walking or changes in wind or water currents during flight or swimming (Reed, 1982). The proprioceptive and vestibular systems are especially important in this regard, but vision and even pressure sensation play their parts as well. When deprived of appropriate sensory feedback, most movements are conspicuously lacking in smoothness (Reed, 1982).

Not all movements use sensory feedback, however. We will cover these briefly before treating the more complex issue of sensory feedback.

Ballistic movements   Some movements, once initiated, are completed without sensory input during their execution. These are called ballistic movements by analogy to bullets, falling acorns, or flying snowballs whose trajectories cannot be corrected in mid-flight. They are also called open-loop behaviors because the feedback "loops," to be discussed in the next section, are disconnected or open.

Ballistic movements are found in diverse species. They are typically quick movements having no time for the extra neural processes required for sensory feedback. Some human eye movements are ballistic (Miles & Evarts, 1979). As mentioned earlier, the semicircular canals constantly monitor changes in the position of the head in space. As the head moves, signals from the semicircular canal receptors are sent to the brainstem where motor neurons are activated, causing contractions of the appropriate extra-ocular muscles, rotating the eyes. This is the vestibulo-ocular reflex (VOR). The VOR rotates the eyes in a direction opposite to the head's movement, thereby keeping the visual image stabilized on the retina (Lisberger, 1988).

Because of its rapidity, the VOR is not highly accurate. Once muscle contraction begins, movement proceeds without regard to what may happen in the meantime. Thus, the final position of the eyes may not correspond precisely with head position. However, another system that is responsive to feedback is also involved and fine-tunes the movement brought about by the VOR (Lisberger, 1988).

Ballistic movements are common in the predatory strikes of several species. The praying mantis, a fascinating insect that hunts other insects, stalks its quarry to within striking distance. Then, with lightning speed, it darts out its specialized front pair of legs toward its target (Roeder, 1970). The strike is so rapid that compensation for prey movement is impossible. A similar process occurs in toads snapping at flies.

Nonballistic movements   Movements that can be corrected mid-course by means of sensory feedback are called nonballistic or closed-loop movements (the feedback loop is closed, meaning that it is operative). Nonballistic movements typically proceed by reducing disparity between the goal and the current limb position (as in reaching out to pick up a small object). Furthermore, the greater the disparity the greater the compensation. This takes time, of course, but that is the price of accuracy.

Eye–hand coordination is an especially obvious example of a closed-loop behavior. However, even in the absence of vision many movements can be directed via sensory feedback from other systems. For instance, the flight movements of young chicks (to be examined later), although requiring no special experience to perform adequately, are nevertheless sensitive to feedback. When one wing is artificially weighted, compensatory movements are initiated, maintaining symmetry of flapping in the two wings, even though they flap more slowly than usual (Provine, 1982).

Ontogeny of Movement Patterns

Neuromuscular systems are involved in all movement patterns. But how do such systems and patterns develop? The answer depends on the movement pattern. In some, the standard developmental processes that regulate neuron growth and synaptic connections seem to be sufficient. (These processes were treated in Chapter 5.) That is, axons of some spinal cord neurons grow out to synapse on specific muscle groups, and neurons within the brain and spinal cord grow toward "target" neurons and synapse with them. In short, developmental events that are standard for the species may be sufficient for the establishment of certain neuromuscular systems (Bekoff, 1978). When such a system is activated by the appropriate stimulus, the complete, well-coordinated movement occurs without the necessity of practice.

Other movements develop only with extensive individual experience. In other words, these movements are due to conditions that are more or less unique to the individual. Further, if those conditions had not been present the behavior would not exist. Handwriting, for example, does not develop as part of the species-typical maturation process. It requires instruction, practice, and reward. (Of course it also depends on development of the basic neuromuscular systems that control movements of the hands and fingers.) Most of us have been exposed to these conditions and thus have handwriting in our behavioral repertoires. Further, the idiosyncratic ways we write are due to individual differences in our experiences (and probably to individual differences in our neuromuscular systems).

This does not imply that all movement systems fall squarely into one or the other category. Rather, it is beneficial to view the development of movement systems as a continuum, ranging from little or no individual experience required to extensive experience required. Some cases along the midpoint will be described shortly. Now we will examine more closely the endpoints of this continuum to gain an idea of the processes involved.

FIXED ACTION PATTERNS

Movement patterns that require little or no specific individual experience for normal execution are called *fixed action patterns* (FAPs). Flight develops in some bird species without practice, although maturation is required (Provine, 1984). In one study, domestic chicks were raised from hatching with elastic cuffs around the body to prevent wing-flapping. When the flap-deprived birds were tested at 13 days of age, they flew as well as nondeprived chicks (Provine, 1981), illustrating that maturation, not practice, is required for this movement to be properly executed. In mammals, the grooming movements of the head and face in mice develop on time even without the forelimbs that are necessary for grooming. Fentress (1973) amputated one or both forelimbs from newborn mice, which later adopted the grooming posture and executed the licking and "arm" movements that are part of grooming, even though they had only ineffective stubs to do the grooming. The mice even closed their eyes at the point in the movement when the limb would have crossed over the eyes. Clearly, no experience, or even sensory feedback, is necessary to establish or maintain this complex movement sequence. Another example of an FAP is smiling in human infants. As Darwin (1872) noted, infants smile without practice or promptings. In fact, even congenitally blind babies smile in species-typical fashion.

Despite the importance of such behavior patterns, behavioral scientists have had difficulty agreeing on the criteria that define FAPs (Dewsbury, 1978; Whalen, 1971; Beach, 1955; Konishi, 1966). Opponents of the notion that behavior can develop without learning confuse the concept even further. First, the criterion that a behavior be performed without the benefit of learning has been used against the FAP concept. If birds fly better after some experience, should flying be considered a fixed action pattern? I think so. It makes a world of difference to show that practice *improves* an already existing behavior versus showing that practice is *necessary* to perform the behavior at all. Second, undue emphasis was placed on the *fixity* of FAPs. Critics found numerous examples of presumed FAPs that were variable, and they attributed the variability to individual differences in experience. Some variability is always to be expected in any phenotype, so finding variability in FAPs should scarcely be surprising. Ethologists tried to

make this explicit (Schleidt, 1974) and even sought to rename the concept *modal action pattern* to reflect the expectation of variability (Barlow, 1977). The term has not caught on, however. Nevertheless, the existence of variability does not necessarily mean that it was due to learning. Individual differences in the form of an FAP can be due to differences in the neuromuscular system that produces the behavior.

In sum, FAPs are movement patterns that are produced without the requirement of practice and which are relatively invariant in form among individuals. These criteria are not absolute, however, so the concept is destined to remain controversial. The best we can do is to recognize that the role of individual experience in the form of a behavior varies from almost none at all to a great deal. If we avoid the trap of trying to dichotomize behavior into learned or unlearned and reserve the FAP designation for the low-experience end of the continuum, confusion and rancor will be minimized.

LEARNING AND MOVEMENT

Learned movements require individual practice which, of course, entails sensitivity to the consequences of the movement. Although the role of learning in movement cannot be disputed, there is some controversy about exactly what is learned (Adams, 1984; Bolles, 1983). For instance, one position is that movement elements are present without practice, but that these elements must be combined into effective sequences by learning processes (reviewed by Adams, 1984). This contrasts with the perspective that even the basic elements must be learned, in addition to effective sequencing.

Once a movement pattern has been learned, it can be performed with little or no attention being paid to it (Kihlstrom, 1987). For example, while learning to type, great attention is paid to the movement of each finger. With practice, however, these movements become virtually automatic. In fact, experienced typists find it difficult to say which finger and movement is required to hit a particular key, but they hit the key without hesitation when sitting at the keyboard!

Lying between the two extremes of FAPs and learned movements is a great middle ground of "semi-learned" behaviors. Walking is a good example. Although neural circuits controlling walking are present at birth or even before (Hofer, 1981), as evidenced by the stepping movements of vertically held infants whose feet are placed in contact with a solid surface, there is no doubt that a great deal of individual practice is required to "get it right." Furthermore, this learning must be continually updated as the body grows, the legs become stronger, and so on.

A well-researched example of this sort of process involves the vestibulo-ocular reflex (VOR) mentioned earlier. The VOR results in eye movements away from the direction of the head movement. If the VOR is of appropriate magnitude, the visual stimulus remains stationary on the retina. If not, the stimulus sweeps across the retina, reducing visual resolution. The VOR is subject to learning (Lisberger, 1988). Monkeys were fitted with lenses that magnified or shrank the visual field (think about looking through binoculars from the correct side vs. backwards). With a magnified image, the normal VOR would not be great enough to stabilize the image; with the reduced image, the normal VOR would be excessive, again destabilizing the image. The monkeys quickly adapted the VOR to suit the new conditions (Lisberger, 1988). Changes of this sort are important, especially when body size changes are occurring and "recalibration" is valuable.

We must address one more topic pertinent to learning of movements. Learning is a change in behavior due to certain forms of experience (see Chapter 8). If performance of a behavior is followed by a reward, the behavior is likely to be repeated. If it is followed by punishment or by lack of reward the behavior is likely to be omitted or changed. The consequences of many behaviors come from external sources such as food, warmth, affection, pain, and so on. The form, frequency, and other aspects of the movement can be shaped by the judicious use of rewards and punishments until the behavior is properly executed. In other words, the environment may "coach" organisms in the form of some movements. The coach can be another individual, or more likely, the environment itself. Squirrels learn the most efficient ways of opening nuts by a lengthy process of trial and error (Eibl-Eibesfeldt, 1963). Presumably, opening a nut is rewarded by consuming its contents, so any behavioral variation that leads to consumption with less delay is rewarded. The behavior is shaped by nonsocial consequences.

Other behaviors seem to be shaped by their approximation to an internalized standard. That is, the organism perceives its own movement and compares it with the standard or template (Bentley & Konishi, 1978). We understand little about how such a process works. However, some movements, particularly the singing of many bird species, seem to fit this model quite well (Marler, 1976b). Young male white-crowned sparrows, for example, listen to and remember the songs of adult males, even though the young males do not sing or attempt to sing at this time. When they are about a year old, however, the young males begin to sing. At first, their attempts are crude, but their singing develops into the adult form within a few weeks, even without the benefit of songs to imitate. Clearly, the memory or template of adult song guided song development (Marler, 1989).

Evolution of Movement Patterns

The evolution of movement patterns is, strictly speaking, the evolution of genes whose products contribute to the neuromuscular apparatus responsible for the movement. The ontogeny of nervous systems has already been examined (Chapter 5) so there is no need to review it here. Suffice it to say that the role of genes in neural development is extensive; thus, changes in genes will affect neuromuscular development and therefore affect behavior.

This section will review some evidence for evolutionary change in movement patterns, especially fixed action patterns. FAPs are convenient for this analysis because their relative stereotypy makes it easier to recognize when relevant genetic changes have occurred. This does not imply that genes are not important in learned behavior. Rather, having observed individual differences in a behavior whose form is heavily dependent on individual experience makes it more difficult for us to detect genetic differences that also influence the form of the behavior. Individual differences in FAPs are more readily attributable to genetic differences.

Before we begin our review of the evolution of behavioral systems, it would be valuable to consider some issues involved in describing and classifying behavior.

DESCRIBING AND CLASSIFYING BEHAVIOR

All sciences depend on description and classification. Description, which can be either verbal, pictorial, or mathematical, is required to define the phenomenon under study. Classification helps to make sense of the phenomena we describe. If we did not group together objects and events that have much in common, we could never derive general principles. We would be forever encountering new phenomena and

having to start from scratch with each. How far could physics go if each falling object had to be studied as a totally unique event?

We face the same problem in the study of behavior. Movements must be described and classified. Aside from the technical difficulties, description of movement is rather straightforward. We must describe the position of each part of the body in space for each instant during the duration of the movement. This is no small task, to be sure, but with high-speed photography and computer technology this essential part of the study of behavior is advancing nicely.

Classification, however, is more difficult. A classification scheme can be based on many different criteria, and it is debatable as to which criterion is best. Further, the resulting classification will differ according to the criteria used. Behavioral scientists have classified behavior in several ways. The first is based on the form of the behavior. Just as animal and plant species are classified according to similarity of anatomical form, behaviors can be classified according to their movement patterns. Another classification scheme addresses the function of the behavior. What does it accomplish and how does it benefit the organism? Third, behaviors are sometimes classified according to the mechanisms that produce them. This section will review classifications based on form, function, and mechanism.

Classification by form   Behavior can be classified according to patterns of movement. Not only are running and walking different behaviors because of their different movement patterns, there are different forms of walking and different forms of running.

The problem with classifying behavior by form is knowing when to stop. Like all phenotypes, behavior is variable, both among individuals, and, for a given individual, from one episode to the next. The classification must not be so exhaustive that it fails to permit unavoidable variation. But when variation occurs, disputes sometimes arise over the classification of particular cases.

Similarly, we must not place two behaviors into the same category just because they tend to occur regularly together. Is there any way to help make these judgments? Careful statistical analysis of behavior can help us deal with inevitable variation within a category and in identifying separable components of behavior (Dawkins, 1983). Consider drinking by chicks. A chick, standing near a cup of water, lowers its head and beak until contact is made with the water, then raises the head and tilts it back allowing the water to flow into the throat. This would seem to be a single behavioral unit because drinking always seems to occur this way. Or does it? Dawkins and Dawkins (1973) used high-speed filming to study chicks' drinking. Their results (Fig. 9-10) show that drinking has two components, head lowering and head raising, which usually, although not always, co-occur. They found that head lowering was more likely to be terminated or interrupted "mid-stream" and to be much more variable than head raising. Head raising was less variable and was rarely inter-

rupted or terminated. Drinking, then, is not one behavior, but two associated behaviors.

Functional classification In this approach, the form of the behavior is of less concern than what the behavior accomplishes. To follow up on an earlier example, human walking varies in its details. Climbing stairs is different from walking on flat ground or trudging through snow. Although the movements differ, however, they share a common function, locomotion, and would therefore be categorized together.

Functional classification is not immune to interpretational problems. If we have established a category called "locomotory behavior" in which walking is placed, we would also have to place running, swimming, and crawling in the same category. Of course, finer-grain functional categories can be established (e.g., "locomotion in water") to alleviate some problems, but then walking through water would be placed in a different category than walking on dry ground. As you can see, there is no easy way to deal with these problems.

Mechanism classifications Some behavior patterns require little or no sensory feedback

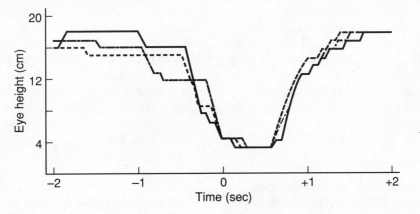

Figure 9.10
Graph of head movement (measured by height of eye above floor) during three drinks in chicks. Note how *the downward movement is much more variable than the upward movement. Time 0 is when the bill struck the water.*

once the behavior begins. Others are utterly dependent on feedback. Some behaviors are initiated by neurons in the brain, some by neurons in the spinal cord. Some are triggered by external stimuli, but others are internally triggered. These dichotomies suggest the range of mechanisms involved in motor behavior, and some experts maintain that these mechanisms should be an important consideration in the classification of behavior units.

Is one classification scheme better than the others? The answer depends on what one wishes to accomplish. Ethologists have traditionally advocated classifying behavior according to form. The rationale was that a complete catalogue of the behavior patterns of a species, called an *ethogram,* would simultaneously define the phenomenon and provide labels that would facilitate communication among behavioral scientists.

These are admirable objectives, but they often go unmet. First, many ethologists incorporated functional terms and issues into their classification based on form, thus confusing the two (Purton, 1978). Second, many ethograms were limited to behaviors that were thought to require little or no individual experience. This practice involved making distinctions among behaviors based on limited information about their ontogeny, and eliminated many behavior patterns from the catalogue, thereby reducing our ability to communicate effectively about them. Classifications based on form, function, and mechanism should be seen as complementary to one another.

BEHAVIOR AND TAXONOMY

Study of the evolution of behavior gained its impetus in the 1930s when Konrad Lorenz published the results of his work on waterfowl (ducks, geese, and swans). Lorenz had been intrigued by waterfowl courtship displays, an assortment of wing flutters, head movements, postures, and vocalizations used by males in the context of attracting mates. Lorenz classified these movements by form and then arranged species into groups according to overall patterns of behavioral similarity. The resulting classification of the waterfowl closely matched classifications based purely on anatomical similarities (Lorenz, 1971). Like bones and blood, behavior changes as genes evolve.

Following Lorenz's groundbreaking work, other researchers have extended the analysis to other organisms and to other problems. For example, the native *Drosophila* (fruit flies) of Hawaii, which number over 500 species, radiated from an original one or two species that arrived there from the mainland. In addition to their diverse anatomical characteristics, their courtship behaviors have diverged enormously (Hoy *et al.,* 1988).

One particularly interesting outcome of behavioral analysis is the discovery of *ethospecies,* groups of two or more species that are indistinguishable anatomically but which nevertheless fail to interbreed because of behavioral differences. Two species of wolf spiders, for example, are so similar anatomically that they were once thought to be a single species. By careful examination of their mating behavior, however, we now know that they are indeed distinct species (Stratton & Uetz, 1981). Females recognize males of their own species by observing the male's courtship behavior, rejecting males of the other species but accepting males of their own species. Males, however, court indiscriminately.

EVIDENCE FOR BEHAVIORAL EVOLUTION

Unfortunately for behavioral scientists, behavior does not fossilize, making the study of behavioral evolution, that is, historical changes in behavior, difficult to study. However, there are some ways of looking into the past to research ancient behaviors.

Fossil correlates of behavior Although behavior itself cannot fossilize, the products of behavior or anatomical features that are correlated with behavior can fossilize, telling us what the behavior must have been like. For instance, there has been some debate about how early in human evolution upright posture and walking emerged. Lovejoy (1988) has approached this problem by conducting comparative analyses of the skeletons of humans and other great apes, the latter, of course, being quadrupedal. There are differences in the structure of the pelvis between bipedal walkers (humans) and quadrupedal walkers (such as chimpanzees). The findings were used to assess the likely walking posture of a fossilized female Australopithecine about three million years old. (*Australopithecus* was a genus of humanlike apes that are thought to be in the evolutionary sequence leading to modern humans.) The fossils pointed to upright walking as their standard mode of locomotion.

Other sorts of fossils offer insights into behavior patterns. Rodent burrows have filled with silt that later turned to stone, allowing reconstruction of this important form of behavior. In other cases fossils provide glimpses into life patterns. For instance, dens of the extinct beardog of the North American plains have been found that contained the skeletons of several individuals, apparently killed at the same time due to inundation with mud (Hunt *et al.*, 1983). Such groupings suggest what the animals' social organization may have been like.

Relict behaviors The behavior patterns of ancestral forms may appear in their descendents. For example, several types of relict behavior can be observed (under certain conditions) in some reproductive behaviors of small parrot species such as lovebirds and cockatiels (Kavanau, 1988). These birds nest in small, bare tree holes, and have apparently done so for millions of years. The earliest-evolved birds were ground nesters, and had a host of behaviors, such as covering the eggs with leaf litter and search patterns for missing eggs, that were clearly adaptive under such conditions (these behaviors are still found in today's ground-nesting birds). The small parrots engage in such behaviors when they are induced to lay eggs on the ground on wood shavings, something they will do only in the laboratory and only if a nest box is not available. These behaviors are relicts of a much earlier period in the birds' evolutionary past.

How do relict behaviors persist? Kavanau (1990) suggests that the systems that produce these behaviors are retained in the nervous system because it is easier to inhibit them than it is to get rid of them. In the laboratory we may expose the animal to conditions that circumvent these inhibitory processes, and the behavior emerges. That these systems are inhibited can be seen in a human example. The familiar palmar (grasping) reflex of neonates is shared with the other primates where it functions in keeping the infant holding to its mother's fur. In humans, it is a nonfunctional relict, which disappears at about three months of age when an inhibitory neural system matures (Swaiman & Wright, 1975). However, in the event of brain damage to these inhibitory systems, the reflex will reappear, even in adults. In fact, there are several reflexes, found normally only in infancy, that are symptomatic of neurological dysfunction when they appear in adults (Kolb & Wishaw, 1985). The significance of such relict behaviors, however, lies in the glimpses they may provide of the behavior of ancient animal species, including human ancestors.

Emotion

At the beginning of this chapter we noted that motor systems include not only movements, but also changes in physiological systems such as hormone secretion and respiration. The study of emotion illustrates this assertion. Emotion involves movement (such as facial expressions and postures), and physiological condition (the status of the autonomic nervous system). Emotion also has important links with integrative systems in that the movements and physiological changes can be instigated or modified by memory of previous events. The physiological changes of emotion can also be affected by cognitive evaluations of the situation in which the individual finds itself. Further, emotion often involves a motivational component in that the individual attempts to make changes in its relationship to the environment. All of these elements are interwoven in ways that make them difficult to study independently of one another (Fig. 9-11). Thus, we should attempt to understand *emotional systems* rather than emotional expressions, states, cognitions, or stimuli (Hinde, 1985).

THE MOTOR ASPECTS OF EMOTION

In his book, *The expression of the emotions in man and animals*, Charles Darwin (1872) emphasized both the movements and physiology of emotion. Thus, the emotion labeled fear involves certain facial expressions, vocalizations, postures, fleeing (if possible), and such internal changes as increased pulse, respiration, dryness of the mouth, and perspiration. The particular form of these changes depends, of course, on the immediacy or strength of the stimuli that elicit them.

Researchers often begin with a list of emotion terms (fear, happiness, anger, and so on) and then proceed to assess the movements and physiological conditions associated with them. The logic is that if two or more emotion labels are associated with the same movements and physiological conditions, then we really have just one emotion. For instance, are fear and anxiety different, or do they differ only in degree? What about anger and fear? Ekman *et al.* (1983) had people contract certain facial muscles (e.g., "lower your brows and pull them together") designed to duplicate the facial expressions commonly found in emotions, but did not tell them the name of the emotion. The researchers simultaneously recorded heart rate, skin temperature, skin resistance, and muscle tension. They found that the physiological changes differed among the six emotions. For example, anger, fear, and sadness all had higher heart rates (compared to the nonemotional baseline condition), but only anger had higher skin temperature. Happiness involved slight increases in heart rate and temperature, but disgust showed slight decreases in both measures (Fig. 9-12). Notice that this research assumes that there is a nonemotional state from which the individual departs, at least on occasion. The changes are part of the emotional response (Zajonc, 1985a). These findings suggest that there are indeed several distinct physiological changes that are involved in emotions. Some researchers had suggested that there were just one or two patterns of physiological change, roughly corresponding to positive emotions such as happiness, versus negative emotions such as fear. Within a group, however, there was thought to be no differentiation (reviewed by McNaughton, 1989). These findings do not imply, however, that there is a unique pattern of physiological changes associated with each emotion label that we might wish to use.

Are there unique facial expressions associated with the physiological changes associated with emotion? The Ekman *et al.* (1983) study is germane to this question because one of the ways that they produced the physiological changes was to portray the facial expression. Smiling, for instance, brought on the physiological changes

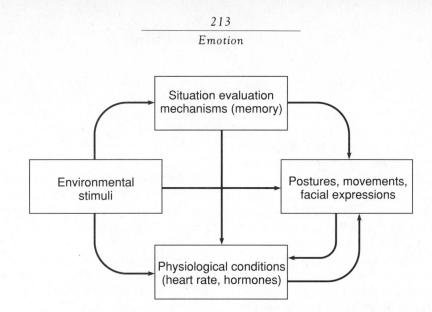

Figure 9.11
Emotion consists of movements and physiological conditions, both of which can be activated directly by environmental stimuli or by situation evaluation mechanisms. Also, movements can influence physiological conditions, and vice versa.

of a slightly faster heartbeat and slightly warmer skin. Burdett (1985) concurs with this relationship.

The muscles of facial expression and the neural structures that influence their movement are among the most sophisticated in the human nervous system (Rinn, 1984). There is abundant evidence that both the pyramidal and extra-pyramidal motor systems (covered above) have independent controls over facial expression. In fact, the two can produce signals that lead to contradictory expressions such as a "half-hearted" smile (happiness and concern). Further, the two systems are not equivalent in terms of symmetric innervation of the face. The often-noted observation that the left side of the face is more expressive than the right is only true for voluntarily produced expressions (controlled by the pyramidal system); the spontaneously produced forms of facial expression that emerge

	Anger	Fear	Sadness	Happiness	Surprise	Disgust
Heart rate change	++	++	++	+	+	−
Skin temperature change	++	−	+	+	−	−

Figure 9.12
Two physiological measures (change in heart rate and skin temperature) can differentiate between emotional states. For instance, anger is accompanied by large increases in both heart rate and skin temperature, whereas surprise has a slight increase in heart rate and a slight decrease in skin temperature. (Data from Ekman et al., 1983.)

from extra-pyramidal activity are much more symmetrical (Rinn, 1984).

The relationship between facial expressions and the physiological changes of emotion are most likely different in those species, such as humans and some great apes, which have extensive innervation of facial muscles, from species with less innervation of the facial musculature. The latter species may have the sorts of physiological changes described above, but they may lack the subtleties of facial expression.

Finally, even in humans, facial expressions may not necessarily accompany physiological changes of emotion. Physiological changes of anxiety, anger, or happiness may occur without facial expressions, for instance. This bears on a controversial issue in emotional research: whether the physiological changes of emotion precede (and cause) the feelings and movements of that emotion, or whether the reverse is true. William James, a nineteenth-century American psychologist, advocated the position that the physiological changes of emotion precede emotional feelings and behavior. In contrast, Walter Cannon, a physiologist, felt that the physiological changes were too slow to precede the feelings and behavior, and that the behavioral changes were the first to occur, with the physiological changes following. (These views are summarized by Petri, 1991.)

There are forms of support for both positions (reviewed by McNaughton, 1989), but rather than dwell on them, trying to find the "right" answer, it may be more valuable to focus on the synergistic relationship between physiological changes and behavioral changes. The Ekman *et al.* (1983) study showed that physiological changes followed the facial expression. However, it is also clear that producing a particular facial expression alone does not produce the emotion in full. Ekman's team reported that the physiological distinctions among the emotions were enhanced by asking the person to "relive" the

emotion, suggesting that induction of the physiological changes can also occur through the activation of integrative systems such as memory of previous emotional situations. Similarly, the quality of the facial expression varies as a function of the individual's internal state. (The smile for the photographer when one does not want to be photographed is likely to be a pale version of the one shown when you hear that you have just won the lottery.) In sum, it appears that various movements can contribute to the physiological changes of emotion, and that physiological changes can lead to behavioral changes.

SITUATIONAL ASPECTS OF EMOTIONAL RESPONSE

Emotional responses commonly occur to environmental stimuli. The flight of sparrows from an approaching hawk, the intense clinging of mother and infant monkeys following a period of separation, and the delighted squeals of a child finding an Easter egg are examples of stimulus-induced emotional responses. In some cases, the relation between stimulus and emotional response (movement and physiology) is rather direct, as is shown in Fig. 9-11. In other cases, the link between environmental stimulus and emotional response is less direct, due to the operation of mechanisms that evaluate the animal's relationship to the stimulus, that is, the situation-evaluation mechanisms of Fig. 9-11.

Let us begin by considering cases in which the detection of certain stimuli may be directly linked with an emotional response. In one study, young rhesus monkeys were raised from birth in social isolation. When older, they were shown slides projected on one wall of their cage. Some of the pictures elicited approaches by the monkeys, but slides of adult males emitting threat displays provoked immediate retreat and cowering. Slides of nonthreatening males had no such effect (Sackett, 1966).

Environmental stimuli do not necessarily produce emotional responses in every case. A threat may be taken very differently by subordinate and dominant individuals. Or a threat from a distance may provoke a weaker or different response than does the same threat given up-close. Further, some previously neutral stimuli may come to be associated with situations that produce emotional responses, and these stimuli may then, by themselves, evoke a conditioned emotional response. For example, if one's job is punishing and stressful, merely seeing the building or thinking about work may evoke comparable emotional responses. Similarly, rats shocked after the sounding of a buzzer eventually exhibit the same responses to the buzzer—suppression of ongoing behavior, urination, heart rate acceleration, and so on—that the shock elicits (Hoffman & Fleshler, 1965). Through such learned associations, both negative and positive, animals come to show emotional responses to a wide variety of situations.

NEUROBIOLOGY OF EMOTION

Emotional responses include both autonomic changes (such as heart rate and blood pressure) and overt behaviors (such as facial expressions). Thus, extensive parts of the nervous system come into play during emotional changes. This section will review the interrelated neural systems involved in the physiology and expression of emotion.

Studies of the hypothalamus have consistently shown its involvement in both behavioral and physiological emotional responses. Electrical stimulation of hypothalamic nuclei bring about such responses as rage in cats, which is characterized by snarling, hissing, fur erection, increased heart rate, and release of epinephrine and norepinephrine (Flynn, 1967). Emotional responses can be caused by hypothalamic stimulation even in animals whose forebrains have been disconnected from the rest of the nervous system, which suggests that the emotional responses themselves are organized at lower levels of the nervous system. The cerebral cortex, however, is certainly involved in emotional behavior in that it participates in directing the responses toward appropriate targets and in performing other evaluative processes. Given the involvement of the hypothalamus in emotion, it should come as no surprise that hypothalamic neurons are intimately involved in motivated behavior, and we will encounter this enormously important small set of neurons in later chapters on sexual behavior, feeding, and aggression.

A group of brain structures, known collectively as the *limbic system*, were thought to be very important in emotional expression. Consisting of the mammillary bodies, midbrain, parts of the thalamus, cingulate gyrus, and hippocampus (Fig. 9-13), the limbic system was thought to control not only the processes of emotional responses but also the evaluation of situations as was discussed above (Shepherd, 1988). Research on the involvement of the limbic structures has cast doubt on whether the hippocampus and thalamus are much involved in emotional responses, but certainly another structure, the amygdala, which is associated with the limbic core, has an important role in certain emotional responses, especially those associated with aggression and fear (Shepherd, 1988).

Evidence for the involvement of limbic structures in emotions comes mostly from clinical cases such as epilepsy, stroke, and tumors. MacLean (1970) has summarized much of this work; he emphasizes several subsystems involved in aggression, pleasurable sensations, and sexual arousal. Snyder (1977) reports that the largest concentration of opiate receptors is found within the limbic system. This may account for mood-affecting qualities of these drugs and their antagonists.

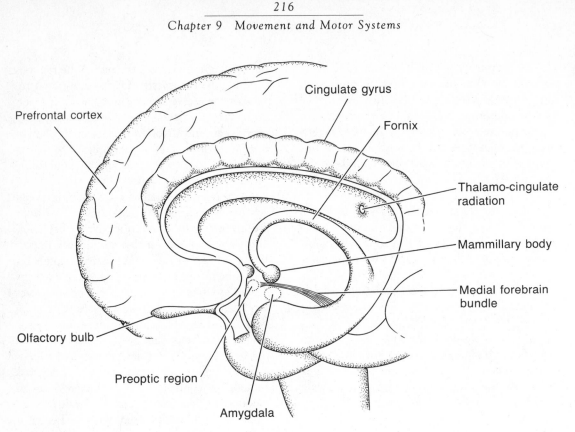

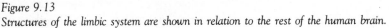

Figure 9.13
Structures of the limbic system are shown in relation to the rest of the human brain.

It should come as no surprise that numerous neural structures contribute to emotion. After all, there are many distinct physiological processes that are part of the emotional response, and numerous muscle groups are involved in the movements of emotion. Further, other structures participate in the decision-making, evaluation, and targeting of emotional responses. The coordination of these diverse structures and processes is poorly understood.

ADAPTIVE SIGNIFICANCE OF EMOTION

The adaptive benefits of emotion and emotional expression come from two routes: bodily preparation for soon-to-occur situations, and communication.

Bodily preparations   The physiological and behavioral changes associated with fear provide a beautiful example of bodily preparations and emotion. A fear-evoking stimulus leads to increased heart rate, constriction of peripheral blood vessels, slowing of gastrointestinal processes, and increased respiration. Fear-inducing stimuli are potentially harmful. Thus, preparation for physical exertion and perhaps injury is highly adaptive. This is the essence of the "fight or flight" expression commonly used to summarize the physiological changes that we call fear or anger.

Another version of the bodily preparation idea was first advanced early this century. Waynbaum, a French physician (Zajonc, 1985a), suggested that regulating cerebral blood flow was important in maintaining normal brain functioning. Because of the anatomy of the vascular system of the head, blood flow can be regulated by squeezing various arteries by contracting sets of facial muscles. With changes in blood flow, or by temperature fluctuations associated with it, the production and release of neurotransmitters could be modified. Despite its plausibility, however, this hypothesis has not been tested and has been criticized (Fridlund & Gilbert, 1985; Izard, 1985).

Communication Although we will study communication in detail in a later chapter, a few words are in order here. Many emotions are evoked by conspecifics. Thus, the individuals involved may have conflicting interests (e.g., two tomcats near a female in heat) and would be expected to behave in ways that are in their own best interests. In some cases this may mean communicating with the other individual, that is, influencing the other's behavior through some signal. For example, an angry facial expression or gesture may accompany the state we call fear. The expression may lead to retreat by the opponent. In other cases the expression may lead to caregiving by the other individual. Crying in infants, for example, is a form of communication that evokes parental attention. Adults who hear infant cries attribute various emotional states to the infants depending on the acoustic qualities of the cries (Green *et al.*, 1987), and whether they are confident about the needs of the infant.

In summary, emotion consists of a complex set of internal physiological conditions that can be provoked by a variety of external stimuli or behaviors. Emotions influence reactions to subsequent stimuli and thereby tend to prepare the body for subsequent action or to communicate with others.

CARROLL IZARD

" . . . *Each emotion serves an important motivational and communicative role in the life of the growing individual.*" [Izard, C. E., & Buechler, S. (1979). Emotional expressions and personality integration in infancy. In C. E. Izard (Ed.), Emotions in personality and psychopathology (pp. 447–472). New York: Plenum (p. 465).]

Summary

Behavior is movement, and movement is produced by muscle contractions. The chapter begins by reviewing neural control of muscle contractions. The neurons that synapse on muscles are themselves controlled by other neurons, and they by others in a neural command hierarchy. Command neurons are found in the vertebrate spinal cord and brain and in various structures of invertebrate nervous systems. Neural structures of vertebrates that participate in movement are reviewed. These include parts of the spinal cord, cerebral cortex, basal ganglia, and cerebellum. Species differences in the anatomy of these structures correspond with differences in motor structures. Primates, for example, have a great deal of motor cortex devoted to the hands.

Motor systems are involved in rhythmic or repetitious behaviors such as the wing-flaps of birds or leg movements of walking. Such movements are largely controlled by oscillators, i.e., command neuron systems that periodically execute signals that bring about the movement. Other movements are episodic, occurring once and then generally not repeating. These, too, are produced by the activities of one or more command neuron systems.

The ontogeny of movement raises questions that are like those concerning ontogeny in general. Some movement patterns (called fixed action patterns) develop with nothing more than the standard developmental conditions that all members of the species are likely to have. That is, individual idiosyncratic experience is not necessary. The grooming movements of mice or the flight patterns of some birds are good examples. Other behaviors require a great deal of individual experience before they can be executed. Many behaviors develop with lesser amounts of individual experience.

Genes that contribute to the neuromuscular systems underlying behavior can and do evolve. The evolution of behavior is studied by comparing the movement patterns of related species. The classification of various duck species, for example, based on similarities and differences in courtship behaviors parallels the standard classification based on anatomic features. Behavioral evolution can also be studied using fossilized products of behavior such as burrows or dens, or skeletal remains that are strongly correlated with certain behaviors. Finally, "relict" behaviors, ones that are "throwbacks" to much earlier evolutionary periods, can shed light on our understanding of behavioral evolution.

Emotions, which are defined by their physiological states and movements, can be evoked by external stimuli directly or through systems that evaluate the situation in which the organism finds itself. Emotional responses, especially the physiological changes, help prepare the body for subsequent activity. Emotional behaviors, such as facial expressions and vocalization, can also benefit the individual through their role in communicating with others.

Recommended Readings

GALLISTEL, C. R. (1980). *The organization of action: A new synthesis.* Hillsdale, NJ: Erlbaum.

KELSO, J. A. S. (1982). *Human motor behavior: An introduction.* Hillsdale, NJ: Erlbaum.

MCNAUGHTON, N. (1989). *Biology and emotion.* Cambridge: Cambridge University Press.

TOWE, A. L., & LUSCHEI, E. S. (1981). *Handbook of behavioral neurobiology. Vol. 5: Motor coordination.* New York: Plenum.

Chapter 10

REPRODUCTION: DEVELOPMENT AND MECHANISMS OF SEXUAL BEHAVIOR

The structure of evolutionary theory is built on a foundation of reproduction. In evolutionary terms, an individual's survival to a ripe old age means very little unless it reproduces. Reproductive success is the means by which genes are perpetuated; thus, characteristics that are involved in reproduction weigh heavily in evolutionary analyses of behavior.

Reproductive success is not simple to achieve. The individual must develop the necessary sexual organs and physiology, acquire a mate, copulate, and, in many species, care for the offspring, sometimes for extended periods. Time and energy must be invested in favorable ways. Finally, an individual's reproductive activities take place within the sociological mating system of its population. These components are closely interwoven, so an important goal of this and the following chapter is to show how they fit together into adaptive "packages."

Hormonal Effects on Reproduction

Hormones influence reproduction in two profound ways. The first is organizational. That is, hormones can influence developmental patterns early in life, some of which influence reproductive organs, physiology, and behavior. The second is an activating, or motivating, effect that occurs later in life, both in adulthood and puberty. But before covering these two processes, we need first to briefly examine the major sex hormones and the processes that regulate their secretion.

The sex hormones are members of the steroid hormone class. Most of them are produced by the gonads (the testes of males and the ovaries of females), but they are also produced in lesser quantities by other glands, especially the adrenals. One group of sex steroids, the androgens, consists of testosterone, dihydrotestosterone, and others. Although generally more common in males, the androgens should not be labeled "male sex hormones" (for reasons that will soon be made clear). Another group of sex steroids, the estrogens, includes estradiol, among others. The estrogens are more common in females, although they are not strictly "female sex hormones." The final class, the progestins, especially progesterone, are more common in females.

The production and release of the gonadal steroids is under the control of other hormones secreted by the pituitary gland at the base of the brain. These hormones, luteinizing hormone (LH) and follicle-stimulating hormone (FSH), are released into the bloodstream where they travel throughout the body, including the gonads. Pituitary hormones that activate the gonads are known as *gonadotropins*, and their release, in turn, is due to the release of gonadotropin-releasing hormone (Gn–RH) from specialized neurons located in the hypothalamus, which is connected to the pituitary gland by a short, tubular stalk. The hypothalamus contains neurons that monitor concentrations of the gonadal hormones; when their concentrations reach certain levels, the release of Gn–RH stops. When gonadal hormone concentration falls, Gn–RH release increases.

The release of Gn–RH occurs in brief pulses, as does the release of gonadotropins and gonadal hormones. The concentration of these hormones can change quite rapidly (within minutes), but they are oftentimes fairly stable for extended periods of time. Typically, male hormone concentrations are more stable over time than are those of females, largely due to the physiological characteristics of the hypothalamus.

ORGANIZATIONAL EFFECTS
OF HORMONES

Chromosomes, hormones, and sexual differentiation   Male and female mammals differ at the chromosomal level. Males have the XY chromosomal pattern and females have the XX pattern (the opposite is true of birds). However, the phenotypic sex may not correspond to the chromosomal sex. In other words, chromosomal males *may* become phenotypic females, and vice versa.

To discover why, we must review the process known as *sexual differentiation*. Early in development the fetus is neither phenotypically male nor female. The internal sex organs exist in a form that can develop into either a male or female. This is due to the presence of two systems, the Müllerian system and the Wolffian system. In most cases one system develops and the other system regresses. Development of the Müllerian system leads to female reproductive organs; development of the Wolffian system leads to male reproductive organs (Fig. 10-1).

What determines which system will develop? The male phenotype depends on two processes. First, a hormone (Müllerian inhibiting substance) actively suppresses the Müllerian system (Wilson *et al.*, 1981). Testosterone production begins when the cells of the testes receive a substance called the H-Y antigen, the production of which is regulated by a gene located on the Y chromosome. H-Y antigen binds with a cytoplasmic receptor and the antigen—receptor complex attaches to sites on the chromosomes, influencing gene expression. Consequently, testicular cells commence testosterone production; testosterone, in turn, affects other cells, including those of the Wolffian system, producing further male-typical development (Wachtel, 1977; Wilson *et al.*, 1981; Haseltine & Ohno, 1981).

Females, lacking the Y chromosome and H-Y antigen, usually have little testosterone. Consequently, the Müllerian system develops into the female reproductive system and the Wolffian system regresses. In other words, nothing additional is required to produce females. The decision rule is this: If testosterone is present a male is produced; if not, a female is produced.

There are two qualifications to this simple decision rule: Testosterone must be present at some minimal level to be effective, and it must be present during a sensitive period of development. A sensitive period is a time span during which the organism is susceptible to certain forms of environmental influence—hormones, temperature, experience, etc.—that have long-lasting effects (see Chapter 2). In the case of sexual differentiation, if testosterone is present during the sensitive period a male phenotype develops (even if the individual is chromosomally female), but if testosterone is not present during the sensitive period, the female phenotype will result (even if the individual is chromosomally male). If testosterone is present too soon or too late, i.e., before or after the sensitive period, the effect is much the same as when testosterone is not present. The chronology of events in human sexual differentiation is shown in Fig. 10-2.

The potential of the embryo to develop male or female internal reproductive organs is matched by its potential to develop male or female external genitalia. Again, from undifferentiated genital tissue, the embryo proceeds to develop the male-typical penis and scrotum, or the female-typical clitoris and labia (Fig. 10-1). The pattern that develops depends, as before, on the presence or absence of tes-

(A)

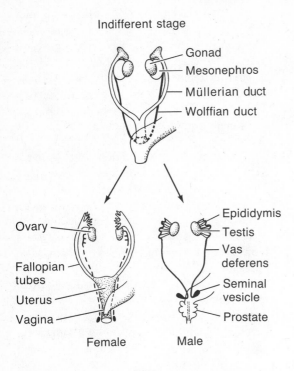

(B)

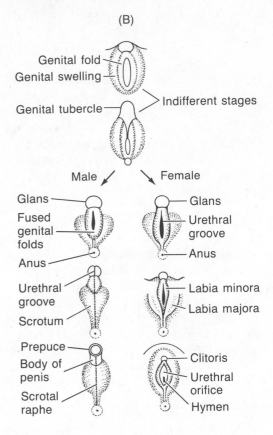

Figure 10.1
Early in development humans and other mammals have the capacity to develop either as a male or a female. The internal reproductive organs (A) develop from the Müllerian or Wolffian duct system. The ex-ternal genitalia (B) develop into the male typical form if testosterone is present in adequate amounts, or into the female-typical form if testosterone is not present in sufficient quantities.

tosterone during a sensitive period. If testosterone is present the male pattern develops; if not, the female pattern develops.

The relationship between hormones, sensitive periods, and sexual phenotype has been worked out during many years of careful research, particularly on laboratory rats. The results of those studies are summarized in Table 10-1, and we review them here.

We begin with newborn rats of male or female chromosomal configurations (XY and XX, respectively). The sensitive period for differentiation in rats occurs shortly *after birth* (about days 1–10, especially days 1–5); so, according to the rule that male phenotypes develop when testosterone is present during the sensitive period, the male phenotype will develop whenever testosterone is present during the first 10 days after birth.

The phenotype that concerns us now is the

copulatory behavior pattern exhibited in adulthood. Briefly, in response to stimulation by a male, female rats exhibit *lordosis*, a copulatory posture in which the female firmly plants her feet, arches her back ventrally, and holds her tail to the side. The male's role involves mounting the female and inserting the penis into her vagina (intromission). Although several features of the individual are influenced by hormones (e.g., external genitalia, brain anatomy, and

reproductive cycling), for now, copulatory behavior will be the phenotype of interest.

Row 1 of Table 10-1 shows that chromosomal males castrated at birth (at the very beginning of the sensitive period) develop into phenotypic females because castration removes the testes, the primary source of testosterone. However, chromosomal males develop into phenotypic males if castration occurs after the sensitive period (row 2), or if replacement doses of

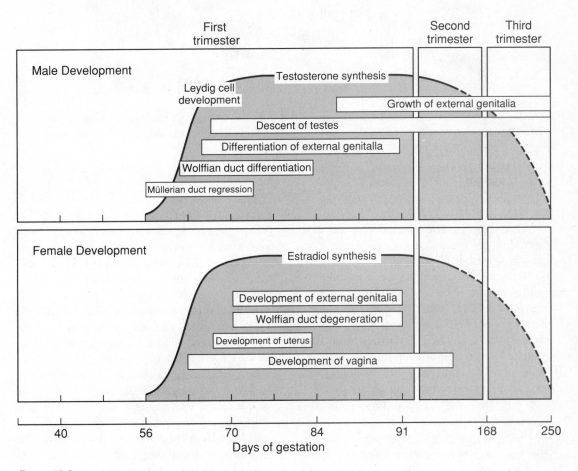

Figure 10.2
Human sexual features develop during certain phases of prenatal growth.

A sexually responsive female rat will respond to stimulation from a male rat by assuming a specific copulatory posture called lordosis, *in which she plants her feet, arches her back, and moves her tail to the side. The male will mount and intromit several times before ejaculating.*

testosterone are given following early castration (row 3).

What about genetic females? Ovariectomy (removal of the ovaries, the female's source of estradiol) at birth leads to the female phenotype (row 4). Remember, estradiol is not required to produce females. Newborn females given testosterone develop into phenotypic males, whether the ovaries are left intact (row 5) or are removed (row 6). However, females given testosterone after day 10 develop into phenotypic females (row 7). Finally, and most puzzling of all, young females given large doses of estradiol develop into phenotypic males (row 8)! So do neonatally castrated males (row 9).

How can estradiol produce males? It appears that estradiol, like testosterone, can influence gene expression. This is why: Testosterone enters cells where it may be converted bio-chemically into several things, one of which is estradiol (McEwen, 1976; Callard *et al.*, 1978). When estradiol binds with special receptor molecules within the cell, the receptor-hormone complex interacts with a segment of the cell's chromosomes, thereby influencing the activity of some genes (O'Malley & Schrader, 1976). It appears that normal masculinization is achieved by estradiol derived from testosterone.

Why aren't all females masculinized by their own or their mother's estradiol? *Alpha-fetoprotein,* a substance produced by both females and males, attaches to estradiol molecules in the bloodstream, preventing them from entering cells and influencing gene expression. However, excessive estradiol "swamps" the available alpha-fetoprotein, allowing some estradiol to enter cells and affect masculinization. Alpha-fetoprotein does not bind testosterone, however,

Table 10-1

SUMMARY OF THE ORGANIZATIONAL EFFECTS OF HORMONES ON ADULT PATTERNS OF
SEXUAL BEHAVIOR

Although the results were obtained with rats, other mammals show similar patterns of sexual behavior

Row	CHROMOSOMAL SEX	SURGICAL PROCEDURE	HORMONE TREATMENT	ADULT SEXUAL BEHAVIOR
1	Male	Castration (at birth)	None	Female
2	Male	Castration (age 14 days)	None	Male
3	Male	Castration (at birth)	Testosterone (days 1–10)	Male
4	Female	Ovariectomy (at birth)	None	Female
5	Female	None	Testosterone (days 1–10)	Male
6	Female	Ovariectomy (at birth)	Testosterone (days 1–10)	Male
7	Female	Ovariectomy (at birth)	Testosterone (day 10 on)	Female
8	Female	None	Extra estradiol	Male
9	Male	Castration (at birth)	Extra estradiol	Male

so genetic females can be masculinized by testosterone. Significantly, production of alpha-
fetoprotein is a short-lived phenomenon (in rats
at least) and begins disappearing toward the end
of the sensitive period (MacLusky & Naftolin,
1981).

Clearly, testosterone and estradiol are not
male and female hormones, respectively. Both
hormones are present and active in both sexes.
Although it is generally true that males have
more androgens than do females, and females
have more estrogens than do males, there are
some vertebrate species in which there is a concentration "reversal" (Callard, 1983).

**Primate and human sexual differentia-
tion** The preceding results came from studies
of rats. What about other mammals, including
humans? The story seems to be much the same
in primates, although the data are not as extensive. Female rhesus monkeys develop masculinized external genitalia and exhibit masculine play behaviors as youngsters if their
mothers are given testosterone during pregnancy

(Goy, 1970; Goy et al., 1988). Unlike rats, the
rhesus monkey's sensitive period for sexual differentiation occurs well before birth (as it does in
humans), so administration of testosterone to
newborn female rhesus monkeys has no mas-
culinizing effect.

In humans, we have only medical evidence
derived from anomalous conditions to shed light
on the question of hormonally induced sexual
differentiation. In *congenital adrenal hyperplasia*
(CAH), genetic females are masculinized by a
condition in which the adrenal glands produce
abnormally large amounts of androgenic hormones (Hines, 1982). The degree of masculinization depends on how much androgen was released and when release occurred relative to the
sensitive period. Other chromosomal females
have been masculinized by administration of
synthetic estrogens such as DES (diethylstilbestrol) to their mothers during pregnancy (Hines, 1982). The synthetic estrogens
are not readily bound by alpha-fetoprotein, but
they do influence gene expression (O'Malley &

Schrader, 1976). Finally, some genetic males have a condition called *androgen-insensitivity syndrome* in which the testes produce normal amounts of testosterone, but cells either lack receptors for the hormone, or the receptors are abnormal (Wilson *et al.*, 1981). Thus, differentiation proceeds in a female-typical pattern. In fact, no one suspects the condition until the "girl" is given a medical exam when she fails to begin menstruation as a teenager. She cannot menstruate, however, because she has no ovaries or uterus. She is a chromosomal male.

Phenotypes influenced by hormonal organization   There are several features of the phenotype that are known to be organized into male-typical and female-typical patterns by steroid hormones, and the list seems to be growing steadily. Although some of the phenotypic features have already been described, a more complete account is called for now.

(1) *Genital traits.* As we saw above, both internal and external genitalia are influenced by the presence or absence of testosterone. The timing of differentiation of these systems differs, with internal genitalia differentiating first (see Fig. 10-2).

The external genitalia of several mammalian species are remarkably similar in both sexes. For example, female spider monkeys have a clitoris that is so large that it resembles a penis. Female laughing hyenas also have an enlarged clitoris that resembles a penis; their labia are fused into a scrotumlike sac which, of course, does not contain testes (Gould, 1981). Combined with the fact that female hyenas are larger than males, the masculinized genitalia means that it is often difficult to tell the sexes apart.

(2) *Neural anatomy and physiology.* In humans, the brain grows especially rapidly during the third trimester of pregnancy, and it is during this time that sexual differentiation of brain tissue is underway. (In rodents, this occurs in the first week or so after birth.) Differentiation occurs when neurons that contain sex hormone receptors bind testosterone or estrogen molecules. Certain neurons, especially those of the hypothalamus, preoptic area, septum, and amygdala seem to be rich in receptors and thus the hormones become concentrated in these areas (Sar, 1984).

Patterns of hormone concentration in the brains of vertebrates are extremely interesting. For example, testosterone is concentrated in brain nuclei controlling bird song and frog croaking, both of which are usually male-only behaviors. Studies of the effects of hormones on these cells indicate that androgens increase the rate of protein synthesis (Konishi & Akutagawa, 1981), induce the growth of dendrites and axons (DeVoogd & Nottebohm, 1981; Toran-Allerand, 1978), and influence the size attained by the neuron (Arnold, 1980). All these changes can affect the physiological activity of the neurons and thus influence behavior. The neural anatomy resulting from early hormones determines to a large extent the form of behavior—male- vs. female-typical—exhibited by an individual.

(3) *Sexual orientation.* There is considerable debate about whether sexual orientation, that is, attraction to the opposite sex for mating (heterosexuality), to the same sex (homosexuality), or to both sexes (bisexuality) is attributable to organizational effects of hormones. This topic is especially problematic in humans. For instance, Gladue *et al.* (1984a) found that male homosexuals responded to an injection of estrogen in a way intermediate to that found in heterosexual men and women. The endocrine response of heterosexual women to the estrogen was a marked increase in luteinizing hormone (LH) that lasted for several days. Heterosexual males showed no increase in LH, but homosexual

males had an increase in LH about half that of heterosexual females (Fig. 10-3). This study has been debated on several points (Herek, 1984; Baum *et al.*, 1985; Gladue *et al.*, 1984b; Gladue, 1985), so the question is far from being resolved.

Hormonal involvement in female homosex-

uality has also been suggested. Ehrhardt *et al.* (1985) discovered that 30 women who had been exposed prenatally to DES, a synthetic estrogen, were significantly more likely to be homosexual or bisexual than were 30 comparable women who had not been subjected to DES, or the sisters of DES women. Still, even among the DES-exposed women, about 75% were heterosexual. Thus, although there may be some effect of early hormones on later sexual orientation, it is not a strong one.

(4) *Other traits.* Sex hormones affect not only genital traits and the nervous system, but several other traits as well. For example, the cessation of bone growth is retarded when testosterone is present, accounting for the generally greater length of male bones. Similarly, sex differences in muscular strength of young children can be traced to prenatal testosterone (Jacklin *et al.*, 1984). Differences in kidney, muscle, and other tissue are also linked to prenatal hormones (Bardin & Catterall, 1981).

It is important to note that different anatomic and behavioral traits have different sensitive periods for development, so an individual can be female in some respects and male in others. For instance, Goy *et al.* (1988) injected pregnant female rhesus monkeys with testosterone either early or late in pregnancy. The early-injected daughters were born with male genitalia, but the late-injected daughters were born with female genitalia. However, the early-injected daughters engaged in play patterns that were like those of untreated females, but the late-injected daughters' play was like that of males. These results indicate that various aspects of the phenotype can develop independently of one another, probably because of differences in sensitive periods. Usually, of course, individuals tend to be consistently masculine or consistently feminine in their anatomy, physiology, and behavior.

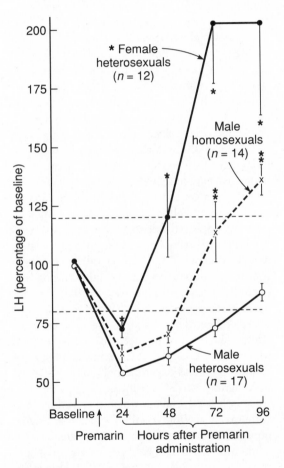

Figure 10.3
Human male homosexuals show an intermediate response to an injection of premarin, an estrogenic compound. This is indicated by the amount of change in luteinizing hormone (LH) in blood serum at various times following the single injection.

Environments, hormones, and sexual development   Much of the evidence linking early hormones with sexual phenotype has been presented as though the outcome was a simple categorical process, male or female. However, phenotypically, there are varying degrees of maleness and femaleness. Moreover, conditions far less drastic than gonadectomy and hormone implants occur naturally and may account for normal variation in maleness and femaleness. For example, several forms of maternal stress demasculinize male rats. Ward (1972; Ward & Weisz, 1980) stressed pregnant female rats by restraining them in a brightly lit cage three times a day for 45 minutes each time. This occurred during the last week of the three-week gestation period. Some newborn males were stressed daily for 10 days after birth. When tested as adults with sexually receptive females, the stressed males were sexually less active, taking longer to mount the female and attaining intromission less often. They were demasculinized by early stress. Stress apparently has this effect because an androgen released by the adrenal glands during stress, androstenedione, reduces secretion of gonadotropin from the pituitary that stimulates secretion of testosterone (Vandenbergh, 1983).

Females are not immune from the effects of stress. Herrenkohl (1979) stressed female rats during their last week of pregnancy. When their daughters became adults and were paired with males, less than half of them became pregnant, whereas 78% of females born to nonstressed mothers became pregnant under the same conditions.

Early stress is not the only way to affect offspring phenotype. Alcohol consumed by the pregnant mother feminizes male offspring and masculinizes female offspring (McGivern et al., 1984; Sparber, 1985; McGivern, 1985). Normally, female rats have a stronger preference for saccharin solutions and have poorer performances on maze learning than do males. However, in rats exposed to alcohol prenatally, these sex differences disappeared. Alcohol is known to reduce testicular production of testosterone, which probably explains the feminization of males, but the mechanism that masculinizes females on these traits is not at all clear.

Prenatal exposure to certain drugs can affect later sexual behavior. Hull et al. (1984) injected female rats with haloperidol, a widely prescribed medication for schizophrenia, during their last week of pregnancy or the first week of lactation, or both. Thus, the drug was passed to their offspring. In tests of sexual performance as adults, the male offspring were shown to have been demasculinized; that is, they achieved significantly fewer ejaculations than comparable males not exposed to the drug. They were still sexually attracted to females, however, and were vigorous and healthy in other respects. Female offspring appeared not to be affected.

Maternal stimulation affects rat pups' later sexual behavior. Mother rats nuzzle and lick their pups, in part because rat pups do not urinate or defecate without such tactile stimulation. Male pups are licked more than female pups, apparently because of the difference in odor, which is influenced by testosterone. Moore (1984) found that when maternal licking of male pups was experimentally reduced, they were significantly slower in their copulatory activities than were males which received normal amounts of licking. Further, providing female pups with extra tactile stimulation increased the amount of *male* sexual behavior performed when they became adults (Moore, 1985)! This is an excellent example of the transactional model of development presented in Chapter 2: A genetic mechanism influences the secretion of a hormone that affects the pup's odor, which influences maternal behavior toward the pup, which in turn affects the pup's later behavior (reviewed by Moore, 1990).

Prepubertal social experience with the mother and siblings or peers seems to be essential in the development of normal copulatory behavior in mammals. Male rats that were raised in an incubator without their mother (the pups were hand-fed) did not copulate with a receptive female when tested as adults. This was aggravated by being raised without littermates, although the absence of the mother was the most important factor (Gruendel & Arnold, 1969). Later social interaction can, with time, produce normal sexual behavior (Moore, 1990).

Finally, maternal odor affects the later copulatory behavior of male rats. Fillion and Blass (1986) swabbed a lemon scent onto the nipples of mother rats each day until weaning. Other mothers were swabbed with saline as a control. The sons were then kept isolated from females and from the scent until they were mature at 3–4 months of age. They were tested with a receptive female who had been swabbed either with lemon scent or with saline. The males who had had infantile experience with lemon scent mated significantly faster with lemon-scented females than with normal females, but the opposite was true of the control males. It appears that an early learning process accounts for these observations.

In conclusion, many forms of prenatal and early postnatal experiences are known to influence later adult sexual behavior. Some of these experiences affect the release of hormones, but others may not. Social experience and social competence are important factors in some species such as cats (Rosenblatt, 1965) and monkeys (Harlow, 1962) apparently without influencing hormones. Much more work needs to be completed to more fully understand these impor-

CELIA MOORE

"Despite the importance of some key factors, behavioral organization at any point in development is shaped by a web of elements and events, some internal and some external to the organism." [Moore, C. (1990). Comparative development of vertebrate sexual behavior: Levels, cascades, and webs. In D. A. Dewsbury (Ed.), Contemporary issues in comparative psychology (pp. 278–299). Sunderland, MA: Sinauer (p. 299).]

tant processes that are so critical to reproductive success.

ACTIVATING EFFECTS OF HORMONES

Being organized in a male- or female-typical fashion generally is not sufficient for the behavioral expression of that phenotype. In many cases, hormones must be present later on to activate the behavior. For example, a male rat organized by neonatal testosterone replacement therapy following early castration will not behave sexually toward a receptive female unless testosterone is present during his exposure to the female. Similarly, the development of secondary sexual characteristics at puberty is dependent on testosterone (males) or estrogens (females). Secondary sexual characteristics include such things as beard growth and deeper voice in men, and breast enlargement in women. In other species, sex differences in coloration, vocal patterns, beak shape, and so on, are secondary sexual characteristics.

There are three features of sexual behavior that can be activated by hormones. Beach (1976) refers to these as attractivity, proceptivity, and receptivity. Although these phenomena apply as well to males as to females, the bulk of the research has been done on females.

Attractivity   Hormonal changes may affect how attractive an individual is to the opposite sex. In female mammals, a wide variety of measures indicate that as estrogens increase, attractiveness to males also increases. Male monkeys, for instance, will work harder to get access to a female with high levels of estrogen than they do when the same female has lower levels of estrogen (Beach, 1976). The attractiveness seems to be primarily olfactory, but some female primates have swellings of the perianal region that are attractive to males. Female chimpanzees and baboons have these swellings, which are pink to red in color, and which are visible at great distances.

Proceptivity   Hormones can influence how attracted the individual is to the opposite sex. Estrogens are associated with how attracted females are to males. Female dogs, primates, and rodents demonstrate greater interest in males when the females have higher concentrations of

estrogen, sometimes in combination with greater amounts of progesterone. Females approach males, engage in precopulatory behaviors, or even mount males under these circumstances.

Receptivity   When a male attempts to copulate, the female may respond in ways that facilitate copulation and ejaculation, or she may resist strenuously. The degree to which an individual tolerates and facilitates copulation attempts is called receptivity. Estrogens, and sometimes progesterone, often bring on sexual receptivity in female mammals.

The phenomena of attractivity, proceptivity, and receptivity are all closely interrelated. *Estrous,* a condition in which female mammals become more attractive to males, are themselves more attracted to males, and are more receptive to copulatory attempts, is largely due to an estrogen surge around the time of ovulation. The fact that all three of these phenomena are largely driven by estrogens does not imply that all three increase and decrease together. More likely, it seems, is that increasing amounts of estrogens are necessary to bring about changes in attractivity, proceptivity, and receptivity. For instance, a slight increase in estrogens may have a positive effect on attractivity, but not on proceptivity. Further, a female with somewhat more estrogen may be attracted to males but will not yet be receptive to copulation. More detailed data are needed on how concentration differences in various hormones influence these three measures of sexuality. Large species differences are expected as well.

Hormonal differences explain only part of the variability in sexual behavior. A large array of purely environmental factors also contribute to sexual behavior (Feder, 1984). The setting, the social environment, and the organism's state with respect to other motivational variables (Chapter 9) all play significant roles in sexual behavior. These other influences may suppress sexual behavior even though the hormones may be present, or they may incite sexual behavior in individuals not particularly hormone-primed. Environmental effects complicate our understanding of hormonal involvement in sexual behavior but they should not be overlooked.

Copulation

The union of male and female gametes can take place externally, as it does in many amphibians and fish that release their eggs and sperm into the water, or it can occur internally as it does in mammals, birds, and many fish and insects. Both forms require precisely timed movement patterns to assure that fertilization occurs. Our examination of copulation will begin with the movement patterns used by mammals. Our discussion will, for the moment, be directed to mammals because mammalian copulatory behavior has been more thoroughly studied than copulatory behavior in other animal groups.

PATTERNS OF COPULATION

The diversity of mammalian copulatory behavior is illustrated by a classification scheme for the copulatory behavior of male mammals (Dewsbury, 1972; Dewsbury & Pierce, 1989). The classification is based on four features that are either present or absent in copulatory behavior. They are: (1) Lock: Some species, such as domestic dogs, exhibit a vaginal lock following ejaculation. The penis swells, making withdrawal difficult or impossible (Fig. 10-4). (2) Thrusting: In some species, such as humans, the penis is repetitively thrust back and forth in the vagina. In others, there is no intravaginal thrusting. (3) Intromission frequency: In some

DONALD DEWSBURY

"Patterns of copulatory behavior vary widely among different species of mammals, but generally are quite stereotyped among individuals within a given species. It would seem reasonable that this . . . might have been brought about by the operation of strong selective pressures for successful reproduction." [Dewsbury, D. A. (1972). Patterns of copulatory behavior in male mammals. Quarterly Review of Biology *47,* 1–33 (p. 1).]

mammals, such as rats, the male mounts the female, intromits the penis into the vagina, and then quickly dismounts. Rats must intromit several times before an ejaculation can occur. Other species need to intromit only once. (4) Ejaculation frequency: In some species, such as baboons, the male typically ejaculates several times per copulation episode. Others usually ejaculate only once. This feature is probably the least clear-cut of the four (Dewsbury & Pierce, 1989).

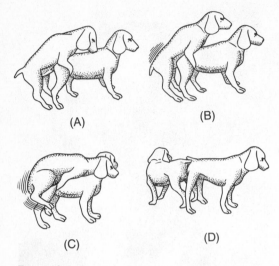

(A)   (B)

(C)   (D)

Figure 10.4
The copulatory behavior of dogs involves mounting (A), thrusting and ejaculation (B, C) followed by a copulatory lock (D).

Each species is classified according to its performance on each of the four variables (Fig. 10-5). Although 11 of the 16 possible categories have been discovered in at least one species, even closely related species may fit into different slots in this system. For example, Dewsbury (1975) found 7 of the 16 categories in his survey of 31 species of small rodent. Primates are less diverse than rodents in their copulatory patterns, with only 3 of the 16 patterns known so far (Dewsbury & Pierce, 1989). Why these species differences exist is not yet known. No ecological correlation of any note has been discovered, and the finding that there is no phylogenetic pattern makes the whole thing even more puzzling. Obviously, more data are necessary to enlighten this issue.

Dewsbury (1979) and his colleagues (e.g., Diakow & Dewsbury, 1978) have begun the process of classifying female mammal copulatory behavior. These efforts have emphasized the be-

haviors used by females to initiate copulation and the female's postures and movements during mounting and intromission. There are species-typical patterns in all these behaviors, but the classification has been applied only to rodent species. Not surprisingly, female behavior patterns complement those of males, so there are species differences in female patterns that parallel those of males. Much more information is needed on female behavior and on the "choreography" of the interaction of male and female during copulation.

Orgasm is a component of female copulatory behavior that has often been thought to occur only in humans. Recent evidence, however, establishes the existence of female orgasm, at least in nonhuman primates, although the physiological details vary among species (Allen & Lemmon, 1981).

Is there any adaptive value to female orgasm? Symons (1979) has argued that female orgasm exists only as a byproduct of male sexual physiology. That is, because male and female sex organs are derived from the same undifferentiated embryonic tissue, females have many of the physiological response characteristics possessed by males, but they evolved because of the selective advantage of male orgasm (ejaculation). Female orgasm, according to this view, is analogous to the presence of nipples in male mammals: a selectively neutral byproduct of a developmental process that is not completely gender-specific.

Others (Allen & Lemmon, 1981) suggest that female orgasm is adaptive in its own right. They point to evidence from humans and other mammals that the vaginal muscle contractions that occur during orgasm may trigger male ejaculation; that semen may be drawn further into the female's reproductive tract, increasing the odds of fertilization; and that, in some cases at least, ovulation may be triggered by orgasm. In

| Lock? | Thrusting? | Multiple intromission? | Multiple ejaculation? | Pattern no. |

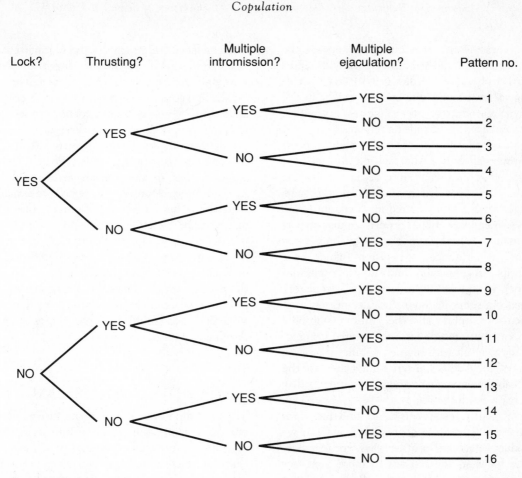

Figure 10.5
Dewsbury's classification scheme for copulatory patterns of male mammals involves four questions. Sixteen patterns result.

other words, although female orgasm may not be necessary for fertilization, it may facilitate fertilization.

QUANTITATIVE DIFFERENCES IN COPULATORY BEHAVIOR

Species whose copulatory patterns fall in the same category often differ quantitatively in their behavioral patterns. For example, the number of intromissions per ejaculation may vary, the aver-age amount of time that elapses between intromissions or ejaculations may differ, and so on. Although both rats and hamsters display pattern number 13 (no lock, thrusting, multiple intromissions, and multiple ejaculations), the average amount of time between mounts with intromission in hamsters is about 10 seconds or less, but in rats this interval is about 50 to 100 seconds (Dewsbury, 1979). Furthermore, the duration of both intromissions and ejaculations is much longer in hamsters than in rats.

These quantitative differences appear to be significant in that they have tie-ins with reproductive physiology. Adler (1979) and his colleagues have found that sperm motility in the female reproductive tract of lab rats is slowed if intromissions are not adequately spaced in time. Similarly, the female's ova will implant into the uterine wall only if the multiple intromission pattern has occurred. This is because the tactile stimulation provided by intromission triggers hormonal changes required for implantation.

Other connections between copulation patterns and reproductive physiology have been found. For instance, in hamsters (which have multiple intromission and multiple ejaculations), it appears that at least four "ejaculatory series" (a series includes the intromission with ejaculation plus all the intromission-only mounts that preceded it) are required for pregnancy to result with high probability (Lanier *et al.*, 1975). Additional series don't increase the probability of pregnancy occurring, nor do they increase the litter size.

Recently, researchers have found that quantitative differences in copulation may foster reproductive success in other ways. For instance, male hamsters that engage in more than five ejaculatory series sire more offspring by that female than do other males that mate with her later. If the first male does not achieve at least five ejaculations, the second male will have equal or greater reproductive success than the first male (Oglesby *et al.*, 1981). Thus, species differences in the probability of a female copulating with more than one male while she is receptive may explain why species differ with respect to number of ejaculations.

Another type of quantitative difference in copulation is just beginning to receive attention. Females may copulate more often or may copulate with more males than would seem to be necessary to become fertilized. After all, why would more than one copulation be needed when males can release millions of sperm in each ejaculation? Small (1988) has suggested that seemingly excessive copulations by females may be advantageous (or even necessary) because the male with whom a female copulates may be temporarily low on sperm because of previous copulations, and because many sperm are defective or have low motility. Hrdy (1981) has also suggested that, in some species, males are more tolerant toward young who were born to females with whom they have copulated. In essence, if a male *could* be the father, he does not mistreat the young. Females who copulate with multiple males may gain by switching off the offspring-destructive tendencies of some males. Both these ideas may, of course, be true of some species but not others. More information will need to be collected before these hypotheses can be thoroughly tested.

FUNCTIONS OF COPULATION

The preceding discussion of quantitative differences in copulatory behavior relating to aspects of female reproductive physiology should suggest that the function of copulation is not solely to place sperm into the female reproductive tract. Let us discuss some of these additional functions.

Facilitating pregnancy   Most mammalian species release eggs (ovulate) spontaneously; that is, hormonal changes in the female run their course without the influence of external conditions. Humans and rats are spontaneous ovulators. Other species are induced ovulators, releasing ova only when mating has taken place. This is due to the tactile stimulation associated with copulation, specifically that applied to the vagina by the penis. Thus, ovulation occurs only when there is a high likelihood of fertilization occurring. Rabbits, cats, and some rodents are induced ovulators.

Other species are intermediate to the two

extremes. Ferguson *et al.* (1984) found that some female red-backed voles (a small, North American rodent) ovulated when housed with a male in a laboratory cage, even though separated from him by wire mesh. Some females even ovulated when housed alone, but in the same room with males. However, the most likely condition for ovulation was when given full access to a male. Thus, induced and spontaneous ovulation are not wholly distinct categories, but represent end-points on a continuum. Nevertheless, copulatory behavior is necessary or highly effective for ovulation in some species.

Another way that copulation facilitates pregnancy is to prepare the uterus for implantation of the fertilized ova. For example, in the absence of the usual copulatory pattern, female rats will slough off fertilized ova because the hormonal changes required for implantation into the uterus have not been induced (Adler, 1979).

Mate recognition A fascinating and apparently unusual function of copulation is to activate an olfactory recognition system in the female. Female mice who had just been mated were placed alone in a cage that contained the odor of a male of the same strain as the stud, or the odor of a different strain. The female was left there for 48 hours and then moved to another cage that housed the stud or a male of the other strain. Pregnancy blockage occurred in those females which were placed with a male of the strain other than the one to whose odor they had been exposed after mating (Keverne & de la Riva, 1982) (Table 10-2). Usually this would be the stud male and the appearance of a stranger male would induce the pregnancy block. Early curtailment of pregnancy under such circumstances is adaptive to the female because the "new" male will most likely kill her pups. Infanticide is generally inhibited after mating (McCarthy & vom Saal, 1986).

Male parental investment In addition to

sperm, males sometimes contribute other substances of reproductive consequence. For example, spermatophores (packets of sperm) of male butterflies contain nutrients that appear in the female's eggs (Boggs & Gilbert, 1979). The same is true in the Mormon cricket (Gwynne, 1981, 1984). Copulation in these species is not only a sexual act, but a parental one as well.

Reducing reproductive competition Female reproductive output is a resource for which males compete. Males who succeed, by whatever means, in acquiring more than an average amount of reproductive success will leave copies of those genes that contributed to that success. Competition for females may occur before mating takes place, a familiar phenomenon, but it may also occur during copulation itself. There are several ways that this may work.

First, copulation in some species involves the male removing sperm that may already be present in the female. In some damselflies (related to dragonflies) the penis is shaped in a way that allows the male to "rake" out sperm from the female's sperm-storage pouches (Waage, 1979; Routman, 1985). The last male to copulate with a female has the advantage, and males often guard females following copulation to prevent other males from removing their sperm.

Second, male semen may harden in the female's reproductive tract, forming a plug that impedes the movement of sperm of males who may copulate later with that female. These plugs have been found in snakes (Devine, 1975), ground squirrels (Murie & McLean, 1980), and other species.

Finally, males may deposit a pheromone (a chemical communication signal) that has an "anti-aphrodisiac" effect on other males. This appears to be the case in garter snakes (Lynch, 1983), some moths (Hirai *et al.*, 1978), and others.

In conclusion, copulatory behavior often does much more than merely get sperm and eggs

Table 10-2
SUMMARY OF THE RESULTS REPORTED BY KEVERNE AND DE LA RIVA (1982)

Female mice were mated to a male of strain A, exposed to the odor of males of strain A or B, and then were placed with a male. If the male was of a strain other than the one whose odor they had lived with, the female usually had a pregnancy block.

STUD MALE STRAIN	STRAIN OF MALE ODOR	EXPOSURE TO MALE	PERCENTAGE SHOWING PREGNANCY BLOCK
A	B	A	75
A	A	A	0
A	A	B	80
A	B	None	0
A	B	B	0

together. These additional functions may set the selective conditions favoring one copulatory pattern over another, or some quantitative variant over another. Perhaps these functions, which are not widely understood, will provide the keys to understanding the distribution of copulatory patterns among mammals.

HORMONAL ACTIVATION OF COPULATORY BEHAVIOR

Sexual behavior generally occurs only when certain hormones are present in sufficient quantities. This section will review data on this issue, both in animals and humans, and in males and females.

Male sexual behavior The motivation of male sexual behavior traditionally has been attributed to testosterone, the assertion being that male sexual motivation increases with greater amounts of testosterone. What evidence is there for such claims? The typical finding is that there is a minimum threshold level of testosterone required to reliably maintain sexual motivation at normal levels. Dropping below this level generally results in reduced sexual motivation.

However, once above the threshold level, sexual motivation often is not correlated with testosterone concentration. In other words, differences among men in testosterone concentration do not correlate with their self-reported sexual activity (Kraemer *et al.*, 1976; Feder, 1984). However, for an individual, there is a positive correlation between testosterone and sex. Each man experiences variation in testosterone concentration, and as his testosterone increases, so do his reports of sexual motivation. But the absolute amount of testosterone does not seem to influence sexual motivation. What may be a high level for one man may be low to another.

Notice that these studies report on correlations between testosterone and sexual motivation. But, of course, correlation does not imply causation, and even if causation does exist, the correlation cannot tell us the direction of the causation. The way around this problem is to perform experiments in which the amount of testosterone is controlled. One way to do this is to eliminate the source of testosterone by surgical castration or by the use of chemicals that reduce testosterone. Generally, procedures that eliminate or greatly reduce testosterone reduce sexual motivation completely or to very low levels. However, when castrated male rats are given replacement doses of testosterone their sexual behavior returns until the dose wears off.

Although the pattern just described seems to hold true in male animals, we have no comparable data on humans. Although human males have been surgically castrated for a variety of reasons, and some, such as convicted rapists, have been required to take anti-androgenic chemicals, the data from such cases are largely useless. This is because the individuals on whom such procedures have been imposed may not be representative of the human male population. One of the most important elements in experimentation is the random assignment of subjects to treatment groups. This is not true in the human research, and should not be done for obvious ethical reasons.

The possibility of obtaining valid experimental data on the issue of testosterone and sexual behavior in men is remote. But can we look for trends in other species for a clue to what may be going on in humans? We can indeed, but heed this caution: Virtually all research on this subject has been conducted on species that have male copulatory patterns (Dewsbury's scheme) and mating systems (see Chapter 11) that differ from those of humans. It may be unwise, or at least premature, to generalize to humans from this data base. Obviously, more work needs to be done here.

Most of the evidence from nonhuman species points to a causal link between testosterone and sexual motivation although it must be remembered that many other factors, such as the male's experience, the social and environmental settings, and the receptivity of females all contribute to the sexual behavior of male mammals. What causes testosterone levels to fluctuate, and why? In many species, breeding is highly seasonal. Neural processes that are sensitive to day length influence sex hormone production in both males and females. In most birds and in many mammals, the longer days of spring increase gonad activity, thus instigating breeding. In other mammals, such as deer and some bats, shorter days have this effect. These species copulate in the fall (reviewed by Bronson, 1989). More details on these processes are provided in Chapter 11.

On a shorter time scale, daily rhythms of testosterone production have been discerned in several species, including humans (Reinberg & Lagoguey, 1978) and nonhuman primates. Typically, testosterone levels peak in the morning (Bernstein, et al., 1974). Sexual behavior itself can also cause increases in testosterone. Kraemer *et al.* (1976) report that testosterone increases for several hours after sexual intercourse or masturbation. This is true of many other mammals as well (Harding, 1981). Moreover, "psychosexual stimulation," such as thinking about sex or viewing erotic material, increases testosterone in men (Pirke *et al.*, 1974).

In nonhuman animals, exposure to a female can cause an increase in testosterone even if the female is not sexually receptive (Harding, 1981). Also, cues associated with copulation can induce hormone release prior to the appearance of a female. Graham and Desjardins (1980) placed male rats in a cage containing a novel odor for 7 minutes before introducing a sexually receptive female. This was repeated daily for 14 days. On day 15 the odor alone was presented and blood serum levels of LH and testosterone were measured. They found increases in both hormones that were similar in magnitude to those found in males presented with a sexually receptive female. This indicates a classically-conditioned anticipatory hormone change. Other research has indicated that hormonally "primed" males are faster and more vigorous in mating activities.

NANCY BURLEY

"If, as hypothesized here, human females have sought to limit their fertility below the biological optimum, natural selection could counter this trend by suppressing cues to ovulation. . . . As human intelligence increased, the signs of ovulation would have become more discreet; any evidence of the event remaining must be subtle enough to escape note and efforts at self-detection." [Burley, N. (1979). The evolution of concealed ovulation. American Naturalist **114,** *835–858 (p. 849).]*

A variety of stressful situations can cause decreases in testosterone. Male mice who are defeated in fights show rapid declines in testosterone that may persist as long as exposure to the dominant male continues (Bronson *et al.*, 1973). In men, increased psychological stress, within the typical day-to-day range, is associated with small declines in testosterone (Chris-

tiansen *et al.*, 1985), but more severe stress can produce significant declines in testosterone (Kreuz *et al.*, 1972). On the other hand, succeeding at some endeavor, such as an athletic contest, can increase testosterone in men (Mazur & Lamb, 1980).

Female sexual behavior   Behavioral endocrinologists have long known about the role of estrogens in female sexual motivation in nonhuman species such as cats, dogs, and rats. These and many other species exhibit estrous ("heat") behavior patterns in which the female not only permits, but actively solicits, sexual intercourse. Estrous normally occurs due to endogenous increases in estrogen, often in conjunction with progesterone, but injections of these hormones will produce estrous at virtually any time.

Given the causal connection between estrogens and estrous in nonhuman mammals, can we safely conclude that variation in women's sexual motivation is due to fluctuations in estrogen? Perhaps, but not necessarily. There are important biological differences between humans (and some other species) on the one hand, and the species on which most of the estrogen–estrous research has been conducted. For instance, human sexual behavior is far less restricted to a single, brief mating period than is the behavior of most other mammals. (The sexual behavior of other monogamous primates is similarly nonrestricted.) Second, human ovulation (when an egg is released and is available for fertilization) is barely discernible from nonovulatory periods (Alexander & Noonan, 1979; Strassmann, 1981; Burley, 1979). In contrast, estrous coincides with ovulation, and nonhuman females often emit olfactory signals that announce their condition to males (Goodwin *et al.*, 1979). Given that women can and do have sexual intercourse at all times, not just around ovulation, it seems unlikely that an estrogen surge around mid-cycle is necessary for sexual motivation.

Perhaps other hormones are involved—or perhaps none. What evidence is there linking women's sexual motivation with hormones?

Udry and Morris (1968) conducted a pioneering study in which they asked women to fill out a brief questionnaire each day as they came to work. They were asked whether they were currently menstruating; whether they had had sexual intercourse within the past 24 hours, and, if so, who initiated it; whether they masturbated or had had erotic thoughts, and so on. When completed, Udry and Morris claimed to find a mid-cycle peak (i.e., midway between menstrual periods) in some of these behaviors, especially intercourse initiated by the woman (Fig. 10-6). Because estrogen concentrations also peak around mid-cycle, they concluded that there is a link between estrogen and sexual motivation in women. They further suggested that the link was causal (reasoning from the animal estrous research described earlier).

An intriguing counterpoint to the Udry and Morris study comes from the suggestion that sexual intercourse may peak at mid-cycle without any hormonal control. Dobbins (1980) conducted a computer simulation study of human sexual behavior using just two assumptions: (1) that the probability of intercourse is very low during the woman's menstrual period, and (2) that the probability of intercourse increases each day since the last intercourse, much like the probability of eating increases with time since one's last meal. Depending on what probability values are assigned, the computer simulation can produce peaks of sexual intercourse at mid-cycle (as Udry & Morris reported), or early or late in the cycle (as others have found).

Finally, Adams *et al.* (1978) conducted a study similar to Udry and Morris's. Again using self-report (questionnaire and interview) information, Adams *et al.* found a peak in female initiated intercourse around the time of ovula-

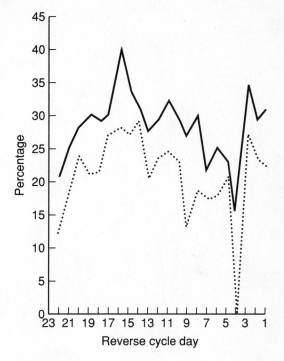

Figure 10.6
Percentage of 40 women who reported having intercourse (solid line) or orgasm (dotted line) according to their stage of the menstrual cycle. The horizontal axis is expressed as days before the beginning of menstruation.

tion (Fig. 10-7). Interestingly, their data also show two other peaks, one shortly after menstruation, and another just before (as the variables in the Dobbins study would predict). Because estrogen is low at both those times, it is obvious that estrogen is not necessary for sexual motivation. However, Adams *et al.* also reported on women who were taking birth control pills that suppress the mid-cycle peak in estrogen. These women had no mid-cycle peak in female-initiated intercourse. In fact, their intercourse rate went down during this time (Fig. 10-7)! To put it

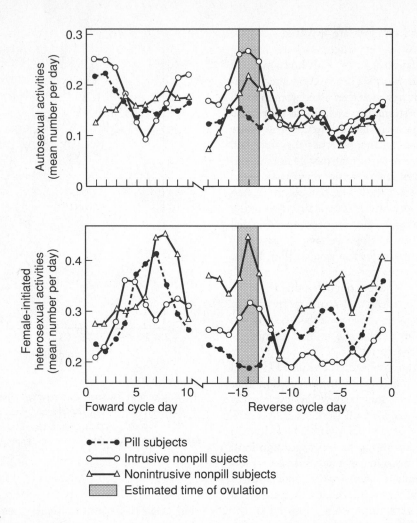

Figure 10.7
The incidence of sexual intercourse (bottom panel) and masturbation (top panel) reported by women varies according to their stage of the menstrual cycle. Some women were using contraceptive pills that suppress the estrogen surge that normally accompanies ovulation. Intrusive nonpill subjects used other forms of contraception. The nonintrusive nonpill subjects used an intrauterine device or male vasectomy for contraception.

mildly, the data on hormonal involvement in the activation of women's sexual behavior is inconsistent and in need of corroboration. It does appear, however, that the role of hormones in motivating the sexual behavior of human females is a small one at best.

NEUROBIOLOGY OF SEXUAL BEHAVIOR

The preceding discussion of hormonal effects on the activation of copulation is only one facet of the mechanism of sexual behavior. Two other aspects will be covered in this section: The role of neurotransmitters, and neural structures associated with copulation.

Neurotransmitters and copulation Work on neurotransmitter effects in males has implicated norepinephrine as a primary activator. Clark *et al.* (1984) gave yohimbine, a drug that enhances the postsynaptic effect of norepinephrine, to sexually naive and to sexually experienced male rats. The drug significantly increased the number of sexually naive males who copulated on their first exposure to a receptive female, and increased the number of mounts in experienced males.

Female copulatory behavior has been linked to ACh, particularly at muscarinic receptors. Drugs that increase or mimic ACh facilitate lordosis in rodents; drugs that are ACh antagonists reduce lordosis. Further, estradiol produces an increase in the number of muscarinic ACh receptors in the hypothalamus of female rats within a few hours after injection (Rainbow *et al.*, 1984). Thus, induction of the proteins required to produce these receptors is a step in the activation of copulation by estradiol.

Female copulatory behavior in rats seems to be inhibited by serotonin. Luine *et al.* (1984) destroyed serotonergic neurons of the hypothalamus of female rats and found that they were more readily induced to perform lordosis when stimulated by tactile contact. They then injected small amounts of serotonin-rich brain tissue from another rat into the hypothalamus of the rats that lacked serotonin. The females' tendency to emit lordosis returned to normal.

Neural structures and copulation Copulation is a complex set of behaviors involving massive sensory and perceptual processes and motor activity. Therefore no single copulatory "center" should be expected. Because we are primarily concerned with motivational issues in this section, emphasis will be given to brain regions underlying sexual motivation.

Emery and Whitney (1985) found that cop-ulatory behaviors of female rats were linked with activity of the pelvic nerve, which transmits sensory information from the vagina, cervix, and perineal regions. Females whose pelvic nerves had been transected spent significantly more time in an arena with sexually active males, posed more often for mounting, and received more intromissions and ejaculations than did females whose pelvic nerves were not cut. These findings suggest that tactile stimulation in this region inhibits copulatory behavior by the female, at least temporarily, and may help regulate the timing of rat copulatory behaviors.

The ventromedial nucleus of the hypothalamus seems to be important to the regulation of female copulatory behavior, at least in the rodent species that have been studied so far. The Luine *et al.* (1984) study mentioned above was focused on this part of the hypothalamus, as was the study by Rainbow *et al.* (1984) on acetylcholine.

The preoptic region of the forebrain, located near the hypothalamus, seems to be critical to male sexual behavior. The copulatory behavior of male rats was facilitated by electrical stimulation of the medial preoptic area (Malsbury, 1971), and severing the axons that leave it reduces copulation in male rats (Conrad & Pfaff, 1976). Finally, Davidson (1980) was able to provoke sexual behavior in male rats who were devoid of testosterone due to adult castration by injecting testosterone into the medial preoptic region.

Spinal cord neurons are also involved in the execution of motor patterns associated with copulation. Hart (1967) found that male dogs whose spinal cords had been cut, thereby disconnecting the spinal cord from the brain, could still get penile erections, show the typical thrusting behavior, and ejaculate.

Unfortunately, very little is known about the neurology of copulation in animals other than rats and dogs. Some neuropsychological data exist on humans, but the effects are difficult to interpret because of the variability in location and extent of the neural damage.

Summary

Our examination of reproductive processes begins with an examination of the hormonal influences on sexual development. Although male and female mammals are, very early in development, indistinguishable anatomically, they quickly differentiate into male and female anatomical forms. Sexual differentiation is due to the presence of testosterone during sensitive periods, producing males, or to the absence of testosterone during the same periods, producing females. There are numerous anatomic features that are organized by hormonal conditions. These include the external genitalia and certain parts of the nervous system. Their sensitive periods occur at different times, so their development is independent of one another.

The development of sexual behavior is influenced by several environmental conditions, such as stress of the mother during pregnancy, maternal consumption of alcohol or other drugs during pregnancy, and treatment of the young by the mother after birth. Because copulation is so critical to reproductive success, developmental processes that affect adult copulatory behavior are extremely important to understand.

Hormones also serve to activate sexual behavior later in development. Hormones are known to influence the attractiveness of individuals to the opposite sex, their attraction to the opposite sex, and their receptivity to copulation.

The behavioral patterns of copulation differ across mammals. Based on the presence or absence of vaginal lock, intravaginal thrusting, multiple intromission, and multiple ejaculation, the copulatory behavior of male mammals falls into 16 separate categories, 11 of which have been noted so far. The copulatory behaviors of female mammals and of nonmammals has not been so thoroughly investigated.

Quantitative differences in copulatory behavior have important implications for reproductive success. Such differences as the number of intromissions and the amount of time between them can affect reproductive physiology, such as implantation of the fertilized ova into the uterus.

Copulation serves several functions besides placing sperm into the female reproductive tract. Copulation may facilitate pregnancy, initiate mate recognition, serve as a form of male parental investment, and even reduce the reproductive success of rival males.

Copulatory behavior is activated by various hormones. Male sexual behavior seems to be tightly linked to testosterone, at least in some species, and female copulation is most consistently associated with estrogen. However, important species differences exist in these processes and there is some danger in generalizing from one species to another in this regard.

Female copulatory behavior has been traced to the ventromedial nucleus of the hypothalamus, which is activated by acetylcholine and inhibited by serotonin. Male copulatory behavior is influenced by neurons of the medial preoptic area.

Recommended Readings

BRONSON, F. H. (1989). *Mammalian reproductive biology*. Chicago: University of Chicago Press.

DALY, M., & WILSON, M. (1983). *Sex, evolution, and behavior*. Boston: Willard Grant Press.

LESHNER, A.I. (1978). *An introduction to behavioral endocrinology*. New York: Oxford University Press.

Chapter 11

 REPRODUCTION:
MATING SYSTEMS,
MATE CHOICE, AND
PARENTAL BEHAVIOR

Successful reproduction often depends on finding,
acquiring, and keeping a mate, sometimes in the
face of vigorous competition. Others in the population are also seeking mates and the resources required to produce and raise offspring. Further,
reproduction must be timed so that offspring

come along in generally favorable conditions and so that there are not too many to care for at the same time. It may even be necessary to cut back on offspring care or to curb it entirely if conditions are such that they cannot be cared for without jeopardizing the parents' future reproductive success. In short, reproduction requires careful "choices" among many options. This chapter explores some of the arenas in which such choices are made.

Mating Systems

Mating systems analysis is concerned with the distribution of mates within a population. Each individual has a finite reproductive capacity (number of offspring that can be produced in a lifetime), and this capacity is a resource that can be utilized by opposite-sex individuals. The study of mating systems is concerned with how this reproductive resource is distributed: with one other individual (monogamy) or with more than one (polygamy). The variations here are numerous, however, so we will begin with a classification of mating systems and a review of the ecological conditions that apparently contributed to their evolution.

CLASSIFICATION OF MATING SYSTEMS

Monogamy   Monogamy is the condition in which one male is mated with only one female. Ideally for our classification, there should be no mating outside the monogamous unit. To the extent that there is, monogamy may grade into the other systems described below.

Only about 3% of mammalian species are monogamous (Kleiman, 1977), but more than 90% of all bird species are monogamous (Lack, 1968).

Dewsbury (1988) has written an excellent review of monogamy, its characteristics, and some associated behaviors. His review emphasizes that no single characteristic defines monogamy, but that the following characteristics tend to occur together in monogamous species: First, male and female reside together in the same home range or territory. Second, there is exclusive or nearly exclusive mating between the paired male and female. Finally, there is usually biparental care of offspring. The other mating systems differ from monogamy in one or more of these characteristics.

Monogamy seems to occur when two full-time parents are required to care for the offspring. In most birds, the mother and father bring food to the nestlings, share incubation duties, and so on. The chance of survival of the offspring are substantially reduced if either parent dies or fails to assist in offspring care. The ecological circumstances associated with monogamy are discussed in detail by Wittenberger & Tilson (1980).

Polygyny   Polygyny is the mating system in which a male is mated with two or more females (we usually call this *polygamy*, although this is less precise). Polygyny occurs because some males are able to exclude other males from breeding (Emlen & Oring, 1977). Thus, in polygynous populations there are usually more unmated males than unmated females (the latter are usually quite rare). Males can exclude other males in three basic ways, described below.

(1) *Resource defense polygyny.* If resources necessary for reproduction are clumped in the habitat, the potential exists for some males to aggressively acquire and defend that resource against other males, but allow access to females

in exchange for mating privileges. An example of resource defense polygyny comes from the bee *Anthidium maculosum.* Females depend on flowering mint for pollen and nectar. The plant grows in clumps and males compete for possession of the plants. When females are ready to breed they visit these flowers to feed, and copulate while there. Successful males mate with several females, but unsuccessful males acquire no mates at all (Alcock, 1980).

(2) *Female defense polygyny.* In some cases females live together in groups because they are safer from predators, or because they can be more successful predators. Regardless of the reason for female clustering, a male that acquires a group of females and prevents other males from copulating with them will have greater reproductive success. This scheme is common among mammals. Male lions fight viciously for possession of "prides" of females, thus leading to a number of lone males without mates (Bertram, 1975). Some deer, horses, and monkeys also engage in female defense polygyny.

(3) *Male dominance polygyny.* Some species, such as baboons, reside in troops consisting of several adult males. However, not all males are equally successful in mating, and differences in success are due to dominance differences. In other words, if some males can aggressively dominate other males, the dominant ones may secure more matings, all at the expense of the subordinate males. The exclusion of some males need not be absolute—even subordinate males may sometimes copulate—but dominance may lead to unequal "consumption" of female reproductive output by males, which is what we define as polygyny. More details on the relationship between dominance and reproductive success are provided in Chapter 12.

Polyandry The opposite of polygyny is polyandry, in which some females utilize the reproductive output of more than one male,

thereby excluding some other females from breeding. Although opposite to polygyny in terms of sex ratios, polyandry has many features in common with polygyny. In some accounts, the two are combined together, in which case they are called *polygamy,* to contrast with monogamy.

Polyandry is a rare mating system. It occurs in a few bird species but apparently not at all in mammals except for a few human societies where it is practiced occasionally and is not the preferred situation. Polyandry seems to occur in situations in which egg or offspring loss to predators is common (Jenni, 1974). Under these circumstances the ability to lay replacement clutches of eggs is highly favored and so females do little nest-tending, spending their time feeding, instead. When a loss occurs the female is able to generate a new clutch in a short time.

Complications A simple classification scheme such as the one above is bound to have some problems, and this one has its share. We will briefly consider two of them.

The first complication deals with the time interval over which the mating system is measured and defined. For instance, if a woman has three husbands in her lifetime, one at a time, and has a child by each of them, should she be considered polyandrous or monogamous? If a man has two wives, but fails to have children by one of them, is he polygynous or monogamous? Clearly, definitions can be stated that can go either way. Some definitions are more concerned with sociological aspects of mating and associated behaviors and would therefore focus on short-term aspects of the system. Birds that are likely to have a new mate each season but which are faithful to that season's mate would be classified as monogamous. Definitions that emphasize the utilization of others' reproductive resources, in contrast, would call the same species polygynous. We must be careful to distinguish between these two time intervals because each may influence various other characteristics of the organism. For instance, a species in which most matings are monogamous, but in which males are more likely to have more mates (in succession) than are females, may have courtship and parental care patterns like those of monogamous species, but may have sex differences in body size or coloration like those of polygynous species (see below).

Another complication involves the "legal" aspects of a mating system and other activities that are outside the main system. A married human couple whose members engage in extramarital intercourse may be considered monogamous by one definition, polygamous by another; polygynous if the man fathers a child by another woman; or polyandrous if the woman bears a child by another man. Further, considering only copulations may yield a different conclusion about the mating system than would consideration of fertilizations. For instance, female baboons may copulate with all or nearly all the males of the troop during their 4- or 5-day estrous periods. However, only a very small number of the males succeed in fertilizing the females. The dominant males are able to sequester females during the times when fertilization is most likely (Hausfater, 1975). The same appears to be true in bighorn sheep (Hogg, 1988). Are these systems polygynous or polygamous? According to the criterion of utilization of the reproductive resource of the other sex, they are polygynous, but such mating behaviors would undoubtedly influence such things as male parental care. A situation in which females copulate with many males is not conducive to the evolution of male parental care (because of low confidence of paternity), but a polygynous system in which females tend to copulate with only one male would be more conducive to parental

investment by males. The issue of male parental care will be covered in more detail later in this chapter.

In conclusion, defining mating systems on the basis of the distribution of lifetime reproductive resources is valuable in some ways, but defining mating systems on the basis of shorter-term patterns of interaction is valuable in other ways.

HUMAN MATING SYSTEMS

Anthropological studies Studies of diverse human societies have always included information on marriage systems. Everywhere, it seems, people have ceremonies and other practices that publicly announce who is married to whom. The results of this work suggest that the majority of human societies permit polygyny and practice it (Fig. 11-1), other societies permit only monogamy, and others permit polyandry or polygyny (Ford & Beach, 1952). One should note, however, that even in polygynous societies the majority of marriages are monogamous. Two or more wives are the province of rich men only. Also, monogamous societies permit remarriage following death of the spouse or following divorce, and extramarital intercourse probably exists in all (although to varying degrees). Remarriage and extramarital intercourse contribute to genetic polygamy even though the society may be legally monogamous.

The evolution of human mating systems Given the diversity that exists in human mating systems it is reasonable to ask whether our ancestors practiced one system more than others. Knowing this might help us understand human sexuality, parental behavior patterns, and relationships between and within the sexes. But how could we ever answer this question? Mating sys-

Figure 11.1
Female defense polygyny means that some males will have reproductive success at the expense of other *males. The competition for females has favored larger size in males, which makes them large relative to females.*

tems do not fossilize, and the vast majority of human history was not recorded in writing. We need an indirect method of studying the effects of mating systems.

There are several ways we can study this issue, all of which depend on the correlational techniques described in Chapter 4. The basic strategy is to assemble data on species whose mating systems are well-known. Then we search for other easily measured attributes that correlate with the mating system. If found, we can then measure that attribute in a species whose mating system we know little about, and make predictions about its likely mating system. Sex difference in body size is one such attribute, as are sex differences in maturation and in reproductive variance.

(1) *Sex differences in body size.* Alexander *et al.* (1979) compiled data from numerous species and found that the more polygynous the species the larger males are relative to females (Fig. 11-2). In monogamous species, males and females are nearly equal in body size. In polyandrous species females are larger than males.

Why are polygyny and polyandry associated with increased body size in males and females, respectively? When there is competition for mates, whatever attributes lead to success in mate acquisition will tend to increase in frequency in the population. In polygynous species, some males are prevented from acquiring even a single mate. Large body size, especially coupled with fighting or bluffing skills, may be advantageous in securing mates under these con-

Figure 11.2
Humans practice several mating systems, and tolerance of polygyny is widespread. This Eskimo man has two wives.

ditions. Thus, competition among males has created the selective condition favoring larger males in polygynous species. Competition among females favors larger females in polyandrous species.

(2) *Maturation rate.* In monogamous species, males and females attain sexual maturity at about the same age. The pattern for polygynous species is for males to mature later than females. Female baboons become sexually mature at about five years of age (Altmann, 1980), but males take about twice as long to become fully mature (Richard, 1985). Males may take longer to mature because of their greater body size.

(3) *Reproductive variance.* Although males and females may have, on average, the same number of offspring, the *variability* in the number of offspring may differ substantially between males and females. In polygynous species, females are less variable than males in the number of offspring produced. This is because some males are excluded from breeding and their "share" is usurped by the successful males. Thus it is common in polygynous species for a small fraction of the males to account for a large fraction of all fertilizations. In elephant seals, for example, 4% of the males apparently fertilized 85% of the females (LeBoeuf & Peterson, 1969). In rhesus monkeys, the variance in reproductive success among males was about three times

greater than among females (Meikle *et al.*, 1984). In monogamous species, reproductive variance is about equal in males and females, but in polyandrous species, female reproductive variance exceeds that of males.

To summarize, males of polygynous species tend to be larger, slower to mature, and more variable in reproductive success than females (Table 11-1). The opposite is true in polyandrous species. In monogamous species the two sexes are nearly equal on all three measures. If we knew only one thing about a species, such as male to female body size, we could predict its mating system with some accuracy.

How do humans rate on these measures? Men are, on average, taller and heavier than women. The difference, however, is not nearly as great as it is in some species. (This does not mean that larger men are more polygynous. We are comparing species here, not individuals.) Males are slower to mature than females in our species, with male puberty occurring about 2 years later than female puberty. Finally, even in our legally monogamous society, men (a) are more likely than women to remarry following divorce or spousal death, (b) are more likely than women to have children by the second or subsequent spouse, (c) have extramarital intercourse more often and with more partners, and (d) are more likely to never marry (Chamie & Nsuly, 1981). These differences tend to make male reproductive variance exceed that of females. In sum, all the available evidence points to the conclusion that humans have, over the bulk of our evolutionary history, been subjected to the same sorts of selection conditions faced by polygynous species. However, because our version of polygyny largely arises through having a succession of monogamous relationships, we expect to find many behavioral characteristics, such as male parental care, that are typically found in purely monogamous species.

ALTERNATIVE MATING STRATEGIES

When a population is said to be monogamous or polygynous, the designation only means that that practice is the typical one in that population. Monogamously-mated individuals may achieve matings with individuals other than their mate, for example. Some of these practices were discussed above. There are, however, some practices that are used by individuals who do not succeed in the course of normal competition for mates. Such individuals do not meekly give up; they may seek alternative ways of achieving reproductive success. These alternative strategies are of basically two forms: surreptitious and forced matings.

Surreptitious matings In Chapter 4 we discussed the case of the female mimicry of some male bluegill sunfish. These males are small, colored like females, and release sperm into the water at the same time that females and territorial males are mating (Dominey, 1980).

Table 11-1

SUMMARY OF CHARACTERISTICS THAT ARE INDICATIVE OF ANIMAL MATING SYSTEMS

MATING SYSTEM	BODY SIZE	MATURATION	REPRODUCTIVE VARIANCE
Monogamy	Equal	Equal	Equal
Polygyny	Males larger	Males slower	Males greater
Polyandry	Females larger	Females slower	Females greater

Female mimicry by males, with accompanying surreptitious mating, is quite common in fish (see Bass, 1990 for additional examples).

Males who do not succeed in acquiring mates through overt competition with other males may nevertheless attempt to copulate with females if they can obtain the opportunity. For example, in the red deer of Scotland, a female-defense polygynous species, males who lose out in the battle for females will nevertheless copulate with females, usually waiting until a dominant male is preoccupied with fighting another male (Clutton-Brock et al., 1982). Similarly, most male bullfrogs attract females by croaking in shallow water, and the best sites for this are fought for by males. Other males, however, assume "satellite" positions, and attempt to mate with females drawn to the area by the croaks of the more dominant males (Howard, 1978). Males who engage in these alternative strategies are not as successful as the males who utilize the "traditional" male strategy, but they are more successful than they would be if they gave up entirely. In some cases these males will use the traditional strategy if they become successful at direct competition with other males.

Forced matings In species in which females exert strong mate choice, some males will not be chosen. Forced matings, which are sometimes referred to as "rape" but which probably should not be (Gowaty, 1982), are quite common among animals. Mallard ducks, for instance, mate monogamously, but there are males that do not acquire mates. These males sometimes forcibly mate with females who are not protected by their mates (Barash, 1977). Although the effectiveness of these forced matings at achieving fertilizations has been questioned (Hailman, 1978; McKinney et al., 1978), there is no doubt that such behavior has at least a small benefit for males who participate in it.

Shields and Shields (1983), analyzing human rape, have suggested that it is an alternative to "honest" courtship and mating that is used when the man judges the benefits to exceed the possible costs. Although they certainly do not condone rape, Shields and Shields emphasize that we gain nothing by viewing such acts as pathological; rather, as long as benefits exceed costs, it will continue. Further, their analysis suggests that males can adopt any of the possible mating strategies facultatively (i.e., depending on the circumstances), much like the male bullfrog or red deer may opt for the traditional or alternative tactic depending on its ability to compete successfully with other males.

In summary, then, the principles of natural selection suggest that individuals will do what they can to achieve reproductive success. In some cases, this may mean being surreptitious in matings, or in forcing matings. What may have evolved is a behavioral mechanism that allows individuals to be flexible in how they pursue reproductive success.

Mate Choice

Mate choice occurs whenever nonrandom mating exists within a population. This term does not imply that a deliberate selection process is occurring, such as among the items on a restaurant menu. Rather, males and females may mate or "pair up" through a sorting process. For example, Berven (1981) reported that large male wood frogs tend to mate with large females and that smaller males tend to mate with smaller females. This is because the larger males are more successful than the smaller males at dislodging males which have grasped a female. In the course of many dislodgings, these frogs sort themselves out according to size. Our interest in this section is on nonrandom mating, regardless of the mechanism that produces it.

In some cases, the processes that determine who mates with whom depend on competition among individuals of the same sex (*intrasexual selection*). The struggles between males for possession of resources or females, mentioned above, are examples of intrasexual selection. In other cases, however, selection is determined by the opposite sex (*intersexual selection*). Darwin (1871) viewed sexual selection as somewhat different from natural selection. However, the evolutionary changes brought about because of the choices of mates is just a special case of natural selection. That is, reproductive success can vary due to individual differences in dealing with predators or finding food, or they can arise because of individual differences in attracting mates. Most of the examples presented in this section will be of intersexual selection.

MATE CHOICE CRITERIA

Potential mates differ from each other in many ways, some of which indicate their quality. Animal behaviorists have studied this issue extensively and in some ingenious ways. Because animals cannot tell us about the criteria used in selecting mates (people can't always do so either!) we must resort to indirect ways to discover which differences are important and which are not. There are numerous criteria used in the mate choice process. We will review some of them now.

Species The most basic criterion for an appropriate mate is that he/she be of the appropriate species. This is not always obvious, however, because very similar species may live in sympatry (co-occur in the same area). When this happens, there are behavioral or other cues that distinguish among them. For example, in Chapter 9 we discussed the case of the two wolf spider species that are so similar that only the

males' courtship behaviors distinguish them. Behavioral differences often serve as reproductive isolating mechanisms, reducing the chances of matings between individuals of different species.

Individual attributes Of greatest interest are the criteria used in choosing among prospective mates of the correct species. Although the details vary, a fair conclusion is that the criteria correspond to attributes that make individuals good mates. These attributes differ among species because their selection conditions vary. A few examples follow.

(1) *Resources.* A common selection criterion is the resource base controlled by an individual. For instance, lark buntings, a small sparrow of the Great Plains, generally build their nests on the ground under a bush, probably because shade reduces the problems of overheating and predation. Female lark buntings choose mates according to the quality of the male's territory, i.e., the presence of appropriate nesting vegetation. Some males have such good territories that they get two or three mates; other males may have only one mate or none (Pleszczynska, 1978). Pleszczynska found that she could make a male more successful at obtaining mates by "planting" some plastic bushes on an otherwise nonattractive territory!

(2) *Parental ability.* Some species choose mates based on attributes that are correlated with parental abilities. For example, male common terns, a gull-like bird, bring fish to females prior to mating Fig. 11-3. Ample providers succeed more often in obtaining a mate than males who do not provide as well. Successful males also benefit from the heavier eggs laid by their mates (which presumably result from the improved nutritional status of well-provisioned females) because large eggs hatch into more vigorous chicks. Moreover, premating fish-provisioning is positively correlated with the male's rate of food provisioning for his young later on; thus, females

Figure 11.3
Male terns present fish to the females they are courting prior to mating. Females tend to select mates on the basis of the quantity of fish that the males provide them. Why? Because the courting behavior of the male is predictive of his parental behavior: Males who bring their prospective mates plenty of fish also tend to do the same for their offspring, thus enhancing the female's reproductive success.

may be choosing among prospective mates on the basis of a trait predictive of male parental skills (Nisbet, 1973).

In moorhens, a European species similar to the North American coot or mudhen, females compete for small, fat males (Petrie, 1983). Males do most of the egg incubation, and fat males can remain on the nest for longer periods, protecting the eggs against potential predators.

(3) *Phenotypic quality.* In species in which one or both sexes provide little or no parental care, mate choice may be based on the mate's genetic quality as judged by its phenotypic quality. For example, only the largest, toughest bull elephant seals succeed in acquiring mates (LeBoeuf & Peterson, 1969). Although females

are sometimes sexually mounted by smaller, subordinate males, the females' loud calls attract the attention of the dominant "beachmaster" male who drives away the interloper (Cox & LeBoeuf, 1977). In this way, females help assure themselves of high genetic quality offspring.

Another example of mate selection for genetic quality occurs in *Colias* butterflies. Individuals differ in a gene that produces an enzyme which supplies energy to the flight muscles. Individuals with a certain combination of alleles have stronger flight, survive longer, and have greater reproductive success than do individuals with other combinations. Females choose males who are persistent in courtship and, because courtship is flight-intensive, males with the best genotype achieve more matings (Watt *et al.*, 1986). Thus, based on a male phenotypic feature, females choose in a way that provides for the best gene quality in their offspring.

Do these examples mean that female elephant seals and butterflies can assess the genes of prospective mates and choose accordingly? No. If a female behaves in such a way as to mate with males who possess certain genotypes, then her offspring will tend to acquire those genes. In all cases, however, the proximate cause of the nonrandom mating is the male phenotype.

The use of phenotypic features that are indicative of genetic quality seems to be most pronounced in those species in which males contribute no parental care or other resources to their mates or offspring. A common phenomenon in such species is known as *lek behavior.* A *lek*

Male sage grouse display at leks, sites where other males and females assemble. Females select males and mate with them, but a small number of males, such as this one, attract and mate with a large number of females. Most males have little or no mating success.

is a site that is used as an assembly area by males for courting and copulating with females. Typically, males compete with each other for the best display sites within the lek, and those sites nearest the center of the lek are the most highly prized. When females are ready for mating, they arrive at the lek, and often spend considerable amounts of time apparently evaluating the males before copulating with one of them (Bradbury, 1977; Wiley, 1978; Emlen, 1976; Bradbury & Gibson, 1983). A relatively small number of males achieve a disproportionate number of matings. For example, about 10% of the males achieve about 90% of the copulations in sage grouse leks (Wiley, 1978).

Lek-breeding species also employ some of the most conspicuous courtship displays in the animal kingdom. Sage grouse males inflate their throat sacs with air, fan their tail feathers and strut before females. Male manikins, small forest birds of the New World tropics, spin around branches with feathers spread while making loud sounds (Foster, 1984). Presumably, such courtship displays are indicative of male genetic quality in some way.

(4) *Phenotypic similarity.* Another criterion, well known in humans and other animals, involves phenotypic similarity. That is, mates often resemble one another in a variety of phenotypic characteristics. This is called *positive assortative mating* (PAM). In humans, PAM has been documented for a wide variety of physical traits such as height, weight, and body proportions, and for personality and cognitive variables (Thiessen & Gregg, 1980; Pennock-Roman, 1984; Zondermann et al., 1977). Married couples are not more similar than expected simply because they have been living together and sharing a common physical, social, and intellectual environment. Newlywed couples and even unmarried couples resemble each other as much as couples married for many years (Pennock-Roman, 1984).

Choosing mates based on phenotypic similarity may benefit the individuals involved in several ways. First, if there are geographic variations in selection conditions, then mating with a similar individual may keep the adaptive alleles together, increasing the odds that the offspring will be adapted to the local conditions. Second, PAM results in offspring that are related to each parent by more than 50%, the expected value if matings occur randomly. Greater parent-offspring relatedness has implications for the degree of parental investment in offspring (Thiessen & Gregg, 1980; also see the section on parental investment, below).

There are limits to the benefits of mating with phenotypically similar individuals. Mating with close relatives can result in *inbreeding depression*, the production of fewer offspring, and offspring with more defects. Inbreeding depression is caused by recessive alleles with deleterious effects appearing in homozygous form when close relatives mate. For example, there are more spontaneous abortions and stillbirths, higher rates of infant mortality, and slower physical maturation in children of first-cousin marriages than in children of less closely related parents (reviewed by Thiessen & Gregg, 1980). Inbreeding also results in lowered IQ in humans (Bashi, 1977; Kamin, 1980). Inbreeding depression is a problem in small, captive animal populations, such as rare species kept in zoos (Ralls et al., 1979) thus providing the impetus for trading of breeding stock among zoos around the world.

There are numerous examples of behavioral mechanisms that reduce the likelihood of inbreeding depression, or, more precisely, that reduce the likelihood of copulation between close relatives. For instance, brother-sister matings might be expected to be very common. Not only would siblings be phenotypically similar (and thus attracted to one another), they would be about the same age and would most likely reside in the same area. Yet brother-sister matings are rare. There seems to exist a mechanism whereby people raised together in the same household are not as attracted to one another as they are to others. A telling case is the phenomenon in Israeli kibbutzim (in which children are raised in age-grouped, mixed-sex communal households) where marriages do not occur among people raised together, even though they are not genetically related (Shepher, 1971). There are no sanctions against these marriages, indeed, they are even encouraged, but they do not occur. Incest avoidance seems to occur in our species through the mechanism of early, close association (Van den Berghe, 1983).

A similar process occurs in chimpanzees. Pusey (1980) reported that prior to attaining sexual maturity, females tend to associate preferentially with their brothers. (Although chimps, like humans, are usually born singly, they maintain close and prolonged associations with their mother. Thus, siblings maintain close contact for several years.) This pattern changes when females become sexually mature. They generally depart for neighboring "communities" of chimpanzees (that probably contain few close relatives), or change their range within their home community, thereby largely avoiding their brothers. Pusey also reports that mother-son copulations are rare.

Inbreeding avoidance also occurs in nonprimates. Acorn woodpeckers of western North America breed in communal groups of two or three monogamous pairs, all of whom lay eggs in the same nest and help rear all the offspring. After returning from their wintering grounds, yearling females return to the nest in which they were raised (yearling males move elsewhere). However, if an adult male who was present the previous year returns to the nest, the young female immediately vacates the area and takes up residence elsewhere. A female thereby avoids breeding with a male who may have been her father (Koenig & Pitelka, 1979).

Inbreeding depression seems to select for individuals who have mechanisms for avoidance of mating with close relatives. A similar though opposite phenomenon is *outbreeding depression*, in which matings of dissimilar individuals produce fewer or lower quality offspring. Cross-species matings are usually sterile, for example, but even within-species matings are not uniformly fertile. Mixed-racial marriages in humans often have lower fertility than do same-race marriages (Bresler, 1982).

Let us try to put all this in perspective. Matings with close relatives may be deleterious, as may matings with others not closely enough related. This has led Bateson (1983b) to suggest his optimal-outbreeding hypothesis: that the best potential mate is one who is similar but not too similar. Experiments with quail suggest that, when given a choice among several opposite-sex strangers, the preference is for first cousins (Bateson, 1978). Siblings, more distantly related kin, and nonkin are significantly less preferred. This does not imply that other variables are not involved in mate choice, but rather, under laboratory conditions in which other information about mate quality is not readily available, slight outbreeding seems to prevail.

To summarize so far, we have seen that many characteristics are used by animals and humans in the process of choosing mates. Some characteristics involve resources, but others, such as food acquisition ability, size, and fighting ability, involve the individual per se. What all these criteria have in common is that they relate, more or less directly, to the reproductive success of the individual who makes the choice. If a safe nesting site is critical to reproductive success, then choosing a mate with a good nesting site is advantageous. If a good provider is needed, then look for signs of a good provider. Reproduction is a costly activity. It takes time and energy, and involves some risk. Thus, successful reproduction is contingent on having a good partner, and discriminative mate choice is widespread.

SEX DIFFERENCES IN MATE CHOICE

Because reproduction is costly and choice of the best available mate helps increase the odds that reproduction will succeed, it follows that if one sex tends to invest more than the other in reproduction, the one that invests more will choose more carefully than the sex that invests less.

In mammals, females tend to invest more than males (due to internal gestation and lactation), and females are generally much more selective than males. Male mammals will nearly always benefit by copulating with any available female because male reproductive success is generally limited by the number of females that they can fertilize. In contrast, females generally have less to gain by seeking additional matings and are therefore more selective about their mates. A good example of sex differences in choosiness occurs in dogs. Beach and LeBoeuf (1967) found that in their colony of beagles, sexually receptive females accepted certain males for copulation more often than others. Although females were often approached by males, many of them were driven away, suggesting selectivity on the part of the females.

The preceding example is not meant to imply that males are not discriminating. Males do have costs involved in mating, even if the ecology is such that males provide no parental care. One cost is sperm depletion. When a male copulates, his sperm supply is decreased. If this expenditure is made on a low-quality female, the male may be giving up the opportunity to mate with a higher-quality female if one is available (Dewsbury, 1982). Of course, the cost of mating in males depends on several variables including sperm production capacity [which is associated with testes size (Harcourt, et al., 1982)] and the probability of encountering another sexually receptive female before sperm are replaced.

Males that have primary care of offspring are quite discriminating in their choice of mates. For instance, male sticklebacks build nests of aquatic vegetation in which females lay their eggs. The male fertilizes the eggs, then spends several days fanning them with his fins to increase oxygenation, driving away predators, etc., and he continues these activities after the eggs hatch. The female does none of this. Male sticklebacks given several prospective mates are quite discriminating in their selection (Li & Owings, 1978).

Parental Behavior

Parental behavior is anything that promotes the survival or well-being of offspring. Enormous variation exists in the preparation and care that parents contribute to their offspring. Some species merely get eggs and sperm together and then leave the embryos to fend for themselves. At the other extreme are those species that carry, feed, teach, clean, discipline, and protect their offspring for many years. In this section we will examine sex differences in parental behavior, the proximate causes of parental care, and finally, the reduction or termination of parental care.

SEX DIFFERENCES
IN PARENTAL BEHAVIOR

As we saw earlier, females often bear the brunt of reproductive costs. But why? Wouldn't it make more sense for males to help out to increase the success of their genes? One reason why males don't give more help involves their confidence of parentage. Females are usually guaranteed of their genetic relatedness to their offspring, but males are rarely sure of their relationship to the offspring. After all, there is usually some chance that the female could have been fertilized by another male. When confidence of paternity is low, males show little if any parental investment in offspring (although they may invest heavily in courting the female). When confidence of paternity is higher, however, males may provide extensive parental care (Ridley, 1978). For example, male cotton-top tamarins, a species of small, New World monkey, carry their heavy sets of twins (Snowdon, 1990) (Fig. 11-4).

The same pattern is shown in humans. In some societies in which sexual promiscuity is common (even while married) men do not extend their fatherly help to their wives' children. Men are fatherly toward their sisters' children, however. A man can be sure that his sisters' children are related to him, but he has no such confidence about his wife's children (Kurland, 1979)!

Let us take a closer look at "confidence of paternity." Does this term imply rather sophisticated cognitive capacities? The answer depends on how the term is used. It can be used without implying a complex psychological mechanism. Think of it this way: Two males, A and B, of a species that fertilizes internally, are courting prospective mates. Both females recently copulated with other males (unbeknownst to A and B). A and B copulate with their mates whereupon eggs are laid and the two couples commence parental duties. After a few days, male B abandons his mate and, in the next week, copulates with two other females. Male A, ever faithful, helps care for the offspring until they become independent. Which male, A or B, is more reproductively successful? Male A may have fathered only 50% of the offspring he helped care for. Male B fathered 50%, too, but may

Figure 11.4
Male parental care is often extensive in monogamous species in which males can be very confident of the offspring being theirs. This male common marmoset does most of the carrying of his heavy set of twins.

have fathered another 50% in each of his other mates. By this count, B would be more successful.

In other words, males vary in the magnitude and duration of their parental behavior. But there is no simple way of knowing whether male parental behavior is adaptive unless we know other relevant conditions. If there is a strong likelihood that the male will end up caring for another male's progeny, a phenomenon known as *cuckoldry*, male parental care may be maladap-

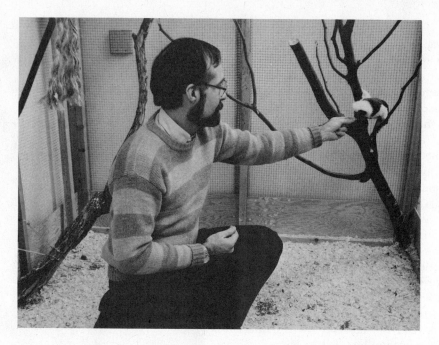

CHARLES SNOWDON

"Monogamy is not a bizarre mating system, nor is paternal care a bizarre behavior. Both are adaptations to an environment where one parent is not sufficient for successful infant rearing." [Snowdon, C. T. (1990).

Mechanisms maintaining monogamy in monkeys. In D. A. Dewsbury, Ed. Contemporary Issues in Comparative Psychology (pp. 225–251). Sunderland, MA: Sinauer (p. 250)].

tive, and searching for another mate rather than behaving parentally may be more successful. On the other hand, if there is little chance of a male caring for another male's offspring, parental care may be the most adaptive option, especially if more offspring survive with biparental care. A cognitive assessment of confidence of paternity is not necessary for such a system to work.

The distribution of male parental care across animal species is rather patchy. Male parental care is fairly common among fish and birds, but in mammals it is less common (Kleiman, 1977). Snowdon (1990) makes a good case for male parental care being most extensive in those species in which biparental care is essential for

raising the offspring. This is usually found in monogamous species (recall that the resource base of monogamous species, in most cases, is such that two parents are required to raise offspring successfully). The tamarins and marmosets of South America usually bear twins. The father—and older siblings if there are any—carries and plays with the youngest offspring, freeing the mother to obtain food necessary for converting to milk.

Not all monogamous species exhibit male parental care, nor do all cases in which confidence of paternity is high. The common factor contributing to male parental care is its *necessity*, usually because of demands on the mother to secure resources for herself and her offspring. This accounts for cultural differences in the involvement of men in childrearing (Snowdon, 1990).

PROXIMATE CAUSES
OF PARENTAL BEHAVIOR

Several internal conditions and external stimuli are known to induce, modify, and direct parental behavior. Although they have been most thoroughly studied in females, a few are also known in males. These proximate causes will be grouped into two categories: hormones and offspring-related stimuli.

Hormonal effects Inexperienced female rats can be induced to behave maternally (retrieving misplaced pups and tending to them in a nest) only with great difficulty. However, the same females are fully maternal toward their first set of pups. This switch can largely be attributed to the combined effects of the steroid hormones estradiol and progesterone, and the pituitary hormone, prolactin. Bridges *et al.* (1985) administered hormone treatments to inexperienced female rats whose ovaries or pituitary gland had been removed. When prolactin and the steroids were all present, the females were fully maternal; the absence of any hormone significantly reduced maternal behavior.

Offspring-related stimuli A variety of sensory stimuli emanating from offspring may initiate or regulate parental attention. An interesting example comes from the physical sensations associated with the birth process itself in mammals. In a study on sheep, Keverne *et al.* (1983) showed that vaginal stimulation, which is normally provided by passage of the lamb down the birth canal, triggers full maternal responsiveness in the ewe. Pregnant ewes adopted newborn lambs following vaginal stimulation with an electric vibrator (no laughs, please!).

Moreover, recently parturient ewes adopted a second lamb following stimulation but not without it. Vaginal stimulation may lead to hormonal release that promptly activates maternal care (licking the lamb, permitting suckling) or it may act directly without hormonal involvement.

Visual stimuli play a role in inducing certain forms of parental care. Human infant faces have proportions that are quite different from those of adults. Sternglanz *et al.* (1977) showed drawings of infant faces, which differed in the proportions of various features, to college students who rated each one on its attractiveness. The maximally attractive infant face was the one with the largest eyes, forehead, and cheeks, and the smallest chin, i.e., those facial features most unlike those of adults (Figure 11-5). This study did not mea-

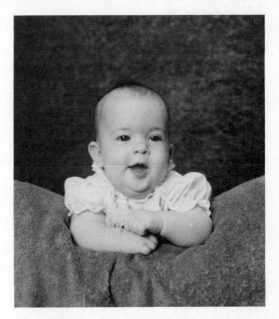

Figure 11.5
The physical features that people find most attractive about babies are those that differ most from adult norms. High forehead, large eyes, and a small chin make babies "cute" and promote adult care-giving.

sure parental behavior, per se, only expressed attractiveness, and therefore falls somewhat short of a measure of parental care.

Finally, auditory cues provided by the offspring can initiate or direct parental care. Young rodents, although usually unable to move about on their own, produce distress vocalizations when they are too cool or hungry, and these calls produce quick responses by mothers or other hormonally primed females (Smotherman *et al.*, 1978). Of course, primate infants are known for their distress cries, which are individually distinctive and highly provocative of parental attentiveness (Gouzoules *et al.*, 1984; Green & Gustafson, 1983; Bell & Ainsworth, 1972). Such cries usually result in prompt attention by the parent.

In conclusion, many stimuli emanating from the infants themselves elicit attention by the parents. Such attention is generally for the good of both the infant and the parents. After all, the parents' reproductive success is tied up in the offspring, and if the parent can successfully gear its attentions in ways that benefit the offspring, so much the better. There are conditions, however, in which the offspring and parents have conflicting goals. These conditions, and their resolutions, will be discussed in the section on terminating investment, below.

CHANGING PATTERNS OF PARENTAL INVESTMENT

Parental investment in offspring is not uniform across the span of time during which care is provided. For example, as the offspring get older and larger, more time and energy may be needed to provide them with food, at least until the offspring can begin to acquire their own food. Eventually the offspring will become independent of the parents. Parents, then, can be thought of as making decisions about how much

to invest in their offspring at any given time, and they may increase or decrease their investment as conditions change. We will begin by examining two perspectives on the basis for decisions about parental investment.

Expected benefits or previous expenditures As their offspring get older, parents are faced with decisions about how much to invest, or whether to continue investing at all. Two hypotheses have been suggested to account for the changes in investment by parents. The expected benefits hypothesis claims that parents assess the number and quality of their offspring and allocate investment accordingly, with more offspring and higher-quality offspring receiving more investment than fewer or lower-quality offspring. In contrast, the previous expenditures hypothesis claims that the greater the amount of previous investment the greater the current investment will be. Parents "protect" their earlier investment by following it up with more, until offspring independence is achieved.

Robertson and Biermann (1979) conducted an experiment to test the merits of these two hypotheses. They started with red-winged blackbird nests that contained the same number of eggs. Thus, they reasoned that the parents had all invested equally to that point. They then removed some eggs from some of the nests and placed them in other nests. When a predatory attack on the nests was arranged (by placing a rubber snake near each one), how strongly did the parents attack? (Antipredator behavior was used as a measure of parental investment.) The vigor of the antipredator response was greater in those parents that had the greater number of eggs. Because the parents had not invested in those additional eggs, Robertson and Biermann reasoned that the birds must have been basing their decisions on the expected benefits of attacking the snake. Saving five eggs had higher expected benefits than did saving two eggs.

Other studies, however, have found support for the previous expenditures hypothesis. Weatherhead (1979), for example, noted that savannah sparrows gave more alarm calls at the approach of a human "predator" the older their nestlings. Nestling age was correlated with previous expenditures because of the greater feeding and incubation investments in older nestlings. A critic, however, would claim that older nestlings provide parents with greater expected benefits, because they are closer to independence and are less likely to perish because of predation or food shortages.

The general consensus seems to be that basing current investment decisions on previous expenditures can be risky business, in that it can sometimes lead to "throwing good money after bad." This approach is sometimes called the "Concorde fallacy" after the multibillion dollar aircraft whose development was plagued by cost overruns. Proponents of the project sought additional funding by using the reasoning that if we don't spend more now to complete the project, our previous spending will be wasted. Dawkins and Carlisle (1976) have argued that on theoretical grounds this strategy is faulty. Instead of looking backward, investors (whether of money or parental care) should look at the expected benefits.

Attainment of offspring independence The typical parental investment pattern involves the parents investing time, effort, and risk until the offspring become independent. During the period of offspring dependency on the parents, it is to the mutual benefit of both parent and offspring for the parents to invest. However, as Trivers (1974) has so compellingly argued, there comes a time when the parents' interests do not coincide with those of the offspring. Parent–offspring conflict is the result.

Consider weaning as an example of parent–offspring conflict. As long as a mother cat con-

ROBERT TRIVERS

*"In general, parent–offspring conflict is expected to increase during the period of parental care, and offspring are expected to employ psychological weapons in order to compete with their parents." [Trivers, R. L. (1972). Parent–offspring conflict. American Zoologist **14,** 249–264 (p. 249).]*

tinues to lactate, she is expending energy on her current litter of kittens that could go toward producing a new litter. Further, lactation may delay the next pregnancy. If her litter could be independent of her, then continuing to feed them is only reducing the mother's lifetime reproductive success. One would expect mother cats to have mechanisms for stopping investment at a time when their kittens could reasonably be expected to fend for themselves. The avoidance or even outright rebuffing of kittens by their mothers at weaning is a perfect example of such processes.

Kin selection theory (Chapter 4) suggests

Parent–offspring conflict. At some point, this mother will wean her kittens. The kittens will resist her rebuffs and attempt to continue nursing because doing so enhances their personal survival and reproductive success.

However, the mother's reproductive success is compromised by nursing past the point at which her offspring are able to exploit other food sources: She could be investing her energy in producing a new litter.

that the kittens should "want" their mother to reproduce again. After all, she will be producing siblings that share genes in common with the kittens. Why, then, do the kittens continue to pester their mother, nursing whenever they can manage to do so? Why don't they accept weaning gracefully and allow their mother to get on with the task of producing more copies of their genes? Although kittens will gain from the mother producing another litter, they have more to gain by protecting their own individual chances of survival and reproductive success. There is a time, then, between the periods when the kittens definitely require maternal care and when they definitely do not require it, that the kittens' individual best interests conflict with the mother's best interest.

Parent–offspring conflict can occur in other arenas besides weaning, of course, and the timing and duration of the conflict will differ among species and type of parental investment. The recognition of the dynamics of parent–offspring conflict permits us a much greater understanding of the processes that lead to the reduction and eventual cessation of parental investment.

Infanticide If too many offspring are born at the same time, or if they overlap too much in time even if born separately, the chances of them all surviving or of maturing into vigorous adults is diminished. Under such circumstances, parents may terminate investment altogether by abandonment or infanticide, or they may terminate investment in some offspring while continuing to invest in others. In humans, infanticide of the latter type is common in cases of multiple births (twins or more) where all but one of the babies are killed outright or are abandoned to die (Dickeman, 1975).

Infanticide or abandonment is more likely when the mother is food-stressed. Wood rats, common grackles (a bird species), lions, and humans, to mention a few, terminate investment in some or all offspring when the mother can not feed all of them without seriously jeopardizing her own health (Howe, 1977; McClure, 1981). Food-deprived female mice who have recently given birth often cannibalize their pups (Bronson & Marstellar, 1985).

Would not abandonment or infanticide be selected against? After all, they appear to reduce reproductive success. Would not those females that produce as many offspring as possible come to predominate in the population? The answer seems to be "no" and this is why: Individuals with maximum *lifetime* reproductive success are the ones that replicate the greatest number of copies of their genes. Infanticide reduces *short-term* reproductive success, but this may translate into long-term benefits, as we have seen. If a female has, let us say, an average of 10 breeding episodes available to her in her lifetime, it would be wise, in the long run, to terminate one episode (if conditions are adverse) so as to protect her options on the remaining episodes. If this is true, a young female (with many episodes remaining) would be more likely to terminate investment than would a female nearing the end of her reproductive career. This is perhaps why species that reproduce only once hold nothing back in their single reproductive act. Salmon literally convert their own muscles into eggs and sperm. They will die anyway, so such extreme measures are adaptive. But species that reproduce several or many times are not as invested in any one reproductive episode, and it may be better to wait for better conditions than to risk overinvestment.

Infanticide does not occur just when there are too many offspring to care for. It also commonly occurs when offspring are malformed, nonresponsive, or otherwise indicate low probability of survival. Under such circumstances, parents may be better off by curtailing investment altogether, saving resources for another breeding attempt. Infanticide in humans, even in societies in which infanticide is severely punished, is far more common among infants with birth defects (Daly & Wilson, 1988c). One of the proximate mechanisms that tends to instigate infanticide or abuse is the infant's cry. Several infantile neurological disorders affect the sound of the cry, making it sound shriller and more piercing (Ostwald & Peltzman, 1974; Lester, 1984; Frodi & Senchak, 1990), contributing to parental stress and increasing the likelihood of abuse (Frodi & Lamb, 1980).

In conclusion, infanticide can be seen as an adaptation for promoting lifetime reproductive success. Long-lived species that can breed many times would be expected to be among those most willing to forego short-term success that jeopardizes the mother, in favor of long-term chances of success.

Temporal Aspects of Reproduction

Reproduction is an expensive proposition. From the production of gametes to the courting of mates, and through the care and protection of offspring, reproduction is costly in terms of energy, nutrients, time, and risk. We expect that adaptations that minimize these costs will evolve, but not to the point of jeopardizing reproductive success. Reproduction is no place for false economy. This section will deal with some "decisions" about when, how often, and how much to invest in reproduction.

TIMING OF REPRODUCTION

Throughout the animal kingdom reproduction is timed so that offspring are born or hatched when it is most conducive to their survival and well being (Bronson, 1989). In many cases, this co-incides with the time of maximum food availability. Among insect-eating birds, for instance, eggs hatch during the early summer when insect abundance is reaching its peak. Grazing mammals give birth in the spring when vegetation is fresh and growing—and highest in protein—which facilitates milk production by the mother. The same species often do not try to reproduce twice in the same season because there is insufficient time to get the offspring through to independence. In more stable habitats, as in many tropical areas, reproduction is not nearly as seasonal (Bronson, 1985).

It is one thing to show that reproduction is timed to occur when offspring survival is greatest, but it is quite another to determine what the proximate mechanisms are that influence the timing of reproduction. After all, with the time that it takes to court and copulate, and then to gestate the offspring, the parents must sometimes begin long before the birth occurs. How do they "know" when to begin?

There are several kinds of proximate mechanisms used to time reproduction (Crews & Moore, 1986). Some mechanisms depend on long-term changes, such as day length, that are predictive of forthcoming conditions. Other mechanisms employ conditions that are predictive, but on a shorter term. For instance, rain may fall sporadically in some deserts, but some of the animals that live there may use rainfall to cue reproduction because the rainfall means that before long the vegetation needed to feed their offspring will be growing (Bronson, 1989). As you might imagine, the predictability of the environment is viewed differently by animals as a function of their average lifespan. To long-lived species, the changing of seasons will happen many times. To something like a small rodent, however, whose lifespan is measured in weeks, seasonal changes may not be relevant. Thus, we find that long-lifespan species tend to use long-term cues but short-lifespan species tend to use cues that are only predictive in the short run (Bronson, 1989).

One of the most common timing mechanisms involves the connection between day length, gonadal hormone production, and copulation. Seasonal changes in day length are known to regulate breeding activity. For example, captive male house sparrows exposed to light for 16 hours per day after having been maintained at 8 to 10 hours per day show prompt enlargement of the gonads, increases in gonadal hormones, and subsequent copulation (Menaker, 1972). This phenomenon occurs even though temperature, food supply, and other factors are held constant. Similarly, Syrian hamsters come into breeding condition when day length is 12.5 hours or longer (Goldman & Darrow, 1983). How does light regulate breeding behavior?

We begin with the retinas. Some optic nerve axons synapse in the suprachiasmatic nuclei of the hypothalamus, located just above the optic chiasm. As long as light strikes the retinas, the suprachiasmatic nuclei are depolarized by arriving action potentials. Neurons of the suprachiasmatic nuclei influence, through some intervening structures, the superior cervical ganglia, part of the sympathetic nervous system. From there, axons extend to the pineal gland located near the center of the brain, where norepinephrine is released. Norepinephrine initiates a series of biochemical processes that convert serotonin to melatonin. The organization of this system is such that melatonin production increases during the dark phase (night). Light inhibits melatonin synthesis, even in nocturnal animals (Binkley, 1979).

Melatonin influences reproduction through its effects on the secretion of other hormones. Some cells of the hypothalamus secrete gonadotropin-releasing hormone (Gn–RH) and the amount of melatonin influences the rate at which Gn–RH is released. As Gn-RH release increases, so does the secretion of luteinizing hormone and follicle-stimulating hormone from the pituitary gland. Finally, these hormones influence the gonads themselves (see Chapter 10).

Melatonin suppresses gonadal activity in some species (Ralph, 1983), but stimulates gonadal activity in others. When Syrian hamsters (the common petshop variety) are given implants of melatonin, the gonads stay undeveloped, even if day length is sufficiently long to trigger gonad development (Goldman & Darrow, 1983). Normally, as day length increases, melatonin production decreases, thereby "liberating" the gonads. The gonads, in turn, produce hormones that act on the brain to activate reproductive behaviors, as we saw earlier. Species with this mechanism are surprisingly sensitive to changes in day length. Syrian hamsters exposed to 12-hour days have regressed gonads, but when they are switched to 12.5-hour days they show full gonadal development (Goldman & Darrow, 1983).

As one might guess, not all species operate this way. Some, such as deer and even another hamster species, have the opposite pattern; that is, melatonin *activates* gonadal processes (by increasing Gn–RH release) that result in breeding. This may account for the "rut" (period of breeding activity) of deer which occurs in the fall when day length is decreasing and melatonin is increasing.

The retina–gonad link as found in mammals is supplemented by hypothalamic receptors in the brains of birds. Although the pineal gland acts as a photoreceptor directly in birds [birds whose optic nerves have been cut still show normal light-associated cycles of activity and reproduction (Menaker, 1972)], even birds whose pineals have been removed sometimes remain responsive to light (Menaker & Binkley, 1981). This appears to be due to the presence of hypothalamic nuclei in birds that are somehow responsive to light (Silver, 1990).

So we seem to have a neat package: Animals often measure the length of their days by the effect of melatonin on the gonads, either suppressing the gonads in spring breeders or activating the gonads in fall breeders. Unfortunately, however, the story is complicated by another factor, endogenous rhythms. That is, under stable conditions that favor gonadal activity in seasonally breeding species, the gonads do not stay in their developed condition permanently. They eventually regress more or less on schedule. However, the gonads will not redevelop without appropriate day length. Therefore, it appears that day length change is necessary to initiate gonadal development, but once developed, the gonads will remain active for only a fixed interval.

Not all species work in the same way with respect to environmental control of breeding. Some species are photoperiodic; i.e., light controls the period of their breeding. Other species are nonphotoperiodic and remain in breeding condition regardless of day length, or cycle in and out of breeding condition under the control of other exogenous factors such as temperature, rainfall, or food (Bronson, 1985, 1989). For example, the montane vole of North America lives in high mountain conditions and breeds seasonally, but the timing of their reproduction is not controlled by light directly, but rather by compounds in the plants that they consume. One of these compounds is found only in green, growing vegetation, and triggers the rodents' reproductive systems. Negus and Berger (1977) were able to induce reproduction in these voles in winter by providing them with green vegetation to eat.

The ecological conditions favoring one mechanism over another have to do with the optimal timing of births. Although in most species this is the spring, this is not always true. Furthermore, differences in gestation length will dictate when copulation must occur in order to achieve optimal birth timing. The deer and the mouse that live in the same meadow breed at very different times: the deer in the fall, the mouse in the spring. However, the deer has a gestation period of about 5 months but the mouse's gestation is only about 3 weeks. Therefore, although both species increase melatonin in the fall (due to shortening days), the melatonin activates the deer's breeding apparatus but suppresses that of the mouse.

SPACING OF OFFSPRING

How much time elapses between births? For many species this is not a concern. Salmon, for instance, reproduce only one time in their life. We will focus instead on those species that can reproduce several or many times within a lifespan. They may produce only one offspring at a time—as in humans, gorillas, and whales—or in litters or clutches, as in most mammals, birds, and fish.

Generally, animals do not commence on a new offspring until nearly finished with the current offspring. This spacing can be accomplished in several ways. First, hormonal changes that occur during pregnancy and lactation (in mammals) inhibit gonadal activity, thereby making reproduction impossible or unlikely. In humans and other mammals the secretion of milk and the suckling of the young leads to a condition known as *lactational amenorrhea*, a period during which ovulation is drastically reduced (Short, 1984; Smith, 1984). Women who breastfeed their babies usually do not resume ovulation for 6 months or more following the birth of their child, but women who only bottle feed resume ovulation within about 3 months after birth (Short, 1984). Furthermore, the frequency and intensity of suckling by the infant affect the duration of lactational amenorrhea. In one human population in which suckling occurs often (the !Kung San bushpeople of southern Africa), the mother does not resume ovulation for about 4 years (Konner & Worthman, 1980) (Fig. 11-6). These women nurse their children about every 13 minutes during the day for about 4 years! American women who nurse do so far less frequently—about every 4 hours—and thus ovulation resumes sooner.

Nutrition also affects the time between births, and ovulation does not recur until the female is in good nutritional condition. In humans, this means having about 35 pounds of stored fat (Frisch, 1980, 1984). Female endurance athletes, who are in excellent health but low on fat, often fail to ovulate, but do so when they reduce their training and fat accumulates (Malina, 1983). Because lactation requires a huge energetic drain [in women this amounts to about 1000 calories per day over the woman's basic requirements (Frisch, 1980)], reproduction may not occur again until the baby is weaned. Thus, two variables conspire to prevent too close spacing of birth in mammals: the hormonal changes produced by lactation, and the energetic drains imposed by lactation. Given this, it seems surprising that so many human cultures have taboos against intercourse during lactation. But to the extent that the taboo is obeyed, it can only increase the spacing of human births.

Figure 11.6
Breast-feeding tends to delay the resumption of ovulation, thus spacing births. In some human populations, as in this Boron woman, lactational amenorrhea may delay births by about four to five years.

What are the consequences of waiting until one offspring (or set of offspring) is finished before commencing with the next? First, the parent may have greater reproductive success. This is because the parent can adequately care for only one offspring (or set) at a time. Having too many mouths to feed might result in underfed offspring that would not be sufficiently healthy and vigorous to survive. This applies to having too large a litter, or to having litters or single births spaced too closely in time.

Summary

The number of opposite-sex mates that individual males and females in a population typically acquire defines the mating system. In monogamy, each male is typically mated to one female. In polygyny, however, males may have two or more mates, and in polyandry, females may have two or more mates. Diverse species have evolved these systems, apparently due to different ecological conditions favoring one system over the others.

Human mating systems differ geographically, but various criteria suggest that humans evolved practicing limited amounts of polygyny. Although most human marriages are monogamous, polygyny occurs in the long run because of the greater likelihood of men remarrying after divorce or death of the spouse. Thus, humans have many characteristics found in purely monogamous species, and some that are found in primarily polygynous species.

Within the context of the mating system, mate choice or nonrandom mating often occurs. The criteria used in mate selection are diverse, but they have in common the finding that the criteria are highly relevant to reproductive success. In cases where one sex invests more in offspring production and care than does the other sex, the sex that invests more is more selective about prospective mates. Although this is usually the female, in some telling cases it is the male.

Parental behavior, when it exists, consists of feeding, care, and defense of the offspring. Generally, females engage in more parental behavior than males, but males are highly parental when their contributions are essential to offspring survival and when the males can be confident of their relatedness to the offspring. Parental behavior is influenced by hormonal regimes brought on by reproduction or by offspring-related cues. Parental behavior can also involve activities that are contrary to the offspring's best interests. Infanticide, for instance, may occur in conditions in which the parents are unable to care for the offspring, due to inadequate resources, or when the offspring are defective. Parenting almost always will involve conflict with the offspring over the amount and timing of parental investment. The stress associated with weaning in mammals is a good example of parent–offspring conflict.

Successful reproduction calls for careful timing of reproduction. Certain mechanisms, most notably seasonal changes in daylength, act to time reproduction so that offspring arrive at times that are conducive to their survival. Other mechanisms help assure that successive offspring do not arrive too soon after the preceding offspring. Although these mechanisms seem, in the short-term, to work against reproductive success, when viewed in the context of the parents' lifetime reproductive success, they may be highly adaptive.

Recommended Readings

BATESON, P.P.G. (1983). *Mate choice*. Cambridge: Cambridge University Press.

BRONSON, F. H. (1989). *Mammalian reproductive biology*. Chicago: University of Chicago Press.

HALLIDAY, T. (1980). *Sexual strategy*. Chicago: University of Chicago Press.

WITTENBERGER, J. F. (1981). *Animal social behavior*. Boston: Duxbury.

Chapter 12

SOCIAL BEHAVIOR
AND ORGANIZATION

Social behavior encompasses anything that animals do in groups of two or more. Some social behavior topics, such as sexual behavior and parenting, have already been addressed. Others, such as communication and aggression, will be encountered in later chapters. However, this chapter will look at social behavior in a more general sense. We will begin by describing social structures and the processes involved in group living. Later, we will examine the ontogeny and evolution of social behavior, and the costs and benefits of group living.

Social Structures and Processes

Social groups have numerous characteristics (*social structures*) that differ from one group to the next. They may have different numbers of individuals, the age or sex distributions of the membership may vary, as may their spacing, division of labor, and so on. In short, social groups are structured in certain ways, and these structures need to be described and understood. Further, there are mechanisms (*social processes*) that produce or maintain social structures. Some primate groups have only a single adult male, for example, and this structure is maintained by the adult male's aggression toward young males when they begin to show signs of sexual maturity.

A complete understanding of sociality can only come about by understanding both social structures and processes (Mason, 1976). *Sociobiology* is the branch of science that seeks to understand the evolution of social structures and their adaptive significance (Wilson, 1975b; Barash, 1982; Trivers, 1985). Sociobiology shares many methods and goals with *behavioral ecology,* which may or may not deal with social issues. The study of social processes has largely been the province of social psychology and ethology, and, to some degree, sociology and anthropology. Although frequently at odds, these two groups have come to see how processes relate to structures and *vice versa,* and the study of sociality is quickly moving to a more integrative approach (e.g., Hinde, 1987; Mason, 1979).

GROUP STRUCTURE

Patterns of affiliation   Consider a troop of 40 to 60 baboons. Although the troop members tend to remain together in the same area for long periods of time, on close inspection there is a finer-grain organization to the troop. Subgroups exist. They may be defined spatially, i.e., some individuals are typically closer to one another than they are to others; or they can be defined behaviorally, i.e., they interact more often with one another than with others, or they interact in different ways. How are subgroups identified and how are their memberships determined?

Identification of subgroups is based upon which individuals spend time together and on the nature of their interactions. Squirrel monkeys, for example, have "huddle groups" composed of individuals who sit close to one another while resting, but who tend not to sit close to other individuals (Leger *et al.*, 1981). Subgroups are also defined according to the type or quality of their interactions. In talapoin monkeys, subgroups based on mutual grooming are easily identified. The monkeys commonly groomed the members of their subgroup but seldom groomed others (Wolfheim, 1977).

How do individuals become members of subgroups? Two routes seem to be most common. First, kinship often leads to social subgroups. The most basic relationship within mammals is that between the mother and her offspring (Altmann, 1980). In primates, the youngster is carried by, rides on, or walks near its mother, and their interactions are largely affiliative. Kin groups can extend beyond the mother–offspring relationship, of course. In chimpanzees, a mother forms the core of a subgroup consisting of herself and her offspring. The offspring, even though born singly and years apart, interact more often with each other than with nonrelatives (Goodall, 1965). Social subgroups consisting of siblings are quite common in primates, lions (Bertram, 1975a,b), and many others, including social insects (Michener, 1985).

Unrelated age peers provide another common source of subgroups. In baboons and macaques, individuals born at about the same time interact playfully at an early age, and these play groups may form the nexus of adult huddle and grooming groups.

The disruption of affiliative groups is frequently associated with behavioral and physiological responses that would help reestablish contact or permit coping with the changed conditions. Infant squirrel monkeys emit large numbers of high-pitched calls and show large increases in cortisol, a hormone released during stress, when their mothers are removed. Although the infants vocalize much less during subsequent short separations, their cortisol levels continue to elevate each time (Hennessy, 1986). Interestingly, the cortisol response, but not the vocalization response, occurs in infant squirrel monkeys whose mother is removed but who are "aunted" by other females of the group (Levine *et al.*, 1987).

Dominance Social groups are commonly organized along the lines of dominance (Bernstein, 1981). This was first described in flocks of hens and was called the "pecking order" because one hen (the most dominant or alpha hen) pecked all others, the second-ranked bird pecked all but the alpha, and so on down to the lowest-ranked hen.

Dominance is a complex phenomenon that cannot be readily equated with any single measurement, and therefore several methods of measurement have been used. First, dominance is commonly measured by the aggressive interactions among the individuals (Francis, 1988). Aggression and dominance are not the same, however, and animals may achieve high status without being highly aggressive (Francis, 1988). Another measure involves competition for scarce or desirable resources. For example, caged groups of squirrel monkeys occasionally were given orange juice in their regular water bottles. There was much pushing, shoving, and chasing, with some monkeys getting far more juice than others (Leger *et al.*, 1981). Other measures of dominance are based on numbers of copulations, or amount of grooming received (Seyfarth, 1977). Finally, studies of who looks at whom, that is, of "attention structure" indicate that some individuals are clearly the focus of attention, while others are barely noticed (Chance, 1967).

All these measures of dominance have an intuitive appeal, but often they do not lead to the same conclusions. An individual may be dominant by one measure, but less dominant by another. Thus, one must be careful to designate the measure used when discussing dominance as a social process (Rowell, 1974).

How does dominance originate in a group? Of course, if aggressive success is the measure of dominance, variables that are related to fighting may be most important to the ranking. Larger or more experienced animals may be the most dominant, as is true in bison (Rutberg, 1986). Similarly, variables that affect the tendency to fight, as the hormone testosterone does in some mammals (see Chapter 15), will also affect an individual's standing in the dominance hierarchy of a group. For instance, castrated male rats who had been dominant in their groups lost their dominance shortly after surgery. They regained it when they were given replacement doses of testosterone (Albert *et al.*, 1986). In other cases, however, there is clear evidence that loss of dominance results in reduced quantities of testosterone. When male tree shrews were placed in the home cage of another male, the resident quickly attacked the intruder and defeated him within a matter of minutes. The subordinate males almost immediately ceased production of gonadotropins and consequently their testosterone levels fell to nearly zero (von Holst, 1985).

Social variables may also play a part in determining social dominance. For instance, in primates such as baboons, offspring usually end up very close in dominance rank to their mothers. This appears to be due to mothers interceding when their offspring are in some sort of conflict. A mother cannot intercede as effectively, however, if the other offspring belongs to a higher-ranking mother. Thus, there tends to be a perpetuation of the dominance *status quo* in some monkey societies (Cheney, 1977; Altmann, 1980).

We should be careful to avoid extrapolating too freely from human to animal forms of dominance. Humans readily recognize transitive relationships among ourselves, such that if A is dominant to B, and B is dominant to C, we fully expect A to dominate C. Furthermore, C probably recognizes the transitive relationship, and will behave subordinately to A even if C has never had the opportunity to interact with A. C recognizes the dominance ranking and behaves accordingly. We do not know whether animal dominance works this way (Altmann, 1981). It appears that the dominance ranking in most nonhuman animals is achieved through a process of interactions among all possible pairs of individuals in the group. C would be subordinate to A only if C had been beaten by A. However, the possibility exists that once beaten a few times, an individual could learn to recognize characteristics in others that are highly predictive of the outcome of a conflict. So, if larger individuals are usually victorious over smaller ones, a small animal could defer to a larger one that it is meeting for the first time.

Reproductive benefits frequently are associated with high dominance rankings. In most studies, both high-ranking males and females have greater lifetime reproductive success than do lower-ranking individuals (e.g., Meikle *et al.*, 1984; Packer, 1979b; D. G. Smith, 1981). Sometimes this is due to higher-ranking males monopolizing access to fertile females (LeBoeuf & Peterson, 1969), or because high-ranking males copulate when females are most fertile (Hausfater, 1975). Similarly, higher-ranking females sometimes prevent other females from copulating, as is true of the cotton-top tamarin, a South American monkey (French *et al.*, 1984), or lower-ranking females may be so harassed that their ovulatory cycles are impaired (Dunbar & Dunbar, 1977).

Finally, recent studies indicate that dominance status may affect certain hormones that influence the activity of the immune system. For example, Sapolsky (1990) found that subordinate male baboons have more cortisol, a hormone that typically increases with stress, than do dominant males. [So do the subordinate male tree shrews discussed above (von Holst, 1985).] Cortisol reduces the effectiveness of the immune system, meaning that subordinate animals may be more prone to disease.

In summary, dominance relationships not only structure the pattern of interactions among group members, they may have implications for access to important resources, reproductive success, and even resistance to disease.

Castes   A specialized form of group structuring exists in some species, especially the social insects. A *caste* is a class within the larger social group that performs specific tasks for prolonged periods of time (E. O. Wilson, 1985a). These "specific tasks" include reproductive activities (queen bees and ants, for instance), foraging, colony defense, or brood care. The reproductives do little but reproduce; the other castes are usually sterile.

Caste differences originate not from genetic differences or even from differences in behavioral experience, but rather from early environmental variables. For instance, army ants have several castes, including several "worker" castes and "soldiers" (Topoff, 1972; Franks, 1989; Fig. 12-1). These castes are probably due to different feeding regimes imposed on newly hatched larvae. A similar mechanism exists in honeybees, in which queens develop from larvae fed "royal jelly," a substance high in sugar content, especially glucose. The workers develop from larvae fed a food that has less sugar overall, and less glucose relative to other sugars. Further, the larvae that will become queens are fed much more frequently than are the workers (Beetsma, 1985). The food seems to affect the secretion of juvenile hormone, which influences growth.

Highly social insects often have several castes, each of which is brought about by environmental factors such as nutrition, temperature, pheromones, or egg size, depending on the species. An individual's caste is determined by its developmental environment, not its genotype (E. O. Wilson, 1985b).

The highly social insects with their sterile castes provide an especially interesting problem for evolutionary theory. If evolution is largely brought about by differences in reproductive success (see Chapter 4), how could sterility evolve? The answer depends on the rather unusual genetic mechanisms of most of these species. Females have the usual diploid chromosomal arrangement; that is, they have two copies of each chromosome. Males, however, are haploid, having only one copy of each chromosome. (Males develop from eggs that are not fertilized by a sperm; females develop from fertilized eggs.) In *haplodiploid* species, the daughters are related

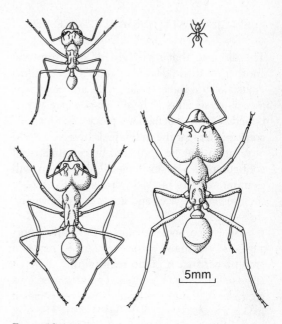

Figure 12.1
Four castes of the ant, Atta laevigata, *illustrate the extreme size differences that can result from variations in developmental conditions. The castes tend to perform specialized tasks within the colony.*

to each other by 0.75, rather than the 0.5 value found in diploid species. This is because all the daughters inherit precisely the same genes from their father (all his sperm are genetically identical), but they inherit varying combinations of the maternal chromosomes and genes. Thus, the daughters get the same 0.5 from the father, but average the same 0.25 from the mother, resulting in average relatedness among daughters of 0.75. (These figures assume that the mother mated with only one male.) The high degree of relatedness among sisters means that the cost of not reproducing directly is countered by the benefits of helping the mother (the queen) produce more sisters.

SPACING PATTERNS AND PROCESSES

The distance that social groups stay from one another, and the distances kept between individuals of the same social group are important aspects of sociality. These distances are maintained by various behavioral processes, and have consequences for the individuals involved. Food acquisition may be optimized by certain spatial configurations, for example. This section will examine some of the ways that animals arrange themselves in space, and attempt to show why they do so.

Spacing of social groups   Group-living organisms maintain some distance between groups, with each group maintaining more or less exclusive use of an area. The area used by a group in the course of its meanderings is called its *home range* (Waser & Wiley, 1979). The part of the home range that is used especially frequently is called the *core area*. The peripheral parts of adjacent groups' home areas may overlap, but core areas tend not to overlap. That part of the home range that is actively defended by the group is known as the *territory.*

How do animal groups space themselves? Two processes seem to be involved: aggression and avoidance (Waser & Wiley, 1979). A common finding among animal species is that the probability of the resident attacking an intruder goes up the closer the intruder is to the resident's core area. On the other hand, the likelihood of retreat by an intruder goes up the farther it is from its own core area (Dunford, 1970). This attack and retreat method of social spacing is direct but costly in terms of energy and time expended and risk of injury.

A more economic mechanism is to merely avoid contact with neighboring groups. This is especially efficient if the animals emit spacing signals that permit neighbors to assess their loca-

tions. Howling by packs of wolves (Harrington & Mech, 1979), "loud calling" by primates (Waser, 1975; Robinson, 1979b), and scent marking by beavers (Butler & Butler, 1979), to name a few, permit neighbors to judge the other's location and distance. When two groups find themselves close together they move off in opposite directions, thereby maintaining their distance without resorting to outright aggression.

Why do groups maintain spacing? Why do not they all converge into one very large group, rather than spending time and energy in spacing? It appears that spacing permits more efficient exploitation of resources, especially food. This is especially true if there is a base that must be maintained, such as a nest, shelter site, or food cache (Waser & Wiley, 1979). When such a base is maintained, it has been shown that the most efficient spacing mechanism is for each group to defend a circular area around its base because this reduces the traveling time and distance required to acquire food or other commodities (C. C. Smith, 1968).

Spacing of individuals within groups   Spacing of individuals within social groups adds another layer of complexity. Fish schools provide an excellent example of the mechanisms involved in maintaining certain distances between individuals. Partridge (1982) has studied the sensory systems involved in spacing in fish schools. He has found that pollock are attracted by the sight of other fish, but the pressure sensations detected by the lateral line organ repel them from one another (Fig. 12-2). The distance that these fish maintain in schools, then, is the balance point between vision-based attraction and lateral-line-based repulsion.

Other within-group spacing examples are far less sophisticated than those involved in fish schools. Nesting colonies of gulls, for instance,

Figure 12.2
The lateral line organ, the dark strip running from the tail to just above the gill, detects pressure in the water. When in proximity to other fish, activity in the lateral line causes the fish to move apart.

maintain regular spacing patterns between nests. The nests are spaced just far enough apart to be out of range of the pecking attempts of neighbors! In populations with less aggression (more tolerance of close neighbors), the birds crowd together more closely (Buckley & Buckley, 1977), probably because the greater population density makes them less vulnerable to predators (Butler & Trivelpiece, 1981).

Dispersal and immigration Social groups do not remain stable in composition for very long. Individuals may leave one group and enter another, sometimes several times during their lives.

A common mammalian pattern is for males to disperse farther than females and to do so at a younger age. This sex-biased dispersal often results in cohesive groups of related females that are accompanied by one or more adult males that immigrate into the group from elsewhere and thus are not related to the females. Although

there are exceptions to this pattern (Frame & Frame, 1976) it is nevertheless true of most mammals. In contrast, in most birds it is the females that are most likely to disperse (Greenwood, 1980).

What are the proximate causes of dispersal? That is, what initiates dispersal and what determines its distance? Let's first consider the initiation of dispersal. In some species, such as the patas monkey, young males are prodded away by the resident adult males(s). As the young male begins to become sexually mature the adult males become increasingly intolerant of his presence. He may be threatened, chased, and attacked. In response to this treatment he disperses (Hall, 1965).

Although hostility is a simple enough proximate cause for dispersal, it does not appear to be the cause in all cases. In Belding's ground squirrels, young males leave the area in which they were born when they grow to a certain size or when they have accumulated a certain amount of fat (Holekamp & Sherman, 1989). Apparently, androgens organize the nervous system in such a way that dispersal occurs when a certain body weight or fat content is achieved: Females injected with testosterone at birth dispersed at about the same time and to the same distance as males, even though normal females rarely disperse.

The second question about dispersal—how far?—also has several answers. In group-living species, such as most primates, dispersing individuals move until they reach another group: they go from one social "island" to another. They may be repulsed by the resident males, however, and move on again before finally settling. In less social species dispersal continues until suitable habitat is encountered. This appears to be the case in arctic lemmings. Contrary to folklore, lemmings do not commit suicide (although many do drown or die of other causes). In fact, if suitable habitat is found lemmings stop and take up residence (Archer, 1970).

Dispersal is risky business. Predators often kill dispersers at a higher rate than residents, probably because the dispersers are less familiar with hiding places, escape routes, and so on. Also, suitable habitat may never be found and the disperser, weakened from his travels, probably undernourished and harassed by residents, falls prey to disease and accident.

So much for "seeking one's fortune." Why does dispersal occur? What is gained? First, dispersal tends to reduce inbreeding depression (see Chapter 11) (Packer, 1979a, 1985). But inbreeding avoidance would not predict that males should disperse in mammals, or females in birds. After all, merely getting opposite-sex relatives apart is all that is required. It may be the case that one sex suffers a greater risk in dispersal and therefore have diminished fitness. Holekamp

and Sherman (1989) suggest, for example, that the need for a good burrow system in which to bear and raise pups is critical to female reproductive success in ground squirrels. If females dispersed, they might find it difficult to find or dig such burrows and their reproductive success would suffer. Males, in contrast, can use most any burrow for their refuge needs, and could disperse without fitness being adversely affected. Because both sexes would suffer from inbreeding, but only females are hurt by moving, males probably became the dispersing sex. Similar types of inequalities in the consequences of dispersal may lead to dispersal in one sex rather than the other.

PATTERNS OF SOCIAL EXCHANGE

Animals live in social groups because the benefits of social life tend to outweigh the costs (Alexander, 1974). Hunting, predator defense, and so on are oftentimes accomplished more efficiently by groups than by individuals (more on this topic later in the chapter). This statement, while generally true, has nothing to say about the interactions among the group members. In other words, although flocking is frequently advantageous for birds (Moriarty, 1976), we still must account for the particular interactions that occur among the flock members. These interactions vary in their outcome for individuals. Contests for food or mates are won and lost, for instance. We need to look at the outcomes of such interactions and their implications for social living.

In a simple sense, interactions can have four outcomes. These are shown in Table 12-1. Let us examine the cells in Table 12-1, clarify their meanings, and consider the evolutionary processes leading to them.

Selfishness   Selfishness occurs when one individual (the actor) does something that re-

Table 12-1

THE FOUR TYPES OF SOCIAL EXCHANGE CAN BE IDENTIFIED BY THE PATTERN OF GAINS
AND LOSSES EXPERIENCED BY THE ACTOR AND RECIPIENT

		RECIPIENT	
		Gains	Loses
ACTOR	Gains	Cooperation	Selfishness
	Loses	Altruism	Spite

sults in a gain to it that causes at least one individual (the recipient) to lose. Examples of selfishness abound in both animal and human behavior. The stag who drives a rival away from his mates, and the kitten who dislodges a sibling from a nipple are both acting selfishly.

Selfishness is a straightforward process. As long as the individual gains some degree of personal fitness (Chapter 4) and the act does not harm its relatives to an appreciable extent, the gene(s) involved in the behavior will tend to become more widespread in the population.

Cooperation Cooperation occurs when both participants gain from the interaction. Fish forming into schools because of reduced predation pressure, and human hunters teaming up to make a kill and share the prey are two of the many examples that could be listed. The benefits accruing to the participants are received simultaneously by each. This is important because this feature makes cooperation a simpler exchange than some forms of altruism, to be discussed next.

A fascinating example of cooperation involving two different species (honeyguides and humans) comes from Kenya. Honeyguides, a bird, are proficient at finding beehives which are sparsely distributed through the savannah. The birds eat bee larvae and the wax of the honeycomb when they can get them. The humans are not so proficient at finding the hives, but are adept at raiding them. Isack and Reyer (1989) report that the natives whistle and shout to attract a honeyguide, which then, Lassie-like, flies in the direction of a hive, returning to its slower accomplices as needed. When it reaches the vicinity of the hive, its calls change. The people then exploit the hive for its honey content, leaving the rest for the honeyguide.

Altruism Altruism, the loss of fitness in the actor accompanied by fitness gains in a recipient, has posed difficult problems for evolutionary biologists. At first glance this sort of exchange would seem doomed. After all, by losing fitness, any genes contributing to such behavior would decline in frequency in the population. Yet, altruism is a common occurrence. Individuals of prey species may signal the presence of a predator to others nearby, thus increasing their own risk of being killed (Sherman, 1977, 1980).

People donate to charitable organizations, shovel snow from their neighbors' sidewalks, and even risk their lives in attempts to rescue someone in danger of drowning.

There are three hypothesized mechanisms for the evolution of altruism (Bertram, 1983). The first, *reciprocal altruism*, asserts that altruism is maintained through a balancing of roles and therefore, costs and benefits. Although a given instance of behavior may be altruistic, if we followed the participants long enough we would find that this interaction was only one in a long series of similar ones, but with roles reversed. In other words, the altruist in one interaction may be the beneficiary in the next.

My favorite example of reciprocal altruism is a rather ghoulish one: the exchange of blood by vampire bats (Wilkinson, 1984). Vampire bats roost in trees in small groups during the day and head out at sundown in search of prey—usually cattle—that they bite to lap up oozing blood. Bats who fail to obtain blood on a given night often receive a regurgitated donation from one who did. The donation is clearly a loss to the donor and a gain to the receiver, but on another day the roles may be reversed.

Reciprocal altruism is like cooperation, except that the benefits are not simultaneous. Sometimes a long wait occurs before the "favor" is returned and because of the delays, problems may surface. Participants must recognize one another as individuals, but also keep track of their exchanges and identify nonreciprocators ("cheaters") for exclusion from future donations. These conditions appear to be met in vampire bats and in others (e.g., Packer, 1977; Lombardo, 1985).

The second hypothesis concerning altruism is compulsion or coercion; that is, the actor makes a sacrifice because it is "forced" to do so, either directly or indirectly. For example, many species of birds and mammals practice some form of "cooperative breeding" in which one or more nonreproductive "helpers" assist the parents in bringing food to the young, defending them, and so forth (Emlen, 1984). To the extent that helpers forego reproduction, their actions are altruistic. However, cooperative breeding typically occurs when the habitat has all the breeding territories filled. Helpers often "inherit" the territory when the breeding adult(s) die (Woolfendon & Fitzpatrick, 1978). Helpers assist as long as they reside on the breeders' territory, and they must reside there if they are ever to acquire a territory and reproduce directly.

Compulsion may be at the root of the social organization of highly social insects, such as bees, mentioned earlier. Queen bees emit a chemical signal that suppresses ovarian activity in workers; consequently, egg-laying by workers is uncommon (Velthuis, 1985). The sterility imposed on the workers makes their participation in brood care and colony defense even more advantageous to them.

The third altruism hypothesis is kin selection. A behavior that reduces an individual's personal fitness may nevertheless increase the individual's inclusive fitness (see Chapter 4 for a more detailed treatment of kin selection). That is, relatives (parents, siblings, cousins) share genes that are identical by descent (Fig. 12-3). When a relative reproduces, their common genes are perpetuated. Anything the altruist does that promotes reproductive success of its kin will be favored, provided the cost to the altruist (in terms of loss of its own reproductive success) is lower than its gain from assisting kin. Because kin differ in fractions of genes held in common, an altruistic act bestowed on a full sibling will have a greater benefit to the altruist than would the same act bestowed upon a niece or nephew. In fact, when there is a choice, altruism is directed toward close relatives. For instance, Emlen and Demong (1984) found that

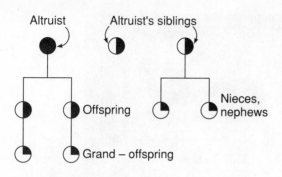

Figure 12.3
Illustration of the genetic relatedness among individuals. The fraction of each circle that is blackened is proportional to the genetic similarity between that individual and the altruist. In general, as genetic relatedness declines, so does helping behavior.

white-fronted bee-eaters, an East African bird, frequently assist relatives in raising offspring, especially in years when food abundance is low. Bee-eaters live in colonies containing many relatives, but when aid is provided it goes to the most closely related individual in the colony who can use the aid.

After its presentation by W. D. Hamilton in 1964, kin selection theory has undergone a number of modifications and embellishments too numerous and detailed to cover here (excellent reviews of these developments can be found in Vehrencamp, 1979, and in Grafen, 1984). However, it is fair to say that Hamilton's original idea still holds true and that it is one of the most important and useful concepts in the study of the evolution of behavior. It has cleared up many difficulties that apparently could not be explained by pure self interest. In essence, it provides a "gene's eye view" of social exchange.

Spite   The last entry in Table 12-1 is spite, a situation in which both the actor and recipient lose. As you might expect, spite is an evolutionary enigma and genes that contribute to it should not increase in frequency. There appear to be no firmly established cases of spiteful behavior (Barash, 1982), although from time to time individuals do things that hurt both themselves and others. Such cases are easily and justifiably attributed to mistakes. The world, as you know, is not perfectly predictable, and what may appear to be a good course of action may turn out to be a disaster. To convincingly demonstrate the existence of spite as an evolved adaptation, one would need to show that it occurs regularly. That sort of demonstration has not yet been made, however.

In summary, the interactions between any two organisms can result in a variety of outcomes for the participants. Further, if the same participants interact repeatedly and can recognize one another individually, the sum of their interaction outcomes over a prolonged period may affect their current behavior. Social interaction has certain game-like characteristics, although the social "game" is often played with life-and-death stakes (Maynard Smith, 1983). The "prisoner's dilemma" game provides a good analogy to summing up social interactions. Both players get a modest gain by cooperating on the same trial. However, if one player "defects," i.e., chooses to be selfish, when the other cooperates, the defector gains a great deal at the expense of the other player. The dilemma is that if both players defect, they both lose a great deal. Over the course of many interactions the best strategy is "tit for tat," that is, start with cooperation, then do whatever the opponent did on the previous trial (Axelrod & Hamilton, 1981). In animal social conditions that approximate the benefits and costs of prisoner's dilemma, the tit-for-tat strategy is employed (Lombardo, 1985). When "played" over a prolonged period, especially with lengthy delays between interactions, with different "opponents" and real gains and losses (not just points tallied on a score sheet), the

KONRAD LORENZ

"One of the reasons greylag geese are such a glorious object for sociological studies is that their filial and social responses can be imprinted to human beings without affecting in any way their choice of object in sexual *behavior." [Lorenz, K. Z. (1981). The Foundations of Ethology. New York: Simon and Schuster (p. 280).]*

stage is set for the evolution of whatever genes lead to the construction of a phenotype that is adept at perceiving, processing, and storing the relevant information. The social "game" may be a powerful selective condition leading to the evolution of advanced cognitive skills (Cheney et al., 1986).

RECOGNITION PROCESSES

Social behavior often requires that a distinction be made between appropriate and inappropriate "partners" in the social interaction. In other words, there is usually some sort of "in-group" and "out-group," or at least some individuals are treated differently from others. The details here vary, of course, from species to species. Ants treat their nest-mates differently from conspecifics of another nest, whom they readily attack (Carlin & Hölldobler, 1983). In other

cases, the distinction is between conspecific and heterospecific, between relatives and nonrelatives, or between individuals A and B. All these cases require recognition and discrimination processes. The recognition may be very broad—conspecific vs. heterospecific—or very narrow—my mother vs. your mother—but in each case a distinction is being made. Let us look at some processes involved in recognition.

Recognition of particular individuals may be due to specific forms of early experience. One well-studied example is called *imprinting*. Imprinting is a specialized form of learning that occurs during a sensitive period, usually early in life. Further, unlike other forms of learning, imprinting is highly persistent and is difficult to modify after it has occurred (Immelmann, 1975). In ducks, geese, sheep and other animals that are mobile and follow the mother shortly after birth, the youngsters must recognize their own mother and distinguish her from others. This is especially beneficial if the offspring intermingle because mothers generally refuse to care for others' offspring.

In ducklings, imprinting on the mother occurs within 48 hours after hatching. Ducklings readily follow large, moving objects and quickly learn their distinguishing features. Ducklings in the lab can be made to imprint on a wide variety of objects including duck models (of their own or another species, male or female), or such unlikely things as shoeboxes or rubber balls (Johnston & Gottlieb, 1981a) provided that the object emits the maternal assembly call, a vocalization given by the hen when she is moving and the ducklings need to follow (Miller & Gottlieb, 1978). In fact, the maternal assembly

call is such a potent stimulus that a duckling that imprinted on a silent object (such as a stuffed mallard) will later abandon its usual preference for that object and switch to something else (such as a stuffed redheaded duck) that emits the assembly call (Johnston & Gottlieb, 1981b).

Imprinting is studied by first hatching duck eggs in a dark incubator, and then exposing the ducklings to an imprinting object sometime later. This is accomplished by placing a duckling in a lighted circular arena (Fig. 12-4) containing a moving duck decoy (or other imprinting object) for about an hour and then being returned to the incubator. A day or two later the duckling is placed back in the arena and the strength of its following response is measured, usually by noting how close it stays to the object. By varying

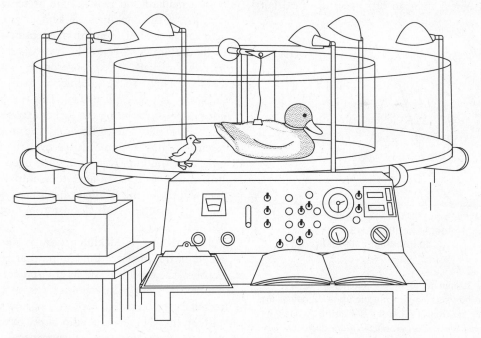

Figure 12.4
The usual apparatus for studying imprinting consists of a round runway. The duck decoy is mounted on a motor-driven rod at the center of the arena.

the amount of time between hatching and first exposure, it has been found that a sensitive period occurs about 5 to 48 hours posthatching. That is, exposure to an appropriate object must occur within this time for a strong following response to occur later (Fig. 12-5). (Numerous studies have investigated ways of extending the sensitive period, with some success. Nevertheless, even "pulling out all the stops" cannot extend the sensitive period beyond a few days of age, still a remarkably short time in which learning must occur.)

Hundreds of experiments have been conducted on imprinting over the past several decades, so the full sweep of this topic cannot be covered here. However, several intriguing findings have emerged. First, although an imprinting object that emits the assembly call is a more potent object than an otherwise identical but silent object, the auditory feature is far more important in some species than in others. Understandably, this occurs in species, such as the wood duck, that nest in dark tree holes (Gottlieb, 1974). These ducklings have only limited abilities to see their mother before leaving the nest, but have ample opportunity to hear her.

A second interesting finding on imprinting concerns the effect of social interactions with siblings on the imprinting process. When ducklings are kept in social isolation after their initial period of exposure to an imprinting object, they fail to discriminate between the original object and another one when given a simultaneous choice. For example, ducklings exposed to a stuffed mallard who are then kept isolated from other ducklings for 24–48 hours will also follow a stuffed redhead duck (a different species) when both a mallard and redhead are presented. In contrast, if the ducklings are kept in groups of eight or more after their initial exposure to the mallard, they will follow only the mallard (Lickliter & Gottlieb, 1985; Johnston & Gottlieb, 1985b). Thus, social interaction with other ducklings is necessary to maintain the preference established during the earlier exposure period. As stated above, however, the maternal assembly call takes precedence over the visual aspects of the imprinting stimulus. Even ducklings raised in isolation after their initial exposure will prefer the familiar object later on if it emits the assembly call (Johnston & Gottlieb, 1985a).

Imprinting in ducklings is an excellent example of the intricate interaction that goes on between the organism and its environment during development. The following response is directed to an object that the duckling encounters early in life. There are certain biases that exist, but even these are affected by nonspecific forms of experience. As stated in Chapter 7, ducklings must hear themselves or other ducklings vocaliz-

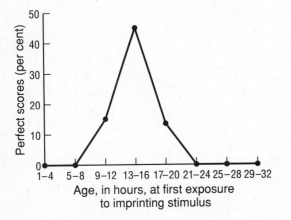

Figure 12.5

After a 20-minute exposure in the imprinting apparatus at posthatching ages ranging up to 32 hours, the following behavior of ducklings is measured a day later. This graph shows the percentage of ducklings that had perfect following scores as a function of their age at first exposure. The sensitive period is between 8 and 24 hours.

ing before they will follow the maternal assembly call. Further, nonspecific forms of experience in the form of social interaction with groups of other ducklings is necessary for maintenance of the preference for (or recall of) the imprinting object. Of course, specific experience with the details of the maternal assembly call emitted by the imprinting object are necessary to establish a discrimination between that particular individual and others that may be emitting the same sort of call. The rapid maturation of these abilities suggests that important changes are occurring in the ducklings' nervous systems. However, very little is known about the neural changes that accompany imprinting (Bischof, 1983).

Long-lasting individual recognition due to a period of early exposure is not limited to offspring learning to recognize the mother. Mothers learn to recognize their offspring, and siblings learn to recognize one another. For example, female Belding's ground squirrels readily retrieve pups raised in their burrows ("familiar" pups) but are slower to retrieve pups from elsewhere ("unfamiliar" pups), even if the unfamiliar pups are their own offspring (some pups were removed from their mothers at birth and exchanged with other pups of the same age) (Holmes, 1984a). In addition, pups raised together in the same litter affiliate more with one another than they do with unfamiliar ground squirrels of the same age even if those unfamiliar squirrels are their biological siblings (again, some offspring were switched at birth) (Holmes & Sherman, 1983). Sibling recognition has also been demonstrated in tadpoles. For example, tadpoles discriminate full-siblings from half-siblings (provided the half-siblings had the same mother) and school preferentially with full siblings (Waldman, 1981). In fact, tadpoles prefer unfamiliar siblings (raised apart) over familiar nonsiblings (Waldman, 1986), indicating a bias for relatedness over familiarity (the opposite pattern is found in ground squirrels). The tadpoles appear to make these discriminations based on odor cues.

Perhaps the most thoroughly studied cases of parental recognition of offspring occur in the swallows. Some swallows nest in colonies and have highly synchronized breeding. Others nest individually or in loose associations, and are not synchronized. Beecher and his colleagues (reviewed by Beecher, 1990) have investigated parent–offspring recognition in these species. They have found that the highly colonial species (bank and cliff swallows) are adept at recognizing their offspring (by their voices) and respond differently to their own and others' offspring. This is particularly pronounced at about the time that the chicks become able to fly because they are far more likely then to get into the wrong nest. Noncolonial species (barn and rough-winged swallows) are not nearly as good at recognizing their own young, although they can do so under certain circumstances. They seem to have little hesitation about behaving parentally toward any chick they find in their nest, even if it is the wrong age. These differences in recognition ability reflect the different selection conditions experienced by colonial and noncolonial swallows: Colonial species face a great deal of potential mixing of offspring and parents who can discriminate their offspring from others and who direct their caregiving activities to only their offspring will have greater reproductive success than those who fail to make such discriminations. Noncolonial species, in contrast, have rarely been faced with such problems, so little or no selective advantage accrues to parents who make such discriminations. Not surprisingly, the vocal cues of the chicks, which parents use in discriminating among offspring, are more individually variable in the colonial species than in the noncolonial species (Beecher, 1982).

Ontogeny of Social Behavior

As expected, there is great diversity in how social behavioral skills are acquired. In some cases the requisite skills may develop with nothing more than nonspecific experience, but in others a long period of individual experience is required for normal social behavior to occur. We will focus on the experience-required species by describing the results of many years of research on the ontogeny of social skills in a monkey, the rhesus macaque.

INFLUENCE OF THE MOTHER

Rhesus monkeys are highly social creatures. When a baby is born, the mother carries it around on her belly, allowing the infant to nurse at its discretion. Although at first the infant is nonresponsive to anything but the mother—and even then all it does is cling to her and suckle— as it matures it begins attending to the actions of others. Later still, the young monkey begins moving away from the mother a short distance to explore its surroundings, including other infants. However, if anything unusual or threatening happens, the baby bolts back to its mother and clings to her. The clinging seems to soothe the infant, and it later moves off again to explore. As it gets older, the periods away from the mother get longer and it moves farther from her. However, she remains a "security blanket" and the youngster seeks her out in times of stress. As the young monkey spends less time with the mother it begins spending more time with its peers. Play becomes more common, and incipient aggression and sexual behavior begin to appear. Gradually, over a period of two to four years, the young monkey becomes independent of the mother and becomes a normal adult (Harlow & Harlow, 1965).

What kinds of experience are required for the rhesus monkey to develop into a normal, functioning adult? These questions can be addressed by systematically altering various aspects of the young monkey's environment.

First, Harlow's group found that depriving young monkeys of their mothers led to serious and long-lasting impairments of the animal's later social behavior. For example, Harlow removed newborn monkeys from their mothers at birth and reared the infants in isolation in wire cages for 6 or 12 months. Although human keepers cared for the animals' basic nonsocial needs such as feeding, warmth, and hygiene, the monkeys developed severely impaired social skills. When exposed to another infant the motherless infants usually cowered in a corner, rocking back and forth. They retreated when approached and seemed to find physical contact terribly aversive (reviewed by Mineka & Suomi, 1978).

Depriving a baby monkey of its mother is a very crude experiment. What is it about a mother that leads to normal social development? Could it be the feeding, the soft warmth of her body, the movement of being carried about, or even the mild punishments doled out as the infant transgresses? One way to find out is to construct artificial mothers that have some of these characteristics but not others. In the first experiments of this sort Harlow raised infant rhesus with a choice of mother surrogates: a wire cylinder covered with terry cloth and topped with a wooden head, or a bare wire cylinder and a head (Fig. 12-6). Harlow found that the soft cloth was preferred by the infants. This was true even if the wire surrogate had a milk-dispensing bottle and the cloth surrogate did not. In this case, infants went to the wire mother long enough to drink the milk, but then returned to the cloth mother to cling. Although neither surrogate condition produced fully normal monkeys, those reared with the cloth surrogate developed further along the normal route (Harlow & Zimmerman, 1959).

Clinging to something soft seems to be essential to normal development, but surely that is not all that a mother provides. Mason and Berkson (1975) extended this finding to include movement of the surrogate. They provided newborn rhesus monkeys with a bleach bottle covered with shaggy carpet. Some of these surrogates were moved by means of an overhead motor and pulley system; the others had an identical but stationary surrogate. The results were dramatic: The movement led to more normal development. The infants did not withdraw from human caretakers, and interacted with other infants in a way much more similar to that of mother-reared infants.

Figure 12.6
Mother surrogates of two types have been used to study emotional attachment in young rhesus monkeys. The monkey is clinging to the cloth-covered surrogate; the wire surrogate was seldom visited.

INFLUENCE OF PEERS

Casual observation of a group of rhesus monkeys reveals that the mother is only one individual of importance to the young monkey (although she is probably the single most important individual). Young monkeys spend increasingly greater amounts of time interacting with peers as they get older. What influence does peer interaction have on social development?

This question has been addressed through several types of experimentation. In one, the infant is reared by the mother without exposure to other infants. Later, the peer-deprived infants are placed with same-age monkeys to ascertain the adequacy of their social skills. In another approach, infants are taken from their mothers at birth and reared in groups of two or four same-age infants. Finally, infants are left with their mothers, but are allowed specific amounts of interaction time each day with peers.

Peer-deprived infants and peer-only infants

did not develop social skills on the same schedule as infants who had both a mother and peers, and, in general, the social competence of peer-deprived and peer-only infants was lower than that of nondeprived monkeys (Harlow & Harlow, 1965). The peer-deprived infants, however, seemed more abnormal than peer-only infants. The latter spent more time clinging to one another than did mother-raised monkeys, and the excessive clinging prevented normal amounts of play and other activities. However, the peer-only monkeys developed adequate social skills

HARRY HARLOW

"It seems possible—even likely—that the infant–mother affectional system is dispensable, whereas the infant–infant system is the sine qua non *for later adjustment in all spheres of monkey life. [Harlow, H. F., & Harlow, M. K. (1962). Social deprivation in monkeys.* Scientific American *207(5), 136–146.]*

more vigorous and prolonged the ensuing play (reviewed by Panksepp *et al.*, 1984). One need only watch a litter of kittens, puppies, or rats for a short time to observe the importance of play. Their time is almost exclusively spent eating, sleeping, and playing.

Social play seems to provide practice in performing the sorts of behavior that will be used as adults. These include aggression, communication, copulation, predation, defense, and others. The practice, however, is performed in a context in which incorrect performance has few adverse effects. Play-deprived individuals are not socially skilled enough to interact adequately with others and therefore may have difficulty incorporating themselves into a social group.

(affiliative, aggressive, and sexual), although they were substantially older than normal before attaining these capacities.

What do peers provide one another that facilitates social development that mothers don't provide? In a word: play. Social play seems to be exceedingly important in the development of many mammals, and play deprivation appears to be as aversive as food or water deprivation. In fact, several mammalian species respond to play deprivation in the same way that they respond to other forms of deprivation. That is, they will perform responses that produce the opportunity to play, they play more vigorously following play deprivation, and the longer the deprivation the

SOCIAL LEARNING AND CULTURE

Ontogeny does not end early in life. All aspects of individual development fall within the domain of ontogeny, and one of the most fascinating subjects in social ontogeny is the learning of social skills from others and the perpetuation of those skills from generation to generation (Galef, 1976).

In a sense we have been dealing with social learning all along. After all, the mechanism whereby interactions with peers brings about normal social behavior is presumably some sort of learning. Let us expand that issue now, however, and describe some examples of social learning that occur later in life that may be equivalent to the sorts of phenomena that anthropologists call "culture."

First, we need to define the limits of what is meant by social learning and culture (Galef, 1976). One important criterion is that the behavior be acquired by means of direct interaction between two individuals, or at least by the observation of one individual by another. Second, the influence should be long-lasting, not temporary. That one hen begins pecking at seed when it observes another doing so would not qualify. However, if hen B began consuming some new type of food as a result of having seen hen A eating it, and B maintained this new behavior even in the absence of A, the behavior would qualify as social learning. Third, the social experience must lead to similarity in behavior of the participants. A dominance interaction between two monkeys will likely result in the development of behavioral differences, not similarities, and would not qualify as an example of culture.

Examples of socially acquired behavior patterns are numerous (Galef, 1976). A few examples will be presented here to illustrate the topic; others will occur in later chapters on communication and feeding.

One of my favorite examples of social learning concerns food preparation in Japanese macaques. A troop of these monkeys was being studied on a small Japanese island and to make observation easier, the researchers began luring the monkeys onto the beach with mounds of sweet potatoes. The monkeys ate them but had to spend much time carefully brushing off the sand that invariably stuck to the potatoes. A young female, Imo, carried some potatoes to a nearby stream where she quickly cleaned them of sand. Washing (first in the stream, later in ocean water) quickly spread through the troop. At first, only Imo's peers imitated her, but gradually their mothers began, too. The old males of the troop were the last to begin the practice (Kawamura, 1959)! Later, when the researchers began providing wheat for the monkeys, Imo again discovered an easier way of separating wheat from sand: She simply dropped a handful of the wheat/sand mixture into the water and quickly skimmed off the floating grain. This practice again spread through the population in

Japanese macaques have devised some clever ways of preparing their food, cleaning it of sand, and even adding salt. These techniques have spread through observation and imitation.

the same order as the potato-washing (Kawai, 1965).

Although cultural or "precultural" behaviors may be most common in mammals, particularly primates, they are found elsewhere, too. French grunts, a coral reef fish, school around coral heads by day, then swim in schools to their feeding sites at dusk and return at dawn. Helfman and Schultz (1984) transplanted some grunts from one site to another and noticed that the transplanted fish swam with the residents along their traditional routes. The transplants quickly learned the route and were able to swim back without the residents. Other transplants

E. O. WILSON

"The principal goal of a general theory of sociobiology should be an ability to predict features of social organization from a knowledge of . . . population parameters combined with information on the behavioral constraints imposed by the genetic constitution of the species." [Wilson, E. O. (1975). Sociobiology: The New Synthesis. *Cambridge, MA: Belkap Press (p. 5).]*

who were not allowed to associate with residents swam off along their own routes.

Another nonmammalian example of cultural transmission occurs in common pigeons. Lefebvre (1986) trained a few pigeons to perform a novel food-acquisition behavior, pecking through a piece of paper covering a grain-filled box. These pigeons were then released into an area in Montreal where these covered boxes were placed. Although no bird discovered on its own how to get to the grain, when the trained birds were seen piercing the paper, others quickly acquired the skill as well. This study is reminiscent of a naturally occurring situation that developed in England in the 1940s: birds began puncturing the covers of milk bottles placed on porches and drinking some of the contents. This behavior, too, spread far and wide, requiring a change in the way milk bottles were capped (Fisher & Hinde, 1949)!

These examples illustrate what is meant by social learning. Animals apparently learn by observing one another (although this part is poorly understood), matching that behavior, and persisting with it after the observation period ends (assuming that the proximate consequences for the individual are positive). The new behaviors become part of the repertoire of animals in the population.

Ecology and Evolution of Sociality

At the beginning of this chapter we covered the concept of social structures, that is, the attributes of social groups. The basic premise of sociobiology and behavioral ecology is that some social structures are more adaptive than others. For example, larger groups may be more advantageous than smaller groups, perhaps because of predator avoidance. We are not claiming that the group is the unit of selection, rather, that the individuals that live in the larger groups leave more offspring than do individuals that live in smaller groups. Ideally, we would like to explore further and discover the individual characteristics that permit them to participate in the more favorable social structures. For example, if large, dense groups were more adaptive than smaller, less dense groups, then those individuals who were behaviorally more tolerant of the close proximity of others would be at an advantage. Adaptive *social* structures can only arise from the interaction of *individuals* with appropriate behavioral attributes. For example, one of the benefits of social life in bees is the ability to regulate temperature. Bees maintain their hive temperature at about 35°C even on the coldest winter nights and the hottest summer days (Heinrich, 1985). They accomplish this amazing feat because of each individual bee doing its best to regulate its own temperature. The bees at the outside of the group press inward as the temperature falls, thereby filling in the heat-robbing air spaces. As the temperature warms, they move apart, allowing more air to flow between them. Finally, in hot conditions, the bees readily accept water droplets from returning workers, which they use in evaporative cooling. The behavioral repertoires of individuals result in a group response that is adaptive to the individuals. The challenge to those who are interested in adaptive social structure is to understand the integration that exists between individual behavior and social organization within the ecological circumstances in which the group exists.

ECOLOGY AND SOCIAL STRUCTURE

Variations in social structure Chimpanzee social groups are described as "fluid." With the exception of mothers and their dependent offspring, who are always together, chimps come and go in groups that vary in number and composition. Sometimes the groups are large, as, for example, when a ripe fig tree is found, but at other times chimps are alone or in groups of two or three (Goodall, 1986).

Gorilla society is much less fluid. Living in groups of about 10 members, gorilla groups are highly stable, modified only intermittently by occasional births, deaths, or a rare immigration or emigration (Schaller, 1963).

Another great ape, the orangutan of southeast Asia, is almost nonsocial. Females live alone or accompanied by their dependent offspring. Except for occasional visits by an adult male for copulation (when the female is receptive), orangutans are essentially "loners" (MacKinnon, 1974).

Three great ape species, three very different social structures. If we expanded our list of species to include other primates, other mammals, other vertebrates and invertebrates, we would quickly discover incredible diversity in social group structuring.

Diversity of social structure also occurs intraspecifically. Some variation is associated with geography, that is, different populations of a species living in different areas may adopt different social structures. For example, spotted hyenas on the Serengeti, where prey animals are sparse, live in small groups and subsist by scavenging corpses of migratory species. Hyenas there are nomadic, following the migratory herds. In contrast, hyenas of the Ngorongoro crater live in large, cohesive groups; they defend a territory all year, and subsist by killing large prey, which they hunt cooperatively (Kruuk, 1972b).

Variation in social structure may also be associated with seasonal changes or changes in the supply of some important resource. For example, coyotes in Wyoming live individually or in pairs during the spring and summer months when they catch and eat small rodents. In the winter, the coyotes form packs and consume the corpses of large animals such as elk (Bekoff & Wells, 1980).

Intraspecific variation in social structure may occur from year to year with variation in some important ecological condition. Acorn woodpeckers drill holes in tree trunks in which they store acorns. In years following heavy acorn production, the woodpeckers breed communally, with several pairs laying their eggs in a

JANE GOODALL

"[Chimpanzees] move in small temporary groups, which may consist of any combination of age/sex classes. Lone males and, occasionally, lone females are also encountered. The only group that is stable over a period of months is a mother with her infant and older offspring." [Goodall, J. (1965). Chimpanzees of the Gombe Stream Reserve. In I. DeVore (Ed.) Primate Behavior: Field Studies of Monkeys and Apes (pp. 425–473). New York: Holt, Rinehart and Winston (p. 430).]

collective nest, and all adults contributing to the care of all the offspring. In years following poor acorn harvests, however, the woodpeckers breed as separate monogamous pairs (Stacey & Bock, 1978).

Mechanisms of intraspecific variation in social structure   The preceding examples are just a few of the hundreds of cases of intraspecific variability in social structure that have been documented. Lott (1984) provides an excellent account of them and emphasizes that we have a poor understanding of the mechanisms that operate in producing a change in social structure. Typically we have merely documented the variations and in some cases have shown how the variants are adaptive given differences in some selective condition. But how are these social variants produced? There are numerous mechanisms at work; a few examples should illustrate the idea.

One mechanism involves the habitat. For example, a species of damselfish that breeds on coral heads may be either monogamous, polygynous, or promiscuous (see Chapter 11). The system varies because the size of the resource (coral head) varies. Small coral heads can support only a single male and female, who thus are monogamous. Large coral heads can support several males and females, who mate promiscuously. Other coral heads are intermediate in size and support one male and a few females. Polygyny is practiced. Thus, variability in an ecological variable leads to social variation (Fricke, 1980).

Variations in amount of defense may affect the spacing of organisms and thus their social system. Many birds scale their defense of an area in proportion to the amount of time they spend in that area (Wiley & Wiley, 1980). If the food supply is good, birds don't have to travel far; if it is poor they will move more widely. However, as they move around more their proclivity to defend space declines. Thus, territorial defense is the norm in good food-supply times and nondefense is the norm in poor food-supply times.

Why does variation in social structure exist? To find out, we need to view social group structures as adaptations to natural selection conditions. In other words, associating with others may help the individuals involved to survive and reproduce. Let us look at some of the ways that ecological conditions may favor sociality. We will begin by listing some of the individual benefits of social living, and then turn to the costs involved.

Benefits and costs of sociality Perhaps the most obvious benefit of living in groups is reduced mortality due to predators. Groups are usually more adept at detecting an approaching predator; groups may counterattack the predator more effectively than individuals can, and escape tactics may work more effectively when they involve many individuals rather than just one. More detailed treatment of these and other social antipredator adaptations can be found in Chapter 14.

Group living may make food acquisition more efficient. A pack of wolves can kill larger prey than can wolves hunting alone or as pairs (Mech, 1966), yielding more meat per animal. Groups may facilitate food-finding by acting as information centers. For example, cliff swallows return to their nesting colonies to feed their young. Because these birds feed only on aerial insects which usually appear in locally dense swarms that last only a few minutes, there is a premium on knowing the location of a swarm. Birds at the colony that were not very successful often follow others that were successful when they return to forage. These roles are frequently reversed, so all benefit from the communal knowledge of constantly changing food locations (Brown, 1986).

Another benefit of sociality comes about through "environmental control." We already saw that honeybees keep their hives warm in winter and cool in summer by the joint actions of their thousands of residents (Morse, 1972). Similarly, clusters of roosting bats maintain a warmer microclimate than when they roost separately, thereby conserving precious energy (Trune & Slobodchikoff, 1976). Army ants, too, control colony temperature within narrow limits by the combined actions of their thousands of members (Franks, 1989).

The list of ways in which group living can benefit the individuals involved is quite long. Not all benefits apply in all cases, however. The challenge to sociobiology is to determine which benefits apply in particular cases and to measure their magnitude. Finally, the benefits need not apply equally to all group members: The subordinate antelope who is kept on the periphery of the herd may be less vulnerable to predators than if

In some species, such as the elephant seal, sociality can have its drawbacks. In this photo, a pup is pinned beneath a bull.

Disease and parasite transmission tend to increase whenever organisms cluster together. Hoogland (1979) found that prairie dog burrows in dense colonies harbored more fleas than did burrows in less dense towns. Fleas transmit diseases that may be fatal to prairie dogs. Similarly, ectoparasites are more numerous in larger bank swallow colonies than in smaller ones (Hoogland & Sherman, 1976).

Larger groups may also be more conspicuous to predators than smaller groups. Although this effect may be offset by the greater ability of large groups to detect predators, it still must be regarded as a cost.

Sociality may even have costs in reproductive success. For example, northern elephant seals breed on small islands along the Pacific coast of North America. Although they are less subject to predation on islands, the crowding on the breeding beaches often leads to high pup mortality caused by the elephant seals themselves. Pups may become separated from their mothers in the herd. Because adult females often repulse others' pups who attempt to nurse, lost pups often die of starvation and injury inflicted by other elephant seals (LeBoeuf & Briggs, 1977). Similarly, the gigantic bulls frequently charge through groups of females and pups to attack rival males. Pups are sometimes run over by the lumbering giants who seem not to notice the frantic squeals of pups pinned beneath them (LeBoeuf & Peterson, 1969).

Finally, the likelihood of misdirected parental care increases when animals live in close proximity. Bank swallows nest in burrows dug into the exposed banks of rivers and streams. These colonies may consist of hundreds of burrows located only a few feet apart. Although bank swallows, like most birds, mate monogamously, mated males still attempt to force copulations with other females. To the extent that

he lived alone, but lions are still more likely to attack him than the more dominant animals in the center of the herd. Differential costs and benefits to the social participants create conflicts of interest that may lead to selfishness (see "Patterns of social exchange," above).

Along with the benefits of group living come a variety of costs. These vary in severity from case to case, but they should always be considered when weighing the pros and cons of group living (Alexander, 1974).

this behavior succeeds, males may end up feeding and caring for other males' offspring (Beecher & Beecher, 1979). Although this would seem not to be a problem for females, in fact they, too, pay a price. Females about to lay eggs are the target of forced copulations by males. Since these attempts usually occur while a female is flying, her foraging efficiency may be greatly reduced. Finally, the tightly packed nests of cliff swallow colonies make it easier for nest parasitism to occur; that is, females may occasionally lay an egg in another's nest (sometimes throwing out one of the resident's eggs first). The resident obviously loses in such cases (Brown, 1984).

The presence of costs means that the evolutionary move toward sociality is not an automatic one. There are always costs of some sort that will mitigate against sociality (Alexander, 1974). Thus, one of the most important and useful exercises in sociobiological research is to construct debit and credit tables for cases of group living. How does one go about such a thing?

The first step, and the most difficult one, is to decide on a unit of measurement. A businessperson would use dollars as a unit for measuring the advantages and disadvantages of a proposed enterprise, but the evolutionist must try to measure costs and benefits in the most fundamental units of evolution: reproductive success. However, as was mentioned in Chapter 4, measuring reproductive success is often extremely difficult. Consequently, we often resort to more easily measured units that seem to correlate with reproductive success. For instance, because many animal species are limited by food availability, we can use caloric intake as a way of measuring costs and benefits. For example, a bird foraging alone may acquire 20 calories per unit time, but the same bird in a flock of ten may acquire 25 calories in the same amount of time. This may be because it "shares" the lookout duties with its flockmates and thus has more time available for food procurement.

Studies on predatory species usually confirm that the number of individuals in a typical hunting group is the number that yields the greatest amount of food for each participant. For example, Harris's hawks hunt cooperatively, flushing their prey, mainly rabbits, into the open where they can be struck by a group member. Following kills, all the hawks in the group share the prey. Based on computations of the energy available in their prey and on hawk energetic requirements, Bednarz (1988) concluded that groups of five would be optimal for the individual hawks. The most common group size was also five. Similarly, individual juncos (a small finch) foraging in a flock spent more time feeding as the number of birds in the flock increased. Each bird spent some time with its head up looking for approaching hawks, but the larger the flock, the less looking-out each individual had to perform (Pulliam *et al.*, 1982).

In sum, then, although there are definite costs associated with social living, there are compensatory benefits. These relationships must not be taken for granted; rather, we must seek to measure the presumed costs and benefits for the group members as a whole, and separately for the various subgroups within it to thoroughly understand the forces that mold social living.

EVOLUTIONARY ROUTES TO SOCIALITY

The complex societies of honeybees, wolves, prairie dogs, and humans presumably did not appear overnight. They were most assuredly a modification from a simpler social organization. Most sociobiologists agree that a "solitary" social organization is most primitive. From that starting point, elaborations evolved if ecological circumstances favored them. There appear to have been two routes taken from the solitary starting point, the familial route and the parasocial route (Vehrencamp, 1979), illustrated in Fig. 12-7. The two routes will be described below, using examples from mammalian species to illustrate the main points.

Familial route   The starting condition, as noted above, is the solitary stage. Here, adults live separately, with males and females coming together only for mating. The female rears the offspring unassisted in most cases. Gophers, leopards, and tigers are some of the many examples of solitary mammals.

The second stage, subsociality, occurs when there is a prolonged association between parent and offspring. That is, instead of the young dispersing when they are weaned, some of them remain in proximity to the mother. This creates an overlap in generations within social groupings.

When animals begin living in groups consisting of kin, the intermediate subsocial stage usually begins. This consists of cooperative activities among group members. For instance, female Belding's ground squirrels settle near their mothers, give alarm calls when one detects a predator, and cooperate in driving off some predators or intruders (Sherman, 1980).

The final stage of the familial route is eusociality. Here, in addition to the cooperative actions described above, there is a reproductive division of labor. That is, there is a lack of correspondence between reproductive effort and reproductive success. In wolves, for example, only one pair breeds, although the other pack members help provision the nursing mother or the cubs (Zimen, 1976).

Parasocial route   As before, the solitary

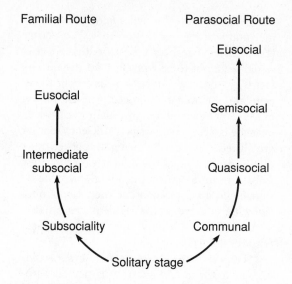

Figure 12.7
The familial and parasocial routes of sociality are thought to begin with a solitary species. The major difference is that groups consist of kin in the familial route, but of nonkin in the parasocial route. Explanations of each level are provided in the text.

stage is the starting point. Next, the communal stage occurs when adults congregate around a limiting resource such as roosting caves for bats. However, the social organization within these groups is minimal and cooperation is not observed.

In the quasisocial stage active cooperation is the rule, with group members gaining equally from the cooperation. Food sharing among vampire bats, mentioned earlier, is a good example.

Finally, the semisocial stage is characterized by a reproductive division of labor, and the eusocial stage occurs when two or more generations co-exist along with reproductive division of labor. There are apparently no cases of semisociality or eusociality in mammals that have evolved along the parasocial route, although there are examples in insects (Vehrencamp, 1979; Wilson, 1975a).

Although the sequences described here are considered to be the normal sequence by which more complex social organizations are derived from less complex forms, there are cases in which transitions may have gone directly from solitary organization to eusociality. For example, Michener (1985) has found that among certain bees, different populations or species are either solitary or eusocial, with no intermediate forms. Further, the changes required to make the transition are fairly simple. For instance, if individual lifespans are long enough, mothers and daughters may co-exist. One of them is dominant and breeds; the subordinant female assists. Their reproductive success is greater as a cooperatively breeding unit than it is as two independent individuals.

In summary, social organization appears to have evolved along two basic routes. The familial route favors sociality by retaining kin to cooperate with one another. In the parasocial route, nonkin associate and cooperate. There is nothing inherently better about later stages than earlier stages; rather, analyses such as these are done with the goal of understanding the historical sequence involved in the evolution of complex societies.

Summary

Many animal species spend much of their time living in social groups. These groups vary from one another in several ways. (1) Group structure varies. For instance, subgroups may exist as defined by the quantity and types of interactions among group members. The group may be organized along a dominance hierarchy or all the individuals may be equivalent. Finally, in some species, castes are noted by the different tasks performed in the group. Castes are especially obvious in the social insects in which sterile castes exist. (2) Groups differ in the degree to which group members maintain spatial distance from one another, or groups from one another. Dispersal of some individuals away from the area in which they were born is also quite common, although usually only one sex disperses. (3) The kinds of interaction that occurs among individuals is very important to the nature of the group. Interactions may be selfish (one gains and the other loses), cooperative (both gain), altruistic (one individual's behavior works to its disadvantage but to the other's gain), or spiteful (both participants lose). The evolutionary routes to selfishness and cooperation are straightforward. Altruism is more difficult, but has been explained through reciprocal altruism (cooperation with delayed benefits to one party); coercion, and kin selection. Spite is extremely rare or nonexistent. (4) Many forms of social exchange require the ability to recognize other individuals. Imprinting is a specialized form of learning that occurs during a sensitive period. Ducklings imprint on their mothers (or mother-substitutes in the lab), and develop preferences for them as indicated by their strong tendency to follow the imprinting object. Parents also learn the idiosyncratic cues of their offspring and direct their parental behavior specifically to their own offspring.

The development of social behaviors can depend on several forms of interaction. The mother is very important in some species, as in most primates. Peers, including siblings, can also be instrumental in the development of normal social behavior. In addition, many behaviors are acquired through social learning, i.e., observations of others performing a behavior. In this way, culture-like processes are known in many animal species besides humans.

The attributes of social groups vary from species to species and even in different populations of the same species. These variations presumably exist because of different ecological conditions favoring some forms of sociality more than others. The nature of the food supply may dictate the sorts of social groups that are advantageous to the individuals; similarly, the benefits of escaping or avoiding predation can favor the evolution of certain social structures. However, in addition to the benefits of sociality, there are often costs, such as increased incidence of disease or parasitic infections, that may work against the evolution of sociality. Social species have evolved from originally-solitary ancestors. This has occurred because of the benefits to the individuals who participate in social groups. In some cases the groups consist of kin, but in others they consist of unrelated individuals.

Recommended Readings

BARASH, D. P. (1982). *Sociobiology and behavior.* New York: Elsevier.

CAIRNS, R. (1979). *Social development: The origins and plasticity of interchanges.* San Francisco: Freeman.

HINDE, R. A. (1987). *Individuals, relationships and culture.* New York: Cambridge University Press.

HÖLLDOBLER, B., & LINDAUER, M. (1985). *Experimental behavioral ecology and sociobiology.* Sunderland, MA: Sinauer.

TRIVERS, R. (1985). *Social evolution.* Menlo Park, CA: Benjamin/Cummings.

WILSON, E. O. (1975). *Sociobiology: The new synthesis.* Cambridge, MA: Belknap/Harvard University Press.

WITTENBERGER, J. F. (1981). *Animal social behavior.* Boston: Duxbury.

Chapter 13

COMMUNICATION AND LANGUAGE

In the introduction to sensory systems in Chapter 7 we stressed the importance of monitoring the environment. Individuals that keep current on environmental matters and behave appropriately as the environment changes have greater reproductive success than those who fail to keep informed. The same reasoning applies to communication because the activities of con-specifics often affect an individual's survival, well-being, and reproductive success. Sensory systems are often exquisitely tuned to the communication signals of conspecifics (Hopkins, 1983).

Communication involves two classes of participants, signalers and receivers, who can, of course, exchange roles rather rapidly. A third party, the observer, must be added to study the interaction. The observer is a critical element in the study of communication because it is through the "filter" of the observer than an understanding of communication is derived. The observer should not influence the participants, but must instead be something of an eavesdropper (Fig. 13-1). The observer's role is especially difficult in the context of studying animal communication. The human observer's sensory systems may not be adequately sensitive to the sounds, odors, or movements of the animal species being studied, and therefore important information may be missed or misinterpreted.

Components of Communication Systems

The goals of communication research include (a) descriptions of signalers, the circumstances in which signaling occurs, and the structure of their signals; and (b) understanding the characteristics of receivers and the determinants of their response to signals.

SIGNALS AND MESSAGES

Signals are behaviors or behavioral products that modify others' behavior in ways that are, on average, advantageous to the signaler. Examples of signals include vocalizations, light reflected during body movements, many odors, and electrical discharges (e.g., electric fishes; Hopkins, 1980; Lissmann, 1963). Although many behaviors and behavioral products modify others' behavior, not all are signals. The critical difference is *function*, meaning that such behaviors evolved because modifying others' behavior was advantageous to the signaler. So, for instance, although hearing someone sneeze may modify one's behavior (saying "gesundheit" or handing over a box of tissue), sneezing is not a signal because it does not function to modify others' behavior. In contrast, a wolf's howl may keep a neighboring wolf pack away from its territory. Consequently, its food supply is protected which leads to enhanced reproductive success. The howl is a signal because it is an adaptation that modifies others' behavior in a way that is advantageous to the signaler.

Does communication require that the signaler *intend* to modify another's behavior? Intent implies that the individual is oriented toward some goal and has some understanding of the processes involved in attaining that goal. Such may not always be the case, but the absence of intent need not mean that communication is not occurring. For example, crickets chirp, frogs croak, and moths release odors and thereby attract mates, but we have no way of knowing whether mate attraction is their goal or intent. Nevertheless, there is no doubt that these be-

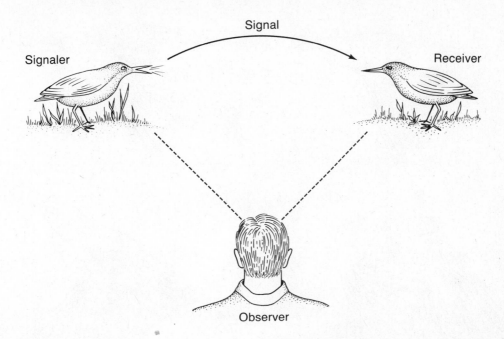

Figure 13.1
The study of communication involves at least three individuals: a signaler, a receiver, and an observer. The observer witnesses signal emission, the signal itself, and responses of receivers, but remains outside the system, like an eavesdropper (as indicated by the dashed lines).

haviors are signals because they do indeed modify others' behavior to the benefit of the signaler (Burghardt, 1970).

The benefit of signaling need not occur in every case. A cricket, chirping on a summer night, may attract a parasite rather than a mate (Cade, 1981) and suffer reduced reproductive success as a result. But, on average, chirping has, during the course of cricket evolution, resulted in greater reproductive success. It is the average net effect of signaling during the evolutionary history of the species that should concern us.

Finally, it is sometimes difficult to determine whether a behavior is a signal or merely affects others incidentally. However, the principle of economy, a basic assumption of evolutionary adaptation, can help us decide. Behaviors are expected to be as efficient (economical) as possible consistent with the function of the behavior (Curio, 1973). We can use violations of the principle of economy to differentiate between signaling and behaviors that provide information only incidentally. For example, male blackbirds must fly around their territories if they are to detect intruders. Females may also notice the male, which may eventually lead to mating. Do males fly to entice females or is female enticement merely a byproduct of the flying necessary to patrol the territory? One way to find out is to look at the effort expended in the flight. If the only function of flight were to get from point A to point B, we would expect to find little wasted movement. And usually, blackbirds fly efficiently. But at other times the flight is not so

Figure 13.2
The display flights (communicative) of male red-winged blackbirds (C) and yellow-headed blackbirds (D) are exaggerated compared to their normal flight movements (A and B, respectively).

economical. The bird appears to "bounce" along, the tail is flared out and down (creating an aerial anchor) and the wings are held awkwardly (Fig. 13-2). Because this form of flight is clearly not efficient from the perspective of pure locomotion, we would probably be correct in concluding that it has some other (or additional) function, perhaps communication for mate attraction.

Signals contain information about the signaler or its surroundings. From the perspective of an observer a signal should increase predictability about the signaler's current or forthcoming behavior, its characteristics, or the external surroundings. The information present in a signal is called its *broadcast information* (Wiley, 1983) or its *message* (W. J. Smith, 1969, 1977).

Behavioral messages A signal may indicate the current behavior of the signaler, or its likely forthcoming behavior. The growl of a dog indicates that it is engaging in aggressive behavior, and may escalate if the interaction continues. The same is true of human speech, of course. The tone or "quality" of the voice is highly indicative of the emotional status of the speaker (Scherer, 1986) and therefore is predictive of forthcoming behavior.

Signaler characteristic messages Some

signals may indicate the signaler's species, age, sex, individual identity, or reproductive status. The songs of many bird species, for example, are sung only by males of that species, are individually different (Beer, 1970), and often only occur during the breeding season when the male is in reproductive condition. Further, the signal may indicate the signaler's distance or direction.

External messages In some cases, especially in human language, signals may refer to objects or events beyond the signaler. That is, they are "about" things other than the signaler itself, or its behavior. Some animal species also signal about external referents. The antipredator calls of some monkeys and ground squirrels, discussed in more detail below, are examples of signals with external messages.

Decoding the message structure of signals is a difficult task for the observer, especially when the subject of study is another species. It is something like observing a conversation between two people speaking a language that one does not understand. But even here the task is easier because at least the observer can be confident that her sensory systems are appropriately tuned to detect the signals and responses. In animal systems this may not be the case (Slater, 1983). Consequently, chemical analysis may need to replace the observer's nose, slow-motion photography may assist her eyes, and sound spectrum analysis may reveal unexpected acoustic structure.

RECEIVER'S RESPONSE

Having detected a signal, the receiver generally will change its behavior. The change may be an overt behavioral one, such as running away or lifting the head, or it may be a physiological response, such as hormone release, that may, in turn, lead to a behavioral change later on.

We will discuss some of the variables that influence responses to signals. These variables fall into two categories: the signals themselves, and the context in which the signals are received.

Signals and the receiver's response It is not at all surprising that the behavior of receivers varies as a function of the signals to which they are exposed. After all, because signals vary with respect to information content and information is crucial to survival and well-being, it follows that differences in signals will produce variation in response.

A nice example of responses changing to reflect signal differences comes from the antipredator signals of vervet monkeys of East Africa and California ground squirrels of western North America. Vervet monkeys have distinct vocalizations that specify their major predators (snakes, eagles, and large carnivores) (Struhsaker, 1967; Seyfarth *et al.*, 1980a, b). When they hear a snake alarm call the monkeys respond by looking around toward the ground. If an eagle alarm is heard, however, the monkeys look up and run into dense brush. The vervet monkeys respond in the same way to playbacks of taperecorded alarm calls as they do to naturally occurring calls (Marler, 1985).

California ground squirrels have a comparable array of antipredator vocalizations (Leger *et al.*, 1980; Owings & Leger, 1980). When a hawk alarm call is heard, the squirrels run toward their burrows and flatten down, a process that reduces their conspicuousness. However, when a mammalian predator alarm occurs, they run to burrows but get up high, either by climbing a rock if one is around, or at least standing upright on their hind legs, resulting in a better view or allowing them to hear better (Owings & Virginia, 1978). Again, squirrels respond to playbacks as they do to naturally occurring calls and to the predators themselves (Leger & Owings, 1978).

The difficulty in studying the effect of signal variation on receiver response is that some forms of signal variation are not important. Human speech is incredibly varied. Different people saying the same word produce different patterns of sound energy; if this were not the case we would not be able to recognize people by their voices. The problem for the observer is to tease apart the variation that is meaningful from variation that is not. We are far from that goal in human speech, and just as far from it in supposedly simpler animal systems.

Context and receiver response   We are all familiar with laments about being quoted out of context. The message of words depends on other words, gestures, facial expressions, and common knowledge shared by the participants. The same is true in the communication systems of animals. Emitting a signal is not equivalent to pushing a button in another individual that sets it off on some predetermined behavioral course. Receivers have several or many behaviors that they can perform, and the choice often depends on many variables, of which signals are only one type. Other events, conditions, and receiver characteristics that affect a receiver's response to a signal are contextual sources of information. A few examples of context follow:

(1) *Receiver sources.* The variables included here are rather diverse, and include the receiver's age or maturational status, physiological condition, ongoing behavior, and previous experience. For example, pea aphids release a chemical "alarm substance" when disturbed. The response of an aphid that detects the alarm substance is heavily dependent on its age: Adults nearly always release their grip on the plant and drop to the ground, but younger aphids rarely drop (Roitberg & Myers, 1978). The adults can more readily reclimb the plant, so dropping for them is a less risky activity.

Physiological condition, especially changes associated with reproduction, often influence receivers. For instance, when presented with a taperecorded infant's cry, women who had recently given birth had different patterns of heart rate change and electrodermal activity than did pregnant women (Bleichfeld & Moely, 1984). Another physiological type of context is hunger. When R. Smith (1981) exposed fish (Iowa darters) to a chemical alarm substance, he found that they took antipredator actions only if they had recently fed. Food deprivation for 48 hours eliminated the antipredator response to the alarm chemical.

(2) *Sources external to the receiver.* Some of the major nonreceiver sources of contextual information include behavior of the signaler that preceded the signal, and aspects of the setting in which communication is occurring.

Examples of this type of context are numerous. In dogs and other carnivores, play is usually initiated by a "play invitation bow," a characteristic posture in which the forelegs are extended forward and pressed against the ground while the hindquarters remain elevated (Fig. 13-3; Bekoff, 1972, 1977). This signal appears to convey the message that everything to follow is "in fun." A growl or bite following a play invitation bow is not treated as an aggressive act, but without the bow they are.

The location of the signaler often has contextual effects. It is well-known in birds that playbacks of a neighbor's song from its territory evoke only weak responses, but when the same songs are played back from outside the singer's usual haunts a full aggressive response ensues (Falls & Brooks, 1975).

Summarizing, the response of a signal receiver depends on the signal itself and on other variables that are referred to as context. It is adaptive for receivers to use context in "choosing" their responses because the costs and bene-fits of responding to a signal vary in complex ways and often depend on other circumstances.

Ontogeny of Communication

An important question often raised about com-munication concerns the role and importance of individual experience in signaling and receiving behavior. Because we have already dealt exten-sively with the role of experience in behavioral development in Chapters 2 and 9, we will not delve deeply into the topic here. Rather, some examples will be presented of the diversity that exists in the role of experience in communica-tion.

Figure 13.3
The "play invitation bow" of carnivores is very similar across species. Here a male lion initiates play with a cub.

MINIMAL EXPERIENCE COMMUNICATION

Signal production Numerous examples exist of signaling behavior that requires little or no experience. That is, first-time performance is comparable to that of others who have had more extensive experience.

Insects present a ready supply of examples. Female fireflies attract males by flashing their abdominal "lanterns" in species-typical pat-terns. They do this perfectly the first time (Carl-son & Copeland, 1978). Similarly, male crickets need no practice to chirp perfectly well, nor do females need experience with the sounds to ap-proach the sound source correctly the first time (Bentley & Hoy, 1974).

Insects are not alone in being able to signal appropriately without specific experience. Song sparrows develop their complex songs without the benefit of hearing the species' typical song (Searcy et al., 1985), and human infants cry, smile, and laugh without practice (Darwin, 1872). Snowdon et al. (1986) have written a

nice account of species differences in the amount of experience required to produce normal sig-nals. In general, primates are less dependent on specific individual experience to produce effec-tive signals than are birds.

Signal perception Perception of certain distinctions in human language is present in very young infants and may not require experience. Eimas (1985) summarizes some fascinating re-search on the categorical perception of human speech sounds, such as the difference between "pin" and "bin." Vocal tract air flow is blocked momentarily in both sounds before air release occurs and the vocal cords commence vibration, a dimension known as voice onset time. How-ever, the vocal cords begin vibration sooner in "bin" than in "pin." Voice onset time varies in a continuous fashion from short to long (up to about 60–70 milliseconds) but we break this continuous range into two categories divided at

PETER MARLER

"In both our species and in certain birds, learning of young from adult plays a major role in the development of natural patterns of vocalizations. In both cases dialects arise as a consequence of that learning. There is in both a certain critical period of life during which the ability for vocal learning is at its maximum." [Marler, P. (1970). Birdsong and speech development: Could there be parallels? American Scientist **58**, 669–673 *(p. 669).]*

about 30 milliseconds. Two examples with voice onset times of 15 and 25 ms are perceived as identical "bins," whereas two examples with voice onset times of 35 and 45 ms are both heard as "pin." Only when two examples come from opposite sides of the perceptual boundary are they heard as different sounds. Infants perceive the same category boundary as adults. This finding extends to several other perceptual distinctions, even ones not used in the language spoken by the infants' parents (Werker, 1989). Categorical perception also occurs in bird song

(Nelson & Marler, 1989) and monkey calls (Pola & Snowdon, 1975).

EXPERIENCE AND THE ONTOGENY OF COMMUNICATION

Individual experience often affects the form of a signal and the circumstances in which signals are emitted (W. J. Smith, 1985a,b). The amount and type of experience required to attain the adult-typical form of the behavior varies a great deal from case to case. Thus, we are dealing with a continuum of experience ranging from virtually none (covered in the preceding section) to a great deal.

Signal form   Bird singing has been the most thoroughly researched case of the role of experience in the ontogeny of communication. Although many species have been studied, the white-crowned sparrow of western North America has a special place for its early and extensive role in this research area. We will briefly cover several types of experience that influence the development of song in this species. Good reviews of this work are available (Kroodsma, 1981; Petrinovich, 1990; Johnston, 1988).

White-crowned sparrow songs vary geographically: each is a sort of "dialect." Elegant work by Peter Marler and his associates has shown that the dialect that a male sings as an adult depends on the dialect he hears much earlier in life, during a sensitive period from about 10 to 50 days posthatching. If a young male white-crown is raised without hearing its species' song during this time, it will produce "songs" that bear little relationship to the songs of wild birds. In contrast, if a male white-crown is allowed to hear tape recordings or live productions of white-crown song during the sensitive period, it will come to sing normal song. Moreover, young males who are exposed to a dialect other than their native one will come to sing the "foreign" dialect perfectly well (Marler & Tamura, 1964). In short, the form of the song depends on the particular experiential history of the singer.

The young male does not sing during the song-exposure period. Instead, when it is about a year old, it begins to sing by first producing a nonmelodious assembly of sounds bearing little relationship to final "crystallized" song, and then gradually refines its output until its song closely approximates the song of its live (or taped) tutor that it heard months before. This suggests that the refinement of its song output is based on a comparison between its current song and its memory of the tutor's song. This memory or "song template" must be quite sharp because each male's song will be a very good match to what it heard earlier.

If the transition from the early versions of song to crystallized song is based on a comparison process, then deafening before crystallized song develops should disrupt the process. Indeed it does. Konishi (1965) deafened male white-crowns after they had been exposed to song but before they began singing. Although they all attempted to sing, none of them produced anything close to a normal song. In contrast, males who were deafened after they had developed crystallized song continued to sing normally, indicating that continued auditory feedback was not required to maintain song in normal form.

The studies above suggest that two types of experience are required in order for white-crowned sparrows to develop song. First, they must hear another white-crown produce song, and they must hear themselves singing so as to modify their output until it matches their memory of song. Will male white-crowns sing any song to which they are exposed during the sensitive period? Early research suggested that they would learn only white-crowned sparrow song. White-crowns raised hearing only the songs of other species produced songs like those of white-crowns raised hearing no songs at all. Even when young males heard white-crowned songs interspersed with the songs of other species, they selectively imitated only the white-crowned songs (Marler, 1970)! These findings suggested that, although young males had to hear white-crowned song in order to sing it later, they somehow could discern their own species' song from those of other species and selectively allow only their own song into memory. How this capability develops is unknown.

More recent work has cast some doubt on the foregoing. First, although a young male white-crown raised hearing only the tape-recorded song of another species will not imitate that song, we now know that if they are raised with a live tutor of another species, they will imitate that species later on (reviewed by Petrinovich, 1990). Further, with a live tutor the sensitive period is nearly twice as long as it is with tape-recordings. Such findings in the laboratory may therefore account for occasional observations of birds in the wild that consistently sing the song of another species even though they are not typically mimics (such birds as mockingbirds and starlings are excellent at copying the sounds of other birds, other animals, or even inanimate sounds).

Although research on white-crowned sparrow song ontogeny is controversial (see Johnston, 1988 and its following commentary) because of inconsistencies about the selectivity of song imitation and the duration of the sensitive period, it seems that white-crowned sparrows indeed treat the song of their own species differently from those of other species. Not only do they readily imitate tape-recorded songs of their species but not others, they are better and faster at learning their own song. Further research on this fascinating little bird will no doubt extend our knowledge of these processes.

MEREDITH WEST   ANDREW KING

" . . . Male cowbirds are open to social influences from their audience and . . . they react to them with vocal modifications." [West, M. J., & King, A. P. (1988). Coming to terms with the everyday language of comparative psychology. In D. W. Leger (Ed.) Comparative Perspectives in Modern Psychology. Nebraska Symposium on
Motivation, Vol. 35 (pp. 51–89). Lincoln: University of Nebraska Press (p. 65).]

Another good example of experiential effects on signal form occurs in the brown-headed
cowbird. Cowbirds are nest parasites; that is,
females lay their eggs in the nests of other species. If the parasitism goes undetected the cowbird egg will be incubated and the nestling fed
and protected by the host adults. From the perspective of a male cowbird, there is no acceptable model from which to learn his song because
he is being raised by another species, perhaps
without other cowbirds in the vicinity. Thus,
the male cowbird requires no experience to sing
a song to which female cowbirds respond (West
et al., 1981), and females require no experience
with male cowbirds or their song to respond
appropriately the first time (King & West,
1977). What, then, is the role of experience in
cowbird song? In a series of intriguing studies,

Meredith West and Andrew King found that the
songs of isolation-reared males differed from
those of socially reared males (West et al., 1979).
But strangely enough, the isolates' songs were
more effective in triggering the female's copulatory response than were the songs of social
males. Why don't all males sing the more potent
isolate song? West and King (1980) discovered
that isolate song led to more attacks by other
males on the singer than did the songs of socially
reared males. In other words, the male cowbird
has the choice of singing a song that is very
attractive to females but which elicits attacks, or
singing a less attractive song that doesn't trigger
violence. As a result of social interaction with
other males, cowbirds come to sing the song type
typical of socially living males.

Another form of experience helps shape the

structure of male cowbird song: the response of females. King and West (1983) raised young male cowbirds of the eastern subspecies with females of their own subspecies or with females of the southern subspecies. As adults, the males sang songs typical of males of the females' subspecies! Although females never sing, they do respond preferentially to songs of their own subspecies (West *et al.*, 1983) so female response to normal variation in males' song shaped males to sing in ways preferred by females (West & King, 1988).

Circumstances of signal emission Even if the form of a signal is little influenced by experience, the circumstances in which it is used may change as experience is acquired. For example, young vervet monkeys give alarm calls in response to potential predators. However, they are considerably more prone than adults to issue alarms to nondangerous animals. They use the "eagle alarm" when they see other large birds or even falling leaves, and the "mammalian predator alarm" when they see a warthog or hare (Seyfarth & Cheney, 1980). As they gain experience they become more discriminating in the use of these important signals.

Communication Channels

Communication channels pertain to the sensory modality in which the signals are received and processed. We will discuss acoustic, optic, and chemical channels, emphasizing the sources of the signals, benefits of using that channel, and how signals may be structured to be most useful given the conditions in which they are employed.

ACOUSTIC CHANNEL

Sources of acoustic signals Acoustic signals are produced in several ways. We are most

familiar with the use of expelled air to produce sound, either by vibrating membranes such as the vocal cords of mammals, or by producing resonance in a tube such as the syrinx of birds (Greenewalt, 1969). Acoustic signals can also be produced by other body parts. Crickets make their stridulation (chirping) sounds by drawing a comb like structure across a ridged "file." The sound occurs when each tooth on the scraper clicks across the file ridges (Fig. 13-4). Other examples include the buzzing sounds produced

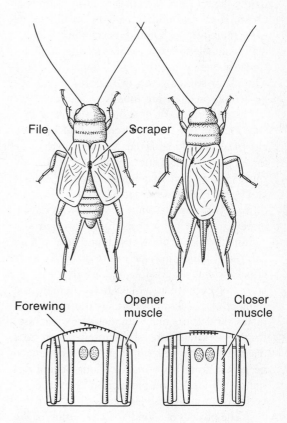

Figure 13.4
Crickets produce their stridulating (chirping) sound by drawing the file across the scraper. Each click of this system produces a sound pulse.

by rapid vibrations of the wings in insects, shaking feathers in some birds, and chattering the teeth in many rodents. Finally, some acoustic signals are produced in conjunction with environmental objects. For example carpenter ants beat their mandibles on thin strips of wood within their nests whenever there has been a breach in nest security (Fuchs, 1976). The drumming activates nest protection behaviors in those that detect it.

Benefits and structure of acoustic signals   There are several benefits to acoustic signaling. First, acoustic signals can be omnidirectional; that is, sounds spread in all directions from their source. Omnidirectionality is especially valuable in circumstances in which a widespread audience must be reached rapidly. This is why alarm signals given in response to an approaching predator are usually acoustic.

Another benefit of acoustic signals is that they can be temporally discrete. Unlike some chemical and optical signals that remain in place for long times, acoustic signals can be readily turned on and off. Therefore, acoustic signals can be modified to correspond to changing conditions. For example, male tungara frogs have a mate-attraction call consisting of two parts: a "whine," which is always used, and one or more "chucks," which may be omitted. Males omit chucks whenever possible because they also attract frog-eating bats. Male frogs increase the number of chucks, however, as the number of males (and thus, mate competition) increases (Ryan, 1990). Temporal discreteness can be a disadvantage, however, if there is any benefit to be gained from continuous or long-lasting signaling because sound production is often energetically very expensive (Gerhardt, 1983).

The physics of sound and the nature of the medium (air, water, soil) through which the sound passes act as selective conditions shaping the characteristics of acoustic signals. For instance, sound loses energy as it spreads away from its source, a phenomenon known as *attenuation*. However, attenuation in a given habitat is generally not uniform across the sound spectrum: Some frequencies attenuate more rapidly than others (Wiley & Richards, 1978; Marten & Marler, 1977). In fact, the habitat may create a "sound window" in which attenuation is minimal in a limited frequency range but much greater for frequencies above and below. Waser and Brown (1984), who were interested in the loud roars, booms, and other long-distance calls of forest monkeys, conducted a study of sound transmission 7 meters up in a Kenyan forest. They found that low-frequency sound (200 Hz) attenuated less rapidly than did higher- and lower-frequency sounds (Fig. 13-5). Not surprisingly, monkeys' "loud calls" fall at about 200 Hz. In general, low-frequency sounds have less attenuation than do high-frequency sounds. Consequently, when long-distance communication is advantageous, as when the receiver is likely to be far off, signals tend to be of low frequency.

On the other hand, if there is an advantage in keeping the signal out of the ears of nonintended receivers, the signal should be relatively high-frequency so that it attenuates rapidly. Snowdon and Hodun (1981) have described a beautiful example of this process. Pygmy marmosets, a species of New World monkey, structure their trill vocalizations according to the distance between the caller and the receiver. When the receiver was nearby, the trills included only high-frequency components. When the receiver was farther away the trills included lower-frequency components. By varying their trills, the marmosets were using the riskier lower-frequency sounds only when absolutely necessary to reach the receiver.

Acoustic signals vary in other ways. Some signals are relatively pure tones (tonal sounds)

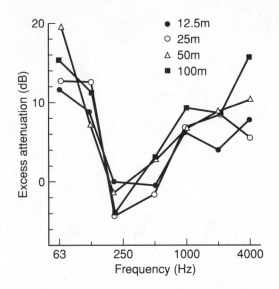

Figure 13.5
Sounds of different frequencies do not retain their energy equally over distance. This graph shows the results of an experiment in which sounds ranging from 63 to 4000 Hz were played through a forest in Kenya and detected by microphones placed at four distances from the speaker. The higher the excess attenuation, the greater the energy loss. The monkeys that live in this forest have loud calls whose frequency is about 200 Hz, the most efficient transmission frequency.

but others have a large range of frequencies that usually sound like clicks, buzzes, rattles, and so forth. The habitat in which communication occurs may favor one type of signal over others in that degradation of one type may exceed that of the other. Degradation refers to the difference between a signal at its source and at its reception point. For instance if a bird signals threat by emitting a series of click like sounds with 100 milliseconds between clicks, and nonaggressive approach with the same sort of click spaced 200 milliseconds apart, the presence of echoes could obscure interpretation by the receiver. Morton (1975) found that forest-dwelling birds in Pan-

ama use few signals in which timing conveyed a message, but instead used more tonal signals and depended on differences in frequency to convey different messages. This was probably due to the problem of echo and scatter in the cluttered forest habitat. In contrast, nearby grassland birds who sing in the open used few tonal sounds but many that used timing (e.g., series of sound pulses). Echoes are not a problem in the open grasslands, but other conditions (wind and temperature gradients) could degrade tonal signals.

Significantly, the pattern that Morton detected between species living in different habitats is paralleled in studies of a single species living in different habitats. For example, the great tit, a chickadee of Europe and Asia, sings tonal songs in forests, but atonal songs in open habitats (Hunter & Krebs, 1979; Fig. 13-6). Finally, the song of Carolina wrens living in a Maryland hardwood forest degraded less there than they did in a Florida scrub pine forest, and vice versa. The songs traveled the same distance in both forests, suggesting that their songs were structured not so much to travel far but to maintain their acoustic structure, which conveys the message of the song (Gish & Morton, 1981).

Finally, acoustic signals are structured by the social situation in which they are used. Morton (1977) reported that the aggressive signals of many vertebrates tend to be low-pitched, harsh or raspy sounds—a dog's growl is a perfect example—but acoustic signals used when the signaler is avoiding attack or when it is affiliating with another individual tend to be higher pitched and of a purer, more tonal quality (also see August & Anderson, 1987). When talking to babies, for example, adults' tones go up (the voice of an angry adult goes down in pitch, of course). Why would these trends—which seem to be found with amazing regularity in diverse vertebrates—be this way? Although the answer is elusive, Morton suggests that animals in an

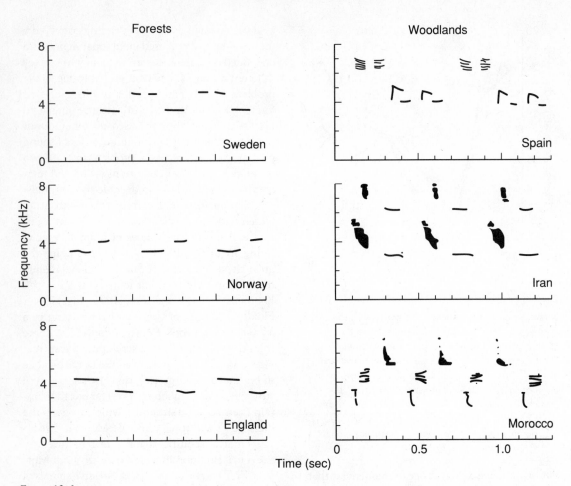

Forests   Woodlands

Figure 13.6
Songs of the great tit, Parus major, *reflect the selective effects of the habitat in which they live. Forests are dense stands of trees, and woodlands are more open areas.*

aggressive interaction do better if they give the illusion of greater size. Mammals and birds tend to erect their fur or feathers during threats, making them appear larger than they actually are, so lowering the voice may be an acoustic analog of hair erection. Larger individuals tend to have deeper voices because as individuals grow the vocal cords lengthen, tending to produce lower frequency sounds, and less pure tones, when vibrated.

OPTICAL CHANNEL

Sources   Most optical signals are produced by reflecting light from the body surface. To this end, the structure of body coverings (hair, feathers, scales) have become specialized for efficient reflection of light (Hailman, 1977). For example, the feathers of the orange-red throat patch of male Anna's hummingbirds are highly irridescent. These birds attempt to maneuver during fights so as to face into the sun, thereby directing a more intense flash at their opponent (Hamilton, 1965).

Movement patterns are exploited for the reflection of light. Stereotyped movements such as those used in courtship are optical signals because they depend on the reflection of light to convey information to the receiver. The repertoires of some lizard species are rich with movements used in courtship and aggression. A lizard will commonly position itself alongside another lizard where it performs an elaborate set of movements including "pushups" (raising and lowering the body by periodic flexions of the legs), head bobs, and extension of the dewlap, a colorful fan-like patch of skin on the throat. Each species has a unique repertoire, and individuals vary the movements or their speed or repetition according to their motivational state (Jenssen, 1977). Human sign language illustrates how rich informative movements can be.

Another source of optical signals is generation of light. Some organisms, such as flashlight fishes (McCosker, 1977a), harbor quantities of light-emitting bacteria. Flashlight fishes (Fig. 13-7) can turn the light signal on and off by dropping a flap of tissue to expose the chamber that contains the bacteria, and by raising the flap to cover the chamber. In this way, they can signal with an optical "Morse code."

Benefits and structure of optic signals Optic signals have two primary benefits. First, they can be constructed to range from very brief (the flash of a firefly or a wink) to very long (the color patterns of many animals are signs that constantly convey species identity messages). Therefore, the "active life" of the signal can be

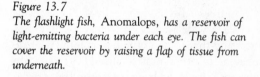

Figure 13.7
The flashlight fish, Anomalops, has a reservoir of light-emitting bacteria under each eye. The fish can cover the reservoir by raising a flap of tissue from underneath.

varied according to the requirements of the situation. Second, even long-lasting optical signals can be inexpensive to produce and maintain (compared with long-lasting acoustic signals). A bird's plumage, for instance, is always signaling (as long as light strikes it) and requires nothing of the energy that singing would expend.

An obvious disadvantage of optical signaling is the requirement that the receiver be properly oriented before signal detection can occur. Reaching a far-flung group of receivers with optical signals would be extremely difficult and time consuming. Another disadvantage of optical signaling is the potential for obstruction by objects in the environment. Although many acoustic signals are not impeded by obstacles, optic signals are. Species that live in cluttered habitats employ few optic signals, and the ones they do use are reserved for close range signaling.

The selective forces exerted by the habitat or medium through which optic signals are propagated has not been studied to the same extent that it has in acoustic signals. However, some interesting cases have been reported. For instance, fireflies use their optic signals in courtship and mate attraction. To be effective these light flashes must contrast with the background, and this they most certainly do. Nearly all species that flash only during twilight have yellow to orange signals. The twilight spectrum at the insects' flying or perching heights is particularly poor in those wavelengths (Lall *et al.*, 1980).

CHEMICAL CHANNEL

Sources   Because the cells of all organisms produce a wide variety of chemicals, it is not surprising that some of them may influence the behavior of other individuals. *Pheromones* are chemicals produced by an organism that are released outside its body that stimulate specific reactions in the receiver (Shorey, 1977). Pheromones must not be confused with hormones, which are kept within the body and influence only other cells of the same individual.

Pheromones are produced by specialized glands that release the chemical directly to the outside of the body or into some product, such as urine, which will then be deposited outside the body. Some insects, such as ants and bees, are veritable pheromone machines, with special glands located throughout the body for this purpose.

It is important to distinguish between pheromones—whose function is to influence another individual—and a wide variety of chemicals produced by the body that affect others only incidentally. Merely deriving information from chemicals emitted by another individual is not sufficient to conclude that the chemical is a pheromone. For instance, it is easy to tell that a person has been exercising on a hot day by the person's perspiration odor. But perspiration is a physiological process necessary for regulating body temperature. Unless it can be shown that the quantity or content of perspiration violates the principle of economy for the thermoregulation function, it is safest to conclude that any information derived from the odor of human perspiration is an incidental byproduct of its production, and is not a true case of communication. Of course, this caution applies to many other purported cases of pheromones in other animals, too.

This sort of argument can be leveled at all the reported cases of human pheromones. Blindfolded humans can tell whether two hands placed in front of the nose for sniffing belong to the same person or to two, especially if one is male and the other female (Wallace, 1977), and they can distinguish vaginal odors according to when they were emitted during the menstrual cycle (Doty *et al.*, 1975). The list goes on for a variety of olfactory tasks. But again, the communicative function of these odors has not been documented. Humans *may* have pheromones, but so far the evidence on this point is lacking.

Benefits and structure of chemical signals   Pheromones are nicely structured to suit the signaling situation. Pheromones vary widely with respect to their volatility, that is, the degree to which they are dispersed in the air or water. Volatility affects fade-out time (Gerhardt, 1983). Some pheromones, such as the alarm pheromones of ants, are extremely volatile and last only a few seconds. Others, such as the waxy castoreum of beavers, are of low volatility but last for many months (Butler & Butler, 1979).

The wide range of volatility permits an elegant match between the signal and the situation in which it is used. Pheromones can be brief like most acoustic signals, or very long-lasting like some optic signals. One situation in which pheromones are nonadvantageous is when the medium is highly turbulent. When turbulence occurs the pheromone has no clear-cut concentration gradient along which others can trace the signal to its source.

Evolution of Communication

As mutations occur in a population, some will undoubtedly affect the systems that produce or influence the emission of communication signals. Some of these systems are neuromuscular and others are motivational. If these alterations of signaling behavior are adaptive, the new alleles will increase in frequency in the population. Thus, the evolution of communication follows precisely the same processes as the evolution of behavior in general.

We have encountered some examples of the evolution of communication in previous chapters; they will be mentioned again here briefly, along with some other cases.

GENETIC BASES OF COMMUNICATION

To evolve, there must be a genetic basis to individual differences in behavior. This has been most frequently studied by means of hybridization experiments, mostly in insects. Bentley (1971; Bentley & Hoy, 1972, 1974) studied the chirps of cricket species and their hybrids. The acoustic patterns of the hybrids' chirps were generally intermediate to those of the parental species, implying that there were several genes involved and that there was no dominance of one parental species' genes over those of the other. Interestingly, the same genes that influence the pattern of male stridulation also affect female preference. Hybrid females approach the playback of the hybrid male pattern more often than they do the patterns of the parental species (Hoy et al., 1976; Pollack & Hoy, 1979).

Similar research has been conducted on the courtship songs of male fruit flies (*Drosophila*).

Genetic mutations are known that alter the acoustic patterns of male courtship songs (von Schilcher, 1977). Species differences in male courtship song are well known, but the song patterns of hybrids are not intermediate to those of the parental species; rather, the hybrids exhibit elements of both parental species (Kyriacou & Hall, 1986). Although hybrid females prefer the songs of hybrid males, the nature of the preference is much more complicated than was the case in crickets. Finally, the many species of *Drosophila* that currently inhabit the Hawaiian Islands are derived from a small number of ancestral species. Nevertheless, extensive species differences in their courtship songs have evolved, probably because there is an advantage to the animals to avoid breeding with the wrong species (Hoy et al., 1988).

Hybridization studies of noninsect species indicate that similar genetic mechanisms may be at work. For example, hybrid treefrogs produce croaking patterns that are intermediate to those of the parental species (Gerhardt, 1974), and hybrid ground squirrels emit alarm calls to predators that have elements of the parental patterns (Koeppl et al., 1978). In primates, the loud calls of hybrid gibbons are intermediate to those of the parental species (Tenaza, 1985). Finally, there are subspecies differences in the acoustic patterns of primates. For example, the red and black-and-white forms of the ruffed lemur of Madagascar have different forms of a loud call (Macedonia & Taylor, 1985), as do some Peruvian tamarins (Hodun et al., 1981).

In summary, the evidence is quite good that species differences in the structure of acoustic signals is largely attributable to genetic differences. Presumably, as populations encountered differing selection conditions, some signal variants proved to be more advantageous than others, and the alleles that contributed to the better forms increased in frequency.

PROCESSES OF EVOLUTIONARY CHANGE

The evolution of communication poses some special problems for evolutionary theory. Because there are at least two participants in communication, there must be receptive mechanisms in place to detect and interpret signals, but how could receptive mechanisms evolve unless the signal was already present, and how could the signal evolve in the absence of the receptive mechanism? How do signals and receptive mechanisms arise from a condition in which neither exists?

As usual, Darwin suggested some answers that are still regarded as correct. Darwin (1872/1965) suggested that communicative signals could originate through modifications of what he called "serviceable associated habits." If animals benefit from monitoring their environments, which includes conspecifics, and if forthcoming behavior of other individuals is predictable from their current behavior, then we expect animals to be closely "tuned" to the actions of conspecifics. Further, if individuals tend to gain by providing clues about their forthcoming behavior, then slight exaggerations of those clues may be advantageous and evolve into signals. For example, in aggressive contexts, carnivores bare their teeth in preparation for biting the opponent. The opponent, seeing the teeth, may withdraw. Exaggerations of the teeth-baring behavior may benefit the animal by capitalizing on this tendency of others to withdraw.

The tooth-baring of the carnivore is an example of an *intention movement,* a form of serviceable associated habit (Daanje, 1950) . Prior to performing a certain behavior pattern, a preparatory activity may be necessary. Cats crouch just before jumping, as do birds just before taking flight. Exaggerations of intention movements may evolve into signals, particularly if the individuals of a population begin to perform the behavior to the same degree. If crouching in birds begins to take on signal properties, then reducing the variability in crouching makes the job of the receiver that much easier, and the signaling that much more effective. The evolutionary change from a situation in which the signal (or incipient signal) is more variable to one in which the signal is less variable is known as *ritualization.*

Once one movement is moving toward ritualization as a signal, the opposite behavioral tendency can be signaled by means of behaviors that are opposite those of the first case (Darwin's "principle of antithesis"). Consider two cats about to fight: Their backs are arched, the ears layed back, the fur is erect, and they hiss and snarl. Any or all of these may serve as signals. Now consider a cat that is "greeting" another cat or human. The ears are up, the fur is sleek, and the cat may even role over onto its back and purr, exactly the opposite of the cat in fighting mode.

Once signaling systems have evolved, they do not necessarily remain static thereafter. As Moynihan (1970) has pointed out, a signal may become overused or used in new contexts through changing its relationship to various motivational systems. The predictability of forthcoming behavior may therefore be reduced, and the signal will become less effective. Therefore, the repertoire of signals within a population may change over time as signals decay, disappear, and get replaced with new ones.

The stability of a signal over time depends on who benefits from emission of the signal: the signaler only, or the signaler and the recipient. Dawkins and Krebs (1978) correctly argued that signaling behavior will not evolve unless the signaler (on average) gains fitness from signaling. Thus, a certain amount of deception or "persuasion" is to be expected even if the receiver loses fitness in the exchange. However, Dawkins and Krebs argued that the consequence to the receiver was irrelevant to the evolution of signaling systems. But receivers are not impartial participants in communication situations. They have their own best interests, too, and they may conflict with those of the signaler. Thus, cases of conflict of interests should favor those receivers who are capable of detecting deception and acting in their own interests. In short, one expects something of an "arms struggle" between signalers and receivers (actually, between signaling systems and reception systems, since each individual is both a signaler and a receiver at various times), such that signals get better at achieving the signaler's goals, and the reception systems get better at detecting deceptive signals. Such a signal–reception system is inherently unstable, and we expect to see relatively rapid change in the nature of the signal repertoire under such circumstances.

In contrast, cases in which the signaler and receiver have compatible interests should produce stable signal–reception systems. For instance, many young birds and mammals emit vocal signals when separated from the parents, and these signals help reunite both parties. Clearly, the young ones benefit by giving signals that are easy to locate and the parent benefits by responding to such signals. Reproductive success hangs in the balance for both. There is no deception and no "probing." Such systems should remain in their current form indefinitely.

In conclusion, communication behaviors are subject to natural selection, which comes primarily from the responses of conspecifics. Genes may change, producing better signals or better reception systems (or both), at least on occasion. Signals appear to have originated from more utilitarian behaviors that others commonly monitored because of the predictability that they

offered of another's behavior. Signals may change over evolutionary time, especially in those cases in which the interests of the signaler and receiver are opposed.

Biology of Human Language

Human language is a special case of communication, and the human species is an especially profligate communicator. But does language as a communication system share much, if anything, in common with the communication systems of other animals? If so, can we learn much about language by studying the songs of birds, the calls of primates, and the pheromones of insects? Does language ontogeny proceed along the lines found in some other species? What neural processes are involved in language production and comprehension, and are these processes specialized for these tasks? These are the sorts of questions to be discussed in this section.

THE EVOLUTION OF LANGUAGE

Human language and animal communication systems cry out for comparison. How are they similar? Different? Two schools of thought have confronted these questions from fundamentally opposed positions. One, held by many linguists, maintains that human language is so unique that there is no useful point to be made in comparing it with the communication of other species (Lenneberg, 1967; John-Steiner & Panofsky, 1987). This position is not antievolutionary. Rather, its proponents argue that human evolution has pushed language processes to such an extreme that its ties to animal communication have been severed. There is a potential danger in this position of closing the question before it is really open. If one decides, in advance, that nonhuman animals lack language (or consciousness, etc.), then we will be blind to its presence even if it does exist (Griffin, 1985). Allen (1987), among others, has taken this perspective.

The second position is more traditionally evolutionary in its approach. Its advocates feel that language is probably the result of a long series of elaborations on a basic mammalian communication system (Lieberman, 1977, 1984). Thus, comparisons of language with animal communication systems should yield a pattern of similarities and differences reflecting our common ancestry and the unique evolutionary history of our species (Steklis, 1985). This position does not imply that language is "just like" animal communication, or even that language is more of the same thing as animal communication. Language may have qualitatively different features. We won't know, however, until after we have studied language—and animal communication—in an unbiased fashion.

Attempting to unravel the evolution of language puts us in the same difficult position we are in whenever we try to trace the history of something that does not fossilize. The only effective strategy is to employ the comparative method: searching for similarities and differences, both in broad form and in detail. We will proceed with this task by comparing the attributes of language with the attributes of other animal communication systems, and by scrutinizing work on attempts to teach great apes to communicate with humans through artificial language systems.

Design Features   A useful way of comparing language with other animals' communication systems is to compile a list of characteristics of human language—design features (Hockett, 1960)—and then survey animal communication systems to determine which features are present and which are absent. Many design features are obviously shared by many other species (see Table 13-1 for a complete listing). For example, language is vocal-auditory, but so is bird song. The last four design features on this list were the last to find animal analogs. We will examine them in some detail.

Displacement refers to the phenomenon of providing information about objects or events that are removed from the signaler in space or time. Human language is full of displacement. We talk of the past and future, of events across town or on the other side of the world. Can animals escape from the here and now? At least one animal system does: the waggle dance of the honeybees (Gould *et al.*, 1985). When a foraging worker returns to the hive after a successful search, she often performs a "dance" on the vertical wall of a honeycomb. Moving in a figure eight (Fig. 13-8) she vibrates her abdomen during one phase. Some dances are oriented vertically: the bee waggles while walking up the face of the comb. Other dances are oriented at other angles, although a particular bee orients at the same angle for many repetitions of the performance. Through some ingenious experiments performed by Karl von Frisch, which, by the way, won him a Nobel prize in 1973, the code of the waggle dance was broken (Lindauer, 1985). The angle of the waggle matched the angle between the sun, the hive, and the food source from which she had returned (see Fig. 13-8). For example, if she waggles while going straight down, the food can be found by flying away from the sun in line with the hive. If she waggles toward "three o'clock" the food is 90 degrees to the right of the sun–hive line. Distance is encoded by the number of vibrations in the waggle. These studies are reviewed by von Frisch (1974). This qualifies as displacement because the bee—in the dark hive—is informing her hive-mates of food that may be several hundred meters away. Moreover, she may continue the dance for hours

Table 13-1
DESIGN FEATURES OF HUMAN LANGUAGE

Vocal-auditory channel: Language is produced vocally and received by means of the auditory system.

Broadcast transmission and directional reception: Being acoustic, language sounds spread in all directions from their source, but the reception device is capable of decoding the direction from which it comes.

Rapid fading: Language sounds are short-lived.

Interchangeability: The same individuals that produce language sounds are also capable of receiving and decoding others' language sounds.

Total feedback: Individuals can detect and decode their own language sounds.

Specialization: Language sounds serve no other function than communication.

Semanticity: Language sounds bear a rather fixed relationship to the objects, events and concepts that they denote.

Arbitrariness: The particular sound that has semantic value bears no physical relationship to its referent. Any sound could have been used.

Discreteness: Slightly different sounds often have very different semantic referents (e.g., "sail" and "mail").

Displacement: The semantic referent of a sound may be distant in time or place from the speaker.

Productivity: Speech sounds can acquire new semantic referents, or combinations of sounds can denote new or different referents. Language is open to change.

Traditional transmission: The details of the language system are acquired individually by each participant through a process of learning.

Duality of patterning: The most fundamental units of speech sound—phonemes—are themselves meaningless, but can be combined in various ways to produce meaningful sounds.

Source: Based on Hockett (1960).

after her return. While doing so she slowly changes the angle of her dance to compensate for the changing angle caused by the earth's rotation!

Another design feature, *productivity,* is the emission of novel signals or novel sequences of signals that are nevertheless understood by receivers. Humans, even young children just learning to speak, exhibit productivity. Productivity may or may not exist in the natural communication systems of animals. Studies of great apes who have learned a form of communication that has been taught to them by humans (such as sign language) commonly exhibit productivity (see below), but critics have argued that productivity in these cases may reflect the design of the communication system as much as it does the animals themselves.

The third design feature, *traditional transmission,* refers to the use of learned conventions in the system. This means that the system requires particular forms of experience to be performed properly. The existence of learned dialects in birds (e.g., Jenkins, 1977) suggests quite

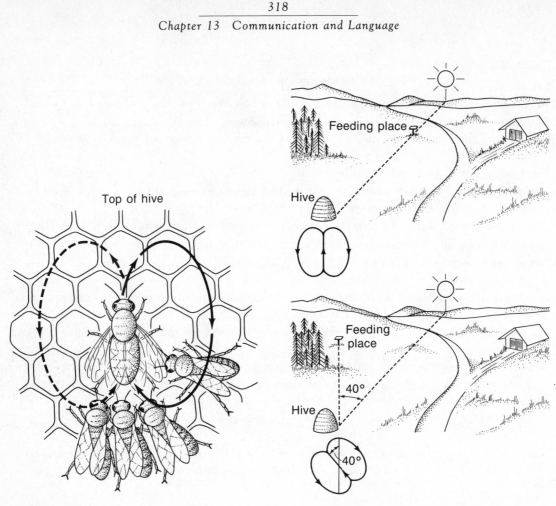

Figure 13.8
The angle at which the waggle portion of the "dance" is performed indicates the angle between the sun, hive, and food source.

strongly that traditional transmission is a widespread feature in animal communication.

The fourth design feature, *duality of patterning*, means that a signal is decomposable into fundamental units (called *phonemes* in human language) that can be rearranged to produce new signals with different message structures. Only a few studies of animal communication have tested for duality of patterning. Some have failed to find it while others have succeeded. The "syllables" that make up the song of the indigo bunting, a New World finch, can be experimentally rearranged and played back to males in the field. Syllable arrangement seems to make no difference (Emlen, 1972), at least in terms of observable responses by male buntings. However, studies of two New World monkeys, the cotton-top tamarin and the titi monkey, indicate that the order in which their calls are arranged is important in determining the message conveyed (Cleveland & Snowdon, 1982; Robinson, 1979a). How extensive this design feature is, however, awaits further research.

In summary, the comparison of human language and animal communication based on design features indicates that many features are shared in common, but that others may not exist in animal communication. In any event, given the small number of species that have been examined, we are far from making any strong conclusions about the similarities that exist. We need more data on more diverse species to begin to see the patterns of distribution of design features in the animal kingdom.

Messages Human language has been thought to differ from animal communication not only in its design features but also in at least two types of message. (Recall that "message" refers to the sort of information conveyed in a signal.)

Signals, roughly classified, are either about the signaler itself or about something in the environment (see the section on signals and messages at the beginning of the chapter). Animal communication traditionally was thought to be limited to internal referents such as the signaler's emotional condition and forthcoming behavior. Accumulating evidence, particularly on nonhuman primates, suggests a view of animal communication that is not nearly so limited (Marler, 1985). We have already seen that vervet monkeys have distinctive calls for each of their classes of predators. Clearly, the monkeys are not merely signaling "I'm terrified." They may be terrified but they are also specifying what they are terrified of. Similarly, the bee dance system provides details of the location of food that cannot be construed solely as the bee's "excitement" about having found a food source.

Another kind of message is one that does not correspond to its referent. A signal suggesting that the signaler is about to attack when in fact it does not, or that it is larger than it is, or is something else entirely are examples of lying or deceit. Humans are not the only species with such messages. Many predators use lures to trick their prey into approaching close enough to be captured. A particularly good example of this occurs in fireflies. Male fireflies emit a species-specific flash code to which receptive females respond with their own "answering" flash pattern. After mating with a male, the females of some species begin mimicking the answering flashes of other species. In this way these "femme fatales" lure other males which they may pounce on and eat (Carlson & Copeland, 1978). Similarly, a South American bird species that is particularly adept at detecting hawks and warning other members of their mixed-species flocks, sometimes emits a hawk alarm call when no hawk is present and while engaged in competition with another bird over an insect. The competitor usually takes evasive action, leaving the bird that "cried wolf" to pursue the insect unimpeded (Munn, 1986).

Do fireflies or other species that do similar things "know" what they are doing? Is it really lying if the organism could do nothing else under the circumstances? People are not accused of lying if the false information they gave was not known by them to be false. Animal communication has been considered to be so automatic that lying could not happen. According to this view, the *femme fatale* firefly is not lying because her physiology is structured in such a way as to switch to another signal after mating. These are reasonable criticisms to make of the proposition that animals lie, at least on occasion. However, if there is flexibility in the signaling system, then the signaling behavior is not rigidly performed and it is appropriate to consider the provision of false information as lying. For instance, male hanging flies often mimic female behavior while approaching a male holding a prey item. If the

SUE SAVAGE-RUMBAUGH

"Apes, then, like children, learn to use symbols as part of social-interaction routines. They are able to discern various sets of circumstances in which the production of various symbols is deemed appropriate and results in obtaining a goal." [Savage-Rumbaugh, E. S., Rumbaugh, D. M., & Boysen, S. (1980). Do apes use language? American Scientist **68,** 49–61 (p. 60).]

mimicry works, the mimic may steal the prey item which is then used in female attraction. But the same male who mimics one time may boldly approach and grapple with the prey owner on another occasion (Thornhill, 1979, 1980).

In summary, it appears that the sorts of messages that commonly appear in language also appear in the natural communication systems of other animals. Some animals communicate about the world around them, and sometimes attempt to deceive others.

Ape language studies One of the great difficulties with comparing language and animal communication comes from our inability to adequately study the signaling systems of other ani-

mals and to discern the nature of the information that they may be providing. We know that our auditory systems are not adequately tuned to the sounds made by many other species, so we may be missing a great deal of what may be present. Further, our olfactory systems are such that many animal pheromones may be missed entirely. Although auditory and chemical analyses may overcome some of these shortcomings, they too have their limitations. Deciphering animal communication systems is an enormous undertaking.

Some animal behaviorists have reasoned that if we can not adequately study animal systems, perhaps animals can be taught language. If a nonhuman species can master language, then it must possess the cognitive skills required in language. If the species can do some things, but not others, we can gain insight into the uniquely human aspects of language. In short, attempts to teach language to apes have been motivated by an interest in the evolution of language, and to see how great a gap in communication processes may exist between humans and our closest relatives.

Shortly after the discovery of the great apes in Africa by European explorers and scientists, the general public was amazed by their similarity to humans. Speculations about chimpanzee language-learning abilities were published as early as 1661 and attempts to teach spoken language to chimpanzees can be traced to nearly a century ago (Rumbaugh *et al.*, 1982).

Attempts to teach spoken language to great apes failed, at least in part, because of the inability of the ape vocal tract to produce human language sounds (Laitman, 1984; Lieberman, 1977). Indeed, the ape vocal apparatus is more like that of infant humans, who are also unable to make many of the sounds found in adult speech. This revelation led to attempts to circumvent the sound-production problem, and subsequent efforts employed sign language or symbol manipulation on keyboards or other devices. How successful have these studies been at teaching apes to communicate using human language processes?

The first major attempt was made using a female chimpanzee named Washoe at the University of Nevada in Reno. Washoe was taught American Sign Language for the Deaf, and with about 4 years of training had acquired well over 100 signs that could be combined in grammatically correct sequences (Gardner & Gardner, 1975). Similar claims were made for other chimpanzees and for a female gorilla, Koko (Patterson, 1978). With respect to productivity, the researchers claimed that the animals began producing sign sequences that were grammatically correct but which had never been formally taught to them. For instance, Koko began signing "You dirty toilet" to her trainers whenever they refused her wishes (Patterson & Linden, 1981)! For a variety of reasons, however, claims about productivity have been criticized (see Ristau & Robbins, 1982).

The excitement about the prospects for ape language were largely chilled when Terrace (Terrace *et al.*, 1979) closely examined data on signing by a young chimp, Nim. Terrace concluded that ape sign language was unlike the language of human children in that the apes were only signing to obtain objects, such as food or toys, that the researchers were offering them. Further, although the chimps sometimes produced strings of signs, the information content did not increase much as a result, primarily because of the repetition of signs within the strings. Terrace and others (e.g., Savage-Rumbaugh, 1984) concluded that although the chimps were clearly producing signs, their understanding of the signs was not what the researchers had thought it was, and their use of signs was not language-like.

The most exciting development in the ape language research field has come from the work of Sue Savage-Rumbaugh (1988), who has studied the language skills of a male bonobo (pygmy chimpanzee) named Kanzi. Kanzi's training differed from that of other apes in that he was not expected to produce language early (he communicates by pressing keys on a special keyboard labeled with various symbols), but he was exposed to language at an early age. Thus, his language ontogeny paralleled that of young children, in which language comprehension precedes language production, often by lengthy periods. Kanzi is highly adept at understanding spoken English. He demonstrates this not only in his responses to words and sentences spoken to him in the informal interactions that go on at the laboratory facility where he lives, but in more formal tests. For example, Kanzi is shown three photographs and hears a tape-recorded sentence that describes one of them, after which he points to one of the pictures. The pictures, and the sentence, are of fairly complex situations. For instance, Kanzi hears the sentence "Bill drinking Coke" and sees a picture of Bill drinking Coke, Mary drinking Coke, and Bill hitting a table with a rock. Kanzi selected the correct picture, as he did on 76% of the 34 problem sets. His performance on single word, single object pictures was even better. Further, Savage-Rumbaugh showed that Kanzi is not responding to intonation patterns, which sometimes complicate animal communication research (say friendly words to your dog in an angry tone and watch the reaction), because he is still highly accurate in his choices even when the word is produced in a monotone, emotion-free form by a computer-driven voice synthesizer! Although other animal species can be trained to discriminate various human speech sounds under carefully controlled conditions (e.g., Kluender *et al.*, 1987), Kanzi's ability is phenomenal and has never been equaled.

The work on Kanzi illustrates that great apes can have rather great comprehension abilities. Their abilities to produce language, however, are not as well demonstrated, and they may indeed not approach those of humans. If we remember, however, that the goal of this research is not to demonstrate that apes *can* communicate with humans using human-designed systems, but rather to determine *to what extent* their perceptual and cognitive systems allow such acquisition, then this research, which has so often been overblown, will begin to shed light on the evolution of language in our species.

In summary, language most certainly excels in the sheer quantity of signals and in the amount of information conveyed. Nevertheless, there are enough similarities between language and animal communication to make further research on animal communication worthwhile from the perspective of increasing our knowledge of language. Of course, animal communication research is valuable in its own right, and adds considerably to our general knowledge of behavioral and evolutionary processes.

ONTOGENY OF LANGUAGE

The ontogeny of human language depends on a complex interplay between the developing sensory, perceptual, and integrative neural systems on the one hand, and language experience on the other. Because language ontogeny involves both language perception and production, our review will be divided in that way.

Language perception   Earlier we discussed the ability of infants to categorize a sound continuum into two discrete classes, ([b] and [p] as in "bin" and "pin") based on voice onset time. However, not all speech sound contrasts are so easy to make, and many are not present until after the child is over a year old, even if the

sounds are a normal part of adult language in the child's society (Lieberman, 1984). Nevertheless, even very young infants make numerous perceptual discriminations, apparently with little or no specific experience with them (Kuhl, 1979). Interestingly, Kuhl and Meltzoff (1982) have shown that infants are adept at determining the synchrony between the facial movements of speech and the acoustic output of speech. They showed videotapes of two female faces, each of whom was speaking a vowel every few seconds (one said [a] as in "pop," the other said [i] as in "peep"). The infants, however, heard only one of the vowels, played from a speaker between the two faces. The infants spent more time looking at the face that registered with the sound than at the other face. This study indicates that both auditory and visual attention is involved in infants' language perception.

Lack of experience with some sounds leads to a loss of perceptual discriminability later on. The best example of this occurs with [r] vs. [l] in Japanese speaking adults. Although the discrimination is made in infancy, because the sounds do not appear in the language, the ability to discriminate them is lost (Eimas, 1975). The same loss occurs in many other nonused contrasts, but adults can regain some of them with extensive practice (Werker, 1989). Because only a few of the many possible phonetic contrasts have been studied in infants (Lieberman, 1984), interesting new findings surely are in store.

Language production   The production side of language can be approached in two stages: the pronunciation of the basic units of speech (syllables), and the arrangement of these units into words and words into sentences.

A once widespread notion was that human infants worldwide produced in their babbling all sounds used in human languages (Lieberman, 1984). We now know this is not true. Some sounds are produced spontaneously, but the full set cannot be produced until the vocal tract matures sufficiently. Another set of sounds is produced through rehearsal, often acquired through imitation games played with the parents or older children.

Some time before their second birthday most children begin the switch from uttering poorly articulated single words to two-word sentences. This is the first of many steps toward adult language. These steps are fascinating in themselves, although space does not permit adequate description of them. A good synopsis is available by Moskowitz (1978). For our purpose the most interesting thing about these steps is their orderliness. Although there are individual differences in the age at which these stages are attained, children go through them in the same order. Furthermore, if a child has not yet acquired a particular stage (such as forming plurals) he or she will be unable to repeat a phrase correctly that contains a plural. The word is repeated in its singular form. This is striking evidence that language does not form by a process of imitation alone (Lenneberg, 1969). Children worldwide are creating utterances not present in the language around them and cannot imitate much of adult language because it consists of so many rules that the child has not yet acquired. However, young children abstract language rules from the adult language around them. They apply these rules in general ways at first, then gradually incorporate refinements and make the necessary exceptions to the rules (Moskowitz, 1978).

Also fascinating is the finding that much of language development is not limited to the vocal-auditory mode. Deaf children developing sign language exhibit many of the same conventions used by hearing children. Thus, surprisingly, children do not need to speak or hear speech for language skills to develop (Goldin-Meadow & Mylander, 1983).

Sensitive periods and language development Language development typically does not begin until the brain has matured to about 65% of its adult size (Lenneberg, 1969). Once begun, however, language development proceeds on pace with brain maturation. Surprisingly, the ability to acquire language declines as brain maturation attains near-adult levels in the early teens. Thus, there is a sensitive period for language acquisition that begins around the first birthday and largely ends about 12 to 13 years later.

There are three forms of evidence that lead to the conclusion about sensitive periods for language development. First, although language production and comprehension regions are located in the left cerebral hemisphere in most people (examined in the next section), the right hemisphere can perform these tasks if the left hemisphere is unable to because of injury or disease. However, the earlier the damage the more complete the recovery due to right hemisphere takeover. Left hemisphere damage in adults leads to nearly irreversible language difficulties. In children there is good prognosis for recovery, and the younger the child the better the prognosis (Vroman, 1987).

Second, the ability to acquire a second language, especially to speak it without an accent, drops substantially after the early teens. This is not to say that additional languages cannot be learned in adulthood. The vocabulary and grammar can be learned, but the ability to make subtle sound contrasts in the new language and to pronounce words like a native speaker become substantially more difficult in adulthood. The best time to learn a second language is in childhood when the brain's language regions are most amenable to the task.

Third, congenitally deaf children who later regain their hearing find it exceptionally difficult to learn language if hearing is restored after the early teens. The younger the child when hearing is achieved the better the prospects for language acquisition.

NEUROBIOLOGY OF LANGUAGE

So far we have largely ignored the role of the brain in the execution of complex forms of communication. Let us turn to that topic now, with special attention to human language. First, this discussion must be prefaced with a caution. Research ethics preclude performing experiments on the brains of humans. Thus, virtually all that we know about the brain's role in human language comes from studies of medically impaired and wounded persons. Many such cases have come to light over the years, however. For example, stroke is unfortunately common, and, depending on the site and severity of the damage, the behavioral symptoms of the afflicted persons can tell us a great deal about the workings of the brain. Nevertheless, no two stroke victims suffer precisely the same amount of damage in the same brain areas, at the same age, and so forth. So we must be careful in drawing general conclusions about brain–language relationships.

Speech production   One of the first brain–language relationships to be discovered was that of speech production. This was worked out by the French anatomist Paul Broca, around 1860. During autopsies, Broca had studied the brains of several people who suffered from *expressive aphasia.* That is, they were severely impaired in their speech production. They could speak only very slowly, often could not pronounce words, and tended to omit many words from their sentences (all these symptoms, of course, varied in severity among patients). Broca found that these people had suffered damage to a part of the frontal lobes (Geschwind, 1972, 1979). Broca reasoned that their language impairment was

due to this damage. Further, he noticed that they all had damage only to the left frontal lobe. Other patients with damage to the corresponding part of the right frontal lobe showed no such language impairment.

Speech perception   About 10 years later, a German neurologist, Carl Wernicke, reported that damage to a specific part of the left temporal lobe produced another sort of aphasia (*receptive aphasia*), associated with the comprehension of speech. In this form of aphasia, the person speaks fluently and pronounces words clearly, but a careful evaluation of the content of the speech indicates severe problems. The speech is essentially a string of unrelated words and phrases and makes little if any sense. Moreover, the person appears not to understand spoken or written instructions.

The brain regions responsible for these processes have come to be called Broca's area and Wernicke's area, respectively (Fig. 13-9). The two areas are connected via a band of axons called the *arcuate fasciculus.* As you might expect, some people suffer strokes that destroy all or part of the arcuate fasciculus. Their symptoms reveal the specialized nature of Broca's and Wernicke's areas. First, the person speaks fluently and pronounces words normally (Broca's area is intact). They also understand spoken and written speech since Wernicke's area is intact. However, what they say often has no relationship to what they hear. This is because the two areas have been disconnected and thus are functioning independently. There are several other forms of aphasia (and many intermediate forms) depending on the site and the severity of the damage (Geschwind, 1972, 1979; Vroman, 1987). The general conclusion to be drawn from these observations, however, is that parts of the brain (almost always on the left side) are specialized for the production and comprehension of language.

How do we know that parts of the left hemi-

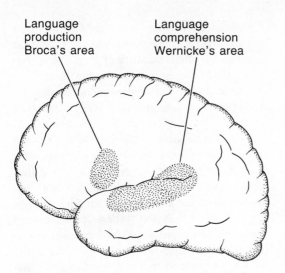

Language production Broca's area

Language comprehension Wernicke's area

Figure 13.9
The left hemisphere has specialized areas for language production (Broca's area) and comprehension (Wernicke's area). The arcuate fasciculus is a band of axons connecting them.

sphere are specialized for language while other parts are not? Perhaps speech comprehension problems are due to general damage to the auditory cortex, and perhaps speech production is impaired because the motor cortex that controls movements of the tongue, mouth, and larynx is damaged. There are several forms of evidence that rule out aphasia as resulting from generalized auditory or motor cortex damage. First, damage to Broca's area does not impair the person's ability to sing. Singing seems to be controlled by the right hemisphere. So the necessary muscles are intact, but the use of these muscles for speech is impaired. This is a good example of a basic motor unit being controlled by two or more command areas (Chapter 9). In this case, the speech command area is damaged but another that controls musical production is not. Second, damage to Wernicke's area alone

does not lead to general hearing difficulty. The person is perfectly capable of hearing human voices and other sounds, but apparently lacks the "decoding device" for comprehending what is heard. So it is indeed the case that Broca's and Wernicke's areas are specialized for the production and perception of speech.

Additional interesting work on the localization of language functions is being conducted without the complications of brain injury. For example, Ojemann and Mateer (1979) applied electrical stimulation to the left hemisphere of people undergoing brain surgery to alleviate their symptoms of epilepsy. They found areas that affect the motor processes of speech (tongue and mouth movements), others that disrupted sound identification, and others that influence short-term verbal memory and grammar. Although the number of subjects was small, this line of work promises to broaden our understanding of the neurobiology of language.

Summary

Communication consists of an individual emitting a signal (a behavior or behavioral product that functions in modifying another's behavior) that results in a change in the behavior of one or more receivers. Signals are best thought of as carriers of information about the signaler or the signaler's environment. The response of the receiver to a signal is determined jointly by the signal's information and by contextual information, i.e., information derived from sources other than the signal itself.

There is great diversity in the ontogeny of communication. Some species signal and respond appropriately without specific individual experience. In contrast, many other communication systems (both human and nonhuman) are only properly executed following extensive individual experience. Experience can alter the form of signals, as it does in human language and some bird songs; in reception of signals; and in the circumstances in which signals are emitted.

Communication occurs in several channels which correspond to the sensory modality (e.g., audition, vision, olfaction) in which the signal is received. The particular structure of a signal (e.g., the pitch of acoustic signals, or the wavelength of reflected light in optic signals) is due to the situations in which signaling typically occurs. For example, acoustic communication over long distances generally leads to the evolution of low-frequency (low-pitch) signals because low-frequency sounds retain their energy over distance better than do higher-frequency sounds. In general, there is an excellent match between signal properties and ecological circumstances.

Communication evolves in the same manner as other behavioral systems. Evidence regarding the effects of genetic differences on signal production and comprehension in insects, frogs, and mammals is reviewed. Communication systems appear to have evolved from the tendency of animals to monitor one another's behavior for signs of forthcoming behavior. Under these circumstances, individuals may have benefited by making these signs more conspicuous and stereotyped.

Human language is a special case of communication, but it has presumably evolved from some other form of communication. Research on the evolution of human language has focused on (a) the attributes or design features of language that may be shared with animal communication systems, (b) the sorts of information that may be present (about external events and objects, and false information), and (c) the language abilities

of great apes. Although it is clear that no other species has a communication system that matches the sheer quantity of language in humans, there are enough intriguing similarities that we can learn a good deal about language by studying the communication systems of other animals.

Human language development is a lengthy and complex process involving extensive environmental inputs interacting with a host of anatomic and physiologic processes that are uniquely geared toward language production and comprehension. Among these processes are brain structures specialized for language, attention to speech sounds and motivation to make speech sounds and to understand them. Language development occurs best during a sensitive period that is approximately the first 12 to 13 years of life. Neural conditions during this period make language acquisition relatively easy; changes in these neural systems thereafter make language acquisition considerably more difficult.

Recommended Readings

HAILMAN, J. P. (1977). *Optical signals: Animal communication and light.* Bloomington: Indiana University Press.

HALLIDAY, T. R. & SLATER, P. J. B. (1983). *Animal behaviour. Vol. 2: Communication.* New York: Freeman.

LIEBERMAN, P. (1984). *The biology and evolution of language.* Cambridge: Harvard University Press.

SMITH, W. J. (1977). *The behavior of communicating: An ethological approach.* Cambridge: Harvard University Press.

Chapter 14

FEEDING, PREDATION, AND ANTIPREDATOR BEHAVIORS

Life does not exist without the utilization of energy. Whether the organism manufactures its own food through photosynthesis, or consumes it in the form of other organisms, the acquisition and utilization of energy are fundamental processes. It should come as no surprise, then, that behavioral, physiological, and anatomical adaptations have evolved because of the necessity of energy acquisition (Pyke *et al.*, 1977).

Avoiding becoming someone else's energy is no less important. Predators may take an important toll on populations of their prey. Because of mortality due to predators, prey have evolved many adaptations for minimizing risk. Thus, predators and prey are locked in struggles with life-or-death stakes, and adaptations by one side are met with counteradaptations by the other. This chapter will review the phenomena involved in food acquisition, feeding, and antipredator activities.

Ontogeny, Experience, and Feeding

We will approach the phenomenon of food acquisition and consumption by examining its developmental aspects. Let us begin with a look at the most fundamental problem, the recognition of food.

FOOD RECOGNITION

Food recognition mechanisms are extremely diverse among animals. At one extreme are those species that seem to require no previous experience with their food to deal with it in a normal fashion. Many insect larvae, such as those of burying beetles, literally hatch out in their food—provided by the parents—and begin eating (Milne & Milne, 1976).

Garter snakes emerge with the behavioral capacity to recognize prey and to avoid nonprey. Arnold (1977) presented prey-naive garter snakes from a coastal population with pieces of slugs, which are abundant in the area. The slugs were readily consumed. Garter snakes from an inland region, where slugs are rare, either consistently ate them or consistently refused to eat them. Further, eating or not eating appeared in all the newborns of a given litter, suggesting either that the response difference was due to genetic differences among litters, or to an unknown environmental variable that differs between coastal and inland areas. Finally, snakes that initially refused to eat slugs never accepted them, even after repeated presentations.

Young mammals demonstrate reflexive sucking movements to a variety of stimuli placed in or near the mouth (Blass & Teicher, 1980). The mother merely presents herself for suckling and the babies take over. Little or no specific individual experience is required, although a familiar odor may be necessary to stimulate suckling the first time in some species (Blass & Teicher, 1980).

Human newborns have some well-developed food-tasting abilities and preferences, but appear to be unable to taste other substances. For instance, neonates prefer a glucose solution over plain water, and more concentrated glucose solutions are preferred over less concentrated solutions. However, they show no ability to taste sodium chloride or even bitter substances. Further, very young human infants and rat pups do not associate sodium chloride or other tastes with illness (Blass & Teicher, 1980), although these abilities develop later, when the youngsters begin consuming foods other than milk.

EXPERIENCE AND FOOD PREFERENCE

Omnivorous species, such as rats, bears, and humans, have many foods available, and they may vary geographically, seasonally, and even hourly in abundance and quality. It is therefore advantageous that omnivorous animals be able to use individual experience in guiding food choice. In some cases the experience is gained passively. For example, in a series of elegant experiments, Galef (1976) found that young rats learn about foods through the tastes that the foods impart to their mother's milk. For omnivorous species like rats, this makes adaptive sense: Anything that the mother is eating is probably good, so persisting in those choices will probably work, too.

Another type of individual experience in food selection comes from the consequences of eating certain foods. In some cases, food may have an adverse effect on the individual. Some foods contain toxins and others may have spoiled. If a food, particularly a novel one, is eaten and the individual later experiences gastrointestinal illness, there is a pronounced tendency to avoid that food thereafter. Garcia *et al.* (1955) demonstrated this by giving rats either a new taste (saccharin in water) or familiar tap water, and, while they drank it, exposed them to radiation. Nausea occurred several hours later. Two days later, after full recovery from their illness, the rats refused to drink the saccharin solution, but continued to drink tap water. The aversion gradually declined, but was still present over one month later. Similar findings have been obtained using other illness-inducing techniques, and in other species, including humans. A good example of taste aversion learning in humans comes from a study of children undergoing chemotherapy for cancer. Some of these children, who were visiting an outpatient clinic for treatment, were given a novel ice cream shortly before their therapy. Most of them became nauseous and vomited after the treatment. When they next visited the clinic and were given a choice of their previous flavor or another new flavor, they almost always avoided the one

ILENE BERNSTEIN

"The demonstration of taste aversions in children receiving chemotherapy treatments may prove to be of importance to physicians who administer treatments which induce nausea and vomiting. Such aversions may be one of the factors contributing to the anorexia and weight loss seen in patients with cancer." [Bernstein, I. (1978). Learned taste aversions in children receiving chemotherapy. Science **200,** *1302–1303 (p. 1303).]*

they had eaten earlier (Bernstein, 1978). Other children who were not being treated were far more likely to ask for the first flavor again. Surprisingly, this aversion occurs even when the person is convinced that the food itself had nothing to do with the illness (Bernstein & Webster, 1980), testifying to the powerful influence of this specialized form of learning.

The "Garcia effect" has been used in a practical fashion to reduce the toll on livestock taken by certain predators, especially coyotes. Gustavson *et al.* (1974) demonstrated that coyotes that ate meat that later made them ill (due to lacing with lithium chloride) would avoid eating that meat thereafter. Ellins and Catalano (1980) found that placing baits with lithium chloride near sheep herds and turkey farms significantly reduced predation rates by coyotes. Coyotes, however, quickly learn to tell whether meat contains lithium chloride by its odor or taste if it is applied too liberally; therefore, the dose has to be small enough that it cannot be detected but large enough to induce illness (Burns, 1980). Controlling livestock depredation through these means is more environmentally sound than killing the predator.

Animals quickly learn to avoid foods that make them sick, but can they learn which foods make them well? There is some evidence that they can. Rozin and Kalat (1971) have reviewed studies on specific hungers and learned food preferences that terminate those hungers. For instance, if a sodium-deprived animal is given a food that contains sodium, it will consume that food until its sodium need is alleviated. The same sort of process occurs for calcium, essential amino acids, and other nutrients. In fact, many of these nutrients are tasteless, and thus the animal must learn about the effects of these foods by attending to the way that it feels after consuming the food. If the individual feels better, it will continue to consume that food (Rozin, 1976). Moreover, if the nutrient deficiency occurs again, the animal will go specifically to the food that alleviates that particular deficiency, not to another that alleviates some other deficiency. Perhaps this "wisdom of the body" is at the root of food cravings that so many people have from time to time.

Although many food choices are based on individuals' experience with those foods, there is a growing body of evidence indicating that food recognition and choice can arise indirectly, by observing others eating certain foods and experiencing the consequences (Galef, 1990). For instance, a rat was given one of two new foods to eat. Afterward, it was placed with another rat for a short time. The second rat was then given a choice, by itself, of the two new foods. Rats overwhelmingly chose the same food that the first rat had eaten. The choice was made on the basis of food odor determined from the first rat's breath (Galef, 1990).

Modeling and imitation are known in several species, including humans and other primates. Young chimpanzees intently watch their mothers as they eat, apparently learning about food through example. The youngsters even sniff the mother's mouth as she chews her food, and may insert a finger into her mouth to sample her food. Humans, of course, are taught explicitly or informally what to eat (and what not to eat!) and strong cultural differences in food preference suggest that what constitutes appropriate foods depends on socially mediated learning or imitation. Although cultural differences in food patterns may seem capricious, in some cases the adaptive value of the choices is clear. For instance, Chinese cuisine contains no milk or milk products. This is probably due to the inability of the vast majority of adult Chinese to digest lactose (milk sugar) for enzymatic reasons (Rozin, 1976). Similarly, starlings lack sucrase, the enzyme required to digest sucrose. If much sucrose is consumed, the bird becomes ill. Consequently, they avoid fruits containing much sucrose, although they readily consume foods with other sugars (Martinez del Rio & Stevens, 1989).

Physiological Mechanisms of Feeding

Given the importance of energy and nutrient balance, numerous regulatory systems have evolved. These systems affect the amount consumed, the timing of food consumption, and energy storage and utilization.

THE DIGESTIVE SYSTEM AND THE CONTROL OF FEEDING

Digestion commences as soon as food enters the mouth, continues in the stomach, and culminates with the absorption of nutrients from food in the intestines. To understand the amount and the timing of food consumption, the digestive system is a likely place to begin.

Let us begin with an animal consuming food. What makes eating stop? There are several mechanisms that contribute to cessation of eating. First, orosensory mechanisms are involved. Animals surgically altered so that swallowed food drops out of a tube leading from the esophagus will eat the usual amount before stopping (Janowitz & Grossman, 1949), indicating that taste, chewing or swallowing, etc., can eventually suppress feeding independently of the stomach and other factors. However, animals prepared in this way begin eating again much sooner than normal: the orosensory mechanisms have only a short-term inhibitory effect.

The stomach also influences the termination of feeding. Early studies concluded that stomach distention was responsible for termination of feeding. This was shown in several ways. Food has been injected into the stomachs of lab animals by means of implanted tubes, thus bypassing the orosensory mechanisms. These animals continued to chew and swallow their own food but ate much less than they normally would (reviewed by Logue, 1986).

The presence of food in the stomach suppresses further eating in two ways. First, there are stretch receptors in the stomach wall that have inhibitory effects on feeding. Activating the stretch receptors by inflating a small balloon within the stomach or by constricting the emptying of food from the stomach both suppress feeding. Signals regarding stomach distention are sent to the brain via the vagus nerve

(Deutsch & Ahn, 1986). However, appetite suppression exerted by nonnutritive processes (balloons, nondigestible "foods," etc.) is relatively short-lived. Second, more complete feeding suppression is due to activation of nutrient receptors embedded in the stomach lining. When nutrients enter the stomach, signals are sent along the splanchnic nerves to the brain, inhibiting further consumption (Deutsch & Ahn, 1986). An extreme example of feeding-induced inhibition of food consumption occurs in the leech, in which a full feeding consisting of about eight times its own weight in blood results in suppression of feeding lasting about a year (Lent & Dickinson, 1988)!

The intestines are the next part of the digestive system to work on the consumed food. The intestines release a hormone, cholecystokinin (CCK), that suppresses appetite, probably by slowing the emptying of food from the stomach (McHugh & Moran, 1985). Injections of CCK into deprived animals greatly reduces the amount of food consumed (Gibbs *et al.*, 1973; Baile *et al.*, 1985).

Finally, the liver is involved in the regulation of feeding. Because its blood supply arrives directly from the intestines, the liver is in a position to monitor the nutrients contained in the blood. Moreover, large quantities of glycogen ("animal starch") are stored in the liver and are drawn upon to help fuel the body. The liver contains receptors for several types of nutrients and their metabolic byproducts. The liver receptors communicate with the brain via the vagus nerve. It appears that these receptors increase their action potential rates when the nutrients they monitor decline in the liver's blood supply. Blocking conduction in the vagus nerve reduces feeding in otherwise hungry animals. This system operates with a longer delay than the orosensory mechanisms or stomach processes because more time is required for digestion to deposit nutrients into the blood supply where they can be detected by the liver. So, after an initial inhibition of feeding by the orosensory mechanisms, stomach, and intestines, the liver can begin influencing the brain in either direction: maintaining satiety if the meal was nutrient rich, or initiating more feeding if nutrients were few.

BRAIN MECHANISMS AND THE CONTROL OF FEEDING

The search for brain mechanisms of feeding control has focused on two hypothalamic regions, the ventromedial hypothalamus (VMH) and the lateral hypothalamus (LH) (Norgren & Grill, 1982). Early studies of the VMH seemed to suggest that it was the site of appetite suppression. Lesions of the VMH led to voracious appetites in lab animals, some of whom doubled their body weight over prelesion weight (Fig. 14-1). The standard interpretation was that VMH had an inhibitory affect on appetite and that removing the inhibition resulted in animals with essentially no control over their intake. In contrast, lesions of LH had the opposite effect: severe reductions in eating and drinking leading to extreme weight loss and even death.

Hundreds of follow up studies on VMH and LH have forced new interpretations of this simple view (Gold, 1973; Stricker, 1983). First, VMH-lesioned rats are clearly not out of control in their eating. They gain weight only if plenty of highly palatable food is available. Further, if they have to work for food by pressing a lever several times for each pellet, they do not work as hard as unoperated rats. Next, if otherwise good food is made to taste bitter, VMH-lesioned animals do not eat as much as normal rats. Finally, VMH-lesioned rats do not gain weight indefinitely, even with palatable, easy-to-obtain food

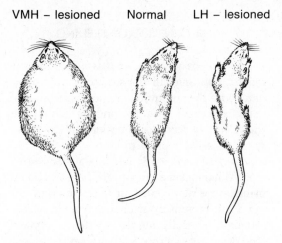

VMH – lesioned   Normal   LH – lesioned

Figure 14.1
Lesions of the ventromedial hypothalamus (VMH) often result in obesity due to overfeeding. In contrast, lesions of the lateral hypothalamus (LH) produce reductions in food consumption and marked weight loss.

in constant supply. They gain to a new, higher body weight and then maintain that weight. The most reasonable conclusion is that lesions of VMH affect palatability (Powley, 1977). Previously good food tastes better than before, but previously disliked food tastes worse than before. These palatability changes affect the amount of food consumed.

VMH lesions also affect body weight indirectly. For instance, VMH-lesioned rats convert more of their food to stored fat, and food is absorbed more rapidly from the gut than in unoperated rats (Duggan & Booth, 1986).

Lesions of LH are more difficult to interpret. Although it appeared at first to be the opposite of VMH, that does not seem to be true. In fact, it may be that LH-lesioned animals are even more finicky than VMH-lesioned animals. LH-lesioned rats can be induced to eat by giving them sweet, soggy food, such as cookies soaked in milk (the LH-lesioned animals drink less, too, making it necessary to obtain water with their food). With time they come to gradually resume their normal diet although they drink only during meals and regulate their body weight at a lower than usual level.

Controversy exists over whether the neurons of LH are really involved in the "LH syndrome." These symptoms can also be produced by lesions of other nuclei, such as the substantia nigra, or the fiber tracts passing near the LH. In fact, a bundle of axons called the nigrostriatal bundle, which use dopamine as their neurotransmitter, are strongly implicated in the LH-lesion syndrome. Dopamine neurons appear to control several active behaviors besides feeding, and treatment with dopamine antagonist drugs results in diminished food intake. In contrast, dopamine agonists increase feeding. Finally, serotonin (5HT) seems to have the opposite effects of dopamine on feeding (Stricker, 1983).

FEEDING, BODY WEIGHT, AND OBESITY

Neural activity in the mouth, stomach, liver, and brain is largely responsible for the initiation and termination of bouts of feeding. Although these processes undoubtedly help explain hour-to-hour variation in food consumption, they do not help as much in accounting for individual patterns of food consumption over a long time or why individuals differ so much in body weight and body composition even when their food consumption is equal. These are the topics we will now address.

First, let us consider body weight regulation. An overwhelming amount of evidence suggests that body weight is regulated by a negative feedback, homeostatic process. The energy "equation" of the body is fairly simple: Energy stored = energy intake − energy expended − nonassimilated energy. Energy expended can be further subdivided into a work component such as muscular contraction during movement, and into a metabolic component involved in the physiological processes of maintaining cells. The two are not completely separate, of course, but the dichotomy is a useful one. Nonassimilated energy is that which passes through the digestive system without being absorbed.

Body weight can be regulated through any part of the equation, but metabolism is very important (Keesey & Corbett, 1984). For example, animals and people who are placed on calorie reduction diets compensate by lowering their metabolic rates, which cuts energy consumption. Resumption of the higher calorie diet leads to resumption of the higher metabolic rate, and an even higher calorie diet increases metabolic rate even further (McMinn, 1984). Metabolic rate cannot be changed enough to prevent weight loss in the low-calorie diet, but it does make the dieter's job more difficult.

Energy assimilation also varies with changing energy intake. When intake is low, the digestive system extracts more of the available energy; when intake increases, a lower percentage is extracted. The person who wants to lose weight needs to make total energy loss (work + metabolism + nonassimilated energy) exceed total energy intake so that fat stores become depleted. Because metabolism and digestive efficiency compensate for decreased energy intake, the only other option is to increase energy consumption in exercise. Ironically, the benefit of exercise in weight loss is due not so much to direct energy utilization in muscle contraction but in its elevation of metabolic rate. That is, the calories used in muscle contractions during a 30-minute run are less than the extra calories consumed by the person's elevated metabolic rate during the other 23.5 hours. In other words, regular exercise increases the basal metabolic rate, probably because of the additional muscle mass generated by the exercise. Thus, the most effective and healthy way to lose weight is to reduce caloric intake slightly and to exercise daily for at least 30 minutes.

What about body composition, that is, the proportions of fat and lean body mass? Individuals of the same height and weight may differ in fat content. Much of the body fat is stored in fat cells of adipose tissue. These "fat pads" are found in several parts of the body, both under the skin (subcutaneous fat) and in the body cavity (abdominal fat). The number and size of the fat cells may help regulate food consumption in a way that influences total fat content. Obese humans tend to have more and larger fat cells than nonobese humans. One of the great difficulties in achieving permanent weight loss for obese people is that even though fat cell size declines, their number does not. As these cells shrink, they apparently signal this to appetite-regulating areas of the brain, leading to intense feelings of hunger (Kolata, 1985). In fact, obese people who have lost weight and are approaching a "normal" weight may show the same symptoms as normals who undergo a severe food shortage: Food cravings become intense, the person feels listless, metabolic rate slows, and women become amenorrheic. Shrunken fat cells in both groups may be at the root of these changes.

If fat cells are important to the regulation of food intake and obesity, we should try to understand what leads to differences in fat cell number and size. Research has focused on nutrition in childhood and in adulthood. Overfeeding in childhood increases fat cell number and size (Sjöström, 1980). Because fat cells shrink in response to a weight-reduction diet, but apparently do not decline in number, early overfeeding may predispose people to a lifelong battle against obesity. What evidence is there for this statement?

First, the most severe cases of obesity begin in early childhood, and obese children more often become obese adults. Carefully controlled laboratory studies of animals suggest that this is only partly true, however. When rats were raised in litters of 4, 9, or 24 pups each, the mother's milk production resulted in overfed, normally fed, and underfed pups, respectively. At weaning the pups from litters of 4 were twice as heavy as pups from litters of 24. When switched to solid food, the difference narrowed somewhat. Later, the rats were switched to a high-fat diet and the initially underfed rats responded by adding relatively more fat to their stores. Although their total body weight was still below that of overfed and normally fed rats, the initially underfed rats had a higher percentage of body fat (Hausberger & Volz, 1984). When pigs were malnourished early in life and then given an ample food supply, they became highly obese (Widdowson, 1974). The same is true of humans (Garn *et al.*, 1975).

The data indicate that early overfeeding and early underfeeding can both lead to later obesity. Perhaps the notion of overfeeding needs to be refined, however. An overfed individual may get many calories, but calories do not build muscle and other lean tissue. That requires protein. It appears that if overfed on a diet with sufficient protein (as Hausberger and Volz's rats were), animals grow large and have an ample amount of lean body tissue. This tissue is metabolically very active, so later consumption of a calorie-rich diet will not result in as much fat deposition. Thus, our principal concern should be about overfeeding a diet that has too much fat and carbohydrate and not enough protein. Moreover, protein will not be used to build muscle unless the muscle is used. Exercise, then, is critical to establish the muscle mass necessary to burn extra calories and avoid obesity.

Patterns of food consumption and exercise in adulthood are better predictors of adult body composition than is food consumption in infancy. If energy intake exceeds output, fat is stored. An enzyme on the surface of fat cells, *lipoprotein lipase,* is responsible for fat storage. People and animals vary in lipoprotein lipase activity, with overweight individuals having more activity than lean individuals. However, previously obese people who have lost significant amounts of fat have lipoprotein lipase activity that is three or four times greater than before weight loss (Schwartz & Brunzell, 1981; Taskinen & Nikkilla, 1981). So, in addition to lowered metabolic rate and increased energy assimilation, the dieter faces the problem of cellular machinery that becomes even more efficient at converting food to fat. Who ever said life was fair?

Behavioral Ecology of Feeding and Predation

Our attention shifts now to the processes and adaptive significance of food acquisition in species-appropriate ecological contexts.

PREY DETECTION, CAPTURE, AND PREPARATION

We will begin with the behavioral adaptations for finding and acquiring prey. In some cases, such as the filter-feeding of barnacles and clams, finding food does not pose a behavioral problem. Large quantities of sea water are pulled in and the edible particles are strained out. The interesting cases occur in those species that must actively search for their food, especially if the food is doing its best not to be found.

Search and detection Searching efficiently is important for keeping food intake above some critical level. Unfortunately, what constitutes an efficient search varies with the kind of food being sought. A few cases should make this clear.

Some food sources are nonmobile and regenerate themselves after being consumed. The nectar contained in flowers is a good example. To be efficient, a nectar-eating animal should not revisit a flower until it has had enough time to replace its depleted nectar stock. Kamil (1978) found that amakihis, a nectar-eating Hawaiian bird, visit the many flowers in their territories in such a way as to avoid revisits until after the full regeneration period has elapsed. Similarly, bees "working" a plant with many flowers follow a regular path, "corkscrewing" up from the bottom, for example (Waddington & Heinrich, 1979). In this way, they do not miss any flowers nor do they revisit flowers.

Efficient search paths can be arranged in other ways. For example, recrossing a path would be inefficient because food would not likely have a chance to regenerate. Flocks of finches foraging for seeds in the Mojave Desert of California rarely recross their own path (Cody, 1971). Other examples of efficient search are provided by Pyke (1978) and Morse (1980)

An efficient search process is a necessary first step in acquiring food. However, it does no good unless prey are detected so that capture can be initiated. Naturally, all the major sensory systems are used in detecting prey, but we will cover only two: visual detection of cryptic prey by birds, and detection by means of soil vibration in scorpions.

Individual experience is extremely important in detection of cryptic prey. The experience may lead to a form of perceptual modification known as a *search image.* Search image formation means that as a result of having found a prey item, the predator then becomes more adept at finding additional prey of that type.

Blue jays searching for cryptic moths have been studied in the process of acquiring search images. In the lab, the jays were shown a series of slides of tree trunks, some of which contained a cryptic moth while others had no moth. The birds were given a food reward for pecking one button if a moth was present or another button if no moth was present. A wrong response was "punished" by turning off the slide followed by a time-out period. The blue jays were slow and error-prone at first, but they gradually became faster and more accurate. However, when two different, cryptic moth species were used, the birds' performance suffered (Pietrewicz & Kamil, 1979).

Prey detection by scorpions presents another interesting case. These arachnids, relatives of spiders, hunt for insects at night in their desert habitat. Their vision and audition are poor, but they have extremely sensitive vibration-sensors located in their "feet" (Fig. 14-2). One kind of sensory receptor detects minute vertical waves in the sand; another type detects horizontal sand movements. Scorpions orient toward the source of a vibration with uncanny accuracy. They do this by comparing the sensory input from their eight legs, using time-of-arrival differences as the primary cue, much like vertebrates do in pinpointing a sound source (Brownell, 1977, 1984). Similarly, some fish have lateral line receptors tuned to movements of their small crustacean prey (Montgomery & McDonald, 1987).

Capture and preparation   Capture can be as simple as a mouse picking up a seed or as complex and time consuming as a pack of wolves hunting caribou. Many species require extensive individual experience before they capture prey effectively. For example, Markstein and Lehner (1980) presented live rats to socially reared but prey-naive coyotes in a large pen. Although

Figure 14.2
Scorpions have two types of vibration-sensing organs on each foot. The slit sensillum detects primarily vertical motion in the soil; the tarsal hairs, in contrast, detect horizontal movements. The scorpion uses these devices to detect and locate prey.

Immediately after striking and envenomating its prey, the rattlesnake releases it. The snake forms an immediate memory of the prey's odor, which it then follows.

The snake continually flicks its tongue, capturing airborne odorous molecules emanating from the dying prey.

hungry, the naive coyotes were inefficient about killing. They "played" with the rat and eventually killed it accidentally. When two naive coyotes were given a rat they competed for it and killed it sooner, but still clumsily. Experienced coyotes, however, dispatched rats in just a few seconds.

Some venomous snakes, such as rattlesnakes, release their prey immediately after striking and envenomating it, apparently because the prey might injure the snake while struggling to escape. The snake, however, must track its prey after releasing it so that it can be consumed. Snakes immediately increase the rate of tongue-flicking after releasing an envenomated prey. Snakes sample the air with their tongues, and bring odorous molecules of the prey to the vomeronasal organ in the roof of the mouth, thus facilitating the chemically-guided search (Golan *et al.*, 1982). Snakes apparently quickly learn the olfactory characteristics of their prey, and may even pass by other freshly-

killed prey that do not match the odor of their own prey (Chiszar *et al.*, 1983). Clearly, acquiring prey sometimes involves more than its initial detection and predatory strike.

Once captured, the food item must often be modified before it can be consumed. This can be a time-consuming process and may be much more difficult than finding and capturing the prey. Squirrels may find an abundant crop of nuts, but each one has to be opened. Young squirrels learn through individual experience how to do this. They begin by gnawing nuts haphazardly. Eventually, the shell is broken and the nut consumed. With experience, the squirrels come to orient their gnawing along certain tracks and open the shell in a fraction of the original time. Because they may consume several types of nut, each with its own best opening technique, the learning process must be repeated for each one (Eibl-Eibesfeldt, 1963). Young oystercatchers, a shorebird that consumes molluscs, also must learn to open their hard-shelled prey and may depend on their parents for instruction (and food supplements) until they are a year old (Norton-Griffiths, 1969).

In some cases, the amount of preparation is varied according to circumstances. Grasshopper sparrows prepare their insect prey by breaking off the relatively inedible or nondigestible parts such as the legs and wings. But the amount of preparation varies with the birds' hunger. A well-fed bird discards virtually everything before consuming the nutritious abdomen, but a hungry bird may dispense with these luxuries and swallow the grasshopper whole (Kaspari, 1990).

CHOICE OF FOOD ITEMS

Assuming that an animal eats several types of food, we need to understand how the various food items are selected. "Choice" does indeed seem to be a good word for this process. In some cases, an individual's diet may consist of large amounts of one prey type, and very little of another. Or, it may eat certain foods in the morning but something else later on. What criteria are used in choosing among foods?

Energy   One of the most important criteria used in food choice is net energy gain. That is, each prey type contains a certain amount of food energy (expressed in calories), but energy and time must be spent in its acquisition. In short, there is a cost/benefit ratio for each potential food. Let us look at the benefit side first. Usually, the caloric value of food is measured in a calorimeter, a device that measures the amount of heat given off when a substance is burned in it. However, this technique only approximates the energy actually obtained from the food by the animal that consumes it. Not all parts of the food may be digestible to the organism. Humans, for instance, cannot digest cellulose, the substance that makes up the cell walls of plants, so we cannot extract all the calories contained in food plants. Also, the digestive system expends energy in processing the food. Thus, net energy of a food is always less than its "raw" energy.

The costs involved in food procurement include search, capture, and handling. Search usually involves the expenditure of energy in moving about the habitat. The capture phase begins when the prey has been detected and the pursuer begins its attempt to acquire the prey. This may be an insignificant event in some cases, as when a bird detects a seed and merely picks it up; but it can be a drawn-out, expensive process in other cases such as when large carnivores (e.g., wolves or lions) chase and grapple with their prey (which does not always result in a kill). Assuming that the prey is captured, handling comes into effect. Handling involves both preparation and consumption. A squirrel that finds an acorn must expend some time and energy opening the shell to expose the nut within. The energy costs involved in search, capture, and handling must be subtracted from the extracted food energy to yield the net benefit of a given type of food.

Food items can be ranked from most to least beneficial on the basis of net energy gained. The most beneficial food item is the one that is the most preferred (i.e., chosen over all others). For example, Davies (1977) studied predation on flies by a European bird, the pied wagtail. First, he found that the size classes of flies consumed by the birds did not closely match the size distribution of flies available in the habitat, indicating that the birds did not merely attack prey as they were encountered. Second, the most preferred size class happened to be the one that yielded the greatest number of calories per unit of time, the second most preferred size class was second most profitable, and so on. Several other studies on birds, fish, and crustaceans have found the same sort of relationship (Krebs, 1978).

Because cost/benefit variables are likely to fluctuate over time, animals should be sensitive to changes in the ranking of food items. As a preferred item becomes depleted, its search cost goes up, making it less desirable than another food item. For example, oystercatchers primarily preyed on large cockles when prey abundance was high, but as the large cockles were depleted, the birds began foraging in previously unused areas and began taking smaller cockles (O'Connor & Brown, 1977). The switch in prey is adaptive because it yields more energy than looking longer for the fewer large prey. Changes in the economics of predation appear to be why food preferences change seasonally or differ microgeographically.

Selection of food based on rankings of the benefit/cost ratios of the choices is not the only way to proceed, and, for some species, may not be the best way, especially if prey are encountered individually with considerable delays between successive appearances. In such cases the best strategy may be to form a simple dichotomy: prey that yield positive energy gain vs. those that do not. For example, flycatchers are small birds that usually capture prey by darting out from their perch to pursue aerial insects. A flycatcher may pursue many species of flying insects in a few hours. If insect density is low, the birds probably cannot afford to "let that one go" so as to wait for a higher ranking prey type to come along. They do let very small insects fly by, unmolested, however, probably because the energy expended in flight would not be compensated for by something as small as a gnat. In general, if search time is high, any profitable prey will be pursued (Collier & Rovee-Collier, 1981).

Nutrients We all have been warned about eating "empty calories," that is, food with energy but little else such as vitamins and minerals. In some cases, food choice is based on the presence of certain nutrients even though the food may provide little caloric value. For instance, in the tundra of northern Canada, sandpipers avidly consume the bones of dead lemmings. The bones are rich in calcium that the birds need for producing eggs (Maclean, 1974). Moose eat large quantities of aquatic vegetation apparently because it contains more sodium than does the land vegetation even though land vegetation yields more energy (Belovsky, 1981). In fact, herbivores and many omnivores are often short of sodium, so taste receptors for sodium develop during an early sensitive period (Hill & Przekop, 1988) and preferences for salt, even excessive amounts of it, can become pronounced (Beauchamp, 1987). Finally, Hill and Hurtado (1989) report that among the Ache hunter-gatherers of Paraguay, departures from expected food choices based on calories alone can be accounted for by taking nutrient content into consideration. For instance, these people go after protein-rich foods even though they may not yield as many calories as carbohydrate-rich foods.

EFFORT, OPPORTUNISM, AND MEAL PATTERNS

When laboratory rats are given free access to unlimited food, they typically eat 10–14 "meals" per day (Johnson *et al.*, 1984). When the amount of effort required to obtain access to food is increased, however, the number, size, and temporal distribution of meals change. These relationships are most readily studied in a laboratory situation in which rats are required to press a small lever a number of times for the opportunity to obtain food. The Johnson *et al.* (1984) study is a good example. Rats began the experiment needing to push the lever only once to obtain access to food. The requirement was gradually increased until they had to push 80 times. As the requirement stiffened the rats consumed fewer meals (i.e., ate less often), but the meals became larger, thus maintaining total daily intake. Collier and Rovee-Collier (1981) have summarized a great deal of research on the relationship between effort and meal patterns. They note that increasing effort in any part of the sequence of feeding behaviors (search, procurement, preparation, consumption) results in a departure from the pattern of many small meals—which exists when food is always available—to a pattern in which fewer but larger meals are consumed. For instance, rats fed sunflower seeds in the shell ate less often than rats fed shelled sunflower seeds.

The relationship between effort and meal patterns suggests that when little or no effort is required, feeding will be quite likely. Such opportunistic feeding (taking advantage of easily obtained food) is common. When animals who work for food delivery in the lab are given "free food," i.e., for little or no work, they actively consume it. Further, some predatory species engage in "surplus killing" when prey are readily available. For example, foxes attempt to prey on nesting gulls or their eggs. Generally, foxes are not overly successful at this because of the antipredator adaptations of the gulls (Kruuk, 1976). However, on particularly dark nights when the birds are unable to see, a fox may kill so many gulls that it cannot begin to eat them all (Kruuk, 1972a).

In reasonably stable food supply conditions, animals typically anticipate their needs and feed before they start running low. This is feed-forward (Chapter 8). Just as motorists begin looking for a gas station before the needle is on empty, animals and people begin searching for food before the need really arises. We all tend to eat at regular times even though we may not feel particularly hungry. But by eating in anticipation of hunger, our nutritional status stays more leveled out over long spans. In natural conditions, food availability is not always predictable, so beginning the search for food well before food is physiologically needed is highly advantageous.

Finally, food storage during times of excess can help level out food availability during lean times (Roberts, 1979). Storage can be in the form of fat, or as the food itself. Acorn woodpeckers, for instance, stash thousands of acorns into small holes chipped into trees, and many rodents collect and cache large quantities of seeds. Storage, energy conservation practices such as hibernation, and other processes help to buffer animals against variations in food supply.

CHOICE OF FORAGING LOCATION

Detecting prey will obviously be easiest when the predator places itself in a place likely to contain prey. If the prey are readily detected this is not an interesting problem. However, if the prey are difficult to detect, some interesting behavioral adaptations must be brought to bear by the predator.

Patch selection   The area in which a predator can detect prey is a "patch." The predator must constantly decide whether to remain in the current patch or to move on. Several hypotheses have been offered to explain movements from patch to patch.

(1) *Simple threshold model.* If prey are not detected at a specified rate, the predator leaves the patch. This implies that some minimum amount of time must be spent in the patch in order to assess prey density. This is analogous to a fisherman who stays in a patch (the area covered by his or her casts) as long as the fish are biting at an acceptable rate, even though fish may be more numerous elsewhere. For an animal, this simple approach to patch selection is acceptable so long as the prey capture rate yields a positive energy balance. Further, it makes few cognitive demands for patch comparison and

may save on time and energy to visit other patches to compare their yields.

(2) *Patch comparison.* By searching for prey in several patches and then comparing their food intake rates, animals can confine their foraging to the most profitable patch. This process is often studied in the lab by presenting the animal with two or more response options (each analogous to a patch). For instance, a pigeon is placed in an experimental chamber with two lighted keys that it can peck for food reinforcement. One key produces food every fiftieth peck (on average) but the other key produces food every hundredth peck (on average). After spending time pecking both keys, the pigeon eventually confines all its pecking to the more profitable key which results in the maximum rate of food intake (Kamil & Roitblat, 1985).

One might argue that this rather simple situation does not do justice to the real world. After all, it seems unlikely the two discrete patches could be so close together and therefore be so easily compared. More realistic simulations can be accomplished by invoking a cost to making a switch from one patch to the next by temporarily instituting a "time-out" from food procurement each time a switch is made. The duration of the time-out period can be varied as a way of simulating travel time (although not energy consumption and risks involved in travel). Increasing the duration of the time-out decreases the rate of switching and increases the amount of effort expended on a patch before making a switch. For example, Cowie (1977) studied chickadees in an aviary by placing mealworms in small, sawdust-filled cups. However, to gain access to the cups the birds had to pry off a cardboard lid. Some of the cups had lids that were tight and took more time and effort to remove, but others had lids that were more easily removed. As expected, the birds spent more time searching within the cup when the effort

was greater. It is as though having expended time and energy one needs to make the most of it. When food is easy to come by, search is less thorough (e.g., Whitham, 1977).

(3) *Marginal value theorem.* The amount of time spent in a patch can often be predicted by the *marginal value theorem* (Charnov, 1976; Krebs, 1978). The basic premise in this theorem is that the foraging animal has sufficient experience with the environment that it has available in memory a representation of the average rate of food intake in its foraging area. Having arrived in a new patch, it begins assessing its current food intake rate. If it is at or above average the animal remains foraging in that patch. As a result of its actions, however, the patch becomes depleted and will eventually decline below the average rate, whereupon the animal leaves to visit another patch.

The marginal value theorem and related ideas require a fair amount of information storage, processing, and retrieval. The foraging animal must continuously update its data on food intake rate. The most common position on this issue is that there is a memory "window" that slides along through time (Crawford, 1983). As new information is added, the oldest information in the window is deleted. If the memory window concept is correct we should expect to find its duration suited to standard foraging conditions. Having too short a window will mean that temporary unusual circumstances will seriously distort the animals' perception of the environment. Too long a window may mean more information processing than is necessary, and could make the animal insufficiently sensitive to changing circumstances (Crawford, 1983).

Although we know relatively little about these processes in animals, some interesting studies are beginning to appear. For example, Milinski and Regelmann (1985) fed *Daphnia,* an aquatic insect, to sticklebacks in two ends of an aquarium (two "patches"). Most of the feeding occurred at one end (patch 1). After a few days of training, the fish were fed ten *Daphnia* in patch 1, then, after a variable delay, were fed five more at the other end (patch 2). They then measured how much time was spent by the fish in the two patches. They found that the longer the delay the less time was spent in patch 1. Delays of 90 seconds or more produced a shift away from patch 1. This experiment suggests that the fish remember prey abundance in patches and behave accordingly.

Antipredator Behaviors

The counterpoint to finding and acquiring food, of course, is to avoid becoming someone else's food. In some respects, the problems of avoiding predation are similar to those of acquiring food: recognizing predators, detecting them, and taking action once detection is made. Let us look at each of these processes.

PREDATOR RECOGNITION AND DETECTION

Predator recognition in some species seems to require no special individual experience. For example, naive goslings fled when the silhouette of a hawk was "flown" over them on a wire. However, the same figure, when moved in the opposite direction, did not elicit escape, probably because it then resembled a goose (Tinbergen, 1948) (Fig. 14-3)! This fascinating observation has been confirmed and extended by others (Green *et al.*, 1968; Mueller & Parker, 1980). Another example in which no individual experience is required comes from another bird species, the great kiskadee of the American tropics. Naive birds in the lab were presented with wooden dowels painted various colors and pat-

terns. These birds eat small snakes, but the dowels painted with red, black, and yellow rings (which resembles the venomous coral snake) were avoided by the birds, even though they avidly pecked at the dowels when they were painted solid colors (S. M. Smith, 1977). Other bird species that do not encounter coral snakes showed no avoidance of the coral snake pattern (Smith, 1980). Some species may recognize predators by means of olfaction. Deer fawns avoided eating from food bowls in which a vial of native predator's urine was placed, but did not avoid bowls containing the urine of nonnative predators such as lion and tiger (Müller-Schwarze, 1972). Still other prey species recognize predators by their sounds. Moths, for instance, begin evasive aerial maneuvers as soon as bat echolocation calls are detected (Roeder, 1965). In summary, many species recognize predators without the necessity of individual experience. This ability, of course, is highly adaptive, because to require experience with predators in order to avoid them may be fatal.

On the other hand, individual experience with predators is sometimes necessary before antipredator behaviors are shown. Curio *et al.* (1978) performed a fascinating experiment indicating that birds could learn to treat as a predator a species that normally does not evoke an antipredator response. Curio housed European blackbirds in two adjoining wire-mesh cages so that they could see and hear each other. Between their cages was a partitioned cubicle in which two stuffed birds were placed such that one blackbird saw a stuffed owl while the other blackbird saw a stuffed Australian bird (obviously not native to Europe, and not a predator). In previous tests Curio had found that blackbirds ignored the stuffed Australian bird. However, blackbirds exhibit strong antipredator behavior toward small owls, one of their common predators. When it saw the owl the blackbird emitted

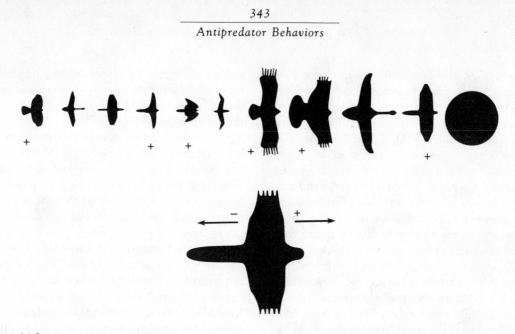

Figure 14.3
Some of these cardboard models evoke escape responses in naive goslings when flown over (from left to right); they are marked "+" and all have short necks. Those that do not evoke escape have long necks. The bottom model evokes escape when flown in one direction, but not in the other.

alarm calls and other antipredator behaviors. The other blackbird witnessed these behaviors but could not see the owl, only the Australian bird. This time, however, it exhibited antipredator behaviors! Furthermore, its behavior could be used to model antipredator behavior in other naive blackbirds. This study shows that social learning or imitation can be used to learn the characteristics of predators.

Predator recognition can be far more subtle and complex than merely recognizing some other species. In fact, some of the most important predators, in terms of the mortality they cause, are members of the same species. Polis *et al.* (1984) list numerous cases of intraspecific predation in mammals, most of which are accompanied by cannibalism. In some human populations, homicide is the leading cause of death (Daly & Wilson, 1988b; Chagnon, 1988). Intraspecific predation poses recognition

problems that transcend those of interspecific predation because the former must depend on assessments of behavioral propensities, and because conspecific predators may be constantly around. Unfortunately, we know relatively little about adaptations for intraspecific predator recognition.

Related to the issue of predator recognition is the process of predator detection. To this end, a variety of forms of vigilance have evolved. Other behaviors are temporarily halted while the individual looks around, takes a long sniff of air, or listens carefully. In social species, these sentry duties are shared by most members of the flock, herd, or school. For instance, ostriches share the vigilance duties, and the larger the flock the less time each bird spends in vigilance (Bertram, 1980). The same is true of sparrows (Barnard, 1980), geese (Dimond & Lazarus, 1974), and other species.

Further, the larger the group the sooner approaching predators are detected. Larger dove flocks were faster at detecting approaching hawks (Siegfried & Underhill, 1975), as were starlings (Powell, 1974). It appears that the more rapid detection of predators by larger groups of prey is not due just to having more eyes and ears "on guard." The sensitivity of the sensory systems may also increase. For instance, Treherne and Foster (1980) noted that larger groups of ocean skaters, a marine insect that rides the water surface, were faster to detect and evade an approaching simulated predator. Further, this was attributed to enhanced visual sensitivity brought about whenever the insects bumped into one another. Because such contacts increase as group size increases, larger groups tend to have more visually sensitive members participating in vigilance.

Vigilance is scaled according to the risk of predation at the time. For instance, finches devote more time to vigilance the farther they are from cover (Caraco *et al.*, 1980), and doves exposed to a weasel shortly before dark are more vigilant during the night than they are when no weasel was exposed (Lendrem, 1984). Similarly, adult squirrel monkeys are more vigilant while their offspring are playing (Biben *et al.*, 1989). Playing youngsters are not only more conspicuous to predators, but they are less able to be vigilant themselves. Thus, the adults increase their vigilance.

ANTIPREDATOR TACTICS

Once a predator has been detected, then what? Several behaviors may occur, including escape, thwarting attack, and counterattack.

Escape   This sounds simple enough, but there are good and bad escape tactics. The best escape is one that minimizes the probability of

capture while simultaneously putting the predator at a safe distance. Consequently, some prey escape using an unpredictable zig-zag course (Humphries & Driver, 1967).

A variant on this strategy that can be used by social groups such as bird flocks, is to scatter simultaneously in many different directions. This forces the predator to single out a target for pursuit. The momentary delay that the decision process requires may provide the necessary margin of safety.

Thwarting attack   Rather than fleeing, another strategy is to "convince" the predator not to attack. This can take the form of "standing one's ground" as musk oxen do when confronted by wolves, or bluffing about one's size or danger. For example, a species of coral reef fish resembles a moray eel from the rear. When in danger, it sticks its head into rock crevices and protrudes its tail mimicking the head of the dangerous eel (McCosker, 1977b).

Counterattack   In some cases, especially if escape fails, the prey may attack the predator, kicking, biting, clawing, or pecking as the case may be. An interesting form of attack on predators is *mobbing* or social harassment. Birds often mob owls and hawks, making special vocalizations that often attract other small birds (Altmann, 1956). They fly toward the owl, either veering away suddenly or sometimes pecking its head or clipping it with the feet. Although mobbing can be dangerous—there are documented cases of mobbers being killed by the predator (Denson, 1979; Myers, 1978; Walker, 1983)—the strategy generally succeeds in driving the predator out of the area.

Several experiments have focused on the stimulus characteristics of predators that provoke mobbing. For instance, a calling owl is more readily detected by small birds than is a quiet owl (Chandler & Rose, 1988), but among the many visible stimuli of an owl, the large eyes are most important (Smith & Graves, 1978). Indeed, eyes and staring are generally important predator features to which prey respond (Scaife, 1976; Kalin & Shelton, 1989).

Many diverse species mob their predators. California ground squirrels mob snakes (see below), penguins have been observed mobbing a major underwater predator, the Weddell seal, and bees and wasps swarm on bears or people that intrude on their hives or nests. The potential for group harassment of predators is one of the main advantages of social living (Chapter 12).

CO-EVOLUTION AND ARMS-RACES

This chapter has focused independently on two highly interdependent processes: adaptations for feeding and predation, and adaptations for avoiding predation. As you might suppose, natural selection has been relentless on both sets of adaptations. But because the interests of one party (the prey) are diametrically opposed to those of the other party (the predator), they exert selection pressures on each other. In other words, predators and prey co-evolve (Sih, 1984). If rabbits become faster runners, new selection pressures will be exerted on foxes, such that they must respond with counteradaptations (e.g., running faster themselves, becoming more stealthy, switching to another prey) or become extinct. In fact, the co-evolutionary process can even result in a reversal of the predator–prey relationship in some cases (e.g., Barkai & Mc-Quaid, 1988). The east-west arms race is an unfortunately convenient metaphor for predator–prey co-evolution (Dawkins & Krebs, 1979). However, it is exceedingly difficult to

Figure 14.4
Rattlesnakes and some other species have heat-sensitive organs, called loreal pits, on the snout. These sensitive receptors can detect warm-blooded prey in complete darkness.

reconstruct the history of adaptations and counteradaptations of predators and prey. The best we can do is carefully study the living products of that evolutionary history.

Such studies, especially when done comparatively, generally illustrate some form of limitation imposed by the predator on the prey, and *vice versa*. For example, male tropical katydids typically emit acoustic signals to attract females for mating, something like the chirping of male crickets. A male katydid stands the best chance of attracting a female if his signals are loud and long-lasting. However, bats use these signals to find and attack katydids, and Belwood and Morris (1987) found that males that signaled in long bursts were quickly attacked. The katydids have adapted to this predicament by signaling in short bursts and by using a tactile signal that bats cannot detect: vibrations of the plant on which they are perched. By setting up tremors that can be felt by the female, males succeed in acquiring mates while minimizing risk of predation. However, these vibrational signals work only at close range, so the use of acoustic signals cannot be eliminated totally. Interestingly, other katydid species that inhabit thorny vegetation that bats avoid use only acoustic signals, as do other species that live in bat-free areas (Belwood & Morris, 1987).

Numerous cases of predator–prey co-evolution have been described. Indeed, one of them, involving bats and moths, was presented in Chapter 7 on auditory systems. Let us review another case, this one involving ground squirrels and snakes.

The California ground squirrel is a colonial, burrowing rodent that co-exists with various snake species including rattlesnakes (venomous) and gopher snakes (nonvenomous), that kill ground squirrels, especially pups.

Although rattlesnakes kill ground squirrels above ground, they do most of their predation in ground squirrel burrows. Here, rattlesnakes appear to have an edge: Although ground squirrels can smell snakes and even discriminate snake species on the basis of odor (Hennessy & Owings, 1978), rattlesnakes have a more acute sense to use underground: they can detect infrared light by means of specialized receptors in pits near the eyes (Fig. 14-4). They can easily use this sense to locate ground squirrels in pitch-black burrows.

Ground squirrels who detect a snake in their burrow often plug the burrow by moving loose soil forward, even tamping it with the head (Coss & Owings, 1978). If this happens on both sides of the snake it may be buried alive.

Above ground, the antipredator options of ground squirrels are more diverse. First, a ground squirrel that detects a snake may give a vocalization that is specific to snakes (Owings & Leger, 1980). This call may lead to the assembly of several more squirrels who join in harassing the snake. Ground squirrels often approach the snake; kick loose soil at it with the forelegs; "bob and weave" nearby, either with the body or by "flagging" the tail; and may even pounce on and bite the snake (see Fig. 14-5). The ground squirrels seem to take turns at being the primary harasser and use tail flagging patterns to coordinate their activity in the vicinity of the snake (Hennessy *et al.*, 1981). This may continue until the snake is driven off (usually down a burrow, which may then be plugged from the surface), covered in soil, or, rarely, killed (Fitch, 1948).

The ground squirrels' behavior seems to match the danger of the snake. Nonvenomous garter snakes are approached more closely, for instance, and large rattlesnakes are treated more cautiously than are smaller ones (Rowe & Owings, 1978). Finally, ground squirrels from areas where rattlesnakes are common require no individual experience to perform the full range of antisnake behaviors (Owings & Coss, 1977).

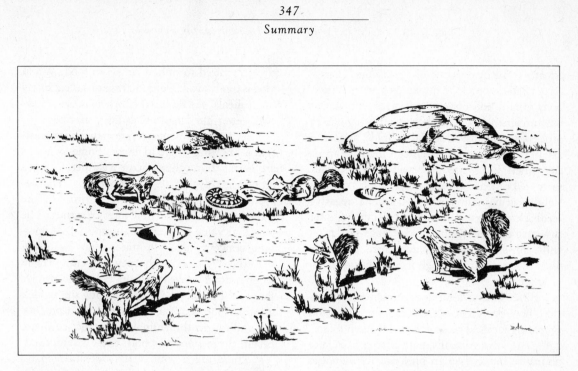

Figure 14.5
California ground squirrels interact with a rattlesnake by approaching, kicking sand at it, flagging their tails, and occasionally pouncing on it. Squirrels typically do not interact with the snake as a group. Rather, when one squirrel moves away, another will replace it. Their movements relative to the snake are predictable by the tail-flagging patterns.

Summary

The analysis of feeding begins with the recognition of food. Techniques range from cases in which recognition of appropriate food items requires no specific individual experience to those in which extensive individual experience is essential. Food choices are often learned through processes that involve monitoring the consequences of consuming the food. Some foods that are associated with illness are thereafter avoided, a phenomenon known as the Garcia effect. Such food aversions can be developed rapidly and are often long-lasting, especially if the food is fairly novel for the individual. Similarly, animals are sensitive to the positive consequences of eating certain foods, especially if they contain nutrients that the individual was lacking, and thereafter will consume that food if the nutritional deficiency redevelops.

The physiological bases of feeding are varied and sometimes complex. Feeding cessation is due to a variety of factors that can operate somewhat independently of one another. Nutrient receptors of the mouth, tongue, and throat can bring a meal to a conclusion independently of the stomach. However, the stomach, intestines, and liver also have the ability to influence the amount of food consumption and its timing. The brain, especially the VMH and LH nuclei of the hypothalamus, also influence feeding patterns. Lesions of these nuclei can have pronounced effects on the quantity of food consumed. Long-term regulation of food intake, and its effects on body weight and body composition, are not as well understood as the shorter-term regulatory processes. Fat cells, which store lipids, appear to signal the brain in ways that can increase appetite when their size decreases. Body weight seems to be rather stable in most people, and this stability is maintained through several negative feedback processes, including metabolic rate, digestive efficiency, and lipid storage in the fat cells. Physical exercise can reduce the body weight "set point" through its impact on metabolic rate.

Several behavioral and perceptual adaptations have evolved for detecting, capturing, and preparing foods. The search paths taken by foraging animals are usually quite efficient, and the ability to detect hidden prey usually increases after having found a few of them. In addition, several sensory and perceptual systems are nicely tuned to the detection of prey. Once detected, the prey must be captured and often prepared. Although these can be quite simple processes, in other cases a great deal of individual experience is required before the individual performs these activities efficiently.

Choice of foods from those available is partly based on the net energy intake. This is in part due to the energy content of the food, but also involves the energy and time spent in finding, capturing, and preparing the food for consumption. Generally, the foods that have the highest net energy intake are the ones that are most highly preferred. However, not all food choices are based on energy: the presence of certain nutrients that are not otherwise readily available can influence food choice regardless of energy content.

The timing and quantity of food consumption depends in large measure on the amount of effort required to obtain access to food. When food is freely available, most organisms eat many small meals. As required effort increases, however, fewer but larger meals are consumed.

An important consideration in food acquisition is knowing where to forage. Some locations are better than others. Most treatments of this process involve "patch" comparisons. That is, evaluating the relative merits of two or more locations in terms of their rates of return. The marginal value theorem is an especially important concept here. It states that organisms should leave the patch they are currently in when its food intake rate drops below the average rate in the habitat. All the foraging site models assume some cognitive or information-processing abilities in the animals that practice them. So far, the evidence supports these assumptions.

There are a wide variety of antipredator adaptations that parallel those for food acquisition. First, predator recognition frequently occurs without individual experience with the predator, but it may also involve an important learned component. An often underestimated predation problem is posed by other individuals of the same species. Recognizing such individuals as predators is more difficult than recognizing other species as predators. A great deal of time is spent in vigilance so that predators may be detected. Vigilance may be shared with other group members. There are several antipredator tactics available to prey species. They include escape, thwarting attack, and counterattacking the predator. Foremost among the latter is the phenomenon known as mobbing, in which several or many prey individuals join in harassing a potential predator.

Predators and their prey frequently coevolve. That is, as predators evolve adaptations for dealing with their prey, the prey generally evolve counteradaptations, and vice versa. Such co-evolutionary processes are illustrated in one particularly interesting predator–prey pair, the rattlesnake and the California ground squirrel.

Recommended Readings

CURIO, E. (1976). *The ethology of predation.* Berlin: Springer-Verlag.

EDMUNDS, M. (1974). *Defence in animals.* New York: Longman.

KAMIL, A. C., & SARGENT, T. D. (1981). *Foraging behavior: Ecological, ethological, and psychological approaches.* New York: Garland STPM Press.

LOGUE, A. W. (1986). *The psychology of eating and drinking.* New York: Freeman.

Chapter 15

AGGRESSION

Instances of aggression are among the most dramatic in all of animal behavior. From the crashing, head-on collisions of big-horn rams, to the silent carnage of ant colony raids, to the chase of one robin by another whose territory has been violated, aggression not only gets our attention, but cries out for adaptive explanations and understanding of mechanisms.

In everyday use, the term "aggression" is used in reference to behavior patterns ranging from physical violence and warfare at one extreme, to simple assertiveness at the other (Hinde & Groebel, 1989). Because of its pervasive and inconsistent use, some scientists avoid the term "aggression" entirely, preferring instead such terms as agonistic behavior or agonism. Agonistic behavior is defined as any social behavior that occurs during conflict between two or more individuals (Scott, 1983). Generally this results in harm (or at least the risk of harm) to the participants. The harm may be injury or death, or it may be loss of some useful or essential resource, such as food, territory, or mates. Agonistic behavior includes not only attack and fighting, but also defensive behaviors, escape, and signals associated with attack and defense. In other words, the topic of agonistic behavior is anything done by the participants in a conflict situation. "Aggression" is limited to those agonistic acts that are intended to inflict injury or harm (Hinde & Groebel, 1989).

Two main themes will emerge from this chapter. First, aggression is not a unitary behavior. That is, there are several or many forms of aggression that differ in terms of their genetics, proximate causes, and evolutionary consequences. We should not expect these various forms to respond in the same way to environ-mental variables. Second, the study of aggression should not become embroiled in issues of morality and ethics. Although it is true that aggression often results in some highly damaging outcomes, and that attempts should be made to limit the damaging consequences, it is nonetheless true that aggressive behavior is a product of natural selection processes and often serves important functions. If control is to be sought, it must be done with the realization that aggression is often adaptive and perhaps cannot be controlled without influencing other aspects of behavior. In any event, control of aggression will only be effective if it comes from a solid comprehension of its behavioral–biological facts.

Ontogeny of Aggression

Individual differences in genes and environmental conditions influence the development of aggression, just as they do all other forms of behavior. We will begin by reviewing evidence on the genetic bases for individual differences in aggression, and then turn to the role of early hormonal profiles on the form and extent of later, adult aggression. Finally, several important environmental and experiential variables will be discussed that influence aggression.

GENES AND AGGRESSION

Genes, through their contribution to the anatomical structure and physiological processes of animals, influence aggressive behavior. This section will review some of the evidence used in the study of genetics and aggressive behavior.

Selective breeding experiments Perhaps the most direct way to show the involvement of genes in aggression is to perform artificial selection experiments. Many such studies have been performed, and researchers have succeeded in separating high aggressive lines from low aggressive lines.

Studies by Ebert (1983) and by Cairns *et al.* (1983) exemplify these findings and are methodologically very sound. Ebert began with a population of wild-trapped house mice. In the lab she placed young females in individual cages and then, 30 days later, placed a female stranger in each cage. The resident female typically directed her behavior toward the "intruder," often attacking and biting her. Ebert bred the most aggressive females with the brothers of other aggressive females, and bred nonaggressive females with the brothers of other nonaggressives. Finally, she bred a line of randomly chosen "controls." In a short time the lines were completely separate (Fig. 15-1), indicating that a large portion of the variability in aggressiveness was due to individual genetic differences. The Cairns *et al.* (1983) study began with an inbred strain of lab mice, but a similar procedure was followed using males as subjects. They also succeeded in producing a quick separation of lines.

Selective breeding experiments on aggression not only demonstrate the involvement of genes in this form of behavior, but they can also provide compelling evidence against the notion that aggression is a unitary trait. Ebert's (1983) research is especially valuable on that issue. In addition to testing resident females against intruder females, Ebert and her colleagues also looked for other forms of aggression in their selected lines. If aggression is a unitary trait, they expected to find elevated aggression in

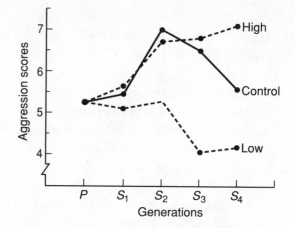

Figure 15.1

Results of selective breeding for high and low aggressiveness in female mice. Lines of high aggressives, low aggressives, and randomly chosen controls were bred for four generations from the same parental stock (P).

other situations besides the one on which they were selecting. First, they found no difference in aggression toward pups in the high- and low-aggressive lines. Second, predatory aggression (i.e., the latency to attack and eat a live cricket) did not differ between the lines. Third, they exposed the brothers of the female subjects to male intruders and found no difference in aggressiveness between the two lines. Finally, they found no weight or other anatomical differences between the lines of females that might make some better fighters than others. In short, their breeding experiment succeeded in isolating interfemale aggression from other forms of aggression.

Strain differences in aggression Many strains of lab mice have been developed over the years for studying diverse biological phenomena ranging from behavior to tumors. Although the strains were not bred for or against aggressivity, they nevertheless exhibit pronounced differences in aggression (Southwick & Clark, 1968). In spite of strain differences in aggressiveness, none is as aggressive as wild mice. Even when researchers have taken the lab-born offspring of wild-trapped mice and handled them daily as young pups (a process that tends to "gentle" animals), the wild-type mice are aggressive, biting the handlers to the point of drawing blood castrated earlier, with the early castrates exhibiting virtually no aggression (Peters *et al.*, 1972). Organization of the neural tissue involved in aggression occurred during the first six days of postnatal life and without such organization intermale aggression did not occur.

Along the same lines, neonatal testosterone treatment of females masculinizes their aggressiveness as adults when activating doses of testosterone are provided (vom Saal, 1983). Females treated with testosterone as newborns even attack intruder males, something nontreated females rarely do (Simon *et al.*, 1984). However, even nontreated females attacked intruder males when the adult females were given testosterone for about 3 weeks prior to the intruder's appearance, suggesting that neonatal testosterone treatments sensitize the animal to adult testosterone if it is present, but that large doses can be effective even in nonsensitized individuals (Simon *et al.*, 1984).

Simon and Whalen (1987) discovered that neonatal hormones sensitize animals to the same type of hormone when it is provided in adulthood, but do not sensitize them to other hormones. Newborn female mice were given either androgens or estrogens. As adults, they were given either the same hormone that they received in infancy, or the other type. When an intruder was placed in their cages, mice who had received the *same* hormone that they were given in infancy were very likely to attack; those mice who received the other hormone were significantly less likely to attack. Hormones early in life therefore seem to affect neural anatomy or physiology in ways that make the individual more responsive to that hormone later in life.

Although the studies described above have demonstrated important links between early hormones and aggressiveness in adulthood, they suffer from their artificial treatment of developmental conditions. Do naturally occurring variations in early hormones affect subsequent aggression? vom Saal and his co-workers have conducted a series of studies in which naturally occurring differences in prenatal hormones are related to aggressiveness in mice (reviewed by vom Saal, 1983). They have found that the position of a mouse fetus in the uterus influences its hormone concentrations (Fig. 15-2). For instance, female fetuses positioned between two males have higher testosterone concentrations than females positioned between two other females. A female fetus positioned between a male and a female has an intermediate level of testosterone. These hormonal differences are not sufficiently large to completely masculinize females; however, the differences in prenatal hormones may account for normal variation that exists among females.

ENVIRONMENTAL VARIABLES AND THE DEVELOPMENT OF AGGRESSION

Prenatal influences Other variables besides prenatal hormonal milieu can affect adult aggressive behavior. Undernutrition in early life leads to increased aggressiveness in rats, presumably due to alterations of normal brain structure (Ebert, 1983). This finding suggests that there may have been some inadvertent selection against aggressiveness in the breeding of lab mice. It is easy to imagine an animal caretaker not moving an aggressive individual to another

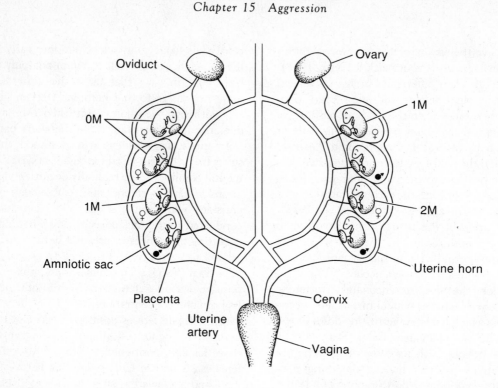

Figure 15.2
The uterine positions of female mice determines their exposure to prenatal testosterone. 2M females are posi- *tioned between two males and have the greatest exposure to testosterone. 0M females have the least exposure.*

cage for breeding purposes and thus gradually eliminating the alleles that contribute to high levels of aggressive behavior.

Chromosomes and human aggression Much has been made of the claim that certain chromosomal abnormalities are more likely to produce aggressiveness than is the standard chromosomal configuration, especially in males. The standard male pattern is XY, but some males have a second Y (XYY), and some have a second X (XXY). Both conditions are rare; others are even rarer.

Attention has focused on XYY males. If being male is associated with increased aggression, and if the Y chromosome is the defining characteristic of maleness, should not men with

two Y chromosomes be more aggressive than men with only one? The incidence of the XYY pattern is about 1 in 1000 (Manning, 1989), but several studies found that prison populations had a higher proportion of XYY males than was found among the population at large. XYY males tend to be taller than average and to have below average IQ scores. The prevailing opinion now is that XYY men are no more likely to commit crimes in general or violent crimes in particular, but they are more likely to be caught, convicted, and incarcerated. Manning (1989) points out that having such a chromosomal arrangement is certainly not strongly predictive of criminality or aggressiveness: more than 99% of the XYY mean have never been incarcerated.

Similarly, men with the XXY chromosome pattern are more common in prison populations. This should not be the case if chromosome pattern is an important factor in aggression. Such men, having an extra female chromosome, should be less likely to commit crimes. This appears not to be the case, however (Mazur, 1983).

ORGANIZATIONAL EFFECTS OF HORMONES

As is true of many forms of behavior, gender differences exist in the form, frequency, and intensity of aggressive behaviors, both in humans and nonhumans. These differences require an explanation. One possibility is that males and females have different early hormone arrays, and thus become structurally and physiologically organized in different ways.

The organizing effects of testosterone on aggressive behavior have been most thoroughly studied in mice, and in many ways the results parallel those of sexual development (Chapter 10). Young male mice were castrated on the day of birth, or 2, 6, 12, or 40 days later. Consequently, they had varying lengths of exposure to testosterone. As adults these males were given an activating dose of testosterone and placed together in groups of four. Wounding was used as evidence of fighting. There was a clear distinction between day 6 to 40 castrates and those tures (Smart, 1981). Moreover, various stressors, such as the application of heat and restraint to pregnant mice, leads to reduced levels of adult aggression in the female offspring (Politch & Herrenkohl, 1979).

Early postnatal influences Although there are strain differences in aggressiveness, we need not conclude that these differences are due solely to genetic differences. In some cases early experience affects later aggression independently of genetic constitution. We know this from cross-fostering studies of mice and rats. For example, Denenberg (1970) showed that when mouse litters are taken from their mothers at birth and raised by lactating rats, the mice are significantly less aggressive than are mice raised by the biological mother or by a mouse foster mother. This effect does not always occur, however. One mouse strain (called C57), which is normally aggressive, is less aggressive when reared by rat mothers, but another mouse strain (Swiss albino), which is not as aggressive as C57, is neither more nor less aggressive when reared by rats (Denenberg, 1973). Much the same result occurs when the normally aggressive grasshopper mouse is raised by foster mothers of the white-footed mouse species: They become less aggressive. But the less aggressive white-footed mouse does not become more aggressive when raised by grasshopper mouse mothers (McCarty & Southwick, 1979). In contrast, in a cross-fostering experiment involving great blue herons and great egrets, the normally less-aggressive herons became more aggressive when raised by egrets, but the egrets failed to become less aggressive when raised by heron parents (Mock, 1984, 1985). Clearly, more work needs to be done to further document the effects of early rearing conditions on later aggressiveness and the means by which these conditions have their effects.

Later postnatal influences The social environment in which animals live is an important determinant of aggressive behavior. Social isolation is a particularly potent condition influencing aggression. For example, social isolation of male mice, even for a few days, results in significantly increased aggression toward strangers compared to males housed in social groups (Ebert, 1983; Cairns *et al.*, 1983). The influence of social isolation is age-dependent, however.

Cairns *et al.* (1985) placed male mice in social isolation for up to 64 days beginning when they were between 21 and 84 days old. (All were living in groups prior to isolation.) The older mice responded to the isolation much sooner than the younger mice. Older males' attack rates on the stranger increased significantly in just 24 hours after isolation, but attack rates by younger males did not increase until they had been isolated for 64 days.

Reinforcement history   Proximate consequences of aggression can influence the individual's later behavior. For example, male mice that have lost fights with other males become very timid when exposed to a new male, but mice who have won fights become more aggressive with each victory (Tellegen *et al.*, 1969). Further, aggressive acts, such as biting in rats or necking in pigeons (both directed toward conspecifics), increased in frequency when such behavior was immediately followed by food or water reinforcement in animals that had been food-or water-deprived (e.g., Azrin & Hutchinson, 1967).

Unfortunately, we do not know how applicable these findings are to real-world aggression. For instance, the form or intensity of attacks that have been subject to positive reinforcement may differ from those subjected to negative reinforcement and both may be strongly influenced by such conditions as season, location relative to a territorial boundary, and so on (reviewed by Archer, 1988).

Mechanisms of Aggression

We now turn our attention to the neural and motivational mechanisms that are responsible for the initiation and regulation of aggressive behavior. These mechanisms are closely linked with stimuli from the surrounding environment that act to provoke aggression, or at least to make it more likely.

NEUROANATOMY OF AGGRESSION

Over the years, a large number of studies have been published on the neurobiology of aggression. Unfortunately, the studies have often yielded inconclusive or inconsistent results. Some of these difficulties can be attributed to differences in species, methods, definitions, and measurements of aggressive behavior (Renfrew & Hutchinson, 1983). This presentation will briefly describe some of the *trends* in this mass of research. We will proceed by discussing three brain regions (hypothalamus, amygdala, and midbrain central gray) and the effects of electrical stimulation or lesion on various forms of aggression. Note, however, that there appear to be no "aggression centers" in the brain; rather, distributed neural systems are involved, with certain areas being perhaps more important than others (Herbert, 1989; Siegel & Pott, 1988).

Hypothalamus   When electrodes are placed in the hypothalamus and the neurons are electrically stimulated, aggressive behaviors are sometimes produced. In cats, for instance, electrical stimulation of the ventromedial region elicits *defensive aggression* (Ursin, 1981), which is characterized by arching of the back, hair erection, snarling, and spitting. If something attackable is nearby, such as a lab rat, another cat, or the experimenter's hand, the cat is likely to attack it in a mauling fashion. Similar behavior is produced by lesions of the medial hypothalamus in several species, including humans (reviewed by Albert & Walsh, 1984). Recall that the ventromedial hypothalamus, when lesioned, produces excessive food consumption under some circumstances (Chapter 14). One human patient with a ventromedial hypothalamic lesion frequently struck and attempted to bite the hospital staff who were treating her! She could be calmed only by allowing her to eat freely, and she consumed 8000–10,000 calories per day (Reeves & Plum, 1969).

Other hypothalamic sites initiate fleeing when stimulated. Fleeing is a component of submissive aggression, which differs from defensive aggression (Adams, 1979) but which may alternate with it. In other hypothalamic nuclei, especially the anterior and lateral regions, a very different behavior, predatory attack, is produced. In this case, the cat looks as though it is stalking prey: it quietly crouches down with its fur sleeked. If a mouse is available, the cat will pounce on it, quickly killing the animal with a lethal bite to the back of the neck (Siegel & Pott, 1988).

Amygdala   Another brain region, the amygdala, located within the temporal lobe, is known to to be involved in submissive and defensive aggression. Both behaviors can be produced by electrical stimulation (Adams, 1979; Ursin, 1981). So far, no evidence for amygdaloid involvement in predatory aggression has been found.

Some intriguing human studies implicated the amygdala in pathological violence. Some habitually violent persons were found to have tumors of the amygdala. However, most violent persons lack such abnormalities, and others who have similar abnormalities exhibit no excessive aggression. Thus, it appears that, in humans at least, abnormalities of the amygdala are neither necessary nor sufficient to provoke violence (Eichelman, 1983).

Midbrain central gray   The central gray matter of the midbrain has been found to be involved in defensive and submissive aggression in rats, cats, and other mammals (Adams, 1979). Although located within the same area, different sets of neurons influence the two forms

of behavior and they exert inhibitory control over one another. Thus, inputs from other brain regions, such as the ventromedial hypothalamus and projections from several sensory systems dictate which of the two behavioral systems will predominate at a given time. Switching from predominantly defensive to submissive aggression (or vice versa) according to changing circumstances would be of decided adaptive value.

Although the hypothalamus, amygdala, and midbrain central gray have been implicated in the expression of various forms of aggressive behavior, it is important to reiterate that aggressive behavior control is distributed among several or many populations of neurons. Further, even though electrical stimulation can produce aggressive behavior, oftentimes such behavior depends on, or is influenced by, contextual environmental stimuli. Siegel and Pott (1988) stress that predatory attack in cats can be produced by electrical or chemical stimulation of several brain structures, but that the degree to which appropriate stimuli, such as a mouse, are needed for normal performance varies between structures. Aggression, especially the sort that might occur between two conspecifics with rapidly changing components of offense and defense, depends on the complex interplay of many brain structures tuned to relevant environmental stimuli.

NEUROTRANSMITTERS AND AGGRESSION

The involvement of neurotransmitters in aggressive behavior is without question; however, the complex nature of their involvement precludes making simple statements about them. Miczek (1983), for example, points out that although there are trends in this area, differences in species and experimental methods have complicated the picture. Thus, the following is a brief account of the trend. More work is required to understand the exceptions.

Defensive aggression   The catecholamines norepinephrine and dopamine are involved in defensive aggression (Eichelman, 1979; Miczek, 1983; Siegel & Pott, 1988). Most of the evidence suggests that procedures that increase norepinephrine enhance defensive aggression, and other treatments that reduce norepinephrine reduce defensive aggression. Interestingly, the psychiatric condition called *mania,* which is characterized by hyperactivity and sometimes verbal and physical assaultiveness, is increased by norepinephrine. Lithium has been used to treat mania for many years. Only recently, however, has it been learned that lithium reduces norepinephrine in human brain tissue (Tosteson, 1981; Schildkraut *et al.,* 1967).

Serotonin and acetylcholine also influence defensive aggression, although apparently in opposite directions. Most treatments that increase acetylcholine at synapses enhance the expression of defensive aggression in cats (Siegel & Pott, 1988). In contrast, serotonin has a generally inhibitory affect on defensive aggression. Lesions of the raphe nuclei deplete serotonin levels and result in more defensive fighting in rats (Jacobs & Cohen, 1976).

Predatory aggression   Muricide, the killing of mice by rats, has received considerable attention. The strongest evidence concerns the inhibitory control exerted by gamma amino butyric acid. Procedures that increase GABA immediately block muricidal behavior, whereas decreases in GABA often produce muricide in rats that normally do not exhibit this behavior. Similarly, decreased serotonin also produces muricide in nonkillers (Mandel *et al.,* 1979). Acetylcholine administered into the lateral hypothalamus facilitates predatory aggression (Bandler, 1970) in rats. Acetylcholine also in-

duces predatory behavior in cats (Bernston & Leibowitz, 1973).

MOTIVATION OF AGGRESSION

In Chapter 8 we examined the principles underlying motivated behavior. In brief, the probability of a behavior occurring, or the intensity with which it is performed, depends on conditions that precede or accompany the behavior, and the consequences of that behavior. This section will focus on those conditions—both antecedents and consequences—that contribute to variations in the behavior of adults over time. That is, at some times an individual may be aggressive (slightly or greatly) and at other times it may be nonaggressive. Why? Several theories have been proposed to account for these behavioral variations.

Aversive stimulation   Perhaps the most common antecedent situation provoking aggression is the application of painful or otherwise aversive stimulation. Laboratory studies on rodents, primates, and birds have consistently shown that attack is likely when an individual is exposed to a painful stimulus such as electric shock or a blow (reviewed by Renfrew & Hutchinson, 1983). If a painful stimulus is reliably preceded by an otherwise neutral stimulus, aggression can be provoked by the onset of that stimulus.

Why would one animal attack another when it is in pain? Perhaps there is a bias toward attributing pain to the actions of another individual, such as a predator or even a conspecific. In any event, aggression can be viewed as a form of escape or avoidance that might decrease the chance of exposure to tissue damage. When placed in the confining situation of a small laboratory cage, aggression is made more likely because other avenues for dealing with the other animal are blocked.

Withdrawal of positive stimuli In many ways, the discontinuance of positive stimuli may be perceived as aversive. When animals are given food reinforcement for performing a behavior, such as lever pressing, and then the reinforcement is withheld (extinction), the most common reaction is to vigorously perform the response, bite the lever, or attack another individual if one is present. Extinction-induced aggression is very common (Azrin *et al.*, 1966). (Think about what people do to vending machines that swallow their coins without returning the desired item.) Social psychologists long ago formulated this sort of motivational model of aggression, where it is known as the *frustration–aggression hypothesis* (Dollard *et al.*, 1939).

The frustration–aggression hypothesis went further than stating that extinction would produce aggressive responses. It suggested that frustration always produces aggression, and that all aggression is linked to frustration. Neither prediction is correct. First, frustration (defined as the thwarting of attempts to achieve a desired goal) can sometimes lead to nonaggressive behavioral changes such as taking a different route, waiting for circumstances to change, or even giving up. Although aggression is a common response to frustrating circumstances, it is certainly not the only response. Second, not all cases of aggression can be attributed to frustration. Some cases of aggression are due to previous reinforcement of aggressive behaviors. The frustration–aggression hypothesis, then, was overly ambitious, but it definitely applies in many instances.

Hydraulic model The responses to aversive stimulation and to withdrawal of positive stimuli are similar in that they are responses to circumstances originating outside the organism.

The hydraulic model of aggression, in contrast, places greater emphasis on internal changes as producers of aggression. Developed in the 1920s and 1930s by ethologists such as Lorenz (1966), the hydraulic model predicts a build-up of *action-specific energy* as time progresses since the behavior last occurred. As this energy attains some threshold level, the individual begins seeking out an opportunity to engage in the behavior. This is the *appetitive phase.* If the opportunity is found, the organism performs the behavior, the so-called *consummatory response.*

Although this model of motivation works reasonably well for such things as feeding and drinking, it has several serious problems when applied to most forms of aggression. First, there seems to be no convincing evidence for an appetitive phase in aggression. Animals generally do not go looking for the opportunity to attack the way they look for food, water, sex partners, or a warm place to sleep. Although some animal species such as Siamese fighting fish will apparently perform behaviors such as traversing a maze or swimming through a hoop for the opportunity to fight an opponent (Hogan, 1967), it is not clear whether aggression *per se* (as opposed to novelty) is what reinforces the behavior (Bols, 1977). Further, the only species in which the appetitive phase *may* occur are those that have been subjected to intense artificial selection for high levels of aggression, so the generality of the observation of an appetite for aggression is questionable. Most researchers of aggressive behavior have reached the conclusion that aggression occurs to escape or avoid detrimental conditions (Archer, 1988). Only predatory behavior, which is, of course, closely linked to feeding, has provided some support for the hydraulic model of aggressive motivation.

Activating effects of hormones Because hormones are known to prime certain other behaviors, it is reasonable to investigate the possible role of hormones in activating aggression. Unfortunately, not nearly as much work has been done on the role of hormones in aggressive behavior as has been done on other behaviors, especially reproduction (Gandelman, 1984). And, as with the neuroanatomical and neurophysiological bases of aggression, the study of hormonal involvement in aggression is clouded by diverse methods of producing and measuring aggression.

Does testosterone or any other hormone activate aggressive behavior? In many cases that appears to be the case, but only under certain circumstances. In mice, males lacking fighting experience will not attack an intruder male unless pretreated with testosterone (assuming normal male organization at an early age). However, testosterone treated males attack only under the strange intruder situation; that is, when they are the resident, not when they are the intruder. Further, males with testosterone rarely attack lactating females, although castrated males do. This has led Johnson and Whalen (1988) to suggest that there is a testosterone-sensitive brain structure or system regulating these two forms of attack. Testosterone activates male-to-male aggression, but inhibits male-to-female aggression.

Among experienced males, testosterone is less important as a determinant of fighting. Dominant males (who have been successful fighters) continue to be aggressive fighters even after their testosterone is removed. Experienced unsuccessful males fail to fight if their testosterone is left alone or even increased. Clearly, experience with fighting and its effects is more important than is an individual's hormone concentration (Herbert, 1989). In fact, Johnson and Whalen (1988) report that the presence of testosterone tends to *reduce* individual differences in aggressiveness of male mice.

In many male mammals, aggression and testosterone increase substantially during the breeding season, suggesting a link between them. However, in at least one species, the dusky-footed wood rat, the rise in breeding season aggression is not due to testosterone. Caldwell *et al.* (1984) castrated male wood rats trapped in the field in late summer when testosterone concentration was very low. They were kept in the lab all winter under natural lighting conditions. In February and March, their breeding season, the castrated males initiated and won as many fights, and provoked as many attacks as did intact males. Clearly, there is no direct causal link between testosterone and aggression in this species; there are probably many others in which this is also true. Perhaps the most reasonable conclusion that can be drawn at this point is that, in some species (perhaps including humans), the presence of testosterone may sensitize the individual to circumstances that may provoke aggression, making aggression more likely or more vigorous than it might otherwise be. However, aggression is highly dependent on external cues and it is to them and to previous experience that we should turn to understand differences in the occurrence of aggression.

Evidence linking testosterone levels with differences in aggression in humans is unconvincing (Mazur, 1983). We are usually interested in a causal connection between the hormone and a behavior, but in humans the evidence is only correlational. For example, one argument goes along these lines: Men have more testosterone than women (true); men engage in more aggressive behaviors (also true); therefore, testosterone causes aggression (perhaps not). Why not? Because demonstrating that two phenomena co-occur (are correlated) cannot be used to conclude that one causes the other. Men also have hairier legs than women. Does that mean that hairy legs cause aggression? In fact, well-documented cases are available of testosterone increases in men that were not associated with aggression, or which were associated with elation. Mazur and Lamb (1980) paid $100 to men who won tennis matches. The men who won decisively had elevated testosterone (compared to prematch levels) and were, according to mood inventories, much happier than the men who lost and whose testosterone remained at prematch levels. Clearly, testosterone can increase without making men surly or otherwise prone to aggression.

The only way to establish a causal relation between a hormone and a behavior is to increase or decrease the hormone in two groups of randomly chosen subjects without their knowledge of what is happening. To allow knowledge would risk that their preconceived notions about hormones would affect their behavior. In most cases, ethical concerns preclude conducting such experiments. Thus, studies in which testosterone concentrations of men convicted of violent crimes are compared with those of nonviolent criminals or noncriminals are not very useful because there is an unknown influence of nonrandomness in selection of men for study. Violent criminals probably differ from noncriminals in many ways besides their hormone concentrations, and even on that count the research is contradictory (reviewed by Sheard, 1979).

What evidence is there for hormonal involvement in female aggression? First, aggression in pregnant female mice is primed by progesterone. Females will attack intruder males only if the female is pregnant or is treated with progesterone. Some strains of mice are more sensitive than others to progesterone and this accounts for the greater aggressiveness of certain strains (Svare, 1988). Second, female rhesus monkeys performed more aggressive acts such as threats and chases during mid-cycle when mating activities were occurring (M. L. Walker *et al.*, 1983). The relationship to hormonal changes was not conclusive, however. Controversy exists over whether women are more irritable and aggressive during the days just before menstruation and the first couple of days of menstruation (the premenstrual syndrome, PMS), and, if so, whether these behavioral changes are due to hormonal changes occurring during that time. Some studies report a greater incidence of aggression premenstrually. For example, Ellis and Austin (1971), studying women in a prison, found significantly more episodes of verbal abuse and physical assault premenstrually than would be expected by chance.

Assuming that irritability and aggressiveness increase premenstrually, can we conclude that the hormonal changes associated with menstruation are responsible for the behavioral changes? Again, showing that hormones and behavior are correlated does not establish a causal relationship (even though one *may* exist). Women may be, as a rule, socialized about how to behave during the menstrual phase and thus their behavior may have little to do with hormonal changes.

Behavioral Ecology of Aggression

Resources (in the form of energy, mates, shelter, etc.) are essential to life or to reproductive success. If such resources are in limited supply, then those characteristics that result in acquisition of those resources will tend to be favored during the course of evolution. There are several ecological circumstances which favor aggression, and within those circumstances there are different ways of attempting to maximize one's success. This section will review some of the circumstances in which aggression may be favored, and the behavioral dynamics that go on during aggression.

ADAPTIVE CONTEXTS FOR AGGRESSION

Resource acquisition and defense It is common for aggression to occur during the acquisition and defense of resources needed for survival and reproduction. For example, bay gobies, a species of small fish that inhabits shallow water along the California coast, fight for burrows in the mud that they use to escape predators and to avoid drying out during low tide (Grossman, 1980). Clearly, aggression is critical for individual survival. However, aggression is not invariably used in resource acquisition and defense, probably because the costs involved (e.g., time, energy, risk of injury) may exceed the gains from possessing the resource. Thus, the concept of *economic defense* has become influential in the analysis of aggressiveness for resources (Davies & Houston, 1984). Some resources, because of their transient nature, are not worth the cost of defense. For instance, bats and birds that feed on aerial insects cannot defend their prey. The insects can quickly disperse and the cost of "riding herd" on such beasts would far exceed the benefits of doing so.

Other resources are economically defendable, however. Birds commonly set up territories in forests, marshes, and other places where they nest, gather food, and rear their young. The resources in these areas are often abundant enough to justify protection, but not so abundant that everyone can have as much as they wish. Thus, aggressive defense helps protect what is necessary for survival and reproduction, even though the result may be that others are excluded, perhaps dying for lack of some essential resource (Marler, 1976a).

Two examples will help clarify this adaptive context. Great egrets and great blue herons share similar habitats for foraging and nesting. In Texas, Mock (1984) found that egret parents bring small fish to their nestlings but heron parents bring large fish to theirs. The egret nestlings were highly aggressive: older, larger nestlings frequently peck at their siblings, and the combination of injury and starvation often results in siblings' deaths. The herons, in contrast, seldom aggressed against their nest mates. Mock hypothesized that egrets are aggressive because aggression made it possible for some chicks to monopolize the food brought to the nest by the parents. Herons, who are brought large prey, cannot monopolize it and therefore aggression would not only be wasted but would damage the potential survival and reproductive chances of siblings, contrary to the expectations of kin selection theory (see Chapters 4 and 12). To test his hypothesis, Mock transferred sets of eggs or newly hatched chicks between species. The birds are about the same size and were readily accepted by the other parents. The heron chicks that were fed small prey by egret parents promptly became aggressive toward nest mates even if the nest was given supplemental food, in the form of small fish, by the experimenter. The egret chicks, however, did not significantly reduce their aggressiveness when reared by heron parents. Mock concluded that egrets have a closed system of aggression, perhaps due to a long evolutionary history of being fed small fish, whereas herons may have a more variable diet and scale aggression according to the resource base.

The second example comes from Hawaiian honeycreepers, small birds that earn a living by consuming flower nectar. When flowers are extremely abundant the birds do not defend them. When flowers are somewhat less abundant, aggressive defense of feeding territories is very common and vigorous. Finally, when flowers are rare, territories are neither established nor defended. Why is this? Aggression, like all behaviors, has costs (energy, risk, and loss of time) and sometimes the costs exceed the benefits. When flowers are highly abundant there is no benefit from aggressively defending them: everyone has plenty. When flowers are rare, however, there is a premium on foraging time. No bird can afford to burn scarce calories defending a territory that has few flowers. But when flowers are at a broad intermediate range of abundance, aggressive defense is beneficial (Carpenter & MacMillan, 1976).

When aggression occurs in defense of resources, one expects it to correspond to the degree of competition for those resources. This appears to be the case. Mockingbirds defend fruit-bearing trees against other bird species in direct proportion to the importance of fruit in the other species' diet. That is, highly frugivorous species were vigorously attacked, but nonfrugivores were not bothered by the mockingbirds, which are themselves highly frugivorous (Fig. 15-3; Moore, 1978).

Reproductive success Aggressive behavior occurs in several situations associated with reproduction. We will discuss aggression that (a) facilitates mate acquisition, (b) protects mates from sexual encounters with other individuals, (c) increases the probability of fertilization by the aggressor, and (d) reduces competition that one's offspring might have for survival.

Mate acquisition is a common context for aggression. For example, bucks may attack other bucks in possession of a group of does (Clutton-Brock *et al.*, 1979), and male Hamadryas baboons sometimes "kidnap" young females from their groups and prevent them from escaping from their control (Kummer, 1968). Humans also engage in aggression for mate acquisition. For example, among the Yanomamo Indians of Venezuela, groups of men from a village conduct raids on other villages, kidnapping women who they bring back with them as wives. Men who have killed rival villagers tend to have more wives than men who have not (Chagnon,

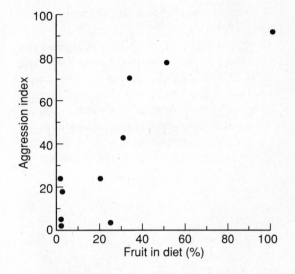

Figure 15.3
The likelihood of mockingbirds attacking other bird species that enter their territory depends on the importance of fruit in the other species diet. Mockingbirds depend on fruit, so other fruit-eaters are more important competitors, and are thus attacked. (Data from Moore, 1978.)

1988), so there is a clear individual reproductive benefit to be gained through successful group aggression. The possibility exists that these people gain food resources through group aggression, but this presently seems unlikely (Chagnon & Hames, 1979).

Having acquired a mate does no good unless the aggressor utilizes the mate's reproductive potential. This means protecting the mate from the sexual advances of others. As we saw in Chapter 11, numerous cases of cuckoldry avoidance have been described. (Cuckoldry is the situation in which a male unknowingly cares for his mate's offspring that were sired by another male.) Male bluebirds attack other males in the vicinity of the mate when she is fertile (Barash, 1976), and bull elephant seals clash with intruding males (LeBoeuf & Peterson, 1969) (Fig. 15-4).

Not surprisingly, much human aggression is concerned with mate protection. Daly and Wilson (1988a, b, also Daly *et al.*, 1982) have reviewed a large body of evidence concerning violence in the context of male sexual jealousy. A large fraction of the murders committed in the United States are provoked when a man concludes that his wife or girlfriend is getting too close to another man, or especially if she is discontinuing their relationship. Of course, nonlethal aggression is very common under the same circumstances.

Aggression can sometimes increase the aggressor's reproductive success by increasing the probability of him fertilizing females, or by fertilizing them sooner than he could have without aggression. Hrdy (1979) studied the behavior of male hanuman langurs, a species of monkey from India, when a small group of males succeeds in ousting the males that had formerly held a troop of females. The new males kill all the offspring who are young enough to still be nursing. Recall that lactational amenorrhea, a period during nursing in which the female fails to ovulate, may last for many months depending on the species. By killing the young offspring, the adult male hurries the resumption of ovulation by the adult females, thereby increasing his reproductive success. These males are committed to killing the offspring, sometimes having to stalk them and their mothers, who attempt to protect their infants, for several days after the takeover. After all have been killed, the males cease their violence, and treat offspring born later with great care. Similar behavior is widely known, occurring in such species as lions, house cats, and mice.

Finally, females sometimes increase their reproductive success through infanticide of others' offspring. Female black-tailed prairie dogs frequently kill some or all of the pups of nearby mothers. By doing so, infanticidal females are more likely to successfully wean their own litters, and they have larger litters at weaning and heavier pups (Hoogland, 1985). These results seem to be due to decreased competition for food on the home territory.

Dominance and social control   Many species, including primates, use aggression to establish and maintain dominance over other individuals. These species often live in groups that

Figure 15.4
Male elephant seals sometimes engage in prolonged fights. The winner gets the opportunity to mate with a large number of females, so fighting ability is highly adaptive.

MARGO WILSON and MARTIN DALY

" . . . *Studies of North American spouse killers indicate that the husband's proprietary concern with his wife's fidelity or her intention to quit the marriage led him to initiate the violence in an overwhelming majority of cases . . . " [Daly, M., & Wilson, M. (1988). Evolutionary social psychology and family homicide. Science 242, 519–524 (p. 521).]*

have stable membership over long periods of time. Dominance rank often translates into priority of access to limited resources, such as food or mates, and thus can be seen as having a generalized function including both resource acquisition and breeding success.

For example, studies of house mice (DeFries & McClearn, 1970), deer mice (Dewsbury, 1984), baboons (Hausfater, 1975), and geladas (a large, Old World monkey related to the baboons, Dunbar & Dunbar, 1977), among others, indicate that the position in a dominance hierarchy is positively correlated with copulatory frequency in males, with copulation frequency during the ovulatory phase of the female's estrous cycle (Chapais, 1983), or with number of births in females (Dunbar & Dunbar, 1977). Although some studies found no such correla-

tions, the preponderance of evidence suggests that dominance—often acquired and maintained through aggression—can yield enhanced reproductive success.

Predatory and antipredator aggression Predation and antipredator behavior were discussed in Chapter 14, so we will not review it in detail here. Probably the most common form of aggression, predation (killing another individual for the purpose of consumption) can be either interspecific or intraspecific.

Predators can be of the same species as their prey (Polis *et al.*, 1984). Consequently, aggressive defense against conspecifics can be thought of as antipredator behavior. Females with vulnerable offspring are especially prone to display such behavior. Female meadow voles who were nursing a litter were significantly more aggres-

SARAH HRDY

" . . . Infant-killing will be directed at offspring unlikely to be direct descendents of the killer, . . . and
. . . elimination of the infant increases the infanticidal
male's own opportunity to breed, typically by shortening the interval until next ovulation in the mother of
the infant killed." [Hrdy, S. B. (1979). Infanticide
among animals: A review, classification, and examination of the implications for the reproductive strategies of
females. Ethology and Sociobiology **1**, 13–40
(p. 17).]

After taking over a troop of females from other males,
male hanuman langurs will kill any offspring who are
being nursed. Doing so hastens ovulation by the
mother, which shortens the time required for the male
to impregnate the mother. Infanticide enhances the new
male's reproductive success.

sive toward juvenile strangers placed in their
cage than were adult males or nonmaternal adult
females (Boonstra, 1984). Strangers may attack
and kill pups, so maternal aggression may protect them from predation.

One tactic that prey sometimes employ
(usually as a last resort) is to attack the predator.
The attack may be made by a group or by an
individual, but it sometimes succeeds in dissuad-
ing the predator, harming it, or even killing it.
Red-winged blackbirds have been observed harassing a kestrel (a species of small falcon) so
intensely that it ended up in a lake and had to
swim out (Smith & Holland, 1974), and Cali-

fornia ground squirrels may pounce on and bite
rattlesnakes, sometimes killing them (Fitch,
1948).

BEHAVIORAL DYNAMICS OF CONFLICT

To behave aggressively is not a simple decision,
especially when one's opponent is capable of
inflicting harm in return. In this section we will
explore some of the factors that would tend to
(a) influence the probability of one individual
initiating aggression against another, (b) change
the intensity of the aggressive behavior (escala-

Behavioral Ecology of Aggression

tion or deescalation) after it has begun, and, finally, (c) terminate the aggressive episode.

Initiating aggression Is the potential gain in resources or reproductive success worth the potential costs of lost energy and time, and risk of injury or predation? Research suggests that animals are sensitive to the costs and benefits of aggression, and that they initiate fights only when they have a good chance of winning. This is clearly illustrated by the red deer of Scotland (Fig. 15-5). This species breeds in the fall and males contest each other for possession of females. Clutton-Brock *et al.* (1979) showed that males were more likely to initiate fights when (a) they held no females, (b) the females were in the peak period of conception, (c) the opponent was smaller, and (d) the opponent was downhill (the bucks push and shove with the antlers and being uphill is advantageous because it gets gravity in one's favor). Although approaches are common, fights are relatively rare.

This suggests that males do not fight without first assessing their prospective opponent. Moreover, fighting has a good chance of success, suggesting that the assessment of the opponent is accurate.

Escalation and de-escalation decisions When an aggressive interaction has begun, how intense does it become? The answer probably depends on some of the same variables mentioned above. The opponent may be a better fighter, or seems more committed than one thought. This brings up an interesting question: If an important part of the intensity decision depends on an assessment of the opponent, why do not animals and humans feign greater fighting ability, defensive commitment, and so forth? Very often, they do. Many animals puff themselves up, perhaps by erecting hairs or feathers, to make themselves appear larger. Their vocal characteristics may also change, usually becoming lower-pitched and harsher (Morton, 1977)

Figure 15.5
Aggressive interactions typically escalate until one participant suddenly gives up, thereby minimizing losses.

thereby appearing more threatening. However, these bluffs can sometimes be discerned by "probes" on the part of the adversary. The probes are generally increases in the intensity of the conflict, gradually testing the capacities of the opponent. Eventually, a bluff may be detected. Gradual escalation of intensity may be beneficial for both adversaries. As intensity increases, so does risk. If one combatant ceases at less than maximal intensity, its opponent obtains its benefit at submaximal risk. On the other hand, the loser who started out at low intensity and then escalated until it became apparent that it would lose will probably suffer less damage than it would have if it had launched a high-intensity attack against a superior force.

Termination of aggression We generally find that agonistic interactions terminate suddenly with the vanquished individual fleeing precipitously. This benefits the loser by not prolonging a contest it is destined to lose and quickly gets it out of harm's way. The victorious individual seldom pursues its escaping foe because there is little to gain from doing so. Because fights are generally over space, resources, or mates, and these have been won, perpetuation of the fight could be disadvantageous to the winner. Its time could be better spent pursuing other activities.

The dynamic nature of agonistic conflicts has led some behavioral ecologists (e.g., Maynard Smith & Price, 1973) to model conflicts using computer simulations. They approach this using game theory, devising various strategies to employ against the opponent's "moves." While unrealistic in detail, these simulations come reasonably close to describing the behavior of real animals. For instance, all-out attack is seldom successful in simulations and is rarely seen among animals, for obvious reasons. In contrast, a more prudent strategy of limited escalations to probe the opponent's ability, with subsequent

behavior based on the opponent's response, generally seems to prevail. This pattern has been found in spiders fighting for territories around webs (Riechert, 1986).

In conclusion, aggressive behavior in animals and humans is not simple in terms of the many variables that are evaluated before and during the encounter. Although the presence of certain hormones and neurotransmitters may make aggression more likely, in virtually every case studied, the participants are highly sensitive to situational cues and other information that is germane to the outcome of the fight (Huntingford, 1989). To understand aggression requires that we explore the role of situational variables and merge their effects along with the previous experience and current physiological status of the participants.

Summary

Aggression or agonism is defined as the set of behaviors that occur in conflict situations. Thus, it includes such behaviors as attack and threat, and defense and escape.

Genetic differences that are relevant to aggression certainly exist. First, selective breeding experiments have been consistently successful in producing high and low levels of certain forms of aggression. Interestingly, selectively breeding for one type of aggression (e.g., attack on same-sex intruders) does not affect other forms of aggression (e.g., predation), suggesting that different forms of aggression are quite distinct at the genetic level. Strain differences also exist in aggressiveness, even when the strains were not bred for aggressiveness. Finally, although chromosomal abnormalities in humans (such as XYY males) were once thought to be associated with heightened aggressiveness in their bearers, this no longer seems to be true.

Aggression develops over the lifespan in much the same way as other behaviors. There are prenatal effects such as hormone concentration, maternal stress, and so on that can affect later adult aggressiveness. Further, postnatal effects, such as handling in rodents, maternal interactions with the pups, and success or failure in aggressive interactions have important implications for the amount of aggression that an individual exhibits.

The physiological mechanisms of aggression are complex and not well-understood. First, there are several brain structures in mammals which are implicated in aggression in its several forms. The hypothalamus, amygdala, and midbrain central gray are some of the more important structures. Electrical stimulation of certain sites within these areas can provoke aggressive behavior (attack, defense, predation) in certain situations. Similarly, some neurotransmitters are known to influence the expression of aggressive behaviors, but these effects are influenced by many other variables.

Studies on the motivational bases of aggression have focused on the role of aversive stimulation and withdrawal of positive stimulation in initiating aggression. That is, pain, discomfort, and inability to acquire positive stimuli frequently evoke aggressive behaviors. Individuals who are reinforced for aggressiveness tend to become more aggressive. The hydraulic model of motivation, which can work reasonably well for other behaviors, does not work well for aggression. This approach sees motivation as being due to the build-up of action-specific energy to the point where the individual shows an appetite for a certain activity and seeks out the opportunity to engage in it. However, there seems to be no good evidence for an appetitive phase with regard to aggression. Finally, hormones sometimes influence the probability, intensity, and form of aggressive behavior. However, the evidence regarding hormonal activation of aggression is mixed in animals, and is rather poor in humans. Linking hormones with human aggression in a causal fashion is especially difficult.

Aggression occurs in several adaptive ecological contexts. Certainly the most common condition involves resource acquisition and defense. When a resource that is necessary or beneficial for survival or reproductive success is economically defendable, that is, when the resource is spatially restricted and is not exceedingly common or rare, aggressive defense is common. Aggression also occurs in several situations associated with breeding success. Finally, aggression occurs in the establishment of social dominance, and in predatory and antipredatory situations. The costs and benefits of aggression are interwoven in complex ways. Thus, we frequently see careful initiation and escalation of aggressive interactions and usually rapid and complete termination of the encounter by one of the participants.

Recommended Readings

ARCHER, J. (1988). *Behavioural biology of aggression*. New York: Cambridge University Press.

GROEBEL, J., & HINDE, R. A. (1989). *Aggression and war: Their biological and social bases*. New York: Cambridge University Press.

LORENZ, K. Z. (1966). *On aggression*. London: Methuen.

SIMMEL, E. C., HAHN, M. E., & WALTERS, J. K. (1983). *Aggressive behavior: Genetic and neural approaches*. Hillsdale, NJ: Erlbaum.

SVARE, B. B. (1983). *Hormones and aggressive behavior*. New York: Plenum.

Chapter 16

SLEEP

To be adaptive, behavior must occur at opportune times with respect to important environmental conditions. Many of these conditions recur cyclically, such as the daily light–dark cycle, and the yearly pattern of the seasons. The amount of activity in most animals rises and falls with the daily light–dark cycle, and the changing seasons are accompanied by periods of reproductive activity, migration, or hibernation, depending on the season, location, and species. In Chapter 11 we examined the mechanisms of seasonal reproduction; in this chapter we will focus on one of the several processes that fluctuate on a daily cycle: sleep.

Rhythms, Clocks, and Behavior

Behavioral cycles　Several types of behavioral cycles can be recognized based on the duration or *period* of the cycle. We are most familiar with *circadian* (daily) cycles of wakefulness and sleep, and with *circannual* (yearly) cycles of reproduction, migration, and hibernation, but behavioral cycles come in periods shorter than one day and longer than one year (Rapp, 1987). At the short end are cycles within human sleep and cognitive performance during wakefulness that each last about 90 minutes (Klein & Armitage, 1979), and tidal or lunar cycles of about 12.4 hours that influence the behavior of marine organisms (Slater, 1976; Palmer, 1990). At the longer end are estrus cycles that occur about every 4 days in rodents, or about monthly in many primates. There are even multiyear cycles such as the emergence every 17 years of certain cicada species. Why do these cycles exist?

There are several adaptive reasons for the existence of cyclical behavioral patterns (Rapp, 1987). Among them are the advantages of anticipating forthcoming events, and of synchronizing otherwise independent processes. For example, the sun rises each morning and sets in the evening. Plants derive their energy from the sun and, in some species, move their leaves during the course of the day, thereby taking full advantage of the available sunlight. At night the leaves move in the direction from which the sun will appear in the morning. The plants maintain this movement rhythm even when kept in darkness (Moore-Ede *et al.*, 1982). An example of the synchronization function is the correspon-

dence between sleep and body temperature. Body temperature is higher during wakefulness than it is during sleep. Body temperature begins to rise just before the end of the sleep phase, and declines again just before sleep begins. Energy is therefore conserved during sleep when behavioral output is minimal (Aschoff, 1970).

How are behavioral cycles regulated such that they occur at the right times? Two possibilities exist. First, the activity could be controlled by regularly occurring external conditions. Wakefulness and sleep could, for example, be timed by the rise and setting of the sun, and activity of animals in the intertidal zone could be controlled by water movement. The second possibility is that cycles are timed internally or endogenously and are not dependent on external variables for the cyclical patterns. Of course, both external and internal processes could be involved in regulating rhythmic patterns of behavior.

The obvious way to determine whether cycles are under external or internal control is to take away the possible external cues. When this is done we often find that the cycle persists on its own, but that the period of the cycle differs from its period found when the external cues are present. For example, when humans live in extremely stable conditions devoid of time cues such as changes in illumination, temperature, noise, and so forth, they tend to fall asleep about every 25 hours (Minors & Waterhouse, 1984). Similarly, fiddler crabs taken from their native beach habitat into the lab away from tidal influences show activity peaks that are close to the tidal cycle that recurs about every 12.4 hours (Palmer, 1990). The presence of endogenous rhythms suggests that there are one or more physiological systems, or biological clocks, that regulate the timing of the activity.

Not all behavioral cycles persist when external cues are removed. For example, ring doves exhibit daily cycles of activity during the day and inactivity during the night. When they are kept in constant dim light, however, these patterns disappear within a few days and the birds begin to intersperse brief periods of activity with brief periods of inactivity (Silver, 1990) (Fig. 16-1).

If activity cycles were entirely controlled by endogenous rhythms whose periods did not match the period of the environmental condition, the behavior would soon become maladaptively desynchronized from external conditions. Biological clocks, however, have a provision for resetting. In the case of clocks controlling sleep and activity in animals, the resetting is accomplished each day by light. A surprisingly short exposure to light suffices to set the clock and prevent it from drifting out of synchrony with external conditions.

In sum, many behavioral cycles are due both to an endogenous rhythm and to external conditions that reset the clock. In the next section we will examine biological clocks in more detail, including the ways by which external variables set the clocks.

Biological clocks   An enormous research effort has been directed at understanding biological clocks. Much of this work has attempted to disrupt the clock so that its mechanism would become more apparent (Johnson & Hastings,

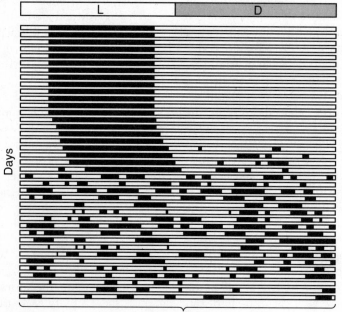

Figure 16.1

The activity patterns of ring doves in captivity are strongly controlled by the light-dark cycle, as shown by the dark horizontal bars, which indicate activity, being confined to the light half of the day. When the birds were switched to constant dim illumination, the activity pattern persisted for a few days, but its period was longer than 24 hours, indicated by the "slant" of the black bars toward the lower right. The free-running pattern disappeared, however, as indicated by the lower part of the record.

1986). Disruption has proceeded through biochemical and anatomical procedures. For example, researchers have cooled parts of the brain, interfered with protein synthesis, modified various neurotransmitters, and placed lesions in brain nuclei. Although there are numerous hypotheses about clock mechanisms, none is very well substantiated (Johnson & Hastings, 1986).

Although we do not know much about how biological clocks operate, we know a fair amount about where they are. There is general agreement that, in mammals, the *suprachiasmatic nuclei* (SCN) play a prominent role in circadian rhythms (Koella, 1984; Minors & Waterhouse, 1986). The SCN are paired structures located just above the optic chiasm. SCN lesions in hamsters disrupt circadian activity cycles (Rusak, 1977), and in other mammals SCN lesions interfere with cycles of hormone release, metabolism, and ingestion of food and water (Minors & Waterhouse, 1986).

A fascinating experiment on hamsters clearly illustrated the role of the SCN in regulating circadian activity. A genetic mutation altered the circadian period of hamsters, such that homozygotes had a period of 20 hours. Homozygous normal hamsters had a period of 24 hours, and heterozygotes had a period of 22 hours. Ralph *et al.* (1990) transplanted SCN tissue from donor animals into hamsters whose SCN had previously been ablated. In about a week the hamsters with the transplants began cycling regularly, with the period of the cycle corresponding to the genotype of the donor, indicating that individual differences in circadian cycle length may be due to individual differences in alleles.

There are undoubtedly other brain structures that contribute to circadian rhythms. Evidence for more than one clock comes from studies of humans and other species maintained in constant conditions (no changes in illumination, noise and so on). Typically, after a few

RAE SILVER

"Most species must adopt a typical temporal niche that complements their ecological spatial niche. Regular daily rhythms of activity increase the likelihood that species can avoid predators and locate food, thereby maximizing the likelihood of survival." [Silver, R. (1990). Biological timing mechanisms with special emphasis on the parental behavior of doves. In D. A. Dewsbury (Ed.) Contemporary issues in comparative psychology (pp. 252–277). Sunderland, MA: Sinauer (p. 252).]

days, physiological and behavioral systems that had been synchronized begin to uncouple and then persist on their own endogenous rhythms independently of one another (Moore-Ede *et al.*, 1982).

When an environmental variable resets a biological clock, we call the process *entrainment* and the environmental variable is a *zeitgeber* ("time-giver"). Although there are many known zeitgebers, we know most about light, and the rest of this section will be devoted to it. How does light entrain biological rhythms?

There are two entrainment pathways used by light. One involves the suprachiasmatic nuclei and the other involves the pineal gland. The suprachiasmatic nuclei receive neural input directly from the retina (Moore & Lenn, 1972; Sadun *et al.*, 1984). Thus, whenever light strikes the retina, the SCN are influenced by axons of the retinohypothalamic tract. Mammals whose optic nerves are cut such that the SCN get no retinal input quickly become desynchronized from the day–night cycle.

Birds, amphibians, and reptiles have an additional pathway for entrainment by light. The pineal gland may be influenced directly by light (Menaker, 1972). Light can penetrate the skull and brain (hold a flashlight behind your hand to see how translucent living tissue is) where it is received by the pineal, which contains a receptor chemical similar to rhodopsin (Somers & Klein, 1984). Birds whose optic nerves have been cut still maintain activity patterns that are synchronized with light, although light intensity must be somewhat greater for them to do so (Menaker, 1972).

Light alters the secretion of melatonin, and this chemical appears to play a prominent role in the entrainment process. Biological rhythms can be entrained by injections of melatonin, and the SCN have receptors for it. Hypothalamic tumors in humans are known to disrupt biological rhythms (Reppert *et al.*, 1988).

Sleep Phenomena

BEHAVIOR

Sleep and behavior may seem like contradictory terms. After all, sleep seems to be the absence of behavior. Not so. Just as musicians' pauses are a component of the performance, pauses from the stream of behavior are a component of the repertoire. The organism "doing nothing" is doing something.

Sleep behavior consists of preparatory activities, adoption of the species-typical sleep posture, the maintenance of the posture for considerable periods, and periodic movements of the body or extremities.

Preparatory activities include searching for an acceptable sleeping site, and modifications of the site prior to sleep. For example, chimpanzees spend time each late afternoon building leaf nests in which to sleep. A sturdy site in a tree is located and then the chimp pulls off leaves and boughs to form a crude mattress. Each nest is used only once (Anderson, 1984). Most carnivores, including cats, prepare for sleep by turning about once or twice before curling up in their characteristic pose.

Each species has a small number of typical sleep postures. Cats sleep either by tucking the forelegs under the ribcage with the tail wrapped close to one side of the body, or by lying on one side with the legs extended (Fig. 16-2). Most rodents curl up in tight little "balls," and birds may balance on one leg, the other pulled up under the feathers. Humans typically lie down to sleep, most commonly on one side with the arms and legs tucked close to the trunk. There are variations on this, of course, but clearly sleep is not done in a wide variety of positions, and positions are usually maintained for fairly long periods of time, and may change with such environmental variables as ambient temperature.

Finally, movements occur during sleep. People change posture, even if that means just changing to the other side, or making adjustments of the arms and legs (Hobson *et al.*, 1978). Other small movements such as chewing motions, facial muscle contractions, and tail flicks are also common.

Figure 16.2
Sleep occurs in species-specific postures. The posture on the left occurs during slow-wave sleep, and the posture on the right occurs during REM sleep.

NEURAL ACTIVITY DURING SLEEP

The most important source of information on neural activity during sleep comes from the electroencephalogram (EEG). The EEG is measured by attaching, with a pasty cream, small circular metal electrodes to various places on the scalp. Wires attached to the electrodes lead to a machine that compares the electrical activity detected by two electrodes. The resulting activity is displayed either by pens inking a moving strip of paper, on an oscilloscope screen, or by feeding directly into a computer for analysis.

When an individual is awake and alert, the EEG is typically desynchronized; that is, the waveforms are of low amplitude, high frequency, and irregular over time (Fig. 16-3). The brain is active, processing much information at many places, giving the EEG a very busy picture. During wakeful relaxation the EEG waves slow in frequency, attain higher amplitude, and become more synchronized (Fig. 16-3). Finally, as drowsiness and sleep ensue, the EEG becomes progressively more synchronized. This is called slow-wave sleep (SWS) or quiet sleep.

Slow-wave sleep in humans and other mammals is usually divided into four stages on the basis of characteristic components of the EEG. Stage 1 is the lightest sleep or drowsiness. The EEG maintains the desynchrony typical of wakefulness interspersed with periods of slow-wave activity (4–6 Hz). Stage 2 is predominantly slow wave with short bursts of higher-frequency activity called sleep spindles, and single, large-amplitude waves called K-complexes. Stage 3 has no spindles or K-complexes and the EEG is of lower frequency, with at least 20% consisting of delta wave activity (less than 4 Hz). Finally, Stage 4 consists of at least 50% delta wave activity.

There is another form of sleep, very different from SWS. This is active sleep or rapid eye

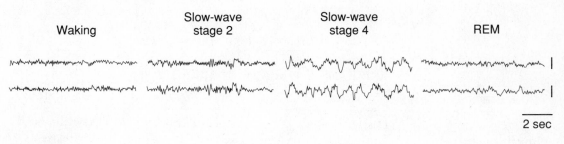

Waking	Slow-wave stage 2	Slow-wave stage 4	REM

2 sec

Figure 16.3
The EEG patterns of wakefulness, slow-wave sleep, and REM sleep differ from one another, as do eye movements and muscle contractions.

movement (REM) sleep. REM sleep is an un-usual phenomenon. Although muscles relax during both types of sleep, the muscles are most relaxed—indeed, virtually paralyzed—during REM sleep (Morrison, 1983). This does not apply to the muscles that rotate the eyes within the sockets, however, nor to some muscles of the extremities. The eye muscles in particular are active and one can see the eyes moving under the closed eyelids of a person in REM sleep (Aserinsky & Kleitman, 1953). The eyes drift about slowly, if at all, during SWS.

The most unusual feature of REM sleep is its EEG pattern. It resembles that of an awake, alert person! The combination of a wakeful EEG and extremely relaxed musculature is highly para-doxical; consequently, many scientists refer to REM sleep as paradoxical sleep.

Another difference between REM and SWS concerns dreaming. People generally report dreaming more often when awakened from REM sleep than from SWS (Aserinsky & Kleitman, 1953), and REM sleep dreams are usually por-trayed as being more vivid (McGinty & Siegel, 1983).

Other differences exist between REM and SWS. For example, thermoregulation is dimin-ished during REM, and body temperature de-clines as REM continues. Growth hormone re-lease occurs predominantly during SWS (Sassin *et al.*, 1969). Autonomic processes also differ, with respiration and heart rate becoming more irregular during REM sleep (McGinty & Siegel, 1983). These differences are summarized in Table 16-1.

A NIGHT'S SLEEP

When first going to sleep a person usually enters SWS-1, later progressing into successively slower SWS stages. Then the process is back-tracked somewhat, usually back to SWS-2 be-fore the first period of REM sleep begins. After REM, the cycle is repeated. A complete sleep cycle takes about 90 minutes in adult humans, so in a typical sleep of about 8 hours, one usually goes through about five complete sleep cycles.

The cycles are not completely uniform, however. The night's first few sleep cycles con-tain little REM sleep, but the later cycles (to-ward morning) may have 30 to 60 minutes of REM sleep (Williams *et al.*, 1973). The com-mon experience of remembering morning dreams is probably due, at least in part, to there being more dreaming in the later cycles (morn-ing) than in the early cycles of the sleep period. In contrast, early cycles contain more slow-wave sleep than do the morning cycles.

Table 16-1

SUMMARY OF FIVE CHARACTERISTICS AS THEY EXIST IN WAKEFULNESS, SLOW-WAVE SLEEP, AND RAPID EYE-MOVEMENT (REM) SLEEP

CHARACTERISTIC	AWAKE	SLOW-WAVE	REM SLEEP
EEG	Desynchronized	Synchronized	Desynchronized
Postural muscles	Tense	Relaxed	Very relaxed
Eye muscles	Active	Inactive	Active
Dreaming	Rare	Infrequent	Frequent
Thermoregulation	Effective	Effective	Ineffective

The characteristics of sleep, including its duration and the timing of REM activity, depend on when it occurs relative to other conditions. For example, Czeisler *et al.*, (1980) reported that people (who were living in conditions devoid of time cues and who could sleep as much as they wanted, whenever they wanted) slept about 8 hours when sleep began at the point of the minimum body temperature cycle. These sleep periods also accumulated REM sleep faster. In contrast, when sleep began near the high-temperature point of the cycle, subjects slept much longer but accumulated REM more slowly.

The characteristics of sleep also vary according to the surrounding (ambient) temperature. Most people regulate the temperature inside their beds to about 30 degrees Celsius by arranging the covers and by the clothing worn. If temperatures are higher or lower than this value, periods of wakefulness become more frequent and longer-lasting. REM sleep duration is reduced in cooler temperatures, but SWS is reduced in warmer temperatures. The reason for the reduced REM in cooler conditions is that the body's thermoregulatory system is not as effective then; that is, the body temperature would tend to drop too low during REM in cold conditions. These and other effects of temperature on sleep characteristics are reviewed by Muzet *et al.* (1984).

ONTOGENY OF SLEEP

Sleep patterns tend to change with age. This includes not only when and how long sleep occurs, but also its internal workings.

Total sleep time Total sleep time decreases with age in humans and in other mammals (Thoman *et al.*, 1979). Newborn babies sleep about 16 to 18 hours of each 24 (Williams

et al., 1973), but this gradually declines to about 8 hours in young adults, and then to 6 or fewer hours in elderly people (Fig. 16-4). However, the general public is so inculcated with the notion that 8 hours of sleep is normal that many elderly people complain of insomnia because they sleep only 4 to 6 hours per night though actually this is entirely within the normal range for persons of that age.

Sleep composition Total sleep time declines with age, as does the proportion accounted for by REM sleep. About 50% of newborn humans' sleep time is spent in REM, and REM constitutes about 75% of the sleep of premature infants (Williams *et al.*, 1973). REM sleep as a fraction of total sleep time declines faster than does total sleep time. Therefore, not only do elderly people sleep less than younger people, the elderly also spend proportionately less time in REM sleep (Roffwarg *et al.*, 1966).

Although SWS almost invariably precedes REM sleep in adults, infants often go from wakefulness directly into REM sleep (Wolff, 1987). This is true in nonhuman mammals as well.

Mechanisms of Sleep

NEURAL MECHANISMS AND SLEEP

The physiological mechanisms of sleep are complex and not thoroughly understood. This is because we have three distinct processes to account for: wakefulness, slow-wave sleep, and REM sleep. Different mechanisms must be coordinated to produce the usual sequence of sleep stages. To complicate matters, some of the methods used to investigate the neural mechanisms of sleep do not always yield clear-cut results. For example, lesions of brain tissue may inadvertently destroy axons passing through the area, cause tissue swelling and other changes

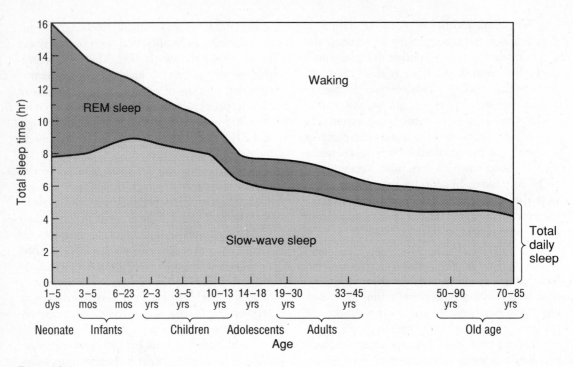

Figure 16.4
Total sleep time declines with age, as does REM sleep as a fraction of total sleep time.

that may affect neural functioning. To attribute control over a sleep process to the lesioned nucleus may not always be justified (McGinty & Siegel, 1983). Consequently, sleep research often produces conflicting results and conclusions, and must therefore be interpreted cautiously. We will examine the evidence regarding sleep mechanisms in two parts: the onset of sleep from waking, and the transitions from SWS to REM and vice versa.

Extending within the brainstem from the medulla through the thalamus is a complex, densely interconnected set of neurons called the *reticular formation* (RF). Moruzzi and Magoun (1949) were the first to describe the effects of the reticular formation on cortical EEG. It is now

well-known that electrical stimulation of the RF results in wakefulness or enhanced alertness and arousal (Koella, 1984). Further, destruction of the RF results in chronic sleep in cats. In short, the reticular formation appeared to be an excellent candidate for a sleep–wake center. But unless the RF possessed its own timing device, it would require input from other brain areas to inhibit its activity so that sleep would ensue. Several structures were soon identified that inhibited the reticular formation when they were stimulated (Lindsley, 1983).

Despite its initial promise, the reticular formation no longer appears to be the sole or even the primary regulator of sleeping/waking patterns. Rather, a nearby set of brainstem nuclei, the *nuclei of raphé*, appears to exert direct effects on cortical neurons. Raphé nuclei contain virtually all the neurons in the brain that release serotonin (Lidov *et al.*, 1980). Jouvet (1969), who was the first to demonstrate the importance of the raphé nuclei to sleep processes, removed large parts of the raphé in cats and noted that sleep was eliminated. Similarly, drugs that block the synthesis of serotonin result in insomnia as long as the drug is active.

Other neural structures also affect the tendency to engage in slow-wave sleep. For instance, the basal forebrain and the nucleus of the solitary tract have been implicated in slow-wave sleep (McGinty & Siegel, 1983). In fact, McGinty and Siegel have concluded that there is no single "executive" structure controlling slow-wave sleep. Rather, there seems to be a more diffuse command system of neural structures responsive to one another, other parts of the brain, and to a variety of chemicals.

Which chemicals participate in the induction of slow-wave sleep? One of the longest-known substances is melatonin. Melatonin synthesis by the pineal gland is inhibited by light (Lewy *et al.*, 1980), which accounts for why one may become sleepy in the dark, even if the darkness occurs during daytime hours. The pineal also seems to have a rhythm that influences the sleep–wakefulness cycle even in conditions of continuous darkness or continuous light, particularly in birds. Another substance, called Factor-S or the sleep factor, appears to facilitate the transition to sleep and accumulates in the cerebrospinal fluid of animals that have gone without sleep (Pappenheimer, 1976). Transferring small amounts of this fluid from sleep-deprived animals to well-rested animals brings on sleep earlier than it would normally occur and causes a longer-lasting sleep, especially of the slow-wave type. Several other chemicals seem to have a natural sleep-inducing

quality (Palca, 1989). Finally, food consumption tends to make conditions conducive to slow-wave sleep. Food consumption leads to the release of cholesystokinin (CCK) from the intestines (see Chapter 14) which has a sedating effect on neural tissue (McGinty & Siegel, 1983).

Our knowledge of the neural processes responsible for REM sleep is quite murky, but it is clear that there is no single structure that regulates the timing or amount of REM sleep. Although there were some exciting leads (Hobson *et al.*, 1975; McCarley & Hobson, 1975), more recent information has led to the conclusion that although many structures are involved in REM sleep phenomena, none of them are known to generate REM sleep (Vertes, 1984).

SLEEP DISORDERS

Complaints about the quantity and quality of sleep are among the most common received by physicians. The use of sleeping medications reflects these complaints. In 1977, about 26 million prescriptions costing over $82 million were written for sleep-inducing drugs (Weitzman, 1981). Although there are numerous sleep disorders, many of which are only poorly understood (Weitzman, 1981), we will confine our discussion to just a few: insomnias, narcolepsy, and disorders of the sleep–wake schedule.

Insomnias Insomnia is a condition characterized by difficulty initiating sleep, or in remaining asleep. Before dealing with these conditions it is important to note that many complaints of insomnia may not be entirely legitimate. Complaints of insomnia increase with age, and sales of sleep-inducing drugs are most common in older age groups (Weitzman, 1981). However, as we noted earlier, there is a natural decline in total sleep time with age; there is also a change

WILLIAM DEMENT

"Excessive daytime sleepiness is the primary and most disabling symptom that characterizes narcolepsy and a host of related problems." [Dement, W. C. (1976). Daytime sleepiness and sleep "attacks." In C. Guilleminault, W. C. Dement, & P. Passouant (Ed.) Narcolepsy (pp. 17–42). New York: Spectrum. .p. 17).]

toward falling asleep earlier and consequently waking earlier (Weitzman, 1981). Common wisdom, however, maintains that 8 hours of sleep is desirable, and thus many elderly people think that there is something wrong because they sleep only 5 hours or less per night. These cases should generally not be considered insomnia any more than infants' 16 hours of sleep

should be considered hypersomnia. Both are age-related normal sleep patterns.

There is another form of pseudo-insomnia in which people complain of getting no sleep or very little sleep, even though there is undeniable EEG evidence that the person slept 6 or 7 hours without interruption or abnormal patterns (Roth *et al.*, 1977).

Although insomnia is the most prevalent sleep disorder, there appear to be different forms of it associated with various other conditions. First, insomnia is commonly associated with depression and other affective (emotional) disorders. The most typical form of insomnia among depressed people involves frequent awakenings from sleep, reduced amounts of stages 3 and 4, and a shortened latency to enter REM. On some nights there is exaggerated REM activity (Gillin *et al.*, 1979).

Second, insomnia is commonly associated with drug and alcohol use. Excessive and sustained alcohol consumption tends to produce brief REM periods, less total REM, and frequent awakenings. Withdrawal from alcohol frequently leads to excessive REM with vivid dreams and sometimes exaggerated amounts of sleep.

Third, insomnia often results from temporary lapses in breathing during sleep. This condition, known as sleep apnea, occurs in most people a few times during every sleep period. However, for about 20 million Americans, apneic periods may number in the hundreds every time they sleep (Palca, 1989). Because apnea is followed by waking, such individuals have severely reduced total sleep time.

Finally, although insomnia is considered to be uncomfortable and disruptive, there are well-documented cases of extreme insomnia in humans who are nevertheless quite healthy (e.g., Jones & Oswald, 1968; Meddis *et al.*, 1973).

Some people have not slept in years; others sleep only an hour or so every few nights. Because these cases are not accompanied by adverse symptoms, they are undoubtedly due to conditions other than the ones discussed above.

Narcolepsy Another sleep disorder, narcolepsy, involves excessive sleep, unavoidable urges to fall asleep during the day, and chronic sleepiness while awake, resulting in personal embarrassment and loss of productivity (Fig. 16-5). Narcolepsy must be distinguished from other conditions that superficially resemble it. Inade-

quate amounts of nighttime sleep can result in daytime sleepiness and napping. After all, sleep seems to be regulated by a homeostatic process, and the system will exert its self-correcting mechanisms if not enough sleep is obtained.

Narcolepsy, which occurs in equal frequency in men and women, is frequently associated with another condition, cataplexy, in which partial or complete muscular weakness occurs, often suddenly. This may make standing or sitting temporarily impossible, resulting in potentially damaging falls. In less severe forms of

Figure 16.5
Narcolepsy is a genetically determined disorder that occurs naturally in dogs. This animal belongs to a colony of narcoleptic dogs at Stanford University used in studying the disorder. This dog is experiencing cataplexy, a state of sudden paralysis, due to the excite-ment of finding some highly preferred food. In humans, cataplexy is normally brought about by laughter, anger, or other strong emotions. Cataplexy may lead to sleep, but in this case the dog is awake during cataplexy, as shown by the second photograph.

cataplexy the person experiences weakness in isolated muscle groups, perhaps leading to slurred speech, dropping objects held in the hands, or slow, labored walking.

Episodes of cataplexy are typically brought on by sudden emotional feelings. One man would drop his fishing rod and nearly fall into the river every time he got a strike; other cataplectics have collapsed in the street when they saw a car coming toward them, and others fall to the floor in response to a good joke.

Narcolepsy and cataplexy seem to be due to a disorder of the REM apparatus. Although the cause of the REM problem is not known, promising leads have been obtained by the finding that there is a genetic proclivity toward narcolepsy–cataplexy in dogs (Kessler, 1976) and apparently in humans (Mamelak *et al.*, 1979). For instance, Mefford *et al.* (1983) have reported that narcoleptic doberman pinschers have lower dopamine utilization than dogs matched for breed and age. Other neurotransmitters, such as serotonin, were equivalent in the two groups.

Disorders of the sleep–wake cycle
Another set of sleep disorders is associated with the timing of sleep during the daily cycle. A common form of this problem is the delayed sleep phase syndrome, characterized by an inability to fall asleep before early morning. Although in itself this is not a problem, the person may get insufficient total sleep if he needs to get up early to go to work or school. This in turn can produce decreased daytime alertness, sleepiness, and other problems. Although little success has been achieved by gradual shifting of bedtime earlier in the night, some success has been achieved by gradual shifting later at night, then delaying it until morning, afternoon, evening, and then night (Czeisler *et al.*, 1979).

Finally, there are some people who apparently cannot be entrained to a 24-hour day, and persist with their own endogenous rhythm which may be 25 or 26 hours long. Thus, the person goes to bed and sleeps about an hour or two later (clock time) than they did the preceding day. This condition is most common among blind people whose blindness is due to retinal or optic nerve damage, in which case the retinohypothalamic tract is disrupted and the suprachiasmatic nuclei do not receive input from the retinas. In a society in which regular habits are valued, such a condition leads to profound problems.

Evolution and Functions of Sleep

PHYLOGENY OF SLEEP PATTERNS

The distribution of sleep through the animal kingdom largely depends on how sleep is defined. If sleep is defined as a circadian period of behavioral quiescence, sleep is widespread among animal species, including insects and other invertebrates. If an EEG definition is assumed, sleep is apparently restricted to vertebrates, but its presence in fish and even reptiles is debatable (Meddis, 1979; see Table 16-2). Moreover, the presence or absence of various components of the EEG corresponds with traditional classifications of vertebrates, including the mammals. For instance, only primates have K-complexes, a characteristic EEG wave pattern found during slow-wave sleep (Table 16-3), and the most primitive mammal, the echidna, lacks REM sleep. However, sleep EEG has not been measured in very many species, and the technique may miss some forms of electrical activity in species, such as reptiles, that have only a small cerebral cortex. Thus, changes in our knowledge of the phylogeny of sleep are inevitable. Presently, however, we know that sleep is an ancient phenomenon as evidenced by its widespread presence across animal species.

Table 16-2

THE DISTRIBUTION OF SLEEP IN VARIOUS ANIMAL GROUPS DEPENDS ON HOW SLEEP IS DEFINED

Behavioral sleep is widespread; various physiological changes are less common.

	PRIMATES	OTHER MAMMALS	MONO-TREMES	BIRDS	REPTILES	AMPHIBIA	FISH	MOLLUSCS	INSECTS
Prolonged period of inactivity	+	+	+	+	+	+	+	+	+
Circadian organization	+	+	+	+	+	+	+	+	+
Raised response thresholds	+	+	+	+	+	+	+	+	+
Specific sleep sites/postures	+	+	+	+	+	+	+	+	+
High-voltage slow waves	+	+	+	+	−	−	−	−	−
Active sleep	+	+	−	+	− ?	−	−	−	−

(Source: Meddis, 1975).

FUNCTIONAL HYPOTHESES

Why do we sleep? At first blush this seems to be a silly question. But because there are many animal species, including some mammals, that apparently never sleep, the question deserves some serious thought. We can take this question further and ask why there are two types of sleep and why their amounts differ among species. Several hypotheses have been suggested to answer these questions. Let us review them.

Recuperative hypothesis When people go for long periods without sleep, a number of deleterious effects occur. These include slowed reaction times, loss of coordination, blurred vision, irritability, and even hallucinations (Horne, 1978). These symptoms are more pronounced and occur earlier if the sleep deprivation is accompanied by vigorous exercise. Observations such as these and ones on the effects of prolonged sleep deprivation in animals (e.g., Rechtschaffen *et al.*, 1983) suggest that a substance accumulates in the body during wakefulness that can be removed only during sleep.

The recuperative hypothesis is appealing and has some support. Several studies have found that total sleep time and SWS increase after a period of exercise. After completing a 92-

Table 16-3

DISTRIBUTION OF SLEEP CHARACTERISTICS ACROSS ANIMAL GROUPS

TAXON	REM	SWS	SPINDLES	K-COMPLEXES
Primates	+	+	+	+
Carnivores	+	+	+	−
Insectivores	+	+	+	−
Birds	+	+	−	−
Reptiles	?	+	−	−

(Source: Meddis, 1979).

km ultramarathon, runners had elevated total sleep time and increased SWS for four nights, especially the first two nights (Shapiro *et al.*, 1981). Other studies, however, claim no sleep changes occur following a period of exercise (Horne & Porter, 1975). The discrepancy can largely be accounted for by differences in the people being studied: Shapiro's group studied well-trained distance runners while the other studies were of sedentary people. People in good shape tend to get more sleep and have more slow-wave sleep than people in poor shape, and the former tend to shift their sleep patterns more readily to suit changing demands (Foret, 1984). It appears, then, that part of the process of becoming physically fit involves modification of sleep processes in addition to the well-known changes of the muscles and cardiovascular system.

Another form of evidence supporting the recuperative hypothesis is the finding that growth hormone secretion is closely linked to SWS (Sassin *et al.*, 1969). Growth hormone stimulates protein synthesis and is essential for restoring damaged tissue as well as the usual wear-and-tear that occurs during wakeful activity.

An interesting aspect of the recuperative process of slow-wave sleep has been proposed by Vertes (1986). During slow-wave sleep, nervous system activity is significantly slower than it is during wakefulness and REM. Vertes has collected evidence that the nervous system may have difficulty coping with sustained periods of inactivity (sudden infant death syndrome cases are most common during sleep, for instance), so REM sleep occurs as a self-protection device, activating the nervous system without breaking the continuity of the sleep period. If Vertes is correct, the recuperative benefits of SWS are obtained at some risk to the sleeper, and REM sleep helps minimize that risk.

Information-processing hypothesis Some evidence suggests that sleep might facilitate learning and memory. Psychologists have known for over a century that a period of sleep following a memorization task facilitates later recall. The traditional explanation of this finding was that sleep puts the individual out of the way of events that might interfere with recall. While this is undoubtedly true, there may be a more direct, physiological reason as well. Fowler *et al.* (1973) have shown that recall following a period of SWS is superior to recall following REM sleep in humans. In fact, they attribute the difference to SWS-4, suggesting that it facilitates memory formation.

In contrast, other studies indicate that REM sleep facilitates learning and memory (reviewed by Pearlman, 1979). C. Smith (1985) has even demonstrated that more REM sleep occurs in animals who have engaged in specific learning tasks and that the increased REM occurs during rather well-defined periods during the sleep phase that follows learning. Depriving animals of REM sleep during those periods often significantly reduces retention of the learned response. Finally, the timing of the enhanced REM period depends on the species and the nature of the learning task. Perhaps this finding may account for some inconsistencies that have appeared in the scientific literature on the effects of REM sleep deprivation on subsequent recall.

Energy conservation hypothesis This hypothesis asserts that sleep is a way of conserving precious energy. Estimates of calorie expenditure during quiet wakefulness, SWS and REM sleep indicate that both forms of sleep are low-energy use times relative to wakefulness. Therefore, if activity is nonadaptive during certain times, switching the metabolic machinery into "idle" would help save energy until activity again becomes profitable.

Three lines of evidence support this hypothesis. First, among warm-blooded animals (birds and mammals), slow-wave sleep reaches appreciable levels only when the infant becomes responsible for maintaining its own body temperature. For example, in the opossum, a marsupial (pouched) mammal, slow-wave sleep does not occur until the babies become capable of regulating their own temperature at about 75 days of age. Because keeping oneself warm on a cold night is energetically demanding, turning down the "thermostat" helps conserve energy (Walker & Berger, 1980).

Second, evidence for this hypothesis has come from the finding that larger mammals tend to sleep less than smaller ones (Zepelin & Rechtschaffen, 1974). Larger mammals also have lower metabolic rates and thus tend to be more energy efficient than smaller species. Small species, then, need to conserve energy and sleep more as a result. Another interpretation, however, is that larger animals need more food than smaller ones and therefore require more time for foraging. Elgar *et al.* (1988) used a statistical procedure to control for body size differences, and found that mammals with higher metabolic rates actually sleep *less* than mammals with lower metabolic rates. Thus, the time needed to acquire food may account for why larger mammals tend to sleep less than smaller mammals.

Third, some species that face extreme energy demands during the day go into torpor at night. Torpor is a physiological state characterized by a drastic lowering of metabolic rate, body temperature, respiration, and heart rate. Hummingbirds burn a tremendous number of calories for their size, but are unable to forage at night. A hummingbird species of the Peruvian Andes spends its nights in caves and often becomes torpid, especially during the winter (Carpenter, 1974). Other bird species, such as doves, become torpid when they are food-deprived and thus need to conserve energy (L. E. Walker *et*

al., 1983). The significance of torpor for our discussion of sleep is that torpor is entered through SWS. That is, torpor seems to be an extension of SWS to levels beyond SWS-4. Likewise, hibernation, which is essentially a deep form of torpor lasting weeks or months, is entered through SWS (Walker *et al.*, 1977) and shares several characteristics with it (Fig. 16-6). Slow-wave sleep, torpor, and hibernation are points on a continuum of energy conservation during more or less difficult times.

Self-protection hypothesis - According to this hypothesis, there are times during which individuals are most vulnerable to attack by predators. Consequently, a good strategy is to curl up somewhere and wait until safer times return. Merely maintaining quiet wakefulness may not suffice because being alert makes remaining quiet more difficult.

Evidence for this hypothesis comes from comparisons among species. Generally speaking, more vulnerable animal species (due to small size and unprotected sleeping sites) sleep more and have more SWS than do less vulnerable species (Meddis, 1975; Webb, 1974; Allison & Cichetti, 1976; Amlaner & Ball, 1983). Elephants, for instance, are not subject to much predation, and sleep only a few hours per night, almost all of which is REM sleep. Smaller and more vulnerable species sleep more hours and spend most of it in SWS.

Differences in sleep according to vulnerability can also be accomplished by individuals. Lendrem (1984) exposed caged Barbary doves to a tame ferret shortly before the birds' normal sleep time. Although the exposure was brief and the ferret never entered the cage, Lendrem found that the birds opened their eyes more often for brief intervals ("peeks") during these sleep episodes than they did on other days when the ferret was not presented. Surprisingly, the birds do not awake during peeks, but instead

Figure 16.6
*Hibernation is entered through slow-wave sleep. Both states save energy and may have
evolved for that reason.*

remain in SWS. They are responsive to what
they see during peeks, however.

Summary of functional hypotheses   Although these hypotheses seem distinct, they are
not necessarily incompatible. For instance, the
energy conservation and self-protection hypotheses are difficult to tease apart because they usually make the same predictions. Small animals
are predicted to sleep more than large ones because small animals are more vulnerable to predators and they tend to lose heat faster. There is
no reason why several things could not be accomplished simultaneously, so we should not
expect to rule out other hypotheses simply because one of them has garnered confirmation.

Summary

Behavioral processes are most adaptive when
they occur properly timed to environmental
conditions. Because certain environmental conditions recur rhythmically, behavioral rhythms
also occur. These may range from a few hours to
multiple years, but most common are rhythms of
a day or year duration. A variety of processes
collectively known as biological clocks are responsible for maintaining these rhythms. In the
complete absence of external cues that might
time these rhythms, several, including sleep,
operate endogenously. The endogenous rhythm
for human sleep seems to be about 25 hours.

However, exogenous conditions, such as light, can time rhythms, a process known as entrainment. Environmental conditions that can entrain rhythms are known as *zeitgebers* or "timegivers."

The phenomenon of sleep consists of certain preparatory behaviors and characteristic sleep postures. Sleep is also characterized by interesting EEG patterns indicative of brain activity. In slow-wave sleep (SWS), the EEG becomes slower but of higher amplitude than it is during wakefulness. In rapid eye movement (REM) sleep, in contrast, the EEG is similar to that observed in awake, alert individuals. A night's sleep consists of cycles of SWS and REM in alternation, with SWS occurring first, and REM following. A typical cycle takes about 90 minutes. Sleep changes considerably with age. Human infants sleep about 16 hours of each 24, but this declines with age until fewer than 6 hours per day is spent asleep in elderly people. Further, REM's portion of total sleep time declines with age.

Although multiple neural structures participate in the phenomena of sleep, no structures have been identified that are central to the onset of either slow-wave or REM sleep. Further, several neurotransmitters and other chemicals affect sleep processes, as do environmental conditions such as light, temperature, and food consumption.

Sleep-associated complaints are among the most common brought to physicians. Sleep disorders are numerous and varied. Among the more important ones (numerically speaking) are insomnia (inability to fall asleep or stay asleep long enough), narcolepsy (characterized by chronic sleepiness and occasionally by sudden loss of muscle tone and onset of REM), and disruptions of the sleep–wake cycle, including such conditions as inability to fall asleep until morning, and the tendency to fall asleep every 25 to 26 hours rather than every 24, which results in lack of coordination with the surrounding society.

The phylogenetic distribution of sleep depends on how one defines sleep. Most organisms exhibit a daily period of behavioral inactivity (behavioral sleep), but only the vertebrates exhibit EEG signs of sleep, and here only the birds and mammals exhibit it commonly. Within even the mammals, however, there are species differences in some of the physiological processes of sleep.

Sleep may have several functions. Recuperation from the day's activities seems to be important. Growth hormone is released only during SWS, and SWS increases following days involving hard physical activity. Lack of sleep is associated with several adverse conditions (loss of coordination, irritability) suggestive of the need to recuperate. Some evidence suggests that sleep may be valuable for memory formation, although whether SWS or REM is most important in this regard is debatable. Sleep may also function in conserving energy during times when the organism is ill-suited for acquiring energy, or in self-preservation during times when the organism may be most prone to predation.

Recommended Readings

DEMENT, W. C. (1976). *Some must watch while some must sleep.* New York: Norton.
MOORE-EDE, M. C., SULZMAN, F. M., & FULLER, C. A. (1982). *The clocks that time us: Physiology of the circadian timing system.* Cambridge: Harvard University Press.

REFERENCES

ADAMS, D. B. (1979). Brain mechanisms for offense, defense, and submission. *Behavior and Brain Sciences* **2,** 201–241.

ADAMS, D. B., GOLD, A. R., & BURT, A. D. (1978). Rise in female-initiated sexual activity at ovulation and its suppression by oral contraceptives. *New England Journal of Medicine* **299,** 1145–1150.

ADAMS, J. A. (1984). Learning of movement sequences. *Psychological Bulletin* **96,** 3–28.

ADLER, N. T. (1979). On the physiological organization of social behavior: Sex and aggression. In P. Marler & J. G. Vandenbergh (Eds.), *Handbook of behavioral neurobiology. Vol. 3: Social behavior and communication* (pp. 29–71). New York: Plenum.

ALBERT, D. J., & WALSH, M. L. (1984). Neural systems and the inhibitory modulation of agonistic behavior: A comparison of mammalian species. *Neuroscience and Biobehavioral Reviews* **8,** 5–24.

ALBERT, D. J., WALSH, M. L., GORZALKA, B. B., SIEMENS, Y., & LOUIE, H. (1986). Testosterone removal in rats results in a decrease in social aggression and a loss of social dominance. *Physiology and Behavior* **36,** 401–407.

ALCOCK, J. (1980). Natural selection and the mating systems of solitary bees. *American Scientist* **68,** 146–153.

ALEXANDER, R. D. (1974). The evolution of social behavior. *Annual Review of Ecology and Systematics* **5,** 325–383.

ALEXANDER, R. D., HOOGLAND, J. L., HOWARD, R. D., NOONAN, K. M., & SHERMAN, P. W. (1979). Sexual dimorphisms and breeding systems in pinnipeds, ungulates, primates, and humans. In N. A. Chagnon & W. Irons (Eds.), *Evolutionary biology and human social behavior: An an-thropological perspective* (pp. 402–435). North Scituate, Mass.: Duxbury.

ALEXANDER, R. D., & NOONAN, K. M. (1979). Concealment of ovulation, parental care, and human social evolution. In N. A. Chagnon & W. Irons (Eds.), *Evolutionary biology and human social behavior: An anthropological perspective* (pp. 436–453). North Scituate, Mass.: Duxbury.

ALI, M. A., & KLYNE, M. A. (1985). *Vision in vertebrates.* New York: Plenum.

ALKON, D. L. (1983). Learning in a marine snail. *Scientific American* **249**(1), 70–84.

ALKON, D. L. (1988). *Memory traces in the brain.* New York: Cambridge University Press.

ALLEN, G. E. (1987). Materialism and reductionism in the study of animal consciousness. In G. Greenberg & E. Tobach (Eds.), *Cognition, language and consciousness: Integrative levels* (pp. 137–160). Hillsdale, NJ: Erlbaum.

ALLEN, M. L., & LEMMON, W. B. (1981). Orgasm in female primates. *American Journal of Primatology* **1,** 15–34.

ALLISON, T., & CICCHETTI, D. Y. (1976). Sleep in mammals: Ecological and constitutional correlates. *Science* **194,** 732–734.

ALLMAN, J. (1982). Reconstructing the evolution of the brain in primates through the use of comparative neurophysiological and neuroanatomical data. In E. Armstrong & D. Falk (Eds.), *Primate brain evolution: Methods and concepts* (pp. 13–28). New York: Plenum.

ALTMANN, J. (1980). *Baboon mothers and infants.* Cambridge: Harvard University Press.

ALTMANN, S. A. (1956). Avian mobbing behavior and predator recognition. *Condor* **58,** 241–253.

ALTMANN, S. A. (1981). Dominance relationships: The Cheshire cat's grin? *Behavior and Brain Science* **4,** 430–431.

ALUMETS, J., HAKANSON, R., SUNDLER, F., & THORELL, J. (1979). Neuronal localisation of immunoreactive enkephalin and B-endorphin in the earthworm. *Nature* **279,** 805–806.

AMLANER, C. J. JR., & BALL, N. J. (1983). A synthesis of sleep in wild birds. *Behaviour* **87,** 85–119.

ANDERSON, J. R. (1984). Ethology and ecology of sleep in monkeys and apes. *Advances in the Study of Behavior* **14,** 166–229.

AOKI, C., & SIEKEVITZ, P. (1988). Plasticity in brain development. *Scientific American* **259,** 56–64.

ARCHER, J. (1970). Effects of population density on behaviour in rodents. In J. H. Crook (Ed.), *Social behaviour in birds and mammals* (pp. 169–210). New York: Academic.

ARCHER, J. (1988). *The behavioural biology of aggression.* New York: Cambridge University Press.

ARMSTRONG, E. (1983). Relative brain size and metabolism in mammals. *Science* **220,** 1302–1304.

ARMSTRONG, E. (1985). Relative brain size in monkeys and prosimians. *American Journal of Physical Anthropology* **66,** 263–273.

ARMSTRONG, E., & FALK, D. (1982). *Primate brain evolution: Methods and concepts.* New York: Plenum.

ARNOLD, A. P. (1980). Sexual differences in the brain. *American Scientist* **68,** 165–173.

ARNOLD, S. J. (1977). Polymorphism and geographic variation in the feeding behavior of the garter snake *Thamnophis elegans. Science* **197,** 676–678.

ARNOTT, H. J., MACIOLEK, N. J., & NICHOL, J. A. C. (1970). Retinal tapetum lucidum: A novel reflecting system in the eye of teleosts. *Science* **169,** 478–480.

ASCHOFF, J. (1970). Circadian rhythm of activity and body temperature. In J. D. Hardy, A. P. Gagge, & J. A. J. Stolwijk (Eds.), *Physiological and behavioral temperature regulation* (pp. 905–919). Springfield, IL: Thomas.

ASERINSKY, E., & KLEITMAN, N. (1953). Regularly occurring periods of eye motility, and concomitant phenomena, during sleep. *Science* **118,** 273–274.

AUGUST, P. V., & ANDERSON, J. G. T. (1987). Mammal sounds and motivation-structural rules: A test of the hypothesis. *Journal of Mammalogy* **68,** 1–9.

AXELROD, R., & HAMILTON, W. D. (1981). The evolution of cooperation. *Science,* **211,** 1390–1396.

AYALA, F. J. (1978). The mechanisms of evolution. *Scientific American* **239**(3), 56–69.

AZRIN, N. H., & HUTCHINSON, R. R. (1967). Conditioning of the aggressive behavior of pigeons by a fixed-interval schedule of reinforcement. *Journal of the Experimental Analysis of Behavior* **10,** 395–402.

AZRIN, N. H., HUTCHINSON, R. R., & HAKE, D. F. (1966). Extinction-induced aggression. *Journal of the Experimental Analysis of Behavior* **9,** 191–204.

BAILE, C. A., DELLA-FERA, M. A., & KRESTEL-RICKERT, D. (1985). Brain peptides controlling behavior and metabolism. *BioScience* **35,** 101–105.

BALKEMA, G. W., MANGINI, N. J., & PINTO, L. H. (1983). Discrete visual defects in pearl mutant mice. *Science* **219**, 1085–1087.

BALTIMORE, D. (1984). The brain of a cell. *Science 84* (Nov.), 149–151.

BANDLER, R. J. (1970). Cholinergic synapses in the lateral hypothalamus for the control of predatory aggression in the rat. *Brain Research* **20**, 409–424.

BANKS, M. S., ASLIN, R. N., & LETSON, R. D. (1975). Sensitive period for the development of human binocular vision. *Science* **190**, 675–677.

BARASH, D. P. (1976). Male response to apparent female adultery in the mountain bluebird (*Sialia currocoides*): An evolutionary interpretation. *American Naturalist* **110**, 1097–1101.

BARASH, D. P. (1977). Sociobiology of rape in mallards (*Anas platyrhynchos*): Responses of the mated male. *Science* **197**, 788–789.

BARASH, D. P. (1982). *Sociobiology and behavior.* New York: Elsevier.

BARDIN, C. W., & CATTERALL, J. F. (1981). Testosterone: A major determinant of extragenital sexual dimorphism. *Science* **211**, 1285–1294.

BARKAI, A., & MCQUAID, C. (1988). Predator-prey role reversal in a marine benthic ecosystem. *Science* **242**, 62–64.

BARLOW, G. W. (1977). Modal action patterns. In T. A. Sebeok (Ed.), *How animals communicate* (pp. 98–134). Bloomington: Indiana University Press.

BARLOW, H. B. (1975). Visual experience and cortical development. *Nature* **258**, 199–204.

BARLOW, H. B. (1982). Physiology of the retina. In H. B. Barlow & J. D. Mollon (Eds.), *The senses* (pp. 102–113). Cambridge: Cambridge University Press.

BARLOW, H. B., & MOLLON, J. D. (1982). *The senses.* New York: Cambridge University Press.

BARNARD, C. J. (1980). Flock feeding and time budgets in the house sparrow (*Passer domesticus* L.). *Animal Behaviour* **28**, 295–309.

BARNES, D. M. (1986). Brain architecture: Beyond genes. *Science* **233**, 155–156.

BASHI, J. (1977). Effects of inbreeding on cognitive performance. *Nature* **266**, 440–442.

BASS, A. H. (1990). Sounds from the intertidal zone: Vocalizing fish. *BioScience* **40**, 249–258.

BATESON, P. (1978). Sexual imprinting and optimal outbreeding. *Nature* **273**, 659–660.

BATESON, P. (1979). How do sensitive periods arise and what are they for? *Animal Behaviour* **27**, 470–486.

BATESON, P. P. G. (1983a). *Mate choice.* Cambridge: Cambridge University Press.

BATESON, P. (1983b). Optimal outbreeding. In P. Bateson (Ed.), *Mate choice* (pp. 257–277). Cambridge: Cambridge University Press.

BAUM, M. J., CARROLL, R. S., ERSKINE, M. S., & TOBET, S. A. (1985). Neuroendocrine response to estrogen and sexual orientation. *Science* **230**, 960–961.

BAYLOR, E. R. (1967). Air and water vision of the Atlantic flying fish *Cypeselurus heterurus. Nature* **214**, 307–309.

BEACH, F. A. (1955). The descent of instinct. *Psychological Review* **62**, 401–410.

BEACH, F. A. (1976). Sexual attractivity, proceptivity, and receptivity in female mammals. *Hormones and Behavior* **7**, 105–138.

BEACH, F. A., & LeBOEUF, B. J. (1967). Coital behavior in dogs. 1. Preferential mating in the bitch. *Animal Behaviour* **15,** 546–558.

BEACH, F. A., & WHALEN, R. E. (1959). Effects of intromission without ejaculation on sexual behavior in male rats. *Journal of Comparative and Physiological Psychology* **52,** 476–481.

BEAUCHAMP, G. K. (1987). The human preference for excess salt. *American Scientist* **75,** 27–33.

BEDNARZ, J. C. (1988). Cooperative hunting in Harris' hawks (*Parabuteo unicinctus*). *Science* **239,** 1525–1527.

BEECHER, M. D. (1982). Signature systems and kin recognition. *American Zoologist* **22,** 477–490.

BEECHER, M. D. (1990). The evolution of parent-offspring recognition in swallows. In D. A. Dewsbury (Ed.), *Contemporary issues in comparative psychology* (pp. 360–380). Sunderland, MA: Sinauer.

BEECHER, M. D. & BEECHER, I. M. (1979). Sociobiology of bank swallows: Reproductive strategy of the male. *Science* **205,** 1282–1285.

BEER, C. G. (1970). Individual recognition of voice in the social behavior of birds. *Advances in the Study of Behavior* **3,** 27–74.

BEETSMA, J. (1985). Feeding behaviour of nurse bees, larval food composition and caste differentiation in the honey bee (*Apis mellifera* L.). In B. Holldobler & M. Lindauer (Eds.), *Experimental behavioral ecology and sociobiology* (pp. 407–410). Sunderland, MA: Sinauer.

BEKOFF, A. (1978). A neuroethological approach to the study of the ontogeny of coordinated behavior. In G. Burghardt & M. Bekoff (Eds.), *The development of behavior: Comparative and evolutionary aspects* (pp. 19–41). New York: Garland.

BEKOFF, M. (1972). The development of social interaction, play, and metacommunication in mammals: An ethological perspective. *Quarterly Review of Biology* **47,** 412–434.

BEKOFF, M. (1977). Social communication in canids: Evidence for the evolution of a stereotyped mammalian display. *Science* **197,** 1097–1099.

BEKOFF, M., & WELLS, M. C. (1980). The social ecology of coyotes. *Scientific American* **242**(4), 130–148.

BELL, S. M., & AINSWORTH, M. D. S. (1972). Infant crying and maternal responsiveness. *Child Development* **43,** 1171–1190.

BELOVSKY, G. E. (1981). Food plant selection by a generalist herbivore: The moose. *Ecology* **62,** 1020–1030.

BELWOOD, J. J., & MORRIS, G. K. (1987). Bat predation and its influence on calling behavior in neotropical katydids. *Science* **238,** 64–67.

BENNETT, K. L., & TRUMAN, J. W. (1985). Steroid-dependent survival of identifiable neurons in cultured ganglia of the moth *Manduca sexta*. *Science* **229,** 58–60.

BENNETT, P. M., & HARVEY, P. H. (1985). Relative brain size and ecology in birds. *Journal of Zoology* **207,** 151–169.

BENTLEY, D. R. (1971). Genetic control of an insect network. *Science* **174,** 1139–1141.

BENTLEY, D. (1975). Single gene cricket mutations: Effects on behavior, sensilla, sensory neurons, and identified interneurons. *Science* **187,** 760–764.

BENTLEY, D. R., & HOY, R. R. (1972). Genetic control of the neuronal network generating cricket (*Teleogryllus gryllus*) song patterns. *Animal Behaviour* **20**, 478–492.

BENTLEY, D., & HOY, R. R. (1974). The neurobiology of cricket song. *Scientific American* **231**(2), 34–44.

BENTLEY, D., & KONISHI, M. (1978). Neural control of behavior. *Annual Review of Neuroscience* **1**, 35–60.

BENZER, S. (1971). From the gene to behavior. *Journal of the American Medical Association* **218**, 1015–1022.

BERGER, P. A. (1978). Medical treatment of mental illness. *Science* **200**, 974–981.

BERNSTEIN, I. L. (1978). Learned taste aversions in children receiving chemotherapy. *Science* **200**, 1302–1303.

BERNSTEIN, I. L., & WEBSTER, M. M. (1980). Learned taste aversions in humans. *Physiology and Behavior* **25**, 363–366.

BERNSTEIN, I. S. (1981). Dominance: The baby and the bathwater. *Behavioral and Brain Science* **4**, 419–457.

BERNSTEIN, I. S., ROSE, R. M., & GORDON, T. P. (1974). Behavioral and environmental events influencing primate testosterone levels. *Journal of Human Evolution* **3**, 517–525.

BERNTSON, G. G., & LEIBOWITZ, S. F. (1973). Biting attack in cats: Evidence for central muscarinic mediation. *Brain Research* **51**, 366–370.

BERTHOLD, P., & QUERNER, U. (1981). Genetic basis of migratory behavior in European warblers. *Science* **212**, 77–79.

BERTRAM, B. C. R. (1975a). The social system of lions. *Scientific American* **232**(5), 54–65.

BERTRAM, B. C. R. (1975b). Social factors influencing reproduction in wild lions. *Journal of Zoology* **177**, 463–482.

BERTRAM, B. C. R. (1980). Vigilance and group size in ostriches. *Animal Behaviour* **28**, 278–286.

BERTRAM, B. C. (1983). Kin selection and altruism. In J. F. Eisenberg & D. G. Kleiman (Eds.), *Advances in the study of mammalian behavior* (pp. 721–737). Special Publication Series: American Society of Mammalogists.

BERVEN, K. A. (1981). Mate choice in the wood frog, *Rana sylvatica. Evolution* **35**, 707–722.

BIBEN, M., SYMMES, D., & BERNHARDS, D. (1989). Vigilance during play in squirrel monkeys. *American Journal of Primatology* **17**, 41–49.

BINKLEY, S. (1979). A timekeeping enzyme in the pineal gland. *Scientific American* **240**(4), 66–71.

BISCHOF, H.-J. (1983). Imprinting and cortical plasticity: A comparative review. *Neuroscience and Biobehavioral Reviews* **7**, 213–225.

BLACK, I. B., ADLER, J. E., DREYFUS, C. F., JONAKIT, G. M., KATZ, D. M., LAGAMMA, E. F., & MARKEY, K. M. (1984). Neurotransmitter plasticity at the molecular level. *Science* **225**, 1266–1270.

BLAKEMORE, C., & COOPER, G. F. (1970). Development of the brain depends on the visual environment. *Nature* **228**, 477–478.

BLASS, E. M., & TEICHER, M. H. (1980). Suckling. *Science* **210**, 15–22.

BLEICHFELD, B., & MOELY, B. E. (1984). Psychophysiological responses to an infant cry: Comparison of groups of women in different phases of the maternal cycle. *Developmental Psychology* **20**, 1082–1091.

BLOOM, F. E. (1981). Neuropeptides. *Scientific American* 245(4), 148–168.

BOGGS, C. L., & GILBERT, L. E. (1979). Male contribution to egg production in butterflies: Evidence for transfer of nutrients at mating. *Science* 206, 83–84.

BOLLES, R. C. (1970). Species-specific defense reactions and avoidance learning. *Psychological Review* 77, 32–48.

BOLLES, R. C. (1983). The explanation of behavior. *Psychological Record* 33, 31–48.

BOLS, R. J. (1977). Display reinforcement in the Siamese fighting fish, *Betta splendens*: Aggressive motivation or curiosity? *Journal of Comparative and Physiological Psychology* 91, 233–244.

BONNER, J. T. (1988). *The evolution of complexity by means of natural selection.* Princeton, NJ: Princeton University Press.

BOONSTRA, R. (1984). Aggressive behavior of adult meadow voles (*Microtus pennsylvanicus*) towards young. *Oecologia* 62, 126–131.

BORG, E., & COUNTER, S. A. (1989). The middle-ear muscles. *Scientific American* 261, 74–80.

BOROWSKY, R. (1978). Social inhibition of maturation in natural populations of *Xiphophorus variatus* (Pisces; Poeciliidae). *Science* 201, 933–935.

BRADBURY, J. W. (1977). Lek mating behavior in the hammer-headed bat. *Zeitschrift für Tierpsychologie* 45, 225–255.

BRADBURY, J. W., & GIBSON, R. M. (1983). Leks and mate choice. In P. Bateson (Ed.), *Mate choice* (pp. 109–138). Cambridge: Cambridge University Press.

BRADFORD, H. F. (1986). *Chemical neurobiology: An introduction to neurochemistry.* New York: Freeman.

BRAMBLE, D. M., & CARRIER, D. R. (1983). Running and breathing in mammals. *Science* 219, 251–256.

BRANDA, R. F., & EATON, J. W. (1978). Skin color and nutrient photolysis: An evolutionary hypothesis. *Science* 201, 625–626.

BRANDON, J. G., & COSS, R. G. (1982). Rapid dendritic spine stem shortening during one-trial learning: The honeybee's first orientation flight. *Brain Research* 252, 51–61.

BRANT, D. H., & KAVANAU, J. L. (1964). "Unrewarded" exploration and learning of complex mazes by wild and domestic mice. *Nature* 204, 267–269.

BRAY, D. (1982). The mechanism of growth cone movements. *Neuroscience Research Program Bulletin* 20, 821–829.

BREEDLOVE, S. M. (1985). Hormonal control of the anatomical specificity of motoneuron-to-muscle innervation in rats. *Science* 227, 1357–1359.

BRESLER, J. B. (1982). Outcrossing in caucasians and fetal loss. *Social Biology* 29, 121–130.

BRIDGES, R. S., DiBIASE, R., LOUNDES, D. D., & DOHERTY, P. C. (1985). Prolactin stimulation of maternal behavior in female rats. *Science* 227, 782–784.

BROCKELMAN, W. Y., & SCHILLING, D. (1984). Inheritance of stereotyped gibbon calls. *Nature* 312, 634–636.

BRONSON, F. H. (1985). Mammalian reproduction: An ecological perspective. *Biology of Reproduction* 32, 1–26.

BRONSON, F. H. (1989). *Mammalian reproductive biology.* Chicago: University of Chicago Press.

BRONSON, F. H., & MARSTELLER, F. A. (1985). Effect of short-term food deprivation on reproduction in female mice. *Biology of Reproduction* **33,** 660–667.

BRONSON, F. H., STETSON, M. H., & STIFF, M. E. (1973). Serum FSH and LH in male mice following aggressive and non-aggressive interactions. *Physiology and Behavior* **10,** 369–372.

BROWER, L. P. (1969). Ecological chemistry. *Scientific American* 220(2), 22–29.

BROWN, C. R. (1984). Laying eggs in a neighbor's nest: Benefit and cost of colonial nesting in swallows. *Science* **224,** 518–519.

BROWN, C. R. (1986). Cliff swallow colonies as information centers. *Science* **234,** 83–85.

BROWN, T. H., CHAPMAN, P. F., KAIRISS, E. W., & KEENAN, C. L. (1988). Long-term synaptic potentiation. *Science* **242,** 724–728.

BROWNELL, P. H. (1977). Compressional and surface waves in sand: Used by desert scorpions to locate prey. *Science* **197,** 479–482.

BROWNELL, P. H. (1984). Prey detection by the sand scorpion. *Scientific American* 251(6), 86–97.

BUCKLEY, P. A., & BUCKLEY, F. G. (1977). Hexagonal packing of royal tern nests. *Auk* **94,** 36–43.

BULLOCK, T. H. (1990). Goals of neuroethology. *BioScience* **40,** 244–248.

BULLOCK, T. H., & HORRIDGE, G. A. (1965). *Structure and function in the nervous systems of invertebrates: Volumes I and II.* San Francisco: Freeman.

BULLOCK, T. H., ORKAND, R., & GRINNELL, A. (1977). *Introduction to nervous systems.* San Francisco: Freeman.

BURDETT, A. N. (1985). Emotions and facial expression. *Science* **230,** 608.

BURGHARDT, G. M. (1970). Defining "com-munication." In J. W. Johnston, Jr., D. G. Moulton, & A. Turk (Eds.), *Advances in chemoreception. Vol. 1: Communication by chemical signals* (pp. 5–18). New York: Appleton-Century-Crofts.

BURLEY, N. (1979). The evolution of concealed ovulation. *American Naturalist* **114,** 835–858.

BURNS, R. J. (1980). Evaluation of conditioned predation aversion for controlling coyote predation. *Journal of Wildlife Management* **44,** 938–942.

BUTLER, R. A. (1975). The influence of the external and middle ear on auditory discriminations. In W. D. Keidel & W. D. Neff (Eds.), *Handbook of sensory physiology, Vol. 5/2* (pp. 247–260). New York: Springer-Verlag.

BUTLER, R. G., & BUTLER, L. A. (1979). Toward a functional interpretation of scent marking in the beaver (*Castor canadensis*). *Behavioral and Neural Biology* **26,** 442–454.

BUTLER, R. G., & TRIVELPIECE, W. (1981). Nest spacing, reproductive success, and behavior of the great black-backed gull (*Larus marinus*). *Auk,* **98,** 99–107.

CADE, W. H. (1981). Alternative male strategies: Genetic differences in crickets. *Science* **212,** 563–564.

CAIRNS, R. B. (1979). *Social development: The origins and plasticity of interchanges.* San Francisco: Freeman.

CAIRNS, R. B., HOOD, K. E., & MIDLAM, J. (1985). On fighting in mice: Is there a sensitive period for isolation effects? *Animal Behaviour* **33,** 166–180.

CAIRNS, R. B., MacCOMBIE, D. J., & HOOD, K. E. (1983). A developmental-genetic analysis of aggressive behavior in mice: 1. Behavioral outcomes. *Journal of Comparative Psychology* **97,** 69–89.

CALDWELL, G. S., GLICKMAN, S. E., & SMITH, E. R. (1984). Seasonal aggression independent of seasonal testosterone in wood rats. *Proceedings of the National Academy of Sciences of the USA* **81**, 5255–5257.

CALLARD, G. V. (1983). Androgen and estrogen actions in the vertebrate brain. *American Zoologist* **23**, 607–620.

CALLARD, G. V., PETRO, Z., & RYAN, K. J. (1978). Conversion of androgen to estrogen and other steroids in the vertebrate brain. *American Zoologist* **18**, 511–523.

CAMHI, J. M. (1980). The escape system of the cockroach. *Scientific American* **243**(6), 158–172.

CAMHI, J. M. (1984). *Neuroethology: Nerve cells and the natural behavior of animals.* Sunderland, MA: Sinauer.

CANADY, R. A., KROODSMA, D. E., & NOTTEBOHM, F. (1984). Population differences in complexity of a learned skill are correlated with the brain space involved. *Proceedings of the National Academy of Sciences of the USA* **81**, 6232–6234.

CAPITANIO, J. P., & LEGER, D. W. (1979). Evolutionary scales lack utility: A reply to Yarczower and Hazlett. *Psychological Bulletin* **86**, 876–879.

CARACO, T., MARTINDALE, S., & PULLIAM, H. R. (1980). Avian time budgets and distance to cover. *Auk* **97**, 872–875.

CARLIN, N. F., & HÖLLDOBLER, B. (1983). Nestmate and kin recognition in interspecific mixed colonies of ants. *Science* **222**, 1027–1029.

CARLSON, A. D., & COPELAND, J. (1978). Behavioral plasticity in the flash communication systems of fireflies. *American Scientist* **66**, 340–346

CARPENTER, F. L. (1974). Torpor in an Andean hummingbird: Its ecological significance. *Science* **183**, 545–547.

CARPENTER, F. L., & MACMILLEN, R. E. (1976). Threshold model of feeding territoriality and test with a Hawaiian honeycreeper. *Science* **194**, 639–642.

CATANIA, A. C. (1984). *Learning.* Englewood Cliffs, NJ: Prentice-Hall.

CATTERALL, W. A. (1984). The molecular basis of neuronal excitability. *Science* **223**, 653–661.

CHAGNON, N. A. (1988). Life histories, blood revenge, and warfare in a tribal population. *Science* **239**, 985–992.

CHAGNON, N. A., & HAMES, R. B. (1979). Protein deficiency and tribal warfare in Amazonia: New data. *Science* **203**, 910–913.

CHALFIE, M. (1984). Genetic analysis of nematode nerve-cell differentiation. *BioScience* **34**, 295–299.

CHAMIE, J., & NSULY, S. (1981). Sex differences in remarriage and spouse selection. *Demography* **18**, 335–348.

CHANCE, M. R. A. (1967). Attention structure as the basis of primate rank orders. *Man* **2**, 503–518.

CHANDLER, C. R., & ROSE, R. K. (1988). Comparative analysis of the effects of visual and auditory stimuli on avian mobbing behavior. *Journal of Field Ornithology* **59**, 269–277.

CHANGEUX, J.-P., DEVILLERS-THIERY, A., & CHEMOUILLI, P. (1984). Acetylcholine receptor: An allosteric protein. *Science* **225**, 1335–1345.

CHAPAIS, B. (1983). Reproductive activity in relation to male dominance and the likelihood of ovulation in rhesus monkeys. *Behavioural Ecology and Sociobiology* **12**, 215–228.

CHARNOV, E. L. (1976). Optimal foraging:

The marginal value theorem. *Theoretical Population Biology* **9,** 129–136.

CHENEY, D. L. (1977). The acquisition of rank and the development of reciprocal alliances among free-ranging immature baboons. *Behavioral Ecology and Sociobiology* **2,** 303–318.

CHENEY, D., SEYFARTH, R., & SMUTS, B. (1986). Social relationships and social cognition in nonhuman primates. *Science* **234,** 1361–1366.

CHISZAR, D., RADCLIFFE, C. W., SCUDDER, K. M., & DUVALL, D. (1983). Strike-induced chemosensory searching by rattlesnakes: The role of envenomation-related chemical cues in the post-strike environment. In D. Müller-Schwarze & R. Silverstein (Eds.), *Chemical signals in vertebrates, Vol. 3* (pp. 1–24). New York: Plenum.

CHRISTIANSEN, K., KNUSSMANN, R., & COUWENBERGS, C. (1985). Sex hormones and stress in the human male. *Hormones and Behavior* **19,** 426–440.

CHUNG, J. M., LEE, K. H., ENDO, K., & COGGESHALL, R. E. (1983). Activation of central neurons by ventral root afferents. *Science* **222,** 934–935.

CIARANELLO, R. D., & BOEHME, R. E. (1982). Genetic regulation of neurotransmitter enzymes and receptors: Relationship to the inheritance of psychiatric disorders. *Behavior Genetics* **12,** 11–35.

CLARK, J. T., SMITH, E. R., & DAVIDSON, J. M. (1984). Enhancement of sexual motivation in male rats by yohimbine. *Science* **225,** 847–849.

CLARKE, B. (1975). The causes of biological diversity. *Scientific American* **233**(2), 50–60.

CLEVELAND, J., & SNOWDON, C. T. (1982). The complex vocal repertoire of the adult cotton-top tamarin (*Saguinus oedipus oedipus*). *Zeitschrift für Tierpsychologie* **58,** 231–270.

CLOPTON, B. M. (1981). Neurophysiological and anatomical aspects of auditory development. In R. N. Aslin, J. R. Alberts, & M. R. Petersen (Eds.), *Development of perception, Vol. 1* (pp. 111–137). New York: Academic Press.

CLUTTON-BROCK, T. H., ALBON, S. D., GIBSON, R. M., & GUINNESS, F. E. (1979). The logical stag: Adaptive aspects of fighting in red deer (*Cervus elaphus* L.). *Animal Behaviour* **27,** 211–225.

CLUTTON-BROCK, T. H., GUINNESS, F. E., & ALBON, S. D. (1982). *Red deer: Behavior and ecology of two sexes.* Chicago: University of Chicago Press.

CLUTTON-BROCK, T. H., & HARVEY, P. H. (1980). Primates, brains and ecology. *Journal of Zoology* **190,** 309–324.

CODY, M. L. (1971). Finch flocks in the Mohave Desert. *Theoretical Population Biology* **2,** 142–158.

COLE, C. J. (1984). Unisexual lizards. *Scientific American* **250**(1), 94–100.

COLGAN, P. (1989). *Animal motivation.* New York: Chapman and Hall.

COLLETT, T. S. (1983). Sensory guidance of motor behaviour. In T.R. Halliday & P. J. B. Slater (Eds.), *Animal behaviour. Vol. 1: Causes and effects* (pp. 40–71). New York: Freeman.

COLLIER, G. H. (1982). Determinants of choice. In H. E. Howe, Jr., & D. J. Bernstein (Eds.), *Nebraska Symposium on Motivation. Vol. 29* (pp. 69–127). Lincoln: University of Nebraska Press.

COLLIER, G. H., & ROVEE-COLLIER, C. K. (1981). A comparative analysis of optimal foraging behavior: Laboratory simulations. In A. C. Kamil, & T. D. Sargent

(Eds.), *Foraging behavior: Ecological, ethological, and psychological approaches* (pp. 39–76). New York: Garland.

COLLIN, S. P., & PETTIGREW, J. D. (1989). Quantitative comparison of the limits on visual spatial resolution set by the ganglion cell layer in twelve species of reef teleosts. *Brain, Behavior and Evolution* **34,** 184–192.

COLOMBO, M., D'AMATO, M. R., RODMAN, H. R., & GROSS, C. G. (1990). Auditory association cortex lesions impair auditory short-term memory in monkeys. *Science* **247,** 336–338.

CONRAD, L. C. A., & PFAFF, D. W. (1976). Efferents from medial basal forebrain and hypothalamus in the rat. I. An autoradiographic study of the medial preoptic area. *Journal of Comparative Neurology* **169,** 185–200.

CONSTANTINE-PATON, M., & LAW, M. I. (1982). The development of maps and stripes in the brain. *Scientific American* **247**(6), 62–70.

COSS, R. G. (1985). Evolutionary restraints on learning: Phylogenetic and synaptic interpretations. In N. M. Weinberger, J. L. McGaugh, & G. Lynch (Eds.), *Memory systems of the brain* (pp. 253–278). New York: Guilford.

COSS, R. G., & GLOBUS, A. (1978). Spine stems on tectal interneurons in jewel fish are shortened by social stimulation. *Science* **200,** 787–790.

COSS, R. G., & GLOBUS, A. (1979). Social experience affects the development of dendritic spines and branches on tectal interneurons in the jewel fish. *Developmental Psychobiology* **12,** 347–358.

COSS, R. G., & OWINGS, D. H. (1978). Snake-directed behavior by snake naive and experienced California ground squirrels in a simulated burrow. *Zeitschrift für Tierpsychologie* **48,** 421–435.

COWAN, W. M. (1979). Development of the brain. *Scientific American* **241**(3), 112–133.

COWAN, W. M., FAWCETT, J. W., O'LEARY, D. D. M., & STANFIELD, B. B. (1984). Regressive events in neurogenesis. *Science* **225,** 1258–1265.

COWIE, R. J. (1977). Optimal foraging in great tits (*Parus major*). *Nature* **268,** 137–139.

COX, C. R., & LEBOEUF, B. J. (1977). Female incitation of male competition: A mechanism in sexual selection. *American Naturalist* **111,** 317–335.

CRAWFORD, L. L. (1983). Local contrast and memory windows as proximate foraging mechanisms. *Zeitschrift für Tierpsychologie* **63,** 283–293.

CREWS, D. (1982). On the origin of sexual behavior. *Psychoneuroendocrinology* **7,** 259–270.

CREWS, D. (1987). Courtship in unisexual lizards: A model for brain evolution. *Scientific American* **257,** 116–121.

CREWS, D., & MOORE, M. C. (1986). Evolution of mechanisms controlling mating behavior. *Science* **231,** 121–125.

CURIO, E. (1973). Towards a methodology of teleonomy. *Experientia* **29,** 1045–1058.

CURIO, E. (1976). *The ethology of predation.* Berlin: Springer-Verlag.

CURIO, E. (1983). Time-energy budgets and optimization. *Experientia* **39,** 25–34.

CURIO, E., ERNST, U., & VIETH, W. (1978). The adaptive significance of avian mobbing. II Cultural transmission of enemy recognition in blackbirds: Effectiveness and some constraints. *Zeitschrift für Tierpsychologie* **48,** 184–202.

CZEISLER, C. A., RICHARDSON, G., COLE-

MAN, R., DEMENT, W., & WEITZMAN, E. (1979). Successful non-drug treatment of delayed sleep phase syndrome with chronotherapy: Resetting a biological clock. *Sleep Research* **8,** 179.

CZEISLER, C. A., WEITZMAN, E. D., MOORE-EDE, M. C., ZIMMERMAN, J. C., & KNAUER, R. S. (1980). Human sleep: Its duration and organization depend on its circadian phase. *Science* **210,** 1264–1266.

DAANJE, A. (1950). On the locomotory movements in birds and the intention movements derived from it. *Behaviour* **3,** 48–98.

DALE, N., SCHACHER, S., & KANDEL, E. R. (1988). Long-term facilitation in *Aplysia* involves increase in transmitter release. *Science* **239,** 282–285.

DALY, M., & WILSON, M. (1983). *Sex, evolution, and behavior.* Boston: Willard Grant Press.

DALY, M., & WILSON, M. (1988a). Evolutionary social psychology and family homicide. *Science* **242,** 519–524.

DALY, M., & WILSON, M. (1988b). *Homicide.* New York: Aldine de Gruyter.

DALY, M., & WILSON, M. (1988c). The Darwinian psychology of discriminative parental solicitude. In D. W. Leger (Ed.), *Comparative perspectives in modern psychology. Nebraska Symposium on Motivation,* Vol. 35. (pp. 91–144). Lincoln: University of Nebraska Press.

DALY, M., WILSON, M., & WEGHORST, S.J. (1982). Male sexual jealousy. *Ethology and Sociobiology* **3,** 11–27.

DARNELL, J. E., JR. (1983). The processing of RNA. *Scientific American* **249**(4), 90–100.

DARNELL, J. E., JR. (1985). RNA. *Scientific American* **253**(4), 68–78.

DARTNALL, H. J. A., BOWMAKER, J. K., &

MOLLON, J. D. (1983). Human visual pigments: Microspectrophotometric results from the eyes of seven persons. *Proceedings of the Royal Society of London* **B220,** 115–130.

DARWIN, C. (1871). *The descent of man, and selection in relation to sex.* London: John Murray.

DARWIN, C. (1872/1965). *The expression of the emotions in man and animals.* Chicago: University of Chicago Press.

DAVIDSON, J. M. (1980). Hormones and sexual behavior in the male. In D. T. Krieger & J. C. Hughes (Eds.), *Neuroendocrinology* (pp. 232–238). Sunderland, MA: Sinauer.

DAVIES, N. B. (1977). Prey selection and social behaviour in wagtails (Aves; Motacillidae). *Journal of Animal Ecology* **46,** 37–57.

DAVIES, N. B., & HOUSTON, A. I. (1984). Territory economics. In J. R. Krebs & N. B. Davies (Eds.), *Behavioural ecology: An evolutionary approach* (pp. 148–169). Sunderland, MA: Sinauer.

DAWKINS, M. S. (1983). The organisation of motor patterns. In T.R. Halliday & P. J. B. Slater (Eds.), *Animal behaviour. Vol. 1: Causes and effects* (pp. 75–99). New York: Freeman.

DAWKINS, R. (1987). *The blind watchmaker.* New York: Norton.

DAWKINS, R., & CARLISLE, T. R. (1976). Parental investment, mate desertion and a fallacy. *Nature* **262,** 131–133.

DAWKINS, R., & DAWKINS, M. S. (1973). Decisions and the uncertainty of behaviour. *Behaviour* **45,** 83–103.

DAWKINS, R., & KREBS, J. R. (1978). Animal signals: Information or manipulation? In J. R. Krebs, & N. B. Davies (Eds.), *Behavioural ecology: An evolutionary ap-*

proach (pp. 282–309). Sunderland, MA: Sinauer.

DAWKINS, R., & KREBS, J. R. (1979). Arms races between and within species. *Proceedings of the Royal Society of London* **B205,** 489–511.

DEFRIES, J. C., HEGMANN, J. P., & HAL-COMB, R. A. (1974). Response to 20 generations of selection for open-field activity in mice. *Behavioral Biology* **11,** 481–495.

DEFRIES, J. C. & MCCLEARN, G. E. (1970). Social dominance and Darwinian fitness in the laboratory mouse. *American Naturalist* **104,** 408–411.

DELCOMYN, F. (1980). Neural basis of rhythmic behavior in animals. *Science* **210,** 492–498.

DEMENT, W. C. (1976). *Some must watch while some must sleep.* New York: Norton.

DENENBERG, V. H. (1970). The mother as a motivator. In W. J. Arnold & M. M. Page (Eds.), *Nebraska Symposium on Motivation, Vol. 18* (pp. 69–93). Lincoln: University of Nebraska Press.

DENENBERG, V. H. (1973). Developmental factors in aggression. In J. F. Knutson (Ed.), *The control of aggression* (pp. 41–57). Chicago: Aldine.

DENSON, R. D. (1979). Owl predation on a mobbing crow. *Wilson Bulletin* **91,** 133.

DEROBERTIS, E. M., OLIVER, G., & WRIGHT, C. V. E. (1990). Homeobox genes and the vertebrate body plan. *Scientific American* **263,** 46–52.

DETHIER, V. G. (1969). Whose real world? *American Zoologist* **9,** 241–249.

DEUTSCH, J. A., & AHN, S. J. (1986). The splanchnic nerve and food intake regulation. *Behavioral and Neural Biology* **45,** 43–47.

DEVINE, M. C. (1975). Copulatory plugs in snakes: Enforced chastity. *Science* **187,** 844–845.

DEVOOGD, T., & NOTTEBOHM, F. (1981). Gonadal hormones induce dendritic growth in the adult avian brain. *Science* **214,** 202–204.

DEWSBURY, D. A. (1972). Patterns of copulatory behavior in male mammals. *Quarterly Review of Biology* **47,** 1–33.

DEWSBURY, D. A. (1975). Diversity and adaptation in rodent copulatory behavior. *Science* **190,** 947–954.

DEWSBURY, D. A. (1978). What is (was?) the 'fixed action pattern'? *Animal Behaviour* **26,** 310–311.

DEWSBURY, D. A. (1979). Description of sexual behavior in research on hormone-behavior interactions. In C. Beyer (Ed.), *Endocrine control of sexual behavior* (pp. 3–32). New York: Raven.

DEWSBURY, D. A. (1982). Ejaculate cost and male choice. *American Naturalist* **119,** 601–610.

DEWSBURY, D. A. (1984). Aggression, copulation, and differential reproduction of deer mice (*Peromyscus maniculatus*) in a semi-natural enclosure. *Behaviour* **91,** 1–23.

DEWSBURY, D. A. (1988). The comparative psychology of monogamy. In D. W. Leger (Ed.), *Comparative perspectives in modern psychology: Nebraska Symposium on Motivation, Vol. 35* (pp. 1–50). Lincoln: University of Nebraska Press.

DEWSBURY, D. A., & PIERCE, J. D., JR. (1989). Copulatory patterns of primates as viewed in broad mammalian perspective. *American Journal of Primatology* **17,** 51–72.

DIAKOW, C., & DEWSBURY, D. A. (1978). A comparative description of the mating behavior of female rodents. *Animal Behaviour* **26,** 1091–1097.

DiBerardino, M. A., Hoffner, N. J., & Etkin, L. D. (1984). Activation of dormant genes in specialized cells. *Science* **224,** 946–952.

Dickeman, M. (1975). Demographic consequences of infanticide in man. *Annual Review of Ecology and Systematics* **6,** 107–137.

Dickerson, R. E. (1978). Chemical evolution and the origin of life. *Scientific American* **239**(3), 70–86.

DiDomenico, R., & Eaton, R. C. (1988). Seven principles for command and the neural causation of behavior. *Brain, Behavior and Evolution* **31,** 125–140.

Diehn, B. (1979). Photic responses and sensory transduction in motile protists. In H. Autrum (Ed.), *Handbook of sensory physiology. Vol. VII/6A* (pp. 23–68). Berlin: Springer-Verlag.

Dill, L. M. (1977). Refraction and the spitting behavior of the archerfish (*Toxotes chatareus*). *Behavioral Ecology and Sociobiology* **2,** 169–184.

Dimond, S., & Lazarus, J. (1974). The problem of vigilance in animal life. *Brain, Behavior and Evolution* **9,** 60–79.

Dixon, L. K., & Johnson, R. C. (1980). *The roots of individuality: A survey of human behavior genetics.* Monterey, CA: Brooks/Cole.

Dobbins, J. G. (1980). Implication of a time-dependent model of sexual intercourse within the menstrual cycle. *Journal of Biosocial Science* **12,** 133–140.

Dobzhansky, T. (1950). The genetic basis of evolution. *Scientific American* **182**(1), 32–42.

Dobzhansky, T., Ayala, F, Stebbins, G., & Valentine, J. W. (1977). *Evolution.* San Francisco: Freeman.

Dodd, J., & Jessell, T. M. (1988). Axon guidance and the patterning of neuronal projections in vertebrates. *Science* **242,** 692–699.

Dollard, J., Doob, L., Miller, N., Mowrer, O., & Sears, R. (1939). *Frustration and aggression.* New Haven: Yale University Press.

Dominey, W. J. (1980). Female mimicry in male bluegill sunfish—a genetic polymorphism? *Nature* **284,** 546–548.

Doolittle, R. F. (1985). Proteins. *Scientific American* **253**(4), 88–99.

Doty, R. L., Ford, M., Preti, G., & Huggins, G. R. (1975). Changes in the intensity and pleasantness of human vaginal odors during the menstrual cycle. *Science* **190,** 1316–1317.

Dowling, J. E. (1987). *The retina: An approachable part of the brain.* Cambridge, MA: Belknap Press.

Duggan, J. P., & Booth, D. A. (1986). Obesity, overeating, and rapid gastric emptying in rats with ventromedial hypothalamic lesions. *Science* **231,** 609–611.

Dumont, J. P. C., & Robertson, R. M. (1986). Neuronal circuits: An evolutionary perspective. *Science* **233,** 849–853.

Dunbar, M. J. (1980). The blunting of Occam's razor, or to hell with parsimony. *Canadian Journal of Zoology* **58,** 123–128.

Dunbar, R. I. M. & Dunbar, E. P. (1977). Dominance and reproductive success among female gelada baboons. *Nature* **266,** 351–352.

Dunford, C. (1970). Behavioral aspects of spatial organization in the chipmunk, *Tamias striatus. Behaviour* **36,** 215–231.

Easter, S. S., Jr., Purves, D., Rakic, P., & Spitzer, N. C. (1985). The changing view of neural specificity. *Science* **230,** 507–511.

Ebert, P. D. (1983). Selection for aggression

in a natural population. In E. C. Simmel, M. E. Hahn, & J. K. Walters (Eds.), *Aggressive behavior: Genetic and neural approaches* (pp. 103–127). Hillsdale, NJ: Erlbaum.

EDMUNDS, M. (1974). *Defence in animals.* New York: Longman.

EHRHARDT, A. A., MEYER-BAHLBURG, H. F. L., ROSEN, L. R., FELDMAN, J. F., VERIDIANO, N. P., ZIMMERMAN, I., & McEWEN, B. S. (1985). Sexual orientation after prenatal exposure to exogenous estrogen. *Archives of Sexual Behavior* **14,** 57–77.

EHRMAN, L., & PARSONS, P. A. (1981). *Behavior genetics and evolution.* New York: McGraw-Hill.

EIBL-EIBESFELDT, I. (1963). Angeborenes und Erworbenes im Verhalten einiger Sauger. *Zeitschrift für Tierpsychologie* **20,** 705–754.

EIBL-EIBESFELDT, I. (1970). *Ethology: The biology of behavior.* New York: Holt.

EICHELMAN, B. (1979). Role of biogenic amines in aggressive behavior. In M. Sandler (Ed.), *Psychopharmacology of aggression* (pp. 61–93). New York: Raven Press.

EICHELMAN, B. (1983). The limbic system and aggression in humans. *Neuroscience and Biobehavioral Reviews* **7,** 391–394.

EIMAS, P. D. (1985). The perception of speech in early infancy. *Scientific American* **252**(1), 46–52.

EISENBERG, J. F., & WILSON, D. (1978). Relative brain size and feeding strategies in the Chiroptera. *Evolution* **32,** 740–751.

EKMAN, P., LEVENSON, R. W., & FRIESEN, W. V. (1983). Autonomic nervous system activity distinguishes among emotions. *Science* **221,** 1208–1210.

ELGAR, M. A., PAGEL, M. D., & HARVEY, P. H. (1988). Sleep in mammals. *Animal Behaviour* **36,** 1407–1419.

ELLINS, S. R., & CATALANO, S. M. (1980). Field application of the conditioned taste aversion paradigm to the control of coyote predation on sheep and turkeys. *Behavioral and Neural Biology* **29,** 532–536.

ELLIS, D., & AUSTIN, P. (1971). Menstruation and aggressive behavior in a correctional center for women. *Justice Criminal Law and Police Science* **62,** 388–395.

EMERY, D. E., & WHITNEY, J. F. (1985). Effects of vagino-cervical stimulation upon sociosexual behaviors in female rats. *Behavioral and Neural Biology* **43,** 199–205.

EMLEN, S. T. (1972). An experimental analysis of the parameters of bird song eliciting species recognition. *Behaviour* **41,** 130–171.

EMLEN, S. T. (1976). Lek organization and mating strategies in the bullfrog. *Behavioral Ecology and Sociobiology* **1,** 283–313.

EMLEN, S. T. (1984). Cooperative breeding in birds and mammals. In J. R. Krebs & N. B. Davies (Eds.), *Behavioural ecology: An evolutionary approach* (pp. 305–339). Sunderland, MA: Sinauer.

EMLEN, S. T., & DEMONG, N. J. (1984). Bee-eaters of Baharini. *Natural History* **93**(10), 50–59.

EMLEN, S. T., & ORING, L. W. (1977). Ecology, sexual selection, and the evolution of mating systems. *Science* **197,** 215–223.

EPSTEIN, R. (1985). Animal cognition as the praxist views it. *Neuroscience and Biobehavioral Reviews* **9,** 623–630.

ERICKSON, J. D. (1978). Down syndrome, paternal age, maternal age and birth order. *Annals of Human Genetics* **41,** 289–298.

ERICKSON, R. P. (1984). On the neural bases of behavior. *American Scientist* **72,** 233–241.

EVANS, E. F. (1982). Functional anatomy

of the auditory system. In H. B. Barlow & J. D. Mollon (Eds.), *The senses* (pp. 307–332). Cambridge: Cambridge University Press.

EVARTS, E. V. (1979). Brain mechanisms of movement. *Scientific American* **241**(3), 164–179.

FALLS, J. B., & BROOKS, R. J. (1975). Individual recognition by song in white-throated sparrows. II. Effects of location. *Canadian Journal of Zoology* **53,** 1412–1420.

FARDE, L., HALL, H., EHRIN, E., & SEDVALL, G. (1986). Quantitative analysis of D2 dopamine receptor binding in the living human brain by PET. *Science* **231,** 258–261.

FAY, R. R., & POPPER, A. N. (1980). Structure and function in teleost auditory systems. In A. N. Popper & R. R. Fay (Eds.), *Comparative studies of hearing in vertebrates* (pp. 3–42). New York: Springer-Verlag.

FEDER, H. H. (1984). Hormones and sexual behavior. *Annual Review of Psychology* **35,** 165–200.

FELDMAN, M. W., & LEWONTIN, R. C. (1975). The heritability hang-up. *Science* **190,** 1163–1168.

FELSENFELD, G. (1985). DNA. *Scientific American* **253**(4), 58–67.

FENTON, M. B., & FULLARD, J. H. (1981). Moth hearing and the feeding strategies of bats. *American Scientist* **69,** 266–275.

FENTRESS, J. C. (1973). Development of grooming in mice with amputated forelimbs. *Science* **179,** 704–705.

FERGUSON, B., WEBSTER, D. G., & DEWSBURY, D. A. (1984). Stimulus control of ovulation in red-backed voles (*Clethrionomys gapperi*). *Bulletin of the Psychonomic Society* **22,** 365–367.

FERGUSON, M. W. J., & JOANEN. T. (1982). Temperature of egg incubation determines sex in *Alligator mississippiensis*. *Nature* **296,** 850–853.

FERNALD, R. D. (1984). Vision and behavior in an African cichlid fish. *American Scientist* **72,** 58–65.

FERRIS, C. F., ALBERS, H. E., WESOLOWSKI, S. M., GOLDMAN, B. D., & LUMAN, S. E. (1984). Vasopressin injected into the hypothalamus triggers a stereotypic behavior in golden hamsters. *Science* **224,** 521–523.

FICKEN, M. S., & FICKEN, R. W. (1967). Singing behavior of blue-winged and golden-winged warblers and their hybrids. *Behaviour* **28,** 149–181.

FILLION, T. J., & BLASS, E. M. (1986). Infantile experience with suckling odors determines adult sexual behavior in male rats. *Science* **231,** 729–731.

FISHER, J., & HINDE, R. A. (1949). The opening of milk bottles by birds. *British Birds* **42,** 347–358.

FITCH, H. S. (1948). Ecology of the California ground squirrel on grazing lands. *American Midland Naturalist* **39,** 513–596.

FLAHERTY, C. F. (1985). *Animal learning and cognition.* New York: Knopf.

FLEISHMAN, L. J., HOWLAND, H. C., HOWLAND, M. J., RAND, A. S., & DAVENPORT, M. L. (1988). Crocodiles don't focus underwater. *Journal of Comparative Physiology A* **163,** 441–443.

FLYNN, J. P. (1967). The neural basis of aggression in cats. In D. C. Glass (Ed.), *Neurophysiology and emotion* (pp. 40–69). New York: Rockefeller University Press.

FORD, C. S., & BEACH, F. A. (1952). *Patterns of sexual behavior.* London: Eyre & Spottiswoode.

FOREE, D. D., & LoLORDO, V. M. (1973). Attention in the pigeon: The differential effects of food-getting vs. shock-avoidance procedures. *Journal of Comparative and Physiological Psychology* **85,** 551–558.

FORET, J. (1984). To what extent can sleep be influenced by diurnal activity? *Experientia* **40,** 422–424.

FOSTER, M. (1984). Jewel bird jamboree. *Natural History* **93**(7), 54–59.

FOWLER, M. J., SULLIVAN, M. J., & EKSTRAND, B. R. (1973). Sleep and memory. *Science* **179,** 302–304.

FOX, R., LEHMKUHLE, S. W., & WESTENDORF, D. H. (1976). Falcon visual acuity. *Science* **192,** 263–265.

FRAME, L. H. & FRAME, G. W. (1976). Female African wild dogs emigrate. *Nature* **273,** 227–229.

FRANCIS, R. C. (1988). On the relationship between aggression and social dominance. *Ethology* **78,** 223–237.

FRANKS, N. R. (1989). Army ants: A collective intelligence. *American Scientist* **77,** 138–145.

FRENCH, J. A., ABBOTT, D. H., & SNOWDON, C. T. (1984). The effect of social environment on estrogen secretion, scent marking, and sociosexual behavior in tamarins (*Saguinus oedipus*). *American Journal of Primatology* **6,** 155–167.

FRICKE, H. W. (1980). Control of different mating systems in a coral reef fish by one environmental factor. *Animal Behaviour* **28,** 561–569.

FRIDLUND, A. J., & GILBERT, A. N. (1985). Emotions and facial expression. *Science* **230,** 607–608.

FRISCH, R. E. (1980). Fatness, puberty, and fertility. *Natural History* **89**(10), 16–27.

FRISCH, R. E. (1984). Body fat, puberty and fertility. *Biological Review* **59,** 161–188.

FRODI, A., & LAMB, M. E. (1980). Child abusers' responses to infant smiles and cries. *Child Development* **51,** 238–241.

FRODI, A., & SENCHAK, M. (1990). Verbal and behavioral responsiveness to the cries of atypical infants. *Child Development* **61,** 76–84.

FUCHS, S. (1976). The response to vibrations of the substrate and reactions to the specific drumming in colonies of carpenter ants (Camponotus, Formicidae, Hymenoptera). *Behavioral Ecology and Sociobiology* **1,** 155–184.

GALEF, B. G. (1976). Social transmission of acquired behavior: A discussion of tradition and social learning in vertebrates. *Advances in the Study of Behavior* **6,** 77–100.

GALEF, B. G., JR. (1990). An adaptationist perspective on social learning, social feeding, and social foraging in Norway rats. In D. A. Dewsbury (Ed.), *Contemporary issues in comparative psychology* (pp. 55–79). Sunderland, MA: Sinauer.

GALLISTEL, C. R. (1980). *The organization of action: A new synthesis.* Hillsdale, NJ: Erlbaum.

GANDELMAN, R. (1983). Gonadal hormones and sensory function. *Neuroscience and Biobehavioral Reviews* **7,** 1–17.

GANDELMAN, R. (1984). Relative contributions of aggression and reproduction to behavioral endocrinology. *Aggressive Behavior* **10,** 123–133.

GARCIA, J., KIMELDORF, D. J., & KOELLING, R. A. (1955). Conditioned aversion to saccharin resulting from exposure to gamma radiation. *Science* **122,** 157–158.

GARCIA, J., & KOELLING, R. A. (1966). Relation of cue to consequence in avoidance learning. *Psychonomic Science* **4,** 123–124.

GARDNER, R. A., & GARDNER, B. T. (1975). Evidence for sentence constituents in the early utterances of child and chimpanzee. *Journal of Experimental Psychology: General* **104**, 244–267.

GARN, S. M., CLARK, D. C., & GUIRE, K. E. (1975). Growth, body composition, and development of obese and lean children. In M. Winick (Ed.), *Childhood obesity* (pp. 23–46). New York: Wiley.

GAZZANIGA, M. S. (1967). The split brain in man. *Scientific American* **217**(2), 24–25.

GAZZANIGA, M. S. (1989). Organization of the human brain. *Science* **245**, 947–952.

GEHRING, W. J. (1985). The molecular basis of development. *Scientific American* **253**, 152–162.

GERHARDT, H. C. (1974). The vocalizations of some hybrid treefrogs: Acoustics and behavioral analysis. *Behaviour* **49**, 130–151.

GERHARDT, H. C. (1983). Communication and the environment. In T. R. Halliday & P. J. B. Slater (Eds.), *Animal behaviour. Vol. 2: Communication* (pp. 82–113). New York: Freeman.

GESCHWIND, N. (1972). Language and the brain. *Scientific American* **226**(4), 76–83.

GESCHWIND, N. (1979). Specializations of the human brain. *Scientific American* **241**(3), 180–199.

GESCHWIND, N., & GALABURDA, A. M. (EDS.). (1984). *Cerebral dominance: The biological foundations.* Cambridge, MA: Harvard University Press.

GIBBS, J., YOUNG, R. C., & SMITH, G. P. (1973). Cholecystokinin decreases food intake in rats. *Journal of Comparative and Physiological Psychology* **84**, 488–495.

GILLIN, J. C., DUNCAN, W., PETTIGREW, K. D., FRANKEL, B. L., & SNYDER, F. (1979). Successful separation of de-

pressed, normal, and insomniac subjects by EEG sleep data. *Archives of General Psychiatry* **36**, 85–90.

GISH, S. L., & MORTON, E. S. (1981). Structural adaptations to local habitat acoustics in Carolina wren songs. *Zeitschrift für Tierpsychologie* **56**, 74–84.

GLADUE, B. A. (1985). Neuroendocrine response to estrogen and sexual orientation. *Science* **230**, 961.

GLADUE, B. A., GREEN, R., & HELLMAN, R. E. (1984a). Neuroendocrine response to estrogen and sexual orientation. *Science* **225**, 1496–1499.

GLADUE, B. A., GREEN, R., & HELLMAN, R. E. (1984b). Values, research questions, and the news media. *Science* **226**, 1142–1144.

GLENNON, R. A., TITELER, M., & MCKENNEY, J. D. (1984). Evidence for 5-HT2 involvement in the mechanism of action of hallucinogenic agents. *Life Sciences* **35**, 2505–2511.

GOLAN, L., RADCLIFFE, C. W., MILLER, T., O'CONNELL, B., & CHISZAR, D. (1982). Prey trailing by the prairie rattlesnake (*Crotalus viridis*). *Journal of Herpetology* **16**, 287–293.

GOLD, P. E. (1987). Sweet memories. *American Scientist* **75**, 151–155.

GOLD, P. E. (1989). Neurobiological features common to memory modulation by many treatments. *Animal Learning & Behavior* **17**, 94–100.

GOLD, P. E., MURPHY, J. M., & COOLEY, S. (1982). Neuroendocrine modulation of memory during development. *Behavioral & Neural Biology* **35**, 277–293.

GOLD, P. E., & STONE, W. S. (1988). Neuroendocrine effects on memory in aged rodents and humans. *Neurobiology of Aging* **9**, 709–717.

GOLD, R. M. (1973). Hypothalamic obesity: The myth of the ventromedial nucleus. *Science* **182,** 488–490.

GOLDIN-MEADOW, S., & MYLANDER, C. (1983). Gestural communication in deaf children: Noneffect of parental input on language development. *Science* **221,** 372–373.

GOLDMAN, B. D., & DARROW, J. M. (1983). The pineal gland and mammalian photoperiodism. *Neuroendocrinology* **37,** 386–396.

GOLDSMITH, T. H. (1980). Hummingbirds see near ultraviolet light. *Science* **207,** 786–788.

GOLDSTEIN, E. B. (1984). *Sensation and perception.* Belmont, CA: Wadsworth.

GOODALL, J. (1965). Chimpanzees of the Gombe Stream Reserve. In I. DeVore (Ed.), *Primate behavior* (pp. 425–473). New York: Holt, Rinehart & Winston.

GOODALL, J. (1986). *The chimpanzees of Gombe: Patterns of behaviour.* Cambridge, MA: Harvard University Press.

GOODWIN, M., GOODING, K. M., & REGNIER, F. (1979). Sex pheromone in the dog. *Science* **203,** 559–561.

GOTTLIEB, D. I. (1988). GABAergic neurons. *Scientific American* **258,** 82–89.

GOTTLIEB, G. (1974). On the acoustic basis of species identification in wood ducklings (*Aix sponsa*). *Journal of Comparative and Physiological Psychology* **87,** 1038–1048.

GOTTLIEB, G. (1981). Roles of early experience in species-specific perceptual development. In R. N. Aslin, J. R. Alberts, & M. R. Petersen (Eds.), *Development of perception, Vol. 1* (pp. 5–44). New York: Academic Press.

GOTTLIEB, G. (1984). Evolutionary trends and evolutionary origins: Relevance to theory in comparative psychology. *Psychological Review* **91,** 448–456.

GOULD, J. L., DYER, F. C., & TOWNE, W. F. (1985). Recent progress in the study of the dance language. In B. Hölldobler & M. Lindauer (Eds.), *Experimental behavioral ecology and sociobiology* (pp. 141–161). Sunderland, MA: Sinauer.

GOULD, J. L., & MARLER, P. (1987). Learning by instinct. *Scientific American* **256,** 74–85.

GOULD, S. J. (1978a). Morton's ranking of races by cranial capacity. *Science* **200,** 503–509.

GOULD, S. J. (1978b). Were dinosaurs dumb? *Natural History* **87**(5), 9–16.

GOULD, S. J. (1978c). Women's brains. *Natural History* **87**(8), 44–50.

GOULD, S. J. (1979). A Darwinian paradox. *Natural History* **88**(1), 32–44.

GOULD, S. J. (1980). Chance riches. *Natural History* **89**(11), 36–44.

GOULD, S. J. (1981). Hyena myths and realities. *Natural History* **90**(2), 16–24.

GOULD, S. J. (1982). Darwinism and the expansion of evolutionary theory. *Science* **216,** 380–387.

GOULD, S. J., & LEWONTIN, R. C. (1979). The spandrels of San Marco and the Panglossian paradigm: A critique of the adaptationist programme. *Proceedings of the Royal Society of London* **B205,** 581–598.

GOUZOULES, S., GOUZOULES, H., & MARLER, P. (1984). Rhesus monkey (*Macaca mulatta*) screams: Representational signalling in the recruitment of agonistic aid. *Animal Behaviour* **32,** 182–193.

GOVIND, C. K. (1989). Asymmetry in lobster claws. *American Scientist* **77,** 468–474.

GOWATY, P. A. (1982). Sexual terms in sociobiology: Emotionally provocative and, paradoxically, jargon. *Animal Behaviour* **30,** 630–631.

GOY, R. W. (1970). Experimental control of psychosexuality. *Philosophical Transactions of the Royal Society* **B259,** 149–162.

GOY, R. W., BERCOVITCH, F. B., & MCBRAIR, M. C. (1988). Behavioral masculinization is independent of genital masculinization in prenatally androgenized female rhesus macaques. *Hormones and Behavior* **22,** 552–571.

GRAFEN, A. (1984). Natural selection, kin selection and group selection. In J. R. Krebs & N. B. Davies (Eds.), *Behavioural ecology: An evolutionary approach* (pp. 62–84). Sunderland, MA: Sinauer.

GRAHAM, J. M., & DESJARDINS, C. (1980). Classical conditioning: Induction of luteinizing hormone and testosterone secretion in anticipation of sexual activity. *Science* **210,** 1039–1041.

GRATTON, A., & WISE, R. A. (1985). Hypothalamic reward mechanism: Two first-stage fiber populations with a cholinergic component. *Science* **227,** 545–548.

GREEN, J. A., & GUSTAFSON, G. E. (1983). Individual recognition of human infants on the basis of cries alone. *Developmental Psychobiology* 16, 485–493.

GREEN, J. A., JONES, L. E., & GUSTAFSON, G. E. (1987). Perception of cries by parents and nonparents: Relation to cry acoustics. *Developmental Psychology* **23,** 370–382.

GREEN, R., CARR, W. S., & GREEN, M. (1968). The hawk-goose phenomenon: Further confirmation and the search for the releaser. *Journal of Psychology* **69,** 271–276.

GREENE, E. (1989). A diet-induced developmental polymorphism in a caterpillar. *Science* **243,** 643–646.

GREENEWALT, C. (1969). How birds sing. *Scientific American* **221**(5), 126–139.

GREENWOOD, P. J. (1980). Mating systems, philopatry and dispersal in birds and mammals. *Animal Behaviour* **28,** 1140–1162.

GRENE, M. (1987). Hierarchies in biology. *American Scientist* **75,** 504–510.

GRIFFIN, D. R. (1976). *The question of animal awareness: Evolutionary continuity of mental experience.* New York: Rockefeller University Press.

GRIFFIN, D. R. (1984a). *Animal thinking.* Cambridge: Harvard University Press.

GRIFFIN, D. R. (1984b). Animal thinking. *American Scientist* **72,** 456–464.

GRIFFIN, D. R. (1985). Animal consciousness. *Neuroscience and Biobehavioral Reviews* **9,** 615–622.

GRILLNER, S. (1985). Neurobiological bases of rhythmic motor acts in vertebrates. *Science* **228,** 143–149.

GROBSTEIN, P., & CHOW, K. L. (1975). Receptive field development and individual experience. *Science* **190,** 352–358.

GROEBEL, J., & HINDE, R. A. (1989). *Aggression and war: Their biological and social bases.* New York: Cambridge University Press.

GROSS, M. R. (1985). Disruptive selection for alternative life histories in salmon. *Nature* **313,** 47–48.

GROSSMAN, G. D. (1980). Food, fights, and burrows: The adaptive significance of intraspecific aggression in the bay goby (Pisces: Gobiidae). *Oecologia* **45,** 261–266.

GRUENDEL, A. D., & ARNOLD, W. J. (1969). Effects of early social deprivation on reproductive behavior of male rats. *Journal of Comparative and Physiological Psychology* **67,** 123–128.

GUILLERY, R. W. (1974). Visual pathways in albinos. *Scientific American* **230**(5), 44–54.

GUSTAVSON, C. R., GARCIA, J., HANKINS, W. G., & RUSINIAK, K. W. (1974). Coyote predation control by aversive conditioning. *Science* **184**, 581–583.

GWYNNE, D. T. (1981). Sexual difference theory: Mormon crickets show role reversal in mate choice. *Science* **213**, 779–780.

GWYNNE, D. T. (1984). Courtship feeding increases female reproductive success in bushcrickets. *Nature* **307**, 361–363.

HAFNER, M. S., & HAFNER, J. C. (1984). Brain size, adaptation and heterochrony in Geomyid rodents. *Evolution* 38, 1088–1098.

HAILMAN, J. P. (1977). *Optical signals: Animal communication and light.* Bloomington: Indiana University Press.

HAILMAN, J. P. (1978). Rape among mallards. *Science* **201**, 280–281.

HAIRSTON, N. G., LI, K. T., & EASTER, S. S., JR. (1982). Fish vision and the detection of planktonic prey. *Science* **218**, 1240–1242.

HALL, K. R. L. (1965). Behavior and ecology of the wild patas monkey, *Erythrocebus patas*, in Uganda. *Journal of Zoology* **148**, 15–87.

HALLIDAY, T. (1980). *Sexual strategy.* Chicago: University of Chicago Press.

HALLIDAY, T. R. & SLATER, P. J. B. (1983). *Animal behaviour. Vol. 2: Communication.* New York: Freeman.

HAMILTON, W. D. (1964). The genetical evolution of social behaviour. I, II. *Journal of Theoretical Biology* 7, 1–52.

HAMILTON, W. J., III. (1965). Sun-oriented display of the Anna's hummingbird. *Wilson Bulletin* **77**, 38–43.

HARCOURT, A. H., HARVEY, P. H., LARSON, S. G., & SHORT, R. V. (1982). Testis weight, body weight and breeding system in primates. *Nature* **293**, 55–57.

HARDING, C. F. (1981). Social modulation of circulating hormone levels in the male. *American Zoologist* **21**, 223–231.

HARLOW, H. F. (1949). The formation of learning sets. *Psychological Review* **56**, 51–65.

HARLOW, H. F. (1962). The heterosexual affectional system in monkeys. *American Psychologist* **17**, 1–9.

HARLOW, H. F., & HARLOW, M. K. (1965). The affectional systems. In A. M. Schrier, H. Harlow, & F. Stollnitz (Eds.), *Behavior of nonhuman primates, Vol. 2* (pp. 287–334). New York: Academic.

HARLOW, H. F., & ZIMMERMAN, R. R. (1959). Affectional responses in the infant monkey. *Science* **130**, 421–432.

HAROSI, F. I., & HASHIMOTO, Y. (1983). Ultraviolet visual pigment in a vertebrate: A tetrachromatic cone system in the dace. *Science* **222**, 1021–1023.

HARRINGTON, F. H., & MECH, L. D. (1979). Wolf howling and its role in territory maintenance. *Behaviour* **68**, 207–249.

HARRIS, D. M. & DALLOS, P. (1984). Ontogenetic changes in frequency mapping of a mammalian ear. *Science* **225**, 741–743.

HARRIS, L. R., BLAKEMORE, C., & DONAGHY, M. (1980). Integration of visual and auditory space in the mammalian superior colliculus. *Nature* **288**, 56–59.

HARRIS, W. A. (1986). Homing behaviour of axons in the embryonic vertebrate brain. *Nature* **320**, 266–269.

HART, B. (1967). Sexual reflexes and mating behavior in the male dog. *Journal of*

Comparative and Physiological Psychology **66,** 388–399.

HARVEY, P. H., & GREENWOOD, P. J. (1978). Anti-predator defence strategies: Some evolutionary problems. In J. R. Krebs & N. B. Davies (Eds.), *Behavioural ecology: An evolutionary approach* (pp. 129–151). Sunderland, MA: Sinauer.

HARVEY, P. H., & KREBS, J. R. (1990). Comparing brains. *Science* **249,** 140–146.

HARWERTH, R. S., SMITH, E. L., III, DUNCAN, G. C., CRAWFORD, M.L. J., & VON NOORDEN, G. K. (1986). Multiple sensitive periods in the development of the primate visual system. *Science* **232,** 235–238.

HASELTINE, F. P., & OHNO, S. (1981). Mechanisms of gonadal differentiation. *Science* **211,** 1272–1278.

HASLER, A. D., SCHOLZ, A. T., & HORRALL, R. M. (1978). Olfactory imprinting and homing in salmon. *American Scientist* **66,** 347–355.

HAUSBERGER, F. X., & VOLZ, J. E. (1984). Feeding in infancy, adipose tissue cellularity and obesity. *Physiology and Behavior* **33,** 81–87.

HAUSFATER, G. (1975). Dominance and reproduction in baboons (*Papio cynocephalus*). *Contributions Primatology* **1,** 1–150.

HEFFNER, H. E., & HEFFNER, R. S. (1984). Temporal lobe lesions and perception of species-specific vocalizations by macaques. *Science* **226,** 75–76.

HEFFNER, R., HEFFNER, H., & STICHMAN, N. (1982). Role of the elephant pinna in sound localization. *Animal Behaviour* **30,** 628–630.

HEFFNER, R. S., & MASTERTON, R. B. (1983). The role of the corticospinal tract in the evolution of human digital dexterity. *Brain Behavior and Evolution* **23,** 165–183.

HEINRICH, B. (1985). The social physiology of temperature regulation in honeybees. In B. Hölldobler & M. Lindauer (Eds.), *Experimental behavioral ecology and sociobiology* (pp. 393–406). Sunderland, MA: Sinauer.

HELFMAN, G. S., & SCHULTZ, E. T. (1984). Social transmission of behavioural traditions in a coral reef fish. *Animal Behaviour* **32,** 379–384.

HENNESSY, D. F. & OWINGS, D. H. (1978). Snake species discrimination and the role of olfactory cues in the snake-directed behavior of the California ground squirrel. *Behaviour* **65,** 115–124.

HENNESSY, D. F., OWINGS, D. H., ROWE, M. P., COSS, R. G. & LEGER, D. W. (1981). The information afforded by a variable signal: Constraints on snake-elicited tail flagging by California ground squirrels. *Behaviour* **78,** 188–226.

HENNESSY, M. B. (1986). Multiple, brief maternal separations in the squirrel monkey: Changes in hormonal and behavioral responsiveness. *Physiology and Behavior* **36,** 245–250.

HERBERT, J. (1989). The physiology of aggression. In J. Groebel & R. A. Hinde (Eds.), *Aggression and war: Their biological and social bases* (pp. 58–71). New York: Cambridge University Press.

HEREK, G. M. (1984). Values, research questions, and the news media. *Science* **226,** 1142.

HERRENKOHL, L. R. (1979). Prenatal stress reduces fertility and fecundity in female offspring. *Science* **206,** 1097–1099.

HILL, D. E. (1979). Orientation by jumping spiders of the genus *Phiddipus* (Araneae: Salticidae) during the pursuit of prey. *Be-*

havioral Ecology and Sociobiology **5,** 301–322.

HILL, D. L., & PRZEKOP, P. R., JR. (1988). Influences of dietary sodium on functional taste receptor development: A sensitive period. *Science* **241,** 1826–1828.

HILL, K., & HURTADO, A. M. (1989). Hunter-gatherers of the New World. *American Scientist* 77, 437–443.

HINDE, R. A. (1985). Was 'the expression of the emotions' a misleading phrase? *Animal Behaviour* **33,** 985–992.

HINDE, R. A. (1987). *Individuals, relationships and culture.* New York: Cambridge University Press.

HINDE, R. A., & GROEBEL, J. (1989). The problem of aggression. In J. Groebel & R. A. Hinde (Eds.), *Aggression and war: Their biological and social bases* (pp. 3–9). New York: Cambridge University Press.

HINES, M. (1982). Prenatal gonadal hormones and sex differences in human behavior. *Psychological Bulletin* **92,** 56–80.

HIRAI, K., SHOREY, H. H., & GASTON, L. K. (1978). Competition among courting moths: Male-to-male inhibitory pheromone. *Science* **202,** 644–645.

HIRSCH, H. V. B., & SPINELLI, D. N. (1970). Visual experience modifies distribution of horizontally and vertically oriented receptive fields in cats. *Science* **168,** 869–871.

HOBSON, J. A., McCARLEY, R. W., & WYZINSKI, P. W. (1975). Sleep cycle oscillation: Reciprocal discharge by two brainstem neuronal groups. *Science* **189,** 55–58.

HOBSON, J. A., SPAGNA, T., & MALENKA, R. (1978). Ethology of sleep studied with time-lapse photography: Postural immobility and sleep-cycle phase in humans. *Science* **201,** 1251–1253.

HOCKETT, C. D. (1960). The origin of speech. *Scientific American* **203**(3), 88–96.

HODOS, W., & CAMPBELL, C. B. G. (1969). Scala naturae: Why there is no theory in comparative psychology. *Psychological Review* **76,** 337–350.

HODUN, A., SNOWDON, C. T., & SOINI, P. (1981). Subspecific variation in the long calls of the tamarin, *Saguinus fuscicollis. Zeitschrift für Tierpsychologie* **57,** 97–110.

HOFER, M. A. (1981). *The roots of human behavior: An introduction to the psychobiology of early development.* San Francisco: Freeman.

HOFFMAN, D. D. (1983). The interpretation of visual illusions. *Scientific American* **249,** 154–162.

HOFFMAN, H. S., & FLEISHLER, M. (1965). Stimulus aspects of aversive controls: The effects of response contingent shock. *Journal of the Experimental Analysis of Behavior* **8,** 89–96.

HOGAN, J. A. (1967). Fighting and reinforcement in Siamese fighting fish *Betta splendens. Journal of Comparative and Physiological Psychology* **64,** 356–359.

HOGG, J. T. (1988). Copulatory tactics in relation to sperm competition in Rocky Mountain bighorn sheep. *Behavioral Ecology and Sociobiology* **22,** 49–59.

HOKFELT, T., JOHANSSON, O., & GOLDSTEIN, M. (1984). Chemical anatomy of the brain. *Science* **225,** 1326–1334.

HOLEKAMP, K. E., & SHERMAN, P. W. (1989). Why male ground squirrels disperse. *American Scientist* 77, 232–239.

HÖLLDOBLER, B., & LINDAUER, M. (1985). *Experimental behavioral ecology and sociobiology.* Sunderland, MA: Sinauer.

HÖLLDOBLER, B. K., & WILSON, E. O. (1977). Weaver ants. *Scientific American* **237**(6), 146–154.

Hölldobler, B., & Wilson, E. O. (1983). The evolution of communal nest-weaving in ants. *American Scientist* **71**, 490–499.

Hollis, K. L. (1982). Pavlovian conditioning of signal-centered action patterns and autonomic behavior: A biological analysis of function. *Advances in the Study of Behavior* **12**, 1–64.

Hollis, K. L. (1984). The biological function of Pavlovian conditioning: The best defense is a good offense. *Journal of Experimental Psychology: Animal Behavior Processes* **10**, 413–425.

Hollis, K. L. (1990). The role of Pavlovian conditioning in territorial aggression and reproduction. In D. A. Dewsbury (Ed.), *Contemporary issues in comparative psychology* (pp. 197–219). Sunderland, MA: Sinauer.

Holmes, W. G. (1984a). Ontogeny of dam-young recognition in captive Belding's ground squirrels (*Spermophilus beldingi*). *Journal of Comparative Psychology* **98**, 246–256.

Holmes, W. G. (1984b). Predation risk and foraging behavior of the hoary marmot in Alaska. *Behavioral Ecology and Sociobiology* **15**, 293–301.

Holmes, W. G. & Sherman, P. W. (1983). Kin recognition in animals. *American Scientist* **71**, 46–55.

Hoogland, J. L. (1979). Aggression, ectoparasitism, and possible costs of prairie dog (Sciuridae, *Cynomys* spp.) coloniality. *Behaviour* **69**, 1–35.

Hoogland, J. L. (1985). Infanticide in prairie dogs: Lactating females kill offspring of close kin. *Science* **230**, 1037–1040.

Hoogland, J. L., & Sherman, P. W. (1976). Advantages and disadvantages of bank swallow (*Riparia riparia*) coloniality. *Ecological Monographs* **46**, 33–58.

Hopkins, C. D. (1980). Evolution of electric communication channels of Mormyrids. *Behavioral Ecology and Sociobiology* **7**, 1–13.

Hopkins, C. D. (1983). Sensory mechanisms in animal communication. In T. R. Halliday & P. J. B. Slater (Eds.), *Animal behaviour. Vol. 2: Communication* (pp. 114–155). New York: Freeman.

Horder, T. J., & Martin, K. A. C. (1979). Morphogenetics as an alternative to chemospecificity in the formation of nerve connections. *Symposium of the Society of Experimental Biology* **32**, 275–359.

Horel, J. A. (1973). The brain and behavior in phylogenetic perspective. In D. A. Dewsbury & D. A. Rethlingshafer (Eds.), *Comparative psychology: A modern survey* (pp. 271–300). New York: McGraw-Hill.

Horne, J. A. (1978). A review of the biological effects of total sleep deprivation in man. *Biological Psychology* **7**, 55–102.

Horne, J. A., & Porter, J. M. (1975). Exercise and human sleep. *Nature* **256**, 573–574.

Horner, J. R. (1984). The nesting behavior of dinosaurs. *Scientific American* **250**(4), 130–137.

Hornykiewicz, O. (1966). Dopamine (3-hydroxytyramine) and brain function. *Pharmacological Review* **18**, 925–964.

Howard, R. D. (1978). The evolution of mating strategies in bullfrogs, *Rana catesbiana*. *Evolution* **32**, 850–871.

Howe, H. F. (1977). Sex ratio adjustment in the common grackle. *Science* **198**, 744–746.

Howell, N. (1979). *Demography of the Dobe !Kung*. New York: Academic.

Hoy, R. R., Hahn, J., & Paul, R. (1976). Hybrid cricket auditory behavior: Evidence for genetic coupling in animal communication. *Science* **195**, 82–84.

HOY, R. R., HOIKKALA, A., & KANESHIRO, K. (1988). Hawaiian courtship songs: Evolutionary innovation in communication signals of *Drosophila*. *Science* **240**, 217–219.

HRDY, S. B. (1979). Infanticide among animals: A review, classification, and examination of the implications for the reproductive strategies of females. *Ethology and Sociobiology* **1**, 13–40.

HRDY, S. B. (1981). *The woman that never evolved*. Cambridge, MA: Harvard University Press.

HUBEL, D. H., & WIESEL, T. N. (1979). Brain mechanisms of vision. *Scientific American* 241(3), 150–162.

HUDSPETH, A. J. (1983). The hair cells of the inner ear. *Scientific American* **248**(1), 54–64.

HUDSPETH, A. J. (1985). The cellular basis of hearing: The biophysics of hair cells. *Science* **230**, 745–752.

HULL, E. M., NISHITA, J. K., BITRAN, D., & DALTERIO, S. (1984). Perinatal dopamine-related drugs demasculinize rats. *Science* **224**, 1011–1013.

HUMPHRIES, D. A. & DRIVER, P. M. (1967). Erratic display as a device against predators. *Science* **156**, 1767–1768.

HUNT, R. M., XUE, X.-X., & KAUFMAN, J. (1983). Miocene burrows of extinct bear dogs: Indication of early denning behavior of large mammalian carnivores. *Science* **221**, 364–366.

HUNTER, M. L., & KREBS, J. R. (1979). Geographical variation in the song of the great tit (*Parus major*) in relation to ecological factors. *Journal of Animal Ecology* **48**, 759–785.

HUNTINGFORD, F. A. (1989). Animals fight, but do not make war. In J. Groebel & R. A. Hinde (Eds.), *Aggression and war:* *Their biological and social bases* (pp. 25–34). New York: Cambridge University Press.

IMMELMANN, K. (1975). Ecological significance of imprinting and early learning. *Annual Review of Ecology and Systematics* **6**, 15–37.

ISACK, H. A., & REYER, H.-U. (1989). Honeyguides and honey gathers: Interspecific communication in a symbiotic relationship. *Science* **243**, 1343–1346.

IVERSEN, L. L. (1979). The chemistry of the brain. *Scientific American* **241**(3), 118–129.

IZARD, C. E. (1985). Emotions and facial expression. *Science* **230**, 608.

JACKLIN, C. N., MACCOBY, E. E., DOERING, C. H., & KING, D. R. (1984). Neonatal sex-steroid hormones and muscular strength of boys and girls in the first three years. *Developmental Psychobiology* **17**, 301–310.

JACOB, F. (1977). Evolution and tinkering. *Science* **196**, 1161–1166.

JACOBS, B. L. (1987). How hallucinogenic drugs work. *American Scientist* **75**, 386–392.

JACOBS, B. L., & COHEN, A. (1976). Differential behavioral effects of lesions of the median or dorsal raphe nuclei in rats: Open field and pain-elicited aggression. *Journal of Comparative and Physiological Psychology* **90**, 102–108.

JACOBS, B. L., & TRULSON, M. E. (1979). Mechanisms of action of LSD. *American Scientist* **67**, 396–404.

JACOBSON, M. (1974). A plentitude of neurons. In G. Gottlieb (Ed.), *Studies on the development of behavior and the nervous system. Vol. 2: Aspects of neurogenesis* (pp. 151–166). New York: Academic Press.

JANE, S. D., & BOWMAKER, J. K. (1988). Tetrachromatic colour vision in the duck (*Anas platyrhynchos L.*): Microspectrophotometry of visual pigments and oil droplets. *Journal of Comparative Physiology A.* **162,** 225–235.

JANOWITZ, H. D., & GROSSMAN, M. I. (1949). Some factors affecting the food intake of normal dogs and dogs with esophagostomy and gastric fistula. *American Journal of Physiology* **159,** 143–148.

JARMAN, P. J. (1982). Prospects for interspecific comparisons in sociobiology. In King's College Sociobiology Group (Eds.), *Current problems in sociobiology* (pp. 323–342). Cambridge: Cambridge University Press.

JENKINS, P. F. (1977). Cultural transmission of song patterns and dialect development in a free-living bird population. *Animal Behaviour* **25,** 50–78.

JENNI, D. A. (1974). Evolution of polyandry in birds. *American Zoologist* **14,** 129–144.

JENSEN, D. D. (1987). Operationism, polytheticism, the biotemporal space, and the empirical integration of ethology, psychology, neuroscience, and sociobiology. *Paper presented at the International Ethological Conference.*, Madison, Wisconsin.

JENSSEN, T. A. (1977). Evolution of anoline lizard display behavior. *American Zoologist* **17,** 203–215.

JERISON, H. J. (1976). Paleoneurology and the evolution of mind. *Scientific American* **234**(1), 90–101.

JERISON, H. J. (1985). Animal intelligence as encephalization. *Philosophical Transactions of the Royal Society of London* **B308,** 21–35.

JOHNSON, C. H., & HASTINGS, J. W. (1986). The elusive mechanism of the circadian clock. *American Scientist* **74,** 29–36.

JOHNSON, D. F., ACKROFF, K. M., COLLIER, G. H., & PLESCIA, L. (1984). Effects of dietary nutrients and foraging costs on meal patterns of rats. *Physiology and Behavior* **33,** 465–471.

JOHNSON, E. M., JR., & YIP, H. K. (1985). Central nervous system and peripheral nerve growth factor provide trophic support critical to mature sensory neuronal survival. *Nature* **314,** 751–752.

JOHNSON, F., & WHALEN, R. E. (1988). Testicular hormones reduce individual differences in aggressive behavior of male mice: A theory of hormone action. *Neuroscience and Biobehavioral Reviews* **12,** 93–99.

JOHN-STEINER, V., & PANOFSKY, C. P. (1987). Human specificity in language: Sociogenetic processes in verbal communication. In G. Greenberg (Ed.) *Cognition, language and consciousness: Integrative levels* (pp. 85–97). Hillsdale, NJ: Erlbaum.

JOHNSTON, T. D. (1988). Developmental explanation and the ontogeny of birdsong: Nature/nurture redux. *Behavioral and Brain Science* **11,** 617–663.

JOHNSTON, T. D., & GOTTLIEB, G. (1981a). Development of visual species identification in ducklings: What is the role of imprinting? *Animal Behaviour* **29,** 1082–1099.

JOHNSTON, T. D., & GOTTLIEB, G. (1981b). Visual preferences of imprinted ducklings are altered by the maternal call. *Journal of Comparative and Physiological Psychology* **95,** 663–675.

JOHNSTON, T. D., & GOTTLIEB, G. (1985a). Development of visually controlled maternal preferences in Peking ducklings. *Developmental Psychobiology* **18,** 23–36.

JOHNSTON, T. D., & GOTTLIEB, G. (1985b). Effects of social experience on visually imprinted maternal preferences in Peking ducklings. *Developmental Psychobiology* **18,** 261–271.

JONES, H. S., & OSWALD, I. (1968). Two cases of healthy insomnia. *Electroencephalography and Clinical Neurophysiology* **24,** 378–380.

JOUVET, M. (1969). Biogenic amines and the states of sleep. *Science* **163,** 32–41.

JULIEN, R. M. (1981). *A primer of drug action.* San Francisco: Freeman.

KALAT, J. W. (1983). Evolutionary thinking in the history of the comparative psychology of learning. *Neuroscience and Biobehavioral Reviews* **7,** 309–314.

KALIL, R. E., JHAVERI, S. R., & RICHARDS, W. (1971). Anomalous retinal pathways in the Siamese cat: An inadequate substrate for normal binocular vision. *Science* **174,** 302–305.

KALIN, N. H., & SHELTON, S. E. (1989). Defensive behaviors in infant rhesus monkeys: Environmental cues and neurochemical regulation. *Science* **243,** 1718–1721.

KAMIL, A. C. (1978). Systematic foraging by a nectar-feeding bird, the amakihi (*Loxops virens*). *Journal of Comparative and Physiological Psychology* **92,** 388–396.

KAMIL, A. C. (1988). A synthetic approach to the study of animal intelligence. In D. W. Leger (Ed.), *Comparative perspectives in modern psychology. Nebraska Symposium on Motivation, Vol. 35* (pp. 257–308). Lincoln: University of Nebraska Press.

KAMIL, A. C., & BALDA, R. P. (1985). Cache recovery and spatial memory in Clark's nutcrackers (*Nucifraga columbiana*). *Journal of Experimental Psychology: Animal Behavior Processes* **11,** 95–111.

KAMIL, A. C., & CLEMENTS, K. C. (1990). Learning, memory, and foraging behavior. In D. A. Dewsbury (Ed.), *Contemporary issues in comparative psychology* (pp. 7–30). Sunderland, MA: Sinauer.

KAMIL, A. C., & ROITBLAT, H. L. (1985). The ecology of foraging behavior: Implications for animal learning and memory. *Annual Review of Psychology* **36,** 141–169.

KAMIL, A. C., & SARGENT, T. D. (1981). *Foraging behavior: Ecological, ethological, and psychological approaches.* New York: Garland STPM Press.

KAMIN, L. J. (1980). Inbreeding depression and IQ. *Psychological Bulletin* **87,** 469–478.

KANDEL, E. R. (1979). Small systems of neurons. *Scientific American* **241**(3), 66–76.

KANDEL, E. R., & SCHWARTZ, J. H. (1982). Molecular biology of learning: Modulation of transmitter release. *Science* **218,** 433–443.

KASPARI, M. (1990). Prey preparation and the determinants of handling time. *Animal Behaviour* **40,** 118–126.

KATZ, M. J., LASEK, R. J., & SILVER, J. (1983). Ontophyletics of the nervous system: Development of the corpus callosum and evolution of axon tracks. *Proceedings of the National Academy of Sciences of the United States of America* **80,** 5936–5940.

KATZIR, G., & INTRATOR, N. (1987). Striking of underwater prey by a reef heron, *Egretta gularis schistacea. Journal of Comparative Physiology A.* **160,** 517–523.

KAVANAU, J. L. (1988). Presumptive relict reproductive behavior in small parrots. *Brain Behavior and Evolution* **32,** 340–352.

KAVANAU, J. L. (1990). Conservative behavioural evolution, the neural substrate. *Animal Behaviour* **39,** 758–767.

KAWAI, M. (1965). Newly acquired pre-cultural behavior of the natural troop of Japanese monkeys on Koshima Inlet. *Primates* **6,** 1–30.

KAWAMURA, S. (1959). The process of sub-culture propagation among Japanese macaques. *Primates* **2**, 43–60.

KEESEY, R. E., & CORBETT, S. W. (1984). Metabolic defense of the body weight set point. In A. J. Stunkard & E. Stellar (Eds.), *Eating and its disorders.* New York: Raven Press.

KELSO, J. A. S. (1982). *Human motor behavior: An introduction.* Hillsdale, NJ: Erlbaum.

KENDRICK, K. M., & BALDWIN, B. A. (1987). Cells in temporal cortex of conscious sheep can respond preferentially to the sight of faces. *Science* **236**, 448–450.

KENNEDY, D., EVOY, W. H., & HANAWALT, J. T. (1966). Release of coordinated behavior in crayfish by single central neurons. *Science* **154**, 917–919.

KESSLER, S. (1976). On genetics of narcolepsy in dogs. In C. Guilleminault, W. C. Dement, & P. Passouant (Eds.), *Advances in sleep research. Vol. 3: Narcolepsy* (pp. 285–300). New York: Spectrum.

KEVERNE, E. B., & DE LA RIVA, C. (1982). Pheromones in mice: Reciprocal interaction between the nose and brain. *Nature* **296**, 148–150.

KEVERNE, E. B., LEVY, F., POINDRON, P., & LINDSAY, D. R. (1983). Vaginal stimulation: An important determinant of maternal bonding in sheep. *Science* **219**, 81–83.

KEYNES, R. D. (1979). Ion channels in the nerve-cell membrane. *Scientific American* **240**(3), 126–135.

KIHLSTROM, J. F. (1987). The cognitive unconscious. *Science* **237**, 1445–1452.

KING, A. P., & WEST, M. J. (1977). Species identification in the North American cowbird: Appropriate responses to abnormal song. *Science* **195**, 1002–1004.

KING, A. P., & WEST, M. J. (1983). Epigenesis of cowbird song—A joint endeavour of males and females. *Nature* **305**, 704–706.

KING, J. L., & JUKES, T. H. (1969). Non-Darwinian evolution. *Science* **164**, 788–798.

KLEIMAN, D. G. (1977). Monogamy in mammals. *Quarterly Review of Biology* **52**, 39–69.

KLEIN, R., & ARMITAGE, R. (1979). Rhythms in human performance: 1½-hour oscillations in cognitive style. *Science* **204**, 1326–1328.

KLUENDER, K. R., DIEHL, R. L., & KILLEEN, P. R. (1987). Japanese quail can learn phonetic categories. *Science* **237**, 1195–1197.

KNOWLES, A. (1982). The biochemical aspects of vision. In H. B. Barlow & J. D. Mollon (Eds.), *The senses* (pp. 82–101). Cambridge: Cambridge University Press.

KNOX, P. (1983). The plasma membrane. *The Biologist* **30**, 159–163.

KNUDSEN, E. I. (1981). The hearing of the barn owl. *Scientific American* **245**(6), 112–125.

KNUDSEN, E. I., & KONISHI, M. (1978). A neural map of auditory space in the owl. *Science* **200**, 795–797.

KOEHN, R. K., & HILBISH, T. J. (1987). The adaptive importance of genetic variation. *American Scientist* **75**, 134–141.

KOELLA, W. P. (1984). The organization and regulation of sleep: A review of the experimental evidence and a novel integrated model of the organizing and regulating apparatus. *Experientia* **40**, 309–338.

KOENIG, W. D., & PITELKA, F. A. (1979). Relatedness and inbreeding avoidance: Counterploys in the communally nesting acorn woodpecker. *Science* **206**, 1103–1105.

KOEPPL, J. W., HOFFMANN, R. S., & NADLER, C. F. (1978). Pattern analysis of acoustical behavior in four species of ground squirrels. *Journal of Mammalogy* **59**, 677–696.

KOLATA, G. (1985). Why do people get fat? *Science* **227**, 1327–1328.

KOLB, B., & WISHAW, I. Q. (1985). *Fundamentals of human neuropsychology*. New York: Freeman.

KONISHI, M. (1965). The role of auditory feedback in the control of vocalization in the white-crowned sparrow. *Zeitschrift für Tierpsychologie* **22**, 770–783.

KONISHI, M. (1966). The attributes of instinct. *Behaviour* **27**, 316–328.

KONISHI, M., & AKUTAGAWA, E. (1981). Androgen increases protein synthesis within the avian brain vocal control system. *Brain Research* **222**, 442–446.

KONNER, M., & WORTHMAN, C. (1980). Nursing frequency, gonadal function, and birth spacing among !Kung hunter-gatherers. *Science* **207**, 788–791.

KORETZ, J. F., & HANDELMAN, G. H. (1988). How the human eye focuses. *Scientific American* **259**, 92–99.

KRAEMER, H. C., BECKER, H. B., BRODIE, H. K. H., DOERING, C. H., MOOS, R. H., & HAMBURG, D. A. (1976). Orgasmic frequency and plasma testosterone in normal human males. *Archives of Sexual Behavior* **5**, 125–132.

KRASNE, F. B., & WINE, J. J. (1977). The control of crayfish escape behavior. In G. Hoyle (Ed.), *Identified neurons and behavior of arthropods* (pp. 275–292). New York: Plenum.

KREBS, J. R. (1978). Optimal foraging: Decision rules for predators. In J. R. Krebs & N. B. Davies (Eds.), *Behavioural ecology: An evolutionary approach* (pp. 23–63). Sunderland, MA: Sinauer.

KREBS, J. R., & DAVIES, N. B. (1987). *An introduction to behavioural ecology*. Sunderland, MA: Sinauer.

KREUZ, L. E., ROSE, R. M., & JENNINGS, J. R. (1972). Suppression of plasma testosterone levels and psychological stress. *Archives of General Psychiatry* **26**, 479–482.

KRIEGER, D.T. (1983). Brain peptides: What, where, and why? *Science* **222**, 975–985.

KROGMAN, W. M. (1951). The scars of human evolution. *Scientific American* **185**(6), 54–57.

KROODSMA, D. E. (176). Reproductive development in a female songbird: Differential stimulation by quality of male song. *Science* 192, 574–576.

KROODSMA, D. E. (1981). Learning and the ontogeny of sound signals in birds. In D. E. Kroodsma, E. H. Miller, & H. Oullet (Eds.), *Acoustic communication in birds.* Vol. 2 (pp. 1–23). New York: Academic.

KRUUK, H. (1972a). Surplus killing by carnivores. *Journal of Zoology (London)* **166**, 233–244.

KRUUK, H. (1972b). *The spotted hyena: A study of predation and social behavior.* Chicago: University of Chicago Press.

KRUUK, H. (1976). The biological function of gulls' attraction towards predators. *Animal Behaviour* **24**, 146–153.

KUFFLER, S. W. (1980). Slow synaptic responses in autonomic ganglia and the pursuit of a peptidergic transmitter. *Journal of Experimental Biology* **89**, 257–286.

KUFFLER, S. W., NICHOLLS, J. G., & MARTIN, A. R. (1984). *From neuron to brain: A cellular approach to the function of the nervous system.* Sunderland, MA:Sinauer.

KUHL, P. K. (1979). The perception of speech in early infancy. In N. J. Lass (Ed.), *Speech and language: Research and theory.* New York: Academic.

KUHL, P. K., & MELTZOFF, A. N. (1982). The bimodal perception of speech in infancy. *Science* **218,** 1138–1141.

KUMMER, H. (1968). *Social organization of hamadryas baboons.* Chicago: University of Chicago Press.

KUPFERMANN, I., & WEISS, K. R. (1978). The command neuron concept. *Behavioral and Brain Sciences* **1,** 3–10.

KURLAND, J. A. (1979). Paternity, mother's brother, and human sociality. In N. A. Chagnon & W. Irons (Eds.), *Evolutionary biology and human social behavior: An anthropological perspective* (pp.145–180). North Scituate, MA: Duxbury.

KYRIACOU, C. P., & HALL, J. C. (1986). Interspecific genetic control of courtship song production and reception in *Drosophila. Science* **232,** 494–497.

LACK, D. (1966). *Population studies of birds.* Oxford: Oxford University Press.

LACK, D. (1968). *Ecological adaptations for breeding in birds.* London: Methuen.

LAITMAN, J. T. (1984). The anatomy of human speech. *Natural History* **93**(8), 20–27.

LAKE, J. A. (1981). The ribosome. *Scientific American* **245**(3), 84–97.

LALL, A. B., SELIGER, H. H., BIGGLEY, W. H., & LLOYD, J. E. (1980). Ecology of colors of firefly bioluminescence. *Science* **210,** 560–562.

LALL, A. B., STROTHER, G. K., CRONIN, T. W., & SELIGER, H. H. (1988). Modification of spectral sensitivities by screening pigments in the compound eyes of twilight-active fireflies (Coleoptera: Lampyridae). *Journal of Comparative Physiology A.* **162,** 23–33.

LAND, M. F. (1981). Optics and vision in invertebrates. In H. Autrum (Ed.), *Handbook of sensory physiology. Vol. VII/6B* (pp. 471–592). Berlin: Springer-Verlag.

LANG, F., GOVIND, C. K., & COSTELLO, W. J. (1978). Experimental transformation of muscle fiber properties in lobster. *Science* **201,** 1037–1039.

LANIER, D. L., ESTEP, D. Q., & DEWSBURY, D. A. (1975). Copulatory behavior of golden hamsters: Effects on pregnancy. *Physiology and Behavior* **15,** 209–212.

LEAHEY, T. H., & HARRIS, R. J. (1989). *Human learning.* Englewood Cliffs, NJ: Prentice-Hall.

LeBOEUF, B. J., & BRIGGS, K. T. (1977). The cost of living in a seal harem. *Mammalia* **41,** 167–195.

LeBOEUF, B. J., & PETERSON, R. S. (1969). Social status and mating activity in elephant seals. *Science* **163,** 91–93.

LEE, T. M., & MOLTZ, H. (1984a). The maternal pheromone and brain development in the preweanling rat. *Physiology and Behavior* **33,** 385–390.

LEE, T. M., & MOLTZ, H. (1984b). The maternal pheromone and deoxycholic acid in relation to brain myelin in the preweanling rat. *Physiology and Behavior* **33,** 391–395.

LEFEBVRE, L. (1986). Cultural diffusion of a novel food-finding behaviour in urban pigeons: An experimental field test. *Ethology* **71,** 295–304.

LEGER, D. W. (1989). The comparative psychology of "us" vs. "them": Language, cognition, and integrative levels. *Contemporary Psychology* **34,** 826–827.

LEGER, D. W., MASON, W. A., & FRAGASZY, D. M. (1981). Sexual segregation, cliques, and social power in squirrel monkey (*Saimiri*) groups. *Behaviour* **76,** 163–181.

LEGER, D. W., & OWINGS, D. H. (1978). Responses to alarm calls by California ground squirrels: Effects of call structure and maternal status. *Behavioral Ecology and Sociobiology* **3**, 177–186.

LEGER, D. W., OWINGS, D. H., & COSS, R. G. (1983). Behavioral ecology of time allocation in California ground squirrels (*Spermophilus beecheyi*): Microhabitat effects. *Journal of Comparative Psychology* **97**, 283–291.

LEGER, D. W., OWINGS, D. H., & GELFAND, D. L. (1980). Single-note vocalizations of California ground squirrels: Graded signals and situation-specificity of predator and socially evoked calls. *Zeitschrift für Tierpsychologie* **52**, 227–246.

LEMEN, C. (1980). Relationship between relative brain size and climbing ability in *Peromyscus*. *Journal of Mammalogy* **61**, 360–364.

LENDREM, D. W. (1984). Sleeping and vigilance in birds, II. An experimental study of the barbary dove (*Streptopelia risoria*). *Animal Behaviour* **32**, 243–248.

LENNEBERG, E. H. (1967). *Biological foundations of language*. New York: Wiley.

LENNEBERG, E. H. (1969). On explaining language. *Science* **164**, 635–643.

LENT, C. M., & DICKINSON, M. H. (1988). The neurobiology of feeding in leeches. *Scientific American* **258**, 98–103.

LENTZ, T. L. (1968). *Primitive nervous systems*. New Haven, CT: Yale University Press.

LESHNER, A. I. (1978). *An introduction to behavioral endocrinology*. New York: Oxford University Press.

LESHNER, A. I. (1979). Kinds of hormonal effects on behavior: A new view. *Neuroscience and Biobehavioral Reviews* **3**, 69–73.

LESTER, B. M. (1984). A biosocial model of infant crying. In L. Lipsett, & C. Rovee-Collier (Eds.), *Advances in infancy research* (pp. 167–212). Norwood, NJ: Ablex.

LESTER, H. A. (1977). The response to acetylcholine. *Scientific American* **236**(2), 106–118.

LESTER, N. P. (1984). The "feed-drink" decision. *Behaviour* **89**, 200–219.

LEVI-MONTALCINI, R. (1987). The nerve growth factor 35 years later. *Science* **237**, 1154–1162.

LEVI-MONTALCINI, R., & CALISSANO, P. (1979). The nerve-growth factor. *Scientific American* **240**(6), 68–77.

LEVINE, J. S., & MACNICHOLL, E. F., JR. (1982). Color vision in fishes. *Scientific American* **246**(2), 140–149.

LEVINE, S., WIENER, S. G., COE, C. L., BAYART, F. E. S., & HAYASHI, K. T. (1987). Primate vocalization: A psychobiological approach. *Child Development*, 58, 1408–1419.

LEVY, J., & LEVY, J. M. (1978). Human lateralization from head to foot: Sex related factors. *Science* **200**, 1291–1292.

LEWIS, A. C. (1986). Memory constraints and flower choice in *Pieris rapae*. *Science* **232**, 863–865.

LEWONTIN, R. C. (1979). Sociobiology as an adaptationist program. *Behavioral Science* **24**, 5–14.

LEWY, A. J., WEHR, T. A., GOODWIN, F. K., NEWSOME, D. A., & MARKEY, S. P. (1980). Light suppresses melatonin secretion in humans. *Science* **210**, 1267–1269.

LI, S. K., & OWINGS, D. H. (1978). Sexual selection in the three-spined stickleback. 1. Normative observations. *Zeitschrift für Tierpsychologie* **46**, 359–371.

LIA, B., WILLIAMS, R. W., & CHALUPA, L. M. (1987). Formation of retinal ganglion cell topography during prenatal development. *Science* **236**, 848–851.

LICKLITER, R., & GOTTLIEB, G. (1985). Social interaction with siblings is necessary for visual imprinting of species-specific maternal preferences in ducklings (*Anas platyrhynchos*). *Journal of Comparative Psychology* **99**, 371–379.

LIDOV, H. G. W., GRZANNA, R., & MOLLIVER, M. E. (1980). The serotonin innervation of the cerebral cortex in the rat—an immunohistochemical analysis. *Neuroscience* **5**, 207–227.

LIEBERMAN, P. (1977). The phylogeny of language. In T. A. Sebeok (Ed.), *How animals communicate* (pp. 3–25). Bloomington: Indiana University Press.

LIEBERMAN, P. (1984). *The biology and evolution of language*. Cambridge: Harvard University Press.

LINDAUER, M. (1985). The dance language of honeybees: The history of a discovery. In B. Hölldobler & M. Lindauer (Eds.), *Experimental behavioral ecology and sociobiology* (pp. 129–140). Sunderland, MA: Sinauer.

LINDSLEY, J. G. (1983). Sleep patterns and functions. In A. Gale & J.A. Edwards (Eds.), *Physiological correlates of human behavior. Vol. 1: Basic issues* (pp. 105–141). London: Academic Press.

LIPPE, W., & RUBEL, E. W. (1983). Development of the place principle: Tonotopic organization. *Science* **219**, 514–516.

LISBERGER, S. G. (1988). The neural basis for learning of simple motor skills. *Science* **242**, 728–735.

LISSMANN, H. W. (1963). Electric location by fishes. *Scientific American*. **208**(3), 50–59.

LLINAS, R. R. (1982). Calcium in synaptic transmission. *Scientific American* **247**(4), 56–65.

LOESER, J. D., & ALVORD, E. C. (1968). Agenesis of the corpus callosum. *Brain* **91**, 553–570.

LOGUE, A. W. (1986). *The psychology of eating and drinking*. New York: Freeman.

LOMBARDO, M. P. (1985). Mutual restraint in tree swallows: A test of the TIT FOR TAT model of reciprocity. *Science* **227**, 1363–1365.

LORENZ, K. Z. (1966). *On aggression*. London: Methuen.

LORENZ, K. Z. (1971). Comparative studies of the motor patterns of Anatinae. In K. Z. Lorenz (Ed.), *Studies in animal and human behaviour, Vol. II* (pp. 14–114). Cambridge: Harvard University Press.

LORENZ, K. Z. (1981). *The foundations of ethology*. New York: Simon and Schuster.

LOTT, D. F. (1984). Intraspecific variation in the social systems of wild vertebrates. *Behaviour* **88**, 266–325.

LOVEJOY, C. O. (1988). Evolution of human walking. *Scientific American* **259**, 118–125.

LUINE, V. N., RENNER, K. J., FRANKFURT, M., & AZMITIA, E. C. (1984). Facilitated sexual behavior reversed and serotonin restored by Raphe nuclei transplanted into denervated hypothalamus. *Science* **226**, 1436–1439.

LYNCH, G., & BAUDRY, M. (1984). The biochemistry of memory: A new and specific hypothesis. *Science* **224**, 1057–1063.

LYNCH, W. (1983). Great balls of snakes. *Natural History* **92**(4), 64–69.

LYTHGOE, J. N. (1979). *The ecology of vision*. New York: Oxford University Press.

MACDONALD, D. W. (1983). The ecology of carnivore social behaviour. *Nature* **301**, 379–384.

MACE, G. M., & EISENBERG, J. F. (1982). Competition, niche specialization and the evolution of brain size in the genus

Peromyscus. Biological Journal of the Linnaen Society **17,** 243–257.

MACEDONIA, J. M., & TAYLOR, L. L. (1985). Subspecific divergence in a loud call of the ruffed lemur (*Varecia variegata*). *American Journal of Primatology* **9,** 295–304.

MACKINTOSH, N. J. (1983). General principles of learning. In T. R. Halliday & P. J. B. Slater (Eds.), *Animal behaviour. Vol. 3: Genes, development and learning* (pp. 149–177). New York: Freeman.

MACKINNON, J. R. (1974). The behaviour and ecology of wild orangutans (*Pongo pygmaeus*). *Animal Behaviour* **22,** 3–74.

MACLEAN, P. D. (1970). The limbic brain in relation to the psychoses. In P. Black (Ed.), *Physiological correlates of emotion* (pp. 129–146). New York: Academic.

MACLEAN, S. F, JR. (1974). Lemming bones as a source of calcium for arctic sandpipers (*Calidris* spp.). *Ibis* **116,** 552–557.

MACLUSKY, N. J., & NAFTOLIN, F. (1981). Sexual differentiation of the central nervous system. *Science* **211,** 1294–1303.

MACPHAIL, E. M. (1982). *Brain and intelligence in vertebrates.* New York: Oxford University Press.

MAGGIO, J. C., & HARDER, D. B. (1983). Genotype and environment interactively determine the magnitude, directionality, and abolition of defensive burying in mice. *Animal Learning and Behavior* **11,** 162–172.

MALINA, R. M. (1983). Menarche in athletes: A synthesis and hypothesis. *Annals of Human Biology* **10,** 1–24.

MALSBURY, C. W. (1971). Facilitation of male rat copulatory behavior by electrical stimulation of the medial preoptic area. *Physiology and Behavior* **7,** 797–805.

MAMELAK, M., CARUSO, V. J., & STEWART, K. (1979). Narcolepsy: A family study. *Biological Psychiatry* **14,** 821–834.

MANDEL, P., MACK, G., & KEMPF, E. (1979). Molecular basis of some models of aggressive behavior. In M. Sandler (Ed.), *Psychopharmacology of aggression* (pp. 95–110). New York: Raven Press.

MANNING, A. (1989). The genetic bases of aggression. In J. Groebel & R. A. Hinde (Eds.), *Aggression and war: Their biological and social bases* (pp. 48–57). New York: Cambridge University Press.

MARKSTEIN, P. L., & LEHNER, P. N. (1980). A comparison of predatory behavior between prey-naive and prey-experienced adult coyotes (*Canis latrans*). *Bulletin of the Psychonomic Society* **15,** 271–274.

MARLER, P. (1959). Developments in the study of animal communication. In P. R. Bell (Ed.), *Darwin's biological work* (pp. 150–206). London: Cambridge University Press.

MARLER, P. (1970). A comparative approach to vocal learning: Song development in white-crowned sparrows. *Journal of Comparative and Physiological Psychology* **71,** 1–25.

MARLER, P. (1976a). On animal aggression: The roles of strangeness and familiarity. *American Psychologist* **31,** 239–246.

MARLER, P. (1976b). Sensory templates in species-specific behavior. In J. C. Fentress (Ed.), *Simpler networks and behavior* (pp. 314–329). Sunderland, MA: Sinauer.

MARLER, P. (1985). Representational vocal signals in primates. In B. Hölldobler & M. Lindauer (Eds.), *Experimental behavioral ecology and sociobiology* (pp. 211–221). Sunderland, MA: Sinauer.

MARLER, P. (1989). Learning by instinct:

Birdsong. *American Speech and Hearing Association Journal,* (May), 75–79.

MARLER, P., & TAMURA, M. (1964). Culturally transmitted patterns of vocal behavior in sparrows. *Science* **146**, 1483–1486.

MARTEN, K., & MARLER, P. (1977). Sound transmission and its significance for animal vocalization. 1. Temperate habitats. *Behavioral Ecology and Sociobiology* **2**, 271–290.

MARTINEZ DEL RIO, C., & STEVENS, B. R. (1989). Physiological constraint on feeding behavior: Intestinal membrane disaccharidases of the starling. *Science* **243**, 794–796.

MARX, J. L. (1985). Proteins for all seasons. *Science* **229**, 638–640.

MASLAND, R. H. (1986). The functional architecture of the retina. *Scientific American* **255**, 102–111.

MASON, J. R., & REIDINGER, R. F. (1982). Observational learning of food aversions in red-winged blackbirds (*Agelaius phoeniceus*). *Auk* **99**, 548–554.

MASON, W. A. (1976). Primate social behavior: Pattern and process. In R. B. Masterton, M. E. Bitterman, C. B. G. Campbell, & N. Hotton (Eds.), *Evolution of brain and behavior in vertebrates* (pp. 425–455). Hillsdale, NJ: Erlbaum.

MASON, W. A. (1979). Ontogeny of social behavior. In P. Marler & J. G. Vandenbergh (Eds.), *Handbook of behavioral neurobiology. Vol. 3: Social behavior and communication* (pp. 1–28). New York: Plenum.

MASON, W. A., & BERKSON, G. (1975). Effects of maternal mobility on the development of rocking and other behaviors in rhesus monkeys: A study with artificial mothers. *Developmental Psychobiology* **8**, 197–211.

MASTERTON, R. B. (ED.). (1978). *Handbook of behavioral neurobiology, Vol. 1: Sensory integration.* New York: Plenum.

MASTERTON, R. B., & IMIG, T. J. (1984). Neural mechanisms of sound localization. *Annual Review of Physiology* **46**, 275–287.

MAYNARD SMITH, J. (1983). *Evolution and the theory of games.* New York: Cambridge University Press.

MAYNARD SMITH, J., & PRICE, G. R. (1973). The logic of animal conflict. *Nature* **246**, 15–18.

MAYR, E. (1961). Cause and effect in biology. *Science* **134**, 1501–1506.

MAYR, E. (1970). *Populations, species, and evolution.* Cambridge: Harvard University Press.

MAYR, E. (1974). Behavior programs and evolutionary strategies. *American Scientist* **62**, 650–659.

MAYR, E. (1978). Evolution. *Scientific American* **239**(3), 46–55.

MAZUR, A. (1983). Hormones, aggression, and dominance in humans. In B. B. Svare (Ed.), *Hormones and aggressive behavior* (pp. 563–576). New York: Plenum.

MAZUR, A., & LAMB, T. A. (1980). Testosterone, status, and mood in human males. *Hormones and Behavior* **14**, 236–246.

MCCARLEY, H. (1970). Differential reproduction in *Spermophilus tridecemlineatus.* *Southwestern Naturalist* **14**, 293–296.

MCCARLEY, R. W., & HOBSON, J. A. (1975). Neural excitability modulation over the sleep cycle: A structural and mathematical model. *Science* **189**, 58–60.

MCCARTHY, M. M., & VOM SAAL, F. S. (1986). Inhibition of infanticide after mating by wild house mice. *Physiology and Behavior* **36,** 203–210.

McCARTY, R., & SOUTHWICK, C. H. (1979). Parental environment: Effects on survival, growth and aggressive behaviors of two rodent species. *Developmental Psychobiology* **12,** 269–279.

McCAULEY, W. J. (1971). *Vertebrate physiology.* Philadelphia: Saunders.

McCLEERY, R. H. (1978). Optimal behaviour sequences and decision making. In J. R. Krebs & N. B. Davies (Eds.), *Behavioural ecology: An evolutionary approach* (pp. 377–410). Sunderland, MA: Sinauer.

McCLEERY, R. H. (1983). Interactions between activities. In T. R. Halliday & P. J. B. Slater (Eds.), *Animal behaviour. Vol. 1: Causes and effects* (pp. 134–167). New York: Freeman.

McCLURE, P. A. (1981). Sex-biased litter reduction in food-restricted wood rats (*Neotoma floridana*). *Science* **211,** 1058–1060.

McCORMICK, D. A., & THOMPSON, R. F. (1984). Cerebellum: Essential involvement in the classically conditioned eyelid response. *Science* **223,** 296–299.

McCOSKER, J. E. (1977a). Flashlight fishes. *Scientific American* **236**(3), 106–114.

McCOSKER, J. E. (1977b). Fright posture of the plesiopid fish *Calloplesiops altivelis*: An example of Batesian mimicry. *Science* **197,** 400–401.

McDONALD, J. F. (1983). The molecular basis of adaptation: A critical review of relevant ideas and observations. *Annual Review of Ecology and Systematics* **14,** 77–102.

McEWEN, B. S. (1976). Interactions between hormones and nerve tissue. *Scientific American* **235**(1), 48–58.

McEWEN, B. S. (1981). Neural gonadal steroid actions. *Science* **211,** 1303–1311.

McFARLAND, D. J. (1977). Decision making in animals. *Nature* **269,** 15–21.

McFARLAND, D. J., & SIBLY, R. M. (1975). The behavioural final common path. *Philosophical Transactions of the Royal Society* **B270,** 265–293.

McGAUGH, J. L. (1983). Hormonal influences on memory. *Annual Review of Psychology* **34,** 297–323.

McGINTY, D. J., & SIEGEL, J. M. (1983). Sleep states. In E. Satinoff & P. Teitelbaum (Eds.), *Handbook of behavioral neurobiology. Vol. 6: Motivation* (pp. 105–181). New York: Plenum.

McGIVERN, R. F. (1985). Androgens and prenatal alcohol exposure. *Science* **229,** 195–196.

McGIVERN, R. F., CLANCY, A. N., HILL, M. A., & NOBLE, E. P. (1984). Prenatal alcohol exposure alters adult expression of sexually dimorphic behavior in the rat. *Science* **224,** 896–898.

McGREGOR, P. K., KREBS, J. R., & PERRINS, C. M. (1981). Song repertoires and lifetime reproductive success in the great tit (*Parus major*). *American Naturalist* **118,** 149–159.

McGUE, M., GOTTESMAN, I. I., & RAO, D. C. (1986). The analysis of schizophrenia family data. *Behavioral Genetics* **16,** 75–87.

McHUGH, P. R., & MORAN, T. H. (1985). The stomach: A conception of its dynamic role in satiety. In J. M. Sprague & A. N. Epstein (Eds.), *Progress in psychobiology and physiological psychology. Vol. 11* (pp. 197–232). Orlando, FL: Academic Press.

McKAY, R. D. G., HOCKFIELD, S., JOHANSEN, J., THOMPSON, I., & FREDERICKSEN,

K. (1983). Surface molecules identify groups of growing axons. *Science* **222,** 788–794.

McKILLUP, S. C. (1983). A behavioural polymorphism in the marine snail *Nassarius pauperatus*: Geographic variation correlated with food availability, and differences in competitive ability between morphs. *Oecologia* **56,** 58–66.

McKINNEY, F., BARRETT, J., & DERRICKSON, S. R. (1978). Rape among mallards. *Science* **201,** 281–282.

McMINN, M. R. (1984). Mechanisms of energy balance in obesity. *Behavioral Neuroscience* 98, 375–393.

McNAUGHTON, N. (1989). *Biology and emotion.* Cambridge: Cambridge University Press.

McNICHOLL, M. K. (1973). Habituation of aggressive responses to avian predators by terns. *Auk* **90,** 902–904.

MECH, L. D. (1966). *The wolves of Isle Royale.* Washington, DC: U.S. Government Printing Office.

MEDDIS, R. (1975). On the functions of sleep. *Animal Behaviour* **23,** 676–691.

MEDDIS, R. (1979). The evolution and function of sleep. In D. A. Oakley & H. C. Plotkin (Eds.), *Brain, behaviour and evolution* (pp. 99–125). London: Methuen.

MEDDIS, R., PEARSON, A. J. D., & LANGFORD, G. (1973). An extreme case of healthy insomnia. *Electroencephalography and Clinical Neurophysiology* **35,** 213–214.

MEFFORD, I. N., BAKER, T. L., BOEHME, R., FOUTZ, A. S., CIARENELLO, R. D., BARCHAS, J. D., & DEMENT, W. C. (1983). Narcolepsy: Biogenic amine deficits in an animal model. *Science* **220,** 629–631.

MEIER, P. T. (1983). Relative brain size within the North American Sciuridae. *Journal of Mammalogy* **64,** 642–647.

MEIKLE, D. B., TILFORD, B. L., & VESSEY, S. H. (1984). Dominance rank, secondary sex ratio, and reproduction of offspring in polygynous primates. *American Naturalist* **124,** 173–188.

MENAKER, M. (1972). Nonvisual light reception. *Scientific American* **226**(3), 22–29.

MENAKER, M., & BINKLEY, S. (1981). Neural and endocrine control of circadian rhythms in the vertebrates. In J. Aschoff (Ed.), *Handbook of behavioral neurobiology: Vol. 4. Biological rhythms* (pp. 243–255). New York: Plenum.

MENZEL, R., & ERBER, J. (1978). Learning and memory in bees. *Scientific American* **239**(1), 80–87.

MERTON, P. A. (1972). How we control the contraction of our muscles. *Scientific American* **226**(5), 30–37.

MEYER, D. B. (1977). The avian eye and its adaptations. In F. Crescitelli (Ed.), *Handbook of sensory physiology, Vol. VII/5* (pp. 549–611). Berlin: Springer-Verlag.

MICHAEL, C. R. (1969). Retinal processing of visual images. *Scientific American* **220**(5), 104–114.

MICHELSEN, A. (1974). Hearing in invertebrates. In W. D. Keidel & W. D. Neff (Eds.), *Handbook of sensory physiology, Vol V/1* (pp. 389–422). Berlin: Springer-Verlag.

MICHENER, C. D. (1985). From solitary to eusocial: Need there be a series of intervening species? In B. Hölldobler & M. Lindauer (Eds.), *Experimental behavioral ecology and sociobiology* (pp. 293–305). Sunderland, MA: Sinauer.

MICZEK, K. A. (1983). Ethopharmacology of aggression, defense, and defeat. In E. C. Simmel, M. E. Hahn & K. Walters (Eds.), *Aggressive behavior: Genetic and neural approaches* (pp. 147–166). Hillsdale, NJ: Erlbaum.

MILES, F. A., & EVARTS, E. V. (1979). Concepts of motor organization. *Annual Review of Psychology* **30,** 327–362.

MILINSKI, M., & REGELMANN, K. (1985). Fading short-term memory for patch quality in sticklebacks. *Animal Behaviour* **33,** 678–680.

MILLER, D. B., & GOTTLIEB, G. (1978). Maternal vocalizations of mallard ducks (*Anas platyrhynchos*). *Animal Behaviour* **26,** 1178–1194.

MILLER, M. W. (1986). Effects of alcohol on the generation and migration of cerebral cortical neurons. *Science* **233,** 1308–1311.

MILNE, L. J., & MILNE, M. (1976). The social behavior of burying beetles. *Scientific American* **235**(2), 84–89

MINEKA, S., & SUOMI, S. J. (1978). Social separation in monkeys. *Psychological Bulletin* **85,** 1376–1400.

MINORS, D. S., & WATERHOUSE, J. M. (1984). The sleep-wakefulness rhythm, exogenous and endogenous factors (in man). *Experientia* **40,** 410–416.

MINORS, D. S., & WATERHOUSE, J. M. (1986). Circadian rhythms and their mechanisms. *Experientia* **42,** 1–13.

MISHKIN, M., & APPENZELLER, T. (1987). The anatomy of memory. *Scientific American* **256,** 80–89.

MOCK, D. W. (1984). Siblicidal aggression and resource monopolization in birds. *Science* **225,** 731–733.

MOCK, D. W. (1985). Knockouts in the nest. *Natural History* **94,** 54–61.

MOEHLMAN, P. D. (1987). Social organization in jackals. *American Scientist* **75,** 366–375.

MOLLON, J. D. (1982). Colour vision and colour blindness. In H. B. Barlow & J. D. Mollon (Eds.), *The senses* (pp. 165–191). Cambridge: Cambridge University Press.

MONTGOMERY, J. C., & MACDONALD, J. A. (1987). Sensory tuning of lateral line receptors in Antarctic fish to the movements of planktonic prey. *Science* **235,** 195–196.

MOORE, C. L. (1984). Maternal contributions to the development of masculine sexual behavior in laboratory rats. *Developmental Psychobiology* **17,** 347–356.

MOORE, C. L. (1985). Development of mammalian sexual behavior. In E. S. Gollin (Ed.), *The comparative development of adaptive skills: Evolutionary implications* (pp. 19–55). Hillsdale, NJ: Erlbaum.

MOORE, C. L. (1990). Comparative development of vertebrate sexual behavior: Levels, cascades, and webs. In D. A. Dewsbury (Ed.), *Contemporary issues in comparative psychology* (pp. 278–299). Sunderland, MA: Sinauer.

MOORE, F. R. (1978). Interspecific aggression: Toward whom should a mockingbird be aggressive? *Behavioural Ecology and Sociobiology* **3,** 173–176.

MOORE, R. Y., & LENN, N. J. (1972). A retinohypothalamic projection in the rat. *Journal of Comparative Neurology* **146,** 1–14.

MOORE-EDE, M. C., SULZMAN, F. M., & FULLER, C. A. (1982). *The clocks that time us: Physiology of the circadian timing system.* Cambridge: Harvard University Press.

MORIARTY, D. J. (1976). The adaptive nature of bird flocks: a review. *Biologist* **58,** 62–79.

MORRISON, A. R. (1983). A window on the sleeping brain. *Scientific American* **248**(4), 94–102.

MORRISON, R. S., KORNBLUM, H. I., LESLIE, F. M., & BRADSHAW, R. A. (1987). Trophic stimulation of cultured neurons from neonatal brain by epidermal growth factor. *Science* **238,** 72–75.

MORSE, D. H. (1980). *Behavioral mechanisms in ecology*. Cambridge: Harvard University Press.

MORSE, R. A. (1972). Environmental control in the beehive. *Scientific American* 226(4), 92–98.

MORTON, E. S. (1975). Ecological sources of selection on avian sounds. *American Naturalist* 109, 17–34.

MORTON, E. S. (1977). On the occurrence and significance of motivation-structural rules in some bird and mammal sounds. *American Naturalist* 111, 855–869.

MORTON, M. L., & SHERMAN, P. W. (1978). Effects of a spring snowstorm on behavior, reproduction, and survival of Belding's ground squirrels. *Canadian Journal of Zoology* 56, 2578–2590.

MORUZZI, G., & MAGOUN, H. (1949). Brain stem reticular formation and activation of the EEG. *Electroencephalography and Clinical Neurophysiology* 1, 455–473.

MOSKOWITZ, B. A. (1978). The acquisition of language. *Scientific American* 239(5), 92–108.

MOYER, K. E. (1980). *Neuroanatomy*. New York: Harper & Row.

MOYNIHAN, M. (1970). Control, suppression, decay, disappearance and replacement of displays. *Journal of Theoretical Biology* 29, 85–112.

MUELLER, H. C., & PARKER, P. G. (1980). Naive ducklings show different cardiac response to hawk than to goose models. *Behaviour* 74, 101–113.

MÜLLER-SCHWARTZ, D. (1972). Responses of young black-tailed deer to predator odors. *Journal of Mammalogy* 53, 393–394.

MUNN, C. A. (1986). Birds that 'cry wolf.' *Nature* 319, 143–145.

MURIE, J. O., & McLEAN, I. G. (1980). Copulatory plugs in ground squirrels. *Journal of Mammalogy* 61, 355–356.

MUZET, A., LIBERT, J.-P., & CANDAS, V. (1984). Ambient temperature and human sleep. *Experientia* 40, 425–429.

MYERS, J. P. (1978). One deleterious effect of mobbing in the southern lapwing (*Vanellus chilensis*). *Auk* 95, 419–420.

NARINS, P. M., & CAPRANICA, R. R. (1976). Sexual differences in the auditory system of the tree frog *Eleutherodactylus coqui*. *Science* 192, 378–380.

NATHANS, J. (1989). The genes for color vision. *Scientific American* 260, 42–49.

NATHANS, J., PIANTANIDA, T. P., EDDY, R. L., SHOWS, T. B., & HOGNESS, D. S. (1986). Molecular genetics of inherited variation in human color vision. *Science* 232, 203–210.

NATHANSON, J. A., & GREENGARD, P. (1977). "Second messengers" in the brain. *Scientific American* 237(2), 108–119.

NAUTA, W. J. H., & FEIRTAG, M. (1986). *Fundamental neuroanatomy*. New York: Freeman.

NEGUS, N. C., & BERGER, P. J. (1977). Experimental triggering of reproduction in a natural population of *Microtus montanus*. *Science* 196, 1230–1231.

NELSON, D. A., & MARLER, P. (1989). Categorical perception of a natural stimulus continuum: Birdsong. *Science* 244, 976–978.

NESTLER, E. J., WALAAS, S. I., & GREENGARD, P. (1984). Neuronal phosphoproteins: Physiological and clinical implications. *Science* 225, 1357–1364.

NICHOLLS, J. G., & VAN ESSEN, D. (1974). The nervous system of the leech. *Scientific American* 230(1), 38–48.

NICOL, S. E., & GOTTESMAN, I. I. (1983). Clues to the genetics and neurobiology of schizophrenia. *American Scientist* 71, 398–404.

NIRENBERG, M., WILSON, S., HIGASHIDA, H., ROTTER, A., KRUEGER, K., BUSIS, N., RAY, R., KENIMER, J. G., & ADLER, M. (1983). Modulation of synapse formation by cyclic adenosine monophosphate. *Science* **222**, 794–799.

NISBET, I. C. T. (1973). Courtship-feeding, egg-size and breeding success in common terns. *Nature* **241**, 141–142.

NOMURA, M. (1984). The control of ribosome synthesis. *Scientific American* **250**(1), 102–114.

NORGREN, R., & GRILL, H. (1982). Brainstem control of ingestive behavior. In D. W. Pfaff (Ed.), *The physiological mechanisms of motivation* (pp. 99–131). New York: Springer.

NORTHCUTT, R. G. (1984). Evolution of the vertebrate central nervous system: Patterns and processes. *American Zoologist* **24**, 701–716.

NORTON-GRIFFITHS, M. (1969). The organization, control and development of parental feeding in the oystercatcher (*Haematopus ostralegus*). *Behaviour* **34**, 55–114.

NOTTEBOHM, F. (1984). Birdsong as a model in which to study brain processes related to learning. *Condor* **86**, 227–236.

NOTTEBOHM, F., STOKES, T. M., & LEONARD, C. M. (1976). Central control of song in the canary, *Serinus canarius*. *Journal of Comparative Neurology* **165**, 457–486.

NUMBERS, R. L. (1982). Creationism in 20th-century America. *Science* **218**, 538–544.

O'BRIEN, D. F. (1982). The chemistry of vision. *Science* **218**, 961–966.

O'CONNOR, R. J., & BROWN, R. A. (1977). Prey depletion and foraging strategy in the oystercatcher, *Haematopus ostralegus*. *Oecologia* **27**, 75–92.

OGLESBY, J. M., LANIER, D. L., & DEWSBURY, D. A. (1981). The role of prolonged copulatory behavior in facilitating reproductive success in male Syrian golden hamsters (*Mesocricetus auratus*) in a competitive mating situation. *Behavioral Ecology and Sociobiology* **8**, 47–54.

OJEMANN, G., & MATEER, C. (1979). Human language cortex: Localization of memory, syntax, and sequential motorphoneme identification systems. *Science* **205**, 1401–1403.

OLDS, J. E., & FOBES, J. L. (1981). The central basis of motivation: Intracranial self-stimulation studies. *Annual Review of Psychology* **32**, 523–574.

OLDS, J., & MILNER, P. (1954). Positive reinforcement produced by electrical stimulation of septal area and other regions of rat brain. *Journal of Comparative and Physiological Psychology* **47**, 419–427.

OLTON, D. S. (1979). Mazes, maps, and memory. *American Psychologist*, **34**, 583–596.

OLTON, D. S., & PAPAS, B. C. (1979). Spatial memory and hippocampal function. *Neuropsychologia* **17**, 669–682.

OLTON, D. S., & SAMUELSON, R. J. (1976). Remembrance of places past: Spatial memory in rats. *Journal of Experimental Psychology: Animal Behavior Processes* **2**, 97–116.

O'MALLEY, B. W., & SCHRADER, W. T. (1976). The receptors of steroid hormones. *Scientific American* **234**(2), 32–43.

OSTER, G. (1984). Muscle sounds. *Scientific American* **250**(3), 108–114.

OSTWALD, P. F., & PELTZMAN, P. (1974). The cry of the human infant. *Scientific American* **230**, 84–90.

OWINGS, D. H., & COSS, R. G. (1977). Snake mobbing by California ground squirrels: Adaptive variation and ontogeny. *Behaviour* **62**, 50–69.

OWINGS, D. H., & LEGER, D. W. (1980). Chatter vocalizations of California ground squirrels: Predator and social-role specificity. *Zeitschrift für Tierpsychologie* **54**, 163–184.

OWINGS, D. H., & VIRGINIA, R. A. (1978). Alarm calls of California ground squirrels (*Spermophilus beecheyi*). *Zeitschrift für Tierpsychologie* **46,** 58–70.

OYAMA, S. (1985). *The ontogeny of information: Developmental systems and evolution.* New York: Cambridge University Press.

PACKER, C. (1977). Reciprocal altruism in olive baboons. *Nature* **265**, 441–443.

PACKER, C. (1979a). Inter-troop transfer and inbreeding avoidance in *Papio anubis. Animal Behaviour* **27,** 1–36.

PACKER, C. (1979b). Male dominance and reproductive activity in *Papio anubis. Animal Behaviour* **27**, 37–45.

PACKER, C. (1985). Dispersal and inbreeding avoidance. *Animal Behaviour* **33**, 676–678.

PAGEL, M. D., & HARVEY, P. H. (1989). Taxonomic differences in the scaling of brain on body weight among mammals. *Science* **244,** 1589–1593.

PAIGE, K. N., & WHITHAM, T. G. (1985). Individual and population shifts in flower color by scarlet gilia: A mechanism for pollinator tracking. *Science* **227**, 315–317.

PALCA, J. (1989). Sleep researchers awake to possibilities. *Science* **245**, 351–352.

PALMER, J. D. (1990). The rhythmic lives of crabs. *BioScience* **40**, 352–358.

PANKSEPP, J., SIVIY, S., & NORMANSELL, L. (1984). The psychobiology of play: Theoretical and methodological perspectives. *Neuroscience and Biobehavioral Reviews* **8,** 465–492.

PANTEV, C., HOKE, M., LUTKENHONER, B., & LEHNERTZ, K. (1989). Tonotopic organization of the auditory cortex: Pitch versus frequency representation. *Science* **246,** 486–488.

PAPPENHEIMER, J. R. (1976). The sleep factor. *Scientific American* **235**(2), 24–29.

PARKER, D. E. (1980). The vestibular apparatus. *Scientific American* **243**(5), 118–135.

PARTRIDGE, B. L. (1982). The structure and function of fish schools. *Scientific American* **246**(6), 114–123.

PASSINGHAM, R. E. (1975). Changes in the size and organization of the brain in man and his ancestors. *Brain, Behavior and Evolution* **11,** 73–90.

PASSINGHAM, R. E. (1979). Brain size and intelligence in man. *Brain, Behavior and Evolution* **16,** 253–270.

PATON, J. A., & NOTTEBOHM, F. N. (1984). Neurons generated in the adult brain are recruited into functional circuits. *Science* **225,** 1046–1048.

PATTERSON, F. (1978). The gestures of a gorilla: Sign language acquisition in another pongid species. *Brain and Language* **5,** 72–97.

PATTERSON, F., & LINDEN, E. (1981). *The education of Koko.* New York: Holt, Rinehart and Winston.

PEARLMAN, C. A. (1979). REM sleep and information processing: Evidence from animal studies. *Neuroscience and Biobehavioral Reviews* **3**, 57–68.

PENNOCK-ROMAN, M. (1984). Assortative marriage for physical characteristics in newlyweds. *American Journal of Physical Anthropology* **64,** 185–190.

PEPPERBERG, I. M. (1983). Cognition in the African Grey parrot: Preliminary evidence for auditory/vocal comprehension of the class concept. *Animal Learning and Behavior* **11**, 179–185.

PETERS, P. J., BRONSON, F. H., & WHITSETT, J. M. (1972). Neonatal castration and intermale aggression in mice. *Physiology & Behavior* **8**, 265–268.

PETRI, H. L. (1991). *Motivation: Theory, research, and applications.* Belmont, CA: Wadsworth.

PETRIE, M. (1983). Female moorhens compete for small fat males. *Science* **220**, 413–415.

PETRINOVICH, L. (1990). Avian song development: Methodological and conceptual issues. In D. A. Dewsbury (Ed.), *Contemporary issues in comparative psychology* (pp. 340–359). Sunderland, MA: Sinauer.

PETTIGREW, J. D. (1986). Flying primates? Megabats have the advanced pathway from eye to midbrain. *Science* **231**, 1304–1306.

PFAFF, D. W. (1982). Motivational concepts: Definitions and distinctions. In D. W. Pfaff (Ed.), *The physiological mechanisms of motivation* (pp. 3–24). New York: Springer-Verlag.

PHOENIX, C. H., COPENHAVER, K. H., & BRENNER, R. M. (1976). Scanning electron microscopy of penile papillae in intact and castrated male rats. *Hormones and Behavior* **7**, 217–222.

PICKLES, J. O. (1988). *An introduction to the physiology of hearing.* London: Academic Press.

PIETREWICZ, A. T., & KAMIL, A. C. (1979). Search image formation in the blue jay (*Cyanocitta cristata*). *Science* **204**, 1332–1333.

PINEL, J. P. J., & TREIT, D. (1978). Burying as a defensive response in rats. *Journal of Comparative and Physiological Psychology* **92**, 708–712.

PIRKE, K. M., KOCKOTT, G., & DITTMAR, F. (1974). Psychosexual stimulation and plasma testosterone in man. *Archives of Sexual Behavior* **3**, 577–584.

PLESZCZYNSKA, W. K. (1978). Microgeographic prediction of polygyny in the lark bunting. *Science* **201**, 935–936.

PLOMIN, R. (1989). Environment and genes: Determinants of behavior. *American Psychologist* **44**, 105–111.

PLOMIN, R. (1990). The role of inheritance in behavior. *Science* **248**, 183–188.

PLOMIN, R., DEFRIES, J. C., & LOEHLIN, J. C. (1977). Genotype-environment interaction and correlation in the analysis of human behavior. *Psychological Bulletin* **84**, 309–322.

PLOMIN, R., DEFRIES, J. C., & MCCLEARN, G. E. (1980). *Behavioral genetics: A primer.* San Francisco: Freeman.

POLA, Y. V., & SNOWDON, C. T. (1975). The vocalizations of pygmy marmosets (*Cebuella pygmaea*). *Animal Behaviour* **23**, 826–842.

POLICANSKY, D. (1982). The asymmetry of flounders. *Scientific American* **246**(5), 116–123.

POLIS, G. A., MYERS, C. A., & HESS, W. R. (1984). A survey of intraspecific predation within the class Mammalia. *Mammal Review* **14**, 187–198.

POLITCH, J. A., & HERRENKOHL, L. R. (1979). Prenatal stress reduces maternal aggression by mice offspring. *Physiology and Behavior* **23**, 415–418.

POLLACK, G. S., & HOY, R. R. (1979). Temporal pattern as a cue for species-specific calling song recognition in crickets. *Science* **204**, 429–432.

POND, C. M. (1977). The significance of lactation in the evolution of mammals. *Evolution* **31**, 177–199.

POSNER, M. I., PETERSEN, S. E., FOX, P. T., & RAICHLE, M. E. (1988). Localization of cognitive operations in the human brain. *Science* **240,** 1627–1631.

POWELL, G. V. N. (1974). Experimental analysis of the social value of flocking by starlings (*Sturnus vulgaris*) in relation to predation and foraging. *Animal Behaviour* **22,** 501–505.

POWLEY, T. L. (1977). The ventromedial hypothalamic syndrome, satiety, and a cephalic phase hypothesis. *Psychological Review* **84,** 89–126.

PROVINE, R. R. (1981). Development of wing-flapping and flight in normal and flap-deprived chicks (*Gallus domesticus*). *Developmental Psychobiology* **14,** 279–291.

PROVINE, R. R. (1982). Pre-flight development of bilateral coordination in the chick (*Gallus domesticus*): Effects of induced bilateral wing asymmetry. *Developmental Psychobiology* **15,** 245–255.

PROVINE, R. R. (1984). Wing-flapping during development and evolution. *American Scientist* **72,** 448–455.

PTASHNE, M. (1989). How gene activators work. *Scientific American,* **260**(1), 40–47.

PULLIAM, H. R., PYKE, G. H., & CARACO, T. (1982). The scanning behavior of juncos: A game-theoretical approach. *Journal of Theoretical Biology* **95,** 89–103.

PURTON, A. C. (1978). Ethological categories of behaviour and some consequences of their conflation. *Animal Behaviour* **26,** 653–670.

PURVES, D., & LICHTMAN, J. W. (1985). *Principles of neural development.* Sunderland, MA: Sinauer.

PUSEY, A. E. (1980). Inbreeding avoidance in chimpanzees. *Animal Behaviour* **28,** 543–552.

PYKE, G. H. (1978). Are animals efficient harvesters? *Animal Behaviour* **26,** 241–250.

PYKE, G. H., PULLIAM, H. R., & CHARNOV, E. L. (1977). Optimal foraging: A selective review of theory and tests. *Quarterly Review of Biology* **52,** 137–154.

QUEVEDO, W. C., JR., FITZPATRICK, T. B., & JIMBOW, K. (1985). Human skin color: Origin, variation and significance. *Journal of Human Evolution* **14,** 43–56.

QUINN, W. G., & GOULD, J. L. (1979). Nerves and genes. *Nature* **278,** 19–23.

RADINSKY, L. (1982). Some cautionary notes on making inferences about relative brain size. In E. Armstrong & D. Falk (Eds.), *Primate brain evolution: Methods and concepts* (pp. 29–37). New York: Plenum.

RAINBOW, T. C., SNYDER, L., BERCK, D. J., & MCEWEN, B. S. (1984). Correlation of muscarinic receptor induction in the ventromedial hypothalamic nucleus with the activation of feminine sexual behavior by estradiol. *Neuroendocrinology* **39,** 476–480.

RAKIC, P. (1985). Limits of neurogenesis in primates. *Science* **227,** 1054–1055.

RAKIC, P., & SIDMAN, R. L. (1973). Weaver mutant mouse cerebellum: Defective neuronal migration secondary to abnormality of Bergmann glia. *Proceedings of the National Academy of Science of the USA* **70,** 240–244.

RALLS, K., BRUGGER, K., & BALLOU, J. (1979). Inbreeding and juvenile mortality in small populations of ungulates. *Science* **206,** 1101–1103.

RALPH, C. L. (1983). Evolution of pineal control of endocrine function in lower vertebrates. *American Zoologist* **23,** 597–605.

RALPH, M. R., FOSTER, R. G., DAVIS, F. C., & MENAKER, M. (1990). Transplanted suprachiasmatic nucleus determines circadian period. *Science* **247,** 975–978.

RAPOPORT, J. L. (1989). The biology of obsessions and compulsions. *Scientific American* **260,** 82–89.

RAPP, P. E. (1987). Why are so many biological systems periodic? *Progress in Neurobiology* **29,** 261–273.

RECHTSCHAFFEN, A., GILLILAND, M. A., BERGMANN, B. M., & WINTER, J. B. (1983). Physiological correlates of prolonged sleep deprivation in rats. *Science* **221,** 182–184.

REED, E. S. (1982). An outline of a theory of action systems. *Journal of Motor Behavior* **14,** 98–134.

REEVES, G. A., & PLUM, F. (1969). Hyperphagia, rage, and dementia accompanying a ventromedial hypothalamic neoplasm. *Archives of Neurology* **20,** 616–624.

REINBERG, A., & LAGOGUEY, M. (1978). Circadian and circannual rhythms in sexual activity and plasma hormones (FSH, LH, testosterone) of five human males. *Archives of Sexual Behavior* **7,** 13–30.

RENFREW, J. W., & HUTCHINSON, R. R. (1983). The motivation of aggression. In E. Satinoff & P. Teitelbaum (Eds.), *Handbook of behavioral neurobiology. Vol. 6: Motivation* (pp. 511–541). New York: Plenum.

REPPERT, S. M., WEAVER, D. R., RIVKEES, S. A., & STOPA, E. G. (1988). Putative melatonin receptors in a human biological clock. *Science* **242,** 78–81.

RICHARD, A. (1985). *Primates in nature.* New York: Freeman.

RIDLEY, M. (1978). Paternal care. *Animal Behaviour* **26,** 904–932.

RIECHERT, S. E. (1986). Spider fights as a test of evolutionary game theory. *American Scientist* **74,** 604–610.

RINN, W. E. (1984). The neuropsychology of facial expression: A review of the neurological and psychological mechanisms for producing facial expressions. *Psychological Bulletin* **95,** 52–77.

RISKA, B., & ATCHLEY, W. R. (1985). Genetics of growth predict patterns of brain-size evolution. *Science* **229,** 668–671.

RISTAU, C. A., & ROBBINS, D. (1982). Language in the great apes: A critical review. *Advances in the Study of Behavior* **12,** 141–255.

ROBERTS, A., & MACKIE, G. O. (1980). The giant axon escape system of a hydrozoan medusa, *Aglantha digitale. Journal of Experimental Biology* **84,** 303–318.

ROBERTS, R. C. (1979). The evolution of avian food-storing behavior. *American Naturalist* **114,** 418–438.

ROBERTSON, D. R. (1972). Social control of sex reversal in a coral-reef fish. *Science* **177,** 1007–1009.

ROBERTSON, R. J., & BIERMANN, G. C. (1979). Parental investment strategies determined by expected benefits. *Zeitschrift für Tierpsychologie* **50,** 124–128.

ROBINSON, D. A. (1972). Eye movements evoked by collicular stimulation in the alert monkey. *Vision Research* **12,** 1795–1808.

ROBINSON, J. G. (1979a). An analysis of the organization of vocal communication in the titi monkey *Callicebus moloch. Zeitschrift für Tierpsychologie* **49,** 381–405.

ROBINSON, J. G. (1979b). Vocal regulation of use of space by groups of titi monkeys *Callicebus moloch. Behavioral Ecology and Sociobiology* **5,** 1–6.

RODIECK, R. W., & BRENIG, R. K. (1983). Retinal ganglion cells: Properties, types, genera, pathways and trans-species comparisons. *Brain, Behavior and Evolution* **23**, 121–164.

ROEDER, K. D. (1965). Moths and ultrasound. *Scientific American* **212**(4), 94–102.

ROEDER, K. D. (1967). *Nerve cells and insect behavior*. Cambridge, MA: Harvard University Press.

ROEDER, K. D. (1970). Episodes in insect brains. *American Scientist* **58**, 378–389.

ROFFWARG, H. P., MUZIO, J. N., & DEMENT, W. C. (1966). Ontogenetic development of the human sleep-dream cycle. *Science* **152**, 604–619.

ROITBERG, B. D., & MYERS, J. H. (1978). Adaptation of alarm pheromone responses of the pea aphid *Acyrthosiphon pisum* (Harris). *Canadian Journal of Zoology* **56**, 103–108.

ROITBLAT, H. L. (1987). *Introduction to comparative cognition*. New York: Freeman.

ROPER, T. J. (1983). Learning as a biological phenomenon. In T. R. Halliday & P. J. B. Slater (Eds.), *Animal Behaviour. Vol. 3: Genes, development and learning* (pp. 178–212). New York: Freeman.

ROSENBLATT, J. S. (1965). Effects of experience on sexual behavior in male cats. In F. A. Beach (Ed.), *Sex and behavior* (pp. 416–439). New York: Wiley.

ROSENZWEIG, M. R. (1984). Experience, memory, and the brain. *American Psychologist* **39**, 365–376.

ROSENZWEIG, M. R., BENNETT, E. L., & DIAMOND, M. C. (1972). Brain changes in response to experience. *Scientific American* **226**(2), 22–29.

ROTH, T., LUTZ, T., KRAMER, M., & TIETZ, E. (1977). The relationship between objective and subjective evaluations of sleep in insomniacs. *Sleep Research* **6**, 178.

ROUTMAN, E. O. (1985). Aspects of the reproductive behavior and morphology of *Perithemis tenera* Say (Odonata:Libellulidae). MS Thesis, University of Nebraska-Lincoln.

ROUTTENBERG, A. (1978). The reward system of the brain. *Scientific American* **239**(5), 154–164.

ROWE, M. P., & OWINGS, D. H. (1978). The meaning of the sound of rattling by rattlesnakes to California ground squirrels. *Behaviour* **66**, 252–267.

ROWELL, T. (1974). The concept of social dominance. *Behavioral Biology* **11**, 131–154.

ROZIN, P. (1976). The selection of foods by rats, humans, and other animals. *Advances in the Study of Behavior* **6**, 21–76.

ROZIN, P. R., & KALAT, J. W. (1971). Specific hungers and poison avoidance as adaptive specializations of learning. *Psychological Review* **78**, 459–480.

RUMBAUGH, D. M., SAVAGE-RUMBAUGH, E. S., & SCANLON, J. L. (1982). The relationship between language in apes and human beings. In J. L. Fobes & J. E. King (Eds.), *Primate behavior* (pp. 361–385). New York: Academic.

RUSAK, B. (1977). The role of the suprachiasmatic nuclei in the generation of circadian rhythms in the golden hamster, *Mesocricetus auratus*. *Journal of Comparative Physiology (A)* **118**, 145–164.

RUSHTON, W. A. H. (1975). Visual pigments and color blindness. *Scientific American* **232**(2), 64–74.

RUTBERG, A. T. (1986). Dominance and its fitness consequences in American bison cows. *Behaviour* **96**, 62–91.

RYAN, M. J. (1990). Signals, species, and sexual selection. *American Scientist* **78**, 46–52.

SACKETT, G. P. (1966). Monkeys reared in

visual isolation with pictures as visual input: Evidence for an innate releasing mechanism. *Science* **154,** 1468–1472.

SADUN, A. A., SCHAECHTER, J. D., & SMITH, L. E. H. (1984). A retinohypothalamic pathway in man: Light mediation of circadian rhythms. *Brain Research* **302,** 371–377.

SALT, G. W. (1979). A comment on the use of the term "emergent properties." *American Naturalist* **113,** 145–148.

SAPOLSKY, R. M. (1990). Stress in the wild. *Scientific American* **262,** 116–123.

SAR, M. (1984). Estradiol is concentrated in tyrosine hydroxylase-containing neurons of the hypothalamus. *Science* **223,** 938–940.

SARNAT, H. B., & NETSKY, M. G. (1981). *Evolution of the nervous system.* New York: Oxford University Press.

SASSIN, J. F., PARKER, D. C., MACE, J. W., GOTLIN, R. W., JOHNSON, L. C., & ROSSMAN, L. G. (1969). Human growth hormone release: Relation to slow-wave sleep and sleep-waking cycles. *Science* **165,** 513–515.

SAVAGE-RUMBAUGH, E. S. (1984). Verbal behavior at a procedural level in the chimpanzee. *Journal of the Experimental Analysis of Behavior* **41,** 223–250.

SAVAGE-RUMBAUGH, E. S. (1988). A new look at ape language: Comprehension of vocal speech and syntax. In D. W. Leger (Ed.), *Comparative perspectives in modern psychology. Nebraska Symposium on Motivation, Vol. 35* (pp. 201–255). Lincoln: University of Nebraska Press.

SCAIFE, M. (1976). The response to eye-like shapes by birds. I. The effect of context: A predator and a strange bird. *Animal Behaviour* **24,** 195–199.

SCHALLER, G. B. (1963). *The mountain gorilla.* Chicago: University of Chicago Press.

SCHELLER, R. H., & AXEL, R. (1984). How genes control an innate behavior. *Scientific American* **250**(3), 54–62.

SCHERER, K. (1986). Vocal affect expression: A review and a model for future research. *Psychological Bulletin* **99,** 143–165.

SCHILDKRAUT, J. J., SCHANBERG, S. M., BREESE, G. R., & KOPIN, I. J. (1967). Norepinephrine metabolism and drugs used in the affective disorders: A possible mechanism of action. *American Journal Psychiatry* **124,** 600–608.

SCHLEIDT, W. M. (1974). How "fixed" is the fixed action pattern? *Zeitschrift für Tierpsychologie* **36,** 184–211.

SCHNAPF, J. L., & BAYLOR, D. A. (1987). How photoreceptor cells respond to light. *Scientific American* **256,** 40–47.

SCHRIER, A. M. (1984). Learning how to learn: The significance and current status of learning set formation. *Primates* **25,** 95–102.

SCHWARTZ, J. H. (1980). The transport of substances in nerve cells. *Scientific American* **242**(4), 152–171.

SCHWARTZ, R. S., & BRUNZELL, J. D. (1981). Increase of adipose tissue lipoprotein lipase activity with weight loss. *Journal of Clinical Investigation* **67,** 1425–1430.

SCOTT, J. P. (1983). A systems approach to research on aggressive behavior. In E. C. Simmel, M. E. Hahn, & J. K. Walters (Eds.), *Aggressive behavior: Genetic and neural approaches* (pp. 1–18). Hillsdale, NJ: Erlbaum.

SEARCY, W. A., MARLER, P., & PETERS, S. S. (1985). Songs of isolation-reared sparrows function in communication, but are significantly less effective than learned songs. *Behavioral Ecology and Sociobiology* **17**, 223–229.

SEEMAN, P., ULPIAN, C., BERGERON, C., RIEDERER, P., JELLINGER, K., GABRIEL, E., REYNOLDS, G. P., & TOURTELLOTTE, W. W. (1984). Bimodal distribution of dopamine receptor densities in brains of schizophrenics. *Science* **225**, 728–731.

SELIGMAN, M. E. P. (1970). On the generality of the laws of learning. *Psychological Review* **77**, 406–418.

SEYFARTH, R. M. (1977). A model of social grooming among adult female monkeys. *Journal of Theoretical Biology* **65**, 671–698.

SEYFARTH, R. M., & CHENEY, D. L. (1980). The ontogeny of vervet monkey alarm calling behavior: A preliminary report. *Zeitschrift für Tierpsychologie* **54**, 37–56.

SEYFARTH, R. M., CHENEY, D. L., & MARLER, P. (1980a). Monkey responses to three different alarm calls: Evidence of predator classification and semantic communication. *Science* **210**, 801–803.

SEYFARTH, R. M., CHENEY, D. L., & MARLER, P. (1980b). Vervet monkey alarm calls: Semantic communication in a free-ranging primate. *Animal Behaviour* **28**, 1070–1094.

SHAPIRO, C. M., BORTZ, R., MITCHELL, D., BARTEL, P., & JOOSTE, P. (1981). Slow-wave sleep: A recovery period after exercise. *Science* **214**, 1253–1254.

SHAPIRO, D. Y. (1983). Distinguishing behavioral interactions from visual cues as causes of adult sex change in a coral reef fish. *Hormones and Behavior* **17**, 424–432.

SHAW, E. A. G. (1974). The external ear. In W. D. Keidel & W. D. Neff (Eds.), *Handbook of Sensory Physiology.* Vol. 5/1 (pp. 455–490). New York: Springer-Verlag.

SHEARD, M. H. (1979). Testosterone and aggression. In M. Sandler (Eds.), *Psychopharmacology of aggression* (pp. 111–121). New York: Raven Press.

SHEPHER, J. (1971). Mate selection among second generation kibbutz adolescents and adults: Incest avoidance and negative imprinting. *Archives of Sexual Behavior* **1**, 293–307.

SHEPHERD, G. M. (1983). *Neurobiology.* New York: Oxford University Press.

SHEPHERD, G. M. (1988). *Neurobiology* (2nd ed.). New York: Oxford University Press.

SHERMAN, P. W. (1977). Nepotism and the evolution of alarm calls. *Science* **197**, 1246–1253.

SHERMAN, P. W. (1980). The limits of ground squirrel nepotism. In G. W. Barlow & J. Silverberg (Eds.), *Sociobiology: Beyond nature nurture?* AAAS Special Symposium 35. Boulder, CO: Westview.

SHERMAN, P. W. (1981). Electrophoresis and avian genealogical analyses. *Auk* **98**, 419–422.

SHERMAN, P. W. (1988). The levels of analysis. *Animal Behaviour* **36**, 616–619.

SHERRY, D. F. (1984). What food-hoarding birds remember. *Canadian Journal of Psychology* **38**, 304–321.

SHERRY, D. F., VACCARINO, A. L., BUCKENHAM, K., & HERZ, R. S. (1989). The hippocampal complex of food-storing birds. *Brain, Behavior and Evolution* **34**, 308–317.

SHETTLEWORTH, S. J. (1972). Constraints on learning. *Advances in the Study of Behavior* **4**, 1–68.

SHETTLEWORTH, S. J. (1983). Memory in food-hoarding birds. *Scientific American* **248**(3), 102–110.

SHETTLEWORTH, S. J. (1984). Learning and behavioural ecology. In J. R. Krebs & N. B. Davies (Eds.), *Behavioural ecology:*

An evolutionary approach (pp. 179–194). Sunderland, MA: Sinauer.

SHIELDS, W. M., & SHIELDS, L. M. (1983). Forcible rape: An evolutionary perspective. *Ethology and Sociobiology* **4**, 115–136.

SHOREY, H. H. (1977). Pheromones. In T. A. Sebeok (Ed.), *How animals communicate* (pp. 137–163). Bloomington: Indiana University Press.

SHORT, R. V. (1984). Breast feeding. *Scientific American* **250**(4), 35–41.

SIEGEL, A., & POTT, C. B. (1988). Neural substrates of aggression and flight in the cat. *Progress in Neurobiology* **31**, 261–283.

SIEGFRIED, W. R., & UNDERHILL, L. G. (1975). Flocking as an anti-predator strategy in doves. *Animal Behaviour* **23**, 504–508.

SIH, A. (1984). The behavioral response race between predator and prey. *American Naturalist* **123**, 143–150.

SILVER, R. (1990). Biological timing mechanisms with special emphasis on the parental behavior of doves. In D. A. Dewsbury (Ed.), *Contemporary issues in comparative psychology* (pp. 252–277). Sunderland, MA: Sinauer.

SILVERMAN, M. S., & CLOPTON, B. M. (1977). Plasticity of binaural interactions I. Effect of early auditory deprivation. *Journal of Neurophysiology* **40**, 1266–1274.

SIMAN, R., BAUDRY, M., & LYNCH, G. (1985). Regulation of glutamate receptor binding by the cytoskeletal protein fodrin. *Nature* **313**, 225–228.

SIMMEL, E. C., HAHN, M. E., & WALTERS, J. K. (1983). *Aggressive behavior: Genetic and neural approaches.* Hillsdale, NJ: Erlbaum.

SIMON, N. G., GANDELMAN, R., & GRAY, J. L. (1984). Endocrine induction of intermale aggression in mice: A comparison of hormonal regimens and their relationship to naturally occurring behavior. *Physiology and Behavior* **33**, 379–383.

SIMON, N. G., & WHALEN, R. E. (1987). Sexual differentiation of androgen-sensitive and estrogen-sensitive regulatory systems for aggressive behavior. *Hormones and Behavior* **21**, 493–500.

SJÖSTRÖM, L. (1980). Fat cells and body weight. In A. J. Stunkard (Ed.), *Obesity.* Philadelphia: Saunders.

SKINNER, B. F. (1981). Selection by consequences. *Science* **213**, 501–504.

SKINNER, B. F. (1987). Whatever happened to psychology as the science of behavior? *American Psychologist* **42**, 780–786.

SLATER, P. J. B. (1976). Tidal rhythm in a seabird. *Nature* **264**, 636–638.

SLATER, P. J. B. (1983). The study of communication. In T. R. Halliday & P. J. B. Slater (Eds.), *Animal behaviour. Vol. 2: Communication* (pp. 9–42). New York: Freeman.

SLATER, P. J. B. (1985). *An introduction to ethology.* London: Cambridge University Press.

SMALL, M. F. (1988). Female primate sexual behavior and conception: Are there really sperm to spare? *Current Anthropology* **29**, 81–100.

SMART, J. L. (1981). Undernutrition and aggression. In P. F. Brain & D. Benton (Eds.), *Multidisciplinary approaches to aggression research* (pp.179–191). Amsterdam: Elsevier/North Holland.

SMITH, C. (1985). Sleep states and learning: A review of the animal literature. *Neuroscience and Biobehavioral Reviews* **9**, 157–168.

SMITH, C. C. (1968). The adaptive nature of social organization in the genus of tree squirrels *Tamiasciurus*. *Ecological Monographs* **38,** 31–63.

SMITH, D. G. (1981). The association between rank and reproductive success of male rhesus monkeys. *American Journal of Primatology* **1,** 83–90.

SMITH, D. G. & HOLLAND, D. H. (1974). Mobbing red-winged blackbirds force American kestrel into water. *Auk* **91,** 843–844.

SMITH, M. J., & GRAVES, H. B. (1978). Some factors influencing mobbing behavior in barn swallows (*Hirundo rustica*). *Behavioral Biology* **23,** 355–372.

SMITH, M. S. (1984). Effects of the intensity of the sucking stimulus and ovarian steroids on pituitary gonadotropin-releasing hormone receptors during lactation. *Biology of Reproduction* **31,** 548–555.

SMITH, R. J. F. (1981). Effect of food deprivation on the reaction of Iowa darters (*Etheostoma exile*) to skin extract. *Canadian Journal of Zoology* **59,** 558–560.

SMITH, S. M. (1977). Coral snake pattern recognition and stimulus generalization by naive great kiskadees (Aves:Tyrannidae). *Nature* **265,** 535–536.

SMITH, S. M. (1980). Responses of naive temperate birds to warning coloration. *American Midland Naturalist* **103,** 346–352.

SMITH, W. J. (1969). Messages of vertebrate communication. *Science* **165,** 145–150.

SMITH, W. J. (1977). *The behavior of communicating: An ethological approach.* Cambridge: Harvard University Press.

SMITH, W. J. (1985a). Consistency and change in communication. In G. Zivin (Ed.), *The development of expressive behavior: Biology-environment interactions* (pp. 51–76). New York: Academic.

SMITH, W. J. (1985b). Comparative study of the ontogeny of communication. In E. S. Gollin (Ed.), *The comparative development of adaptive skills: Evolutionary implications* (pp. 173–205). Hillsdale, NJ: Erlbaum.

SMITH-GILL, S. J. (1983). Developmental plasticity: Conversion versus phenotypic modulation. *American Zoologist* **23,** 47–55.

SMOTHERMAN, W. P., BELL, R. W., HERSHBERGER, W. A., & COOVER, G. D. (1978). Orientation to rat pup cues: Effects of maternal experiential history. *Animal Behaviour* **26,** 265–273.

SNOWDON, C. T. (1983). Ethology, comparative psychology, and animal behavior. *Annual Review of Psychology* **34,** 63–94.

SNOWDON, C. T. (1990). Mechanisms maintaining monogamy in monkeys. In D. A. Dewsbury (Ed.), *Contemporary issues in comparative psychology* (pp. 225–251). Sunderland, MA: Sinauer.

SNOWDON, C. T., FRENCH, J. A., & CLEVELAND, J. (1986). Ontogeny of primate vocalizations: Models from bird song and human speech. In D. M. Taub & F. A. King (Eds.), *Current perspectives in primate social dynamics* (pp. 389–402). New York: Van Nostrand Reinhold.

SNOWDON, C. T., & HODUN, A. (1981). Acoustic adaptations in pygmy marmoset contact calls: Locational cues vary with distances between conspecifics. *Behavioral Ecology and Sociobiology* **9,** 295–300.

SNYDER, S. H. (1977). Opiate receptors and internal opiates. *Scientific American* **236**(3), 44–56.

SNYDER, S. H. (1980). *Biological aspects of mental disorder.* New York: Oxford University Press.

SNYDER, S. H. (1984a). Drug and neurotransmitter receptors in the brain. *Science* **224,** 22–31.

SNYDER, S. H. (1984b). Medicated minds. *Science 84*, (Nov.), 141–142.

SNYDER, S. H. (1985). The molecular basis of communication between cells. *Scientific American* 253(4), 132–141.

SNYDER, S. H., BANERJEE, S. P., YAMAMURA, H. I., & GREENBERG, D. (1974). Drugs, neurotransmitters, and schizophrenia. *Science* 184, 1243–1253.

SOHN, J. J. (1977). Socially induced inhibition of genetically determined maturation in the platyfish, *Xiphophorus maculatus. Science* 195, 199–201.

SOMERS, R. L., & KLEIN, D. C. (1984). Rhodopsin kinase activity in the mammalian pineal gland and other tissues. *Science* 226, 182–184.

SOUTHWICK, C. H., & CLARK, L. H. (1968). Interstrain differences in aggressive behavior and exploratory activity of inbred mice. *Communications in Behavioral Biology* IA, 49–59.

SPARBER, S. B. (1985). Androgens and prenatal alcohol exposure. *Science* 229, 195.

SPECTOR, R., & JOHANSON, C. E. (1989). The mammalian choroid plexus. *Scientific American* 261, 68–74.

SPERRY, R. W. (1963). Chemoaffinity in the orderly growth of nerve fiber patterns and connections. *Proceedings of the National Academy of Science of the USA* 50, 703–710.

SQUIRE, L. R. (1987). *Memory and brain.* New York: Oxford University Press.

STACEY, P. B., & BOCK, C. E. (1978). Social plasticity in the acorn woodpecker. *Science* 202, 1298–1300.

STADDON, J. E. R. (1983). *Adaptive behavior and learning.* New York: Oxford University Press.

STAHL, F. W. (1987). Genetic recombination. *Scientific American* 256, 90–101.

STEBBINS, G. L. (1982). *Darwin to DNA, molecules to humanity.* San Francisco: Freeman.

STEBBINS, W. C. (1983). *The acoustic sense of animals.* Cambridge: Harvard University Press.

STEIN, G. S., STEIN, J. S., & KLEINSMITH, L. J. (1975). Chromosomal proteins and gene regulation. *Scientific American* 232(2), 46–57.

STEIN, P. S. G. (1978). Motor systems, with specific reference to the control of locomotion. *Annual Review of Neuroscience* 1, 61–81.

STEKLIS, H. D. (1985). Primate communication, comparative neurology, and the origin of language re-examined. *Journal of Human Evolution* 14, 157–173.

STERNGLANZ, S. H., GRAY, J. L., & MURAKAMI, M. (1977). Adult preferences for infantile facial features: An ethological approach. *Animal Behaviour* 25, 108–115.

STEVENS, C. F. (1984). Biophysical studies of ion channels. *Science* 225, 1346–1350.

STRASSMANN, B. I. (1981). Sexual selection, parental care, and concealed ovulation in humans. *Ethology and Sociobiology* 2, 31–40.

STRATTON, G. E., & UETZ, G. W. (1981). Acoustic communication and reproductive isolation in two species of wolf spiders. *Science* 214, 575–577.

STRICKBERGER, M. W. (1986). The structure and organization of genetic material. *American Zoologist* 26, 769–780.

STRICKER, E. M. (1983). Brain neurochemistry and the control of food intake. In E. Satinoff & P. Teitelbaum (Eds.), *Handbook of behavioral neurobiology. Vol. 6: Motivation* (pp. 329–366). New York: Plenum.

STRUHSAKER, T. T. (1967). Auditory communication among vervet monkeys (*Cercopithecus aethiops*). In S. A. Altmann (Ed.), *Social communication among primates*. Chicago: University of Chicago Press.

STRYER, L. (1987). The molecules of visual excitation. *Scientific American* **257,** 42–50.

SUGA, N. (1990). Biosonar and neural computation in bats. *Scientific American* **262**(6), 60–68.

SVARE, B. B. (ED.). (1983). *Hormones and aggressive behavior*. New York: Plenum.

SVARE, B. (1988). Genotype modulates the aggression-promoting quality of progesterone in pregnant mice. *Hormones and Behavior* **22,** 90–99.

SWAAB, D. F., & FLIERS, E. (1985). A sexually dimorphic nucleus in the human brain. *Science* **228,** 1112–1115.

SWAIMAN, K. F., & WRIGHT, F. S. (1975). *The practice of pediatric neurology*. St. Louis: Mosby.

SYMONS, D. (1979). *The evolution of human sexuality*. New York: Oxford University Press.

TAKEDA, Y., OHLENDORF, D. H., ANDERSON, W. F., & MATTHEWS, B. W. (1983). DNA-binding proteins. *Science* **221,** 1020–1026.

TASKINEN, M.-R., & NIKKILLA, E. A. (1981). Lipoprotein lipase of adipose tissue and skeletal muscle in human obesity: Response to glucose and semistarvation. *Metabolism* **30,** 810–817.

TELLEGEN, A., HORN, J. M., & LEGRAND, R. G. (1969). Opportunity for aggression as a reinforcer in mice. *Psychonomic Science* **14,** 104–105.

TENAZA, R. (1985). Songs of hybrid gibbons (*Hylobates lar* x *H. muelleri*). *American Journal of Primatology* **8,** 249–253.

TERRACE, H. S. (1985). On the nature of animal thinking. *Neuroscience and Biobehavioral Reviews* **9,** 643–652.

TERRACE, H. S., PETTITO, L. A., & BEVER, T. G. (1979). Can an ape create a sentence? *Science* **206,** 891–900.

THIESSEN, D., & GREGG, B. (1980). Human assortative mating and genetic equilibrium: An evolutionary perspective. *Ethology and Sociobiology* **1,** 111–140.

THOMAN, E. B., WAITE, S. P., DESANTIS, D. T., & DENENBERG, V. H. (1979). Ontogeny of sleep and wake states in the rabbit. *Animal Behaviour* **27,** 95–106.

THOMPSON, R. F. (1985). *The brain: An introduction to neuroscience*. New York: Freeman.

THOMPSON, R. F. (1986). The neurobiology of learning and memory. *Science* **233,** 941–947.

THOMSON, K. S. (1984). Reductionism and other isms in biology. *American Scientist* **72,** 388–390.

THORNHILL, R. (1979). Adaptive female-mimicking behavior in a scorpionfly. *Science* **205,** 412–414.

THORNHILL, R. (1980). Sexual selection in the black-tipped hangingfly. *Scientific American* **246**(6), 162–172.

TIERNEY, A. J. (1986). The evolution of learned and innate behavior: Contributions from genetics and neurobiology to a theory of behavioral evolution. *Animal Learning and Behavior* **14,** 339–348.

TIMBERLAKE, W. (1990). Natural learning in laboratory paradigms. In D. A. Dewsbury (Ed.), *Contemporary issues in comparative psychology* (pp. 31–54). Sunderland, MA: Sinauer.

TINBERGEN, J. M. (1981). Foraging decisions in starlings (*Sturnus vulgaris* L.). *Ardea* **69,** 1–66.

TINBERGEN, N. (1948). Social releasers and

the experimental method required for their study. *Wilson Bulletin* **60,** 6–52.

TINBERGEN, N. (1951). *The study of instinct.* New York: Oxford University Press.

TINBERGEN, N. (1963). On aims and methods of ethology. *Zeitschrift für Tierpsychologie* **20,** 410–433.

TOATES, F. (1980). *Animal behaviour: A systems approach.* Chichester, England: Wiley.

TOATES, F. M. (1983). Models of motivation. In T. R. Halliday & P. J. B. Slater (Eds.), *Animal behaviour. Vol. 1: Causes and effects* (pp. 168–196). New York: Academic.

TOATES, F. M., & ARCHER, J. (1978). A comparative review of motivational systems using classical control theory. *Animal Behaviour* **26,** 368–380.

TOLMAN, E. C. (1948). Cognitive maps in rats and men. *Psychological Review* **55,** 189–208.

TOLMAN, E. C., RITCHIE, B. F., & KALISH, D. (1946). Studies in spatial learning I. Orientation and the short-cut. *Journal of Experimental Psychology* **36,** 13–24.

TOPOFF, H. R. (1972). The social behavior of army ants. *Scientific American* **227**(5), 70–79.

TOPOFF, H. (1984). Invasion of the booty snatchers. *Natural History* **93(10),** 78–85.

TORAN-ALLERAND, C. D. (1978). Gonadal hormones and brain development: Cellular aspects of sexual differentiation. *American Zoologist* **18,** 553–565.

TOSTESON, D. C. (1981). Lithium and mania. *Scientific American* **244**(4), 164-

TOWE, A. L., & LUSCHEI, E. S. (EDS.). (1981). *Handbook of behavioral neurobiology. Vol. 5: Motor coordination* (p. 174). New York: Plenum.

TRANEL, D., & DAMASIO, A. R. (1985).

Knowledge without awareness: An autonomic index of facial expression in prosopagnosics. *Science* **228,** 1453–1454.

TREHERNE, J. E., & FOSTER, W. A. (1980). The effects of group size on predator avoidance in a marine insect. *Animal Behaviour* **28,** 1119–1122.

TRIVERS, R. L. (1974). Parent-offspring conflict. *American Zoologist* **14,** 249–264.

TRIVERS, R. (1985). *Social evolution.* Menlo Park, CA: Benjamin/Cummings.

TRUNE, D. R., & SLOBODCHIKOFF, C. N. (1976). Social effects of roosting on the metabolism of the pallid bat (*Antrozus pallidus*). *Mammalogy* **57,** 656–653.

TULVING, E. (1989). Remembering and knowing the past. *American Scientist* **77,** 361–367.

TULVING, E., & SCHACTER, D. L. (1990). Priming and human memory systems. *Science* **247,** 301–306.

TUTTLE, M. D., & RYAN, M. J. (1981). Bat predation and the evolution of frog vocalizations in the neotropics. *Science* **214,** 677–678.

UDRY, J. R., & MORRIS, N. M. (1968). Distribution of coitus in the menstrual cycle. *Nature* **220,** 593–596.

UNWIN, N., & HENDERSON, R. (1984). The structure of proteins in biological membranes. *Scientific American* **250**(2), 78–94.

URSIN, H. (1981). Neuroanatomical basis of aggression. In P. F. Brain & D. Benton (Eds.), *Multidisciplinary approaches to aggression research* (pp. 269–293). New York: Elsevier/North Holland.

VALE, J. R. (1980). *Genes, environment, and behavior: An interactionist approach.* New York: Harper & Row.

VALE, J. R., RAY, D., & VALE, C. A. (1974). Neonatal androgen treatment and sexual behavior in males of three inbred strains of mice. *Developmental Psychobiology* **7**, 483–488.

VAN ABEELEN, J. H. F., & VAN DER KROON, P. H. W. (1967). Nijmegen waltzer—a new neurological mutant in the mouse. *Genetical Research* **10**, 117–118.

VANDENBERGH, J. G. (1983). The role of hormones in synchronizing mammalian reproductive behavior. In J. F. Eisenberg & D. G. Kleiman (Eds.), *Advances in the study of mammalian behavior* (pp. 95–112). Special Publications Series, American Society of Mammalogists.

VAN DEN BERGHE, P. L. (1983). Human inbreeding avoidance: Culture in nature. *Behavioral and Brain Science* **6**, 91–123.

VANDER WALL, S. B. (1982). An experimental analysis of cache recovery in Clark's nutcracker. *Animal Behaviour* **30**, 84–94.

VAN DYKE, C., & BYCK, R. (1982). Cocaine. *Scientific American* **246**(3), 128–141.

VEHRENCAMP, S. L. (1979). The roles of individual, kin, and group selection in the evolution of sociality. In P. Marler & J. G. Vandenbergh (Eds.), *Handbook of behavioral neurobiology. Vol. 3: Social behavior and communication* (pp. 351–394). New York: Plenum.

VELTHUIS, H. H. W. (1985). The honeybee queen and social organization of her colony. In B. Hölldobler & M. Lindauer (Eds.), *Experimental behavioral ecology and sociobiology* (pp. 343–357). Sunderland, MA: Sinauer.

VERTES, R. P. (1984). Brainstem control of the events of REM sleep. *Progress in Neurobiology* **22**, 241–288.

VERTES, R. P. (1986). A life-sustaining function for REM sleep: A theory. *Neuroscience and Biobehavioral Reviews* **10**, 371–376.

VOM SAAL, F. S. (1983). Models of early hormonal effects on intrasex aggression in mice. In B. B. Svare (Ed.), *Hormones and aggressive behavior* (pp. 197–222). New York: Plenum.

VON BEKESY, G. (1957). The ear. *Scientific American* **197**(2), 66–78.

VON FRISCH, K. (1974). Decoding the language of the bee. *Science* **185**, 663–668.

VON HOLST, D. (1985). Coping behaviour and stress physiology in male tree shrews (*Tupaia belangeri*). In B. Hölldobler & M. Lindauer (Eds.), *Experimental behavioral ecology and sociobiology* (pp. 461–470). Sunderland, MA: Sinauer.

VON HOLST, E., & VON SAINT PAUL, U. (1962). Electrically controlled behavior. *Scientific American* **206**(3), 50–59.

VON SCHILCHER, F. (1977). A mutation which changes courtship song in *Drosophila melanogaster*. *Behavioral Genetics* **7**, 251–259.

VROMAN, G. M. (1987). Aphasia as a communicative disorder: Application of the levels concept. In G. Greenberg, & E. Tobach (Eds.) *Cognition, language and consciousness: Integrative levels* (pp. 99–116). Hillsdale, NJ: Erlbaum.

WAAGE, J. K. (1979). Dual function of the damselfly penis: Sperm removal and transfer. *Science* **203**, 916–918.

WACHTEL, S. (1977). H-Y antigen and the genetics of sex determination. *Science* **198**, 797–799.

WADDINGTON, K. D., & HEINRICH, B. (1979). The foraging movements of bumblebees on vertical inflorescences: An experimental analysis. *Journal of Comparative Physiology* **134**, 113–117.

WAHLSTEN, D. (1977). Heredity and brain structure. In A. Oliverio (Ed.), *Genetics, environment and intelligence* (pp. 93–115). Amsterdam: North Holland.

WALDMAN, B. (1981). Sibling recognition in toad tadpoles: The role of experience. *Zeitschrift für Tierpsychologie* **56**, 341–358.

WALDMAN, B. (1986). Preference for unfamiliar siblings over familiar non-siblings in American toad (*Bufo americanus*) tadpoles. *Animal Behaviour* **34**, 48–53.

WALDVOGEL, J. A. (1990). The bird's eye view. *American Scientist* **78**, 342–353.

WALKER, D. G. (1983). Golden eagle killing mobbing carrion crows. *British Birds* **76**, 312.

WALKER, J. M., & BERGER, R. J. (1980). The ontogenesis of sleep states, thermogenesis, and thermoregulation in the Virginia opossum. *Developmental Psychobiology* **13**, 443–454.

WALKER, J. M., GLOTZBACH, S. F., BERGER, R. J., & HELLER, H. C. (1977). Sleep and hibernation in ground squirrels (*Citellus* spp.): Electrophysiological observations. *American Journal of Physiology* **233**, 213–221.

WALKER, L. E., WALKER, J. M., PALCA, J. W., & BERGER, R. J. (1983). A continuum of sleep and shallow torpor in fasting doves. *Science* **221**, 194–195.

WALKER, M. L., WILSON, M. E., & GORDON, T. P. (1983). Female rhesus monkey aggression during the menstrual cycle. *Animal Behaviour* **31**, 1047–1054.

WALLACE, P. (1977). Individual discrimination of humans by odor. *Physiology and Behavior* **19**, 577–579.

WARD, I. L. (1972). Prenatal stress feminizes and demasculinizes the behavior of males. *Science* **175**, 82–84.

WARD, I. L., & WEISZ, J. (1980). Maternal stress alters plasma testosterone in fetal males. *Science* **207**, 328–329.

WARD, S. (1977). Invertebrate neurogenetics. *Annual Review of Genetics* **11**, 414–450.

WASER, P. M. (1975). Experimental playbacks show vocal mediation of avoidance in a forest monkey. *Nature* **255**, 56–58.

WASER, P. M., & BROWN, C. H. (1984). Is there a "sound window" for primate communication? *Behavioral Ecology and Sociobiology* **15**, 73–76.

WASER, P. M., & WILEY, R. H. (1979). Mechanisms and evolution of spacing in animals. In P. Marler & J. G. Vandenbergh (Eds.), *Handbook of behavioral neurobiology. Vol. 3: Social behavior and communication* (pp. 159–223). New York: Plenum.

WASSERSUG, R. (1986). How does a tadpole know when to metamorphose? A theory linking environmental and hormonal cues. *Journal of Theoretical Biology* **118**, 171–181.

WATSON, J. D., & CRICK, F. C. (1953a). Molecular structure of nucleic acids: A structure for deoxyribose nucleic acids. *Nature* **171**, 737–738.

WATSON, J. D., & CRICK, F. C. (1953b). Genetical implications of the structure of deoxyribonucleic acid. *Nature* **171**, 964–967.

WATT, W. B., CARTER, P. A., & DONOHUE, K. (1986). Females' choice of "good genotypes" as mates is promoted by an insect mating system. *Science* **233**, 1187–1190.

WEALE, R. A. (1974). Natural history of optics. In H. Davson & L. T. Graham, Jr. (Eds.), *The eye: Comparative physiology, Vol. 6* (pp. 1–110). New York: Academic.

WEATHERHEAD, P. J. (1979). Do savannah sparrows commit the Concorde fallacy? *Behavioral Ecology and Sociobiology* **5**, 373–381.

WEBB, W. B. (1974). Sleep as an adaptive

process. *Perceptual and Motor Skills* **38,** 1023–1027.

WEBSTER, D. B., & WEBSTER, M. (1980). Morphological adaptations of the ear in the rodent family Heteromyidae. *American Zoologist* **20,** 247–254

WEISKRANTZ, L. (1980). Varieties of residual experience. *Quarterly Journal of Experimental Psychology* **32,** 365–386.

WEITZMAN, E.D. (1981). Sleep and its disorders. *Annual Review of Neuroscience* **4,** 381–417.

WERKER, J. F. (1989). Becoming a native listener. *American Scientist* **77,** 54–59.

WEST, M. J., & KING, A. P. (1980). Enriching cowbird song by social deprivation. *Journal of Comparative and Physiological Psychology* **94,** 263–270.

WEST, M. J., & KING, A. P. (1988). Coming to terms with the everyday language of comparative psychology. In D. W. Leger (Ed.), *Comparative perspectives in modern psychology. Nebraska Symposium on Motivation, Vol. 35* (pp. 51–89). Lincoln: University of Nebraska Press.

WEST, M. J., KING, A. P., & EASTZER, D. H. (1981). The cowbird: Reflections on development from an unlikely source. *American Scientist* **69,** 57–66.

WEST, M. J., KING, A. P., EASTZER, D. H., & STADDON, J. E. R. (1979). A bioassay of isolate cowbird song. *Journal of Comparative and Physiological Psychology* **93,** 124–133.

WEST, M. J., KING, A. P., & HARROCKS, T. J. (1983). Cultural transmission of cowbird song (*Molothrus ater*): Measuring its development and outcome. *Journal of Comparative Psychology* **97,** 327–337.

WEVER, E. G. (1974). The evolution of vertebrate hearing. In W. D. Keidel & W. D. Neff (Eds.), *Handbook of sensory physiology, Vol V/1* (pp. 423–454). Berlin: Springer-Verlag.

WHALEN, R. E. (1971). The concept of instinct. In J. L. McGaugh (Ed.), *Psychobiology* (pp. 53–72). New York: Academic.

WHALEN, R. E., & SIMON, N. G. (1984). Biological motivation. *Annual Review of Psychology* 35, 275–276.

WHITHAM, T. G. (1977). Coevolution of foraging in *Bombus*-nectar dispensing *Chilopsis*: A last dreg theory. *Science* **197,** 593–596.

WIDDOWSON, E. M. (1974). Changes in pigs due to undernutrition before birth, and for one, two, and three years afterward, and the effects of rehabilitation. *Advances in Experimental Medical Biology* **49,** 165–181.

WIESEL, T. N. (1982). Postnatal development of the visual cortex and the influence of environment. *Nature* **299,** 583–591.

WILEY, R. H., JR. (1978). The lek mating system of the sage grouse. *Scientific American* **238**(5), 114–125.

WILEY, R. H. (1983). The evolution of communication: Information and manipulation. In T. R. Halliday & P. J. B. Slater (Eds.), *Animal behaviour. Vol. 2: Communication* (pp. 156–189). New York: Freeman.

WILEY, R. H., & RICHARDS, D. G. (1978). Physical constraints on acoustic communication in the atmosphere: Implications for the evolution of animal vocalizations. *Behavioral Ecology and Sociobiology* **3,** 69–94.

WILEY, R. H., & WILEY, M. S. (1980). Territorial behavior of a blackbird: mechanisms of site-dependent dominance. *Behaviour* **73,** 130–154.

WILKINSON, G. S. (1984). Reciprocal food

sharing in the vampire bat. *Nature* **308,** 181–184.

WILLIAMS, G. C. (1966). *Adaptation and natural selection.* Princeton, NJ: Princeton University Press.

WILLIAMS, H. L., HOLLOWAY, F. A., & GRIFFITHS, W. J. (1973). Physiological psychology: Sleep. *Annual Review of Psychology* **24,** 279–316.

WILSON, A. C. (1985). The molecular basis of evolution. *Scientific American* **253**(4), 164–173.

WILSON, E. O. (1975a). Slavery in ants. *Scientific American* **232**(6), 32–36.

WILSON, E. O. (1975b). *Sociobiology: The new synthesis.* Cambridge: Belknap/Harvard.

WILSON, E. O. (1985a). The principles of caste evolution. In B. Hölldobler & M. Lindauer (Eds.), *Experimental behavioral ecology and sociobiology* (pp. 307–324). Sunderland, MA: Sinauer.

WILSON, E. O. (1985). The sociogenesis of insect colonies. *Science* **228,** 1489–1495.

WILSON, J. D., GEORGE, F. W., & GRIFFIN, J. E. (1981). The hormonal control of sexual development. *Science* **211,** 1278–1284.

WILSON, R. S. (1978). Synchronies in mental development: An epigenetic perspective. *Science* **202,** 939–948

WINGFIELD, J. C., BALL, G. F., DUFTY, A. M., JR., HEGNER, R. E., & RAMENOFSKY, M. (1987). Testosterone and aggression in birds. *American Scientist* **75,** 602–608.

WINICK, M. (1980). Nutrition and brain development. *Natural history* **89**(**12**), 6–13.

WISE, S. P., & DESIMONE, R. (1988). Behavioral neurophysiology: Insights into seeing and grasping. *Science* **242,** 736–741.

WITELSON, S. F. (1985). The brain connection: The corpus callosum is larger in left-handers. *Science* **229,** 665–668.

WITTENBERGER, J. F. (1981). *Animal social behavior.* Boston: Duxbury.

WITTENBERGER, J. F., & TILSON, R. L. (1980). The evolution of monogamy: A theoretical overview. *Annual Review of Ecology and Systematics* **11,** 197–232.

WOLFF, P. H. (1987). *Behavioral states and the expression of emotions in early infancy: New proposals for investigation.* Chicago: University of Chicago Press.

WOLFHEIM, J. H. (1977). A quantitative analysis of the organization of a group of captive talapoin monkeys (*Miopithecus talapoin*). *Folia Primatologica* **27,** 1–27.

WOOLFENDON, G. E., & FITZPATRICK, J. W. (1978). The inheritance of territory in group-breeding birds. *Bioscience* **28,** 104–108.

WYNNE-EDWARDS, V. C. (1962). *Animal dispersion in relation to social behaviour.* Edinburgh: Oliver & Boyd.

WYNNE-EDWARDS, V. C. (1964). Population control in animals. *Scientific American* **211**(2), 68–75.

YAGER, D. D., & HOY, R. R. (1986). The cyclopean ear: A new sense for the praying mantis. *Science* **231,** 727–729.

YARCZOWER, M., & HAZLETT, L. (1977). Evolutionary scales and anagenesis. *Psychological Bulletin* **84,** 1088–1097.

YARCZOWER, M., & YARCZOWER, B. S. (1979). In defense of anagenesis, grades, and evolutionary scales. *Psychological Bulletin* **86,** 880–883.

YOUNG, J. Z. (1967). Some comparisons between the nervous systems of cephalopods and mammals. In C. A. G. Wiersma (Ed.), *Invertebrate nervous systems: Their significance for mammalian neu-*

References

rophysiology (pp. 353–362). Chicago: University of Chicago Press.

ZAJONC, R. B. (1985a). Emotion and facial efference: A theory reclaimed. *Science* **228**, 15–21.

ZAJONC, R. B. (1985b). Emotions and facial expression. *Science* **230**, 608–610.

ZEPELIN, H. (1983). Normal age related change in sleep. In M. H. Chase & E. D. Weitzman (Eds.) *Sleep disorders: Basic and clinical research* (pp. 431–444). New York: Spectrum.

ZEPELIN, H., & RECHTSCHAFFEN, A. (1974). Mammalian sleep, longevity, and energy metabolism. *Brain, Behavior and Evolution* **10**, 425–470.

ZIMEN, E. (1976). On the regulation of pack size in wolves. *Zeitschrift für Tierpsychologie* **40**, 300–341.

ZONDERMAN, A. B., VANDENBERG, S. G., SPUHLER, K. P., & FAIN, P. R. (1977). Assortative marriage for cognitive abilities. *Behavioral Genetics* **7**, 261–271.

ZUCKER, R. S., KENNEDY, D., & SELVERSTON, A. I. (1971). Neuronal circuit mediating escape responses in crayfish. *Science* **173**, 645–650.

ZUCKER, R. S., & LANDO, L. (1986). Mechanism of transmitter release: Voltage hypothesis and calcium hypothesis. *Science* **231**, 574–579.

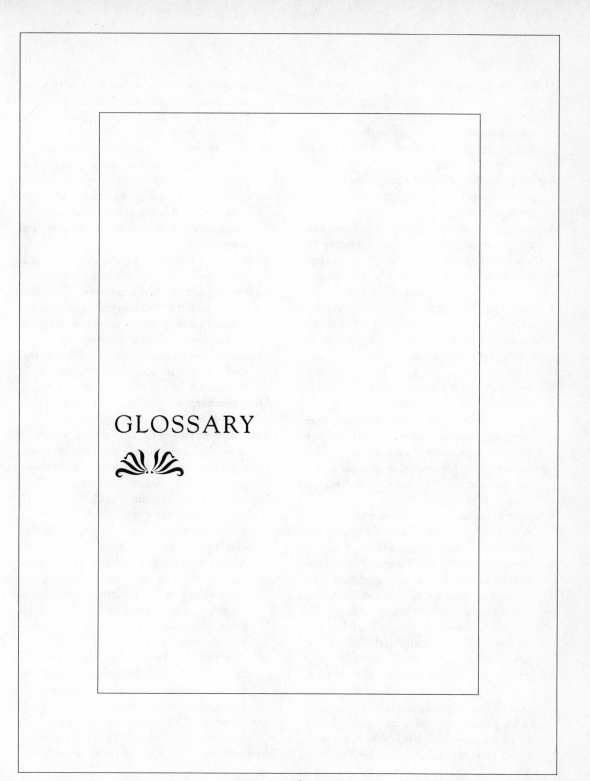

GLOSSARY

Absorption spectrum The quantity of light absorbed by a particular photopigment across the visible spectrum.

Accommodation Changing the shape of the lens of the eye to focus on light sources at different distances.

Action potential A brief change in polarity that travels, in a nondecremental fashion, along an axon.

Action-specific energy A motivational concept in which an individual increases its proclivity toward a certain action as time passes since it last engaged in that action. Also see *hydraulic model.*

Acuity The ability of a visual system to resolve detail.

Adaptation (1) Any feature of the phenotype (anatomic, physiologic, or behavioral) that tends to enhance fitness. (2) The process that leads to the evolution of an advantageous phenotypic feature.

Adaptive neutrality The persistence of a trait over time because it neither increases nor decreases reproductive success.

Aggression Any behavior that intends to inflict harm on another individual. Also see *agonistic behavior.*

Agonistic behavior Any behavior that occurs in a conflict situation, including both aggressive and defensive actions.

All-or-none-law A characteristic of action potentials in which the full magnitude and duration of polarity change occurs if and only if a critical threshold level of depolarization is achieved. If the threshold is not reached, an action potential will not be generated.

Allele A form of a gene that arises through mutation and which produces a different form of the original protein.

Alpha-fetoprotein A protein found in very young mammals that binds to estrogen molecules preventing their entry into cells.

Alpha motor neurons Neurons that produce contractions of skeletal muscle cells.

Altruism Any behavior that is beneficial to another but is costly to the actor.

Amino acid A class of compounds containing a carboxyl group and an amino group. Amino acids are assembled to form proteins.

Amygdala An assembly of nuclei in the temporal lobe. Among other functions, the amygdalas are involved in memory and emotion.

Anagenesis The theory that evolution proceeds from the simple to the complex.

Androgen insensitivity syndrome A condition in which a chromosomal male does not respond to androgenic hormones, and thus develops female characteristics.

Androgens A class of steroid hormone typically found in greater concentration in males than in females.

Anthropomorphism The attribution of humanlike traits to other species.

Appetitive phase The time during which an individual seeks out the opportunity to engage in a certain behavior, or to obtain a particular commodity. Also see *consummatory response; hydraulic model.*

Approach—avoidance conflict A situation in which an individual is attracted to a particular object or situation because of its beneficial attributes, and simultaneously avoids it because of its detrimental attributes.

Artificial selection Long-lasting changes in gene frequencies produced by breeding a group of organisms for a particular trait.

Associative conditioning Learning processes that link two or more stimuli with each other, stimuli with responses, or responses with consequences. Also see *classical conditioning; operant conditioning.*

Attenuation The dissipation of energy in a sound as it spreads away from its source.

Attractivity The state of being attractive to

individuals of the opposite sex. Also see *proceptivity; receptivity.*

Audiogram A graph showing the relationship between sound frequency and the minimum intensity required for detection.

Auditory nerve The axons that travel between the cochlea and brainstem. Part of the vestibulocochlear nerve, a cranial nerve.

Autonomic nervous system The portion of the peripheral nervous system that inervates the visceral organs.

Axon A filamentous extension from a neuron's cell body that conveys action potentials toward other cells.

Axon collateral A branch of an axon.

Ballistic movement A behavior that, once begun, can not be modified during the course of its performance.

Basal ganglia A collection of cerebral nuclei that function in motor control. The basal ganglia include the caudate, putamen, and globus pallidus.

Basilar membrane A membrane in the cochlea to which hair cells are attached. Movements of the basilar membrane displace the hair cells relative to the tectorial membrane, stimulating the hair cells.

Behavior The self-produced movements and postures of an animal that influence the animal's relationship to its environment.

Behavioral disorder Any form of behavior that tends to reduce the ability of the individual to cope with environmental demands.

Behavioral ecology The science that seeks to understand how behavior aids the adaptation of animals to their environments. Also see *sociobiology.*

Biotemporal space A scheme illustrating the two dimensions of biological science, the temporal (cause and consequence) and the level of organization (molecular to molar).

Caste A group of individuals of a certain age or anatomical form that differs from other such groups and that is behaviorally specialized.

Cataplexy A disorder in which the individual shows sudden loss of muscle tone, leading to collapse. Often accompanied by narcolepsy.

Catecholamines A class of neurotransmitter that contains dopamine, epinephrine, and norepinephrine.

Cell body The part of a cell that contains the nucleus.

Center-surround organization A characteristic of some visual neuron receptive fields in which light striking the central portion of the field has an effect on the neuron that is opposite to that found in the more peripheral parts of the field.

Central canal A tube extending the length of the spinal cord that contains cerebrospinal fluid.

Central nervous system The brain and spinal cord. Also see *peripheral nervous system.*

Central oscillator A neuron or group of neurons that control a repetitive movement, such as wing movements of flight.

Cerebellum A large, convoluted hindbrain structure, especially noted for its role in the coordination of movement and balance.

Cerebral cortex The outer layers of the cerebrum.

Cerebral hemispheres The two sides of the cerebrum.

Cerebral lobes Regions of the cerebrum defined by certain convolutions or neuron cell structure.

Cerebral ventricles Chambers within the brain that contain cerebrospinal fluid.

Cerebrospinal fluid The liquid, similar to blood plasma, that fills the cerebral ventricles, the central canal of the spinal cord, and the space between the brain and spinal cord and the inner surface of skull or spinal column.

Cerebrum The most anterior portion of the brain, divided into two hemispheres. The cerebrum participates in a wide variety of sensory, motor, and integrative processes.

Chain reflexes A series of motor neuron–muscle–sensory neuron units which, when stimulated, produces a rhythmic or repetitive movement.

Choroid plexus Capillary-rich tissue in the cerebral ventricles from which cerebrospinal fluid is secreted.

Chromosome Self-replicating structures consisting of DNA and proteins bound to it.

Circadian cycle A pattern of activity of a behavioral or physiological system that recurs approximately every 24 hours.

Circannual cycle A pattern of activity of a behavioral or physiological system that recurs approximately every year.

Classical conditioning A form of learning in which a neutral stimulus comes to evoke a response as a result of the neutral stimulus being paired with another stimulus that naturally evokes that response.

Closed phenotypic system Phenotypic characteristic whose form is only slightly affected by normal variations in environmental conditions.

Cochlea The organ that transduces sound into neural activity and begins the processing of information contained in sound.

Cochlear duct A fluid-filled chamber extending the length of the cochlea that lies between the vestibular and tympanic canals. Within it is the organ of Corti.

Cochlear nucleus The paired sets of neurons of the brainstem involved in auditory perception.

Command neurons Individual neurons or small sets of neurons which, when stimulated, initiate complete movement patterns or portions of such patterns.

Communication The production of informative signals and their reception and decoding by another individual.

Communication channel The sensory modality (such as audition, vision) in which communication occurs.

Comparative method A technique in which the similarities and dissimilarities of two or more species are evaluated in order to understand their evolutionary relationships.

Comparative psychology The branch of science that seeks to understand species differences in behavior. Also see *ethology*; *behavioral ecology*; *sociobiology*.

Conditioned response In classical conditioning, the behavioral or physiological response that comes to be evoked by a previously neutral stimulus, the conditioned stimulus.

Conditioned stimulus In classical conditioning, the previously neutral stimulus that is paired with an effective unconditioned stimulus.

Cones A class of photoreceptor that contains iodopsin. Cones are used in wavelength discrimination (color vision).

Congenital adrenal hyperplasia A condition in which female fetuses are masculinized by the androgens produced by the mother's adrenal glands.

Consummatory response The culmination of a behavioral sequence which, once performed, tends to lessen the probability of the behavior recurring in the near future. Also see *hydraulic model*.

Context Information (not contained in a signal) that is used by the recipient in its response to the signal.

Convergent evolution A type of evolutionary change in which two or more unrelated species evolve similar characteristics due to similar selection conditions.

Conversion A developmental process in which some feature of the phenotype can take on qualitatively distinct forms depending on the environmental conditions influencing the organism.

Cooperation Activities by two or more individuals that tend to result in greater average gains to participants than could be expected from individual efforts.

Copulation Sexual intercourse.

Core area The part of an individual's home range that is most heavily used.

Cornea The clear, outer structure of the eye, often rounded to accomplish refraction of incoming light.

Corpus callosum The large band of axons that cross the midline of the brain, connecting the cerebral hemispheres.

Correlational method A procedure for studying adaptation in which variations in environmental conditions are measured and compared to various forms of a phenotypic characteristic. The results do not imply that one variable causes the other, only that the variables are related.

Corticospinal tracts Bundles of axons that originate in primary motor cortex and which synapse on motor neurons of the spinal cord.

Cranial nerves The 12 pairs of nerves that exit from, or lead into, the vertebrate brain.

Cuckoldry The condition in which a male unknowingly cares for his mate's offspring who were sired by another male.

Cytoplasm The material comprising the interior of a cell. Also see *extracellular fluid*.

Deactivating enzyme An enzyme that removes or decomposes a neurotransmitter, curbing its effect on a postsynaptic neuron.

Defensive aggression Any action that lessens the chance of personal injury or resource loss to an aggressive competitor. Also see *agonistic behavior.*

Delayed sleep phase syndrome A condition in which an individual falls asleep on a period greater than 24 hours due to an inability to entrain to daily cues such as light.

Dendrite A short branchlike projection from the cell body of a neuron that specializes in the reception of signals from other neurons.

Dendritic spine Locations on dendrites that are adjacent to terminal buttons, forming the postsynaptic surface.

Depolarization A reduction in polarity of a neuronal membrane from its resting potential.

Design features Attributes of human language.

Development The age-related changes in the anatomy, physiology, and behavior of an individual during its lifespan.

Diethylstilbestrol (DES) A synthetic estrogen.

Differentiation In development, the process of tissue changing from being uniform in structure and function to being more specialized.

Directional selection A process in which individuals at one end of the phenotypic distribution have greater reproductive success than individuals at the other end of the distribution.

Displacement The ability of human language and some animal communication systems to provide information about objects or events that are distant in time or space.

Disruptive selection A process in which individuals with intermediate forms of a phenotype have lower reproductive success than do individuals at both extremes, producing a bimodal distribution.

Divergent evolution A situation in which two or more similar species evolve different characteristics due to different selection conditions.

DNA A molecular structure capable of replicating itself and which forms the core of the chromosomes and directs the synthesis of proteins.

Dorsal horn The upper (toward the back) portions of spinal cord grey matter. Most dorsal horn neurons are sensory.

Duality of patterning A characteristic of human language in which the smallest "particles" of speech (phonemes) can be rearranged to produce intelligible words.

Economic defense Protection of resources in such a way that the cost of defense is less than the benefits of the resource.

Electroencephalogram (EEG) Recordings made of the electrical activity of the brain by means of scalp electrodes.

Emergent property A characteristic of a structure or process that is not predictable from knowledge of its lower-level components.

Emotion A physiological state of an organism that prepares it for forthcoming actions. Behavioral changes (e.g., facial expressions, "freezing") often accompany the physiological state.

Encephalization quotient The ratio of an animal's brain size to body size relative to a typical animal of that body size.

Endplate potentials The polarity changes that occur on muscle cells when they are contacted by a neurotransmitter.

Entrainment The process by which an environmental stimulus resets a biological rhythm. Also see *zeitgeber.*

Enzyme A molecule that promotes a particular biochemical reaction.

Estradiol A type of estrogenic hormone.

Estrogens A class of steroid hormone typically found in greater concentration in females than in males.

Estrous The period of intense sexual motivation shown periodically by females of some mammalian species.

Ethogram A detailed list and description of the behavior patterns of a species.

Ethology The study of behavior, particularly as it naturally occurs in its ecological context. Also see *comparative psychology; behavioral ecology; sociobiology.*

Ethospecies Species that can be discriminated from one another only by means of their behavioral differences.

Eusociality A form of social organization in which there are one or more sterile castes.

Evolution A series of long-lasting transformations of the genetic composition of a population.

Evolutionary grade An arrangement of various forms of a phenotypic feature according to some criterion.

Evolutionary stable strategy A behavioral characteristic that cannot be bettered by some other form of that behavior.

Excitatory postsynaptic potential (EPSP) A depolarizing graded potential.

Experimental method A procedure for studying adaptation in which the phenotypic or selection variable is manipulated and the effect of the manipulation is measured.

Expressive aphasia A disorder in which a formerly fluent person is severely impaired in his or her ability to speak.

External auditory canal The opening between the outer ear and the tympanic membrane.

Extracellular fluid The liquid that surrounds the cells. Also see *cytoplasm.*

Extrafusal fiber The portion of muscle responsible for contraction. Also see *intrafusal fiber; muscle spindle.*

Extrapyramidal motor system The set of motor system structures other than motor cortex. Also see *basal ganglia; cerebellum.*

Familial route An evolutionary process in which complex social organizations originated due to interactions among closely related individuals.

Feedback effects (of hormones) A change in the concentration of certain hormones following the performance of a behavior pattern. Such changes may influence the probability or vigor of subsequent behaviors.

Feedforward A motivational process in which organisms anticipate departures from set point, and act in such a way as to avoid them.

Fitness An individual's reproductive success relative to the average reproductive success in the population.

Fixed action pattern A behavior pattern that is widespread in the population and that appears in complete or nearly complete form without the necessity of specific individual experience. Also see *instinct; modal action pattern.*

Founder population A small group that becomes separated from the main population and whose genes constitute the gene pool of the new population.

Fovea The central portion of the retina with greatest acuity. Also see *retinal periphery.*

Frequency The number of cycles per second of a waveform phenomenon such as sound.

Frequency-dependent selection A situation in which the average fitness of the bearers of a given phenotype depends on the commonness of the phenotype in the population. The more common the form, the lower the fitness.

Frustration–aggression hypothesis The notion that being thwarted in attainment of a goal results in aggression, and that all aggression can be traced to frustration.

Gamma motor neuron A class of motor neuron that regulates muscle length.

Ganglia Clusters of nerve cell bodies lying outside the central nervous system. Exceptions to this definition include the basal ganglia of the brain.

Ganglion cells Cells forming a retinal layer that receives input from intermediate cells and whose axons form the optic nerve.

Gap junction Sites where the axon of one neuron is connected, via protein tubes, with the membrane of another neuron.

Garcia effect The avoidance of certain foods, tastes, or odors that have been associated with gastrointestinal illness.

Gene-environment interaction A process in which an environmental variable has one phenotypic outcome in individuals with a certain gene, but a different outcome in individuals with a different gene.

General process theory The position that all cases of a certain form of conditioning obey the same basic mechanisms.

Genetic drift A cause of evolution due to the random assortment of chromosomes and their accompanying genes during sexual reproduction.

Glial cells Nonneural cells of the nervous system that support the structure and activities of neurons.

Golgi tendon organ A sensory receptor located in tendons that monitors tendon stretch.

Gonadotropins Hormones secreted by the pituitary gland that inflence the sex organs (gonads).

Graded potential Changes of polarity that occur on neurons in response to neurotransmitter release. Graded potentials may be excitatory or inhibitory. Also see *excitatory postsynaptic potential; inhibitory postsynaptic potential.*

Grey matter Parts of the nervous system that consist primarily of neuron cell bodies, dendrites, and unmyelinated axons. Also see *white matter.*

Group selection The competition between groups for genetic representation in the following generation.

Growth cone The flattened tip of growing axons that forms temporary adhesions with surrounding tissue, thus "pulling" the axon along.

Habituation A form of nonassociative learning in which there is a reduction of response to a repeated inconsequential stimulus.

Hair cells Cells of the vestibular and auditory systems that transduce movements of their hairlike extensions into polarity changes.

Haplodiploid A condition in which males develop from unfertilized eggs (containing only one set of chromosomes, the haploid number) and females develop from fertilized eggs (containing two sets of chromosomes, the diploid condition).

Heritability The proportion of variance in the phenotypes of population members that is attributable to their genetic differences.

Heterozygote An organism that possesses two different alleles of a particular gene.

Heterozygote advantage A situation in which an individual having two dissimilar alleles has greater reproductive success than an individual with two copies of the same allele.

Hibernation A state characterized by long-lasting, extensive reductions in body temperature, energy consumption, and movement.

Hippocampus A structure of the cerebral hemispheres that appears to play a critical role in the learning and memory of spatial relationships.

Homeostasis The steady state of a physiological system, such as body temperature.

Homozygote An organism that has two identical alleles of a particular gene.

Hormone A chemical produced by cells that influences cells elsewhere in the body.

Huntington's chorea A degenerative disease of the nervous system that results in motor impairments and death.

Hybrid An offspring of two parents who are of different species, subspecies, or strains.

Hydraulic model A theory that motivation for a behavior occurs as the result of building of "energy" for that behavior. The behavior then relieves that pressure. Also see *action-specific energy; consummatory response.*

Hyperpolarization A graded potential that has an inhibitory effect on a neuron, making it less likely to generate an action potential.

Hypothalamus A multinucleus region of the basal forebrain that monitors and controls numerous physiological systems, most notably the secretion of various hormones.

Imprinting A specialized form of learning that occurs early in life during a sensitive period and which is resistant to change.

Inbred strain A group of individuals that arose from only brother–sister matings for at least 20 generations, resulting in phenotypically identical individuals.

Inbreeding depression The increased likelihood of detrimental characteristics in offspring of closely related parents.

Inclusive fitness The sum of an individual's personal reproductive success plus its effect on the reproductive success of its relatives.

Individual selection Individual differences in lifetime reproductive success.

Induced ovulation The release of eggs for potential fertilization only following copulatory behavior. Spontaneous ovulators release eggs without the necessity of copulation.

Inhibitory postsynaptic potential (IPSP) A hyperpolarizing graded potential. Results in reduced chance of the cell reaching its action potential threshold.

Insomnia A condition in which an individual is unable to sleep adequately, resulting in impaired behavioral performance.

Instinct Any behavior that develops without the necessity of specific individual experience. Also see *fixed action pattern*.

Integral protein Protein molecules embedded in the membranes of cells.

Intention movement A behavior that is immediately preparatory to the execution of another behavior (e.g., the crouch of a cat about to jump).

Interneuron See *internuncial neuron*.

Internuncial neuron A spinal cord neuron that receives its synaptic input from sensory neurons and synapses on motor or other neurons.

Intersexual selection Mate choice of one sex by the other.

Intrafusal fiber Muscle fibers involved in regulating muscle stretch or length. Also see *extrafusal fiber; gamma motor neuron*.

Intrasexual selection Differences in reproductive success among individuals of one sex due to their competition for mates.

Invasion In neural evolution, the appearance of a structure or organization that was not found in the ancestral species.

Iodopsin The photosensitive molecules of cones. Also see *rhodopsin*.

Ion An electrically charged atom.

Ion channel A type of integral protein that regulates the movement of ions through a cellular membrane.

Iris The muscular structure that changes the size of the pupil, thereby influencing the amount of light that enters the eye.

Kin selection Gene perpetuation due to an individual's contribution to the reproductive success of its relatives. Also see *inclusive fitness*.

Lactational amenorrhea Reduced fertility of female mammals who are nursing offspring.

Lateral geniculate nuclei Nuclei of the thalamus that get their input from the optic nerves, and send their axons to visual cortex.

Lateral line system A sensory system found in fish that detects changes in water pressure and currents.

Lateralization The state of being bilaterally asymmetrical, either anatomically or functionally. Handedness is an example of lateralization.

Learning The ability to modify one's behavior based on experience.

Lek A traditional site used by males for courting females for breeding.

Lek behavior Activities that are usually limited to a lek area, such as courtship displays, intermale competition, and mate choice.

Lens The transparent structure inside the eye that refracts incoming light onto the retina.

Limbic system A group of structures of the forebrain, thought to regulate emotional responses.

Lipid bilayer membrane The double-layered membrane of cells consisting of lipid (fat) molecules.

Lipoprotein lipase An enzyme on the surface of adipose tissue cells that stores lipids within the cells.

Lordosis A copulatory position adopted by female four-legged mammals.

Mania A disorder characterized by hyperactivity and often grandiose activity and aggressiveness.

Marginal value theorem The theory that optimal foragers will leave a food-containing area when the food value of that area declines to the average value of the feeding areas in the animal's home range.

Mechanism The physiological processes of an organism and its interactions with the environment that regulate behavior.

Medial forebrain bundle A set of axons that pass through the hypothalamus that may be involved in the perception of certain positive sensations.

Medial geniculate nuclei Paired thalamic nuclei involved in processing of auditory information.

Medulla oblongata Portion of the brainstem immediately anterior to the spinal cord.

Meiosis The process of producing gametes with half the complement of chromosomes from cells with the full complement.

Melatonin A pineal gland hormone that, in some species, participates in coordinating reproduction with seasonal changes in day length.

Meninges The three tissue layers lying between the outer surface of the brain and spinal cord and the overlying bone.

Message or broadcast information The information contained in a communicative signal.

Microtubules A proteinaceous tube system that extends from the cell body into the dendrites and axon. Various substances, including neurotransmitters or their precursors, move in both directions through these tubes.

Midbrain A subdivision of the vertebrate brain consisting of the superior and inferior colliculi and their underlying structures.

Modal action pattern Similar to fixed action pattern, but with the explicit recognition that differences among individuals are expected.

Modulation A developmental process in which some phenotypic characteristic varies among individuals according to differences in their environmental conditions. The phenotypic differences are a matter of degree. Also see *conversion*.

Monogamy A mating system in which a male mates with only one female, the mated pair resides together, and jointly cares for offspring.

Morgan's canon The philosophical position that the best explanation for a phenomenon is the simplest explanation that accounts for the phenomenon.

Motivation Any goal-directed state of an animal. Such states influence the probability, frequency, form, direction, or intensity of associated behaviors.

Motor unit A motor neuron and the set of muscle fibers on which it synapses.

Müllerian system The embryonic tissues that give rise to female reproductive organs.

Muscle spindles A sensory receptor that monitors muscle stretch or length. Also see *intrafusal fiber*.

Mutation Any change in the base sequence of DNA or RNA.

Myelin The insulating covering on some axons formed by wraps of certain glial cells.

Narcolepsy A disorder in which the individual is chronically sleepy.

Natural selection A process whereby genes that lead to more reproductively successful phenotypic forms increase in frequency in subsequent generations.

Negative feedback A control system in which deviations from a set point activate processes that return the system to the set point.

Negative reinforcement An increase in the rate of a response that leads to avoidance or escape from aversive stimuli.

Nerve growth factor A protein secreted by some nonneural cells that directs the growth of some axons toward those cells.

Neural plate An embryonic structure from which the nervous system develops.

Neuromodulator Chemicals released at synapses that have effects on the postsynaptic cell lasting seconds or longer. Also see *neurotransmitter*.

Neuromuscular junction The synapse between a neuron and a muscle cell.

Neuropsychology The branch of psychology that attempts to relate behavioral or cognitive disorders to neurological damage or dysfunction.

Neurotransmitter A chemical that diffuses across the synaptic cleft and that acts on the membrane of the receptor dendrite to change its polarity.

Node of Ranvier The bare segments of axon between adjacent myelin sheaths.

Nonassociative conditioning Any behavioral change brought about by exposure to a stimulus, even without linkage to another stimulus or consequence. Also see *habituation; sensitization*.

Nonballistic movement A behavior whose direction or speed can be changed once the behavior has begun. Reaching toward a moving target is an example. Also see *ballistic movement*.

Nondecremental conduction A characteristic of action potentials in which the rate and magnitude of polarity change remains constant as it moves along the axon.

Nucleus In a cell, the organelle that contains the chromosomes. In the nervous system, an assembly of neuron cell bodies.

Oligodendrocyte A type of glial cell in the central nervous system that wraps around axons insulating them with myelin sheaths.

Ommatidia The photosensitive units of the compound eyes of some invertebrates. Many ommatidia collectively form an eye.

Ontogeny See *development*.

Open phenotypic system Phenotypic traits whose developmental outcomes are sensitive to environmental conditions.

Operant conditioning A learning process in which the frequency of a behavior pattern is changed due to the consequences of the behavior.

Optic chiasm The cross-over point of the left and right optic nerves between the retina and the thalamus.

Optic disc The portion of the retina that is devoid of receptors due to the optic nerve fibers that leave the retina at that point.

Optic nerve The bundle of ganglion cell axons that connect the retina with the brain.

Optimality method A method of studying adaptation in which the most advantageous form of the phenotype, according to theoretical expectations, is compared with the real life form of the phenotype.

Organizational effect Any long-lasting change in the anatomy or physiology of an organism brought about by the secretion of a hormone or by some environmental condition.

Orthogenesis The notion that evolution proceeds in a unilinear fashion from a simple organism through to humans.

Ossicles The series of small bones that connect the tympanic membrane with the oval window of the cochlea.

Otolith receptors A component of the vestibular system consisting of crystals resting on a "carpet" of hair cells. The hair cells signal head movement.

Outbreeding depression Reduced fertility experienced by individuals who mate with others who are distantly related.

Oval window A membrane at the base of the cochlea that is compressed by movements of the tympanic membrane via the ossicles. Also see *round window.*

Parasocial route An evolutionary sequence leading to complex social organization that involved cooperation among unrelated individuals. Also see *familial route.*

Parasympathetic nervous system A subdivision of the autonomic division of the peripheral nervous system having a slowing or inhibitory effect.

Parkinson's disease A motor disorder due to inadequate amounts of dopamine. Its symptoms consist of difficulty initiating movements, tremor, and rigidity.

Pavlovian conditioning See *classical conditioning.*

Period The amount of time between successive peaks of activity of a recurring behavior or physiological process. Also see *circadian; circannual.*

Peripheral nervous system That portion of the nervous system other than the brain and spinal cord.

Phenotype Any attribute of an organism other than its genetic material. These attributes include anatomy, physiology, and behavior.

Pheromone A chemical produced and released by one individual that influences the behavior of another individual.

Phoneme The most basic unit of sound in human language.

Phylogeny The evolutionary history of a species.

Pinna The external ears.

Place theory The theory that the point along the basilar membrane of maximal vibration varies according to the frequency of the sound entering the ear and determines the pitch heard.

Pleiotropism A phenomenon in which a single gene's product influences more than one trait.

Polarity The difference in electrical charge across a membrane.

Polyandry The mating system in which a mated female has more than one mate.

Polygamy A generic term referring to non-monogamous mating systems. Also see *polyandry; polygyny.*

Polygenic inheritance Inheritance of numerous genes and alleles that contribute to a phenotype.

Polygyny The mating system in which a mated male has more than one mate.

Positive assortative mating A mate choice process in which individuals mate with others who resemble themselves phenotypically.

Positive feedback A motivational phenomenon in which performing a behavior temporarily increases the probability and vigor of that behavior.

Positive reinforcement A process in which the arrival of a stimulus contingent on the emission of a behavior increases the frequency of that behavior.

Postsynaptic membrane The portion of the membrane of a neuron that lies adjacent to a terminal button. Also see *dendritic spine.*

Preferred orientation The angle of a bar of light that produces maximal change in action potential rate in a simple cell of visual cortex.

Preparedness The degree to which a species' neural systems permit certain learned associations to be formed.

Presynaptic membrane The portion of a terminal button from which neurotransmitter is released into the synaptic cleft.

Primary motor cortex   The precentral gyrus of the cerebral cortex that contains many motor neurons, producing movements of the contralateral side of the body.

Primary visual cortex   Occipital lobe tissue that receives direct synaptic input from the lateral geniculate nuclei.

Priming effects (of hormones)   Hormonal changes usually brought about by environmental conditions (such as changing day length) that affect the probability of certain behaviors.

Principle of equipotentiality   The notion that all stimulus–response pairs (that an animal can perceive and produce) are equally likely to become associated.

Proceptivity   The condition of being sexually attracted to individuals of the opposite sex.

Productivity   The ability to emit novel signals or combinations of signals that are nevertheless capable of being understood by the audience.

Proliferation   The increase in the number of neurons during development.

Propagation   The movement of action potentials along a neuronal membrane such as an axon.

Proximate cause   Anything that initiates, directs, or controls behavior and that occurs directly before the behavior.

Proximate consequence   Anything that results from the execution of a behavior; the consequences may be beneficial or adverse and have some effect on the individual's well-being, survival, and reproductive success.

Punishment   The application of an aversive stimulus contingent on a particular behavior. Punishment generally reduces the probability of that behavior.

Pupil   The opening in the iris through which light enters the eye.

Pyramidal motor system   The motor control system consisting of cerebral cortical motor neurons and their connections in lower portions of the brain and upper spinal cord.

Rapid eye movement sleep (REM)   A form of sleep characterized by rapid eye movements, active EEG, reduced muscle tone in the trunk, and dreaming.

Receptive aphasia   A disorder in which a person loses the ability to understand his or her spoken language even though no hearing loss has occurred.

Receptive field   The set of receptor cells from which a neuron receives its input, often indirectly.

Receptivity   The condition in which an individual permits another to engage it in copulation.

Receptor site   A location on a molecule to which another molecule (e.g., neurotransmitter, hormone, drug) attaches or with which another molecule interacts.

Reciprocal altruism   A form of social exchange in which one individual bestows aid to another at some cost to itself; later, the roles are reversed.

Recombination   A chromosomal event in which pieces of different chromosomes break off and are exchanged with other chromosomes.

Refraction   The change in direction of light when it moves from one medium into another, such as from air to water.

Regulator/enhancer gene   A gene that produces proteins that activate or suppress other genes.

Reinforcement   The application of consequences following behavior that results in increasing the frequency of the behavior.

Reissner's membrane   The membrane separating the cochlear duct from the vestibular canal.

Relative refractory period   The time immediately following an action potential during which another action potential can be generated, but more depolarization is required to do so.

Relict behaviors Behaviors that were performed by an ancestral species, but which may reappear under unusual circumstances in more modern forms.

Resting membrane potential The polarized state of a neuron when it is neither conducting or receiving action potentials.

Retina The layer of cells at the back of the eye that contains cells that transduce light and others that do some processing of light information.

Retinal convergence The number of receptors of the retina that are indirectly connected to a ganglion cell.

Retinal periphery The portions of the retina other than the fovea(s).

Rhodopsin A two-part photopigment in rod receptor cells of the retina which, when struck by light, changes the rod's permeability to sodium.

Ribosome Organelle within a cell in which RNA translation into proteins occurs.

Ritualization The evolutionary process in which a signal behavior is derived from a movement with nonsignal functions.

RNA Assembled by a DNA molecule, this molecule translates a DNA code into protein.

Rods The class of photoreceptor that contains rhodopsin. Rods are used in perception of light intensity. Also see *cone.*

Round window The membrane at the base of the cochlea that flexes in and out, compensating for movements of the oval window.

Saltatory conduction The manner by which an action potential moves along a myelinated axon. The action potential "jumps" from one node of Ranvier to the next.

Search image A perceptual learning phenom-

enon in which a predator becomes more adept at locating its prey as a result of having encountered that prey.

Second messenger system A process by which the polarity of a neuron is modified by a neuromodulator-activated enzyme which causes an ion channel to stay open for a longer period of time.

Selective breeding A process by which a person breeds a group of organisms for a particular desired trait.

Selfishness Any act that tends to benefit the actor at the expense of others.

Semicircular canals Three ringlike tubes of the vestibular system whose sensory receptors monitor head movement.

Sensitive period A stage of life in which some feature of the phenotype is most strongly influenced by particular forms of environmental conditions.

Sensitivity The degree to which a sensory system can detect low energy levels (e.g., of light, sound, or chemicals).

Sensitization An increase in general responsivity due to the application of some stimulus.

Sex steroid hormones The set of hormones produced by the gonads, including androgens, estrogens, and progestins.

Sexual differentiation The process of an individual becoming phenotypically male or female from a previously indifferent state.

Sign stimulus Any stimulus that reliably initiates fixed action patterns.

Signal Any behavior or product of behavior that is specialized for the transmission of information from one individual to another.

Simple cell A form of neuron, found in visual cortex, whose receptive field is elongate and exhibits center-surround organization.

Sleep apnea A disorder in which breathing is temporarily suspended during sleep.

Slow-wave sleep The state characterized by

slow EEG activity, and lowered body temperature and other vital functions. Also see *rapid eye movement sleep (REM)*.

Social process The mechanism that brings about or maintains social patterns.

Social structure Any attribute of a social group.

Sociobiology The branch of biology that studies the evolution and adaptive significance of social behavior. Also see *behavioral ecology*.

Sodium–potassium pump An enzyme embedded in the cell membrane that actively transports sodium ions out of the cell while simultaneously transporting potassium ions into the cell.

Somatic nervous system The portion of the peripheral nervous system responsible for the body wall, both motor and sensory.

Spatial summation Phenomenon in which graded potentials occurring at the same time on a cell's membrane are added together.

Spinal cord The portion of the nervous system lying within the vertebral column.

Spinal nerves The bundles of axons protruding from the spinal cord.

Stabilizing selection The process in which individuals with median forms of a phenotype have greater reproductive success than individuals with more extreme forms of the phenotype.

State-space A motivational concept that an animal can be characterized by its status on each of many physiological variables. Its position in this multivariate "space" contributes to its behavioral decisions.

Strabismus A condition in which the eyes cannot be simultaneously focused on the same spot.

Superior colliculus Paired midbrain nuclei involved in visual processing, especially involving control of eye movements.

Superior olivary nuclei Auditory system nuclei of the brainstem responsible for binaural comparisons.

Sympathetic nervous system The division of the autonomic nervous system that generally produces physiological changes associated with arousal. Also see *parasympathetic nervous system*.

Synapse A junction between the terminal button of an axon of one neuron and the dendrite or cell body of another neuron.

Synaptic cleft The narrow space separating the terminal button from the postsynaptic membrane.

Synaptic potential See *graded potential*.

Tapetum lucidum A layer of reflective material behind the retinas of nocturnal animals. It reflects light back into the receptor cell layer.

Tectorial membrane A structure in the cochlear duct to which the projections of some hair cells are attached. Also see *basilar membrane*.

Tectum The portion of the midbrain that includes the superior and inferior colliculi.

Temporal summation The process in which successive graded potentials are added together, thereby enhancing polarity change.

Terminal button A swelling at the tip of an axon that releases neurotransmitter when an action potential arrives. See also *synapse*.

Territory An area that is actively defended against competitors of the same or other species.

Testosterone An androgenic hormone, primarily produced by the testis of males, but also found in females.

Thalamus A large set of nuclei, near the center of the brain, that are involved in sensory processing and some motor control.

Thought Any self-contained activity of the nervous system of which one is aware.

Tonotopic organization The spatial arrangement of neurons in any part of the auditory system in such a way that it corresponds to sound frequency.

Torpor   A condition resembling sleep in which body temperature falls and most physiological processes are greatly slowed. Also see *hibernation.*

Traditional transmission   A characteristic of human language involving learning of arbitrary associations between sounds and their referents (objects, actions, etc.).

Transcription   The synthesis of RNA from DNA.

Transduction   The process by which energy is transformed from one form to another. The process by which sensory receptors change physical energy to neural activity.

Translation   The construction of a protein according to the code specified by RNA.

Transmitter agonist   A drug that mimics the effect of a neurotransmitter.

Transmitter antagonist   A drug that blocks or reduces the effect of a neurotransmitter.

Traveling wave   The "ripple" that occurs on the basilar membrane due to movements of the oval window.

Trophic substance   A chemical secreted by certain cells that, when taken in by certain neurons, keeps them alive and functional.

Tympanic canal   A fluid-filled cochlear chamber separated from the cochlear duct by the basilar membrane. Also see *vestibular canal.*

Tympanic membrane   The eardrum. The tympanic membrane moves in response to sound pressure striking it.

Ultimate cause   Past experiences, conditions, and genetic material that affects the individual's current behavior.

Ultimate consequence   The long-term effect of an individual's behavior on survival and reproduction.

Unconditioned response   In classical conditioning, the response (behavioral or physiological) that occurs when a specific stimulus strikes the organism. The unconditioned response occurs without prior learning.

Unconditioned stimulus   In classical conditioning, the stimulus that evokes a behavioral or physiological response without the necessity of learning. This response is the unconditioned response.

Ventral horn   The lower portions of the spinal cord's grey matter. Most ventral horn neurons are involved in motor control processes. Also see *dorsal horn.*

Vesicle   A "packet" containing neurotransmitter in terminal buttons.

Vestibular canal   A fluid-filled cochlear chamber separated from the cochlear duct by Reissner's membrane. Also see *tympanic membrane.*

Vestibuloocular reflex   Eye movements that are generated to automatically compensate for movements of the head.

Voltage gating   A phenomenon that occurs in ion channels of membranes in which the attainment of a particular polarity value "locks" the channel in a fully open or fully closed position.

Wavelength   In waveform phenomena, such as sound, the distance between successive wave peaks.

White matter   Neural tissue containing large quantities of myelin, giving it a whitish, shiny appearance. Also see *grey matter.*

Wolffian system   The embryonic tissues that give rise to male reproductive organs.

Zeitgeber   Any environmental stimulus that is capable of resetting biological clocks. Also see *entrainment.*

PICTURE
CREDITS

❧

by the American Association for the Advancement of Science. Used with the permission of the AAAS; p. 29, redrawn from Richard H. Scheller and Richard Axel (1984). "How genes control an innate behavior." *Scientific American* **250**(3), 54–62. Copyright © 1984 by Scientific American, Inc. All rights reserved; p. 30, © George Roos/Animals Animals; p. 31, Wellcome Institute Library, London; p. 34, redrawn from R. Tenaza (1985). "Songs of hybrid gibbons (*Hylobates lar* × *H. muelleri*." *American Journal of Primatology* **8**, 249–253. Copyright © 1985 Wiley-Liss, Inc., a division of John Wiley and Sons, Inc.; p. 35, redrawn from W. H. Cade (1981). "Alternative male strategies: genetic differences in crickets." *Science* **212**, 563–564. Copyright © 1981 by the American Association for the Advancement of Science. Used with the permission of the AAAS and William Cade

CHAPTER 3: (*opener*) p. 38, © Stephen Krasemann/Valan; p. 40, © Wilf Schurig/Valan; p. 42, courtesy of Charles Pfizer & Co., Inc.; p. 46, © Dennis W. Schmidt/Valan; p. 50, The Rockefeller Archive Center; p. 51, [baboon] © Don and Pat Valenti/f-Stop Pictures, [bear] © Leonard Lee Rue III/Visuals Unlimited, [musk oxen] © Fred Bruemmer/Valan; p. 53, redrawn from A. I. Leshner (1979). "Kinds of hormonal effects on behavior: a new view." *Neuroscience and Biobehavioral Reviews* **3**, 69–73. Used with permission of Pergamon Press and Alan I. Leshner; p. 54, from C. H. Phoenix, K. H. Copenhaver, and R. M. Brenner (1976). "Scanning electron miscrocopy of penile papillae in intact and castrated male rats." *Hormones and Behavior* **7**, 217–222. Copyright © 1976 by Academic Press, Inc. Reprinted by permission of Academic Press and Charles Phoenix. Photograph courtesy of Charles Phoenix; p. 55, courtesy of Dr. Michael Gazzaniga

CHAPTER 4: (*opener*) p. 57, © Irene Vandermolen/Visuals Unlimited; p. 60, © Thomas Kitchin/Tom Stack & Associates; p. 65, courtesy of W. D. Hamilton; p. 68, © Fred Bruemmer/Valan; p. 72, Darwin Museum, Down House, Downe, Kent; p. 73, redrawn with permission from P. K. McGregor, J. R. Krebs, and C. M. Perrins (1981). "Song repertoires and lifetime reproductive success in the great tit (*Parus major*)." *American Naturalist* **118**, 148–159. Copyright © 1981 by the University of Chicago Press; p. 79, courtesy of Dr. Francois Jacob; p. 80, © Mantis Wildlife Films/Animals Animals

CHAPTER 5: (*opener*) p. 84, Carolina Biological Supply Co.; p. 86, redrawn with permission from D. Purves and J. W. Lichtman (1985). *Principles of Neural Development*. Copyright © 1985 by Sinauer Associates, Inc.; p. 88, AP/Wide World; p. 92, courtesy of Professor Mark Rosenzweig; p. 95 [Figs. 5.3 and 5.4] adapted from *Neuroanatomy* by K. E. Moyer. Copyright © 1980 by K. E. Moyer. Used by permission of HarperCollins Publishers; p. 97, adapted from *Principles of Anatomy and Physiology*, 5th ed., by Gerard J. Tortora and Nicholas Anagnostakos. Copyright © 1987 by Biological Sciences Textbooks, Inc., A&P Textbooks, Inc., and Elia-Sparta, Inc. Used with permission of HarperCollins Publishers; pp. 98, 99, adapted from *Neuroanatomy* by K. E. Moyer. Copyright © 1980 by K. E. Moyer. Used with permission of HarperCollins Publishers; p. 106, redrawn with permission from Charles F. Stevens (1979). "The neuron." *Scientific American* **241**(3), 54–65. Copyright © 1979 by Scientific American, Inc. All rights reserved.

CHAPTER 6: (*opener*) p. 116, © 1990 Custom Medical Stock Photo; p. 117, courtesy of the Department of Neuroscience, University of California; p. 118, redrawn with permission from Jeffrey M. Camhi (1980). "The escape system of the cockroach." *Scientific American* **243**(6), 158–172. Copyright © 1980 by Scientific American, Inc. All rights reserved; p. 120, redrawn with permission from David H. Hubel (1979). "The brain." *Scientific American* **241**(3), 44–53. Copyright © 1979 by Scientific American, Inc. All rights reserved; p. 122, redrawn from H. J. Jerison (1969). "Brain evolution and dinosaur brains." *American Naturalist* **103**, 575–588. Used with permission of University of Chicago Press; p. 129, redrawn from Lee C. Drickamer and Stephen H. Vessey (1986). *Animal Behavior: Concepts, Processes, and Methods.* Boston: PWS Publsihers. Used with permission of the authors.

CHAPTER 7: (*opener*) p. 130, © Albert Kuhnigk/Valan; p. 133, redrawn from L. M. Dill (1977). "Refraction and the spitting behavior of the archerfish (*Toxotes chatareus*)." *Behavioral Ecology and Sociobiology* **2**, 169–184. Copyright © 1977 by Springer-Verlag. Used with permission of Springer-Verlag and L. M. Dill; p. 134, redrawn with permission from J. A. Waldvogel (1990). *American Scientist* **78**, 342–353; p. 135, adapted from J. E. Dowling and B. B. Boycott (1966). "Organization of the primate retina: electron microscopy." *Proceeding of the Royal Society of London B* **166**, 80–111. Copyright © 1966 The Royal Society. Used with permission of The Royal Society and John Dowling; p. 136, redrawn from W. Buskist and D. W. Gerbing (1991). *Psychology: Boundaries and Frontiers.* Copyright © 1991 HarperCollins Publishers; p. 148, [top] Harvard University News Office, [bottom] Harvard University News Office; p. 152, redrawn from Lee C. Drickamer and Stephen H. Vessey (1986). *Animal Behavior: Concepts, Processes, and Methods.* Boston: PWS Publishers. Used with permission of the authors;

pp. 154–155, adapted from Gerard J. Tortora and Nicholas Anagnostakos (1987). *Principles of Anatomy and Physiology*, 5th ed. Copyright © 1987 by Biological Sciences Textbooks, Inc., A&P Textbooks, Inc., and Elia-Sparta, Inc. Used with permission of HarperCollins Publishers; p. 157, redrawn with permission from J. Tonndorf (1960). "Shearing motion in scala media of cochlear models." *Journal of the Acoustical Society of America* **32**, 238–244. Copyright © 1960 by the American Institute of Physics; p. 158, redrawn from M. B. Sachs, N. K. Woolf, and J. M. Sinnott (1980). "Response properties of neurons in the avian auditory system: comparisons with mammalian homologues and consideration of the neural encoding of complex stimuli." In A. N. Popper and R. R. Fay (eds.). *Comparative Studies of Hearing in Vertebrates.* New York: Springer-Verlag. Copyright © 1980 by Springer-Verlag. Used with permission of the publisher and Murray B. Sachs; p. 159, redrawn with permission from W. C. Stebbins (1983). *The Acoustic Sense of Animals.* Cambridge, MA: Harvard University Press. Copyright © 1983 by the President and Fellows of Harvard College; p. 161, courtesy of Masakazu Konishi; p. 162, redrawn with permission from P. Marler (1959). "Developments in the study of animal communication." In P. R. Bell (ed.). *Darwin's Biological Work: Some Aspects Reconsidered.* New York: Cambridge University Press (pp. 150–206). Copyright © 1959 Cambridge University Press; p. 164, redrawn with permission from K. D. Roeder (1963). *Nerve Cells and Insect Behavior.* Cambridge, MA: Harvard University Press. Copyright © 1963 by the President and Fellows of Harvard College

CHAPTER 8: (*opener*) p. 167, © Mickey Gibson/Animals Animals; p. 170, © Joe McNally; p. 173, redrawn with permission from R. G. Coss and A. Globus (1979). "Social experience affects the development of dendritic spines and branches on tectal interneurons in the jewel fish." *Developmental Psychobiology* **12**, 347–358. Copyright © 1979 by John Wiley and Sons, Inc.; p. 175, redrawn from G. Lynch and M. Baudry (1984). "The biochemistry of memory: a new and specific hypothesis." *Science* **244**, 1057–1063. Copyright © 1984 by the American Association for the Advancement of Science. Used with permission of the AAAS and Gary Lynch; p. 176, Dr. James Olds; p. 177, redrawn from D. S. Olton and R. J. Samuelson (1976). "Remembrance of places past: spatial memory in rats." *Journal of Experimental Psychology: Animal Behavior Processes* **2**, 97–116. Copyright © 1976 by the American Psychological Association. Used with permission of the APA and David Olton; p. 180, courtesy Department of Psychology, University of Toronto; p. 181, courtesy of Al Kamil, Department of Psychology, University of Massachusetts; p. 183, redrawn from Sara J. Shettleworth (1983). "Memory in food-hoarding birds." *Scientific American* **248**(3), 102–110. Copyright © 1983 Scientific American, Inc. All rights reserved; p. 184, © Arthur Gloor/Animals Animals; p. 188, redrawn with permission from N. P. Lester (1981). "The 'feed-drink' decision." *Behaviour* **89**, 200–219. Copyright © 1981 by E. J. Brill; p. 189, © John Shaw/Tom Stack & Associates

CHAPTER 9: (*opener*) p. 192, © Len Rue, Jr./Visuals Unlimited; pp. 193, 197, 202, 203, adapted from Gerard J. Tortora and Nicholas Anagnostakos (1987). *Principles of Anatomy and Physiology*, 5th ed. Copyright © 1987 by Biological Sciences Textbooks, Inc., A&P Textbooks, and Elia-Sparta, Inc. Used with permission of HarperCollins Publishers; p. 209, redrawn with permission from R. Dawkins and M. S. Dawkins (1981). "Decisions and the uncertainty of behaviour." *Behaviour* **45**, 83–103. Copyright ©

1981 by E. J. Brill; p. 216, adapted from K. E. Moyer (1980). *Neuroanatomy.* Copyright © 1980 by K. E. Moyer. Used with permission of HarperCollins Publishers; p. 217, University of Delaware, Newark/Jack Buxbaum

CHAPTER 10: (*opener*) p. 219, © Gary W. Griffen/Animals Animals; pp. 222, 223, redrawn from J. D. Wilson (1981). "The hormonal control of sexual development." *Science* **211**, 1278–1284. Copyright © 1981 by the American Association for the Advancement of Science. Used with the permission of the AAAS and Jean Wilson; p. 224, courtesy of S. Schwartz-Giblin and A. Robbins, Rockefeller University; p. 227, redrawn from B. A. Gladue, R. Green, and R. E. Hellman (1984). "Neuroendocrine response to estrogen and sexual orientation." *Science* **225**, 1496–1499. Copyright © 1984 by the American Association for the Advancement of Science. Used with the permission of the AAAS and Brian Gladue; p. 229, courtesy of the Department of Psychology, University of Massachusetts; p. 231, courtesy of the Department of Psychology, University of Florida, Gainesville; p. 232, redrawn from B. Hart (1967). "Sexual reflexes and mating behavior in the male dog." *Journal of Comparative and Physiological Psychology* **66**, 388–399. Copyright © 1967 by the American Psychological Association. Used with the permission of the APA and Benjamin Hart; p. 233, redrawn with permission from D. A. Dewsbury (1972). "Patterns of copulatory behavior in male mammals." *Quarterly Review of Biology* **47**, 1–33. Copyright © 1972 University of Chicago Press; p. 238, University of Illinois; p. 239, redrawn from J. R. Udry and N. M. Morris (1968). "Distribution of coitus in the menstrual cycle." *Nature* **220**, 593–596. Copyright © 1968 Macmillan Magazines Limited; p. 240, redrawn with permission from D. B. Adams, A. R. Gold, and A. D. Burt (1978).

"Rise in female-initiated sexual activity at ovulation and its suppression by oral contraceptives." *The New England Journal of Medicine* **299,** 1145–1150

CHAPTER 11: (*opener*) p. 243, © Don and Pat Valenti/f-Stop Pictures; p. 247, © Leonard Lee Rue III/Visuals Unlimited; p. 248, Photri; p. 252, © Robert Maier/Animals Animals; p. 253, © Leonard Lee Rue III/Visuals Unlimited; p. 257, © Gary Milburn/Tom Stack & Associates; p. 258, University of Wisconsin, Madison/Michael Kienitz; p. 259, © Daniel Leger; p. 261, University of California, Santa Cruz/Don Harris; p. 262 © M. J. Johnson/Valan; p. 267, © Frances Schroeder/SuperStock International, Inc.

CHAPTER 12: (*opener*) p. 269, © Animals Animals; p. 273, redrawn with permission from George F. Oster and Edward O. Wilson (1978). *Caste and Ecology in the Social Insects.* Princeton, NJ: Princeton University Press. Copyright © 1978 Princeton University Press; p. 275, © John D. Cunningham/Visuals Unlimited; p. 280, © 1965 Time Inc./Nina Leen; pp. 281, 282, redrawn from E. H. Hess (1959). "Imprinting." *Science* **130**, 133–141. Copyright © 1959 by the American Association for the Advancement of Science; p. 285, © Harlow Primate Center, University of Wisconsin, Madison; p. 286, courtesy of University of Wisconsin Photographic Media Center; p. 287, © Dominique Braud/Tom Stack & Associates; p. 288, Harvard University News Office/Jane Reed; p. 290, AP/Wide World; p. 292, Jack D. Swenson/Tom Stack & Associates

CHAPTER 13: (*opener*) p. 297, © Daniel Leger; p. 300, redrawn from G. H. Orians and G. M. Christman (1968). "A comparative study of the behavior of red-winged, tricolored, and yellow-headed blackbirds." *University of California Publications in Zoology* **84**, 1–81. Used with permission of the University of California Press; p. 303, redrawn with permission from G. B. Schaller (1972). *The Serengeti Lion: A Study of Predator–Prey Relations.* Copyright © 1972 by The University of Chicago Press; p. 304, The Rockefeller Archive Center; p. 306, courtesy of Department of Psychology, Indiana University, Bloomington; p. 307, redrawn from D. Bentley and R. R. Hoy (1974). "The neurobiology of cricket song." *Scientific American* **231**(2), 34–44. Copyright © 1974 by Scientific American, Inc. All rights reserved; p. 309, redrawn from P. M. Waser and C. H. Brown (1984). "Is there a 'sound window' for primate communication?" *Behavioral Ecology and Sociobiology* **15**, 73–76. Copyright © 1984 Springer-Verlag. Used with permission of Springer-Verlag and Peter M. Waser; p. 310, redrawn with permission from M. L. Hunter and J. R. Krebs (1979). "Geographical variation in the song of the great tit (*Parus major*) in relation to ecological factors." *Journal of Animal Ecology* **48**, 759–785. Copyright © 1979 by Blackwell Scientific Publications, Limited; p. 311, © R. F. Myers/Visuals Unlimited; p. 318, redrawn with permission from K. von Frisch (1974). "Decoding the language of the bee." *Science* **185**, 663–668. Copyright © 1974 by the Nobel Foundation; p. 320, courtesy Sue Savage-Rumbaugh, Associate Professor of Biology at Georgia State University; p. 324, adapted with permission from K. E. Moyer (1980). *Neuroanatomy.* New York: HarperCollins

CHAPTER 14: (*opener*) p. 327, © Warren Garst/Tom Stack & Associates; p. 329, courtesy of Ilene L. Bernstein, Ph.D.; p. 336, © Cleveland P. Hickman, Jr./Visuals Unlimited; p. 337, © Aubrey Lang/Valan; p. 343, redrawn from N. Tinbergen (1948). "Social releasers and the experimental method required for their study." *The*

Wilson Bulletin **60**, 6–52. Used with the permission of the Wilson Ornithogical Society; p. 345, © Leonard Lee Rue III/Animals Animals; p. 347, redrawn with permission from D. F. Hennessy, D. H. Owings, M. P. Rowe, R. G. Coss, and D. W. Leger (1981). "The information afforded by a variable signal: constraints on snake-elicited tail flagging by California ground squirrels." *Behaviour* **78**, 188–226. Copyright © 1981 by E. J. Brill

CHAPTER 15: (*opener*) p. 350, © Len Rue Jr./Visuals Unlimited; p. 352, redrawn with permission from P. D. Ebert and J. S. Hyde (1976). "Selection for agonistic behavior in wild female *Mus musculus*." *Behavior Genetics* **6**, 291–304. Copyright © 1976 Plenum Publishing Corporation; p. 354, redrawn from F. S. vom Saal (1983). "Models of early hormonal effects on intrasex aggression in mice." In B. B. Svare (ed.). *Hormones and Aggressive Behavior*. New York: Plenum Press (pp. 197–222). Used with permission of the publisher and Frederick S. vom Saal; p. 364, © Kevin Schafer/Tom Stack & Associates; p. 365, courtesy of Department of Psychology, McMaster University, Hamilton, Ontario; p. 366 [left], courtesy of the Department of Anthropology, University of California, Davis, [right] © Michael Dick/Animals Animals; p. 367, © Kevin Jackson/Animals Animals

CHAPTER 16: (*opener*) p. 370, Dr. A. Farquhar/Valan; p. 372, redrawn from R. Silver (1990). "Biological timing mechanisms with special emphasis on the parental behavior of doves." In D. A. Dewsbury (ed.). *Contemporary Issues in Comparative Psychology*. Sunderland, MA: Sinauer Associates (pp. 252–277). Used with permission of the publisher and Rae Silver; p. 373, courtesy Rae Silver; p. 375 [Fig. 16.3] redrawn with permission from F. R. Freemon (1972). *Sleep Research: A Critical Guide*. Springfield, IL: Charles C. Thomas; p. 378, adapted from H. P. Roffwarg, J. N. Muzio, and W. C. Dement (1966). "Ontogenetic development of the human sleep-dream cycle." *Science* **152**, 604–619. Copyright © 1966 by the American Association for the Advancement of Science. Used with permission of the AAAS and H. P. Roffwarg; p. 380, Stanford University News Service; p. 381, courtesy of Dr. Seiji Nishino, Nishino, et al., Shinkei; Keukyu No Shinpo (1990); p. 383 [Table 16.2] reprinted with permission from R. Meddis (1975). "On the function of sleep." *Animal Behavior* **23**, 676–691. Used with permission of Academic Press, Inc. (London), [Table 16.3] reprinted from R. Meddis (1979). "The evolution and function of sleep." In D. A. Oakley and H. C. Plotkin (eds.). *Brain, Behavior, and Evolution*. London: Methuen (pp. 99–125). Reprinted by permission of the publisher; p. 386, © Leonard Lee Rue III/Visuals Unlimited

INDEX